THE BEST

# FISHING STORIES

## EVER TOLD

# THE BEST
# FISHING STORIES
## EVER TOLD

EDITED AND INTRODUCED BY
## NICK LYONS

FOREWORD BY
## DAVID HALBERSTAM

Skyhorse Publishing

Skyhorse Publishing books may be purchased in bulk at special discounts for sales promotion, corporate gifts, fund-raising, or educational purposes. Special editions can also be created to specifications. For details, contact the Special Sales Department, Skyhorse Publishing, 555 Eighth Avenue, Suite 903, New York, NY 10018 or info@skyhorsepublishing.com.

www.skyhorsepublishing.com

10 9 8 7 6 5 4 3 2 1

The authors and texts included in this book represent more than a century of literature. The integrity of their individual styles, including spelling, punctuation, and grammar, has been respected. The stories reflect the attitudes of their times, and do not necessarily represent the views or opinions of Skyhorse Publishing, Inc.

This book is a condensation of the previously published volume *The Gigantic Book of Fishing Stories*.

Library of Congress Cataloging-in-Publication Data is available on file.

ISBN: 978-1-61608-056-3

Printed in the United States of America

# CONTENTS

# FOREWORD—A MEMOIR

## DAVID HALBERSTAM

I am a fisherman and thus a dreamer of a certain quite precise kind, almost always when I am on the water; in my day job I am the most skeptical of men in one of the most skeptical of professions in a world which regrettably holds out fewer and fewer dreams the older I get. But on the water, fly rod in hand, my dreams never desert me; I can look out and even when the river water is murky and deep and running too fast, I can visualize a trout, always of a goodly size, rising to my fly, or if it's a clear day in the Caribbean, I can see a handsome bonefish moving steadily on its anointed course toward our boat, at the last second breaking off the requisite two feet to hit my fly. On the water, as I am never without dreams, I am never without hope.

The dreams began long ago, in 1940, when I was a boy, and I worked our old family row boat, caulked and recaulked as it was (mostly by me), and dreamed of what seemed back then like the rarest of rewards, a legal-sized bass (that is one at least ten inches long). And now that I am a man and a septuagenarian to boot, I still dream many of the same dreams, changed little over the years in subject matter, albeit expanded greatly in scope. Highland Lake, where the dreams began, was just two miles from downtown Winsted, Connecticut, a mill town where I spent the best part of my boyhood. It was in truth a terrible fished-out lake, but who dares tell a young and eager boy that, that his passion to fish might be at this moment ill-considered and more or less hopeless and that he would be better off concentrating on his swimming? To the contrary, my dreams were all the more important, my hopes for what would happen each time I fished inevitably greater than the reality of what did happen. I fished Highland Lake almost every day of every summer from roughly 1940 to 1948, starting when I was six, and ending when I was fourteen. I fished it mostly with worms which I dug myself; on occasion, after it had rained, with night crawlers; sometimes with crawfish (almost as much fun to catch in their rock-covered hideaways as the fish themselves); and on rare occasion, when either my uncle or my father was with my brother and me and we were being rather fancy, with live bait.

More often than not, I fished with a clunky old metal telescopic rod—the promise had been made (but no exact date set) that when I got older there would be a bamboo rod for me. In addition, I had an old casting rod and reel; this was the era just before the arrival of spinning gear when you could still get a world class backlash—an entire morning often devoted to the untangling—with the wrong kind of cast. In those days, I could cast, with surprising distance for someone so young, a red-headed white-bodied Jitterbug, and sometimes a black skeletal Heddon River Runt, and occasionally a Hawaiian Wiggler (you could easily change the rubber skirt on the Wiggler), or, most simple of all, a red and white spoon. I have not touched a casting rod in sixty years, and sitting here writing about those days, I am stunned that I still remember the names of the different plugs, and can still see myself casting with that surprisingly short and stiff rod, and can even remember the rare strike of a bass or pickerel on the surface with the Jitterbug.

I was a fully committed fisherman as a boy. I read *Field & Stream* faithfully—I loved the byline of Ted Trueblood (was there ever a sportsman more appropriately named?), a man always, it seemed, on the case of some giant lunker that lurked in the most inaccessible of places. I admired as well the sketches that came with the articles, depicting huge record-breaking bass or muskie exploding out of deep weed patches, and dreamt that one day I too would catch my own lunkers. In those days, my brother and I—he was two years older and an accomplice in all this, though I do not think quite as passionate as I—not only fished every day, but we lingered in Mr. Rank's store in downtown Winsted, a place where fishing and hunting gear was sold. I loved Rank's—I did not then and do not now know his first name, for he was always Mr. Rank to us—and I loved the sense that, unlike any other store in Winsted, his had been designed for someone like me, a store stocked for a boy's fantasy world, stacks of rods, some of them bamboo, perhaps one of them one day mine, and different reels, all carefully set out, row on row of them, and a vast variety of lures, surely all of them magical, sure to find the hidden lunkers of that world. In addition, Mr. Rank was the local tobacconist, and there was a marvelous smell of pipe tobacco in that shop. On those days when my brother and I missed the school bus because we were playing baseball or football after school and walked the two miles back to our house on the lake, we almost always stopped at Rank's, lingering as long as we dared, the time passed there in inverse proportion I am sure to the tiny scale of our purchases (a few Eagle Claw hooks perhaps). I liked everything about the store, except for the fact that Mr. Rank called me Sonny; I did not then, and do not now, think of myself as a Sonny, and I felt it demeaned me as a serious customer.

Highland Lake had three bays and we lived right on the lake in my uncle's house on First Bay—my father was off in the war—and I fished the lake every day. Each summer my hands were quickly hardened with the calluses that came from rowing our boat. Highland Lake was, truth to be told, rarely if ever restocked, and I was lucky if I caught two or three legal-sized bass a year. I think in all those years I caught one truly large bass, perhaps two or three pounds, but I can remember my father's warning when it struck—one of those warnings you hear and never forget, good for all occasions and all kinds of larger fish still to come—Never horse a bass! Up in Third Bay—I could row there, although in time we were given what I remember as a five-horsepower, extremely temperamental Evinrude motor, which started almost as often as it did not—there was an area filled with lilies which we called the Pickerel Grounds, which somehow promised (though rarely produced) more big fish, and I would row there, perhaps two miles each way, with higher hopes than when I fished First Bay.

I did not realize this at the time, but from the start, I was always at peace with myself when I fished. Back then, I loved every moment on the water, the days when I caught nothing, and the days when we caught the rare bass and perch, and the days when we caught rock bass and pumpkinseed, some of them surely for the umpteenth time that summer. I am sure as well that from the start, fishing gave me a wonderful sense of expectation, the belief that the next cast will be the best, and the fact that the last cast of the day is surely going to be the best one. I think back now, so many years later, and I cannot think of myself ever returning to our house and being unhappy—rather simply more determined than ever to do it again the next day.

The promised bamboo rods never materialized in my childhood. My father died when I was young, and as such I moved away from fishing for a long time. My career took over my life; journalists when they are young do not control their itineraries—they go where they are sent, to places like the Congo and Vietnam where even Ted Trueblood had probably never fished. But then in my mid-Thirties I bought a house in Nantucket, and came back to fishing. My friend Dick Steadman and I bought a twenty-foot Mako, and there were years when he and I and our friend David Fine fished two and three times a week, using very light spinning tackle and going after blues, the most savage of predators, and stripers, usually one hook, no barb. Though I had not fished in twenty years, it was as if I had never been away, the pleasure was so acute. Often there were days when I caught more big fish—ferocious ones; if they shook the hook during the struggle, they would often strike again—in one afternoon than I had caught in an entire summer as a boy. It was as if all those boyhood hopes and dreams had finally been fulfilled, or at least partially fulfilled.

And so I had, without consciously seeking to, come back to fishing and returned as well to a critical part of my boyhood. Now as I get older it has become an ever more important part of my life. The truth is, I suppose, that the thrill of it, that great sense of anticipation for every cast, the belief that this is the day that it will all happen, never went away. Late in life, a little restless with the self-imposed limits of fishing on Nantucket, I started to fly fish. We all, I suspect, need enablers in life to push us to do the things we want and need to do, and when I was in my sixties I found my enabler, a friend named Richard Berlin— we became connected through our daughters, who were pals at boarding school. He is the most serious of fishermen. He had asked me when we first met, because of my Nantucket connection, if I was a fisherman, and with that the connection was made. His boyhood as a fisherman was as different from mine as it possibly could have been: it was spent with gifted guides at some of the world's great fishing lodges, significant skills honed long before there was a chance to learn how to do things the wrong way. When I was catching and recatching the same sunfish throughout the long summers of my boyhood, he was working great Canadian rivers like the Miramichi, catching monster Atlantic salmon.

He is not merely a very gifted fisherman, but even more important, he has impeccable fishing manners: he is generous, tuned to how other, less skilled friends are doing and how much fun they are having, and never worried about his own success; he is good enough to know that he will get his rightful share of big fish. And in time—for it was never deliberate, just something that happened—he started putting together a group of us, drawn from different parts of his life, unlikely friendships for all of us on our normal scale of palship, our politics and professions as different as it is possible to be, but joined by one thing, the sheer madness or the sheer logic of fishing, whichever it really is, the easy camaraderie that comes with unhurried time on the water, all of us with very different stories of how we got to be there, and always the sweetness of going off some great distance to fish together, with nothing else on the agenda, the comforting days on the water blended as it were with the occasional raucous noise of the lodge at the end of the day. Some of the men I fish with are truly gifted; they started young, had a natural grace and never stopped getting better. They cast with a certain artistry and there are moments when I am fishing that I stop for a time and steal a glance, admiring the skill in the way they cast, and admiring as well their modesty when we are back at the lodge, the fact they never boast about how well they have done, their awareness that it is all in the doing, and if they do it well there is no need to tell someone else that they have done it well. The trips we have made, aided by so many accumulated airline miles, strike me in retrospect as beyond exotic: the Rio Grande in Tierra del Fuego, the Zhupanova in Kamchatka, and a number of islands in the Caribbean, places I suspect beyond the reach of even the mighty Ted Trueblood. Sometimes now when I try to understand the passion I retain for fishing, my willingness to go halfway around the world, I trace it back to Highland Lake, to the fact that fishing there was so hard, that I am still, late in life looking for the rewards denied me when I was a boy; some of my friends, I think, still fish because of what they caught when they were boys—I fish, in no small part, because of what I didn't catch as a boy.

I was not good with a fly rod in the beginning and it was frustrating at first, but year after year, the more I practice, the better I've become, and I like that— it's a rare thing, to feel that you're getting better at something in your sixties and even in your seventies; mostly the opposite is true, the things you did so easily when you were young fade from your mastery. My equipment has gotten better, lighter and whippier. The telescopic rods of my childhood are but a distant memory (I do remember, as I write this, oiling those rods with three-in-one oil, so that they would not rust) relegated to an imaginary place that all of us have, the museum of childhood things, a place of memories rather than objects, and a reminder of how lucky I've been and how far I've come and how I do things now that once seemed so far out of reach. The venues, even as I visit them, stagger me, for their geographic reach—I who read *Field & Stream* faithfully as a boy, and thought that anyone who fished in Canada for salmon or in northern Minnesota for musky was blessed, now fly halfway around the world to fish. But the pleasures, I think, are much the same as the pleasures first discovered by that boy in Winsted more than sixty years ago. I remain forever a dreamer on the water, believing still, often against impressive evidence, that on the last cast of the day

I will beget my best strike, and even when that does not happen, that tomorrow will always be better than today.

**David Halberstam** was the winner of the 1964 Pulitzer Prize for international reporting. In the fall of 2007, his twenty-first book, *The Coldest Winter*, about the Chinese entry into the Korean War, was published by Hyperion. His prior fourteen books, starting with *The Best and the Brightest*, have been national bestsellers. He passed away in April 2007.

# INTRODUCTION

What a lot of fun I've had collecting the stories, memoirs, articles, and poems in this book. It is probably the largest, fullest, and most diverse collection of this sort ever compiled. And its very diversity and fullness are what excite me most—and what I predict will appeal to the vast number of people who share a love of fishing.

Surely there is a bond—too little acknowledged, I fear—between the catfish angler and the fly fisher. Both pursue a creature from that mysterious element, water, with some sort of bait, lure, or feathered thing. People have been fishing for a long time and parts of the practice have changed radically. Still, the early fish-hook (about which you can read an excellent essay in this book) persists, albeit in subtle new variations. The fishing done by a boy sometimes remains the same or sometimes evolves into one of many new forms. In this anthology, you will find both tradition and change—and some wonderful surprises, too.

There are selections from and about the earliest days of angling. There is a long section on warm-water fishing that includes some of James Henshall's classic writing about the small and largemouth basses and has John McPhee on shad, "the founding fish"; Ted Leeson on bluegill; James Prosek on eels; and John James Audubon on fishing for catfish in the Ohio River. Muskies, pike, bow-fin, pickerel, and carp are not wanting here, either.

A special section on salt-water angling includes writing about fishing for bonefish, sharks, tuna, weakfish, and the great tarpon. A longer section covers the trout and the variety of ways we fish for it (a good deal of the time with flies). Paul O'Neil's brilliant, often overlooked, essay "In Praise of Trout—And Also Me," caps this section. It was originally published in *Life* Magazine and is surely one of the best modern pieces of its kind; I'm proud to include it.

Howell Raines contributes a wonderful adventure narrative from his new book, *The One That Got Away*, and John Bryan's "The Miramichi it ain't"— which takes place much closer to home, in New York's Hudson River—is a wonderful example of how exciting and adventuresome fishing nearby can be. You don't have to go to the Himalayas for mahseer for real adventure—though that's here too.

There is much here about the variety of folks who fish—the famous (like Zane Grey, various presidents, and the great Norman Maclean) and the not-so-famous (but perhaps more addicted) people who bottom fish, fish with worms or fish with flies—and their passions, foibles and ways of doing this thing so many of us love.

And at the end I've included over twenty of my favorite stories, by de Maupassant, Kipling, John Taintor Foote, G. E. M. Skues and others. Forgive me if I've slipped in one I wrote, which rarely gets republished.

I hope you have as much fun reading this collection as I had bringing its pieces together from the vast world of writing about fishing. I hope you will be inspired to find more writings by the authors you most enjoy here, a good number of whom you'll probably be reading for the first time.

We spend more time off the water than on it. I hope you'll find those days at home a bit more enjoyable in the company of these memorable authors, anglers all.

*Nick Lyons*

THE BEST
# FISHING
# STORIES
EVER TOLD

# PART I

# EARLY
# DAYS—OF
# IT AND US

# THE PRIMITIVE FISH-HOOK

### BARNET PHILLIPS

I have before me an illustrated catalogue of modern fish-hooks and angling implements, and in looking over its pages I find an *embarrass de choix*. I have no need for rods, for mine, like well-kept violins, have rather improved by age. A lashing may be frayed, or a ferrule loose, but fifteen minutes' pleasant work will make my rods all right again. Lines are sound, for I have carefully stretched them after use. But my hooks! They are certainly the worse for wear. I began my season's fishing with a meager stock. Friends borrowed from me, and in replenishing my fly-book in an out-of-the-way place, the purchase was unsatisfactory. As I lost more than one fish from badly tempered or worse fashioned hooks, I recalled a delightful paper by Mr. Froude. Rod in hand, he was whipping some pleasant trout stream, near an historic site, the home of the Russells, and, breaking his hooks, commenced from that very moment to indulge in the gloomiest forebodings as to the future of England.

Fairly familiar with the general character of fishing-gear, either for business or amusement, I see in my book, Kirby, Limerick, Dublin, O'Shaughnessy, Kinsey, Carlisle, Harrison, Central Draught, as somewhat distant families of hooks, used for sea or river fishing, and from these main stocks there grow many varieties, with all conceivable twists, quirls, and crookednesses. I discard all trap-hooks, infernal machines working with springs, as only adapted for the capture of land animals. Somehow I remember an aggressive book, given to me at an early age, which, containing more than one depressing passage, had one of extraordinary malevolence. This was couched nearly as follows: "Suppose you were translated only some seven hundred years back, then, pray, what would you be good for? Could you make gunpowder? You have, perhaps, a vague idea that sulfur, saltpeter, and charcoal are the component parts, but do you know where or how they are procured?" I forget whether this dispiriting author was not equally harrowing in regard to the youthful reader's turning off a spectroscope at a minute's notice, or wound up with the modest request that you should try your hand among the Crusaders with an aneroid barometer of your own special manufacture.

Still this question arises: Suppose you were famishing, though fish were plenty in a stream, and you had neither line nor hook, What would you do? Now, has a condition of this kind ever occurred? Yes, it has, and certainly thousands of times. Not so many years ago, the early surveyors of the Panama route suffered terrible privations from the want of fishing implements. The rains had rendered their powder worthless; they could not use their guns. Had they only been provided with hooks and lines, they could have subsisted on fish. Then there are circumstances under which it would be really necessary for a man to be somewhat of a Jack-of-all-trades, and to be able to fashion the implements he might require, and so this crabbed old book might, after all, act in the guise of a useful reminder. There was certainly a period, when every man was in a condition of comparative helplessness, when his existence depended on his proficiency in making such implements as would catch fish or kill animals. He must fashion hooks or something else to take fish with, or die.

Probably man, in the first stage of his existence, took much of his food from the water, although whether he did or not might depend upon locality. If on certain portions of the earth's surface there were stretches of land intersected by rivers, dotted by lakes, or bordering on the seas, the presence of shell-fish, the invertebrates or the vertebrates, cetaceans and fish, to the exclusion of land animals, might have rendered primitive man icthyophagous, or dependent for subsistence upon the art of fishing. But herein we grapple at once with that most abstruse of all problems, the procession of life. Still, it is natural to suppose, so far as the study of man goes, when considered in relation to his pursuits, that in the early dawn of humanity, mammals, birds, and fish must have been synchronous.

After brute instinct, which is imitativeness, then came shiftiness and adaptiveness. The rapid stride of civilization, considered in its material sense, is due solely to the use of such implements as are specially adapted for a particular kind of work. With primitive man, this could never have been the case. Tools of the Paleolithic or Neolithic age (which terms indicate stages of civilization, but are not chronological), whether they were axes, hammers, or arrows, must have served river-drift or cave-men for more than a single purpose. People with few tools do manage by skill alone to adapt these to a variety of ends. The Fijian and the Russian peasant, one with a stone adze, the other with a hatchet, bring to their trades the minimum of tools. The Kafir, with his assegai, fights his battles, kills cattle, carves his spoons, and shaves himself. It was only as man advanced that he devised special tools for different purposes.

According to our present acquaintance with primitive habits, if man existed in the later Miocene age, and used a lance or spear for the killing of land animals, he probably employed the same weapons for the destruction of the creatures—possibly of gigantic form—inhabiting the seas, lakes, and rivers. The presence of harpoons made of bone, found in so many localities, belonging to a later period, may not in all cases point to the existence of animals, but to the presence of large fish.

Following, then, closely the advance of man, when his fishing implements are particularly considered, we are inclined to believe that he first used the spear for taking fish; next, the hook and line; and, lastly, the net. There might have been an intermediate stage between the spear and the hook, when the bow and arrow were used.

Interesting as is the whole subject of primitive fishing, we are, however, to occupy ourselves principally with the form of the primitive fish-hook. To-day, there are some careful archaeologists who are not willing to accept that particular form which is presented below. I believe, from the many reasons which can be advanced, that this simple form was the first device used by man in taking fish with a line. The argument I shall use is in some respects a novel one.

These illustrations, exactly copied to size, represent a small piece of dark, polished stone. It was found in the valley of the Somme, in France, and was dug out of a peat-bed twenty-two feet below the surface. The age of this peat-bed has been variously estimated. M. Boucher de Perthes thought that thirty thousand years must have elapsed since the lowest layer of peat was formed. The late Sir Charles Lyell and  Sir John Lubbock, without too strict an adherence to date, believed that this peat-bed represented in its formation "that vast lapse of time which began with the commencement of the Neolithic period." Later authorities deem it not older than seven thousand years B. C.

Wonderful changes have come to pass since this bit of polished stone was lost in what must have been a lake. Examining this piece of worked stone, which once belonged to a prehistoric man living in that valley, we find it fairly well polished, though the action of countless years has slightly "weathered" or disintegrated its once smooth surface. In the center, a groove has been cut, and the ends of the stone rise slightly from the middle. It is rather crescent-shaped. It must have been tied to a line, and this stone gorge was covered with a bait; the fish swallowed it, and, the gorge coming crosswise with the gullet, the fish was captured.

The evolution of any present form of implement from an older one is often more cleverly specious than logically conclusive; nevertheless, I believe that, in this case, starting with the crude fish-gorge, I can show, step by step, the complete sequence of the fish-hook, until it ends with the perfected hook of to-day. It can be insisted upon even that there is persistence of form in the descendants of this fish-gorge, for, as Professor Mitchell writes in his "Past in the Present," "an old art may long refuse to disappear wholly, even in the midst of conditions which seem to be necessarily fatal to its continued existence."

In the Swiss lakes are found the remains of the Lacustrine dwellers. Among the many implements discovered are fish-gorges made of bronze wire. When these forms are studied, the fact must be recognized at once that they follow, in shape and principle of construction, the stone gorges of the Neolithic period.

Now, it is perfectly well known that the early bronze-worker invariably followed the stone patterns. The Lacustrine gorges have had the name of *bricole* given them. This is a faithful copy of a bronze bricole found in the Lake of Neufchatel. It is made of bronze wire, and is bent in the simplest way, with an open curve allowing the line to be fastened to it. The ends of the gorge are very slightly bent, but they were probably sharpened when first made.

This bricole varies from the rather straight one found in the Lake of Neufchatel, and belongs to a later period. It is possible to imagine that the lake-dweller, according to his pleasure, made one or the other of these two forms of fishing implements. As the double hook required more bronze, and bronze at first was very precious, he might not have had material enough in the early period to make it. This device is, however, a clever one, for a fisherman of to-day who had lost his hook might imitate it with a bit of wire. Had any member of the hungry Isthmus party before mentioned known this form of Lacustrine hook, he might have twisted some part of a suspender buckle, providing there were no thorny plants at hand, and have caught fish.

When we compare the four forms, showing only their outlines, the evolution of the fish-hook can be better appreciated. Returning to the stone fish-gorge, the work of the Neolithic period, it is evident that the man of that time followed the shape handed down to him by his ancestors; and as this fashioned stone from the valley of the Somme is of a most remote period, how much older must have been the Paleolithic fish-gorge of rough stone. It might have been with a splinter of flint attached to some tendril, in lieu of a line, that the first fish was taken.

It is very curious to learn that in France a modification of this gorge-hook is in use to-day for catching eels. A needle is sharpened at its eye-end, a slight groove is made in the middle of it, and around this some shreds of flax are attached. A worm is spitted, a little of the line being covered with the bait.

Not eels alone are taken with this needle, for M. de la Blanchere informs us that many kinds of fish are caught with it in France.

Any doubts as to the use of the Neolithic form of fish-gorge must be removed when it can be insisted upon that precisely this form of implement was in use by our Indians not more than forty years ago. In 1878, when studying this question of the primitive hook, I was fortunate enough to receive direct testimony on the subject. My informant, who in his younger days had lived among the Indians at the head-waters of Lake Superior, said that in 1846 the Indians used a gorge made of bone to catch their fish. My authority, who had never seen a prehistoric fish-gorge, save the drawing of one, said that the Indian form was precisely like the early shape, and that the Chippewas fished some with the hook of civilization, others with bone gorges of a primitive period.

In tracing the history of the fish-hook, it should be borne in mind that an overlapping of periods must have taken place. By this is meant, that at one and the same time an individual employed tools or weapons of various periods. To-day, the Western hunter lights his fire with a match. This splinter of wood, tipped with phosphorus, the chlorates, sulfur, or paraffin, represents the progress made in chemistry from the time of the alchemists. But this trapper is sure to have stowed away in his pouch, ready for an emergency, his flint and steel. The Esquimau, the Alaskan, shoots his seal with an American repeating rifle, and, in lieu of a knife, flays the creature with a flint splinter. The net of the Norseman is to-day sunk with stones or buoyed with wood,—certainly the same devices as were used by the early Scandinavian,—while the  net, so far as the making of the thread goes, is due to the best modern mechanical appliances. Survival of forms requires some consideration apart from that of material, the first having the much stronger reasons for persistence. It is, then, very curious to note that hooks not made of iron and steel, but of bronze, or alloys of copper, are still in use on the coast of Finland, as I have quite recently obtained brass hooks from Northern Europe such as are commonly in use by fishermen there.

The origin of the double hook having been, I believe, satisfactorily explained, to make the barb on it was readily suggested to primitive man, as he had used the same device on fish-spears and harpoons.

This double-barbed hook from the Swiss lakes is quite common. Then, from the double to the single hook the transition was rapid. Single bronze hooks of the Lacustrine period sometimes have no barb. Such differences as exist are due to the various methods of attaching the line.

In Professor A. M. Mayer's collection there is a Lacustrine bronze hook, the shank of which is bent over parallel with the stem of the hook. This hook is a large one, and must have been used for big fish—probably the trout of the Swiss lakes.

Hooks made of stone are exceedingly rare, and though it is barely possible that they might have been used for fish, I think this has not been conclusively shown. Wilson gives, in his work, drawings of two stone hooks which were found in Scandinavia. Though the theory that these stone objects were fashioned for fishing is supported by so good an authority as Mr. Charles Rau, the archaeologist of the United States National Museum at Washington, it does not seem to me possible that these hooks could have been made for fishing. Such forms, from the nature of the material, would have been exceedingly difficult to fashion, and, even if made, would have presented few advantages over the primitive gorge.

This, however, must be borne in mind: in catching fish, primitive man could have had no inkling of the present curved form of fish-hook, which, with its barb, secures the fish by penetration. A large proportion of sea-fish, and many river-fish, swallow the hook, and are caught, not by the hook entering the jaws of the fish, but because it is fastened in their stomachs. In the Gloucester fisherman's language of to-day, a fish so captured is called "poke-hooked"; and accordingly, when the representative of the Neolithic period fished in that lake in the valley of the Somme, all

the fish he took must have been poke-hooked. A bone hook, excellent in form, has been found near the remains of a huge species of pike (*Esox*). Hooks made of the tusks of the wild boar have also been discovered with Lacustrine remains.

In commenting on the large size of the bone hook figured in Wilson's work, its proximity to the remains of large fish was noticed. When the endless varieties of hooks belonging to savage races are subjects of discussion, the kind of fish they serve for catching should always be cited. In the examples

of hooks which illustrate works of travel, a good many errors arise from the simple fact that the writers are not fishermen. Although the outline of a hook be accurately given, the method of securing it to the line is often incorrectly drawn.

In the engraving on this page, an Alaskan halibut-hook is represented.

The form is a common one, and is used by all the savage races of the Pacific; but the main interest lay in the manner of tying the line to this hook. Since the fish to be caught was the halibut, the form was the best adapted to the taking of the *Hippoglossus Americanus*; but had the line been attached in any other way than exactly as represented, this big fish could hardly have been caught with such a hook.

In the drawing, the halibut-hook hangs but slightly inclining toward the sea-bottom, the weight of the bait having a tendency to lower it. In this position it can be readily taken by the fish; but should it be suspended in a different way, it must be at once seen how difficult it would be for the fish to swallow it. In this Alaskan hook must be recognized the very first idea of what we call to-day the center-draught hook. A drawing is also given of a steel hook of a peculiar form coming from Northern Russia. The resemblance between the Alaskan and this Russian hook is at first apparently slight, but they both are, nevertheless, constructed on the same principle. When this Russian hook is seized by the fish, and force is applied to the line by the fisherman, the point of the barb and the line are almost in one and the same direction. Almost the same may be said

of the Alaskan hook. Desirous of testing the capabilities of this hook, I had a gross made after the Russian model, and sent them to Captain J. W. Collins, of the United States Fish Commission, stationed at Gloucester, requesting him to distribute them among the fishermen. While writing this article, I am in receipt of a letter from Captain Collins, informing me that these hooks are excellent, the captains of fishing-smacks reporting that a great many deep-sea fish were taken with them.

A study of these hooks—the Alaskan and the Russian—with reference to the

method of attaching the line, explains, I think, the peculiarity of certain shell-hooks of great antiquity found in California which have puzzled archaeologists. These hooks, the originals of which are to be found in the National Museum at Washington, are shown in the following engravings. The notch cut in one of the hooks seems to show that the line was attached at that place. Hang the hooks in any other position and they would catch no fish, for one could hardly suppose that the blunt barb could penetrate the mouth of the fish.

If there be some doubt entertained by American archaeologists as to the use of these shell-hooks, there can be none in regard to their having barbs. The barbs turn outward, in which respect they differ from all the primitive European hooks I have seen. In confirmation of the idea advanced as to the proper place of attaching the line, Professors C. C. Abbott and F. W. Putnam, in a chapter entitled "Implements and Weapons made of Bone and Wood," in the United States Geographical Survey, west of the hundredth meridian, write, referring to these hooks: "These hooks are flattened and are longer than wide . . . The barbs in these specimens are judged by fishermen of to-day to be on the wrong side of a good fish-hook, and the point is too near the shank. By having the line so fastened that the point of tension is at the notch at the base of the shank, instead of at the extreme end of the stem, the defect of the design of the hook would be somewhat remedied, as the barb would be forced down, so that it might possibly catch itself in the lower jaw of the fish that had taken the hook." The summing up of this is, I think, that in an imperfect way the maker of this Santa Barbara hook had some idea of the efficiency of a center-draught hook. As the first step in manufacturing this hook, a hole was drilled in the shell, and the hook finished up afterward by rounding the outside. Dr. West, of Brooklyn, has a series of such primitive work in his collection.

To advance the idea that in all cases hooks have been improved by slightly increased culture among semi-civilized races would be a source of error. It is quite possible that in many instances there has been retrogression from the better forms of fishing implements once in use. This relapse might have been brought about, not so much by a decrease of intelligence, as changes due to fortuitous causes. A fishing race might have been driven away from a shore or a river-bank and replaced by an inland people.

Some primitive races still use a hook made from a thorn, and in this practice we find to-day a most wonderful survival. On the coast of France, hooks made of thorns are still used to catch fish, the fishermen representing that they possess the great advantage of costing nothing and of not fouling on the sea-bottom. The Piutes take the spine of a cactus, bending it to suit their purpose, and very simple barbless hooks of this kind may be seen in the collections of the National Museum at Washington.

Undoubtedly, in primitive times, hooks of a compound character were used. Just as men tipped a deer's antler with a flint, they combined more than one material in the making of their hooks, lashing together a shank of bone or wood with a bronze barb. It would be almost impossible in a single article to follow all the varieties of hooks used and the ingenuity displayed in their manufacture. Occasionally, a savage will construct a lure for fish which rivals the daintiest fly ever made by the most fastidious of anglers. In Professor Mayer's collection there is an exceedingly clever hook, coming from the North-western coast, which shows very fine lapidary work. A small red quartoze pebble of great hardness has been rounded, polished, and joined to a piece of bone. The piece is small, not more than an inch and three-quarters in length, and might weigh an ounce and a half. In the shank of bone a small hook is hidden. It somewhat imitates a shrimp. The parts are joined together by lashings of tendon, and these are laid in grooves cut into the stone. It must have taken much toil to perfect this clever artificial bait, and, as it is to-day, it might be used with success by a clever striped-bass fisherman at Newport.

In this necessarily brief study of primitive fishing, I have endeavored to show the genesis of the fish-hook, from the stone gorge to the more perfected implement of to-day. Simple as it may seem, it is a subject on which a good deal of research is still requisite. "It is not an acquaintance with a single series of things which can throw light on any subject, but a thorough comparison of the whole of them." If in the Swiss lakes there are found bronze hooks of a very large size, out of proportion to the fish which swim there to-day, it is but just to suppose that, many thousands of years ago, long before history had its dawn, the aquatic fauna were then of greater bulk than in 1883. Considerations of the primitive form of the fish-hook must even comprehend examination of prior geological conditions, differences of land and water, or such geographical changes as may have taken place. Then ichthyology becomes an important factor, for by the character of the hook, the kind of fish taken, in some instances, may be understood. We are fast coming to this conclusion: that, putting aside what can only be the merest speculations as to the condition of man when he is said to have first diverged from the brute, he was soon endowed with a wonderful degree of intelligence. And, if I am not mistaken, primitive man did not confine himself in his fishing to the rivers and lakes alone, but went out boldly to sea after the cod.

# ÆLIAN—THE MACEDONIAN INVENTION, OR THE FIRST MENTION OF AN ARTIFICIAL FLY

## WILLIAM RADCLIFFE

"They knew 'e stole; 'e knew they knowed;
  They did not tell, or make a fuss,
But winked at Ælian down the road,
And 'e winked back—the same as us!"[1]

Ælian (170–230 A. D.), who, though born in Italy and brought up in the Latin tongue, acquired so complete a command of Greek that he could speak it as well as an Athenian gentleman (hence his sobriquet μεʹγλωττος), composed his works in Greek.

---

[1]    After Kipling.

His *Natural History*[2] soon became a standard work on Zoology, although in arrangement it is very defective: for instance, he skips from elephants (XI. 15) to dragons in the very next chapter, and from the livers of mice in II. 56 to the uses of oxen in II. 57. This treatment of things, ποικ'ιλα ποικ'ιλως, is asserted by the author to be intentional, so as to avoid boring the reader. For his part he avows that he prefers observing the habits of animals and fish, listening to the nightingale, or studying the migration of cranes, to heaping up riches![3]

Whether as a naturalist Ælian possesses any value, whether his work is "scrappy and gossiping, and largely collected from older and more logical writers,"[4] or "from the industry displayed, despite deficiency in arrangement, a valuable collection in Natural History," to us fishermen matters little, for unto him has been ascribed the great glory of being the first author of all ages and of all countries specially to mention and roughly describe an Artificial Fly.

And not only is he the first, but also (with possibly one exception) the only author during fourteen hundred years, who makes any reference to any such fly.[5] From Ælian until the *Treatyse of Fysshynge with an Angle* we find no mention of, or allusion to, the Artifical Fly, but that it was well known as a method of angling is easily deduced from the authoress's abrupt introduction of the subject, "These ben the xij flies or dubbes with which ye shall angle."[6]

The usually accurate *Bibliotheca Piscatoria* of Westwood and Satchell states under heading of 'Ælian,' that Stephen Oliver (Mr. Chatto), in his *Scenes and Recollections of Fly Fishing*, first pointed out this remarkable passage. Now the first edition of Oliver's book is dated 1834; so, if the *Bibliotheca Piscatoria* be correct,

---

[2]  Περ'ι Ζ'ωων 'ι'οι'οτηος.

[3]  See Smith's *Dict. Gk. And Rom. Biog. And Myth., s.v. 'Aelian.'*

[4]  Perizonius has proved that Aelian transferred large portions of the *Deipnosophistæ* of Athenaeus to his *Varia Historia,* a robbery which must have been committed almost in the lifetime of the pillaged author: that Aelian extended such transference to his *Natural History* also, his story of the *Pinna*, and others would seemingly demonstrate. Sir J. E. Sandys, *A History of Classical Scholarship*, ed. 2 (Cambridge, 1906), i. 336, goes so far as to say: "He is the author of seventeen books *On Animals*, mainly borrowed from Alexander of Myndos (first century A.D.)."

[5]  Dr. W. J. Turrell, *op. cit.*, XI., states that a Latin poem written by Richard de Fournival, about the thirteenth century, alludes incidentally to fishing, and from this it appears that the fly and the worm were among the lures then used by anglers, but does not state expressly whether Fournival's *fly* was natural or artificial.

[6]  Cf. H. Mayer, *Sport with Rod and Line*, Barnet and Phillips, New York.

Ælian's statement apparently remained unknown to Anglers for nearly eighteen centuries.

I purposely set out a translation of the whole passage in Ælian, XV. 1, because short extracts are usually given, and because these vary greatly on a very important point. I adopt with some alterations the translation by Mr. O. Lambert in his *Angling Literature in England* (1881).

"I have heard of a Macedonian way of catching fish, and it is this: between Beroea and Thessalonica runs a river called the Astraeus, and in it there are fish with speckled skins; what the natives of the country call them you had better ask the Macedonians. These fish feed on a fly peculiar to the country, which hovers on the river. It is not like flies found elsewhere, nor does it resemble a wasp in appearance, nor in shape would one justly describe it as a midge or a bee, yet it has something of each of these. In boldness it is like a fly, in size you might call it a midge, it imitates the color of a wasp, and it hums like a bee. The natives generally call it the *Hipporous*.

"These flies seek their food over the river, but do not escape the observation of the fish swimming below. When then the fish observes a fly on the surface, it swims quietly up, afraid to stir the water above, lest it should scare away its prey; then coming up by its shadow, it opens its mouth gently and gulps down the fly, like a wolf carrying off a sheep from the fold or an eagle a goose from the farmyard; having done this it goes below the rippling water.

"Now though the fishermen know of this, they do not use these flies at all for bait for fish; for if a man's hand touch them, they lose their natural color, their wings wither, and they become unfit food for the fish. For this reason they have nothing to do with them, hating them for their bad character; but they have planned a snare for the fish, and get the better of them by their fisherman's craft.

"They fasten red (crimson red) wool round a hook, and fix on to the wool two feathers which grow under a cock's wattles, and which in color are like wax. Their rod is six feet long, and their line is the same length. Then they throw their snare, and the fish, attracted and maddened by the color, comes straight at it, thinking from the pretty sight to get a dainty mouthful; when, however, it opens its jaws, it is caught by the hook and enjoys a bitter repast, a captive."

The lines which describe the making up of the fly—τ῿ω αγκίστρω περιβάλλουσιν ῾εριον φοινικόυν, ῾ηρμοστάι τε τ῿ω εριω δ῾υο πτερά ῾αλεκτρυόνος ῾υπό τοῖς καλλάισις πεφυκότα καί κηρ῾ωτ῾ην χρ῾υαν προσεικασμένα[7] are translated in Westwood and Satchell's *Bibl. Pisc.*, and by Mr. Lambert quite differently.

---

[7]  Jacobs adopts κηρ῾ω, instead of Gesner's χρυσ῾ω, chiefly because it is written thus quite clearly in the Codex Augustanus. It also seems to fit the context better.

*In the Bibl. Pisc.:*

"Round the hook they twist scarlet wool, and two wings are secured on this wool from the feathers which grow under the wattles of a cock, brought up to the proper color with wax."

In Lambert:

"They fasten red wool round a hook and fit on the wool two feathers which grow under a cock's wattles, and which in color are like wax."

It is asserted in the *Bibl. Pisc.* that the whole passage is therein "for the first time, accurately, translated," but this proud boast must take a back seat, for Mr. Lambert translates with far nearer accuracy. One grave error springs from mistranslation in the former of προσεικασμ'ενα as "brought up to," instead of "like," a meaning very common in Greek writers in the second and third century.

But, apart from the question which of the two be better rendering, no doubt whatever can exist which of the flies described would be found the better, if not the only, killer. Application of wax to the hackles of a cock would certainly cause the fiber to stick together, entirely destroy their free play in the water, and render them useless as wings.

This passage, ever since its rediscovery by Oliver in 1834, has been acclaimed by most writers on Fishing as (A) being the first instance in literature, or for that matter in art, of the Artificial Fly, and as (B) ascribing to the Macedonians the credit of a "new invention" in Angling.

It is undoubtedly the first and only express mention of a specially made-up Artificial Fly down to 500 A.D., and probably even down to Dame Juliana's Book (*c.* 1500). But I suggest and believe that this passage is intended, not as a description of a "new invention," or of a striking departure from old methods of Angling. It merely instances the Macedonian's adaptability to his environment, and his imitative skill in dressing from his wools and feathers a fly to resemble as closely as possible the natural fly on which the fish were feeding, a practice very common among anglers of the present day.

So far from the Artificial Fly being a "new invention," it seems to me to have been for a long time in more or less regular use. The materials necessary or employed for dressing flies are set forth in two other places by Ælian in this same work. The Macedonian fly is described at length and in special detail, probably because it marked an advance in making up a fly.

I have not been able so far to find the passages in Bk. III. 43, and Bk. XV. 10, mentioned (except in Blümner's general list of fishing weapons under *"Fischfang"*[8])

---

[8]    Die römischen Privataltertümer (Munich, 1911), pp. 529–530.

or alluded to in connection with fly-making, much less brought into the prominence which their special pertinence of a surety deserves and demands.

This omission may be due to previous writers being content with the authority and researches of Oliver and of Westwood and Satchell, and on the line of least exertion not pursuing the subject any further even in the pages of Ælian himself. If they had so pursued, they would have discovered in the first passage in Bk. XII. 43, which is separated by only three books, and in the second passage in Bk. XV. 10, which is separated by only nine chapters from the *locus classicus* in Bk. XV. I, strong inventions for qualifying their statement as to the Macedonian "invention."

In Bk. XII. 43, Fishing is divided into four kinds—by Nets, Spears, Weels, and Hooks; that by hooks (αγκιστρε'ια) is adjudged "the most skilful, and most becoming for free men," that by Weels (κυρτε'ια) the least so. In each class Ælian carefully enumerates the articles necessary or generally used.

The list of those necessary for fishing with hooks, or Angling, recounts "natural horsehair, white, and black, and flame-colored, and half-grey; but of the dyed hair, they select only those that are grey, or of true sea-purple, for the rest, they say, are pretty poor. They use, too, the straight bristles of swine, and thread, and much copper and lead, and cords." Now follow the important words—"and feathers, chiefly white or black, or various. They use two wools, red and blue."[9]

Further requirements are "corks, and wood, and iron, and of things they need, are reeds well-grown, and nets, and soaked rushes, a shaved wand, and a dog-wood Rod, and the horns and hide of a she-goat." The equipment is as ample as amazing. What use, in the name of every fishing Deity, unless the author is referring to Oppian's method, did the *Angler* make of the "horns and hide of a she-goat"?

Ælian concludes with αλλος δ'ε'αλλω το'υτων ιχθ'υς αιρε'ι ται, which antedates the tale of the millionaire, who, reproached with having brought a thousand times too many flies, ejaculated, "With some of these, if I can't get a salmon, maybe I'll strike a sucker!"

In XV. 10, which deals with the capture of pelamyde or young tunny fish, one of the crew sitting at the stern lets down on either side of the ship lines with hooks. On each hook he ties a bait (perhaps not a bait in our modern technical

---

[9] Κα'ι πτεροις, μ'αλιστα μ'εν λευκοις κα'ι ποικ'ιλοις. Χρ'ωντα'ι γε μ'ην ο'ι 'αλιεις κα'ι φοινικο'ις'ερ'ιοις κα'ι αλουργ'εσι, κ.τ.λ.

sense, but rather a lure) wrapped in wool of Laconian red, and to each hook attaches the feather of a seamew.[10]

Let us set aside, because of Ælian's haphazard method of arrangement, any argument which might otherwise fairly be adduced from the following facts. (A) He expressly sets forth in XII. 43 (three books before he mentions the Macedonian device) *red and other wools and feathers* as part of the *ordinary tackle* of an Angler—most probably in river or lake, for here, unlike XV. 10, where the prey is a sea-fish, we have no mention of a ship, oars, etc. (B) When he does mention the Macedonian device, he does not announce it in any way as a new invention or a striking departure from the old methods of fishing, but quite simply, in the words: "I have heard of the Macedonian way of fishing, and it is this."

Setting aside, I repeat, any arguments thus to be deduced, we are face to face with the hard and curious fact, that in all three passages the materials, out of which the lures are constructed, *are the same*; they are wools of various colors, and feathers taken from birds, in XV. I, from a cock, in XV. 10, from a seamew.

Any assertion or suggestion that these wools and feathers were used, and are specially stated to have been used for tying only the Macedonian fly, and that this special statement of such uses is meant expressly to differentiate the Macedonian from all other ways of fishing, and thus constitutes the first mention of an Artificial Fly, I counter by a couple of queries.

Why in XII. 43, and XV. 10, are these self-same wools and feathers set out among the necessary ordinary requisite tackle of a fisherman, if they were not used for dressing a fly, perhaps more primitive but still Artificial? And, if they were not so used, to what other fishing purpose can they be fairly applied?

Again, let us for a moment grant that the Macedonian device was the absolutely new invention or the striking departure from all preceding angling methods, which, had artificial flies not previously been well known, it most certainly would have been. In this case, surely Ælian, meticulous in his examination and classification of the tackle, etc., needed for each of the four stated kinds of fishing, would have employed, when about to tell of this invention, words calling more instant attention to and far worthier of this great revolution than the simple, "I have heard of the Macedonian way of fishing, and it is this!"

As supporting my contention, a further point must be noted. In the list of tackle in XII. 43, wools and feathers are mentioned in a general manner, but in XV. 1, their use is particularized and elaborated. Similarly in the first passage

---

[10] κα'ι πτερ'ον'εκ'ασν λ'αρον 'εκ'αστω 'αγκ'ιστ ρω προσ'ηρτηται.

the making and material of Rods are given, but in the second (and here only) the particular length of rod is stated.

It is on these passages (XII. 43, and XV. 10) and on their natural implication, that I chiefly found my conclusion that (A) the practice of making up and fishing with some kind of artificial fly had been in more or less general use for a long time previous to the Macedonian device, and (B) that the device is quoted merely as an instance of a special, local, and improved adaptation of such usage—in a word as *le dernier cri* in flies![11]

If in Martial (*Ep.*, V. 18. 8) *musco*, not *musca*, should be read, then to Ælian would belong the credit of being the first to mention not only the use of the artificial fly, but also the use of the natural fly.

In XIV. 22, we read of the *Thymalus* (a kind of grayling), which alone of all fishes gives out after capture no fishy smell, but rather so fragrant an odor that one would almost swear that in his hand he held a freshly gathered bunch of thyme ("that herb so beloved by bees"), instead of a fish. Ælian then lays down that, while it is easy to catch this fish in nets, it is impossible to do so with a hook baited with *anything* except the κ′ωνωψ, *i.e.* the gnat, or more probably from the vivid description by one who has evidently suffered, the mosquito, "that horrid insect, a foe to man, both day and night, alike with his bite and his buzz."[12]

Here then, in XIV. 22, we get, if the conjecture *musco* should be held to deprive Martial of his priority, the first mention of angling with a *natural* fly.

The difficulty, obvious at once to the practical angler, of how the ancients (or even the moderns with all the elaborate perfections of Redditch) could manufacture a hook little enough to impale a mosquito did not escape Aldrovandi.[13] But the κ′ωνωψ, said to spring from the σκ′ωληκες, *i.e., larvæ* found in the sediment of vinegar, was apparently even smaller than his brother mosquito, the εμπ′ις.[14]

As not only with great care, and even then only on very fine wire, can the smallest modern hook, No. 000, be coaxed to impale a big gnat, the problem

---

[11]  If Sandys (antea, 185, note 4) be right about Ælian's work being "mainly borrowed from Alexander of Myndos," first century A.D., the artificial fly was probably well known in Martial's time.

[12]  πονηρ′ω μ′εν ζ′ωω κα′ι μεθ ′ημ′εραν κα′ι ν′υκτωρ ′ανθρ′ωποις κα′ι δακε′ιν κα′ι βο′ησαι.

[13]  For size of hooks, see *antea*, p. 157 and note 1.

[14]  Cf. Arist., *N. H.*, V. 19. The σκ′ωληξ of Aristotle is an immature product of generation which grows and finally becomes a pupa, or (so Aristotle believed) an egg giving birth to the perfect animal.

before the Ancients of impaling with a hook one, and this not even the largest, of the mosquito tribe seems insoluble. But perhaps Ælian's κ'ωνωψ (as probably also his ιππουρος) was far larger than its descendant of the present day, or perhaps our author has substituted by mistake the mosquito for some larger but similar gnat.

# THE COMPLEAT ANGLER
# (SELECTIONS)

## IZAAK WALTON AND CHARLES COTTON

Now for the art of catching fish, that is to say, how to make a man that was none to be an angler by a book, he that undertakes it shall undertake a harder task than Mr. Hales, a most valiant and excellent fencer, who, in a printed book called "A Private School of Defence" undertook by it to teach that art or science, and was laughed at for his labor. Not but many useful things might be learnt by that book, but he was laughed at because that art was not to be taught by words, but practice: and so must angling. And in this discourse I do not undertake to say all that is known or may be said of it, but I undertake to acquaint the reader with many things that are not usually known to every angler; and I shall leave gleanings and observations enough to be made out of the experience of all that love and practice this recreation, to which I shall encourage them. For angling may be said to be so like the mathematics that it can never be fully learnt; at least not so fully, but that there will still be more new experiments left for the trial of other men that succeed us.

But I think all that love this game may here learn something that may be worth their money, if they be not poor and needy men: and in case they be, I then wish them to forbear to buy it; for I write not to get money, but for pleasure, and this discourse boasts of no more; for I hate to promise much, and deceive the reader.

And however it proves to him, yet I am sure I have found a high content in the search and conference of what is here offered to the reader's view and censure. I wish him as much in the perusal of it. And so I might here take my leave, but will stay a little and tell him that whereas it is said by many that in fly-fishing for a trout, the angler must observe his twelve several flies for the twelve months of the year; I say he that follows that rule shall be sure to catch fish and be as wise as he that makes hay by the fair days in an almanac, and no surer; for those very flies that used to appear about and on the water in one month of the year may the following year come almost a month sooner or later, as the same year proves colder or hotter; and yet in the following discourse I have set down the twelve flies that are in reputation with many anglers, and they may serve to give him some light concerning them. And he may note that there are in Wales and other countries peculiar flies, proper to the particular place or country; and doubtless, unless a man makes a fly to counterfeit that very fly in that place, he is like to lose his labor, or much of it; but for the generality, three or four flies neat and rightly made, and not too big, serve for a trout in most rivers all the summer. And for winter fly-fishing it is as useful as an almanac out of date. And of these (because as no man is born an artist, so no man is born an angler) I thought fit to give thee this notice.

∽∾

And for you that have heard many grave, serious men pity anglers; let me tell you, Sir, there be many men that are by others taken to be serious and grave men which we condemn and pity. Men that are taken to be grave, because nature hath made them of a sour complexion, money-getting men, men that spend all their time first in getting, and next in anxious care to keep it, men that are condemned to be rich, and then always busy or discontented. For these poor-rich-men, we anglers pity them perfectly, and stand in no need to borrow their thoughts to think ourselves happy. No, no, Sir, we enjoy a contentedness above the reach of such dispositions, and as the learned and ingenuous Montaigne says, like himself freely, "When my cat and I entertain each other with mutual apish tricks, as playing with a garter, who knows but that I make my cat more sport than she makes me? Shall I conclude her to be simple, that has her time to begin or refuse sportiveness as freely as I myself have? Nay, who knows but that it is a defect of my not understanding her language (for doubtless cats talk and reason with one another) that we agree no better? and who knows but that she pities me for being no wiser, and laughs and censures my folly for making sport for her when we two play together?"

Thus freely speaks Montaigne concerning cats, and I hope I may take as great a liberty to blame any man, and laugh at him too, let him be never so serious, that hath not heard what anglers can say in the justification of their art and recreation. Which I may again tell you is so full of pleasure that we need not borrow their thoughts, to think ourselves happy.

⟡

PISCATOR. O, sir, doubt not but that angling is an art! Is it not an art to deceive a trout with an artificial fly? a trout! that is more sharp-sighted than any hawk you have named and more watchful and timorous than your high-mettled merlin is bold! And yet I doubt not to catch a brace or two tomorrow, for a friend's breakfast. Doubt not, therefore, Sir, but that angling is an art and an art worth your learning. The question is rather whether you be capable of learning it! for angling is somewhat like poetry, men are to be born so. I mean, with inclinations to it, though both may be heightened by practice and experience; but he that hopes to be a good angler must not only bring an inquiring, searching, observing wit, but he must bring a large measure of hope and patience and a love and propensity to the art itself; but having once got and practiced it, then doubt not but angling will prove to be so pleasant that it will prove to be, like virtue, a reward to itself.

VENATOR. Sir, I am now become so full of expectation, that I long much to have you proceed and in the order that you propose.

PISCATOR. Then first, for the antiquity of angling, of which I shall not say much but only this: some say it is as ancient as Deucalion's Flood; others, that Belus, who was the first inventor of godly and virtuous recreations, was the first inventor of angling; and some others say, for former times have had their disquisitions about the antiquity of it, that Seth, one of the sons of Adam, taught it to his sons, and that by them it was derived to posterity; others say that he left it engraven on those pillars which he erected and trusted to preserve the knowledge of mathematics, music, and the rest of that precious knowledge and those useful arts, which by God's appointment or allowance and his noble industry were thereby preserved from perishing in Noah's Flood.

These, sir, have been the opinions of several men, that have possibly endeavored to make angling more ancient than is needful or may well be warranted; but for my part, I shall content myself in telling you, that angling is much more ancient than the incarnation of our Savior; for in the Prophet Amos mention is made of fish-hooks; and in the Book of Job—which was long before the days of Amos, for that book is said to have been writ by Moses—mention is made also of fish-hooks, which must imply anglers in those times.

But, my worthy friend, as I would rather prove myself a gentleman, by being learned and humble, valiant and inoffensive, virtuous and communicable, than by any fond ostentation of riches, or, wanting those virtues myself, boast that these were in my ancestors—and yet I grant that where a noble and ancient descent and such merit meet in any man it is a double dignification of that person—so if this antiquity of angling—which for my part I have not forced—shall, like an ancient family, be either an honor or an ornament to this virtuous art which I profess to love and practice, I shall be the gladder that I made an accidental mention of the antiquity of it; of which I shall say no more, but proceed to that just commendation which I think it deserves.

And for that I shall tell you that in ancient times a debate hath risen, and it remains yet unresolved—whether the happiness of man in this world doth consist more in contemplation or action.

Concerning which some have endeavored to maintain their opinion of the first, by saying, "that the nearer we mortals come to God by way of imitation the more happy we are." And they say, "that God enjoys himself only by a contemplation of his own infiniteness, eternity, power, and goodness," and the like. And upon this ground many cloisteral men of great learning and devotion prefer contemplation before action. And many of the fathers seem to approve this opinion, as may appear in their commentaries upon the words of our Savior to Martha, Luke 10:41, 42.

And on the contrary there want not men of equal authority and credit that prefer action to be the more excellent, as namely "experiments in physic and the application of it, both for the ease and prolongation of man's life"; by which each man is enabled to act and do good to others, either to serve his country or do good to particular persons; and they say also "that action is doctrinal and teaches both art and virtue and is a maintainer of human society"; and for these and other like reasons to be preferred before contemplation.

Concerning which two opinions I shall forbear to add a third by declaring my own, and rest myself contented in telling you, my very worthy friend, that both these meet together, and do most properly belong to the most honest, ingenuous, quiet, and harmless art of angling.

And first, I shall tell you what some have observed, and I have found to be a real truth, that the very sitting by the river's side, is not only the quietest and fittest place for contemplation but will invite an angler to it. And this seems to be maintained by the learned Pet. du Moulin, who, in his discourse of the Fulfilling of Prophecies, observes that when God intended to reveal any future event or high notions to his prophets, he then carried them either to the deserts or the sea-shore, that having so separated them from amidst the press of people and business and the cares of the world he might settle their mind in a quiet repose, and make them fit for revelation.

༄༅

And for the lawfulness of fishing, it may very well be maintained by our Savior's bidding St. Peter cast his hook into the water and catch a fish for money to pay tribute to Caesar. And let me tell you that angling is of high esteem and of much use in other nations. He that reads the voyages of Ferdinand Mendez Pinto shall find that there he declares to have found a king and several priests a-fishing.

And he that reads Plutarch shall find that angling was not contemptible in the days of Marc Antony and Cleopatra and that they in the midst of their wonderful glory used angling as a principal recreation. And let me tell you that in the Scripture angling is always taken in the best sense and that though hunting may be sometimes so taken, yet it is but seldom to be so understood. And let me add this more. He that views the ancient ecclesiastical canons shall find hunting to be forbidden to churchmen, as being a toilsome, perplexing recreation; and shall find angling allowed to clergymen, as being a harmless recreation, a recreation that invites them to contemplation and quietness.

༄༅

My next and last example shall be that undervaluer of money, the late Provost of Eton College, Sir Henry Wotton, a man with whom I have often fished and conversed, a man whose foreign employments in the service of this nation and whose experience, learning, wit, and cheerfulness made his company to be esteemed one of the delights of mankind. This man, whose very approbation of angling were sufficient to convince any modest censurer of it, this man was also a most dear lover and a frequent practice of the art of angling; of which he would say, " 'Twas an employment for his idle time, which was not then idly spent"; for angling was, after tedious study, "a rest to his mind, a cheerer of his spirits, a diverter of sadness, a calmer of unquiet thoughts, a moderator of passions, a procurer of contentedness; and that it begot habits of peace and patience in those that professed and practiced it." Indeed, my friend, you will find angling to be like the virtue of humility, which has a calmness of spirit and a world of other blessings attending upon it.

Sir, this was the saying of that learned man, and I do easily believe, that peace and patience and a calm content did cohabit in the cheerful heart of Sir Henry Wotton, because I know that when he was beyond seventy years of age, he made this description of a part of the present pleasure that possessed him, as he sat quietly in a summer's evening on a bank a-fishing. It is a description of the spring, which, because it glides as soft and sweetly from his pen as that river does at this time, by which it was then made, I shall repeat it unto you:

This day Dame Nature seemed in love;
The lusty sap began to move;
Fresh juice did stir th' embracing vines,
And birds had drawn their valentines.
The jealous trout, that low did lie,
Rose at a well-dissembled fly;
There stood my friend with patient skill
Attending of his trembling quill.

Already were the eaves possessed
With the swift pilgrim's daubed nest;
The groves already did rejoice,
In Philomel's triumphing voice,
The showers were short, the weather mild,
The morning fresh, the evening smiled.
Joan takes her neat-rubbed pail, and now
She trips to milk the sand-red cow;

Where, for some sturdy foot-ball swain,
Joan strokes a syllabub or twain;

The fields and gardens were beset
With tulips, crocus, violet;

And now, though late, the modest rose
Did more than half a blush disclose.
Thus all looks gay, and full of cheer,
To welcome the new-liveried year.

These were the thoughts that then possessed the undisturbed mind of Sir Henry
Wotton. Will you hear the wish of another angler, and the commendation of his
happy life, which he also sings in verse; *viz.* Jo. Davors, Esq.?

Let me live harmlessly; and near the brink
Of Trent or Avon have a dwelling place,
Where I may see my quill or cork down sink
With eager bite of perch, or bleak, or dace;
And on the world and my Creator think;
Whilst some men strive ill-gotten goods t'embrace;
And others spend their time in base excess
Of wine or worse, in war and wantonness:

Let them that list these pastimes still pursue,
And on such pleasing fancies feed their fill,
So I the fields and meadows green may view,
And daily by fresh rivers walk at will
Among the daisies and the violets blue,
Red hyacinth, and yellow daffodil,
Purple Narcissus like the morning rays,
Pale gander-grass, and azure culver-keys.

I count it higher pleasure to behold
The stately compass of the lofty sky;
And in the midst thereof, like burning gold,
The flaming chariot of the world's great eye;
The watery clouds that in the air up-rolled,
With sundry kinds of painted colors fly;
And fair Aurora, lifting up her head,
Still blushing rise from old Tithonus' bed;

The hills and mountains raisèd from the plains,
The plains extended level with the ground,
The grounds divided into sundry veins,
The veins enclosed with rivers running round;
These rivers making way through nature's chains,
With headlong course into the sea profound;
The raging sea, beneath the valleys low,
Where lakes and rills and rivulets do flow;

The lofty woods, the forests wide and long,
Adorned with leaves, and branches fresh and green,
In whose cool bowers the birds with many a song
Do welcome with their quire the summer's queen;
The meadows fair where Flora's gifts among
Are intermixed with verdant grass between;
The silver-scalèd fish that softly swim
Within the sweet brook's crystal watery stream.

All these, and many more, of his creation
That made the heavens, the angler oft doth see,
Taking therein no little delectation,
To think how strange, how wonderful they be,
Framing thereof an inward contemplation,
To set his heart from other fancies free;
And whilst he looks on these with joyful eye,
His mind is rapt above the starry sky.

PISCATOR. The Trout is a fish highly valued, both in this and foreign nations. He may be justly said, as the old poet said of wine and we English say of venison, to be a generous fish; a fish that is so like the buck, that he also has his seasons; for it is observed that he comes in and goes out of season with the stag and buck. Gesner says his name is of a German offspring, and says he is a fish that feeds clean and purely, in the swiftest streams, and on the hardest gravel, and that he may justly contend with all fresh water fish, as the mullet may with all sea fish, for precedency and daintiness of taste; and that being in right season, the most dainty palates have allowed precedency to him.

And before I go farther in my discourse, let me tell you that you are to observe that as there be some barren does that are good in summer, so there be some barren trouts that are good in winter; but there are not many that are so; for usually they be in their perfection in the month of May and decline with the buck. Now you are to take notice that in several countries, as in Germany and in other parts, compared to ours, fish do differ much in their bigness and shape, and other ways; and so do trouts. It is well known that in the Lake Leman, the Lake of Geneva, there are trouts taken of three cubits long, as is affirmed by Gesner, a writer of good credit, and Mercator says the trouts that are taken in the Lake of Geneva are a great part of the merchandise of that famous city. And you are further to know that there be certain waters that breed trouts remarkable both for their number and smallness. I know a little brook in Kent that breeds them to a number incredible, and you may take them twenty or forty in an hour, but none greater than about the size of a gudgeon. There are also in divers rivers, especially that relate to, or be near to the sea, as Winchester or the Thames about Windsor, a little trout called a samlet or skegger Trout, in both which places I have caught twenty or forty at a standing, that will bite as fast and as freely as minnows; these be by some taken to be young salmons, but in those waters they never grow to be bigger than a herring.

There is also in Kent, near to Canterbury, a trout called there a Fordidge trout, a Trout that bears the name of the town where it is usually caught, that is accounted the rarest of fish, many of them near the bigness of a salmon, but known by their different color, and in their best season they cut very white; and none of these have been known to be caught with an angle, unless it were one that was caught by Sir George Hastings, an excellent angler, and now with God; and he hath told me, he thought that trout bit not for hunger but wantonness; and it is the rather to be believed, because both he then and many others before him have been curious to search into their bellies, what the food was by which they lived; and have found out nothing by which they might satisfy their curiosity.

Concerning which you are to take notice that it is reported by good authors that grasshoppers and some fish have no mouths, but are nourished and take breath by the porousness of their gills, man knows not how; and this may be believed, if we consider that when the raven hath hatched her eggs, she takes no further care, but leaves her young ones to the care of the God of nature, who is said, in the Psalms, "to feed the young ravens that call upon him." And they be kept alive and fed by a dew, or worms that breed in their nests, or some other ways that we mortals know not. And this may be believed of the Fordidge Trout which, as it is said of the stork that he knows his season, so he knows his times, I think almost his day, of coming into that river out of the sea, where he lives, and, it is like, feeds, nine months of the year, and fasts three in the River of Fordidge. And you are to note that those townsmen are very punctual in observing the time of beginning to fish for them; and boast much that their river affords a trout that exceeds all others. And just so does Sussex boast of several fish, as namely a Shelsey cockle, a Chichester lobster, an Arundel mullet, and an Amerly trout.

And now, for some confirmation of the Fordidge trout, you are to know that this Trout is thought to eat nothing in the fresh water; and it may be the better believed because it is well known that swallows, which are not seen to fly in England for six months in the year but about Michelmas leave us for a hotter climate, yet some of them that have been left behind their fellows have been found many thousands at a time in hollow trees, where they have been observed to live and sleep out the whole winter without meat; and so Albertus observes that there is one kind of frog that hath her mouth naturally shut up about the end of August and that she lives so all the winter; and though it be strange to some, yet it is known to too many among us to be doubted.

And so much for these Fordidge trouts, which never afford an angler sport, but either live their time of being in the fresh water by their meat formerly gotten in the sea, not unlike the swallow or frog, or by the virtue of the fresh water only; or as the birds of paradise and the chameleon are said to live, by the sun and the air.

There is also in Northumberland a trout called a bull-trout, of a much greater length and bigness than any in these southern parts; and there is in many rivers that relate to the sea salmon-trouts, as much different from others both in shape and in their spots, as we see sheep in some countries differ one from another in their shape and bigness, and in the fineness of the wool; and, certainly, as some pastures breed larger sheep; so do some rivers by reason of the ground over which they run breed larger trouts.

Now the next thing that I will commend to your consideration is that the trout is of a more sudden growth than other fish. Concerning which you are also to take notice that he lives not so long as the perch and divers other fishes do, as Sir Francis Bacon hath observed in his History of Life and Death.

And next you are to take notice that he is not like the crocodile, which if he lives never so long, yet always thrives till his death; but 'tis not so with the trout, for after he is come to his full growth, he declines in his body, and keeps his bigness or thrives only in his head till his death. And you are to know that he will about (especially before), the time of his spawning get almost miraculously through weirs and flood-gates against the stream, even through such high and swift places as is almost incredible. Next, that the trout usually spawns about October or November, but in some rivers a little sooner or later. Which is the more observable because most other fish spawn in the spring or summer when the sun hath warmed both the earth and water and made it fit for generation. And you are to note that he continues many months out of season; for it may be observed of the trout that he is like the buck or the ox that will not be fat in many months, though he go in the very same pastures that horses do which will be fat in one month; and so you may observe that most other fishes recover strength and grow sooner fat and in season than the trout doth.

And next you are to note that till the sun gets to such a height as to warm the earth and the water the trout is sick and lean and lousy and unwholesome; for you shall in winter find him to have a big head and then to be lank and thin and lean; at which time many of them have sticking on them sugs, or trout-lice, which is a kind of worm in shape like a clove or pin with a big head, and sticks close to him and sucks his moisture; these, I think, the trout breeds himself, and never thrives till he free himself from them, which is till warm weather comes; and then, as he grows stronger, he gets from the dead, still water into the sharp streams and the gravel and there rubs off these worms or lice, and then as he grows stronger, so he gets him into swifter and swifter streams, and there lies at the watch for any fly or minnow that comes near to him; and he especially loves the May-fly, which is bred of the cod-worm or caddis; and these make the trout bold and lusty, and he is usually fatter and better meat at the end of that month than at any time of the year.

Now you are to know that it is observed that usually the best trouts are either red or yellow, though some, as the Fordidge trout, be white and yet good; but that is not usual. And it is a note observable that the female trout hath usually a less head and a deeper body than the male trout, and is usually the better meat. And note that a hog-back and a little head to any fish, either trout, salmon, or other fish, is a sign that that fish is in season.

But yet you are to note that as you see some willows or palm-trees bud and blossom sooner than others do, as some trouts be in some rivers sooner in season; and as some hollies or oaks are longer before they cast their leaves, so are some trouts in some rivers longer before they go out of season.

And you are to note that there are several kinds of trouts. But these several kinds are not considered but by very few men; for they go under the general name of trouts; just as pigeons do in most places, though it is certain there are tame and wild pigeons; and of the tame there be helmits and runts and carriers and croppers, and indeed too many to name. Nay, the Royal Society have found and published lately that there be thirty and three kinds of spiders; and yet all, for aught I know, go under that one general name of spider. And it is so with many kinds of fish, and of trouts especially, which differ in their bigness and shapes and spots and color. The great Kentish hens may be an instance, compared to other hens; and doubtless there is a kind of small trout which will never thrive to be big that breeds very many more than others do that be of a larger size. Which you may rather believe, if you consider that the little wren and titmouse will have twenty young ones at a time, when usually the noble hawk or the musical throstle or blackbird shall exceed not four or five.

And now you shall see me try my skill to catch a trout; and at my next walking, either this evening or tomorrow morning, I will give you directions how you yourself shall fish for him.

VENATOR. Trust me, master, I see now it is a harder matter to catch a trout than a chub; for I have put on patience and followed you these two hours and not seen a fish stir, neither at your minnow nor your worm.

PISCATOR. Well, scholar, you must endure worse luck sometime, or you will never make a good angler. But what say you now? There is a trout now, and a good one too, if I can but hold him; and two or three turns more will tire him. Now you see he lies still, and the sleight is to land him. Reach me that landing-net. So, Sir, now he is mine own. What say you now? is this not worth all my labor and your patience?

VENATOR. On my word, master, this is a gallant trout; what shall we do with him?

PISCATOR. Marry, e'en eat him to supper. We'll go to my hostess from whence we came; she told me, as I was going out of door, that my brother Peter, a good angler and a cheerful companion, had sent word he would lodge there tonight and bring a friend with him. My hostess has two beds, and I know you and I may have the best. We'll rejoice with my brother Peter and his friend, tell tales, or sing ballads, or make a catch, or find some harmless sport to content us, and pass away a little time without offence to God or man.

VENATOR. A match, good master, let's go to that house, for the linen looks white and smells of lavender, and I long to lie in a pair of sheets that smell so. Let's be going, good master, for I am hungry again with fishing.

PISCATOR. Nay, stay a little, good scholar. I caught my last trout with a worm, now I will put on a minnow and try a quarter of an hour about yonder tree for another, and so walk towards our lodging. Look you, scholar, thereabout we shall have a bite presently, or not at all. Have with you, Sir! On my word, I have hold of him. Oh, it is a great logger-headed chub! Come, hang him upon that willow twig, and let's be going.

⌒⊙⌒

VENATOR. Well now, good master, as we walk toward the river, give me direction, according to your promise, how I shall fish for a trout.

PISCATOR. My honest scholar, I will take this very convenient opportunity to do it.

The trout is usually caught with a worm or a minnow, which some call a penk, or with a fly, *viz.* either a natural or an artificial fly. Concerning which three I will give you some observations and directions.

And, first, for worms. Of these there be very many sorts, some bred only in the earth, as the earth-worm, others of or amongst plants, as the dug-worm, and others bred either out of excrements or in the bodies of living creatures, as in the horns of sheep or deer, or some of dead flesh, as the maggot or gentle, and others.

Now these be most of them particularly good for particular fishes. But for the trout the dew-worm, which some also call the lob-worm, and the brandling are the chief; and especially the first for a great trout, and the latter for a less. There be also of lob-worms some called squirrel-tails, a worm that has a red head, a streak down the back, and a broad tail, which are noted to be the best because they are the toughest and most lively and live longest in the water; for you are to know that a dead worm is but a dead bait and like to catch nothing, compared to a lively, quick, stirring worm. And for a brandling he is usually found in an old dunghill or some very rotten place near to it, but most usually in cow-dung or hog's-dung, rather than horse-dung, which is somewhat too hot and dry for that worm. But the best of them are to be found in the bark of the tanners which they have cast up in heaps after they have used it about their leather.

There are also divers other kinds of worms which for color and shape alter even as the ground out of which they are got; as the marsh-worm, the tag-tail, the flag-worm, the dock-worm, the oak-worm, the gilt-tail, the twachel or lob-worm, which of all others is the most excellent bait for a salmon, and too many to name, even as many sorts as some think there be of several herbs or shrubs or of several kinds of birds in the air. Of which I shall say no more but tell you that what worms so ever you fish with are the better for being long kept before they are used. And in case you have not been so provident, then the way to cleanse and scour them quickly is to put them all night in water if they be lob-worms, and then put them into your bag with fennel. But you must not put your brandlings above an hour in water and then put them into fennel, for sudden use; but if you have time and purpose to keep them long, then they be best preserved in an earthen pot, with good store of moss, which is to be fresh every three or four days in summer and every week or eight days in winter; or at least the moss taken from them and clean washed and wrung betwixt your hands till it be dry, and then put it to them again. And when your worms, especially the brandling, begins to be sick and lose of his bigness, then you may recover him by putting a little milk or cream, about a spoonful in a day, into them by drops on the moss; and if there be added to the cream an egg beaten and boiled in it, then it will both fatten and preserve them long. And note that when the knot which is near to the middle of the brandling begins to swell, then he is sick; and if he be not well looked to, is near dying. And for moss you are to note that there be divers kinds of it which I could name to you, but I will only tell you that which is likest; a buck's-horn is the best, except it be soft white moss that grows on some heaths and is hard to be found. And note that in a very dry time when you are put to an extremity for worms walnut-tree leaves squeezed into water, or salt in water to make it bitter or salt, and then that water poured on the ground where you shall see worms are used to rise in the night will make them to appear above ground presently.

And now, I shall show you how to bait your hook with a worm so as shall prevent you from much trouble and the loss of many a hook too, when you fish for a trout with a running line, that is to say, when you fish for him by hand at the ground. I will direct you in this as plainly as I can, that you may not mistake.

Suppose it be a big lob-worm. Put your hook into him somewhat above the middle and out again a little below the middle. Having so done, draw your worm above the arming of your hook; but note that at the entering of your hook it must not be at the head-end of the worm but at the tail-end of him, that the point of your hook may come out toward the head-end. And having drawn him above the arming of your hook, then put the point of your hook again into the very head of the worm till it come near to the place where the point of the hook first came out. And then draw back that part of the worm that was above the shank or arming of your hook, and so fish with it. And if you mean to fish with two worms, then put the second on before you turn back the hook's-head of the first worm. You cannot lose above two or three worms before you attain to what I direct you; and having attained it, you will find it very useful, and thank me for it. For you will run on the ground without tangling.

Now for the minnow, or penk, he is not easily found and caught till March, or in April, for then he appears first in the river, nature having taught him to shelter and hide himself in the winter in ditches that be near to the river, and there both to hide and keep himself warm in the mud or in the weeds, which rot not so soon as in a running river, in which place if he were in winter, the distempered floods that are usually in that season would suffer him to take no rest, but carry him headlong to mills and weirs to his confusion. And of these minnows, first, you are to know that the biggest size is not the best; and next, that the middle size and the whitest are the best; and then you are to know that your minnow must be so put on your hook that it must turn round when 'tis drawn against the stream, and, that it may turn nimbly, you must put it on a big-sized hook, as I shall now direct you, which is thus: put your hook in at his mouth, and out at his gill; then, having drawn your hook two or three inches beyond or through his gill, put it again into his mouth, and the point and beard out at his tail; and then tie the hook and his tail about very neatly with a white thread, which will make it the apter to turn quick in the water; that done, pull back that part of your line which was slack when you did put your hook into the minnow the second time; I say, pull that part of it back so that it shall fasten the head so that the body of the minnow shall be almost straight on your hook; this done, try how it will turn, by drawing it across the water or against a stream; and if it do not turn nimbly, then turn the tail a little to the right or left hand, and try again till it turn quick; for if not, you are in danger to catch nothing; for know, that it is impossible that it should turn too quick. And you are yet to know that in case you want a minnow, then a small loach, or a stickleback, or any other small fish will serve as well. And you are yet to know that you may salt them and by that means keep them fit for use three or four days or longer; and that of salt, bay-salt is the best.

And here let me tell you, what many old anglers know right well, that at some times and in some waters a minnow is not to be got; and therefore let me tell you I have (which I will show to you) an artificial minnow that will catch a trout as well as an artificial fly. And it was made by a handsome woman that had a fine hand, and a live minnow lying by her: the mould or body of the minnow was cloth and wrought upon or over it thus with a needle; the back of it with very sad French green silk, and paler green silk towards the belly, shadowed as perfectly as you can imagine, just as you see a minnow; the belly was wrought also with a needle, and it was, a part of it, white silk; and another part of it with silver thread; the tail and fins were of a quill which was shaven thin; the eyes were of two little black beads; and the head was so shadowed and all of it so curi-ously wrought and so exactly dissembled that it would beguile any sharp-sighted trout in a swift stream. And this minnow I will now show you, and if you like it, lend it you to have two or three made by it; for they be easily carried about an angler, and be of excellent use; for note that a large trout will come as fiercely at a minnow as the highest-mettled hawk doth seize on a partridge, or a greyhound on a hare. I have been told that one hundred sixty minnows have been found in a trout's belly. Either the Trout had devoured so many, or the miller that gave it a friend of mine had forced them down his throat after he had taken him.

Now for flies, which is the third bait wherewith trouts are usually taken. You are to know that there are so many sorts of flies as there be of fruits. I will name you but some of them: as the dun-fly, the stone-fly, the red-fly, the moor-fly, the tawny-fly, the shell-fly, the cloudy or blackish-fly, the flag-fly, the vine-fly; there be of flies, caterpillars and canker-flies, and bear-flies; and indeed too many either for me to name, or for you to remember. And their breeding is so various and wonderful that I might easily amaze myself and tire you in a relation of them.

And yet I will exercise your promised patience by saying a little of the caterpillar, or the palmer-fly or worm, that by them you may guess what a work it were in a discourse but to run over those very many flies, worms, and little living creatures with which the sun and summer adorn and beautify the river-banks and meadows, both for the recreation and contemplation of us anglers, and which, I think, myself enjoy more than any other man that is not of my profession.

Pliny holds an opinion that many have their birth or being from a dew that in the spring falls upon the leaves of trees, and that some kinds of them are from a dew left upon herbs or flowers; and others from a dew left upon coleworts or cabbages. All which kinds of dews, being thickened and condensed, are by the sun's generative heat most of them hatched and in three days made living creatures; and these of several shapes and colors; some being hard and tough; some smooth and soft; some are horned in their head, some in their tail, some have none; some have hair, some none; some have sixteen feet, some less, and some have none, but (as our Topsel hath with great diligence observed) those which have none move upon the earth or upon broad leaves, their motion being not unlike to the waves of the sea. Some of them he also observes to be bred of the eggs of other caterpillars and that those in their time turn to be butterflies; and again that their eggs turn the following year to be caterpillars. And some affirm that every plant has its particular fly or caterpillar which it breeds and feeds. I have seen, and may therefore affirm it, a green caterpillar, or worm, as big as a small peascod, which had fourteen legs, eight on the belly, four under the neck, and two near the tail. It was found on a hedge of privet, and was taken thence and put into a large box and a little branch or two of privet put to it, on which I saw it feed as sharply as a dog gnaws a bone. It lived thus five or six days and thrived and changed the color two or three times, but by some neglect in the keeper of it, it then died and did not turn to a fly. But if it had lived, it had doubtless turned to one of those flies that some call flies of prey, which those that walk by the rivers may in summer see fasten on smaller flies and I think make them their food. And 'tis observable that as there be these flies of prey which be very large, so there be others, very little, created I think only to feed them, and bred out of I know not what; whose life, they say, nature intended not to exceed an hour, and yet that life is thus made shorter by other flies, or accident.

'Tis endless to tell you what the curious searchers into nature's productions have observed of these worms and flies. But yet I shall tell you what Aldrovandus, our Topsel, and others say of the palmer-worm or caterpillar: that whereas others content themselves to feed on particular herbs or leaves (for most think those very leaves that gave them life and shape give them a particular feeding and nourishment and that upon them they usually abide), yet he observes that this is called a pilgrim or palmer-worm for his very wandering life and various food; not contenting himself, as others do, with any one certain place for his abode nor any certain kind of herb or flower for his feeding, but will boldly and disorderly wander up and down and not endure to be kept to a diet or fixed to a particular place.

Nay, the very colors of caterpillars are, as one has observed, very elegant and beautiful. I shall, for a taste of the rest, describe one of them which I will some time the next month show you feeding on a willow-tree, and you shall find him punctually to answer this very description: his lips and mouth somewhat yellow, his eyes black as jet, his forehead purple, his feet and hinder parts green, his tail two-forked and black, the whole body stained with a kind of red spots which run along the neck and shoulder-blade, not unlike the form of St. Andrew's cross or the letter X made thus crosswise, and a white line drawn down his back to his tail; all which add much beauty to his whole body. And it is to me observable that at a fixed age this caterpillar gives over to eat, and towards winter comes to be covered over with a strange shell or crust called an aurelia, and so lives a kind of dead life without eating all the winter. And as others of several kinds turn to be several kinds of flies and vermin the spring following, so this caterpillar then turns to be a painted butterfly.

⚬⚬⚬

VENATOR. Master, I can neither catch with the first nor second angle. I have no fortune.

PISCATOR. Look you, scholar, I have yet another. And now, having caught three brace of trouts, I will tell you a short tale as we walk towards our breakfast: a scholar—a preacher I should say—that was to preach to procure the approbation of a parish that he might be their lecturer had got from his fellow-pupil the copy of a sermon that was first preached with great commendation by him that composed and preached it; and though the borrower of it preached it word for word as it was at first, yet it was utterly disliked as it was preached by the second. Which the sermon-borrower complained of to the lender of it; and was thus answered: "I lent you, indeed, my fiddle, but not my fiddle-stick; for you are to know that everyone cannot make music with my words, which are fitted for my own mouth." And so, my scholar, you are to know that as the ill pronunciation or ill accenting of words in a sermon spoils it, so the ill carriage of your line or not fishing even to a foot in a right place makes you lose your labor. And you are to know that though you have my fiddle, that is, my very rod and tacklings with which you see I catch fish, yet you have not my fiddle-stick, that is, you yet have not skill to know how to carry your hand and line nor how to guide it to a right place. And this must be taught you—for you are to remember I told you angling is an art—either by practice or a long observation or both. But take this for a rule: when you fish for a trout with a worm, let your line have so much and not more lead than will fit the stream in which you fish; that is to say, more in a great troublesome stream than in a smaller that is quieter; as near as may be, so much as will sink the bait to the bottom and keep it still in motion, and not more.

But now, let's say grace, and fall to breakfast. What say you, scholar, to the providence of an old angler? Does not this meat taste well? and was not this place well chosen to eat it? for this sycamore-tree will shade us from the sun's heat.

VENATOR. All excellent good, and my stomach excellent too. And now I remember and find that true which devout Lessius says, "That poor men and those that fast often have much more pleasure in eating than rich men and gluttons, that always feed before their stomachs are empty of their last meat and so rob themselves of that pleasure that hunger brings to poor men." And I do seriously approve of that saying of yours, "That you had rather be a civil, well-grounded, temperate, poor angler than a drunken lord." But I hope there is none such. However, I am certain of this, that I have been at many very costly dinners that have not afforded me half the content that this has done, for which I thank God and you.

And now, good master, proceed to your promised direction for making and ordering my artificial fly.

PISCATOR. My honest scholar, I will do it, for it is a debt due unto you by my promise. And because you shall not think yourself more engaged to me than indeed you really are, I will freely give you such directions as were lately given to me by an ingenious brother of the angle, an honest man, and a most excellent fly-fisher.

You are to note that there are twelve kinds of artificial-made flies to angle with upon the top of the water. Note, by the way, that the fittest season of using these is in a blustering windy day, when the waters are so troubled that the natural fly cannot be seen, or rest upon them. The first is the dun-fly in March; the body is made of dun wool, the wings, of the partridge's feathers. The second is another dun-fly; the body of black wool, and the wings made of the black drake's feathers and of the feathers under his tail. The third is the stone-fly in April; the body is made of black wool made yellow under the wings and under the tail and so made with wings of the drake. The fourth is the ruddy-fly in the beginning of May; the body made of red wool, wrapt about with black silk, and the feathers are the wings of the drake, with the feathers of a red capon also, which hang dangling on his sides next to the tail. The fifth is the yellow or greenish fly, in May likewise; the body made of yellow wool; and the wings made of the red cock's hackle or tail. The sixth is the black-fly, in May also; the body made of black wool, and lapt about with the herle of a peacock's tail, the wings are made of the wings of a brown capon, with his blue feathers in his head. The seventh is the sad yellow-fly in June; the body is made of black wool, with a yellow list on either side, and the wings taken off the wings of a buzzard, bound with black braked hemp. The eighth is the moorish-fly; made with the body of duskish wool, and the wings made of the blackish mail of the drake. The ninth is the tawny-fly, good until the middle of June; the body made of tawny wool, the wings made contrary one against the other, made of the whitish mail of the wild drake. The tenth is the wasp-fly in July; the body made of black wool, lapt about with yellow silk, the wings made of the feathers of the drake or of the buzzard. The eleventh is the shell-fly, good in mid-July; the body made of greenish wool, lapt about with the herle of a peacock's tail, and the wings made of the wings of the buzzard. The twelfth is the dark drake-fly, good in August; the body made with black wool, lapt about with black silk, his wings are made with the mail of the black drake, with a black head. Thus have you a jury of flies likely to betray and condemn all the trouts in the river.

I shall next give you some other directions for fly-fishing such as are given by Mr. Thomas Barker, a gentleman that hath spent much time in fishing; but I shall do it with a little variation.

First, let your rod be light, and very gentle. I take the best to be of two pieces. And let not your line exceed, especially for three or four links next to the hook, I say, not exceed three or four hairs at the most, though you may fish a little stronger above, in the upper part of your line. But if you can attain to angle with one hair, you shall have more rises, and catch more fish. Now you must be sure not to cumber yourself with too long a line, as most do. And before you begin to angle, cast to have the wind on your back; and the sun, if it shines, to be before you, and to fish down the stream; and carry the point or top of your rod downward, by which means the shadow of yourself and rod too will be the least offensive to the fish; for the sight of any shade amazes the fish and spoils your sport, of which you must take great care.

In the middle of March—till which time a man should not in honesty catch a trout—or in April, if the weather be dark or a little windy or cloudy, the best fishing is with the palmer-worm, of which I last spoke to you; but of these there be divers kinds, or at least of divers colors. These and the May-fly are the ground of all fly-angling. Which are to be thus made:

First, you must arm your hook with the line in the inside of it; then take your scissors and cut so much of a brown mallard's feather as in your own reason, will make the wings of it, you having withal regard to the bigness or littleness of your hook; then lay the outmost part of your feather next to your hook; then the point of your feather next the shank of your hook; and having so done, whip it three or four times about the hook with the same silk with which your hook was armed; and having made the silk fast, take the hackle of a cock or capon's neck or a plover's top, which is usually better; take off the one side of the feather, and then take the hackle, silk, or crewel, gold or silver thread; make these fast at the bent of the hook, that is to say, below your arming; then you must take the hackle, the silver or gold thread, and work it up to the wings, shifting or still removing your finger as you turn the silk about the hook and still looking at every stop or turn that your gold or what materials soever you make your fly of do lie right and neatly; and if you find they do so, then when you have made the head, make all fast; and then work your hackle up to the head, and make that fast; and then with a needle or pin divide the wing into two; and then with the arming silk whip it about cross-ways betwixt the wings; and then with your thumb you must turn the point of the feather towards the bent of the hook; and then work three or four times about the shank of the hook; and then view the proportion; and if all be neat and to your liking, fasten.

I confess no direction can be given to make a man of a dull capacity able to make a fly well. And yet I know this, with a little practice, will help an ingenious angler in a good degree. But to see a fly made by an artist in that kind is the best teaching to make it. And then an ingenious angler may walk by the river and mark what flies fall on the water that day, and catch one of them, if he sees the trouts leap at a fly of that kind: and then having always hooks ready-hung with him and having a bag always with him with bear's hair or the hair of a brown or sad-colored heifer, hackles of a cock or capon, several colored silk and crewel to make the body of the fly, the feathers of a drake's head, black or brown sheep's wool, or hog's wool, or hair, thread of gold and of silver; silk of several colors, especially sad-colored, to make the fly's head; and there be also other colored feathers, both of little birds and of speckled fowl—I say, having those with him in a bag and trying to make a fly, though he miss at first, yet shall he at last hit it better even to such a perfection as none can well teach him. And if he hit to make his fly right and have the luck to hit also where there is store of trouts, a dark day, and a right wind, he will catch such store of them as will encourage him to grow more and more in love with the art of fly-making.

VENATOR. But, my loving master, if any wind will not serve, then I wish I were in Lapland, to buy a good wind of one of the honest witches that sell so many winds there and so cheap.

PISCATOR. Marry, scholar, but I would not be there, nor indeed from under this tree. For look how it begins to rain, and by the clouds, if I mistake not, we shall presently have a smoking shower, and therefore sit close. This sycamore-tree will shelter us. And I will tell you, as they shall come into my mind, more observations of fly-fishing for a trout.

But first for the wind, you are to take notice that of the winds the south wind is said to be best. One observes that

when the wind is south,
It blows your bait into a fish's mouth.

Next to that the west wind is believed to be the best. And having told you that the east wind is the worst, I need not tell you which wind is the best in the third degree. And yet, as Solomon observes, that "he that considers the wind shall never sow"; so he that busies his head too much about them, if the weather be not made extreme cold by an east wind, shall be a little superstitious. For as it is observed by some that "There is no good horse of a bad color"; so I have observed that if it be a cloudy day and not extreme cold, let the wind sit in what corner it will and do its worst. And yet take this for a rule, that I would willingly fish standing on the lee-shore. And you are to take notice that the fish lies or swims nearer the bottom and in deeper water in winter than in summer; and also nearer the bottom in any cold day, and then gets nearest the lee-side of the water.

But I promised to tell you more of the fly-fishing for a trout; which I may have time enough to do, for you see it rains May butter. First for a May-fly, you may make his body with greenish-colored crewel, or willowish color, darkening it in most places with waxed silk, or ribbed with black hair, or some of them ribbed with silver thread, and such wings for the color as you see the fly to have at that season, nay, at that very day on the water. Or you may make the oak-fly, with an orange-tawny and black ground, and the brown of a mallard's feather for the wings. And you are to know that these two are most excellent flies, that is, the May-fly and the oak-fly. And let me again tell you that you keep as far from the water as you can possibly, whether you fish with a fly or worm, and fish down the stream. And when you fish with a fly, if it be possible, let no part of your line touch the water, but your fly only; and be still moving your fly upon the water, or casting it into the water, you yourself being also always moving down the stream. Mr. Barker commends several sorts of the palmer-flies, not only those ribbed with silver and gold, but others that have their bodies all made of black, or some with red, and a red hackle. You may also make the hawthorn-fly, which is all black, and not big, but very small, the smaller the better. Or the oak-fly, the body of which is orange color and black crewel, with a brown wing. Or a fly made with a peacock's feather is excellent in a bright day. You must be sure you want not in your magazine-bag the peacock's feather and grounds of such wool and crewel as will make the grasshopper. And note that usually the smallest flies are the best; and note also that the light fly does usually make most sport in a dark day, and the darkest and least fly in a bright or clear day; and lastly note that you are to repair upon any occasion to your magazine-bag: and upon any occasion vary and make them lighter or sadder according to your fancy or the day.

And now I shall tell you that the fishing with a natural fly is excellent, and affords much pleasure. They may be found thus: the May-fly usually in and about that month near to the river-side, especially against rain; the oak-fly on the butt or body of an oak or ash from the beginning of May to the end of August; it is a brownish fly and easy to be so found, and stands usually with his head downward, that is to say, towards the root of the tree; the small black-fly, or hawthorn-fly, is to be had on any hawthorn bush after the leaves be come forth. With these and a short line, as I showed to angle for a chub, you may dape or dop, and also with a grasshopper, behind a tree or in any deep hole; still making it to move on the top of the water as if it were alive and still keeping yourself out of sight, you shall certainly have sport if there be trouts; yea, in a hot day, but especially in the evening of a hot day.

And now, scholar, my direction for fly-fishing is ended with this shower, for it has done raining. And now look about you, and see how pleasantly that meadow looks; nay, and the earth smells so sweetly too. Come let me tell you what holy Mr. Herbert says of such days and flowers as these, and then we will thank God that we enjoy them, and walk to the river and sit down quietly, and try to catch the other place of trouts.

Sweet day, so cool, so calm, so bright,
The bridal of the earth and sky,
Sweet dews shall weep thy fall tonight,
For thou must die.

Sweet rose, whose hue, angry and brave,
Bids the rash gazer wipe his eye,
Thy root is ever in its grave,
And thus must die.

Sweet spring, full of sweet days and roses,
A box where sweets compacted lie;
My music shows you have your closes,
And all must die.

Only a sweet and virtuous soul
Like seasoned timber never gives,
But when the whole world turns to coal,
Then chiefly lives.

VENATOR. I thank you, good master, for your good direction for fly-fishing and for the sweet enjoyment of the pleasant day, which is so far spent without offence to God or man; and I thank you for the sweet close of your discourse with Mr. Herbert's verses, which, I have heard, loved angling; and I do the rather believe it, because he had a spirit suitable to anglers and to those primitive Christians that you love and have so much commended.

∽

No life, my honest scholar, no life so happy and so pleasant as the life of a well-governed angler; for when the lawyer is swallowed up with business and the statesman is preventing or contriving plots, then we sit on cowslip-banks, hear the birds sing, and possess ourselves in as much quietness as these silent silver streams which we now see glide so quietly by us. Indeed, my good scholar, we may say of angling as Dr. Boteler said of strawberries, "Doubtless God could have made a better berry, but doubtless God never did"; and if so I might be judge, God never did make a more calm, quiet, innocent recreation than angling.

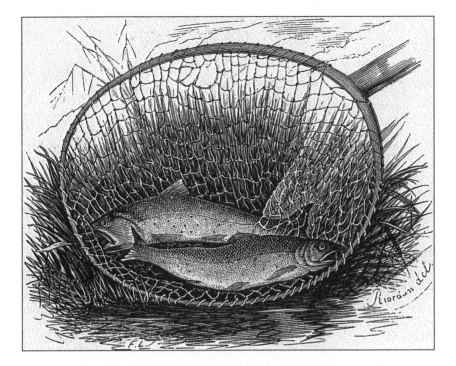

# TROUT: MEETING THEM ON THE "JUNE RISE"

## "NESSMUK"

There is a spot where plumy pines
O'erhang the sylvan banks of Otter;
Where wood-ducks build among the vines
That bend above the crystal water.

And there the blue-jay makes her nest
In thickest shade of water beeches;
The fish-hawk, statuesque in rest,
Keeps guard o'er glassy pools and reaches.

'Tis there the deer come down to drink,
From laurel brakes and wooded ridges;
The trout, beneath the sedgy brink,
Are sharp on ship-wrecked flies and midges.

And of the scores of mountain trout-streams that I have fished, the Otter is associated with the most pleasant memories.

It is, or was, a model trout-stream; a thing to dream of. Having its rise within three miles of the village, it meandered southward for ten miles through a mountain valley to its confluence with the second fork of Pine Creek, six miles of the distance being through a forest without settler or clearing.

The stream was swift, stony, and exceptionally free of brush, fallen timber and the usual *debris* that is so trying to the angler on most wooded streams. Then, it was just the right distance from town. It was so handy to start from the village in the middle of an afternoon in early summer, walk an hour and a half at a leisurely pace, and find one's self on a brawling brook where speckled trout were plenty as a reasonable man could wish.

Fishing only the most promising places for a couple of miles always gave trout enough for supper and breakfast, and brought the angler to the "Trout-House," as a modest cottage of squared logs was called, it being the last house in the clearings and owned by good-natured Charley Davis, who never refused to entertain fishermen with the best his little house afforded. His accommodations were of the narrowest, but also of the neatest, and few women could fry trout so nicely as Mrs. Davis. True, there was only one spare bed, and, if more than two anglers desired lodgings, they were relegated to the barn, with a supply of buffalo skins and blankets. On a soft bed of sweet hay this was all that could be desired by way of lodgings, with the advantage of being free from mosquitoes and punkies. The best of rich, yellow butter with good bread were always to be had at Charley's, and his charges were 12½ cents for meals, and the same for lodgings.

The two miles of fishing above the "Trout-House" led through clearings, and the banks were much overgrown with willows, making it expedient to use bait, or a single fly. I chose the latter; my favorite bug for such fishing being the red hackle, though I am obliged to confess that the fellow who used a white grub generally beat me.

But the evening episode was only preliminary; it meant a pleasant walk, thirty or forty brook-trout for supper and breakfast, and a quiet night's rest. The real angling commenced the next morning at the bridge, with a six-mile stretch of clear, cold, rushing water to fish. My old-fashioned creel held an honest twelve pounds of dressed trout, and I do not recollect that I ever missed filling it, with time to spare, on that stretch of water. Nor, though I could sometimes fill it in a forenoon, did I ever continue to fish after it *was* full. Twelve pounds of trout is enough for any but a trout-hog.

But the peculiar phase of trout lore that most interested me, was the "run" of trout that were sure to find their way up stream whenever we had a flood late in May or the first half of June. They were distinct and different from the trout that came up with the early spring freshets. Lighter in color, deeper in body, with smaller heads, and better conditioned altogether. They could be distinguished at a glance; the individuals of any school were as like as peas in color and size, and we never saw them except on a summer flood. The natives called them river trout. They came in schools of one hundred to five times as many, just as the flood was subsiding, and they had a way of halting to rest at the deep pools and spring-holes along their route. Lucky was the angler who could find them at rest in a deep pool, under a scooped out bank, or at the foot of a rushing cascade. At such times they seemed to lose their usual shyness, and would take the fly or worm indifferently, until their numbers were reduced more than one-half. To "meet them on the June rise" was the ardent desire of every angler who fished the streams which they were accustomed to ascend. These streams were not numerous. The First, Second, and Third Forks of Pine Creek, with the Otter, comprised the list so far as I know. And no man could be certain of striking a school at any time; it depended somewhat on judgment, but more on luck. Two or three times I tried it on the Otter and missed; while a friend who had the pluck and muscle to make a ten-mile tramp over the mountain to Second Fork took forty pounds of fine trout from a single school. It was a hoggish thing to do; but he was a native and knew no reason for letting up.

At length my white day came around. There was a fierce rain for three days, and the raging waters took mills, fences and lumber down stream in a way to be remembered. Luckily it also took the lumbermen the same way, and left few native anglers at home. When the waters had subsided to a fair volume, and the streams had still a suspicion of milkiness, I started at 3 PM of a lovely June afternoon for the Trout-House. An easy two hours walk, an hour of delightful angling, and I reached the little hostelry with three dozen brook trout, averaging about seven inches in length only, but fresh and sweet, all caught on a single red hackle, which will probably remain my favorite bug until I go over the last carry (though I notice it has gone well out of fashion with modern anglers).

A supper of trout; an evening such as must be seen and felt to be appreciated; trout again for breakfast, with a dozen packed for lunch, and I struck in at the bridge before sunrise for an all day bout, "to meet 'em on the June rise." I didn't do it. I took the entire day to whip that six miles of bright, dashing water. I filled a twelve-pound creel with trout, putting back everything under eight inches. I put back more than I kept. I had one of the most enjoyable days of my life; I came out at the lower bridge after sundown—and I had not seen or caught one fresh-run river trout. They were all the slender, large-mouthed, dark-mottled fish of the gloomy forest, with crimson spots like fresh drops of blood. But I was not discouraged. Had the trout been there I should have met them. I walked half a mile to the little inn at Babb's, selected a dozen of my best fish for supper and breakfast, gave away the rest, and, tired as a hound, slept the sleep of the just man.

At 4 o'clock the next morning I was on the stream again, feeling my way carefully down, catching a trout at every cast, and putting them mostly back with care, that they might live; but for an hour no sign of a fresh-run river trout.

Below the bridge there is a meadow, the oldest clearing on the creek; there are trees scattered about this meadow that are models of arborial beauty, black walnut, elm, ash, birch, hickory, maple, etc. Most of them grand, spreading trees. One of them, a large, umbrageous yellow-birch, stood on the left bank of the stream, and was already in danger of a fall by

"The swifter current that mined its roots."

It was here that I met them on the June rise.

I dropped my cast of two flies just above the roots of the birch, and on the instant, two fresh-run, silver-sided, red-spotted trout immolated themselves, with a generous self-abnegation that I shall never forget.

Standing there on that glorious June morning, I made cast after cast, taking, usually, two at each cast. I made no boyish "show" of playing them. They were lifted out as soon as struck. To have fooled with them would have tangled me, and very likely have scattered the school.

It was old-time angling; I shall not see it again.

My cast was a red hackle for tail-fly, with something like the brown hen for hand-fly. I only used two, with four-foot leader; and I was about the only angler who used a fly at all in those days, on these waters.

I fished about one hour. I caught sixty-four trout, weighing thirteen and three quarter pounds. I caught too many. I was obliged to *string* some of them, as the creel would not hold them all. But my head was moderately level. When I had caught as many as I thought right I held up; and I said, if any of these natives get on to this school, they will take the last trout, if it be a hundred pounds. And they will *salt them down*. So when I was done, and the fishing was as good as the start, I cut a long "staddle," with a bush at the top, and I just went for that school of trout. I chevied, harried and scattered them, up stream and down, until I could not see a fish. Then I packed my duffle and went to the little inn for breakfast. Of course every male biped was anxious to know "where I met 'em." I told them truly; and they started, man and boy, for the "Big Birch," with beech rods, stiff linen lines, and a full stock of white grubs.

I was credibly informed afterwards, that these backwoods cherubs did not succeed in "Meeting 'em on the June rise." I have a word to add, which is not important though it may be novel.

There is a roaring, impetuous brook emptying into Second Fork, called "Rock Run." It heads in a level swamp, near the summit of the mountain. The swamp contains about forty acres, and is simply a level bed of loose stones, completely overgrown with bright green moss.

"Rock Run" heads in a strong, ice-cold spring, but is soon sunken and lost among the loose stones of the swamp. Just where the immense hemlocks, that make the swamp a sunless gloom, get their foothold, is one of the things I shall never find out. But, all the same, they are *there*. And "Rock Run" finds its way underground for 80 rods with never a ray of sunlight to illuminate its course. Not once in its swamp course does it break out to daylight. You may follow it by its heavy gurgling, going by ear; but you cannot see the water. Now remove the heavy coating of moss here and there, and you may see glimpses of dark, cold water, three or four feet beneath the surface. Drop a hook, baited with angleworm down these dark watery holes, and it will be instantly taken by a dark, crimson-spotted specimen of simon pure *Salmo fontinalis*. They are small, four to six inches in length, hard, sweet; the *beau ideal* of mountain trout. Follow this subterranean brook for eighty rods, and you find it gushing over the mountain's brink in a cascade that no fish could or would attempt to ascend. Follow the roaring brook down to its confluence with Second Fork, and you will not find one trout in the course of a mile. The stream is simply a succession of falls, cascades, and rapids, up which no fish can beat its way for one hundred yards. And yet at the head of this stream is a subterranean brook stocked with the finest specimens of *Salmo fontinalis*. They did not breed on the mountain top. They *cannot* ascend the stream. Where did they originate? When, and how did they manage to get there? I leave the questions to *savants* and *naturalists*. As for myself, I state the fact—still demonstrable—for the trout are yet there. But I take it to be one of the conundrums "no fellah can ever find out."

P.S.—A word as to bugs, lures, flies, etc. Now I have no criticism to offer as regards flies or lures. I saw a Gotham banker in 1880, making a cast on Third lake, with a leader that carried *twelve flies*. Why not? He enjoyed it; and he caught some trout. Even the guides laughed at him. I did not: he rode his hobby, and he rode it well. Fishing beside him, with a five-dollar rod, I caught two to his one. What did he care? He came out to enjoy himself after his own fashion, and he did it. Like myself, he only cared for the sport—the recreation and enough trout for supper. (I cannot cast twelve flies.)

Now my favorite lures—with forty years' experience—stand about thus. Tail fly, red hackle; second, brown hen; third, Romeyn. Or, tail fly, red ibis; second, brown hackle; third, queen of the waters. Or, red hackle, queen, royal coachman. Sometimes trout will *not* rise to the fly. I respect their tastes. I use then—tail fly, an angle worm, with a bit of clear pork for the head, and a white miller for second. If this fails I go to camp and sleep. I am not above worms and grubs, but prefer the fly. *And I take but what I need for present use.* Can all brother anglers say the same?

# TROUTING ALONG THE CATASAUQUA

## FRANK FORESTER

"And this 'clattering creek,' what sort of water is it?" asked Frank; "that I may learn at once the whole lay of the land."

"A real mountain burn."

"I'm thinking of trying it myself tomorrow," said Robins. "Mr. Langdale tells me it can only be fished with bait, and that's what I'm best at. Besides, there are bigger fish in it."

"But fewer," answered Langdale. "No, Robins, I'd advise you to stick to the 'Stony,' unless you'll try a cast of the fly with us over the pool and down the Catasauqua."

"No, no," replied St. Clair, half indignantly, "none of your flies for me, and no canoe-work. But why do you advise me against it? You said there were no trees, bait-fishing and big fish. What is there against it?"

"The toughest crag-climbing and the most difficult fishing you ever tried."

"What like fishing is it, Lancelot?" asked Frank.

"Exactly what that capital sportsman, Colquhoon of Luss, describes in his excellent book, the 'Moor and Loch,' under the title of 'Moorburn'."

"I remember," replied Frank. "Is it as bad as that?"

"Worse; but the fish much larger. I have caught them up to two pounds."

"I should like to hear about that. Can't you read it to me?" asked the Wall-street man, eager for information.

"I've no objection," said Langdale, "if Frank has not. HE has read it fifty times already."

"I'm convenient," answered Frank, laying down his knife and fork, the last duck having disappeared.

"Well, then, here goes. Now, Scipio, look alive and clear away the table; bring us our pipes and our coffee; and then we'll to bed, for we must be afoot by day-break."

And with the word he rose, and, after turning over a few volumes on his crowded shelves, brought down the volume in question, with its pages under-lined, and interlined, and filled with marginal notes and references. This done, he ensconced himself in the chimney corner, threw on a fresh log, and read as follows:

" 'In most of the small Highland burns, there is a succession of cataracts and pools, with a parapet of rock rising perpendicularly on each side, and often scarcely footing enough for a dog to pass. The greater proportion of picturesque-looking brethren of the angle would almost start at the idea of continuing their pastime under such disadvantages. They therefore make a circuit, and come down again upon the burn, where it is more easy to fish, and the ground less rugged. The trout in these places are thus left until many of them grow large, and each taking possession of a favorite nook, drives all the smaller fry away. The difficulty of reaching these places is, I admit, often great, the angler having sometimes to scramble up on his hands and knees, covered with wet moss or gravel, and then drag his fishing-rod after him. These lyns should always be fished up-stream, otherwise the moment you appear at the top of the water-fall or rock, the trout are very like to see you, and slink into their hiding-place. The burn, however, must always be low, as at no other time can you distinguish the snug retreat of these little tyrants, which, indeed, they often leave, during the slightest flood, in search of prey. By fishing up the stream, your head will be on a level with the different eddies and pools, as they successively present themselves, and the rest of your person out of sight. Hold the baited hook with the left hand, jerking out the rod, underhanded, with your right, so as to make the bait fall softly at the lower end of the pool. The trout always take their station either there or at the top where the water flows in, ready to pounce on worms, snails, slugs, etc., as they enter or leave the pool. Should a trout seize the bait, a little time may be given to allow it to gorge, which it will most likely do without much ceremony. If large, care must be taken to prevent it from getting to the top of the lyn, which may probably harbor another expectant. The best plan is, if possible, to persuade it to descend into the pool below. Having deposited the half-pounder in your creel, you will now crawl upon hands and knees, just so near the top of the lyn as will enable you to drop the bait immediately below the bubbling foam, nearly as favorite a station for an overgrown, monopolizing trout as the other. Except in such situations, the burn trout seldom exceeds a quarter of a pound, and may be pulled out with single gut, without much risk of breaking it. In these lyns, however, I have occasionally taken them upward of a pound, which is easily accounted for. As soon as the trout grows to a sufficient size to intimidate his pigmy neighbors, he falls back into the best pool for feeding, not occupied by a greater giant than himself, and as these lyns are almost always in precipices very difficult of access, he remains undisturbed and alone, or with a single companion, driving all others away, until he may at last attain to a pound weight.'

"Now, I fear, brother angler, that you are in some respects what the indefatigable Gael would call a 'picturesque angler'; so I advise you in good faith, stick to the 'Stony Brook'; fish it from the long fall carefully down. Scipio shall attend you with the landing-net and plenty of worms and minnows; the last, hooked through the lip and back fin, will do you yeoman service in the lower pools; and Frank and I will join you in the afternoon."

"Agreed," said Mr. Robins; "I'll take your advice, I believe; and now I guess I'll turn in. Good night."

"Time, too," said Frank, laughing. "He was beginning to get a little white about the gills. Could that be his old Otard; he did not drink so much of it."

"Lord help you, no! he'd drink a gallon of it and no hurt. No! But he will persist in smoking Cavendish tobacco and kinnikinnic, because he has seen me do it, and, I believe, imagines that it confers some special powers of trout-catching. But come, suppose we turn in, too; you'll be tired after your journey, and a good night's rest will give a steady hand and clear eye tomorrow."

"*Volontiers.*"

So they incontinently joined the Wall-street man, who declared, half asleep, that the bed was not so very bad, after all; while Frank, once ensconced in the fragrant sheets, swore, by the great god Pan, patron of hunters, that never had bed so sweet, so soft, so warm, in every way so excellent, received the limbs of weary hunter. And so, indeed, it proved; for, until Scipio made his entree, with his announcement that breakfast was ready, no one stirred or spoke during the livelong night.

Thereon they all turned, like the Iron Duke, not over, but out. Their sporting toilets were soon made; but Frank and Lancelot, in their old shepherd's plaid jackets and trews and hob-nailed fishing shoes, could not but exchange glances and smiles at the elaborate rig of their friend, which some Broadway artist had, it was evident, elaborated from a Parisian fashion-plate, the high boots of exquisitely enameled leather, the fine doeskin trousers, the many-pocketed, pearl-buttoned shooting jacket of fawn-colored silk plush, the batiste neckerchief and waistcoat, point device, with green and silver fishes embroidered on a blue ground, and, to complete the whole, a cavalier hat, in which, but that it lacked the king's black feather, Rupert might well have charged at Marston Moor or Naseby. He seemed, however, so happy, that it would have been as useless as ill-natured to indoctrinate him; for evidently, as an angler, the man was hopelessly incurable, though, as Frank observed, for Wall-street, he was wonderfully decent.

His weapon was a right good Conroy's general-fishing rod, but without reel, and having its line, an unusually stout silk one, with a superb salmon-gut bottom, which, in good hands, would have held a twenty-pounder, made carefully fast to the top funnel; eschewing all use of the ring and destroying all chance of the rod's regularly bending to its work. But again, to counsel would have been to offend; so our friends held their peace.

The smoked venison ham, broiled troutlings, dry toast and black tea, which furnished their morning meal, were soon finished; and forth they went into the delicious, breezy air of the quiet summer morning, not a sound disturbing the solitude, except the plash and rippling of the rapid waters, the low voices of the never-silent pine-tops, and the twittering of the swallows, as they skimmed the limpid pool.

Up the gorge of the Stony Brook, followed by Scipio, with bait of all kinds enough to have kept the kraten fat for one day at least, a large creel at his back, and gaff and landing-net in hand, away went St. Clair Robins, gay and joyous and confident; and then, but not till then quoth Forester—

"And whither we?"

"To the other side of the pool. You may see the big fish rising under the alders, there, in the shadow of the big hill, from this distance. That shadow will hang there until noon, while all this side of the basin will be in blazing sunshine. Not a fish will bite here, I warrant me, until three o'clock, while we'll fill our basket there with good ones, certain. The best fish in the pool lies under that round-headed stone, just in the tail of the strong eddy, where the 'Clattering Creek' comes in, in the broken water. I rate him a six-pounder, and have saved him for you all the spring. As soon as the sun turns westward, and the hemlocks' shadows cross the white water, you shall kill him, and then we'll away to the Wall-street man"; and therewith the larger birch canoe was manned, paddled gently over to the shady side of the pool and moored in about twenty-foot water, and then, the rods being put together, the reels secured, and the lines carried duly through the rings, the following colloquy followed:

"What flies do you most affect here, Lancelot?" asked Frank.

"Any, at times, and almost all," answered Langdale. "In some weather I have killed well with middle-sized gaudy lake flies; but my favorites, on the whole, are all the red, brown, orange, and yellow hackles, and the blue and yellow duns. And yours?"

"My favorite of all is a snipe feather and mouse body; next to that the black and the furnace hackles."

"And will you use them today?"

"I will; the snipe wing for my stretcher. I mean to kill the big chap with him this evening."

"Be it so! to work."

And to work they went; but, though most glorious the sport to enjoy, or even to see performed gnostically, to read of it described, is as little interesting as to decribe it is difficult. Suffice it to say, that before the sun had begun to turn westward, sixteen brace and a half were fairly brought to basket by our anglers, one a three-pound-and-a-halfer, three two-pounders, there or there about; not a fish under a pound, all smaller were thrown back unscathed, and very few so small as that, all beautifully fed fish, big-bellied, small-headed, high in color, prime in condition. At one o'clock, they paddled leisurely back to the cabin, lunched frugally on a crust of bread and a glass of sherry, and awaited the hour when the hemlock's shadow should be on the white water.

At the moment they were there; and lo! the big trout was feeding fiercely on the natural fly.

"Be ready, Frank, and when next he rises drop your fly right in the middle of his bell."

"Be easy, I mean it." His line, as he spoke, was describing an easy circle around his head; the fish rose not. The second revolution succeeded; the great trout rose, missed his object, disappeared; and, on the instant, right in the centre of the bell, ere the inmost circle had subsided, the snipe feather fell and fluttered. With an arrowy rush, the monster rose, and as his broad tail showed above the surface, the merry music of the resonant click-reel told that Frank had him. Well struck, he was better played, killed unexceptionably; in thirteen minutes he lay fluttering on the greensward, lacking four ounces of a six-pounder. The snipe feather and mouse body won the day in a canter. So off they started up the Stony Brook, to admire the feats of P. St. Clair Robins. It was not long ere they found him; he had reached the lower waters of the brook, full of beautiful scours, eddies, whirlpools and basins, and was fishing quietly down it, wading about knee deep with his bait, he was roving with a minnow, some ten yards down the stream, playing naturally enough in the clear, swirling waters. Some trees on the bank hung thickly over his head; a few yards behind him was a pretty rocky cascade, and above that an open upland glade, lighted up by a gleam of the westering sun; and, altogether, with his gay garb, he presented quite a picturesque, if not a very sportsmanly appearance.

"After all," said Frank, as unseen themselves, they stood observing him, "he does not do it so very badly as one might have expected."

But before the words had passed his lips, a good fish, at least a pounder, threw itself clear out of the water and seized his minnow. In a second, in the twinkling of an eye, by a movement never before seen or contemplated by mortal angler, he ran his right hand up to the top of the third joint of his rod, which he held perpendicularly aloft, and with his left grasped his line, mid length, and essayed to drag the trout by main force out of his element. The tackle was stout, the stream strong, the bottom slippery, the fish active, and, before any one could see how it was done, hand and foot both slipped, the line parted, the rod crashed in the middle, the fish went over the next fall with a joyous flirt of his tail, and the fisherman, hapless fisherman, measured his own length in the deepest pool of the Stony Brook.

He was soon fished out, equipped in dry rigging, comforted with a hot glass of his favorite cognac; but he would not be consoled. He was off at daylight the following morning, and, for aught that I have heard, Cotton's Cabin beheld him nevermore.

# SOME MEMORIES OF EARLY DAYS

## LORD GREY OF FALLODEN

E very angler must have some account to give of the beginning of his keenness for angling. Some of us remember it as the great excitement of our
boyhood, whilst others have only discovered its existence in later years of life. I
think, however, that the keenest anglers are born and not made; that the passion
is latent in them from the beginning, and is revealed sooner or later according to
opportunity. In some cases it may be that the passion perishes unsuspected and
unrevealed, because there is no opportunity of indulging or discovering it, till too
late in life. The longer we live the deeper becomes the groove or the rut in which
our life moves, and the more difficult it becomes to go outside it. To me the
opportunity for fishing came early, and the passion for it awoke suddenly. I was
about seven years old, and was riding on a Shetland pony by the side of a very
small burn. A mill was working higher up the stream, and the water was full
of life and agitation, caused by the opening of the sluice of the mill pond above.
I had seen small trout caught in the burn before, but now, for the first time and
suddenly, came an overpowering desire to fish, which gave no rest till some very

primitive tackle was given me. With this and some worms, many afternoons were spent in vain. The impulse to see the trout destroyed all chance of success. It did not suit me to believe that it was fatal to look into the water before dropping a worm over the bank, or that I could not see the trout first and catch them afterwards, and I preferred to learn by experience and disappointment rather than the short, but unconvincing, method of believing what I was told.

For some years this burn fishing was all that I knew. It was very fascinating, though the trout were so small that one of four ounces was considered a good one, whilst the very largest ran to six ounces. These larger trout taught me a second lesson—self-restraint. The first lesson was, as has been said, to learn to refrain from looking into the water before I fished it: all the trout of every size combined to teach this. The second difficulty was to restrain the excitement when I had a bite. The natural impulse then was to strike so hard as to hurl the fish into the air overhead: this answered very well with trout of two or three ounces, though once a small one came unfastened in the air, flew off at a tangent into the hay behind, and could not be found. But with six ounce trout this violent method did not answer so well; neither the angler, nor the rod, nor the tackle, was always strong enough to deal with them so summarily. Catastrophes occurred, and by slow degrees and painful losses I learnt the necessity of getting keenness under control. After I had improved in these matters there still remained the hardest trial of all, which has to be undergone by all anglers, namely, how to face the disappointment of losing a fish. Many of us must have known what it is in boyhood to suffer anguish after losing an unexpectedly large fish. The whole of life then seems laid waste by despair; the memory of past joys counts for nothing; one is sure that no future success can ever compensate for the present loss; and one rails against the established order of everything, and is indignant that any human being should ever have been born to undergo such intolerable misery. Even in later years we cannot hope to face the loss of very large fish with equanimity. Nobody can become perfect in bearing what is unbearable, and it may be counted to our credit if in these very bitter moments silence descends upon us, and we preserve outward appearances. Here is a saying that is very relevant: "When things can neither be cured nor endured, one has to pretend."

Burn fishing is not without its charm even in later years, and is a peculiar form of angling separate from all others. I am thinking now of those north country burns too small for fly fishing, which run in narrow stony channels between overgrown banks. Here one must fish with a worm and a short line, and the difficulty consists in getting the worm into the water without any part of oneself being seen by the trout. The usual method is to advance stealthily, sometimes stooping, sometimes on one's knees, sometimes at full length, according to the necessities of the case, pushing the rod in front, and at last swinging the worm gently on a short line over the edge of the bank and lowering it into the water. When the angler knows the burn well he goes at once from place to place, approaching the bank afresh at each spot which he knows to be suitable. If he does not know the burn he most reconnoiter from a distance to see the sort of water that is before him. It does not do to drop a worm blindly over the bank without knowing where it will fall, as the hooks are sure in this case to become mixed up sooner or later with a bush or a heap of sticks.

One burn I used to fish flowed through a wood of high trees down a steep rocky channel. Here it was possible, at least for a small boy, to keep out of sight by walking up the bed of the burn itself, stooping low, jerking the worm up into little pools and cascades above, and lifting the trout out down stream on to the bank. This was very pretty work. I remember once getting several trout quickly one after the other in this place, and then they suddenly stopped taking. One little favorite pool after another produced nothing, and a fear of something unknown came over me; the gloom and stillness of the wood made me uneasy, everything about me seemed to know something, to have a meaning, which was hidden from me; and I felt as if my fishing was out of place. At last I could resist the feeling of apprehension no longer; I left the rod with the line in a pool to fish for itself, and went up to the edge of the wood to see what was happening in the open world outside. There was a great storm coming up full of awful menace, as thunderclouds often are. It filled me with terror. I hurried back for my rod, left the burn and the wood, and fled before the storm, going slow to get breath now and then, and continually urged to running again by the sound of thunder behind me.

Burn trout are wayward little things. Sometimes they take a worm greedily on the brightest days in low clear water, rushing to it directly it falls into the pool, or seizing it as it travels down the stream, and being hooked without trouble. On these days all the angler need do is wait for four or five seconds after he knows, by the stopping or the trembling of the line, that the worm has been taken, and then strike sharply but not violently. If the trout is very small it may be lifted out at once, but if it is four ounces' weight or heavier it is safer to let it do some splashing and struggling in the water, to wait till it is still, and then to lift it out with an even movement, quickly but without any sudden jerk. If there is a clear space without branches or bushes in the way, this can be done without the trout struggling in the air. It is always unsafe to lift a fish which is in the act of struggling, for the jerks of the fish, added to the dead weight of its body in the air, greatly increase the risk either of the line breaking or of the hooks coming out. If the trout exceeds six ounces, I play it with as much respect as if it were a salmon, and choose a shallow landing-place, and draw it on to that without lifting it at all. The feeling of losing a trout in the air is familiar to burn anglers. The fish falls back into the water with a splash, the line flies up into the air, often becoming hopelessly entangled in a tree; and before it is extricated the angler has frightened all the other fish in the pool, and is convinced that the trout and the branches and the rod and line and hooks are all in a conspiracy against him. I use the word "hooks," as I have found small Stewart or Pennell worm tackle much the best for trout fishing: it is easily baited, and with it the angler can, if he likes, strike directly the worm is taken, though it is better to wait just long enough to let the trout get all the worm well into its mouth, and not long enough to let the worm be swallowed.

On some days burn trout are very aggravating, and will take the worm and chew it without being hooked. The angler waits and then strikes, and feels that he has just touched a fish and no more, and this happens time after time. He tries the effect of waiting longer before striking, and then finds either that he still just misses the fish, or else that the fish has taken the worm off the hooks or left the worm altogether; or that a very small trout not worth killing has swallowed the hooks, and wasted its own life and his time and trouble. I suppose on these days the trout are not really hungry, and begin to chew the worm instead of trying to swallow it at once. They then discover the presence of the hooks, and either reject the whole thing, or try to separate the worm from the hooks with their lips, which results in the angler's touching without hooking them when he strikes. There are other days when burn trout dash at the worm and endeavor to make off with it immediately at speed. On these occasions the angler feels a quick tug and all is over before he can strike; he probably does strike too late, and his line having no resistance at the end is jerked out of the water into a bush, if there is one near.

Three other moods are common to burn trout; they are those of indifference, suspicion, and abnormal fright. When the trout are indifferent, they simply ignore the worm, and appear not to notice its presence: one might think from their behavior either that they were blind, or that they habitually lived with worms before their eyes. When they are suspicious, they will, on the contrary, swim up to the worm and investigate it as if they had never seen such a thing before, or dash about it as if its presence excited them. On other days, and these are not necessarily the brightest, it is almost impossible to keep out of sight of the trout, which seem to be watching for the least hint of the approach of an angler; and even when the angler succeeds in concealing himself, they fly from the sight of the rod, or the gut, however quietly it is put before them. All these things make burn fishing an interesting and delicate sport. The drawback to it is that the constant stooping and crawling become so much harder as years go on. Joints ache and crack, and the continual effort of keeping a stiff and full-grown body out of sight is difficult and painful. Some of the crouching may be avoided by using a long rod, but among bushes and trees a long rod is an awkward instrument, and one cannot guide the line so accurately among the branches. To dodge bushes and leaves and twigs successfully, the angler must use a short stiff rod and a short line. He can then not only guide the line and drop the worm more accurately with the rod, but after fishing each place can catch the end of the short line with one hand, while still holding the rod with the other, and so make his way through the trees to the next pool, without having to put the rod down and alter the length of the line. A well wooded burn is the nicest of all. It has places where the angler can watch the trout and see his worm taken, while he is hidden behind leaves, or lying in tall meadow-sweet or some such undergrowth of herbs. Even if he does not feel the thrill and the rapt excitement, which he felt as a boy when his line stopped and trembled in the stream with a bite, or when he saw a trout open its mouth and take his worm, he can still remember what he used to feel in those early days, and "beget that golden time again." He can enjoy, too, more than he ever did before, the light playing through the leaves upon the still water of a clear pool, the running water sparkling in the sun, the tinkling sound of little streams, and the shade and the hot summer's day. And even yet there is some satisfaction, when the burn is low and clear, in outwitting the trout, small as they are, for it is not to be done without care, difficulty, and effort.

I need hardly add that fine drawn gut is proper for burn fishing: in small burns two or three feet of gut is enough, as the water is shallow, the line is kept more perpendicular than horizontal, and but little of it falls into the water. The special merits of brandling worms were so impressed upon me from the first that I have never been content to use any other kind. They are certainly good both in color and size. The objection to them is that they are rather soft, but for burn fishing, where the worm is dropped rather than cast into the water, this does not matter so much. Brandling worms, however, are not to be found in common earth, nor in every heap of decaying manure or rubbish. Kitchen garden refuse is a valuable ingredient, but it is not the only one, and the heaps must be of the right material in the right stage of decay; young anglers of intelligence and observation make it their business to know the best places for brandling worms, so that they may be sure of getting a good supply whenever they want it. The brandlings are best after being kept for a day or two in clean moss, but trout take them well enough when they are fresh.

Very wonderful is the perspective of childhood, which can make a small burn seem greater than rivers in after life. There was one burn which I knew intimately from its source to the sea. Much of the upper part was wooded, and it was stony and shallow, till within two miles of its mouth. Here there was for a child another world. There were no trees, the bottom of the burn was of mud or sand, and the channel was full of rustling reeds, with open pools of some depth at intervals. These pools had a fascination for me, there was something about them which kept me excited with expectation of great events, as I lay behind the reeds, peering through them, and watching the line intently. The result of much waiting was generally an eel, or a small flat fish up from the sea; or now and then a small trout, but never for many years one of the monsters which I was sure must inhabit such mysterious pools. At last one evening something heavy really did take the worm. The fish kept deep, played round and round the pool and could not be seen, but I remember shouting to a companion at a little distance, that I had hooked a trout of one pound, and being conscious from the tone of his reply that he didn't in the least believe me, for a trout of one pound was in those days our very utmost limit of legitimate expectation. There was a mill pond higher up in which such a weight had been attained, and we who fished the burn could talk of trout of that size, and yet feel that we were speaking like anglers of this world. But this fish turned out to be heavier even than one pound, and when at last it came up from the depth into my view, I felt that the great moment had come which was to make or mar my happiness for ever. I got into the shallow water below the fish, and after great anxieties secured with the help of my hand a fresh run sea trout of three pounds. Never was a dead fish treated with more care and honor. It had swallowed the hooks, and rather than risk spoiling its appearance in getting them out, the gut was cut and they were left inside. The small trout and eels and flounders were turned out of my basket and put into my companion's, so that the great sea trout might lie in state. It was felt that the expectation of years was justified, that the marvelous had become real, that the glory which had been unseen was revealed, and that after the present moment the hope of great things in the future would live for ever. A few years ago there was published a delightful book called *The Golden Age* in which the author describes the world of childhood as it has been to all of us—a world whose boundaries are unknown, where everything is at the same time more wonderful and more real than it seems afterwards, and where mystery is our most constant companion. So it was with me, especially in the places where I fished. I used to go to the lower part of this burn in the charge of an old gamekeeper, and after a long journey through pathless open fields, we seemed to reach a distant land where things happened otherwise than in the world nearer home. At the end of the walk it was as if we had reached another country, and were living in another day under a different sky. The gamekeeper fished more leisurely than I, and sometimes he would be lost among the windings of the burn, to be found again by the sight of the smoke from his pipe rising gently from behind a whin bush. When I now recall that distant land, I see always somewhere among the whin bushes a little curl of thin smoke, and no other sign of an inhabitant.

In course of time there came experience of a fine Highland river, and lochs near it and of fly fishing in them in August. The trout did not always rise very well in August, but many of them were three-quarters of a pound in weight, a few were even larger, and the sport seemed to me magnificent. Three great days happened all in different years on this river and its lochs. Once the trout took exceptionally well in the loch, and instead of the usual number of twenty or less I landed forty-eight, averaging about three to the pound. Another day there was a little fresh water in the river, and I tried an artificial minnow. First a trout of about two pounds, larger than any trout ever hooked by me before, was lost. While I was still in the agony of disappointment, a second weighing three pounds and a quarter was hooked and eventually landed, and directly after that a third trout of about the same size was hooked and lost, when it was in full view and half in the landing net. Then nothing more would take, and I spent the rest of the day without further incident, trying to think of the fish landed and not of the ones lost.

But the greatest day of all was the third. I was standing at the end of a pier built for salmon fishing, casting out into the smooth strong stream, when a sort of wave seemed to come suddenly and swallow the top fly, and a large heavy body went down stream pulling out the line. I shouted, "A salmon!" and the old gillie came hurrying to my side. His first words were, "We shall never get him," against which I protested with rage, and he partially retracted and set to work to advise me. We could not follow the fish downward, but it hove to about twenty years below us and hung steady in the stream. We turned the trout rod up stream and held it still, keeping a steady strain upon the fish, and waited for what seemed an age without result; but the good old man encouraged me when I grew faint-hearted, and kept me patient. Eventually the fish began to yield. We gained line foot by foot, and more than once got the fish up stream nearly opposite the pier, but it saw us and dropped back each time to the old place down stream. At last amid great excitement it was coaxed past the pier, in a moment was in the backwater above, and to my astonishment was then almost at once exhausted and landed. It was a grilse of about six pounds, and rather red, but the distinction between grilse and salmon, between red fish and fresh run fish, was nothing to me. That same day another grilse of about four pounds took the same fly. This second fish took with a splash, ran freely and was landed without difficulty. In the course of many seasons I must have had dozens of days' trout fishing in that same river at the same time of year, but never on any other day did I hook or even rise a grilse or salmon with a trout fly.

These were the triumphs of luck, but they came at an age when youth, not from conceit, but from sheer gladness and simplicity, does not discriminate between luck and skill. The first temptation to become proud of possessing skill came later, and after the use of the dry fly had been learnt at Winchester. It was not on the Itchen that any pride was felt, for I was only a learner there, improving year by year, but with examples of greater skill and success than mine constantly before me. In the holidays, however, I took away with me from the Itchen to distant rivers the art of the dry fly, which was then not nearly so widely known as it has come to be in the last twenty years. So it happened that on west or north country streams, or in Ireland, or on dark smooth water in the Highlands, I was sometimes the first to introduce the dry fly, with results which astonished the trout and the local anglers, and were very gratifying to myself. In the Highland river spoken of above there was a long dark stretch, bordered by rocks and trees, where the river flowed with a deep even stream, carrying a few thin flecks of slow-moving foam upon its surface, but without a ripple. Here, especially in the evening, some of the best trout used to rise. You might fish every day for a week in the rougher water and never hook a trout of one pound weight with a fly and be very grateful for half-pounders, but in this smooth deep part many of the trout were upwards of one pound; and the average weight was about three-quarters of a pound. Often had I tried them with March-browns, and small Heckum Peckums and the various patterns which are attractive in the Highlands, but not one of these particular trout would stand the sight of my flies. I continued to visit that river in my summer holidays, and the time came when I brought with me some drawn gut, some small olive and red quills, and a single-handed rod with which to cast them lightly. A pupil on the Itchen was a master among these Highland trout, and in the still hour of sunset on many an August evening I used to endure the torment of the midges and find a rich reward. A struggle with a trout of one pound and a half hooked on Itchen tackle in that fine flow of deep water, among the rocks and trees, was no mean affair.

In the Easter holidays I went alone once or twice to the Dart. I do not know how the Dart fares now, for it is nearly twenty years since I have seen it; but in those days there was beautiful trout water between Staverton and Buckfastleigh, which could be fished by ticket, and if one was not disappointed with trout of less than half a pound, there was very good sport to be had. I remember once fishing a part of the river where there was a succession of streams, which towards the middle of the day seemed alive with little trout, rising actively all over the water at natural flies. It was one of those maddening days when the trout rise in quantities and take no notice of artificial flies. I could do nothing, and the other anglers above and below me, of whom two or three were in sight, were not doing very much better. At last in despair I waded to the bank, and went down to a smooth piece of the river between wooded banks. In this place the water was clear, and varied from a foot to perhaps three feet in depth. No one was fishing, and there were trout rising in shoals and very quietly. A stout March-brown, such as I had been using above, would have put them all to flight, but the trouble of using a dry fly for such separate trout seemed out of proportion to the size of the fish. Yet as I wanted very much to save an empty basket, I gave up the hope of counting trout that day by the dozen, put on one small olive quill and waded in quietly below the rising fish. They took the little dry fly as if they were pleased to see it, and when the rise was over I waded out with thirty-one trout in my basket. The old angling diary to which I have referred gives the weight of the largest as eight ounces. It does not give the total weight, but I remember congratulating myself on the fact that the average size of my trout was at least equal to the size of those generally caught with fly in April in the more favorite streams above. As I emerged from the trees on the bank, I met one of the best of the local anglers returning from above with a lighter basket than usual. He stopped me and asked what I had done. I opened my basket. "You can't have caught those to-day with fly," he said. "Yes," I replied; "I caught them with a dry fly." "Dry fly," he said very sternly, "we know nothing about a dry fly here." Then he went on his way, with thoughts, I fear, that were not very kind.

The next reminiscence goes back to about 1880, and has to do with a river in Ireland. The first time I saw this river was late in August. There were said to be trout, and good ones, and it was believed to be possible to catch some with fly earlier in the season, when the water was in order. The river had in parts a very wide bed, which when low it did not nearly fill. The water ran in all sorts of channels between beds of bright green weeds. Here and there was a long stream with a stony bottom, free from weeds, and now and then there would be a huge pool, full of peaty-colored water of unknown depth, in which one or two salmon lay. One could wander for miles all day about the most extraordinary variety of water. The river was full of pike, and it was said, probably with truth, that the inhabitants of the district forked trout out of the weeds in low water with various agricultural implements. But there were trout enough for dry fly fishing. Half a dozen or so might be found rising near together, and then perhaps one would have to go several hundred yards before another one was found; a little sound would be heard presently, as if a small pebble had dropped in somewhere without a splash, and heard perhaps two or three times before the rise could be seen in such a large and curious river. Then there was a different stalk, probably through water and weeds, with the chance of going overhead into a big hole unawares.

I was warned that at this season of the year, when the water was low, I must not expect to catch any of these fish, but I cared nothing for warnings. The trout were there, and were rising, and though I saw at once that it was a case for dry fly and for that only, I had by this time been taught to believe that any one, who could catch Winchester trout, could catch rising trout anywhere. These trout, however, at first upset my calculations. They brought me face to face with a difficulty which did not exist on the ticket water at Winchester—they were unapproachable. Never was an angler more put upon his mettle. There were trout visibly and audibly rising, which had never seen an artificial dry fly, and would probably take it at once. They were evidently also big trout. There was splendid sport to be had, and reputation and glory to be won in catching even one of them, and yet so shy were they, that I could not get my dry fly to them.

For two days they defeated me utterly. I walked and knelt and waded and labored and perspired under an August sun without success. Some of the trout were put down by my approach, some were scared by the first waving of the rod, and some, which had been successfully stalked, turned tail and fled when the gut floated over them without even the last drag; at last, on the second evening in a fading light, I hooked a fish which went off up stream at once with a mighty rush, and came to rest somewhere out of sight at the end of a lot of line. I waded carefully up in the twilight, keeping a tight line by reeling up as I went till I was over a great bed of strong weeds. Into this one hand carefully felt its way along the casting line, and touched at last the side of a great fish. Nothing could be seen for it was getting dark, and the weeds were too thick for a landing net to be used in them. I tried with one hand to arrange a grip on the trout, and very broad and hard he felt; but at the critical moment he made the most violent commotion in the weeds and dashed of somewhere. When all was still I felt again and found in the weeds only the end of broken gut. There was nothing more to be done that evening, and I waded out and lay on the bank in the dusk. On the whole, I think that was the bitterest moment I have ever known in angling. To have come so near to success, and to have it snatched from me at the last moment, after keenness and effort had been sustained at the very highest pitch for two whole days, was more than could be borne.

But success did come afterwards, and in broad daylight; I found a place where, by wading and kneeling in the river on the shallow side, it was possible to get within reach of and *opposite* to rising trout without frightening them. Then the fly could be thrown some way above them with an underhand cast, so as not to show the rod; and being opposite and not below, I could let the fly float down a few inches on the near side of a rising trout, so that only the fly and none of the gut was seen. In this way I at last caught one or two trout, and then somehow, when the frost of failure had once broken up, it seemed more easy to succeed all over the river.

These trout were the shyest I have ever known. They were more difficult to approach and more easily scared by rod or gut than any others I ever fished for; but if the fly could be floated to a rising fish without frightening it, the fly was generally taken. On the best day that I had there I caught eleven fish. None of these weighed three pounds, but the first two were each over two pounds and three-quarters. For such shy fish really fine gut had to be used, and there were many disasters in the weeds, but also many splendid struggles fought out in pools which were far too deep for any vegetation. It was the wildest and most exciting and most fascinating dry fly fishing that I have ever had. My experience of it has only been during late August or early September, but I can imagine that in May and in June it might be the finest dry fly fishing in the United Kingdom.[1]

---

[1]   The river was the Suir, and the part of it described was at Graiguenoe, not far from Thurles. Before 1880 I do not think any one had ever fished it with a dry fly. I was never there after 1886, but I heard that the merits of the water for dry fly fishing were afterwards much appreciated by many anglers.

# FISHING WITH MY DADDY

## JIMMY CARTER

A few miles north of the Okefenokee was the small village of Hortense, not far from where the Little Satilla River joins the Big Satilla. This was one of my father's favorite fishing spots; he tried to go there every year with some of his associates in the farming, peanut, and fertilizer business. On two occasions he took me with him, when I was about ten or twelve years old.

We stayed in a big and somewhat dilapidated wood-frame house, on a small farm near the banks of the Little Satilla. The house had been built to accommodate at least three generations of a family, but now there was just a man named Joe Strickland, his wife, Shug, and two daughters, one a pretty girl in her teens named Jessie. Joe was the guide for our group of about six people. The women cooked our meals and plowed mules in the small fields during the day while we were fishing. It was the first time I had seen women plowing, which I found quite surprising, but they all seemed to take it as a matter of course.

The Little Satilla is a serpentine stream in the flattest part of Georgia's coastal plain, weaving back and forth from one bend to another. A number of oxbow lakes had been left behind when the river changed its course. We fished in the area of what was called Ludie's Lake. On the outside of almost every bend of the stream there was a deep hole, often cut into a steep bank, and on the opposite side of the river was usually a sand bar. There were not as many bushes and snags in the water as we had around Plains, and the bottom was sandy and firm.

I had never done this kind of fishing before. We spent our time in the stream, wading halfway across it to fish in the deep water under the overhanging banks, using the longest cane poles we could handle. I wore cutoff overall pants with no shirt, and tied my fish stringer to one of the belt loops. Joe and I were the only ones barefoot; all the other men had on old tennis shoes or brogans to protect their tender feet. We fished with large pond worms and caught mostly "copperheads," which were very large bluegill bream whose heads, when mature, assumed a bronze color, perhaps from the tannin stain in the water.

The group of us would string out along the river, my daddy and I usually fishing within sight of each other. We always had a fairly good idea of what luck each fisherman was having. For some reason I never understood, the men would shout "Billy McKay!" when they had on a nice fish. The words would roll through the woods as all of us smiled; the enthusiasm of the voices was contagious. Each night after supper I went to bed early, but the men stayed up to play poker and to have a few drinks. Sometimes they made enough noise to wake me up, but I didn't mind. It seemed to make me more a member of the party if they weren't trying to stay quiet just for me. Most often I was tired enough to go right back to sleep.

While we were in the river Joe moved quietly from one of us to another, just to make sure we were properly spaced and to give advice about the water and some of the bypasses we had to take around obstacles. He tried—successfully— to build up a reputation as something of a character and always gave the group something to talk about during the months between our visits to Hortense.

Once we were walking single file along a path toward the river and Joe called, "Watch out for the barbed wire!"

One of the men said, "Joe, you didn't look down. How do you know wire's there?"

Joe said, "My feet will flatten briers or thorns, but I can feel barbed wire when I step on it."

Another time, when we had to cross the river, Joe walked down the bank, entered the water with his pole and lunch over his head, and moved smoothly across toward the other side with the water never higher than his armpits. The next man, whom I called Mr. Charlie, was the oldest in the group, and he stepped off in the water and immediately went down out of sight. He came up sputtering, and shouted, "Joe, how deep is it here?"

Joe replied, "Oh, I reckon it's about fifteen foot." Joe could tread water like a duck, and just wanted to demonstrate his prowess so that none of us would forget.

Then came my most memorable day. Late one afternoon, after a good day of fishing, Daddy called me over and asked me to keep his string of fish while he went up the river to talk to one of his friends. I tied it on with mine on the downstream side of me while I kept fishing, enjoying the steady pull of the current on our day's catch. It wasn't long before I watched my cork begin to move slowly and steadily up under a snag and knew I had hooked a big one. After a few minutes I had a large copperhead bream in my hands, but as I struggled with it and wondered how I was going to hold the fish while untying the stringer, a cold chill went down my spine. I realized that the tugging of the current on the stringers was gone, as were all our fish! My belt loop had broken.

I threw my pole up on the nearest sandbar and began to dive madly into the river below where I had been standing.

Then I heard Daddy's voice calling my nickname. "Hot," he said, "what's wrong?"

"I've lost the fish, Daddy."

"All of them? Mine too?"

"Yes, sir." I began to cry, and the tears and water ran down my face together each time I came up for breath.

Daddy was rarely patient with foolishness or mistakes. But after a long silence, he said, "Let them go." I stumbled out on the bank, and he put his arms around me.

It seems foolish now, but at that time it was a great tragedy for me. We stood there for a while, and he said, "There are a lot more fish in the river. We'll get them tomorrow." He knew how I felt and was especially nice to me for the next couple of days. I worshipped him.

At Joe's home we ate fish and whatever was in season. Both times I went, our breakfasts consisted of biscuits, grits, green beans, and fried fish. It was the first time I had eaten green beans early in the morning, but soon it seemed like a normal thing to do. With plenty of butter and sugar-cane syrup to go with the piles of hot biscuits, we never got up from the table hungry.

When I left Joe's place to come home, his daughter Jessie told me that she had brought me a going-away present. She then handed me a baby alligator about a foot long, whom I immediately named Mickey Mouse. When I returned to our house I installed him inside a large truck tire, partially buried in the ground and covered with boards. For a number of weeks I fed him earthworms, crickets, wasp larvae, and anything else he would eat. My friends were quite envious of my new pet. Unfortunately, the cats and dogs around the farm were also interested. One morning I went out to feed Mickey and found the boards pushed aside and the little alligator missing. Daddy was very considerate and said he was sure the 'gator had escaped into the nearest swamp. I was not quite naïve enough to believe him, but from then on I stayed on the lookout for my 'gator whenever I was fishing or exploring along the neighborhood creeks.

Almost fifty years later, after I left the White House, I stopped by Hortense, Georgia to try to find the place we used to visit. I couldn't remember the roads or even Joe's last name when I inquired of some folks in the service station. I did recall the pretty daughter, but one of the men told me, "We had a lot of pretty daughters around here." At least I remembered the bare feet, barbed wire, good catches, lost fish, Mickey Mouse, and green beans for breakfast. When I described some of these things to the postmistress, she said, "You must mean Joe Strickland. Miss Jessie still lives at the same place, but in a new house." I followed her directions and found the cottage in what had been the large yard of the old house, just a few steps from the Little Satilla River.

Miss Jessie responded to our knock on her door, saying, "Won't y'all come in!" even before she knew who we were. We had a good time reminiscing about old times. Both her parents had died long ago, and she was intrigued that I remembered so much about them. She said that she remembered my visits: "I told a lot of people while you were in the White House that the President had fished with my daddy."

To which I replied, "When I was in the White House, I told several people the same thing about yours. Many of the most highly publicized events of my presidency are not nearly as memorable or significant in my life as fishing with my daddy or yours when I was a boy. Certainly, almost none of them was as enjoyable!"

# THE RIVER GOD

## ROLAND PERTWEE

When I was a little boy I had a friend who was a colonel. He was not the kind of colonel you meet nowadays, who manages a motor showroom in the West End of London and wears crocodile shoes and a small mustache and who calls you "old man" and slaps your back, independent of the fact that you may have been no more than a private in the war. My colonel was of the older order that takes a third of a century and a lot of Indian sun and Madras curry in the making. A veteran of the Mutiny he was, and wore side whiskers to prove it. Once he came upon a number of Sepoys conspiring mischief in a byre with a barrel of gunpowder. So he put the butt of his cheroot into the barrel and presently they all went to hell. That was the kind of man he was in the way of business.

In the way of pleasure he was very different. In the way of pleasure he wore an old Norfolk coat that smelt of heather and brine, and which had no elbows to speak of. And he wore a Sherlock Holmesy kind of cap with a swarm of salmon flies upon it, that to my boyish fancy was more splendid than a crown. I cannot remember his legs, because they were nearly always under water, hidden in great canvas waders. But once he sent me a photograph of himself riding on a tricycle, so I expect he had some knickerbockers, too, which would have been that tight kind, with box cloth under the knees. Boys don't take much stock of clothes. His head occupied my imagination. A big, brave, white-haired head with cherry-red rugose cheeks and honest, laughing, puckered eyes, with gunpowder marks in their corners.

People at the little Welsh fishing inn where we met said he was a bore; but I knew him to be a god and shall prove it.

I was ten years old and his best friend.

He was seventy something and my hero.

Properly I should not have mentioned my hero so soon in this narrative. He belongs to a later epoch, but sometimes it is forgivable to start with a boast, and now that I have committed myself I lack the courage to call upon my colonel to fall back two paces to the rear, quick march, and wait until he is wanted.

The real beginning takes place, as I remember, somewhere in Hampshire on the Grayshott Road, among sandy banks, sentinel firs and plum-colored wastes of heather. Summer-holiday time it was, and I was among folks whose names have since vanished like lizards under the stones of forgetfulness. Perhaps it was a picnic walk; perhaps I carried a basket and was told not to swing it for fear of bursting its cargo of ginger beer. In those days ginger beer had big bulgy corks held down with a string. In a hot sun or under stress of too much agitation the string would break and the corks fly. Then there would be a merry foaming fountain and someone would get reproached.

One of our company had a fishing rod. He was a young man who, one day, was to be an uncle of mine. But that didn't concern me. What concerned me was the fishing rod and presently—perhaps because he felt he must keep in with the family—he let me carry it. To the fisherman born there is nothing so provoking of curiosity as a fishing rod in a case.

Surreptitiously I opened the flap, which contained a small grass spear in a wee pocket, and, pulling down the case a little, I admired the beauties of the cork butt, with its gun-metal ferrule and reel rings and the exquisite frail slenderness of the two top joints.

"It's got two top joints—two!" I exclaimed ecstatically.

"Of course," said he. "All good trout rods have two."

I marveled in silence at what seemed to me then a combination of extravagance and excellent precaution.

There must have been something inherently understanding and noble about that young man who would one day be my uncle, for, taking me by the arm, he sat me down on a tuft of heather and took the pieces of rod from the case and fitted them together. The rest of the company moved on and left me in Paradise.

It is thirty-five years ago since that moment and not one detail of it is forgotten. There sounds in my ears today as clearly as then, the faint, clear pop made by the little cork stoppers with their boxwood tops as they were withdrawn. I remember how, before fitting the pieces together, he rubbed the ferrules against the side of his nose to prevent them from sticking. I remember looking up the length of it through a tunnel of sneck rings to the eyelet at the end. Not until he had fixed a reel and passed a line through the rings did he put the lovely thing into my hand. So light it was, so firm, so persuasive; such a thing alive—a scepter. I could do no more than say "Oo!" and again, "Oo!"

"A thrill, ain't it?" said he.

I had no need to answer that. In my new-found rapture was only one sorrow—the knowledge that such happiness would not endure and that, all too soon, a blank and rodless future awaited me.

"They must be awfully—awfully 'spensive," I said.

"Couple of guineas," he replied offhandedly.

A couple of guineas! And we were poor folk and the future was more rodless than ever.

"Then I shall save and save and save," I said.

And my imagination started to add up twopence a week into guineas. Two hundred and forty pennies to the pound, multiplied by two—four hundred and eighty—and then another twenty-four pennies—five hundred and four. Why, it would take a lifetime, and no sweets, no elastic for catapults, no penny novelty boxes or air-gun bullets or ices or anything. Tragedy must have been writ large upon my face, for he said suddenly, "When's your birthday?"

I was almost ashamed to tell him how soon it was. Perhaps he, too, was a little taken aback by its proximity, for that future uncle of mine was not so rich as uncles should be.

"We must see about it."

"But it wouldn't—it couldn't be one like that," I said.

I must have touched his pride, for he answered loftily, "Certainly it will."

In the fortnight that followed I walked on air and told everybody I had as good as got a couple-of-guineas rod.

No one can deceive a child, save the child himself, and when my birthday came and with it a long brown paper parcel, I knew, even before I had removed the wrappers, that this two-guinea rod was not worth the money. There was a brown linen case, it is true, but it was not a case with a neat compartment for each joint, nor was there a spear in the flap. There was only one top instead of two, and there were no popping little stoppers to protect the ferrules from dust and injury. The lower joint boasted no elegant cork hand piece, but was a tapered affair coarsely made and rudely varnished. When I fitted the pieces together, what I balanced in my hand was tough and stodgy, rather than limber. The reel, which had come in a different parcel, was of wood. It had neither check nor brake, the line overran and backwound itself with distressing frequency.

I had not read and reread Gamages' price list without knowing something of rods, and I did not need to look long at this rod before realizing that it was no match to the one I had handled on the Grayshott Road.

I believe at first a great sadness possessed me, but very presently imagination came to the rescue. For I told myself that I had only to think that this was the rod of all other rods that I desired most and it would be so. And it was so.

Furthermore, I told myself that, in this great wide ignorant world, but few people existed with such expert knowledge of rods as I possessed. That I had but to say, "Here is the final word in good rods," and they would accept it as such.

Very confidently I tried the experiment on my mother, with inevitable success. From the depths of her affection and her ignorance on all such matters, she produced:

"It's a magnificent rod."

I went my way, knowing full well that she knew not what she said, but that she was kind.

With rather less confidence I approached my father, saying, "Look, father! It cost two guineas. It's absolutely the best sort you can get."

And he, after waggling it a few moments in silence, quoted cryptically:

"There is nothing either good or bad but thinking makes it so."

Young as I was, I had some curiosity about words, and on any other occasion I would have called on him to explain. But this I did not do, but left hurriedly for fear that he should explain.

In the two years that followed I fished every day in the slip of a back garden of our tiny London house. And, having regard to the fact that this rod was never fashioned to throw a fly, I acquired a pretty knack in the fullness of time and performed some glib casting at the nasturtiums and marigolds that flourished by the back wall.

My parents' fortunes must have been in the ascendant, I suppose, for I call to mind an unforgettable breakfast when my mother told me that father had decided we should spend our summer holiday at a Welsh hotel on the river Lledr. The place was called Pont-y-pant, and she showed me a picture of the hotel with a great knock-me-down river creaming past the front of it.

Although in my dreams I had heard fast water often enough, I had never seen it, and the knowledge that in a month's time I should wake with the music of a cataract in my ears was almost more than patience could endure.

In that exquisite, intolerable period of suspense I suffered as only childish longing and enthusiasm can suffer. Even the hank of guilt that I bought and bent into innumerable casts failed to alleviate that suffering. I would walk for miles in a moment's delight captured in gluing my nose to the windows of tackleists' shops in the West End. I learned from my grandmother—a wise and calm old lady—how to make nets and, having mastered the art, I made myself a landing net. This I set up on a frame fashioned from a penny schoolmaster's cane bound to an old walking stick. It would be pleasant to record that this was a good and serviceable net, but it was not. It flopped over in a very distressing fashion when called upon to lift the lightest weight. I had to confess to myself that I had more enthusiasm than skill in the manufacture of such articles.

At school there was a boy who had a fishing creel, which he swapped with me for a Swedish knife, a copy of the *Rogues of the Fiery Cross*, and an Easter egg which I had kept on account of its rare beauty. He had forced a hard bargain and was sure he had the best of it, but I knew otherwise.

At last the great day dawned, and after infinite travel by train we reached our destination as the glow of sunset was graying into dark. The river was in spate, and as we crossed a tall stone bridge on our way to the hotel I heard it below me, barking and grumbling among great rocks. I was pretty far gone in tiredness, for I remember little else that night but a rod rack in the hall—a dozen rods of different sorts and sizes, with gaudy salmon flies, some nets, a gaff and an oak coffer upon which lay a freshly caught salmon on a blue ashet. Then supper by candlelight, bed, a glitter of stars through the open window, and the ceaseless drumming of water.

By six o'clock next morning I was on the river bank, fitting my rod together and watching in awe the great brown ribbon of water go fleetly by.

Among my most treasured possessions were half a dozen flies, and two of these I attached to the cast with exquisite care. While so engaged, a shadow fell on the grass beside me and, looking up, I beheld a lank, shabby individual with a walrus mustache and an unhealthy face who, the night before, had helped with our luggage at the station.

"Water's too heavy for flies," said he, with an uptilting inflection. "This evening, yes; now, no—none whateffer. Better try with a worrum in the burrun."

He pointed at a busy little brook which tumbled down the steep hillside and joined the main stream at the garden end.

"C-couldn't I fish with a fly in the—the burrun?" I asked, for although I wanted to catch a fish very badly, for honor's sake I would fain take it on a fly.

"Indeed, no," he replied, slanting the tone of his voice skyward. "You cootn't. Neffer. And that isn't a fly rod whateffer."

"It is," I replied hotly. "Yes, it is."

But he only shook his head and repeated, "No," and took the rod from my hand and illustrated its awkwardness and handed it back with a wretched laugh.

If he had pitched me into the river I should have been happier.

"It is a fly rod and it cost two guineas," I said, and my lower lip trembled.

"Neffer," he repeated. "Five shillings would be too much."

Even a small boy is entitled to some dignity.

Picking up my basket, I turned without another word and made for the hotel. Perhaps my eyes were blinded with tears, for I was about to plunge into the dark hall when a great, rough, kindly voice arrested me with:

"Easy does it."

At the thick end of an immense salmon rod there strode out into the sunlight the noblest figure I had ever seen.

There is no real need to describe my colonel again—I have done so already—but the temptation is too great. Standing in my doorway, the sixteen-foot rod in hand, the deer-stalker hat, besprent with flies, crowning his shaggy head, the waders, like seven-league boots, braced up to his armpits, the creel across his shoulder, a gaff across his back, he looked what he was—a god. His eyes met mine with that kind of smile one good man keeps for another.

"An early start," he said. "Any luck, old fellar?"

I told him I hadn't started—not yet.

"Wise chap," said he. "Water's a bit heavy for trouting. It'll soon run down, though. Let's vet those flies of yours."

He took my rod and whipped it expertly.

"A nice piece—new, eh?"

"N-not quite," I stammered; "but I haven't used it yet, sir, in water."

That god read men's minds.

"I know—garden practice; capital; nothing like it."

Releasing my cast, he frowned critically over the flies—a Blue Dun and a March Brown.

"Think so?" he queried. "You don't think it's a shade late in the season for these fancies?" I said I thought perhaps it was. "Yes, I think you're right," said he. "I believe in this big water you'd do better with a livelier pattern. Teal and Red, Cock-y-bundy, Greenwell's Glory."

I said nothing, but nodded gravely at these brave names.

Once more he read my thoughts and saw through the wicker sides of my creel a great emptiness.

"I expect you've fished most in southern rivers. These Welsh trout have a fancy for a spot of color."

He rummaged in the pocket of his Norfolk jacket and produced a round tin which once had held saddle soap.

"Collar on to that," said he; "there's a proper pickle of flies and casts in that tin that, as a keen fisherman, you won't mind sorting it out. Still, they may come in useful."

"But, I say, you don't mean—" I began.

"Yes, go in; stick to it. All fishermen are members of the same club and I'm giving the trout a rest for a bit." His eyes ranged the hills and trees opposite. "I must be getting on with it before the sun's too high."

Waving his free hand, he strode away and presently was lost to view at a bend in the road.

I think my mother was a little piqued by my abstraction during breakfast. My eyes never, for an instant, deserted the round tin box which lay open beside my plate. Within it were a paradise and a hundred miracles all tangled together in the pleasantest disorder. My mother said something about a lovely walk over the hills, but I had other plans, which included a very glorious hour which should be spent untangling and wrapping up in neat squares of paper my new treasures.

"I suppose he knows best what he wants to do," he said.

So it came about that I was left alone and betook myself to a sheltered spot behind a rock where all the delicious disorder was remedied and I could take stock of what was mine.

I am sure there were at least six casts all set up with flies, and ever so many loose flies and one great stout, tapered cast, with a salmon fly upon it, that was so rich in splendor that I doubted if my benefactor could really have known that it was there.

I felt almost guilty at owning so much, and not until I had done full justice to everything did I fasten a new cast to my line and go a-fishing.

There is a lot said and written about beginners' luck, but none of it came my way. Indeed, I spent most of the morning extricating my line from the most fearsome tangles. I had no skill in throwing a cast with two droppers upon it and I found it was an art not to be learned in a minute. Then, from overeagerness, I was too snappy with my back cast, whereby, before many minutes had gone, I heard that warning crack behind me that betokens the loss of a tail fly. I must have spent half an hour searching the meadow for that lost fly and finding it not. Which is not strange, for I wonder has any fisherman ever found that lost fly. The reeds, the buttercups, and the little people with many legs who run in the wet grass conspire together to keep the secret of its hiding place. I gave up at last, and with a feeling of shame that was only proper, I invested a new fly on the point of my cast and set to work again, but more warily.

In that hard racing water a good strain was put upon my rod, and before the morning was out it was creaking at the joints in a way that kept my heart continually in my mouth. It is the duty of a rod to work with a single smooth action and by no means to divide its performance into three sections of activity. It is a hard task for any angler to persuade his line austerely if his rod behaves thus.

When, at last, my father strolled up the river bank, walking, to his shame, much nearer the water than a good fisherman should, my nerves were jumpy from apprehension.

"Come along. Food's ready. Done any good?" said he.

Again it was to his discredit that he put food before sport, but I told him I had had a wonderful morning, and he was glad.

"What do you want to do this morning, old man?" he asked.

"Fish," I said.

"But you can't always fish," he said.

I told him I could, and I was right and have proved it for thirty years and more.

"Well, well," he said, "please yourself, but isn't it dull not catching anything?"

And I said, as I've said a thousand times since, "As if it could be."

So that afternoon I went downstream instead of up, and found myself in difficult country where the river boiled between the narrows of two hills. Stunted oaks overhung the water and great boulders opposed its flow. Presently I came to a sort of natural flight of steps—a pool and a cascade three times repeated—and there, watching the maniac fury of the waters in awe and wonderment, I saw the most stirring sight in my young life. I saw a silver salmon leap superbly from the caldron below into the pool above. And I saw another and another salmon do likewise. And I wonder the eyes of me did not fall out of my head.

I cannot say how long I stayed watching that gallant pageant of leaping fish—in ecstasy there is no measurement of time—but at last it came upon me that all the salmon in the sea were careering past me and that if I were to realize my soul's desire I must hasten to the pool below before the last of them had gone by.

It was a mad adventure, for until I had discovered that stout cast, with the gaudy fly attached in the tin box, I had given no thought to such noble quarry. My recent possessions had put ideas into my head above my station and beyond my powers. Failure, however, means little to the young and, walking fast, yet gingerly, for fear of breaking my rod top against a tree, I followed the path downstream until I came to a great basin of water into which, through a narrow throat, the river thundered like a storm.

At the head of the pool was a plate of rock scored by the nails of fishermen's boots, and here I sat me down to wait while the salmon cast, removed from its wrapper, was allowed to soak and soften in a puddle left by the rain.

And while I waited a salmon rolled not ten yards from where I sat. Head and tail, up and down he went, a great monster of a fish, sporting and deriding me.

With that performance so near at hand, I have often wondered how I was able to control my fingers well enough to tie a figure-eight knot between the line and the cast. But I did, and I'm proud to be able to record it. Your true-born angler does not go blindly to work until he has first satisfied his conscience. There is a pride, in knots, of which the laity knows nothing, and if, through neglect to tie them rightly, failure and loss should result, pride may not be restored nor conscience salved by the plea of eagerness. With my trembling fingers I bent the knot and, with a pummeling heart, launched the line into the broken water at the throat of the pool.

At first the mere tug of the water against that large fly was so thrilling to me that it was hard to believe that I had not hooked a whale. The trembling line swung round in a wide arc into a calm eddy below where I stood. Before casting afresh I shot a glance over my shoulder to assure myself that there was no limbo of a tree behind me to foul the fly. And this was a gallant cast, true and straight, with a couple of yards more length than its predecessor, and a wider radius. Instinctively I knew, as if the surface had been marked with an X where the salmon had risen, that my fly must pass right over the spot. As it swung by, my nerves were trained like piano wires. I think I knew something tremendous, impossible, terrifying, was going to happen. The sense, the certitude was so strong in me that I half opened my mouth to shout a warning to the monster, not to.

I must have felt very, very young in that moment. I, who that same day had been talked to as a man by a man among men. The years were stripped from me and I was what I was—ten years old and appalled. And then, with the suddenness of a rocket, it happened. The water was cut into a swath. I remember a silver loop bearing downward—a bright, shining, vanishing thing like the bobbin of my mother's sewing machine—and a tug. I shall never forget the viciousness of that tug. I had my fingers tight upon the line, so I got the full force of it. To counteract a tendency to go headfirst into the spinning water below, I threw myself backward and sat down o the hard rock with a jar that shut my teeth on my tongue—like the jaws of a trap.

Luckily I had let the rod go out straight with the line, else it must have snapped in the first frenzy of the downstream rush. Little ass that I was, I tried to check the speeding line with my forefinger, with the result that it cut and burnt me to the bone. There wasn't above twenty yards of line in the reel, and the wretched contrivance was trying to be rid of the line even faster than the fish was wrenching it out. Heaven knows why it didn't snarl, for great loops and whorls were whirling, like Catherine wheels, under my wrist. An instant's glance revealed the terrifying fact that there was not more than half a dozen yards left on the reel and the fish showed no sign of abating his rush. With the realization of impending and inevitable catastrophe upon me, I launched a yell for help, which, rising above the roar of the waters, went echoing down the gorge.

And then, to add to my terrors, the salmon leaped—a winging leap like a silver arch appearing and instantly disappearing upon the broken surface. So mighty, so all-powerful he seemed in that sublime moment that I lost all sense of reason and raised the rod, with a sudden jerk, above my head.

I have often wondered, had the rod actually been the two-guinea rod my imagination claimed for it, whether it could have withstood the strain thus violently and unreasonably imposed upon it. The wretched thing that I held so grimly never even put up a fight. It snapped at the ferrule of the lower join and plunged like a toboggan down the slanting line, to vanish into the black depths of the water.

My horror at this calamity was so profound that I was lost even to the consciousness that the last of my line had run out. A couple of vicious tugs advised me of this awful truth. Then, snap! The line parted at the reel, flickered out through the rings and was gone. I was left with nothing but the butt of a broken rod in my hand and an agony of mind that even now I cannot recall without emotion.

I am not ashamed to confess that I cried. I lay down on the rock, with my cheek in the puddle where I had soaked the cast, and plenished it with my tears. For what had the future left for me but a cut and burning finger, a badly bumped behind, the single joint of a broken rod and no faith in uncles? How long I lay there weeping I do not know. Ages, perhaps, or minutes, or seconds.

I was roused by a rough hand on my shoulder and a kindly voice demanding, "Hurt yourself, Ike Walton?"

Blinking away my tears, I pointed at my broken rod with a bleeding forefinger.

"Come! This is bad luck," said my colonel, his voice grave as a stone. "How did it happen?"

"I c-caught a s-salmon."

"You what?" said he.

"I d-did," I said.

He looked at me long and earnestly; then, taking my injured hand, he looked at that and nodded.

"The poor groundlings who can find no better use for a river than something to put a bridge over think all fishermen are liars," said he. "But we know better, eh? By the bumps and breaks and cuts I'd say you made a plucky fight against heavy odds. Let's hear all about it."

So, with his arm round my shoulders and his great shaggy head near to mine, I told him all about it.

At the end he gave me a mighty and comforting squeeze, and he said, "The loss of one's first big fish is the heaviest loss I know. One feels, whatever happens, one'll never—" He stopped and pointed dramatically. "There it goes—see! Down there at the tail of the pool!"

In the broken water where the pool emptied itself into the shallows beyond, I saw the top joints of my rod dancing on the surface.

"Come on!" he shouted, and gripping my hand, jerked me to my feet. "Scatter your legs! There's just a chance!"

Dragging me after him, we raced along by the river path to the end of the pool, where, on a narrow promontory of grass, his enormous salmon rod was lying.

"Now," he said, picking it up and making the line whistle to and fro in the air with sublime authority, "keep your eyes skinned on those shallows for another glimpse of it."

A second later I was shouting, "There! There!"

He must have seen the rod point at the same moment, for his line flowed out and the big fly hit the water with a plop not a couple of feet from the spot.

He let it ride on the current, playing it with a sensitive touch like the brushwork of an artist.

"Half a jiffy!" he exclaimed at last. "Wait! Yes, I think so. Cut down to that rock and see if I haven't fished up the line."

I needed no second invitation, and presently was yelling, "Yes—yes, you have!"

"Stretch yourself out then and collar hold of it."

With the most exquisite care he navigated the line to where I lay stretched upon the rock. Then:

"Right you are! Good lad! I'm coming down."

Considering his age, he leaped the rocks like a chamois.

"Now," he said, and took the wet line delicately between his forefinger and thumb. One end trailed limply downstream, but the other end seemed anchored in the big pool where I had had my unequal and disastrous contest.

Looking into his face, I saw a sudden light of excitement dancing in his eyes.

"Odd," he muttered, "but not impossible."

"What isn't?" I asked breathlessly.

"Well, it looks to me as if the joints of that rod of yours have gone down-stream."

Gingerly he pulled up the line, and presently an end with a broken know appeared.

"The reel knot, eh?" I nodded gloomily. "Then we lose the rod," said he. That wasn't very heartening news. "On the other hand, it's just possible the fish is still on—sulking."

"Oo!" I exclaimed.

"Now, steady does it," he warned, "and give me my rod."

Taking a pair of clippers from his pocket, he cut his own line just above the cast.

"Can you tie a knot?" he asked.

"Yes," I nodded.

"Come on, then; bend your line onto mine. Quick as lightning."

Under his critical eye, I joined the two lines with a blood knot. "I guessed you were a fisherman," he said, nodded approvingly and clipped off the ends. "And now to know the best or the worst."

I shall never forget the music of that check reel or the suspense with which I watched as, with the butt of the rod bearing against the hollow of his thigh, he steadily wound up the wet slack line. Every instant I expected it to come drifting downstream, but it didn't. Presently it rose in a tight slant from the pool above.

"Snagged, I'm afraid," he said, and worked the rod with an easy straining motion to and fro. "Yes, I'm afraid—no, by Lord Bobs, he's on!"

I think it was only right and proper that I should have launched a yell of triumph as, with the spoken word, the point at which the line cut the water shifted magically from the left side of the pool to the right.

"And a fish too," said he.

In the fifteen minutes that followed, I must have experienced every known form of terror and delight.

"Youngster," said he, "you should be doing this, by rights, but I'm afraid the rod's a bit above your weight."

"Oh, go on and catch him," I pleaded.

"And so I will," he promised; "unship the gaff, young un, and stand by to use it, and if you break the cast we'll never speak to each other again, and that's a bet."

But I didn't break the cast. The noble, courageous, indomitable example of my river god had lent me skill and precision beyond my years. When at long last a weary, beaten, silver monster rolled within reach of my arm into a shallow eddy, the steel gaff shot out fair and true, and sank home.

And then I was lying on the grass, with my arms round a salmon that weighed twenty-two pounds on the scale and contained every sort of happiness known to a boy.

And best of all, my river god shook hands with me and called me "partner."

That evening the salmon was placed upon the blue ashet in the hall, bearing a little card with its weight and my name upon it.

And I am afraid I sat on a chair facing it, for ever so long, so that I could hear what the other anglers had to say as they passed by. I was sitting there when my colonel put his head out of his private sitting room and beckoned me to come in.

"A true fisherman lives in the future, not the past, old man," said he; "though for this once, it 'ud be a shame to reproach you."

I suppose I colored guiltily—at any rate, I hope so.

"We got the fish," said he, "but we lost the rod, and a future without a rod doesn't bear thinking of. Now"—and he pointed at a long wooden box on the floor, that overflowed with rods of different sorts and sizes—"rummage among those. Take your time and see if you can find anything to suit you."

"But do you mean—can I—"

"We're partners, aren't we? And p'r'aps as such you'd rather we went through our stock together."

"Oo, sir," I said.

"Here, quit that," he ordered gruffly. "By Lord Bobs, if a show like this afternoon's don't deserve a medal, what does? Now, here's a handy piece by Hardy—a light and useful tool—or if you fancy greenheart is in preference to split bamboo—"

I have the rod to this day, and I count it among my dearest treasures. And to this day I have a flick of the wrist that was his legacy. I have, too, some small skill in dressing flies, the elements of which were learned in his company by candlelight after the day's work was over. And I have countless memories of that month-long, month-short friendship—the closest and most perfect friendship, perhaps, of all my life.

He came to the station and saw me off. How I vividly remember his shaggy head at the window, with the whiskered cheeks and the gunpowder marks at the corners of his eyes! I didn't cry, although I wanted to awfully. We were partners and shook hands. I never saw him again, although on my birthdays I would have colored cards from him, with Irish, Scotch, Norwegian postmarks. Very brief they were: "Water very low." "Took a good fish last Thursday." "Been prawning, but don't like it."

Sometimes at Christmas I had gifts—a reel, a tapered line, a fly book. But I never saw him again.

Came at last no more cards or gifts, but in the *Fishing Gazette*, of which I was a religious reader, was an obituary telling how one of the last of the Mutiny veterans had joined the great majority. It seems he had been fishing half an hour before he died. He had taken his rod down and passed out. They had buried him at Totnes, overlooking the River Dart.

So he was no more—my river god—and what was left of him they had put into a box and buried it in the earth.

But that isn't true; nor is it true that I never saw him again. For I seldom go a-fishing but that I meet him on the river banks.

The banks of a river are frequented by a strange company and are full of mysterious and murmurous sounds—the cluck and laughter of water, the piping of birds, the hum of insects, and the whispering of wind in the willows. What should prevent a man in such a place having a word and speech with another who is not there? So much of a fishing lies in imagination, and mine needs little stretching to give my river god a living form.

"With this ripple," says he, "you should do well."

"And what's it to be," say I—"Blue Upright, Red Spinner? What's your fancy, sir?"

Spirits never grow old. He has begun to take an interest in dry-fly methods—that river god of mine, with his seven-league boots, his shaggy head, and the gaff across his back.

# PART II

# THE WARM WATER MIX

# "THEY'RE IN THE RIVER"

## JOHN MCPHEE

Among the spectators on the bridge, a cop appeared. He shouted, "Does one of you guys down there own a green Jeep?"

Ed Cervone shouted back, "Yes, Officer, I do."

"Well," the cop continued, with the slightest pause. "Your wife called. She wants you home. She thinks you're dead."

Laughter on the bridge—9:50 PM.

It was not true that Marian Cervone was concerned about her husband. By her own account, the man is too unpredictable to worry about. She wasn't worried about Edmund, either. It was my wife, Yolanda Whitman, whose mind had been crossed by the ultimate possibility. This was a few years before the sudden bloom of cellular phones. I had no way to tell her why I was late, and deliberately breaking off that fish never crossed my mind.

Yolanda seems to remember the evening with total recall. For one thing, it was my turn to cook. "By nine o'clock, I was just plain mad," she has said for the record. "You were dithering too long. I was waiting for my dinner. You were taking your sweet time, failing in your responsibilities."

Yes.

"At some point after that, I shifted from mad to concern. You had fallen out of the boat. Gone through the rapids."

The rapids, not far from the bridge, cross a diabase ledge and are tumultuous in spring.

"It was pitch black. Cold. I imagined you with hypothermia in the river. So I called Marian. I told her I was worried because your absence was 'out of character.'"

Marian must have marveled that someone could seriously use a phrase like that about a husband. Marian said she would call back if she learned anything. After hanging up, she called the Lambertville police. She said her husband and son and a friend were out in a boat and had not returned "way beyond the time" she expected them. Would the police check the boat-launch parking lot and see if a green Jeep was there? The woman on the other end of the line said the police surely would.

A while later, the police called Marian, and Marian called Yolanda, who continues the narrative: "While I waited, a tear or two actually squeezed out. I had let myself wander into the impossible. Perhaps I was madder at Ed than at you—who knows? After Marian called back, I was again spitting mad. She said, 'They're still fishing.'"

Two hours, thirty minutes. At last the fish had come up enough in the river so that the people on the bridge caught glimpses of it as, now and again, it canted—silver flashing—and changed direction. We heard them go "Ooh!" We heard them shout, "Wow, what a huge fish!" When we, in the boat, finally got a glimpse of it, we thought it enormous, too. Toward the end, I kept pressing it, tightened the drag even more, a risky, foolish thing to do. I just hoped it would not make a sudden run. If it did so, at least I had turned off the anti-reverse button, and the reel could spin free.

The fish was close now. When it saw the boat, it dived. After it came up, and saw the boat again, it took off for the bottom of the river, slowly to rise once more. At some point in the last five minutes, Edmund tried for it with the boat net and missed. I finally worked it up to the side of the boat. It was still swimming, unspent. It did not roll over. It never gave up. On the second try, Edmund got it into the net, and the dart dropped out of its mouth. He brought into the boat a four-and-three-quarter-pound roe shad.

I still have the dart—secured with monofilament to a small piece of cedar shingle. It was only the second dart I had ever retired. On a bookshelf, I propped it up beside a dart of the same weight and colors, with which, on an upriver day the spring before, I had caught seventeen shad without changing or losing the lure. The chemically sharpened hook was a novelty I had succumbed to in a catalogue. That shipment of hooks was uneven, to say the least. Some of them were so weak they were bent out straight by the force of tugging shad. But not this one. Despite two hours and thirty-five minutes in the shad's mouth, the curve of the black steel looked as it had when I made the dart and festooned it with bucktail in a vise. At home, I studied the fish with a magnifying glass. It had not been hooked on the top of the head or in any other place on the outside. It was not foul-hooked. It was hooked in the roof of the mouth, very near the front, slightly off the midline, to the right. I saw a narrow hole there, and I put a toothpick in it, which did not come through to the outside. The connection of hook and shad had been something like a trailer hitch.

Mindful of the species' paper jaw and its legendary fragility, I would one day lay a shad on a dissecting table at the University of Massachusetts and show Willy Bemis just where my fish had been hooked.

"How would you describe that, Willy?"

"It's the ethmoid cartilage of the braincase. It's the part of the braincase that everyone would understand as, regionally, the nose. One solid cartilaginous structure forms the braincase during early development. This is the anterior tip of it. The brain is back in the center of the head. Most of the braincase is protected by bone, which would make it a very tough place for a hook to latch on to. But once you've got a hook past the bone and into that little piece of cartilage, it doesn't come out. If a hook goes through that, it's going to hook on to the fish in a very serious way. There's no way that fish is ever going to throw that hook."

The monofilament felt sandpapery. When I took it off the reel, it contracted instantly into coils from a hundred and fifty-five minutes of twisting. A thick mass of bunched contracted circles hopelessly intertwined, it looked like something an owl dropped.

I sent the reel to the Daiwa Corporation, in California, for an assessment. They wanted $54.40 to fix it, because the shad had bent the pinion gear, the shad

had bent the drive gear, the shad had damaged the oscillating system and gone a long way toward wearing out the drag system. The reel required two new gears, a new pawl, a new worm shaft, and three new drag washers.

I still have some of the scales. They report the shad's age as three. For a female that young to be on the spawning run is more than uncommon. It's rare. The scales record strong growth in the river in the first summer, as the egg turned into a larva, and the larva into a juvenile. They record normal growth in the ocean in each of the following years. Then they show the shad coming back into the river—two years earlier than most females do.

Soon after that evening in Lambertville, I told this story to Richard St. Pierre, of the U.S. Fish and Wildlife Service. Headquartered in Harrisburg, on the Susquehanna River, he is a shad specialist, who has worked as a shad consultant on the Hudson River, the Columbia River, and the Yangtze. He said that it must have been a letdown for me to learn that the fish was not a striped bass or a sturgeon or a muskellunge "but just a shad."

It was not in any sense a letdown, I told him. I'm a shad fisherman. I was fishing for American shad.

# THE BLACK BASS AS A GAME FISH

## JAMES A. HENSHALL

*"He is a fish that lurks close all winter; but is very pleasant and jolly after mid-April, and in May, and in the hot months."*—Izaak Walton

Those who have tasted the lotus of salmon or trout fishing, in that Utopian clime of far away—while reveling in its aesthetic atmosphere, and surrounded by a misty halo of spray from the waterfall, or enveloped by the filmy gauze and iridescent tomes, sung idylls, chanted paeans, and poured out libations in honor and praise of the silver-spangled salmon, or the ruby-studded trout, while it is left to the vulgar horde of black bass anglers to stand upon the mountain of their own doubt and presumption, and, with uplifted hands, in admiration and awe, gaze with dazed eyes from afar upon that forbidden land— that *terra incognita*—and then, having lived in vain, die and leave no sign.

It is, then, with a spirit of rank heresy in my heart; with smoked glass spectacles on my nose, to dim the glare and glamour of the transcendent shore; with the scales of justice across my shoulder—*M. salmoides* in one scoop and *M. dolomieu* in the other—I pass the barriers and confines of the enchanted land, and toss them into a stream that has been depopulated of even fingerlings, by the *dilettanti* of salmon and trout fishers; for I would not, even here, put black bass in a stream inhabited by salmon or brook trout.

While watching the plebeian interlopers sporting in an eddy, their bristling spines and emerald sides gleaming in the sunshine, I hear an awful voice from the adjacent rocks exclaiming: "Fools rush in where angels fear to tread!" Shade of Izaak Walton defend us! While appealing to Father Izaak for protection, I quote his words: "Of which, if thou be a severe, sour complexioned man, then I here disallow thee to be a competent judge."

Seriously, from Izaak Walton to the present day, the salmon and trout of Great Britain have been sung in song and story as game-fishes, and it is sufficient to say that they deserve all the praise bestowed upon them. And as our ideas of fish and fishing have derived mostly from English authors, it follows that many American writers and anglers have been obsessed by their teaching, even down to the present day, as in dry fly-fishing.

Now, while we have in America the same salmon as in Great Britain, and several species of trout equally as good or better than the brown trout, we also have many other game-fishes equally worthy, and among them the black bass.

I feel free to assert, that, were the black bass a native of Great Britain, it would rank fully as high in the estimation of British anglers as either the trout or the salmon. I am borne out in this by the opinions of British sportsmen whose statements have been received without question.

W. H. Herbert (Frank Forester) writing of the black bass, says:

> "This is one of the finest of the American fresh-water fishes: it is surpassed by none in boldness of biting, in fierce and violent resistance when hooked, and by a very few only in excellence upon the board." (Fish and Fishing, 1850.)

Parker Gillmore ("Ubique") says:

> "I fear it will be almost deemed heresy to place this fish (black bass) on a par with the trout; at least, some such idea I had when I first heard

the two compared; but I am bold, and will go further. I consider he is the superior of the two, for he is equally good as an article of food, and much stronger, and untiring in his efforts to escape when hooked." (*Prairie and Forest*, 1874)

In regard to the comparative gameness of the black bass and the brook trout the following opinions of American anglers are added. Seth Green, one of the fathers of fish-culture and a lifelong angler for trout, among other fishes, has this to say:

"This is among the finest sporting as well as food fish in America. Bites fiercely at fly or trolling spoon; makes a vigorous fight for life, liberty and happiness, showing a perfect willingness 'to fight it out on that line if it takes all summer,' and at last when subdued and brought to the table does honor to the cook who prepares it, and pleasure to the palate that enjoys it." (*Fish Hatching and Fish Catching*, 1879)

Robert B. Roosevelt, who, with Seth Green, was a Fish Commissioner of New York, and co-author of *Fish Hatching and Fish Catching*, and a notable angler for salmon and trout, says of the black bass:

"A fish that is inferior only to the salmon and trout, if even to the latter; that requires the best of tackle and skill in its inveiglement, and exhibits courage and game qualities of the highest order." (*Superior Fishing*, 1865)

E. E. Millard, a veteran fly-fisher for trout for fifty years, who has camped many summers on the famous Nipigon, and who is a true and faithful lover of the brook trout, has this to say in comparing the trout and the black bass as game-fishes:

"When the acrobatic bass approaches with every spine bristling it signifies fight, and he dies battling face to the foe—not that the trout tamely submits at the first prick of the steel; far from it. He is a fighter, though not a scientific one, having no appreciation of the finer and more artistic points of the game. He looks the fighter, having the neck and shoulders of the pugilist, but is rather too beautiful, which, however, does not always follow, and there is lacking a little of the Irish in his composition, though when put to the crowning test, he hangs on with bulldog tenacity, lacking only the resourcefulness of the small-mouth bass, the generally recognized champion of finny warriors, and of whom I can well believe that, inch for inch and pound for pound, he is the gamest fish that swims." (*Days on the Nipigon*, 1917)

Now, while salmon fishing is, unquestionably, the highest branch of piscatorial sport; and while trout fishing in Canada, Maine, and the Lake Superior region justifies all the extravagant praise bestowed upon it, I am inclined to doubt the judgment and good taste of those anglers who snap their fingers in contempt of black bass fishing, while they will wade in a stream with brush and logs, catch a few trout weighing six or eight to the pound, and call it the only artistic angling in the world! While they are certainly welcome to their opinion, I think their zeal is worthy of a better cause.

The black bass is eminently an American fish, and is truly representative in his characteristics. He has the faculty of asserting himself and making himself completely at home wherever placed. He is plucky, game, brave, and unyielding to the last when hooked. He has the arrowy rush and vigor of the trout, the untiring strength and bold leap of the salmon, while he has a system of fighting tactics peculiarly his own.

Among anglers, the question is often raised as to what constitutes a game-fish, and what particular species are to be considered best among game-fishes. In coordinating the essential attributes of game-fishes, each inherent trait and quality must be duly and impartially considered. Their habits and habitat; their aptitude to rise to the artificial fly; their manner of resistance and struggle for freedom when hooked; their finesse and intelligence; and their excellence as food must all be taken into account and duly weighed.

The black bass is more advanced in the scheme of evolution, and exhibits traits of a higher organization than either the salmon or trout. It is worthy of note that the highest development of fishes is shown in those with spiny-rayed fins as in the black bass, striped bass, channel bass, etc., while those of a lower development have soft-rayed fins as in the salmon, trout, whitefish, pike, etc.

In the animal creation the highest intelligence is exemplified by the parental instinct or care of the young. This is shown in the highest degree among mammals, next among birds, in but few reptiles, and scarcely at all among fishes. In the two hundred, or more, families of fishes, those that evince any parental instinct or manifest any care of their young can be counted on the fingers of one hand. The black bass stands pre-eminent in this respect, and is a bright and shining example to all the finny tribe in its habit of watching and guarding its nest and caring for its young brood when hatched.

Most fishes in fresh and salt water abandon their eggs as soon as emitted and fertilized. The salmon and trouts deposit their eggs in the shallowest water and leave them to the tender mercies of predatory fish, birds, and reptiles during an incubation of two or three months.

The black bass will rise to the artificial fly as readily as the salmon or the brook trout, under the same conditions; and will take the live minnow, or other live bait, under any and all circumstances favorable to the taking of any other fish. I consider him, *inch for inch* and *pound for pound*, the gamest fish that swims. The royal salmon and the lordly trout must yield the palm to a black bass of *equal weight*.

That he will eventually become the leading game-fish of America is my oft-expressed opinion and firm belief. This result, I think, is inevitable; if for no other reasons, from a force of circumstances occasioned by climatic conditions and the operation of immutable natural laws, such as the gradual drying up and dwindling away of the small trout streams, and the consequent decrease in brook trout, both in quality and quantity; and by the introduction of predatory fish in waters where the trout still exists.

Another prominent cause of the decline and fall of the brook trout, is the erection of dams, saw-mills, and factories upon trout streams, which, though to be deplored, cannot be prevented; the march of empire and the progress of civilization can not be stayed by the honest, though powerless, protests of anglers.

But, while the ultimate fate of the brook trout is sealed beyond peradventure, in open, public waters, we have the satisfaction of knowing that in the black bass we have a fish equally worthy, both as to game and edible qualities, and which at the same time is able to withstand and defy many of the causes that will, in the end, effect the annihilation and extinction of the brook trout.

As to a comparison of game qualities as between the small-mouth bass and the large-mouth bass, I hold that, other things being equal, and where the two species inhabit the same waters, there is no difference in game qualities; for, while the small-mouth is probably more active in its movements, the large-mouth bass is more powerful; and no angler can tell from its manner of resistance whether he is fast to one or the other.

Both species of black bass rise equally well to the artificial fly; though, if there be any difference in this respect, I think the large-mouth bass has the advantage. In a letter Count Von dem Borne, of Germany (who was very successful in introducing and propagating the black bass in that country), wrote me that the large-mouth black bass rose better to the artificial fly than the small-mouth bass. My own experience rather favors this view, and it has likewise been brought to my notice by anglers in various parts of the country.

The current but erroneous opinion that the small-mouth bass exceeds the large-mouth bass in game qualities, has been very widespread, and has been much enhanced by the endorsement of several of our best ichthyologists, who unfortunately, however, are not, and do not pretend to be, anglers, but who imbibed this opinion second-hand from prejudiced anglers who ought to have known better. But as the black bass is becoming better known, and fly fishing for the species is being more commonly practiced, this unfair and unmerited comparison is fast dying out.

Fish inhabiting swiftly-running streams are always more vigorous and gamy than those in still waters, and it is probable that where the large-mouth bass exists alone in very shallow and sluggish waters, of high temperature and thickly grown with algae, it will exhibit less combative qualities, consequent on the enervating influences of its environment; but where both species inhabit the same waters, and are subject to the same conditions, I am convinced that no angler can tell whether he has hooked a large-mouth or a small-mouth bass, from their resistance and mode of fighting, provided they are of equal weight, until he has the ocular evidence.

I use the expression "equal weight" advisedly, for most anglers must have remarked that the largest bass of either species are not necessarily the hardest fighters; on the contrary, a bass of two or two and a half pounds' weight will usually make a more gallant fight than one of twice the size, and this fact, I think, will account in a great measure for the popular idea that the small-mouth bass is the "gamest" species for this reason:

Where the two species co-exist in the same stream or lake, the large-mouth bass always grows to a larger size than the other species, and an angler having just landed a two-pound small-mouth bass after a long struggle, next hooks a large-mouth bass weighing four or five pounds, and is surprised, probably, that it "fights" no harder or perhaps not so hard as the smaller fish—in fact, seems "logy"; he, therefore, reiterates the cry that the small-mouth bass is the gamest fish.

But, now, if he next succeeds in hooking a large-mouth bass of the same size as the first one caught, he is certain that he is playing a small-mouth bass until it is landed, when to his astonishment it proves to be a large-mouth bass; he merely says, "he fought well for one of his kind," still basing his opinion of the fighting qualities of the two species upon the first two caught.

Perhaps his next catch may be a small-mouth bass of four pounds, and which, though twice the weight of the large-mouth bass just landed, does not offer any greater resistance, and he sets it down in his mind as a large-mouth bass. Imagine the angler's surprise, then, upon taking it into the landing net, to find it a small-mouth bass, and one which, from its large size and the angler's preconceived opinion of the species should have fought like a Trojan.

Now, one would think that the angler would be somewhat staggered in his former belief; but no, he is equal to the occasion, and in compliance with the popular idea, he merely suggests that "it was out of condition, somehow," or "was hooked so as to drown it in the struggle"; and so, as his largest fish will necessarily be big-mouth bass, and because they do not fight in proportion to their size, they are set down as lacking in game qualities—of course, leaving the largest small-mouth bass out of the calculation.

Gentle reader, this is not a case of special pleading, nor is the angler a creation of the imagination lugged in as an apologist for the large-mouth bass; he is a veritable creature of fish and blood, of earth earthy, and with the self-conceit, weaknesses and shortcomings characteristic of the genus *homo*. I have met him and heard his arguments and sage expressions scores of times, and if the reader will reflect a moment I am sure he will recognize him.

Many years ago I was at Gogebic Lake, Wisconsin, where, among a number of prominent anglers, were Dr. F., and Dr. T., both of New York City. Dr. F. had a very extensive angling experience in all parts of the country, and Dr. T. was well known as a participant in the fly- and bait-catching contests in the tournaments of the National Rod and Reel Association of that day.

Dr. T. was a firm believer in the superior game qualities of the small-mouth bass, and declared that he could invariably tell what species of black bass he had hooked, from its manner of "fighting." Dr. F. was confident he could not do so. The matter was finally put to a practical test, when Dr. T. was forced to acknowledge himself vanquished, and that he nor any other angler could make the distinction, for one fish was as "gamy" as the other. I might add that this result will be obtained wherever the two species exist in the same waters.

Mr. S. C. Clarke, a veteran angler of sixty years' experience, and whose opinion is titled to great weight, says:

> "I will say that, from an acquaintance with both species for more than forty years, from Minnesota to Florida, I have found little or no difference between them. I have taken them with fly, spoon, and bait, as many as fifty in a day (in early times), and up to six and a half pounds' weight."

A few years before his death, Fred Mather wrote as follows:

"A bad name, given to the big-mouth bass when black bass first began to attract the attention of anglers, has stuck. It may interest a younger generation of anglers to know that forty years ago these gamy fishes were hardly known to anglers, and as soon as they began to attract attention some persons, to show their exquisite discrimination, began to praise one to the detriment of the other. Dr. Henshall and I have had the courage to fight this, and to say that in game qualities there is little difference, and that what there is depends on the weight of the fish, two pounds being its fighting weight. Further than to say that the big-mouth is not so capricious about taking the fly as his brother—*i.e.*, will usually take it more freely—I have not room to go into this subject here. I have written all this before and intend to keep at it until justice is done to a noble game-fish."

Mr. Henry Talbott, an angler of wide experience, and who has written so entertainingly and instructively on black bass angling in the Potomac, says:

"There are some anglers who consider there is but one black bass, the small-mouth, and that the other is useless for food, lacking in gamy qualities and only fished for by the misguided. In this they are mistaken, and it is a theory they will abandon and resent when their experience is wider.

"It is possible that in the Florida lakes they may be tame sport, and there seems to be a general agreement that in some of the swamps of Ohio the big-mouth is an inferior fish, but there is yet to be found his superior where he has a fair chance.

"Taking the two fish at their best, there is no man living can tell the difference in their taking the fly, in their fight to the boat, or on the platter, by any other sign than that one has a more capacious smile than the other; and by the same token he is just a little the better jumper and will leave the water oftener after being hooked, and is as long in coming to the net as his cousin."

Owing to my admiration for the black bass as a game-fish, and my championship of its cause for many years, and my efforts to place it in the front rank of game-fishes, and my desire to have it placed in new waters, I am sometimes, thoughtlessly and unjustly, accused of being opposed to the brook trout, and of advising the stocking of trout streams with my "favorite" fish. Nothing can be further from the truth.

I am utterly opposed to the introduction of black bass into waters in which there is the remotest chance for the brook trout or rainbow trout to thrive. I yield to no one in love and admiration of the brook trout. I was perfectly familiar with it before I ever saw a black bass; but I am not so blinded by prejudice but that I can share that love with the black bass, which for several reasons is destined to become the favorite game-fish of America. "My offending hath this extent, no more."

Let us look this thing squarely in the face. I do not wish to disturb anyone's preference, but I do want to disabuse the minds of anglers of all prejudice in the matter. The brook trout must go. It has already gone from many streams, and is fast disappearing from others. It is sad to contemplate the extinction of the "angler's pride" in public waters, but the stern fact remains that in this utilitarian age its days are numbered and its fate irrevocably sealed. As the red man disappears before the tread of the white man, the "living arrow" of the mountain streams goes with him.

The trout is essentially a creature of the pine forests. Its natural home is in waters shaded by pine, balsam, spruce, and hemlock, where the cold mountain brooks retain their low temperature, and the air is redolent of balsamic fragrance; where the natural food of the trout is produced in the greatest abundance, and where its breeding grounds are undisturbed.

But the iron has entered its soul. As the buffalo disappears before the iron horse, the brook trout vanishes before the axe of the lumberman. As the giants of the forest are laid low, and the rank and file decimated and the wooden walls of the streams battered down, the hot, fiery sun leaps through the breaches, disclosing the most secret recesses of forest and stream to the bright glare of midday. The moisture of the earth is dissipated, the mosses and ferns become shriveled and dry, the wintergreen and partridge-berry, the ground pine and trailing arbutus struggle feebly for existence; the waters decrease in size and increase in temperature, the conditions of the food supply and of the breeding grounds of the brook trout are changed; it deteriorates in size and numbers and vitality, until finally, in accordance with the immutable laws of nature and the great principle of the "survival of the fittest" (not the fittest from the angler's point of view, but the fittest to survive the changes and mutations consequent on the march of civilization), it disappears altogether.

Much has been said about the "trout hog" in connection with the decrease of the trout. But while he deserves all the odium and contempt heaped upon him by the honest angler, the result would be the same were the trout allowed undisturbed and peaceable possession of the streams, so far as the fish-hook is concerned, while the axe of the lumberman continues to ring its death knell.

Let us, then, cherish and foster and protect the crimson-spotted favorite of our youthful days as long as possible in public waters, and introduce the rainbow trout, the Dolly Varden, the steelhead, the red-throat trout, or the English brown trout, when he has disappeared; and when all these succumb, then, and not till then, introduce the black bass. But let us give these cousins of the brook trout a fair trial first, and without prejudice. There are plenty of lakes, ponds, and large streams in the eastern states into which the black bass can be introduced without interfering with trout waters.

For many years to come brook trout will be artificially cultivated, and the supply thus kept up in preserved waters by wealthy angling clubs; but by the alteration of the natural conditions of their existence they will gradually decrease in size and quality, until finally they will either cease to be or degenerate to such a degree as to forfeit even this praiseworthy protection.

I must dissent from the statement sometimes made that the black bass is the blue-fish of fresh waters. The black bass is voracious—so are all game-fishes—but not more so than the brook trout. The character of a fish's teeth determines the nature of its food and the manner of its feeding. The bluefish has the most formidable array of teeth of any fish of its size—compressed, lancet-shaped, covered with enamel, and exceedingly strong and sharp, in fact, miniature shark teeth—while the black bass has soft, small, brush-like teeth, incapable of wounding, and intended only for holding its prey, which is swallowed whole. The brook trout has longer, stronger and sharper teeth than the bass, and a large, long mouth, capable of swallowing a bigger fish than a black bass of equal weight. The mouth of the bass is very wide, for the purpose of taking in crawfish with their long and aggressive claws, and not, as supposed by some, for the swallowing of large fishes. The black bass gets the best of other game-fishes, not by devouring the fishes themselves, but by devouring their food. For this reason, more than any other, they should not be introduced into the same waters with brook trout. The pike or pickerel is the bluefish of fresh waters, and in dental capacity and destructive possibilities is not far behind it.

The brook trout, I think, is the most beautiful of all fishes, as a fresh-run salmon is the handsomest and most perfect in form. The salmon is a king, the brook trout a courtier, but the black bass, in his virescent cuirass and spiny crest, is a doughty warrior whose prowess none can gainsay.

I have fished for brook trout in the wilds of Canada, where a dozen would rise at every cast of the fly, and it would be a scramble as to which should get it—great lusty trout, from a half-pound to two pounds in weight—but the black fly made life a burden by day, and the mosquito by night. The glory and beauty of the madly rushing stream breaking wildly over the great black rocks, and the quiet, glassy pools below reflecting the green spires of spruce and fir, availed nothing to swollen eyelids and smarting brow.

I have cast from early morn till dewy eve, on a good salmon stream in New Brunswick, for three days in succession without a single rise. I have cast standing in a birch-bark canoe until both arms and legs were weary with the strain, and then rested by casting while sitting—but all in vain. The swift-flowing, crystal stream reflected back the fierce glare of the northern sun and flowed on in silence toward the sea. The fir-clad hills rose boldly on either side, and stood in silent, solemn grandeur—for neither note of bird or hum of bee disturbed the painful silence of the Canadian woods.

At such times would flash on memory's mirror many a fair scene of limpid lake or rushing river, shadowed by cool, umbrageous trees, and vocal with myriads of voices—where the black bass rose responsive to the swish of the rod and dropping of the fly. Or, should the bass be coy and shy, or loth to leave his lair beneath some root or shelving rock—the melody of the birds, the tinkle of a cow-bell, the chirp of a cricket, the scudding of a squirrel, filled up the void and made full compensation.

The true angler can find real pleasure in catching little sunfish, or silver-sides, if the stream and birds, and bees and butterflies do their part by him; while the killing of large or many fish, even salmon or trout, in silence and solitude, may fail to fully satisfy him.

I can find something beautiful or interesting in every fish that swims. I have an abiding affection for every one, from the lowly, naked bull-head, the humble scavenger of the waters, to the silver-spangled king who will not deign to soil his dainty lips with food during his sojourn in crystal streams, and I love the brook trout best of all. But, as an angler, I can find more true enjoyment, more blessed peace, in wading some rushing, rocky stream, flecked by the shadows of over-hanging elm and sycamore, while tossing the silken gage to the knight in Lincoln-green, my ears conscious of the rippling laughter of the merry stream, the joyous matin of the woodland thrush, the purring undertone of the quivering leaves—my eyes catching glimpses of hill and meadow, wren and robin, bee and bittern, fern and flower, and my breath inhaling the sweet fragrance of upland clover and elder-blossom—I say I can find more true enjoyment in this—than paying court to the lordly salmon in his drear and silent demesne, or in wooing the lovely trout with anointed face, gloved hands, and head swathed in gauze.

If this be treason, my brother, make the most of it. I am content. It is my honest conviction. After killing every species of game-fish east of the Rocky Mountains, from Canada to Florida, and some in foreign lands, I find the knightly bass and his tourney-field all sufficient.

## THE CAPTURE OF THE BASS

My brother of the angle, go with me
This perfect morning in the leafy June,
To yonder pool below the rapid's foot.
Approach with caution; let your tread be soft;
Beware the bending bushes on the brink.
Disturb no branch, nor twig, nor leaf, my friend,
The finny tribe is wary.

Rest we here.
Behold the lovely scene! The rippling stream,
Now dancing, sparkling, in the morning sun;
The blue-eyed violet nodding at your feet;
The red-bird, all ablaze, with swelling throat,
The dreamy, droning hum of insect wings
Is mingled ever with the rustling leaves.
Sleek, well-fed cattle there contented stand,
On gravelly shoal beneath the spreading beech.
Across the narrow stream a sycamore,
A weather-beaten giant, old and gray,
With scarr'd arms stretching o'er the silent pool,
With gnarl'd and twisted roots bathed in the flood
For, lo, these hundred years.

Beneath those roots
With watchful eye—proud monarch of the pool—
A cunning bass doth lie, on balanced fin,
In waiting for his prey.

And now with rod,
With faithful reel, and taper'd line of silk,
With mist-like leader and two fairly flies—
Dark, bush hackles, both—I make a cast.

With lengthen'd line I quickly cast again,
And just beneath the tree the twin-like lures
As gently drop as falling autumn leaves;
And half-submerged, like things of life they seem,
Responsive to the rod and line.
But look!
Saw you that gleam beneath the flood? A flash—
A shadow—then a swirl upon the pool?
My hand, responsive to the sudden thrill,
Strikes in the steel—the wary bass is hooked!
And now with lightning speed he darts away
To reach his lair—his refuge 'neath the roots.
The singing reel proclaims him almost there—
I "give the butt"—the ever-faithful rod
In horse-shoe curve checks his headlong flight.
Right lustily he tugs and pulls, Egad!
But still the barb is fast.

The hissing line—
The rod now bending like a slender reed
Resists the tight'ning strain. He turns his course—
In curving reaches, back and forth, he darts,
Describing arcs and segments in the pool.
Ha! nobly done! as with a mighty rush
He cleaves the crystal stream, and at one bound,
Full half a fathom in the realm above
He nimbly takes an atmospheric flight—
His fins extended, stiff with bristling points—
His armor brightly flashing in the sun—
His wide-extended jaws he shakes in rage
To rid him of the hook.

And now I lower
The pliant rod in court'sy to the brave.
The line relieved, somewhat, of steady strain,
Outwits the wily bass—the hook holds fast!
Now back again he falls with angry splash
To seek the aid of snag, or root of tree;

For thus, my friend, he oft escapes, I trow,
By fouling line or hook—

He never sulks!
Not he; while life remains, or strength holds good,
His efforts never cease. Now up the stream—
Now down again—I have him well in hand.
Now reeling in, or erstwhile giving line;
He swims now fast or slow—now high or low.
The steady strain is still maintained, you see!
The good rod swaying like a wind-blown rush—
He surges thro' the flood.

Another leap!
Ye Gods! How like an angry beast he shakes
His brisling mane, and dives below again!
And did you mark, my friend, his shrewd intent,
As when he fell upon the slacken'd line?
If then he'd found it stretched and taut, I ween,
He would have made his safe and sure escape.
But haply then the tip was slightly lowered—
And so, with yielding line, the hook held fast.
Now truly, friend, he makes a gallant fight!
In air or water—all the same to him—
His spiny crest erect; he struggles still.
No sulking here! but like a mettl'd steed
He champs the bit, and ever speeds the best
With firm-held, tighten'd rein.

He's off again!
Now down the stream he flashes like a shaft
From long-bow swiftly sped—his last bold spurt—
The effort cost him dear—his worsted strength
Is ebbing fast. And now in lessening curves
He feebly swims, and labors with the tide.
And as I reel the line he slowly yields,
And now turns up his breast-plate, snowy white—
A vanquished, conquered knight.

And now my friend
The landing-net. With firm and cautious hand
Beneath the surface hold it. Take him in.
Now lift him out and gently lay him down.
How bright his tunic, bronze and glossy green!
A fitting rival to the velvet sward.
And see the ragged rent the hook hath made!
You marvel how it held him safe and fast!
'Twas by the equal and continual strain
Of supple rod and ever-faithful reel.
'Twas work well done.

Oh valiant, noble bass!
Fit dweller of the merry, brawling stream.
Thy once-loved pool beneath thy giant tree,
Thy fancied stronghold 'neath its tangled roots,
Shall know thee never more. Thy race is run!

Now in thy creel,
My doubting friend, we'll gently lay him down
Upon a bed of cool and graceful ferns,
Yet sparkling with the early morning dew—
A warrior in repose!

# RED, WHITE, AND BLUEGILL

## TED LEESON

Among angling aristocrats, Atlantic salmon have long been celebrated as "the fish of kings," no doubt because the two have so much in common: the aloof arrogance and inflated sense of self-worth, a fussiness about habitat, expensive tastes. And as far as I'm concerned, they deserve each other. Give me a panfish any day—a fish of the people, blue-collar rather than blue blood, a working-class fish, a fish for a great republic. I've never understood how the bald eagle, a scavenger and a thief, could have been chosen as our national symbol, whereas the honest, sweat-of-the-brow bluegill never even made the shortlist. I guess the Founding Fathers didn't fish much.

Panfish, of course, doesn't denote a particular species but a loosely defined assemblage with varying regional representatives—a little like Congress but harder working and better behaved. The core of the group comes from the Centrarchidae family—the sunfishes—itself a kind of melting pot whose chief ingredients include bluegills, pumpkinseeds, redears, redbreasts, green sunfish, warmouths, rock bass, and white and black crappies. A kind of odd-man-out, the yellow perch is not a sunfish but no less a panfish wherever it is found. I'm not aware of any single place that's home to all these species at once. They crop up in various mixes and proportions in different geographical areas, and membership in the category of panfish (or "bream" or "brim," depending on where you live) has always been a matter of shifting local interpretations, further complicated by a host of colloquial names: shellcracker, stumpknocker, goggle-eye, sun perch, longear, speckled perch, white bass, and so on. In practice, the term ultimately falls into that set of expressions, like "I'll do it in a minute" or "I have strong feelings for you," that are universally understood but not necessarily taken to mean exactly the same thing by everyone.

Fishermen don't trouble themselves much about such discrepancies, instead focusing on the collective virtues of the fish. And foremost among their merits is a relentless availability. Like the other indispensables of American life—duct tape, canned chili, and WD-40—panfish can be obtained virtually everywhere. I've taken them in creeks and rivers, brackish water and fresh, 10,000-acre lakes and quarter-acre stock tanks, old quarry pits, prairie potholes, golf-course water hazards, abandoned strip mines, backyard ponds, irrigation ditches, and once, the ornamental fountain pool behind a fancy hotel. As a group, they are America's most widespread and abundant gamefish. And they are nothing if not game. I've caught them by accident and on purpose, on handlines, trotlines, poles cut from tree limbs, garage-sale spincast outfits, fly tackle that cost slightly less than my car, and every kind of gear in between. I've grabbed a few by hand and (in a mercifully brief period of angling dementia) jigged them up through 2 feet of ice. Equally ready for a few casual casts after work or the formalities of an organized expedition, panfish are a fish-of-all-trades, up for anything, anytime. They are a welcome counterweight to the forces of high-tech angling and a persistent reminder that fishing is finally about fish, not equipment.

Accommodating and enthusiastic, genial and cooperative, panfish are custom-cut for the neophyte. In the angling universe of my youth, they were the force of gravity that held everything together. The ones I could catch whetted my skills and honed my instincts. Those that proved better at being fish than I did at being a fisherman gave me a continuing sense of purpose. Without panfish, I might well have sunk into juvenile delinquency, or golf. The pinnacle of every summer was the day my father, a man who did not readily leave the house, squeezed our whole family into a station wagon and endured the eight-hour drive to a lake in northern Wisconsin. He herded us directly from the car into a rowboat where, except for a few moments stolen to dig more worms, we spent a week or two yarding in unimaginable numbers of perch and rock bass and bluegills. The little ones bit readily. And the bigger ones proved just discriminating enough to teach you something but still catchable enough that you could learn the lesson. At a time of life as yet uncorrupted by a lust for magazine-cover specimens, panfish fulfilled the greatest promise in all of angling—pure action.

We ate them too, by the stringerful, with butter and lemon and onions, fried, baked, broiled, and grilled, and best of all, without guilt. Even today, in a time when quality angling for high-profile species increasingly hinges on catch-and-release, you can still sit down to a plate of bluegills or crappies without the slightest twinge of conscience or the fear of a second-rate meal. They come by their name honestly, for a pan is the highest destiny of these sweet-eating fishes. Bony? Sure, a little. And a steamed crab is mostly shell. Who's that going to stop?

Once you've got panfish in your soul, they never really leave. Not many seasons ago, a friend and I extorted an invitation to a pay-to-play trophy trout lake in the high desert of eastern Washington. The morning's fishing, though not fast, produced some remarkable trout, among the biggest of my life. Noon found us prospecting the lower end of the lake. Approaching deeper water near an earthen dam, we suddenly doubled up—smaller fish, it was clear, but dogged and determined fighters. To our utter disbelief, they turned out to be a pair of identical yellow perch a full pound apiece, with deep blue-green backs and lemon-lime flanks that shaded into fat, cantaloupe bellies. With no real idea how they got there, but a pretty good one about how to get them out, we burned up half a box of trout flies and a whole afternoon happily catching perch in a $200-a-day lake where a 5-pound rainbow scarcely elicits a yawn. That evening when our host, proud of his fishery and eager for a report, asked how we'd done, we just told him, "Couldn't have been better."

And we meant it. In this age of scientific fisheries control, of measurements and projections that produce finely calibrated angling regulations, panfish may well be the last unmanaged gamefish in America, left to themselves, on their own as they've always been and doing just fine, thank you. It's ironic that a whole sector of the fishing industry now thrives on whisking anglers off for remote and pristine destinations to experience sport of unspoiled abundance, fishing "the way it used to be." Any 8-year-old kid with a cane pole, a bike, and panfish in his heart can lead you to just such a place.

And maybe that's what I like best about them: Panfish are the most democratic of gamefish. They do not care who fishes them and bite equally for everyone. They're unimpressed by the cost of your tackle, indifferent to the methods you use, unconcerned about the bait you favor, and sometimes, whether there's any bait at all. Panfish are angling's version of the single-shot .22—sturdy and dependable, workmanlike and unpretentious. If panfish formed a baseball team, they'd be the Cubs; if you could play them on a jukebox, they'd be Hank Williams tunes; if panfish were a beer, they'd be whatever's on sale.

Oh, and there's one last thing. Except for the more cosmopolitan perch, panfish are pure homegrown. Though, like much in American life, they've been exported around the world, panfish are indigenous only to North America, native to no other part of the globe. So picture this for a moment—a red-and-white bobber twitching above the slab of a sunset-colored bluegill. Now there's something worth printing on the back of a dollar bill.

# SACRED EELS

## JAMES PROSEK

*We have not attained to the full solution of the exceedingly difficult eel problems,*
*but the steady progress of the last twenty years is full of promise for the future . . .*
*Altogether the whole story of the eel and its spawning has come to read almost like a romance,*
*wherein reality has far exceeded the dreams of fantasy.*

—Dr. Johannes Schmidt, 1912

My early encounters with eels were awkward, confused. My friends and I caught them by accident while fishing for trout or bass with worms. We never stopped to admire them; we were too shocked by their energy, frustrated by our inability to hold onto their slimy bodies, and just wanted our hooks back.

One December in Italy eight years ago, I stood at the edge of a lake next to my friend Larry Ashmead. A line of slender poles was sticking out of the water along the shore. A man nearby said the poles marked traps for catching eels, and I began to tell Larry what little I knew of the life history of freshwater eel.

Like those slender fish on the other side of the Atlantic, the eels in this lake were born in the middle of the Atlantic Ocean, somewhere east of the Bahamas, maybe several thousand feet deep. The discovery of the eels' spawning place was made in the early 1900s by the Danish oceanographer Johannes Schmidt, who caught thousands of specimens of the larval stage of the eel in fine mesh nets in an amorphous region of the North Atlantic, several million square miles, called the Sargasso Sea. Observing these larvae, only a few millimeters long and a few days old, drifting in the surface of the ocean currents, Schmidt concluded that the adult eels had recently spawned, somewhere beneath his nets. News of the find, one of the most exciting in marine biology in the twentieth century, was published widely, in such magazines as *National Geographic*, in 1913, and the journal *Nature*. But it soon became clear that although Schmidt had solved a part of the "eel problem," he had merely stoked the fire. Although they knew at the surface where the eels spawned, no one had witnessed the adults spawning. It became then, perhaps, an even greater marine mystery.

Before the twentieth century, scientists both amateur and professional had concocted numerous explanations about how eels reproduced, many of them harebrained: that they were generated from horse hairs, or drops of dew, that they mated with snakes on the banks of rivers, or emerged from the carcasses of dead animals or the mud. It was not even known whether eels were asexual or had gender and reproductive organs until Sigmund Freud as a young medical student published the first paper on the location of the eel's gonads. As it turns out, the reproductive organs were virtually invisible until the fish began its journey in the sea. The larval stage of the eel—which looks nothing like the adult itself, but more like a leaf-shaped fish with fangs—was indeed known for centuries, named its own species, *Leptocephalus breverostris*. But until two Italian biologists in the late 1800s observed these fish metamorphosing into eels we didn't know the eel had a larval stage at all. Schmidt was determined to find out where these larvae, caught in the open ocean, came from. But even after Schmidt's discovery of the general vicinity of the Atlantic eels' spawning place, to this day, no one has witnessed an adult eel spawning in the sea, or seen an adult eel much beyond the river mouth on their way to the spawning grounds. His findings merely opened a larger can of eels.

"After the young are born in the ocean as little leaf-shaped fish," I said to my friend Larry, "they are spread randomly by ocean currents to the coasts of the Atlantic. After twenty years or so in freshwater, the adults return to the ocean to spawn and then die."

The eel is one of the few fishes that are catadromous—that is, it spends its adult life in freshwater but reproduces in salt. This life history is the opposite of that of the salmon, for instance, an anadromous fish, which spends its adult life in the sea but reproduces in freshwater. There are several other populations of catadromous eels around the world that spawn in other oceans but carry out very similar lives to the Atlantic eel.

Larry found all this hard to believe. Until his moment of doubt, I hadn't really stopped to consider what the eels went through to get to and from the small brooks and lakes where they spent their adult lives. The place where they would reproduce, and probably die, was thousands of miles away.

Some weeks later, Larry came across a 1941 story by Rachel Carson from *Under the Sea Wind*, called "Odyssey of the Eel." It is a tale written largely through the eyes of a female eel named Anguilla (the genus name for catadromous eels), inspired by Schmidt's discovery. The story begins by describing juvenile eels swimming to a small body of water called Bittern Pond, two hundred miles from the sea, "like pieces of slender glass rods shorter than a man's finger." And then, one dark rainy night in autumn, many years after she first entered freshwater, Anguilla leaves the pond, beginning her long journey back to the Sargasso.

Anguilla is drawn almost magnetically toward that place of warmth and darkness hundreds of feet below the surface of the ocean where she was born. Beyond that, the author imagines the rest, because once Anguilla leaves the mouth of the river, her life in the ocean is entirely a mystery: "No one can trace the path of the eels that left the salt marsh at the mouth of the bay on that November night when wind and tide brought them the feeling of warm ocean water—how they passed from the bay to the deep Atlantic basin that lies south of Bermuda and east of Florida half a thousand miles."

We don't know much more of the eel's life history today, nearly a century after Schmidt's discovery. What remains consistent about the eel is its ability to avoid our gaze. That ultimately was what attracted me to the eel.

It's not easy to get to like, or to know, the eel. It is dark and slippery, and not particularly beautiful at first glance. For me, the eel began as an idea. The idea was of the unseen journey, and the eel's intangible determination to reach a destination, a destiny that ends with death, and life. I'm still trying to figure out what to do with that idea, and whether trying to make sense of its ethereal qualities would somehow break the beauty of its incomprehensibility. In the course of my time spent with eels, I met other people who were as interested in eels as I was, people whose lives cross paths with the eel. Fishermen, scientists, slippery lovers of darkness themselves, who I began to call, in jest, "eelians."

Many eelians live lives like the eel, unseen, quiet, under the radar. For me, the unexpected paths that led to these people became wrapped in the original idea. One, Ray Turner, an eel fisherman of the Catskill Mountains in New York State, became a kind of prophet to me, who spoke in aphorisms that appeared alternately meaningless and prophetic, depending on the circumstances and delivery. "It's not the journey, it's the road," he once told me. Or, "Art is reality out of proportion." But the elusiveness of the eel was its beauty.

All around the world, the eel inspires fear, awe, and respect. Humans seem to have some visceral reaction to this minimalist fish, as they do the snake, a tempter of the innocent and virginal, an erotic symbol, a food source, a god. In some cultures the eel fills both the well of human spirituality and the stomach. The spawning areas and much of the life history of the world's catadromous eels is still a mystery, one that may be, as the indigenous people of New Zealand believe, best left unsolved. But it would be unfortunate if the opportunity to know the eel became lost. All around the world, catadromous eel populations are in serious decline. The causes are many and not always easily defined. If we do lose the eel, however, before we witness its spawning or know more about what fuels its determination to make the journey, or how it navigates in its migration, then, as the poet Wallace Stevens once wrote, "farewell to an idea."

I began my work on eels around 1998, and, as is the case when I dig into a topic, I mentioned my interest in eels with anyone who came within talking distance. I brought up eels in conversation with family, editors, artists, therapists, my barber, and one day with a friend named David Seidler, a screenwriter friend in Santa Monica. He asked me if I'd heard of the sacred eels in New Zealand. I had not, nor had I read anything about how important eels were to the culture and traditions of the Maori, the native Polynesians of New Zealand. There was, I would discover, a reason for this—Maori stories and traditions are passed on orally, and only between Maori.

As I found out on my first visit to New Zealand a few years before, a post-college trout-fishing trip with my friend Taylor, the Maori are genial, but don't go out of their way to share anything. Taylor and I saw Maori men in bars after their long days at work in the sawmills or slaughterhouses, but not much more than a grunt or nod passed between us. We trekked on Maori tribal land, hiked trails through old growth forests, fished crystal clear rivers with tall fern trees shading emerald pools, caught trout introduced by the British, and hung out with naturalized British people. But overall, the experience, though visually and physically fulfilling, felt superficial. I left New Zealand feeling empty, knowing that I was glimpsing only one small part of that country and little of its soul; in other words, its people. It was the first time in my travels that a pretty landscape was not enough for me.

As David told me more about the giant eels in New Zealand, I remembered then, while eating lunch on the bank of a remote river on that first trip with Taylor, that a slender dark shape, five feet long and big around as my arm, had come out of the shadows to eat a piece of the sandwich that I'd thrown in the water. I saw it so briefly that I wasn't sure I'd seen it at all. But as David spoke over the phone, it registered in my mind that the big dark fish had been perhaps the only native fish I'd seen on that trip, an eel.

David told me that it is a tradition of the Maori to keep ponds with sacred eels. The Maori feed the eels and protect them and in turn the eels protect the *iwi*, or tribe. The eels can be huge—six, seven feet—and feed right out of one's hands. The Maori say some of these eels are over 300 years old.

David, who grew up in America, knew the land of Kiwis from his years living there married to a Maori woman named Titihuiarangimoana, whom he met while working for a television company in Australia. His marriage gave him access to a world usually closed to pakeha, or white people. His introduction to the New Zealand wilds, or "bush" as it's called, was through fly-fishing for trout with a Maori man named DJ.

"I've seen some huge ones while trout fishing, mate," David said. "I was fishing in this mountain lake one day, wading through the shallows and went to step over this big log when . . . the log moved! It was a giant eel—big around as the fattest part of my leg. There was no stream running out of the lake, so I don't know how this eel would get to the sea to spawn, but they say that some small eels get up to high lakes when there's a typhoon, and they'll stay up there, sometimes over a hundred years, until the next big typhoon comes and washes them down the mountain."

David sent an e-mail to his friend DJ on the North Island in autumn of 2002, inquiring about eels on my behalf. DJ said he knew a thing or two about eels, but would try to find someone who might have more to say than he did on the importance of eels in Maori culture. Eventually, it was decided that the best person to lead me around New Zealand in search of eels was a twenty-three-year-old half-Maori woman named Stella August. Stella had just finished her graduate work at Waikato University in Hamilton. The subject of her thesis was the spring migration of glass eels on the Tukituki River, which flows toward the eastern coast of the North Island, near her family's tribal land in Hawke Bay.

A few e-mail correspondences later, Stella agreed to set up an itinerary for me and to be my eel guide on a trip to New Zealand. Our trip was scheduled for February of 2004, summertime in the southern hemisphere.

In the meantime, in my research, I came across some Polynesian myths that involved eels, in the work of Joseph Campbell. Campbell explains in his book, *The Masks of God: Creative Mythology,* how the creation myth in India involving the snake made its way through Indonesia and was eventually inherited by the Polynesians, who replaced the snake, which was unknown in the islands, with the indigenous eel. "East of Indonesia, Melanesia, and Australia, throughout the island-studded triangle of Polynesia—which has Hawaii at its apex, New Zealand at one angle, and Easter Island at the other—the mythological image of the murdered divine being whose body became a food plant has been adjusted to the natural elements of an oceanic environment," Campbell wrote. "The voluptuous atmosphere of the lush Polynesian adventure will be different, indeed, from the grim holiness of the rabbinical Torah; nevertheless, we are certainly in the same old book—of which, so to say, all the earliest editions have been lost."

In several stories throughout the region, particularly in Samoa, a small eel is taken as a pet by a girl named Sina. Sina raises the eel in a coconut shell until it becomes too big, at which point she lets it go in a spring, but continues to feed it. One day when she's bathing in the spring the eel tries to pierce her vagina with its tail. The eel is killed and the head is buried, where a coconut tree grows. The nut of the coconut bears the mark of the eel's eyes and mouth. The story of the eel as a creature both loved but feared, and as a kind of detached phallus with a mind of its own, in consistent throughout the region.

Another Polynesian story, of which there are many variations, concerns a monster eel called Te Tuna, and the seduction of the god Maui's wife, Hine. Campbell likens Maui to a kind of Hercules of Polynesia. When Maui finds the giant eel Te Tuna in bed with his wife one night, he cuts off the eel's head with a hatchet. In the story, the head of the eel becomes all the saltwater eels of the world, and the tail becomes all the freshwater eels of the world.

It is not surprising, perhaps, that in the South Pacific region the word for eel, *tuna,* is a synonym for penis. There are many variations of stories of eels seducing women by a spring while they're washing clothes, or in their sleep, as well as stories of eels as monsters, but I found nothing specifically about the Maori and eels, or about sacred eels at all, until I stumbled onto the works of Elsdon Best.

Best was born in Tawa Flat, New Zealand, in 1856, the son of British immigrants. He is considered to be the foremost ethnographer of Maori society, which was diminishing rapidly even in the late nineteenth century. In his work, it is evident from the sheer proportion of pages devoted to the eel in his book, about two-thirds, that the eel was once the greatest inland food source for the Maori. He listed over two hundred local Maori names for the freshwater eel in his *Fishing Methods and Devices*. If the number of different words used to describe the nuances of an object in a language—like snow to the Eskimo—is evidence of its importance in a culture, then this fact alone, for me, confirmed the importance of eels in Maori life.

It was also in Best's work where I first read about the Maori monster called the *taniwha*, which most commonly takes the form of a giant eel.

In Maori Myth and Religion Part II, Best describes how Captain Cook, on his third voyage to New Zealand in 1777, gave us the first written record of what the natives there called *taniwha*: "We had another piece of intelligence from him, more correctly given, though not confirmed by our own observations, that there are snakes and lizards there of enormous size. He described the latter as being eight feet in length and big around as a man's body. He said they sometimes devour men."

Best, commenting on Cook's account, points out that the Maori man telling the story to Cook would certainly have known a lizard—though no eight-foot lizards exist in New Zealand—but would have never seen a snake. What the native described to Cook was the longfin eel of their freshwater rivers, *Anguilla dieffenbachii*, capable of growing to eight feet long and confirmed to live well over eighty pounds and a hundred years. Best also wrote that large eels were sometimes tamed and regularly fed. Offerings were sometimes made to these eels, and thought to be "sacred," they were respected like gods.

These Polynesian myths and traditions in the works of European writers, as they related to eels, were interesting to me, but at times dry. This was in part because the people who recorded them were not the authentic tellers of the tales. There was no Polynesian Homer to write them down. The soul of these stories was yet unwritten, was still in the minds of Maori elders in seaside and mountain villages in New Zealand. Because they were nature-based stories, they felt deflated and pale when told outside of any other context than the environment they came from. I slowly learned when I returned to New Zealand, the dangers that face the so-called pagan faiths. If the nature was endangered, the culture and ideas were as well.

Stella August was twenty-four years old when I visited New Zealand in 2004. Her mother is British, and her father was Maori. Stella's mother left home when Stella was nine, and she lived with her younger sister Wiki and their father on their tribal land on Kairakau Beach, a remote windswept coastline at Hawke Bay. Stella learned of her affinity for the sea and rivers through her father, and it was the sea that took him in a boating accident when a rogue wave overturned his skiff. He drowned, just off the beach near their home. Stella was sixteen at the time.

When her father died, Stella contacted her mother and asked if she would return to their tribal land to live with her and Wiki and help out on the farm. The mother had not set foot there since she'd left, years before. She agreed to return and has lived there ever since, tending to a herd of sheep and cows with her boyfriend Ray, and the help of cigarettes and cold Lion's Red beer to pass the time.

Drinking was just another part of living out there, a good hour and a half from the nearest supermarket.

Since Stella's father died, the elders of Ngati Kahagnunu had looked after her. Because of her love for the sea, she studied marine biology in college on a fellowship from her *iwi*, Ngati Kahanunu. When I met up with her, she had just handed in her master's thesis, was working part time in a coffee shop, and was organizing what she'd termed an "eel adventure" throughout New Zealand, for me.

Our scheduled meeting point was a Burger King on the second roundabout in Hamilton about a two-hour drive south of Auckland. She was wearing board shorts and a sweatshirt with surfer logos, and would not look directly into my eyes.

"You brought the sun," she said.

It had been raining for three weeks straight and New Zealand waterways had experienced some of the biggest floods in a lifetime. It was good weather, I supposed, for an eel.

We talked briefly about our itinerary there in the parking lot. Toward the end of our trip, I'd arranged for us to stay at a fishing lodge on the Mohaka River called Poronui Ranch. "That will be a good chance for us to sit down and make sure we both know where we're coming from," Stella said, with slight severity. "About what you're going to write."

I assured Stella that I would be sympathetic to the Maori culture. But she worried me when her tone turned defensive. She mentioned that the stories we would hear during our eel adventure were the "intellectual property" of her people. The Maori people had a right to be wary, even protective—the English colonists had lied to them, stole their language, customs, their spirituality (replacing it, with mixed results, with Christianity), and land. The latest assault in the eyes of some Maori, was the success of the film *Whale Rider*, about a young Maori girl learning the indigenous customs from her grandfather. Hollywood had made all kinds of money on this "intellectual property," and the Maori people hadn't received any measurable compensation. It was clear that Stella was conflicted about being my guide. She seemed happy that I'd shown interest in learning about her culture and sharing it with whoever cared to read, but also reticent about making known what was sacred and very personal, and being paid, though not much, to do so.

The movie *Whale Rider*, Stella agreed, was actually a very realistic portrayal of modern Maori life, especially in the instance of a young girl inheriting the culture from her reluctant grandfather, who traditionally would have passed that knowledge orally to a boy. But the boys in the modern Maori culture had no patience, they had attention problems, were fidgety, and more often than not got into trouble with drugs and alcohol. It was young women like Stella and her sister who were inheriting the faith and staging a cultural revival.

"I'm here," I said, repeating sentiments I'd shared in numerous e-mails over the previous months, "because of a genuine fascination for a very strange and fascinating fish."

She paused before answering. "Well, you and I are alike, then," she said. "But I didn't always like them. Eels. When my father brought them home, I wouldn't go near them. But my interest in fish is definitely because of my father." A lot of people were suspicious of me, Stella said, when she rang them up and told them she wanted to bring an American by to do research on eels in Maori culture. "The first thing they said was, 'Why does he want to know?' They've got a lifetime of experience, which traditionally is shared with those in their *hapu*, or sub-tribe, within the *iwi*. They're suspicious of science."

"I'm not a scientist," I protested.

She knew that, she said, but there was something she wanted me to understand about her culture. "I went to this big eel conference where the leading eel experts in New Zealand had gathered. Don Jellyman, a pakeha, probably the most famous, he's at NIWA"—the National Institute of Water and Atmosphere—"and was delivering a paper on his attempts to track eight large migrant eels from the river mouth to their spawning grounds with radio transmitters. He explained that all sign of the radio transmitters had been lost once the eels reached the edge of the trench off the east coast of the South Island. When Don sat down, Kelly Davis, who I hope will be available to see us, got up to represent the Maori. He addressed Don directly, saying, in front of everyone, 'Why do you need to know where they go? The juvenile eels come up the river in spring, the adults migrate out in the fall. My people have known this forever. What good will it do the fish to find the house where they breed?' Don was speechless."

I listened. And I learned not to assert too much, to ask too many questions, and to listen as best I could to what these individuals on our eel adventure had to share. Not an hour went by that Stella did not remind me that we would be meeting with the most knowledgeable people on eels in all New Zealand, that I was privileged to have time with them. As she advised, I had brought *koha*, or personal gifts, to give to them all: small art works I'd made, signed books.

Over lunch at her flat, Stella told me more about her love of eels, and about the time she spent with them. "Why do we have to try to understand everything that isn't understandable? Everyone wants to unlock everything. I'm conflicted because I'm Maori: I don't want to know where they go, and yet I've studied their movements in the rivers in a scientific way."

Our conversation returned to the idea of the *taniwha*, that important element of Maori stories. In the *Reed Dictionary of Modern Maori*, the translation of *taniwha* is "water monster, powerful person, ogre." It can make itself known at certain times to certain people, sometimes to warn them of danger. Stella pointed out that the most common form in which a *taniwha* shows itself is an eel. Usually a large eel.

"If you spear an eel that's a *taniwha*, or catch it in a net, it will cry like a baby or bark like a dog, or even change colors," Stella said. "If you killed a *taniwha*, you'd have a *matuku*, or curse, and start going crazy, like you're possessed."

In that case, she added, it meant you had broken *tapu*—something sacred, or off-limits.

Three weeks later, Stella and I were huddled in a tent, stranded in the bush with DJ. He had taken us up a small tributary of the Mata River he called Stony Creek, in the northeast corner of the North Island, so we might fish for trout and search for the big eels that often live in the headwaters of streams. The creek was in a remote piece of tribal land, thick with punga, the exotic looking New Zealand fern tree, the fronds of which hung over emerald plunge pools inhabited by large trout and eels. We'd been dropped off via helicopter four days before. In a driving rain, the river in the canyon rising, we waited for the weather to clear so we could be picked up at the appointed time. A day later, we were still in the tent, wet as water rats, hoping for a break in the rain so we could try to start a fire.

After four days in the bush, DJ was just starting to get comfortable enough with me to tell me what was really on his mind. He was, like all Maori I had come into contact with, a little reserved at first, even intimidating in his silence. His stature was imposing, tall and thin with dark skin, but strong, like a Native American cowboy. He had a long sage nose and a casual swagger and wore a silver pocket watch in a leather sack on his belt. The rain let up and, toward evening, the sky began to clear. Relieved that we'd probably fly out in the morning, we slipped from our tent, stretched our legs, and, after some effort, got a fire started. DJ pulled out his skillet to cook the two remaining steaks we'd brought. "I've seen some crazy things out here," he said, poking the fire, making a spot over the coals for the skillet to sit. "But it's more the things I've felt and haven't seen that stick with me."

DJ started to talk about the skillet and its history. He called it his family heirloom but with his Kiwi accent it sounded more like "hair-loom." His short "a" and "i" sounds were long and drawn out, pronounced like "ee"'s. I asked DJ if he had any stories of *taniwha*. I was eager to know more. But, as I was learning, he wouldn't be rushed.

"This was my dad's skillet," DJ said. "Most of the places I take people fishing and hunting in the bush are places I went hunting with my father as a boy. If I'm in an area I don't know I ask local people in the pub, the bros, or I have a yarn with the publican. I never take my white clients along, 'cause if I do, the bros won't talk. They won't even move their leeps, mate." DJ stoked the fire with a stick. A cool wind blew down the river valley.

One time, he said, he was up in the bush with friends on horseback, pig hunting. "We'd camped under this permanent shelter that heed been there foreever. We'd had a long day of hunting and we were cooking a big feed and all of a sudden the bush weent silent. You normally hear all these noises, the crickets and that, like now. Well, it all weent quiet, and then the horses started acting up, and then the dogs weent balleestic. We're told, you know, don't ever camp on the track, you're neever supposed to, but we deed, we were set up right on it." DJ flipped the steaks.

"I'm always trying to reason, and I thought, there's a logical reason why the horses are acting up. An expeerienced horseman could ride up in the dark and spook the horses. People do it all the time. It's possible. I waited for that horseman, but he neever came."

Stella asked if he had grabbed a gun.

"What good's a gun?" DJ asked. "I was in my sleeping bag with the top pulled over my heed. And then come this roar. I don't know how to describe eet, and I never heard eet since, and I'm not superstitious, but I have no way of explaining eet. Eet was like a jeet eengine, and loud, like deefening. I don't know what to call it, like a *taniwha* or what."

DJ split the steaks three ways and we sat on logs and ate. We made the fire bigger and were soon dry. To hear a personal *taniwha* story from DJ made me think. This wasn't a dry story told by a European ethnographer, it was an account told in the element from which it was derived. And the impact of the experience was as loud as the monster in his story. It was more impactful than a ghost story at a campfire, because you knew for sure by his tone and seriousness that DJ had experienced it, and had no logical reason to explain it. But in his spirit, in his Maori spirit, he believed it was a *taniwha*.

DJ knew I'd come to New Zealand to learn about eels in Maori culture. He'd been waiting for the right moment to tell me his version of things.

"The way I see eet," he said, salting his steak and taking a bite, "there are three players in a New Zealand river: the rainbow trout, the brown trout, and the eel. The eel is the cultural factor. The eel is the Maori factor. The trout is the British colonist. Everyone forgets about the eels because you don't see them. They're out at neeght mostly. You don't see the eel, but he's theere, and he's releentless in his eefforts to catch the trout. He's always stalking them. Ultimately he's the survivor. He can take the other two out eeny time. He might wait years to catch theem. 'Til they geet old and weak. The eel's got time. The eels been theere long before the British put theem in the rivers," DJ threw the gristle from his steak in the fire, "they'll be there eefter. We call that *morehu*, the survivor."

DJ's was a common sentiment among Maori in the early twenty-first century. The culture, buried underground for the better part of a hundred years, was re-emerging with a vengeance, and sometimes with some resentment for the descendents of the British colonists. The eel, I would come to find, was not only "sacred," but one of the most important creatures in Maori culture for a host of reasons—the lubricious creature seducing the wife of gods, a synonym of the penis, a protector, and the main traditional food source for the inland Maori. But most importantly, the eel was a symbol of what we were losing, the world over—that the loss of nature would equal a loss of culture, especially indigenous "pagan" culture, a loss of connection to the earth, and loss of soul.

This new world was not one I wanted to live in. And I began to rethink the assumptions I'd made about indigenous people from the things I'd read in the work of Campbell and Elsdon Best. I'd treated the stories about *taniwha* in the way that they were presented, as myth. But from the seriousness of tone in my conversations with Stella and DJ and others, I was finding out that what I had perceived as "mythology" was indeed very much a part of the spiritual reality of the Maori. And in many ways, the eelian thinking about nature, as an idea that couldn't be, and didn't need to be, pinned down, that would persevere, began to make a lot of sense.

As far as spirituality went, the idea at the source of, for instance, the Christian faith was much more portable and versatile than the core of the nature-based faith. The success of the Christian "myth" it occurred to me, sitting in that tent in the rain, listening to DJ's story, was its versatility, malleability, and portability. The Christian religion was based on the belief that the son of God, in human form, came to earth to take away our sins; this can be understood by any human anywhere in any environment in the world. The concepts of the Christian religion are promoted both in buildings built by people and in the open air. The difference with a nature-based faith like that of the Maori (and other indigenous peoples around the world) is that once you lose the Nature that the spiritual system is based on, you are also in danger of losing spirituality. If the eel is endangered is the Maori sense of spirituality also endangered? If a young Maori boy does not see a giant eel, is not awed by that six-foot writhing pile of muscle, can he have faith, truly, in a *taniwha*? What has happened to a large extent in the Maori culture is that the British immigrants began to destroy the foundation of the Maori faith. The Acclimitization Society (the established Department of Wildlife if you will) introduced trout to make the streams friendly for settlers from England, and they trapped the large eels, leaving them stranded on the bank, because they saw them as a threat to the introduced fish. Kelly Davis, an old Maori I spoke to later in the trip, said that he used to walk the banks of the river with his dad, kicking these large stranded eels back into the river. The British knew the quickest way to eradicate an indigenous culture, remove the creatures that are spiritually and gastronomically closest to them. The end of the eel for the Maori (and the whale and the kiwi) was the end of an idea. It is precisely what the Europeans did to the American plains Indians when they slaughtered hundreds of thousands of bison. Is there a connection between the loss of such natural wonders in New Zealand and the disillusioned youth of the Maori, especially the boys, who are turning to drugs and mischief instead of nature? When their energies and aggressions are not spent running around fishing and hunting do they turn to hostility? Toward their spouses, toward the government, toward everything? What becomes clearer and clearer to our 21st century society, with all our wisdom and reason, is that, although it is harder to imagine myth as a spiritual reality, we do need some form of spirituality. I found when I was in New Zealand, that when I let my "reason" fade, and imagined a giant eel living in a deep pool, one that warned off children from a dangerous current, or protected the surroundings of a place, or heard stories of areas of forest that were sacred, where there is a spiritual silence, where "no birds sing," I felt whole, I felt motivated, and I felt human.

# THE 'LUNGE

## STEWART EDWARD WHITE

Dick and I traveled in a fifteen-foot wooden canoe, with grub, duffel, tent, and Deuce, the black-and-white setter dog. As a consequence we were pretty well down toward the water-line, for we had not realized that a wooden canoe would carry so little weight for its length in comparison with a birchbark. A good heavy sea we could ride—with proper management and a little baling; but sloppy waves kept us busy.

Deuce did not like it at all. He was a dog old in the wisdom of experience. It had taken him just twenty minutes to learn all about canoes. After a single tentative trial he jumped lightly to the very centre of his place, with the lithe caution of a cat. Then if the water happened to be smooth, he would sit gravely on his haunches, or would rest his chin on the gunwale to contemplate the passing landscape. But in rough weather he crouched directly over the keel, his nose between his paws, and tried not to dodge when the cold water dashed in on him. Deuce was a true woodsman in that respect. Discomfort he always bore with equanimity, and he must often have been very cold and very cramped.

For just over a week we had been traveling in open water, and the elements had not been kind to us at all. We had crept up under rock-cliff points; had weathered the rips of white water to shelter on the other side; had struggled across open spaces where each wave was singly a problem to fail in whose solution meant instant swamping; had baled, and schemed, and figured, and carried, and sworn, and tried again, and succeeded with about two cupfuls to spare, until we as well as Deuce had grown a little tired of it. For the lust of travel was on us.

The lust of travel is a very real disease. It usually takes you when you have made up your mind that there is no hurry. Its predisposing cause is a chart or map, and its main symptom is the feverish delight with which you check off the landmarks of your journey. A fair wind of some force is absolutely fatal. With that at your back you cannot stop. Good fishing, fine scenery, interesting bays, reputed game, even camps where friends might be visited—all pass swiftly astern. Hardly do you pause for lunch at noon. The mad joy of putting country behind you eats all other interests. You recover only when you have come to your journey's end a week too early, and must then search out new voyages to fill in the time.

All this morning we had been bucking a strong north wind. Fortunately, the shelter of a string of islands had given us smooth water enough, but the heavy gusts sometimes stopped us as effectively as though we had butted solid land. Now about noon we came to the last island, and looked out on a five-mile stretch of tumbling seas. We landed the canoe and mounted a high rock.

"Can't make it like this," said I. "I'll take the outfit over and land it, and come back for you and the dog. Let's see that chart."

We hid behind the rock and spread out the map.

"Four miles," measured Dick. "It's going to be a terror."

We looked at each other vaguely, suddenly tired.

"We can't camp here—at this time of day," objected Dick, to our unspoken thoughts.

And then the map gave him an inspiration. "Here's a little river," ruminated Dick, "that goes to a little lake, and then there's another little river that flows from the lake and comes out about ten miles above here."

"It's a good thirty miles," I objected.

"What of it?" asked Dick, calmly.

So the fever-lust of travel broke. We turned to the right behind the last island, searched out the reed-grown opening to the stream, and paddled serenely and philosophically against the current. Deuce sat up and yawned with a mighty satisfaction.

We had been bending our heads to the demon of wind; our ears had been filled with his shoutings, our eyes blinded with tears, our breath caught away from us, our muscles strung to the fiercest endeavor. Suddenly we found ourselves between the ranks of tall forest trees, bathed in a warm sunlight, gliding like a feather from one grassy bend to another of the laziest little stream that ever hesitated as to which way the grasses of its bed should float. As for the wind, it was lost somewhere away up high, where we could hear it muttering to itself about something.

The woods leaned over the fringe of bushes cool and green and silent. Occasionally through tiny openings we caught instant impressions of straight column trunks and transparent shadows. Miniature grass marshes jutted out from the bends of the little river. We idled along as with a homely rustic companion through the aloofness of patrician multitudes.

Every bend offered us charming surprises. Sometimes a muskrat swam hastily in a pointed furrow of ripple; vanishing wings, barely sensed in the flash, left us staring; stealthy withdrawals of creatures, whose presence we realized only in the fact of those withdrawals, snared our eager interest; porcupines rattled and rustled importantly and regally from the water's edge to the woods; herons, ravens, an occasional duck, croaked away at our approach; thrice we surprised eagles, once a tassel-eared Canada lynx. Or, if all else lacked, we still experienced the little thrill of pleased novelty over the disclosure of a group of silvery birches on a knoll; a magnificent white pine towering over the beech and maple forest; the unexpected aisle of a long, straight stretch of the little river.

Deuce approved thoroughly. He stretched himself and yawned and shook off the water, and glanced at me open-mouthed with doggy good-nature, and set himself to acquiring a conscientious olfactory knowledge of both banks of the river. I do not doubt he knew a great deal more about it than we did. Porcupines aroused his special enthusiasm. Incidentally, two days later he returned to camp after an expedition of his own, bristling as to the face with that animal's barbed weapons. Thenceforward his interest waned.

We ascended the charming little river two or three miles. At a sharp bend to the east a huge sheet of rock sloped from a round grass knoll sparsely planted with birches directly down into a pool. Two or three tree trunks jammed directly opposite had formed a sort of half dam under which the water lay dark. A tiny grass meadow forty feet in diameter narrowed the stream to half its width.

We landed. Dick seated himself on the shelving rock. I put my fish-rod together. Deuce disappeared.

Deuce always disappeared whenever we landed. With nose down, hind quarters well tucked under him, ears flying, he quartered the forest at high speed, investigating every nook and cranny of it for the radius of a quarter of a mile. When he had quite satisfied himself that we were safe for the moment, he would return to the fire, where he would lie, six inches of pink tongue vibrating with breathlessness, beautiful in the consciousness of virtue. Dick generally sat on a rock and thought. I generally fished.

After a time Deuce returned. I gave up flies, spoons, phantom minnows, artificial frogs, and crayfish. As Dick continued to sit on the rock and think, we both joined him. The sun was very warm and grateful, and I am sure we both acquired an added respect for Dick's judgment.

Just when it happened neither of us was afterwards able to decide. Perhaps Deuce knew. But suddenly, as often a figure appears in a cinematograph, the diminutive meadow thirty feet away contained two deer. They stood knee-deep in the grass, wagging their little tails in impatience of the flies.

"Look a' there!" stammered Dick aloud.

Deuce sat up on his haunches.

I started for my camera.

The deer did not seem to be in the slightest degree alarmed. They pointed four big ears in our direction, ate a few leisurely mouthfuls of grass, sauntered to the stream for a drink of water, wagged their little tails some more, and quietly faded into the cool shadows of the forest.

An hour later we ran out into reeds, and so to the lake. It was a pretty lake, forest-girt. Across the distance we made out a moving object which shortly resolved itself into a birch canoe. The canoe proved to contain an Indian, an Indian boy of about ten years, a black dog, and a bundle. When within a few rods of each other we ceased paddling, and drifted by with the momentum. The Indian was a fine-looking man of about forty, his hair bound with a red fillet, his feet encased in silk-worked moccasins, but otherwise dressed in white men's garments. He smoked a short pipe, and contemplated us gravely.

"Bo' jou', bo' jou'," we called in the usual double-barreled North Country salutation.

"Bo' jou', bo' jou," he replied.

"Kée-gons?" we inquired as to the fishing in the lake.

"Áh-hah," he assented.

We drifted by each other without further speech. When the decent distance of etiquette separated us we resumed our paddles.

I produced a young cable terminated by a tremendous spoon and a solid brass snell as thick as a telegraph wire. We had laid in this formidable implement in hopes of a big muscallunge. It had been trailed for days at a time. We had become used to its vibration, which actually seemed to communicate itself to every fiber of the light canoe. Every once in a while we would stop with a jerk that would nearly snap our heads off. Then we would know we had hooked the American continent. We had become used to that also. It generally happened when we attempted a little burst of speed. So when the canoe brought up so violently that all our tinware rolled on Deuce, Dick was merely disgusted.

"There she goes again," he grumbled. "You've hooked Canada."

Canada held quiescent for about three seconds. Then it started due south.

"Suffering serpents!" shrieked Dick.

"Paddle, you sulphurated idiot!" yelled I.

It was most interesting. All I had to do was to hang on and try to stay in the boat. Dick paddled and fumed and splashed water and got more excited. Canada dragged us bodily backward.

Then Canada changed his mind and started in our direction. I was plenty busy taking in slack, so I did not notice Dick. Dick was absolutely demented. His mind automatically reacted in the direction of paddling. He paddled, blindly, frantically. Canada came surging in, his mouth open, his wicked eyes flaming, a tremendous indistinct body lashing foam. Dick glanced once over his shoulder, and let out a frantic howl.

"You've got the sea-serpent!" he shrieked.

I turned to fumble for the pistol. We were headed directly for a log stranded on shore, and about ten feet from it.

"Dick!" I yelled in warning.

He thrust his paddle out forward just in time. The stout maple bent and cracked. The canoe hit with a bump that threw us forward. I returned to the young cable. It came in limp and slack.

We looked at each other sadly.

"No use," sighed Dick at last. "They've never invented the words, and we'd be upset if we kicked the dog."

I had the end of the line in my hands.

"Look here!" I cried. That thick brass wire had been as cleanly bitten through as though it had been cut with clippers. "He must have caught sight of you," said I.

Dick lifted up his voice in lamentation. "You had four feet of him out of water," he wailed, "and there was a lot more."

"If you had kept cool," said I, severely, "we shouldn't have lost him. You don't want to get rattled in an emergency. There's no sense in it."

"What were you going to do with that?" asked Dick, pointing to where I had laid the pistol.

"I was going to shoot him in the head," I replied with dignity. "It's the best way to land them."

Dick laughed disagreeably. I looked down. At my side lay our largest iron spoon.

We skirted the left-hand side of the lake in silence. Far out from shore the water was ruffled where the wind swept down, but with us it was as still and calm as the forest trees that looked over into it. After a time we turned short to the left through a very narrow passage between two marshy shores, and so, after a sharp bend of but a few hundred feet, came into the other river.

This was a wide stream, smoothly hurrying, without rapids or tumult. The forest had drawn to either side to let us pass. Here were the wilder reaches after the intimacies of the little river. Across stretches of marsh we could see an occasional great blue heron standing mid-leg deep. Long strings of ducks struggled quacking from invisible pools. The faint marsh odor saluted our nostrils from the point where the lily-pads flashed broadly, ruffling in the wind. We dropped out the smaller spoon and masterfully landed a five-pound pickerel. Even Deuce brightened. He cared nothing for raw fish, but he knew their possibilities. Towards evening we entered the hilly country, and so at the last turned to the left into a sand cove where grew maples and birches in beautiful park order under a hill. There we pitched camp, and, as the flies lacked, built a friendship-fire about which to foregather when the day was done.

Dick still vocally regretted the muscallunge as the largest fish since Jonah, so I told him of my big bear.

One day, late in the summer, I was engaged in packing some supplies along an old fur trail north of Lake Superior. I had accomplished one back-load, and with empty straps was returning to the cache for another. The trail at one point emerged into and crossed an open park some hundreds of feet in diameter, in which the grass grew to the height of the knee. When I was about halfway across, a black bear arose to his hind legs not ten feet from me, and remarked *Woof!* in a loud tone of voice. Now, if a man were to say *woof!* to you unexpectedly, even in the formality of an Italian garden or the accustomedness of a city street, you would be somewhat startled. So I went to camp. There I told them about the bear. I tried to be conservative in my description, because I did not wish to be accused of exaggeration. My impression of the animal was that he and a spruce tree that grew near enough for ready comparison were approximately of the same stature. We returned to the grass park. After some difficulty we found a clear footprint. It was a little larger than that made by a good-sized coon.

"So, you see," I admonished, didactically, "that 'lunge probably was not quite so large as you thought."

"It may have been a Chinese bear," said Dick, dreamily—"a Chinese lady bear of high degree."

I gave him up.

*Scale of Inches.*

THE CARP FAMILY.—1. Golden Carp, or Goldfish, *Cyprinus auratus.* 2. The Roach, *Leuciscus rutilus.* 3. The Loach, or Beardie, *Cobitis barbatula.* 4. The Tench, *Tinca vulgaris.* 5. The Barbel, *Barbus vulgaris.* 6. New York Shiner, *Cyprinus crysoleucas.* 7. Common Carp, *Cyprinus carpis.* 8. Common New York Sucker, *Catostomus communis.*

# CARP FISHING

## FRANK FORESTER

This, I confess, I regard as very miserable sport; for though the fish is shy and wary, the difficulty in taking him arises only from his timidity and unwillingness to bite, and he is as lazy when hooked as he is slow to bite.

His proper haunts are deep, stagnant, slow-flowing streams, or ponds with muddy bottoms; and he lies under weeds, and among the stems and flat leaves of water-lilies, flags, and marsh-grasses.

Not indigenous to this country, he has been naturalized in the waters of the Hudson, where he is, for the present, protected by severe legislative enactments.

He will doubtless, ere long, become very plentiful; and as he is a rich fish when cooked *secundum artem*, and by many esteemed a great delicacy, he is likely enough to become a favorite with the angler.

Hofland thus describes the method of baiting the ground and fishing for Carp in England, and his directions are the best I have seen; they may be followed with implicit confidence:

"In rivers, the Carp prefer those parts where the current is not too strong, and where the bottom is marly, or muddy; and in lakes or ponds are to be found near beds of water-lilies, and other aquatic plants. Old Carp are very crafty and wary, and will not easily be taken by the angler; but young ones, when a pond is well stocked, may be easily taken in great quantities.

"Notwithstanding these instances of familiarity, it is by no means easy to make a large Carp familiar with your bait: to do this, the greatest nicety and caution must be observed; but if the young angler, who has been often foiled in his attempts, will patiently and implicitly follow my instructions, he will become a match for this cunning fish.

"Use a strong rod with running-tackle, and have a bottom of three yards of fineish gut, and a hook No. 9 or 10; use a very light quill-float, that will carry two small shot, and bait with a well-scoured red worm.

"Now plumb the depth with the greatest nicety, and let your bait just touch, or all but touch, the bottom; but you are not yet prepared; for a forked stick must be fixed into the bank, on which you must let your rod rest, so that the float will fall over the exact spot you have plumbed. Now throw in a sufficient quantity of ground-bait, of bread and bran worked into a paste, and made into little balls; or, in want of these, throw in the garbage of chickens or ducks; and all this is to be done on the evening of the day before you intend to fish.

"The next morning, if in summer, be at the pond-side where you have baited and plumbed your depth, by four o'clock at least, and, taking your rod and line, which is already fixed to the exact depth, bait with a small, bright, red, worm; then approach the water cautiously, keeping out of sight as much as possible, and drop your bait exactly over the spot you plumbed over night; then rest part of your rod on the forked stick, and the bottom of it on the ground.

"You must now retire a few paces, keeping entirely out of sight, but still near enough to observe your float; when you perceive a bite, give a little time; indeed, it is better to wait till you see the float begin to move off, before you strike, which you may then do smartly; and, as the Carp is a leather-mouthed fish, if you manage him well, there is no fear of losing him, unless the pond is very weedy. Be careful to have your line free, that, if a large fish, he may run out some of your line before you attempt to turn him; as he is a very strong fish, and your tackle rather light, you must give him careful play before you land him.

"The extreme shyness of the large Carp makes all this somewhat tedious process necessary to insure success; but I can safely assert, that I scarcely ever took this trouble in vain. Various baits are recommended for Carp,—such as green peas parboiled, pastes of all descriptions, gentles, caterpillars, &c.; but I have found the red worm the best, and next to this, the gentle, and plain bread-paste. Those who prefer a sweet paste may dip the bread in honey. Paste and gentle will answer better in autumn than spring. April and May are, in my opinion, the best months for Carp fishing; and very early in the morning, or late in the evening, is the best time for pursuing your sport."

The above mode of baiting bottom-grounds, and of fishing with the worm, in all its particulars, may be pursued with perfect success in all ponds and slow-running streams, for all the many species of the Carp family, which are, for the most part, the least carnivorous of fishes, and consequently the most difficult to allure, as the Bream, Roach, Dace, Chub, and Shiner, as they are provincially termed, though by no means identical with the European fishes of the same names. The Suckers (*Catastomi*), a sub-genus of the same family, will hardly take any bait whatsoever.

While fishing, as above described, both small river Perch and Eels of all sizes are likely to be hooked, as the baited bottom-ground allures all those species which seek their food at the bottom to its vicinity.

# BOW-FIN FISHING IN THE SOUTH SLANG

### ROWLAND E. ROBINSON

S am Lovel and Antoine Bisette were taking after-dinner ease in a comfortable smoke at their summer camp near the mouth of Little Otter, and their talk was mostly of fishing.

"Ah'll tol' you what, Sam," said Antoine, reaching out lazily from his recumbent position, to the nearest stone, and knocking the ashes from his pipe, "Ah'll b'lieved dey ant no funs for feeshin' lak he was raght all raound here, me." Then getting to a sitting posture he tucked his legs crosswise after the not-latest fashion of a tailor, and began whittling a fresh charge from a plug of black tobacco. " 'Cause you see, de feesh was so variety of it," he continued, looking askance at Sam to note whether this newly-acquired word was comprehended. "Dar was peekerel an' pikes an' shad Ah ant ketch 'cause he come honly on de seine, an' basses, two kan' of it, Ah guess, tree, prob'ly, an' de sheephead you'll ant see yet an' de heel, he mek mah mout tase good when Ah'll tink of it, an' de bull-paout mos' as mooch an' de mud-turkey more as bose of it. Dey was all good feesh, for mek mans felt plump when he ketch or heat it.

"Den dey was bow-fins an' leeng mek you lot o' fun for ketch, but, bah gosh! you ant want heat it an' say he good 'less you want tol' lie; no sah!

"Den dey was parches an' punkin' seed an' lot o' leetly feller dat was mek fer give de boy some funs, an' come in pooty good for mans when he can' ketch de beeg feller an' de bes' feller, an' he ant so bad for heat as no feesh 't all or bow-fins or clam.

"Bah gosh! Ah'll lak for see boy ketch all he can't carry of it an' feel so bigger as mans wid sturgeon, sem Ah'll was be feel when Ah was leetly boy in Canada an' carry home for show mah mudder all de ponkin seed Ah'll got.

"Ah'll weesh Ah'll can feel so beeg one tam more, but Ah'll can't 'f Ah ketch whale. Ah'll grow so modesty wid mah grow hol', an' Ah'll can't brag some more."

"It raly is tu bad 'baout you, Antwine," Sam remarked; "you'd orter git red o' your bashfulness."

"Ah'll can't help it, Sam. Dat was what Ah'll got for leeve wid Yankee so longs.

"But Ah'll tol' you, Sam, it mek me laft for hear dem feller up to Danvit brag when he come home wid string of traout baout half so longer as you finger of it, an' tol' all haow he ketch it an' when he ketch it, sem lak some mans tol' haow fas' hees hol' plug trot dat can't go so fas' as you roll barrel pot-ashins.

"What dem fellers tink dat go feeshin' for traout minny in brooks dey can step over, 'f dey feesh in waters lak dis, was so wide you can't holler crost it, an' ketch one feesh, dey mos' can't lift him?"

"Wal, I don't go altogether agin, nor with, what you're sayin', Antoine. The' is heaps o' fun in wrastlin with an' ol' lunker of a pickerel or pike, an' a bass is the beater o' the hull caboodle, fer he's julluk an' ol' sollaker of a traout, full o' fight an' tricks. But I hain't goin' tu go agin the fishing 'at I was brung up on, an' it makes me feel most as good as it did the fust time, when I go traoutin' along a lunsome brook with nobody anigh me but the birds a stoppin' their jinglin' tu watch me whilst I snatch aout the traouts, handsomer, 'f they be little, 'an any o' these mud-loafers.

"An' the smell o' the spruce an' balsam, sweeter 'n any these mashes affords 'cepten' them pond lilies, an' the wind a sythin' 'mongst 'em an' the brook allus a singin' an' invitin' you furder, to where it starts from, or to where it goes.

"An' if you're dry, you can flop yourself an' git a drink anywheres, 'at won't make ye stomerk sick, like this stuff. By the gret horn spoon! I wish't I hed a quart o' Stunny Brook this minute. I wish't the brook was beddin' right in my insides."

"Ah don't b'lieved water was very heal'ty for drink. It was bes' for feesh in, an' for whoman wash his close, Ah guess, an' bile patack. Ah tink some tam haow tire feesh mus' git for drink water, water all de tam. Prob'ly dat what mek him bit, fer git pull off of it. Bah gosh! Ah'll glad Ah'll ant feesh, but can git once a gret many while, leetly drops whiskee."

"Better stick tu what the fish du, Antwine, an' not hanker arter nothin' else. They don't."

"Ah'll don't b'lieve dat, Sam. Sometam, when Ah'll ketched hol' buster feesh, an' pull up mah leetly jaug fer treat mahsef, Ah'll seen heem ope hees mout an' look so wishin' as if he'll askin' for jes' one jaw-fulls."

"Did ye ever try if one on 'em would take a snort?"

"No, sah!" Antoine answered, emphatically. "Ah'll ant goin' treat feller can't say 'Salut,' 'sides of dat, Ah'll ant never got more as Ah'll want mahsef—not quat so moch now," he added with a sigh, and then applied himself to lighting his pipe with a coal raked from the smoldering fire.

The fumes of the kindling tobacco seemed to inspire an idea. "Say, Sam, le's go up to Saou' Slang an' ketch some bow-fins, hein? Ah'll ketch some fraug an' we go have it some funs jes' for funs!" He rose quickly and made a motion as if to lead the way to the landing.

"Wal, I don't care," Sam assented, arising more deliberately, "Any fishin's better'n none," and he followed the Canadian toward the Creek.

When they reached the level ground of the shore, Antoine was alert for frogs, and was presently in pursuit of one that made flying leaps in the direction of the water. Locating the fugitive in a cluster of rushes, he made a clutch at him and secured him writhing in the midst of a handful of marsh herbage. Live bait not being required for the purposed fishing, Antoine ended the struggles of the captive by a rap on the head, and so caught and killed others till, when they neared the boats, he had a dozen dangling by their hind legs from his left hand. Here another broke cover and made for the safer shelter of the creek.

Antoine, dropping his bunch of dead frogs, made after this lively one. Running at full speed with hands uplifted to pounce upon his prey at its first brief halt, he was close to the water-line, vaguely defined among the growth of weeds, when his foot caught on a hidden stick of driftwood, and he fell headlong, ploughing half his length through weeds, water and mud. As he struggled upright from the ooze and floundered to firmer footing, all the expletives which he had gathered from two languages poured from his lips faster than the water and black mud of the marsh dripped from his garments. He rained imprecations on all the frogs that ever lived, and particularly on the one that caused his mishap, and grieved that those he had captured were not alive, that he might wreak vengeance on them; on the whole expanse of Little Otter's marshes, and on bow-fins, and on himself for being such a "sacre damn hol' foolish for go hunt dat cussed leetly jompey-jomp frawg for ketch some ant good for dev' bow-fins."

He had so far relieved himself, when he reached dry land, that Sam ventured to ask out of his laughter, "Did ye ketch the frawg, Antwine?"

"Ketch it? no!" sputtered the Canadian; " 'less Ah'll ketch in mah mout. Ah'll ant ex-amine for see. Mebby Ah'll swaller. Bah gosh! 'f Ah tink he in mah stomach, Ah'll took vomitic for punish it."

He did not mind the wetting, for the shallow water was as warm as the weather, and he would not have minded it in a colder temperature if it had been in a better cause. So when he had cleared his clothes of mud, by scraping and ablution, and his burdened spirit by vigorous use of French and English, he was restored to good humor and enthusiasm in the prospective sport.

He took the oars, and, while Sam steered with a paddle, sent the scow surging upstream, noisily parting the quiet waters with her broad bow, and setting all the rushes of the marsh on either hand, and behind, aquiver with her wake. The water fowl, whose summer home was in the marshes, set up a clamor of strange cries as the boat's passage alarmed them or aroused their curiosity, but kept ever out of sight.

"Ah'll ant never see noting for belong to dat nowse," said Antoine, listening with uplifted oars. "Ah do' know 'f he was be bird or beas' or watry snaike. Ah guess he don't mud turkey, ant it? Ah'll hear folks said snaike mek nowse, but Ah'll ant mos' b'lieved it, 'less dis was snaike hollerin. He saound mos' hugly 'nough for it."

"Folks that lives here says it's birds; coots or fool-ducks some calls 'em, an' ma'sh chickens, an' they sca'cely ever see 'em till the last o' summer or int' the fall. But there's a reg'lar duck an' her hull fam'ly," said Sam, pointing forward with his paddle, and Antoine turning his head, saw a wood duck with her callow brood, a pretty fleet sailing in line along the rush border of the channel, faster than the scow, but with silent, arrowy wake. But their progress was not swift enough for the anxious mother, and she took wing, her ducklings following her low flight, running on the surface with a prodigious splashing and flutter of pinionless wings till they disappeared around the next bend.

When the scow rounded it, a broad landscape was disclosed, stretching to the mountains that lifted their blue peaks against the paler blue of the sky. Grandest of them all, the leonine front of Camel's Hump towered above its neighbors, and further southward the voyagers saw with a twinge of home-yearning their own as ill-named peak of Tater Hill, far beyond the strange homesteads and green fields of the lowland country.

Entering the narrow channel of the South Slang, the scow moved now more slowly. Her bow disturbed now and then some large fish that, making a gulp that sounded like plunging an inverted tumbler into the water, moved sluggishly off, marking its way with a slow under-water wake.

"Dat was bow-fins," Antoine explained. "He was here waitin' for us, an' when he mek dat nowse Ah spec he was smack hees mout for dis frawg. Ah wish he'll gat dat feller Ah'll ant ketch, bah gosh!"

Not far up stream they found a stake which marked a favorite fishing-ground, and making the boat fast to it made ready for fishing. Their rods were not made of lancewood, greenheart, nor split bamboo, in fact were not made at all, but had grown at their own will from chance sown seeds of iron-wood, and were not rods, but only stout and rather crooked poles. The lines were such as carpenters used for chalking, with hooks as stout, and sinkers that might have served for plummets. Antoine skinned the hind legs of a frog, placed the tempting bait on his hook, and made a splashing cast that would have scared a wary fish out of the Slang. Sam followed his example, and both began the patient waiting which gives the angler time for the contemplation which so distinguishes his pastime.

A throng of swallows wheeled in swift circles around them or skimmed the quiet water, scarcely ruffling it where swallow and mirrored double briefly met. High above them a fish-hawk swung with moveless wing, in his lofty course. A king-fisher clattered along the channel's curves; a bittern gulped up his lugubrious strain in a marshy nook; a flicker cackled and drummed on a distant tree, and from further meadows came the jangle of bobolinks, and the clear, long drawn notes of meadow larks.

The marsh was alive with sunfish and perch, snapping eagerly at the swarming insects, but for a long half-hour nothing was allured by the angler's baits; nothing came to their line but the steel blue dragon flies that alighted one above another along the cotton cord, their slender bodies at right angles with it, as if it was a magnetized wire and they insects of steel. Sam amused himself with trying to duck them, but whether the line sank swift or slow not one glittering body or gauzy wing suffered wetting.

As he raised his pole slowly, after one of these futile attempts, it was as slowly but very strongly drawn down, till its tip touched the water, by a heavy, downright pull. Sam struck, and his line began to cut the water in a wide, deep sweep, singing as it went, and making the tough iron-wood writhe and tremble as the fish moved steadily toward the weeds.

"You'll gat it, Sam!" Antoine shouted. "Ah'll know it sem Ah'll see it was bowfins. Hang hol' of it! Kept it off de ma'sh 'less he ketch all de weed grow for ten rod!"

Sam held on stoutly and the fish gained no headway but what the spring of the pole gave him, while it bent till it almost cracked as he bored to right and left among the bottom weeds. At last he began to show signs of weakening, and Sam began towing him toward the boat, along with a great raft of up-torn weeds. But just as his uncouth form became discernible among the moving mass of vegetation, the strain proved too great for a weak spot in the line. It parted midway between hook and tip, and with dismay Sam saw the severed part trailed out of sight.

"Oh, bah gosh!" Antoine groaned, "dat was too bad for los' you fus' bowfins, too bad! too bad! But he an't wort' notings only funs an' you had some wid heem, 'f he'll did had de mos' an' laft at you naow. Fix off you line an' try 'gin, dey was more of it."

Sam unwound from his pole line enough to make up for the lost portion, tested every foot of it with pulls across his knee, bent on another hook, and was presently fishing again. It was soon Antoine's fortune to strike a big fish, which he handled with the skill born of experience, and with little ceremony brought to boat the wide-mouthed, small-eyed fellow, before half the fight was out of him.

"He'll ant han'some but he'll strong, as de dev' say, when he'll sew hees tore trauser wid lawg chain," Antoine remarked, as he unhooked his prize.

Indeed, this survival of the first form of fishes is no beauty, but he is a vigorous fighter, as tenacious of life as a turtle, and, when he can be found without his usual environment of weeds, might afford good sport with light rod and tackle. The fish seemed to have fallen into the mood of biting now, and the two anglers took several in rapid succession without further mishap to their stout tackle. As Sam unhooked an eight-pounder, as they guessed his weight, he noticed another line hanging from his broad jaws, and upon examination found it be the lost portion of his own, readily identified by the sinker and the hook which was fast in the fish's maw.

"By the gret horn spoon!" Sam remarked, "That feller's ekal to Bifmouthed Sile Baily 'at swallered his fork when he was eatin' in a hurry, an' then tucked his knife in tu keep it comp'ny."

"He want all de line you gat, Sam. He tryin' for stop de en' of dis bowfins feeshin' prob'ly."

When their bait was spent they had had enough of the sport, and, casting loose from the stake, took their way toward camp, while the shadows of the western shore slanted far across the deepened green of the marsh and the darkening water.

"What be we goin' tu du wi' these 'ere fish naow we've got 'em?" Sam asked, regarding the catch, as the scow slid up the shelving shore. "If we've got tu heave 'em away, seems tu me it's kinder useless fishin'."

"Wal, Sam, Ah do' know. We'll had de funs an' dat was what bowfins be mek for, prob'ly. Sartin he ant be made for han'some, or for heat. Ant you do not'ing honly for heat sometings? What you shoot skonk for, hein? You ant heat it, you ant peel hees skin for sol' it?"

"Skunks eat pa'tridges an' suck the 'aigs."

"Bowfins heat better feesh as he was," Antoine answered as laconically. "But if you feel so bad for t'row it, Ah'll streeng all dat bowfins and hitch heem in de water for some hol' bowfins heatin' mans come 'long for give it. Dey leeve week, prob'ly all summer so, till some mans come for give it. Der was hole feller leeve up de creek salt all he can't heat naow, for winter, sem lak codfeesh. An' some mans feed hawg of it."

So the fish were tethered to the edge of the marsh to await the coming of some appreciative native, and the anglers, wending their way to camp, rekindled the fire and soon had a fine pike-perch of the morning's fishing in the pan.

The shadows of night crept around them, darkening all their surroundings but the radiant circle of the camp fire, and still as they smoked the last pipe, Antoine discoursed of the pleasures of bowfin angling.

"Wal, arter all," Sam said, as he knocked the ashes from his pipe, "I'd ruther be a ketchin' them leetle traouts, Antwine." And who would not?

# A BIG MUSKELLUNGE

## W. N. HULL

The summer days began to drag. The brick walls of the city glimmered in the hot sunshine. Offices were like bake-ovens.

"Let's escape to the country," said Bob, fanning himself vigorously and mopping the perspiration from his jolly fat face.

"I know what's on your mind, Bob; you want another dog-fish."

"Let's go this time for muskellunge."

It was scarcely necessary for him to make the suggestion; I was ready to do anything to escape the terrible heat.

Next evening found us on board one of the boats of the Goodrich Line, steaming slowly out of the Chicago River and cutting a passage through the black veil of night which hung like a pall over the lake.

After a more refreshing sleep upon the cool waters of the lake than the summer had so far granted us, we landed next morning at Grand Haven. We transferred to a smaller steamer, and in two hours more we found ourselves fanned by the cool air of the upper lakes, and we turned into the Muskegon River and ran up to the city of Muskegon.

How delightful it is on a hot summer day to sit forward upon the upper deck of a lake steamer and be fanned by the rushing air as the boat speeds along!

We hire an electric launch to take us over to the other side of the bay, and there engage a man with a rowboat to row us up the bay while we take turns trolling for the muskellunge.

Our line is at least three hundred feet long and a good strong one. On the end is a monster spoon-hook, gaily ornamented with gaudy feathers. We want a large fish or none.

Bob now has the line on the stern seat, Charley is at the oars, and I am the gentleman at the bow. The gaff-hook lies near me, and I may have one stroke of skillful work to do. We are about fifty feet from the shore. Bob plays out two hundred feet of line, and Charley is rowing so slowly that there is scarcely a move of the water. The wind has risen slightly and raises a ripple upon the lake. This is favorable for a good catch.

An hour passes, and we have not had a strike. Charley says the fish are here, and we must be patient and keep a sharp lookout. We talk in low voices, and the fish are not frightened by anything uncommon among them this beautiful summer morning.

We started in at nine o'clock, and it is now ten. The movement and work are lazy and monotonous, and day-dreaming is creeping over the rower and the gentleman in the bow.

But Bob is alert. He has the business end of the expedition. He is an old fisherman and a true lover of the sport. He draws upon the line, causing the spoon to revolve more swiftly, and again lets it out, giving the spoon a slower movement.

Memory goes wool-gathering and roams across the continent. Again I am at Pacific Cottage on the Atlantic shore and the delightful days pass all too quickly; but my dreams are almost broken and we are almost upset by Bob, who springs to his feet shouting, "A strike! A strike!"

Sure enough, the line is playing out fast, and the "whale," as Charley calls him, is taking—we were about to say a bee-line, but probably it would be more correct to call it a fish-line—for his haunts in deep water. Bob holds him with a firm and skillful hand.

"He's well hooked," says Charley. "There's plenty of sport ahead for you city chaps. Ten to one you don't land him."

"I take you," says Bob, but does not take his eye off the line, nor his hands from the push and pull.

Now the fish changes his mind and shoots for the shore, but finding himself in shallow water, he turns again. In the shallow water we have caught glimpses that lead us to believe he is a rare fish.

"How much will he weigh, Charley?" I ask.

"With his own scales?" says Charley interrogatively, with a cunning look.

"Any way," I answer, and feel I have silenced Charley with my witty gun, but his reply takes a more practical turn:

"Don't count your chickens before they are hatched, nor weigh your fish till he is caught," and he slowly turns the boat as he sees the fish make a break up the lake.

"The line is all out, and he is actually pulling us along." It does seem so, and naturally we wonder if the line will stand the strain.

"Turn again, Charley; he's running down the lake," and Bob reaches rapidly hand over hand upon the slacking line.

The muskellunge is called the "wolf of the waters" and is the hardest fighter ever hooked. Bob's fish thrashes the waters like a mad bull. He jumps and he turns. He strikes with his tail, and whirls with a sudden wrench upon the line that tests its strength and his own jaws. But every effort and every swift run weakens him. He cares less and less for escape, and comes nearer the boat.

I have the gaff-hook ready.

"Pull him a little nearer, Bob," I shout.

"I can't do it," says Bob, "let him go again."

But he does not turn very far. Again Bob pulls him toward the boat, in and out, in and out for at least an hour and a half.

In the meantime Charley is telling how, away up in the mountain streams, two men in a canoe, with pole and reel, have great sport catching these big fellows that have crept up, like the salmon of the Pacific, as far as possible, to spawn.

"Strike him! Yank him in!" shouts Bob.

I am standing in the boat, keeping it as steady as I can, as I watch my chance. A wrong blow may break the hook or line and the fish will be lost.

"Next time, sure," I reply.

Now he comes so near that his whole body is seen, and he seems to be pausing to take breath. I take a careful blow with the gaff-hook and a sudden pull toward the boat. The fish comes in.

"Jump on him! Where's the hatchet?" shouts Bob. "He's the wolf of the waters, and will fight to the bitter end."

The hatchet lies at Charley's feet. He seizes it and with one blow with the sharp edge he splits the captive's head almost open, and the fish is surely ours; he quivers a little, and gives up his life.

"How much will he weigh now, Charley?"

"Thirty pounds," says Charley.

Later the scales reveal the fact that Charley was excited eight pounds, for the fish actually weighs but twenty-two pounds.

Bob's face is flushed with excitement. He chuckles and laughs, still keeping his eye upon the fish and stroking him occasionally all the way down to dinner.

"Isn't he a beauty?"

"Looks much like a pickerel."

"He is broader and more chunky."

"Tell you how we'll have him cooked. We'll have him stuffed, covered with slices of salt pork, and baked."

"If we had him down at the office we could bake him without an oven."

"Now, don't say office here; it sickens me to think of it."

But when we did return to the office, of all the stories Bob told to the calling friends, this is the one that he lingered longest over and made the most of. He always affirms that this was one of the best sporting events of his life.

# THE SHANTY

## JERRY GIBBS

The ice was dead gray. It stretched as far as you could see looking north up the big, ragged lake. Snow that had once brightened the surface had melted into hills of slush or two-inch-deep sheets of water that the wind riffled passing through. Beneath the water the ice showed bleakly. It was still safe, still over a foot thick, far from the blackness that would herald its final rottenness.

At the access parking lot stood remnants of a once-bustling ice-fishing village, shanties that had been hastily pulled during the thaws to prevent them being locked in when the weather turned again. The few ice houses still on the lake were owned by hard-core regulars who would fish them daily or nightly keeping watch on the weather.

It was the worst time of year in the North Country. Roads crumbled or turned to mud. Shrinking snow revealed mounds of preserved winter litter. Trees stood exhausted and bare. The crows had returned, though, and their sharp rasping knifed across the woodland valleys. You could say it was spring, the way it is spring in the North.

The two men and the big black Labrador retriever were 50 yards out heading south on the ice toward a long point guarding the entrance to a bay. The dog ran ahead, quartering, returning to check. Its owner, Bud Tuttle, pulled the sled that carried most of their equipment. The dog was very happy.

"Ought to harness your energy, foolish dog," Tuttle told the Lab. "This sled is getting waterlogged and heavy."

"Let me haul it for awhile," the other man said. He was a little shorter, but broader than Bud. His name was Earl Waite. The two were old friends who had not seen one another for some time.

"Nah," Bud told him. "I only let friends haul coming back—when I'm beat from digging holes."

"Right," Earl laughed.

Far off the point were several ice fishermen. Some had set out tip-ups but most worked short jigging rods or sticks for yellow perch.

"Don't know why they keep fishing out that far," Bud Tuttle said. "Those schools of yellows are moving in here by now. Those fish want deeper water they can find it off the point. Then it shallows fast soon as you get to the bay mouth. Course there's a better chance at a passing trout or salmon outside, but I pick up trout right at the drop, too."

Around the point, not far from it, stood a fragile shanty of wood framing and black roofing paper. "Look at that shack," Bud continued. "That's old René Tatro's. He's in there most all the time day or night. Anybody catches fish through a hole in the ice, it's him."

They sloshed a little way on without talking, then Earl said, "I haven't had a good perch feed in so long, almost forgot how they taste."

"Should get them," Bud said.

Earl took the auger and started the first hole. Bud set a jig rod and a Styrofoam cup of live maggot bait near the drilling, then dragged the sled through the slush-water angling toward the point. The dog splashed ahead like a spring colt. The first hole done, Earl walked over and the two men grabbed the auger together, alternating grips along the handle to cut the second hole fast. Then Earl returned to the first hole. He freed the hookless attractor spoon and ice flies secured to the jig rod guides and baited the fly hooks. He sent the silver spoon followed by the flies on droppers above it down the hole, found bottom and cranked up a few turns.

"Work from the bottom up, you never know where you'll hit them," Bud called over. "I'll be in a little deeper water here."

"You using the same rig?"

"I put on one of those Rapala jigs—you know, the things that swim around in little circles. Never can tell when a stray trout or pike might eat. I got the flies on above it."

It was quiet across the lake, then came the floating strains of a song sung in a dry, cracking voice.

"Who's singing?" Earl called over.

"That'll be old René in his shack," Bud laughed. "All the time he spends in there, guess he gets lonely. Keeps a bottle a rum for company. If he gets really tuned we'll have some music."

The first holes produced nothing and the two moved just off the point, drilling at new spots, Earl farther out, Bud closer in. Strains of a song in Quebec French came across to them from the shanty.

"He hasn't got started," Bud said. "You'll see. He switches back to English sometimes."

The dog appeared around the corner of the musical shanty, snuffling its edges.

"Ace, get over here," Bud yelled. The dog came up panting, nuzzled Tuttle's leg. "Good boy." He rubbed the dog's ears. "You leave the old man's shack alone, hear." Then he straightened. "Old Tatro's got a smelt system in there. Got a whole long trench he keeps open; a bunch of fishing lines spaced along it on a rack. Lines come off little wood spools, go through open brackets. Fish hits, he just plucks the line off, hand-over-hands it in unless it's a big one. They use the same thing up to the St. Lawrence fishing Tommy cod. Slick as owl dung in the rain. He won't get smelt now, though. Perch are just fine with him, too."

"Sounds like a production line," Earl said.

"He catches 'em, old geezer. I worry one day he'll slip through that trench after enough a that rum."

Earl counted off line in two-foot pulls. "It's deep," he said to himself. He cranked up until he figured he was at 15 feet. Overhead, streaks of thin clouds backed by a high, gray dome gave the sky the look of cool, polished tombstone. Far to the north the lake was empty. It seemed a very lonely place and Earl was glad he had company.

After a time, his second hole producing nothing, Earl started in. Bud had done no better. With Ace leading they headed around the point to the bay side closer to the old man's shanty. The black and gray shack sagged toward the left. "He builds it up new every year," Bud said. "It's not the strongest thing."

They drilled new holes inside the drop edge where the bottom rose from 40 to 18 feet. They drilled closer together, more for company than any insight into fish location.

René's shanty had been quiet for some time. Suddenly the old man's disembodied voice boomed across the ice. He sang in English this time, high in his nose in grand country fashion. First something about Texas ladies, then he segued into "90 miles an hour down a dead-end road . . . You gotta be bad to have a good time . . ." It was all delightfully incongruous for the time and place. Then Earl felt a peck and he struck with the jig rod.

He used the tip of the rod and his non-rod hand in a kind of alternating cat's cradle to pick up line and bring the fish in. He dropped the monofilament on the ice, the perch following.

"Nice," he said, "nice perch."

The fish was fat, gleaming brassy-gold, its black vertical bars vivid. It splayed its sharp-pointed gill covers, arched its spiny dorsal. Earl brought it to the bucket on the sled.

Hearing excitement Ace trotted back from one of his circuits, coming up just as a fish hit Bud's rig. "Just a couple feet off bottom," he said happily.

"That's where mine hit."

The dog danced, lunged for Bud's fish. "Ace, back!" Tuttle ordered. The dog backed reluctantly, wanting the fish. "You'll get fin-pricked," Bud grumbled affectionately, "not to mention slobbering dinner."

They took two more fish each but it was not fast and they spread out, drilling new holes, looking for the main school. They tried shallower, drilling a hole line, then moved out on the drop again and here they hit the school.

The fish were so tightly concentrated that holes a couple of yards apart meant the difference between an occasional fish or rapid action. They ended with four holes drilled in a cluster, alternating between them as one cooled and another became productive.

In his shack old René started in again singing ". . . we got winners we got losers, we got bikers we got truckers . . . an' the girls next door dress up like movie stars . . . I love this bar, I love this bar. . . ."

"He's getting there," Bud laughed.

"So are we," Earl said sticking another fish.

"Let's string out these holes and connect them," Bud said. "Make a trench like old René's so we can keep moving right on top of the fish."

They augered new holes, connected the old ones. Then Bud grabbed the long steel ice spud from his sled and widened the slot. The opening was a long, rough rectangle.

Ace stayed with them now, feinting at each new fish, whining happily. Over in his shack René had launched into a sad-sweet ballad in Quebec French. Two crows circled overhead eyeballing for scrap bait. Just then Bud struck but this time his little jigging rod bowed over, line tearing from the reel with a soft zipping sound. "No perch!" he yelled.

Quickly Earl reeled in, ran over. The fish finished its first run and Bud was getting line back now, reeling smoothly. Then the fish went again. It was a shorter run but deeper, and when the fish was turned it came only a little way before going a third time, this run toward the point and just beneath the ice. Bud thrust his rod half down into the trench. "He's awfully close to the top. He'll cut me off on the ice edge if I let him."

Ace danced close, tail wagging, excited as the men.

"I got him coming," Bud said. He reeled faster now, gaining line. Then they saw the fish.

"Trout! Nice rainbow," Earl said. He raced for the sled. "You got a net?"

"Ah, no," Bud said worriedly. The fish was at the surface. It thrashed, showering Bud on his knees, reaching for it. Then it ran again forcing him to punch the rod into the trench.

"I have heavy line," Bud said. "If I can get him to hold on top a second I can scoop him with one hand, just swing him over."

The fish came. It lay on the surface, Bud holding it with raised rod, reaching under its belly with his other hand, scooping it, the fish arcing brightly through the air to the ice, gleaming, bold magenta stripe on its side. It arched its body, hard muscles lifting it from the ice. Earl grabbed it but instantly it slipped away. The fish spun on the ice, flopped, and Ace was on it but not fast enough. The rainbow's last effort took it from between the dog's feet back into the trench, the Lab after it, hitting the frigid water, diving.

"Ace!" Bud bellowed. He pounded with his boot heel on the ice. Earl jabbed his own jig rod under, searching. Bud ran to the sled, came back with the ice sieve, dropped to his belly. His arm up to the shoulder in the water, Bud swung the sieve in wide circles under water searching frantically for the dog.

"Ace, Ace!" he called. "Oh the damned, stupid . . ." He rolled over on the ice, his hand gone angry red. "I can't hold on to this scoop."

"Here give it to me." Earl grabbed the sieve. He was down now scooping at the other end of the wide trench.

A scream sliced the air. They saw René's shanty rock once before one black paper wall exploded, flimsy framing splintering, spewing the old man in green suspenders and baggy wool trousers. His white hair flared in ragged streamers, his eyes rolled madly, and from his sunken cavern-dark mouth came a wavering, tortured wail. René Tatro hit the ice running. He slipped to all fours, regained his feet, staggering for shore, not seeing the anglers, not seeing anything now but the safety of shore.

"La bête . . . sauvage!" he screamed, "the beast, the beast!"

He reached the shore, crashed into the woods. The two anglers were running now, heading for the destroyed shanty, reaching it, staring in. Inside was a shambles. Tackle was strewn everywhere. A half-filled can of corn had scattered kernels like confetti. Bits of lunch joined the yellow niblets. An empty rum bottle lay on its side. And in the middle of it all was Ace, tail beating as he wolfed down everything edible.

"Ace you fool!" Bud told the dog. "Come here." The dog even gave up eating to come. Bud grabbed the Lab around the shoulders and Ace shook his hindquarters showering both men.

"Can't believe this," Earl said.

"Oh yeah, it's real. Look at that setup. Ace must have boiled right up the middle of René's ice trench looking like the devil himself."

They both began laughing. They sat in the debris and could not stop laughing.

"That poor geezer. If he didn't think it was old Ned he likely thought it was the lake monster we're supposed to have," Bud said wiping tears from his eyes.

"Oh, I remember that—like the one in Loch Ness," Earl said.

"Ace you are a monster all right. Nothing's hurt with the fishing setup anyway," Bud pointed. "But the shack's sure finished."

"I'm shutting down this stove," Earl said. Ace squirmed to get back at the food.

"No more, you. You've done enough for the day," Bud told the dog. "I'm gonna call poor René. He won't believe me. Maybe I shouldn't tell him the truth. I bet he goes on the wagon for a while. Got to fix his shack for him. I wonder if I can ever get him back on the ice again."

"We better get out of here before we freeze," Earl said. "I'm starting to feel it."

"Same here. I think my arm's frozen," Bud said.

They staggered to the sled, started back fast toward the access, looking at one another, beginning to laugh again so hard that walking became difficult. The dog ran in front pleased with it all.

Finally Earl said, "You know, along with everything we have enough fish for supper."

"Good thing," Bud told him. "Nobody'll believe the rest."

Overhead along the shoreline two crows headed north into the silence of spring.

# FISHING IN THE OHIO

## JOHN JAMES AUDUBON

I t is with mingled feelings of pleasure and regret that recall to my mind the many pleasant days I have spent on the shores of the Ohio. The visions of former years crowd on my view, as I picture to myself the fertile soil and genial atmosphere of our great western garden, Kentucky, and view the placid waters of the fair stream that flows along its western boundary. Methinks I am now on the banks of the noble river. Twenty years of my life have returned to me; my sinews are strong, and the "bowstring of my spirit is not slack"; bright visions of the future float before me, as I sit on a grassy bank, gazing on the glittering waters. Around me are dense forests of lofty trees and thickly tangled undergrowth, amid which are heard the songs of feathered choristers, and from whose boughs hang clusters of glowing fruits and beautiful flowers. Reader, I am very happy. But now the dream has vanished, and here I am in the British Athens, penning an episode for my *Ornithological Biography*, and having before me sundry well-thumbed and weather-beaten folios, from which I expect to be able to extract some interesting particulars respecting the methods employed in those days in catching Cat-fish.

But, before entering on my subject, I will present you with a brief description of the place of my residence on the banks of the Ohio. When I first landed at Henderson in Kentucky, my family, like the village, was quite small. The latter consisted of six or eight houses; the former of my wife, myself, and a young child. Few as the houses were, we fortunately found one empty. It was a log-*cabin*, not a log-*house*; but as better could not be had, we were pleased. Well, then, we were located. The country around was thinly peopled, and all purchasable provisions rather scarce; but our neighbors were friendly, and we had brought with us flour and bacon-hams. Our pleasures were those of young people not long married, and full of life and merriment; a single smile from our infant was, I assure you, more valued by us than all the treasures of a modern Croesus would have been. The woods were amply stocked with game, the river with fish; and now and then the hoarded sweets of the industrious bees were brought from some hollow tree to our little table. Our child's cradle was our richest piece of furniture, our guns and fishing-lines our most serviceable implements, for although we began to cultivate a garden, the rankness of the soil kept the seeds we planted far beneath the tall weeds that sprung up the first year. I had then a partner, a "man of business," and there was also with me a Kentucky youth, who much preferred the sports of the forest and river to either day-book or ledger. He was naturally, as I may say, a good woodsman, hunter, and angler, and, like me, thought chiefly of procuring supplies of fish and fowl. To the task accordingly we directed all our energies.

Quantity as well as quality was an object with us, and although we well know that three species of Cat-fish existed in the Ohio, and that all were sufficiently good, we were not sure as to the best method of securing them. We determined, however, to work on a large scale, and immediately commenced making a famous "trot-line." Now, reader, as you may probably know nothing about this engine, I shall describe it to you.

A trot-line is one of considerable length and thickness, both qualities, however, varying according to the extent of water, and the size of the fish you expect to catch. As the Ohio, at Henderson, is rather more than half a mile in breadth, and as its fishes weigh from one to a hundred pounds, we manufactured a line which measured about two hundred yards in length, as thick as the little finger of some fair one yet in her teens, and as white as the damsel's finger well could be, for it was wholly of Kentucky cotton, just, let me tell you, because that substance stands the water better than either hemp or flax. The main line finished, we made a hundred smaller ones, about five feet in length, to each of which we fastened a capital hook of Kirby and Co.'s manufacture. Now for the bait!

It was the month of May. Nature had brought abroad myriads of living beings: they covered the earth, glided through the water, and swarmed in the air. The Cat-fish is a voracious creature, not at all nice in feeding, but one who, like the vulture, contents himself with carrion when nothing better can be had. A few experiments proved to us that, of the dainties with which we tried to allure them to our hooks, they gave a decided preference, at that season, to *live toads*. These animals were very abundant about Henderson. They ramble or feed, whether by instinct or reason, during early or late twilight more than at any other time, especially after a shower, and are unable to bear the heat of the sun's rays for several hours before and after noon. We have a good number of these crawling things in America, particularly in the western and southern parts of the Union, and are very well supplied with frogs, snakes, lizards, and even crocodiles, which we call alligators; but there is enough of food for them all, and we generally suffer them to creep about, to leap or to flounder as they please, or in accordance with the habits which have been given them by the great Conductor of all.

During the month of May, and indeed until autumn, we found an abundant supply of toads. Many "fine ladies," no doubt, would have swooned, or at least screamed and gone into hysterics, had they seen one of our baskets filled with these animals, all alive and plump. Fortunately we had no tragedy queen or sentimental spinster at Henderson. Our Kentucky ladies mind their own affairs, and seldom meddle with those of others farther than to do all they can for their comfort. The toads, collected one by one, and brought home in baskets, were deposited in a barrel for use. And now that night is over, and as is the first trial we are going to give our trot-line, just watch our movements from that high bank beside the stream. There sit down under the large cotton-wood tree. You are in no danger of catching cold at this season.

My assistant follows me with a gaff hook, while I carry the paddle of our canoe; a boy bears on his back a hundred toads as good as ever hopped. Our line—oh, I forgot to inform you that we had set it last night, but without the small ones you now see on my arm. Fastening one end to yon sycamore, we paddled our canoe, with the rest nicely coiled in the stern, and soon reached its extremity, when I threw over the side the heavy stone fastened to it as a sinker. All this was done that it might be thoroughly soaked, and without kinks or snarls in the morning. Now, you observe, we launch our light bark, the toads in the basket are placed next to my feet in the bow; I have the small lines across my knees all ready looped at the end. Nat, with the paddle, and assisted by the current, keeps the stern of our boat directly down stream; and David fixes, by the skin of the back and hind parts, the living bait to the hook. I hold the main line all the while, and now, having fixed one linelet to it, over goes the latter. Can you see the poor toad kicking and flouncing in the water? "No"—well, I do. You observe at length that all the lines, one after another, have been fixed, baited, and dropped. We now return swiftly to the shore.

"What a delightful thing is fishing!" have I more than once heard some knowing angler exclaim, who, "with the patience of Job," stands or slowly moves along some rivulet twenty feet wide, and three or four feet deep, with a sham fly to allure a trout, which, when at length caught, weighs half a pound. Reader, I never had such patience. Although I have waited ten years, and yet seen only three-fourths of the *Birds of America* engraved, although some of the drawings of that work were patiently made so long ago as 1805, and although I have to wait with patience two years more before I see the end of it, I never could hold a line or a rod for many minutes, unless I had—not a "nibble," but a hearty bite, and could throw the fish at once over my head on the ground. No, no—if I fish for trout, I must soon give up, or catch, as I have done in Pennsylvania's Lehigh, or the streams of Maine, fifty or more in a couple of hours. But the trot-line is in the river, and there *it* may patiently wait, until I visit it toward night. Now I take up my gun and note-book, and, accompanied by my dog, intend to ramble through the woods until breakfast. Who knows but I may shoot a turkey or a deer? It is barely four o'clock; and see what delightful mornings we have at this season in Kentucky!

Evening has returned. The heavens have already opened their twinkling eyes, although the orb of day has yet scarcely withdrawn itself from our view. How calm is the air! The nocturnal insects and quadrupeds are abroad; the bear is moving through the dark cane-brake, the land crows are flying towards their roosts, their aquatic brethren towards the interior of the forests, the squirrel is barking his adieu, and the Barred Owl glides silently and swiftly from his retreat, to seize upon the gay and noisy animal. The boat is pushed off from the shore; the mainline is in my hands; now it shakes; surely some fish have been hooked. Hand over hand I proceed to the first hook. Nothing there! But now I feel several jerks stronger and more frequent than before. Several hooks I pass; but see, what a fine Cat-fish is twisting around and round the little line to which he is fast! Nat, look to your gaff—hook him close to the tail. Keep it up, my dear fellow!—there now, we have him. More are on, and we proceed. When we have reached the end many goodly fishes are lying in the bottom of our skiff. New bait has been put on, and, as we return, I congratulate myself and my companions on the success of our efforts; for there lies fish enough for ourselves and our neighbors.

A trot-line at this period was perfectly safe at Henderson, should I have allowed it to remain for weeks at a time. The navigation was mostly performed by flat-bottomed boats, which during calm nights floated in the middle current of the river, so that the people on board could not observe the fish that had been hooked. Not a single steamer had as yet ever gone down the Ohio; now and then, it is true, a barge or a keel-boat was propelled by poles and oars; but the nature of the river is such at that place, that these boats when ascending were obliged to keep near the Indian shore until above the landing of the village (below which I always fixed my lines), when they pulled across the stream.

Several species or varieties of Cat-fish are found in the Ohio, namely the Blue, the White, and the Mud Cats, which differ considerably in their form and color, as well as in their habits. The Mud Cat is the best, although it seldom attains so great a size as the rest. The Blue Cat is the coarsest, but when not exceeding from four to six pounds, it affords tolerable eating. The White Cat is preferable to the last, but not so common; and the Yellow Mud Cat is the best and rarest. Of the blue kind some have been caught that weighed a hundred pounds. Such fishes, however, are looked upon as monsters.

The form in all the varieties inclines to the conical, the head being dispro-portionately large, while the body tapers away to the root of the tail. The eyes, which are small, are placed far apart, and situated as it were on the top of the forehead, but laterally. Their mouth is wide, and armed with numerous small and very sharp teeth, while it is defended by single-sided spines, which when the fish is in the agonies of death, stand out at right angles, and are so firmly fixed as sometimes to break before you can loosen them. The Cat-fish has also feelers of proportionate length, apparently intended to guide its motions over the bottom, whilst its eyes are watching the objects passing above.

Trot-lines cannot be used with much success unless during the middle stages of the water. When very low, it is too clear, and the fish, although extremely vora-cious, will rarely risk its life for a toad. When the waters are rising rapidly, your trot-lines are likely to be carried away by one of the numerous trees that float in the stream. A "happy medium" is therefore best.

When the waters are rising fast and have become muddy, a single line is used for catching Cat-fish. It is fastened to the elastic branch of some willow several feet above the water, and must be twenty or thirty feet in length. The entrails of a Wild Turkey, or a piece of fresh venison, furnish good bait; and if, when you visit your line the next morning after you have set it, the water has not risen too much, the swinging of the willow indicates that a fish has been hooked, and you have only to haul the prize ashore.

One evening I saw that the river was rising at a great rate, although it was still within its banks. I knew that the White Perch were running, that is, ascending the river from the sea, and anxious to have a tasting of that fine fish, I baited a line with a crayfish, and fastened it to the bough of a tree. Next morning as I pulled in the line, it felt as if fast at the bottom, yet on drawing it slowly I found that it came. Presently I felt a strong pull, the line slipped through my fingers, and next instant a large Cat-fish leaped out of the water. I played it for a while, until it became exhausted, when I drew it ashore. It had swallowed the hook, and I cut off the line close to its head. Then passing a stick through one of the gills, I and a servant tugged the fish home. On cutting it open, we, to our surprise, found in its stomach a fine White Perch, dead, but not in the least injured. The Perch had been lightly hooked, and the Cat-fish, after swallowing it, had been hooked in the stomach, so that, although the instrument was small, the torture caused by it no doubt tended to disable the Cat-fish. The perch we ate, and the cat, which was fine, we divided into four parts, and distributed among our neighbors. My most worthy friend and relative, Nicholas Berthoud, Esq., who formerly resided at Shippingport in Kentucky, but now in New York, a better fisher than whom I never knew, once placed a trot-line in "the basin" below "Tarascon's Mills," at the foot of the Rapids of the Ohio, I cannot recollect the bait which was used; but on taking up the line we obtained a remarkably fine Cat-fish, in which was found the greater part of a suckling pig!

PART III

# A TOUCH
# OF SALT

# THE ANGLER AND THE WEAKFISH

## CHARLES BRADFORD

"The boats are in the breezy bay,
Fast by some point that juts its bar.

Or by some river mouth that pours
Its affluent current by the shores,
The fisher casts his baited line
To tempt the weakfish of the brine."
ISAAC McLELLAN

The doctor has come to my camp on the tiny island in the Great South Bay almost against his will—I forced the outing upon him by constant praising of the wild spot—and I feel that I must first make him comfortable and then show him the fishing. He is not at all himself. The long sail from the mainland, he says, has destroyed his usual good nature, but I tell him that it is hunger that makes him surly. "Living unnaturally, as you do in the city, Doctor, has destroyed your sense of appetite, and it has been so long a time since you were really hungry that you've forgotten what hunger is; you can't recognize it when, by a few hours of natural life, it returns to you, and you very naturally call your ailment by another name and attribute its origin to a false cause. I'll open some Little Necks for you, and while you eat them I'll broil you a sea bass." And I handed the old man a cup of sherry.

"Oh, I'll have none of your hungry yarn, nor any of your other yarns. I guess I know a little more about myself than you do," and the doctor looked real angry. "I couldn't eat in town, where I have every luxury; I couldn't sleep there, where I have a decent bed and decent roof over my head; and from what I see of this place I guess I'll starve outright or die of exposure here. I was a fool to listen to you. Why, this is the very worst sort of thing a man in my state of health should do—come out to a rough-and-tumble place like this. I wish I had gone back with the captain; that old numbskull, too, should have known better. Where are the decent things you said you had out here—the soft, clean beds, the fine stove, and all the other things?"

"Oh, don't fret so, Doctor. Everything will come in its order," I say to him. "Drink some sherry—it'll calm you. Here's your clams; now for a nice sea bass."

The shanty is not so bad as my visitor paints it. It has given me firm shelter for years, and some of the happiest days of my life have been spent within sight of its homely portal. Its island lies abreast of Bellmore, six miles distant on the mainland. The little house faces the ocean, whose breakers can be seen and heard rolling in on the wild beach a quarter of a mile to the south.

"Who owns this old place and what's it all about?" asks the doctor, the eating of the little clams and the sight of a fine sea bass giving battle at the end of my line reviving his spirits.

"I don't know the owner, Doctor. I took possession one summer's day some years ago—made for the open door during a terrific thunderstorm that overtook me in a small sailboat out there in the channel—and have never been disturbed, though spending several weeks here twice a year ever since."

The doctor is beginning to act agreeably. He offers to clean the sea bass while I catch another, but I hand him the rod and I set about cleaning the fish and building the drift-chip fire.

I could arrange for the doctor to take a nice weakfish, but decide it is better to first have the supper over and the beds made before we become really interested in the angle. So I let the dear old fellow take a two-pound bass, and then entice him from the play by putting the broiled fish on his knee.

The fish is cooked whole—head, tail, fins, and all—and I centre it in a great white platter, with thin slices of red pickled beet and a border of willow-green eel-grass.

"Well, you've proven three of your statements, at least," says the old man, pitching into the juicy flakes of the bass with the first natural hunger that has crossed his stomach in years, as he himself confesses; "I am hungry, as you said I'd be; fish are caught easily at the very door of the camp, and you really do cook and serve decently."

"And is not everything here really more pleasant than I described it?" I ask. "To-morrow at this time, my friend, you will admit as much."

The doctor is persuaded to eat the other bass and some thin strips of bacon, two huge potatoes roasted in the hot ashes, and a quantity of steamed soft clams raked out of a hotbed of seaweed.

"Now, Doctor, light your cigar and adjust your rod, and while you ply it upon the weakfish I'll clear away the supper mess and lay you a night couch where your sleep will prove 'sweeter and sounder, lighter and more luxurious than princes catch on beds of eiderdown and velvet'—here's your bait."

The day is nearing its end. The red sun is just dropping behind the fringe of dark-green upland, and already the flashes of Fire Island light pierce the gray shadows that gather in the east. The green herons are flying toward the island to roost, and the night herons are coming out to feed. The gulls gather on the loamy flats and exposed sandbars, and their restrained screams mingle with the cluck of the clapper rail, the whistle of the curlew, and the loud but mellow call of the golden plover and yellow shank, as they wing over the surf and meadow land.

The doctor, a few minutes before so surly with the world and himself, is now as calm and sweet-tempered as the tiny marsh wren that swings on the frail grassy stem at his feet, pouring out her evening hymn.

My companion stands on the sod banks and casts his crab bait into the tide, the green water now rushing in from the ocean, on whose plain the bounding whitecaps are made beautiful by the background of dark sky and the sunlit western heavens toward which they roll. Soon the tide will creep over the sod and flood the very island, but we shall not suffer any inconvenience. The little house rests high upon sturdy hardwood posts, and I have gathered up the out-door cooking utensils, staked the boat safely, cut the salt hay for our beds, and gathered the chip-wood for the breakfast fire.

"You must cast out farther in the channel, Doctor," I call to my old friend, "or fish at the mouth of the little creek to your right. The sea bass, fluke, and blackfish frequent the spot you are attending, but the weakfish do not come in so close."

A cunning smile and a peculiar nod of the old angler's head tells me my advice will be heeded, but not upon the instant; he has something at his bait—a large fluke it proves to be—and he is playing the fish skillfully, for his tackle is delicate and his footing none too secure. The fish tugs heavily and, to the old man's astonishment, actually leaps out of the water and skims over the surface like a huge flat stone that is thrown to perform this service ere its weight will make it sink from sight. The fluke and the man battle for twenty minutes, but the angler gains the victory, and I tell him we shall have broiled flatfish if not planked weakfish for our morning meal.

Now the doctor removes his ounce dipsy and flails in the milder water at the creek mouth, and the crab meat, unhampered by any weight save that of itself and the hook, swirls with the current just as it might flow along at its own free will. It barely hides itself beneath the surface ere it is snapped by the game the doctor seeks, and the old man's rod again bends to the play, more violently now and with quicker movements than when the fluke tested its resiliency. We use the landing-net to secure this weakfish, because the locality does not permit of its being guided over the sod bank to the angler's footing, as the fluke was conquered. Here the bank is as yet a full foot out of water, while the spot where the great flatfish was landed allowed of the game being floated quite to the doctor's ankles.

My friend is now at the height of good nature, brought about by honest excitement, and as I take his rod and lead him toward the shanty, now without apparent foundation beyond the water that has flooded the whole meadow land, and appearing for all the world like a diminutive ark on stilts, I fancy I feel a slight quivering in his arm—the tremble of invigoration, not collapse.

"We'll go out in the boat and catch one more," says the doctor; "I'll handle the boat and let you take the fish."

"No, not to-night," I reply; "to-morrow, yes; and we'll make a glorious day of it, old friend; but no more tonight. You are tired, and that's all you can reasonably ask."

"But I'm not as tired to-night as I have been every night in town for the past half year."

"Ah, Doctor, your town tiredness is a different condition. There, 'mid the noise, the smoke, the frantic crowd, and all the unnatural disturbances of so-called civilization, you become fatigued, not really tired. Fatigue is killing; an honest tired feeling is health-giving. Fatigue is born of abuse; tiredness of exhilaration."

We go into the little house, now aglow with a bright, sweet-smelling wood fire, and the doctor's happy frame of mind goes on soaring higher and higher with every revealment. He sees the clean beds, made of rough pine wood and built against the wall one above the other like the berths of a steamship; the little shelves and cupboards in all the glory of their charges—tin tobacco boxes filled with every sort of spice and cooking condiment, and the hundred other homely but inviting articles stored here and there. Four square holes, one at each quarter of the dwelling, let in cool sea air on hot summer days, and stout wooden blinds protect these openings during storms.

The doctor and I talk a long time as we sit about the cozy fire, more than once filling the room with tobacco smoke so that we are obliged to open the door and fan the place with our coats.

I tell the old man all I know about the fishing and the natural history of the great lagoon, and he is a willing audience.

"The baymen, Doctor, say the Great South Bay is ninety miles long, six miles wide, and two feet deep. This is their deduction, and it is about correct, though, of course, in some places it is narrower than six miles and deeper, much, than two feet. There are channels twenty feet deep and open spots fully sixty feet in depth."

"Is flood tide the best for weakfish?" asks the doctor.

"Sometimes and in some places," I answer, remembering the reply of the bayman when I asked the same question years ago. "Most of my best fishing has been done just as the tide turns to run out and until it is about half out, though I have caught some nice fish on the incoming tide, as you took your four-pound fish this evening."

And so we chat until the doctor is made miserable by repeated efforts to keep awake; then we seek the berths, the old man being snugly housed in the lower one, and I blanketed to my chin in the one above him. Here we pass the night in sweet repose, lulled betimes by the booming of the surf, the splashing of the high tide, the leaping of heavy fish, the murmur of the mild wind, and the cry of the night bird.

"I may, peradventure, give you some instructions that may be of use even in your own rivers; and shall bring you acquainted with more flies than Father Walton has taken notice of in his *Compleat Angler*."

CHARLES COTTON.

# SHARKS ON THE SHELL BARS

## VEREEN BELL

We went for reds. But we hadn't been trolling more than fifteen minutes when we saw two triangular dorsal fins easing through the water near a shell bar a hundred yards away. That's when we forgot about the red fish . . .

We've done considerable coast fishing together, the six of us—Fondron and Emmett and I, and our wives—and we've learned some things. The main thing we've learned is that you can fish and be comfortable too. Some people think it's acceptable sport to spend six hours under a blistering Florida-coast sun in a small boat rank with old fish bait and ankle-deep in dirty brine. And, I might as well admit it, I'm one of them—if I can't do any better.

But we knew how to do better. From one of Panacea's mullet fishermen we rented a seine boat. Price, one dollar for the day. This boat is about twenty-four feet long, with plenty of width, a dry bottom, a six-foot seine deck at the stern end, and infinite seaworthiness. Room for portable ice boxes full of mullet and beer, vacuum jugs, gasoline cans, tackle boxes, a dozen rods, and reels of all sizes. Room for six people to fish without slapping one another in the face with bait slabs. Room to get up and move around and prevent *rigor mortis* from setting in. And finally, room for three motors—yes, three—on the capacious stern board.

After daylight the cars wound through the palmetto flatland bordering the broad, black Ochlockonee River mouth, and stopped beside an unoccupied fisherman's shack surrounded by tin cans. Floating serenely forty feet from shore was our yacht. Emmett shouldered his motor and waded out to it. When he had gunned the boat to the beach we loaded up.

Then we mounted the motors. My motor, a 9-horsepower one, went in the middle of the stern board. Emmett and Fondron had 4's, which they mounted on either side of mine. We shoved out a bit, then pulled the three starting cords simultaneously, and the three motors burst into life on the first pull. These modern motors don't have to be cajoled; they *go*. We nudged the levers open and the throbbing hum of the motors rose in harmony. Probably the people of the countryside muttered something about a distant squadron of naval planes from Pensacola and went back to sleep.

An incoming tide flooded upriver from the bay, and the wind that came with it chopped the black water, but the boat rode steady, and the battery of motors thrust it rapidly into the teeth of the tide. Fondron and the feminine element rigged redfish spoons while Emmett and I manned the outboards, steering with the larger motor. We knifed between the piles of the new Ochlockonee Bay bridge without slowing, and presently the water began taking on a greenish tinge. We were in the bay.

When we reached the shell bars we killed two of the motors and uptilted them, using one of the 4's for trolling. The three girls let out spoons astern. The water was shallow, only four or five feet deep. Startled mullet darted away over the shoals. Ahead, an occasional smear of white splash seemed to indicate striking reds.

About that time Flonnie, my wife, yelled, then tugged her line and said, "Shucks. Just raked bottom, I guess."

Life moved in the bay. Yonder in the shallows near the shore, white spray fanned upward where porpoises were giving the mullet hell. Once, not far astern, a tarpon rolled, showing his flag and for a few moments we held our breath, waiting for him to lam into one of the cruising spoons. But he either didn't see them, or didn't want them. Later, a hundred yards gulfward, a big whip ray leaped eight feet clear, flinging spray. For a monster of such personal ugliness, a whip ray takes the air with incredible grace. He leaps to rid himself of remoras, the little striped hitch hikers that cling to big fish by means of handy suction disks on their heads.

Suddenly Fondron, who had his 260 pounds up front to watch for shell banks, shouted, "Look!"

We looked—and saw two good-size sharks cruising around in a horseshoe formed by oyster bars. That's when we forgot about the reds.

We took off the spoons, and eased into the horseshoe's shallows. I had 15-thread line on my reel, about 150 yards of it, with a test pull of 456 pounds, while both of the fins we saw indicated sharks of 300 pounds plus. Emmett's line was bigger, being about a 24 thread. Fondron's had been on his reel so long he'd forgotten what it was. We quickly fastened big hooks onto eight-foot piano-wire leaders, baited up with half mullets, yelled "Duck!" to the excited girls, and let fling toward the spot we'd last seen the sharks. My mullet-head cast was about fifty feet.

Then we waited. Nothing happened. Maybe we had scared the sharks away. But that didn't seem likely. Sharks aren't likely to frighten easily . . .

Somebody hissed. Down to the right, a fin showed. Back of us, forty yards or more, were two other fins. The place was infested.

One of the fish turned our way, cruising lazily along the bar in water not three feet deep, with his tail waving leisurely back and forth. Emmett reeled in hurriedly, wound up, and hurled the big bait sixty feet through the air. The mullet plunked about four yards to the left of the shark. The dorsal fin swerved— toward the bait!

"He's going for it!" I whispered.

"Take it, boy, take it!" Emmett urged hoarsely.

The fin submerged. Our throats got tight, waiting. Three pieces of mullet out, and a hungry shark not ten feet from the farthest! You could hear the girls almost moaning with excitement, and my own pulse was tom-tomming. It was like sitting on a time bomb, wondering if this was the appointed moment for the explosion, or the next.

Still nothing happened. We knew the shark had by now passed Emmett's offering. Mine was close. Then Fondron grunted. His line was inching out. He braced himself and yanked the hook hard. And that set off the explosion!

"*Got him!*" Fondron yelled.

We knew that. We could see the line, taut as a fiddle string, razoring through the brine. We could hear the reel singing out. Emmett and I, on the raised stern deck, saw something else. The shark was angling sharply astern, and going like hell. We had a split second to realize that we both would have to try to jump that cleaving line. I had a momentary glimpse of myself clumping around on my knees, selling pencils. At the second the line would have attempted to cut our legs from under us, it went limp . . .

Broken line!

Fondron made a futile tug, then took a deep, shuddering breath and began coloring the clear air with a purple haze. I afterward noticed that the paint was blistered on his side of the boat. The girls didn't mind his language much—within another four months they were speaking to him again as if nothing had happened.

As for Emmett and me, we tried hard to sympathize with him, but we were so relieved not to be swept overboard or amputated at mid-thigh that I'm afraid we didn't sound sincere.

We cast baits out again.

Emmett said, "Fon, how you expect to catch a shark with an old piece of grocery string?"

I don't know what Fondron muttered, but it cooked the piece of mullet in his hand. He wound up and cast the bait, still smoking slightly, halfway to the shell bar.

"You own a whole hardware store full of fishing tackle," I put in, "and come off with line that—"

A shock ran up my line and jolted against my backbone. The reel hummed. Forgetting I was using a reel with no leather guard, I jammed my thumb against the wildly whirring spindle and lost about a square inch of skin. Finally I found the star drag.

"Crank up!" I yelled to Emmett.

He jumped to the motors. My line was melting fast. I was afraid I'd have none left by the time Emmett got a motor in the water and going. Then my rod tip ducked, something snapped, and I exhaled wearily and began winding in. The shark had rolled on my leader, kinked it, and broken it.

I sat down and called for a bottle of beer, while the others told me how I could have held him.

The crabs began finding our mullet. Every two or three minutes we'd have to reel in and shake a couple of them off. Virginia and Flonnie, who would sell their birthrights for a mess of deviled crabs, stood it as long as humanly possible.

"Let's get some of those crabs," they said. "We could catch dozens."

They rigged up a couple of fresh-water casting reels, baiting with mullet, and went to fishing. They caught several crabs immediately. Getting no further action from sharks, and seeing none rambling around, we watched the crabbing.

Abruptly Virginia's line went taut, and the little rod almost leaped out of her hand. She had several hundred pounds of shark on a freshwater casting outfit!

"What'll I do?" she cried above the throb and bump of the racing reel.

Not one of us could tell her anything to do, except hang on and yell, and she was already doing that. It ended soon—though not soon enough for Virginia—with a snapped line.

Not three minutes later my line tightened.

"This time you'll stick!" I vowed, and set the hook. Instantly the line began ripping out, whining hotly against the rod guides. "Crank up!"

The line evaporated off the drum, dancing and leaping. I heard one of the motors hiss, then break into a welcome hum. We had to get out of the horseshoe before the shark, already out of it, could cut back and take my line across the shell bar.

"Give it the gun!" Fondron yelled.

Then the reel drum ceased whirring. The terrific tug faded. And I knew I had an empty line. The shark was gone. When I reeled the 100 yards of line in, nothing was broken. Everything except the bait was there. And something else was there—the twenty yards of line that had been snapped off Fondron's rig earlier was tangled around my leader. Problem: was it the same shark? And did I hang him with my own hook, or did my tackle get tangled with the broken line that trailed from the shark's mouth? Or did I merely drag the loose line in as I recovered my own? Your guess is as good as mine. It only goes to prove that you can't tell what will happen when you're fooling with sharks.

Emmett hung one next, and lost him. Then we saw another shark lazing along the bars, looking for trouble. He took Emmett's bait. And he got his trouble. Emmett leaned on his rod with a back yank that would have sunk the hook into a coconut. The shark raced for the open end of the horseshoe.

Fondron spun the motor. It broke into life. Virginia, up front, manfully hoisted the anchor—she was the only one who could get to it. We slid out of the shell bars just before the shark would have taken the last of Emmett's line.

For fifteen minutes the shark ran wildly, with almost the abruptness of a tarpon—and with a lot more sheer horsepower. When he finally settled down to a steady pull we killed the motor.

Standing now on the bow, Emmett fought the shark, inching in a little line when he could, losing it back when the big fish wanted it. And all the time that mulelike shark towed a 24-foot seine boat with six people in it. He didn't knife it through the water. But he kept it following him. You could feel it moving, and behind there was a gentle wake. Sharks may not walk on their tails, or arch in the sunlight like some of our flashier game fish, but they don't have to apologize for brute pulling power.

Half an hour passed. I opened a bottle of cold beer and handed it to the sweating Emmett.

Fifteen minutes later Emmett gasped, "He's tiring!"

That was surprising. We had guessed it would take at least an hour and a half to bring him in.

Emmett fought all the line in except about ten yards. In the shimmering green water, a gray-white shape moved. Then a mighty thrash of the fish's tail showered spray over the boat, and he was running again.

A few minutes later, though, he was close once more. We had no gaff—we hadn't come for big fish. So Fondron got out the Colt Woodsman .22 automatic pistol.

The shark broke water five yards away. And then we saw why he had become quickly exhausted. He was hooked, not in the mouth, but in the left pectoral fin. He had been forced to swim unnaturally, against a terrific side pull.

A bullet from the little gun galvanized him into furious action, and again the reel whined. But it didn't last long. Emmett pumped him up again. Presently he was alongside, his movements increasingly feeble.

The little gun spat. The shark convulsed considerably and, dying, rolled belly up. That upside-down position, the only one he hadn't tried, did the trick— it tore the hook out of the fin. The shark slid bottomward, headfirst, and we followed his descent until he gradually faded out of sight in the murky greenness— and became just another big one that got away.

We came back that afternoon with nothing to show for our trouble except a dozen crabs that could have been bought in town for twenty-five cents the lot. And they, it turned out, were dead and therefore no good. Not worth while, you say?

We planned to go back the next weekend.

But when we went looking for sharks, we never seemed to find them. So we went fishing for other things, with a crafty eye peeled for cruising dorsal fins, and we always took some bigger tackle along. No really heavy tackle. I had a reel that held about 140 yards of 18-thread line. I lost one shark because I had forgotten to wet the line beforehand, and it hung and broke.

When you hang a shark of 200 pounds on fairly light tackle like that, it's absolutely necessary to haul in the anchor and follow him a way. Otherwise he'll take out all your line, snap it, and keep helling it on away from there without any please-excuse-its. Once when I had a shark strike, there was some trouble with the anchor. My line was melting fast, so I tried tightening the drag a bit to slow him. I lost that shark too.

That night I removed the little wire spring that controlled the drag, making a no-drag reel of it, and put on a leather thumb guard. And that was the shape of my reel when I hung my next shark.

This time we went for sea trout. There were four of us now, so we used a smaller boat and two motors instead of three on the stern board. The day was hotter than the inside of a Bessemer converter. Fondron, in his bathing trunks, scoffed at the heat and made bold talk to the bubbling sun. "Shine on down, Josh, you might as well be shining on a lightwood knot."

Sea trouting on the coast is drift fishing. You drift over the shallow, grassy flats, then crank up and drift again. It was at the end of a drift, just on the edge of deep water, that we lost interest in the trout. Something took Fondron's trout bait and sprung his light casting rod into a bow. Just before the knifing line snapped, a big angry tail roiled the water ten feet behind the line, and we knew we had found sharks again. We wound in the trout line and rigged up the bigger outfits with eight-foot leaders. I put a mullet head on a 6/0 hook, and made my cast.

My bait waited about three minutes. Then a shark took it and said aloha. When I tried to set my hook my line went limp. The hook was too small. I put on one nearly twice as big, baited it with half a mullet, and cast.

Presently my line started leaping out again. I gave the rod a stiff back-yank—more, really, than was necessary, because a shark's mouth is meaty and it's usually easy to set the hook.

"Crank up!" I said. "I got him!"

Fondron leaped astern, gave the cord handle a hurried pull, and we were off. Meantime, though, the shark was racing seaward, whipping my line off as he went. The thumb guard, pressed hard against the whirring spindle, got so hot I could hardly keep my thumb on it. Before the first fifteen minutes of that fight were gone, I regretted my hasty action in removing the star drag.

It was forty-five minutes before the shark broke water, some sixty yards ahead of the boat. In that brief second he looked brown in the sun-drenched water. Finally, with arms aching and warm sweat rolling into my mouth, I inched him toward the boat. Again we had brought no gaff, so the little automatic .22 was used. At the impact of the first hollowpoint he made a mad run, and I had to pump him in again. Seven shots seemed to have no effect. About the tenth, he began to weaken, and went down. When I started pumping again, there was a leaden weight and I knew he was dead.

We lashed him to the bow with the anchor line, and headed for shore. It was a long way in, even with both motors humming.

Hot? I sat up front with a cigarette and a bottle of beer, resting and sweating. Both the wives seemed half-stupefied by the heat.

Eventually the boat grounded on the beach at Ball Point. Fondron, with a sun-benumbed lack of expression on his face, murmured, "Thank the Lord!" He climbed out of the boat, but not on the land side. He stepped into the water and waded unsteadily out into the receding tide. Then he lay down with his face submerged and tried to cool his heat-soaked head.

"Shine on, Josh," his wife said, loud enough for Fondron, if not the sun, to hear. "You might as well be shining on a lightwood knot."

# THE SAGA OF THE YELLOWFIN

## MARK SOSIN

It wasn't my idea. The late Joe Brooks, a friend, master fly fisherman, and one of the first inductees into the IGFA Hall of Fame, spent time convincing me. "You can do it," he insisted. "You're young and strong with plenty of endurance." Joe felt that the time had come to catch a husky yellowfin tuna on fly and the place to do it was Bermuda. Without waiting for an answer, he simply said he would set up the trip.

Pete Perinchief, who never failed to let you know that he was On Her Majesty's Service and whose family had lived in Bermuda for three or four centuries, handled visiting fishermen. He was skeptical that anyone could catch a yellowfin on fly (which they call Allison tuna in Bermuda), so he brought his good friend Louis Mowbry with him to watch the attempt. Louis was the curator of the Bermuda aquarium and a man with impeccable credentials. My wife, Susan, and another friend of Pete's made up the party.

On July 3, 1969, we set sail for Challenger Bank aboard Captain Boyd Gibbons' Coral Sea. His brother, Terry, served as mate. The procedure is to anchor the boat in the shallower water of the bank and let out enough anchor line so the stem of the boat was near the dropoff to deeper water. The current would carry the chum over the edge and attract a variety of fish including the prized Allison tuna. Hog-mouthed fry was the chum of choice, a small silvery fish that flashed and radiated in the exceptionally clear water.

The tuna did not appear for a considerable amount of time, so everyone busied themselves catching a variety of other species. Suddenly, they were there, big, torpedo-shaped brutes moving swiftly through the slick as they feasted on the free food being drifted back to them.

Pete Perinchief changed his mind. Instead of letting me cast a fly to the tuna, he announced that all of us on board would catch one first on conventional tackle. To say I was disappointed was an understatement, but I remained silent. Pete, Louis, and their friend all caught a tuna, with only one man fishing at a time. It takes time to land an Allison on a 30-pound outfit. My concern was that the small school would leave our chum slick and my chance with the flyrod would be gone.

When the three men had caught their fish, Pete told me I had to catch one on regulation gear first. By the time I battled that tuna into submission, I wasn't so sure I could land one on fly. It was a tough fish and I was a bit winded when I finally brought that critter to boatside.

It's important to understand that state-of-the-art saltwater fly tackle in 1969 was not even close to what we use today. The rod was made from the traditional E-glass and would be considered a less desirable version of the modern 10-weight. Flylines were catalogued by letters in those days instead of numbers. The line was a GAAF which is about what a 10-weight is today. The late Myron Gregory had not yet sold his system of standardizing flylines with a numbering system. My reel was a Seamaster spooled with 275 yards of 30-pound test Dacron backing and the full flyline. The class tippet on the leader tested less than 12-pounds with a short, 30-pound test abrasion tippet that measured less than 12-inches.

A few tuna still fed aggressively in the slick when Pete suggested that now was the time to try one on fly. The flies I had tied for this undertaking were a combination of polar bear hair and Mylar, giving them that shiny appearance in the water that would hopefully attract a tuna. I'm a right-handed caster, yet they gave me the left side of the cockpit, so I had to release each cast on the backcast. The fly landed among the tuna and I started to strip it in short, sharp jerks. The tuna kept swimming around it, eating dead fry instead of the tempting polar bear and Mylar fly.

Frustration began to build. I was convinced that a tuna would grab the fly on the first cast and inhale it. It didn't happen. And, it didn't happen on the next dozen casts. I had come all this way to catch a tuna on fly and the ugly face of failure was staring right at me. My father cast and retrieved flies in chum slicks since the early 1940s and he caught fish. I did, too, under those circumstances, but then I never cast to a tuna before.

Finally, in pure desperation, I asked Terry Gibbons to toss a handful of fry right behind the boat. He did and I cast the fly in the middle of it. Instead of retrieving the fly, I let it drift with the chum. To this day, I can still see that tuna eat the fly going away from the boat and I vividly recall the flyline shooting off the deck the instant I set the hook. Until that moment, I had never read or heard of anybody else dead drifting a fly in a chum slick. Today, it is common practice.

The first run was devastating. That tuna kept going and going as the reel handle spun in reverse and backing disappeared at an alarming rate. The fish wasn't going to stop. We were anchored and no one was about to chase the fish with the boat. This was going to be a dead boat battle and I began to realize I was about to lose the tuna because the reel did not hold enough backing. You could see the gold of the reel spool between the remaining coils of Dacron. It was only seconds before it would end as abruptly as it started.

Not knowing what to do, I smacked the rod butt three or four times with my right hand. The fish stopped with a half-dozen turns of backing still on the reel. The tuna reversed direction and swam toward me. Now, I had to crank all the line back on the flyreel with a one-to-one retrieve.

Just when I thought things were under control, the tuna streaked for the horizon again. I could hear Pete Perinchief with his distinctive accent muttering his famed *Good God Miss Agnes* in the background. Once again, it appeared that I would be spooled, so I started hitting the rod butt again and it worked a second time. The fish stopped, turned around, and started swimming toward me.

As the fortunes of war changed and the result of the battle seemed to shift, the others on board began a discussion of how to handle this fish near the boat if I did in fact manage to land it. While I was in the throes of fighting that fish, my wife, an observer all day, heard them talk about grabbing the flyline, pulling the fish toward the boat, and gaffing it. She knew this was wrong and began to plead with them to talk to me first before they did anything. Fly fishing for big fish was new to them. Finally, she said, "You're going to break the fish off if you touch the leader, please don't do anything until you ask Mark."

They listened to her. I explained to Terry Gibbons that he had to free gaff the fish without touching line or leader. Equally important was how he gaffed the fish. "You want the fish swimming in a circle and moving away from the boat at the instant of gaffing," I explained. "Come up from behind the fish so the gaff does not pass in front of the line. That way, if you miss, the fish does not swim under the boat and break off and the leader does not break against the gaff."

Terry Gibbons gaffed that fish perfectly on his first attempt and threw it on the deck. I never physically touched the fish, allowing Pete and Louis to put it on ice and to weigh it back at the dock. The fish weighed 53 pounds 6 ounces on an officially certified scale and was the first tuna ever taken chumming. Obviously, it was a world record. For a long time, Pete Perinchief and Louis Mowbry erroneously concluded that the fish had to be sick for me to be able to land it. They later realized that the fish was perfectly healthy and that what they had witnessed pushed the frontiers of fly fishing that much further toward the horizon.

That catch is still considered by many to be a significant angling achievement.

# KEEPING BUSY WHEN NOT ON THE CASTING DECK

## LEFTY KREH

I t's more fun and certainly you'll catch more fish if you and your companion in a flats boat work as a team. While one stands on the platform, ready to throw at the next fish, his companion should be just as busy, maybe more so, than the person in the ready-to-fish position.

A major problem for the person on the bow is that the line remains free of tangles and obstructions. Wind blows the line around. It can slide unknowingly underfoot, or it can catch on a rod holder or a piece of gear in the boat, spoiling a cast. Because the fly fisherman is concentrating on seeing the fish and then making a good presentation, he is often unaware that disaster lurks nearby.

Sitting in the boat, the companion can observe what is happening to the line. He constantly makes sure all line is tangle-free. When the angler is false casting prior to throwing to a fish, his friend can alert him that his foot is on the line. If the caster or the boat changes position this can affect how the line is lying on the deck. His teammate constantly monitors the line to make sure it is okay to cast.

The companion can have ready additional flies and leader material. If the angler breaks off his fish either on a hook-up or during the fight, the companion has a leader tippet and fly ready. It is much quicker for him to repair the leader and attach the fly than the man standing on the bow.

Quite often one pattern isn't drawing strikes and a change in flies is needed. The friend can have several flies ready. He can quickly snip off one fly and tie on another. I make it a practice that anytime I miss on two hookups, I check the hook point for sharpness. If the man sitting behind the caster has a file ready, he can check the point and hone it in seconds.

If a fish is hooked and the companion sees that a knot is developing in the line, there is often time for him to remove the knot before the escaping fish pulls the line through the guides. I know of several times when my friend saved a fish by such quick action.

If a fish is hooked and there is some rough water, the friend can often step to the platform and help stabilize the fisherman as he fights his quarry.

Each time you reach a new fishing location line has to be pulled from the reel. This can be time consuming for the angler. But, if the companion will pull the line hand-over-hand from the reel, the chore can be accomplished in seconds. Sometimes the fly line has coils in it that can spoil the cast. *Again,* the companion can stretch the line to remove them.

Many fish are difficult to see on a flat. A snook hiding among the mangrove roots can be near impossible to spot. Despite its size, a permit can often be difficult to see—even for the guide on the poling platform. There are many indicators that help locate a fish on the flats. It can be a silvery flash in the water. A small shower of minnows indicates something chasing them. A subtle mud puff could tip off the anglers to a feeding bonefish. A tail that appears above the surface for only a moment can lead to a catch. A bird flying low over the flats will often briefly frighten a permit, bonefish, redfish, or tarpon. The guide and the angler are looking for all of these indicators. But, so can the companion. Many times it is the person that is not fishing that first locates a fish.

The guide usually stands on the poling platform, which is elevated above the deck. When the angler hooks a fish and brings it to the boat, the guide must stow the pole and climb off the platform to land the fish. All of this takes time and the boat either has to be staked out or anchored or is not under control during this time. Instead, the guide can maintain the boat if the companion will land the fish for his friend.

And, once the fish has been landed, the angler often wants a photograph of it. Many guides, especially outside the United States, know little or nothing about handling a camera or taking a good photo. This is where a friend can really help out.

Several years ago I realized something that took a long time to understand. I began to carry a fly swatter on flats boats. In Florida and the tropics there are biting flies that really hurt. These stinging bloodsuckers have caused many fish to escape, as the angler is distracted trying to kill the pests. Some of these flies are tough. I have knocked them unconscious with my hat, only to see them revive later and fly away. No so with a fly swatter. The companion can carry a fly swatter at the ready. Not long ago Mike O'Brien, a fishing buddy and I killed so many flies with my swatter that we actually wore it out. I piled a big number of their carcasses on the deck, laid the ruined swatter beside it and took a picture of what I called a "fly cemetery." The companion not only can keep these pesky critters from bothering either him or the fisherman, but it sure helps to pass the time when not fishing. And, I might add, there is a certain satisfaction in killing them.

I have seen many pairs of fly fishermen in a flats boat. One stands on the platform, ready to fish. The other person simply sits back and relaxes.

But the person who becomes a team player will get more fun out of the day, and both of them will probably catch more fish.

# THE TARPON OF TURNER'S RIVER

## A. W. DIMOCK

**M**arco is the name of a post office, but the place is called Collier's. Ask any child on the West Coast of Florida about Marco and he will shake his head, but mention Collier and the infant will brighten up and say: "Dat's Tap'n Bill!"

Island, bay, hotel, houses, boat-building plant, and even the atmosphere are, and always have been, Collier's. When Ponce de Leon was cavorting about the peninsula pestering the inhabitants with his inquiries about a spring, he stopped at Collier's. Everybody who goes down the coast stops there. The only way to avoid a long detour around the Cape Romano Shoals is to go through Collier's Bay to Coon Key, and one cannot pass through Collier's Bay without calling at the store.

Summer is the time to visit Collier. When the little mail boat lands me with my family at the dock Captain Bill meets me with:

"Well, how are you? The hotel isn't open, you know."

"Glad of it. That's why I am here. Where's that baggage truck?"

Then I wheel our baggage to the hotel, we select the choice rooms, and spread our belongings all over the place as if we owned the whole business. When the dinner bell rings we sit down with the family and occasional tramps like ourselves who stop in on their way down the coast. Instead of the colorless crowd of tourists who occupy the tables when the hotel is open, we meet itinerant preachers and teachers, lighthouse keepers and land seekers, scientists and Seminoles.

We take possession of the island, and wandering forth with big baskets return laden with a score of varieties of fruits from avocado, pears, bananas, and cocoanuts down through the alphabet to sapadilloes and tamarinds.

As evening approaches we sit on the sheltered piazza that overlooks the bay, and, if the tide favors, watch the porpoises at play, and, more rarely, we witness the dizzy leaps of a dozen or a score of tarpon each minute.

From Collier's Bay to Coon Key the channel twists and turns among sand flats and oyster reefs, between wooded banks and around tiny keys without blaze or buoy, stake, or sign to point out the path. After years of observation and practice I can take a boat over the course, if the day is clear, without running on a bank more than once in three trips.

Yet a boy to the manner born has piloted me through the maze on a night so dark that I could scarcely see his face as I sat beside him. He chatted with me throughout the trip with his hand resting carelessly on the wheel which he idly swung to and fro without apparent thought or purpose. His every act was so casual that I had just figured out that we were hopelessly lost somewhere in the Ten Thousand Islands when he leaned past me to shut off the gasoline from the motor. A minute later the boat rubbed gently against some object that I couldn't see.

"Where are we?" I asked.

"At your own dock," was the amazing reply.

My captain carried us over the same course in the same mysterious manner and I was only sure we had passed Coon Key through the broader sweep of the wind and the gentle rise and fall of the boat on the slight swell from the Gulf. Going down the coast I got my bearings and felt rather than saw its familiar features. I was conscious of the nearness of Horse and Panther Keys, and off

Gomez Point I had a mental picture of the old man for whom it was named as I last saw him at his home. He was then well along in his second century, and year by year his recollection of the first Napoleon, under whom he served, became clearer and of the details of their intimacy more distinct.

Sand-fly Pass, leading to Chokoloskee Bay, was our goal for the night, and nothing but a nose was needed to find it even in Cimmerian darkness. Its mouth was guarded by a pelican key, from which a rookery of the birds sent forth lines of stench as a Fresnal lens radiates light.

In the morning we entered Chokoloskee Bay, and crossing it anchored within the mouth of Allen's River, near the Storter store.

For nearly two miles Allen's River is a considerable stream. Beyond that distance it divides and spreads over flats until it is only navigable to a light draft skiff. Near the mouth of the river we caught and released a few tarpon of good size, but when a mile up the stream I struck a ten-pound fish I returned to the *Irene* and rigged up an eight-ounce fly rod. The fish rose best to a tiny strip of mullet, cast and skittered along the surface, or trolled. They preferred light flies to those of more brilliant coloring. Yet their tastes changed as often as the colors of a chameleon, and they turned up their noses to-day at the lure that best pleased them yesterday.

The light fly rod is too flexible to fasten the hook in the hard mouth of the tarpon with any approach to certainty. In the beginning the fly fisherman will fail, nine times out of ten, to fasten the hook in the mouth of the striking tarpon. Then he will learn to thrust the butt of his rod away from the fish when it seizes the bait, and clutching the line or reel bring a strong, straight pull to bear on the hook in the mouth of the fish.

My first fish on the fly rod in Allen River weighed about four pounds, but it took longer to land than its predecessor of twenty times that weight. It led me into a narrow creek where an out-thrusting branch from the bank forced me to step out of the canoe in water waist deep. I followed the fish up the shallowing stream, walking on the bank when the bushes permitted and wading in the channel when trees came to the water's edge.

When the tarpon had had fun enough with me in shallow water it led me back to the deeper river. I nearly capsized the canoe as I got aboard while playing the fish, which cavorted up and down and across the stream, leaping several feet in the air every minute or two for a quarter of an hour before yielding.

In two days I had a score of strikes and landed half that number of tarpon after an average contest of an hour with each. The largest one was four feet long and weighed therefore about thirty-two pounds, but it was an exceptionally active fish and wore itself out in half an hour. By a series of frantic leaps, one of which took it over the bow of the canoe within reach of my hand.

During the two days' fishing there was seldom an interval of ten minutes between the landing of one tarpon and the strike of its successor. On the third day the tarpon were as abundant as ever and jumped all around the canoe, but not a strike could I get. If Solomon had ever fished for tarpon he would have added the way of a tarpon in the water to that of an eagle in the air, a serpent on a rock, and the other things that were beyond his comprehension.

We sailed to the south end of Chokoloskee Bay, where Turner's River connects it with the network of waterways through which tidal water flows in all directions around the big and little keys of the Ten Thousand Islands which extend from Cape Romano to Sable. Channels navigable to tarpon of the greatest draft connect Turner's River with the Gulf of Mexico, while from scores of tiny streams and shallow watercourses it collects the output of many tarpon nurseries.

I began business on Turner's River with an eight-ounce fly rod, and soon was fast to a ten-pound tarpon which thirty minutes later was captured and freed half a mile up the stream. Scarcely had a fresh lure been thrown out when there was a tug on my line and, as I believe, the largest tarpon that was ever caught on a fly rod shot a dozen feet in the air. Three times in quick succession it leaped violently, shaking its head to dislodge the hook.

Down the river the tarpon dashed till only a few feet of line was left on my little reel. The slight strain I could put on the line wouldn't have feazed a fish one tenth the size of the one to which I was fast. I needed more yards than I had feet of line to offer a chance of tiring this creature whose length exceeded mine by a foot. One more stroke of that propeller tail and my goose would be cooked.

I yelled to the captain to paddle for his life, regardless of the fact that he was already putting in licks that endangered it. Soon he was gaining faster than I could take in line and I shouted to him to slow up, changing the next instant to a cry to go ahead. When the trouble was over I asked the captain if I had screamed at him very often.

"Most all the time, but I didn't mind. I knew you was excited and didn't rightly know what you said," was his reply.

The line never again ran so low as in that first dash of the tarpon. Yet a hundred times the end of our hopes seemed near, but always the fish swam slower, or the captain paddled faster. The wild leaps of the creature were startling but welcome, for they tired the tarpon without carrying away line. We had followed the fish up, down, and across the river, and after an hour's struggle were well out in the bay, yet at all times we had kept within two hundred feet of our quarry.

Always we feared the tarpon's getting too far away. Sometimes the danger was of its coming too near, and more than once it sprang at us with wide-open jaws, falling short of the canoe by inches only, and once it sprang fairly against the captain, neatly capsizing the craft.

The sport of fishing is in inverse ratio to the size of the tackle compared with the activity, strength, and weight of the fish. Linus Yale, as skillful with trout as he was ingenious with locks, used to hitch his horse to a tree by a mountain brook near his New England home and forget for the day the anxieties of the inventor and the burdens of the manufacturer.

All trouble was left behind as he constructed a line from hairs in his horse's tail, attached a hook of his own forging, tinier than was ever made before, with an almost microscopic fly, and with a reedlike rod, made on the ground, captured the wariest trout in the brook. When with this flimsy tackle he landed a trout of large size he rejoiced more than when picking the Hobbs lock gave him world-wide fame.

As I followed my big fish the game increased in interest. It was more like chess than fishing. Strength availed little, for the utmost strain I could put on the line through the light rod was no restraint on the powerful tarpon. The creature must be made to tire itself out and do the chief work in its own capture and at the same time be kept within the narrow limits that the shortness of my line established.

When the reel was nearly empty the line was held lightly, while the captain paddled strongly. As we neared the quarry a quick twitch of the line usually sent the tarpon high in the air and off on another dash. As the reel buzzed the captain invited apoplexy by his efforts, while I encouraged him to increase them.

At times the fish seemed to be on to our game and refused to jump when called on. It even became immune to the splash of the paddle and made an ingenious move that threatened checkmate. The tarpon was beside us and the line short when it dived beneath the canoe and swam swiftly away on the other side. There is only one move to meet that attack, and it usually ends in a broken rod and a lost fish. I dropped the rod flat on the water, thrusting it beneath the surface elbow deep, while my finger kept a light pressure on the line. Happily the tip swung to the tarpon without breaking and the fish was played from a rod under water until the captain had turned the canoe around.

The strain of a single pound on a fly rod is more exhausting to the fisherman than ten or even twenty times that pull on a tarpon rod, and I was glad when the camera man said he had used his last plate and offered to change places with me. Usually when plates were out we got rid of the fish as soon as we could, but this was an unusual fish, destined to hold long the record for an eight-ounce rod capture, if once we could slide it over the side of the little canoe. The craft might be swamped the next minute, but the record would be safe.

The tarpon noticed the new hand at the bellows and went over his repertoire brilliantly. He traveled a mile up the river in search of a place to hide from the human gadfly that worried him and sulked under a bank for some minutes before allowing himself to be coaxed out. He pranced down the stream to the hay, with occasional leaps by the way, and the captain struggled mightily every foot of the course to keep within the limits of the line. In the bay a new terror possessed him and he dashed about as if crazy.

He saw his fate in the thing that he couldn't shake off, as the creature of the forest knows when the wolf is on his track, and he exhausted himself in his panic. Then he rolled over and lay quietly on his back with gasping gills in apparent surrender while the canoe was paddled beside him.

"I'm afraid we'll capsize if I take it aboard," said the captain.

"Get it in the canoe first and capsize afterwards all you want, only don't move till I measure it," replied the camera man.

After the tarpon had been found to measure six feet six inches, the captain got a grip on the corner of its mouth, and lifting its head over the side of the canoe was about to slide it inside when a powerful stroke of the fish's rail sent the head outboard and the captain was given his choice between swamping the canoe or releasing the fish. He let the tarpon go, for which I abused him at the time, but forgave him later when I saw that the hook was still fast in the creature's mouth. It was many minutes before the captain got another chance at the fish, but when he had renewed his hold and was ready to haul it aboard he sang out to me:

"I'll hang on to him this time if he lands me in—Halifax, so look out for the pieces of your canoe!"

But the tarpon slid into the canoe without a flutter, and slipping under the thwarts lay flat in the bottom. The trouble came later when, the rod having been laid aside, camera man and captain worked together to get the slippery thing out from under the thwarts and overboard. They would probably have swamped the canoe anyhow, but the tarpon made the thing sure and secured his revenge by a flap of his tail that landed him in the bay with his tormentors. It was a fitting end to the adventure, for, after the final scrimmage, canoe and canoe men sadly needed the scrubbing they got in the nearby shallow water to which they swam.

We hit the top of the tarpon season at Turner's River, on the West Coast of Florida, and for three days the fish stood in line, waiting their turn like metropolitans seeking good seats at the opera or holding their places in the bread line. No sooner had we turned loose an exhausted tarpon than a fresh one presented itself for the vacant chair. Twenty tarpon a day was our score, of fish that ran from ten to thirty pounds each. Most of them were taken on the fly rod, for which they were too large, as their weight was light for a heavy rod in such blasé hands as ours were becoming by that time.

Much of the action of a fly rod is wasted with a fish of the tarpon type weighing over five pounds, and much time lost from the camera standpoint, since it is hard to hold the fish near the canoe. A stiff, single-action, tournament style of fly rod fits the agile baby tarpon down to the ground, while a withy, double-action article couldn't follow for a minute the fish's changes of mind.

"These fish are too little for the big rod, too big for the little rod, and we have nothing between," I observed to the camera man just after landing on a tarpon rod a ten-pound fish in as many minutes.

"Let's go down the coast," was the reply. "There are big fish in the big rivers and babies in the creeks at the head of Harney."

I agreed to this as I threw out a freshly baited hook and trolled for another ten pounder. But it was a tarpon of ten stone or more that struck before twenty feet of line had run out, and as the creature shot up toward the sky I shouted:

"There's a seven-footer for you, the biggest tarp of the trip!"

It may have been the biggest, but I shall never know for sure. I threw myself back on the rod with a force that would have slung a little fish to the horizon and my guaranteed rod snapped like glass. I hung on to the broken rod and the tarpon played me for a few minutes, after which he sailed away with half of my line as a trophy.

Before running down the coast we went back to the Storter store in search of a substitute for the broken rod. The captain said he could make a better rod than the old one out of anything, from a wagon tongue to a flag pole. We bought a heavy hickory hoe handle which looked unbreakable, and furnished it with extra fittings which I had on hand. As we sailed down the coast I mended the broken rod and we entered on the new campaign with three heavy tarpon rods in commission.

We were cruising in the land of the crustacean. There were reefs of oysters along the coast. Oyster bars guarded the mouths of the rivers and great bunches of the bivalves clung like fruit to the branches of the trees. Beneath us was one vast clam bed, and dropping our anchor we drove poles in the mud down which we climbed and to which we clung with one hand while digging clams out of the mud with the other. We gathered a hundred or more, as many as the most sanguine of us believed we could eat. They ranged in size from that of the little neck of New York to giant quahaugs, of which single specimens weighed over five pounds.

Our anchorage that night was beside the little pelican key that separates the mouths of Broad and Rodger's rivers, and we roasted clams on the beach beside the latter. It was the toss of a copper which stream we should fish in the morning. Their sources and mouths were the same in each caw and a creek united their middles like the band of the Siamese twins. We chose Rodger's River because of its beauty, the great palms that adorned it, and the legends connected with its abandoned plantation, rotting house, and overgrown graves.

Big herons rose sluggishly from flooded banks before us and with hoarse cries flew up the river, dangling their preposterous legs. Fly-up-the-creeks flitted silently away, while lunatic snake birds, made crazy by worms in their brains, watched us from branches that overhung the stream, and when we were almost beneath them dropped into the water as awkwardly as if they had been shot.

We admired beautiful trees, great vines, fragrant flowers, and blossoming orchids as the tarpon bait was trolled from the trailing canoe, and from the mouth of the river to the cut-off no tarpon disturbed our meditations. Hurrying sharks showed huge fins above the surface, slowly rolling porpoises turned teen eyes upon us as they passed, otters lifted their little round heads, and a great manatee, frightened by a sudden glimpse of our outfit, left a long wake of swirls like those of an outgoing liner.

Crossing to Broad River by the crooked cut-off, we traveled a mile and a half to gain a third of that distance. Projecting roots held us back, overhanging branches brushed us harshly, while with bare faces we swept away scores of great spider habitations, suspended from bridges which their occupants had engineered across the stream. Yet I had little cause of complaint, since the only spiders that ran down my neck were the few that escaped the camera man, whose position in the bow of the leading craft gave him the first chance at the arachnids, or vice versa.

As there wasn't a tarpon in Rodger's River, we looked upon trolling down its companion stream as a mere formality, yet no sooner had I put out my line after turning down Broad River than the bait was seized by a splendid specimen of the silver king. The camera man missed the early leaps, for he had been slow in getting out his artillery, but after it had been brought into action he was kept busy. We were carried up into Broad River Bay, where the channels were so overhung with manatee grass that at every turn my line was loaded almost to the breaking point.

When the motor boat, maneuvering for position, got out of the middle of the channel, the propeller twisted a wad of the grass about the shaft and the motor stopped. Then Joe leaned over the stern of the boat, with head and arms under water as he tore at the clinging mass, while the camera man relieved his mind by energetic exhortation.

The tarpon led us through Broad River Bay to a series of deep channels which we had long known as the home of the manatee, several specimens of which we had captured there. The surrender of our quarry came after we had entered the broad, shallow, island-dotted bay that stretches from the heads of Broad, Rodger's, and Lossman's rivers across to the narrow strip of swamp prairie and forest that separates it from the Everglades.

After releasing the tarpon I fished no more till we were back in Broad River, when, again, on putting out my line, the bait was seized by a tarpon whose length we estimated at five feet since we never had a chance to measure it. The fish attended strictly to business, and after a few brilliant preliminary jumps, made straight for the cut-off, where, after turning a few corners and tying the line around some snags, it leaped joyously high in air, free of all bonds and in full possession of a valuable tarpon hook and a goodly section of costly line.

We traveled a mile down the river before throwing out another lure, and found ourselves in a tarpon town meeting. There were scores of them, leaping and cavorting, dashing hither and yon, and behaving as if at a big banquet, but it was a Barmecide feast, for not a food fish could be seen.

"Hang to 'em, if you can," called out the camera man as I baited my hook, "for I've had bad luck with the fish so far to-day."

"The next tarpon stays with me, or I go with him," was my reply, and the next minute one of the family was over my head, fiercely shaking his wide-open jaws to get rid of the hook. But the hook was fast and I hung to the line through the tarpon's first run, though the canoe was nearly capsized before the captain could head it for the flying fish. The thwarted creature, after three wild leaps, headed straight for the canoe, and diving under it brought the strain of his weight on the tip of the rod, which broke in two parts. I clung to the butt, and as the fish was of medium size soon brought it to the captain's hand, despite the broken tip.

We had now no rod nearer than the *Irene*, which was five miles distant, but the fish were in biting humor and the opportunity was not to be lost. There was a hand line in the motor boat, and I handed it to the captain, for my muscles were aching, and I thought to rest them with the paddle. The broken rod was left with the camera man, for both the hand line and the captain were strong, mix-ups with big tarpon certain, and a swim in the river the probable outcome.

One tarpon turned back so quickly, after towing us steadily for a quarter of a mile or so, that I couldn't change the course of the canoe till the fish had torn a dozen yards of line from the captain's hands and was that far behind us. The captain pulled fiercely, and the creature turned again and seemed to leap at me with wide-open jaws. Its weight fell on my arm and the side of the canoe, which would have capsized but for some quick balancing by my companion. Thereafter that afternoon the captain played the fish a bit less savagely, for which I was not sorry.

I had no dread of being swamped by a tarpon. It had happened before and would happen again, probably that very day, but I wanted it over, and expecting it every minute for hours got on my nerves.

It was late when the crisis came and we were near the mouth of the river, for each fish we struck had carried us down the stream with the ebbing tide. It was a tarpon of the largest size that turned away from an approaching hammerhead shark, and swimming beside the canoe shot high in the air directly above it.

I held my paddle without moving, waiting, waiting for the canoe to sink under me as it had done before. The captain rose to his feet as the tarpon turned in the air, and by a seeming act of volition threw himself clear of the craft.

"Glad I didn't wait for the spill," said the camera man as he turned the plate holder in his camera, "but I don't see how he missed you. What's become of the fish? Can't you get him to do it again?"

The tarpon had escaped. He had given the line a turn about the canoe, and of course it had broken.

The *Irene* was in sight of the mouth of the river as I tied a new hook on the broken line and told the captain I would troll until we reached the boat. But a tarpon lay in wait for me among the oyster reefs, and after he was fast, started back up the river. He was a hard fighter and so erratic in his dashes as he tacked up the stream that every few minutes I had to give him line to keep from capsizing.

"Can't you get that fish nearer the canoe?" shouted the camera man. "How can I photograph him when you're a mile apart?"

"I'll take him inside the canoe, if you want," I replied, though I had no notion of doing it.

I hauled on the line till the fish was twice his length from me and was trying to hold him there when the creature dived till the line ran straight down. Then it loosened, and like an arrow from a bow something shot up from the depths, dashing gallons of water in my face as it passed. I couldn't look up, but I wondered what would happen. Just as I concluded that this tarpon, like the last, had cleared the canoe in his fall, the craft gave a twist, a roll, and plunged me, shoulder first, beneath the surface!

It was a few yards' swim to an oyster reef, where the captain and I reembarked and were soon paddling for the *Irene*. It isn't worth while to change the few garments one wears when fishing for tarpon just because one has been overboard, so we sat on the deck as we were and ate clams on the half shell while Joe made clam stew for a second course and gave us our choice of stewed smoked turtle or clams for the next one.

# THE ISLAND

## MARGOT PAGE

The Atlantic Ocean off Cape Cod is virtually boiling with fish, the brownish striped bass rolling slowly on their sides as they gulp the bait they have trapped on the surface. A layer of bluefish slash just underneath. A glint in the high summer sun, seagulls hover excitedly twenty feet above the water, one to a fish, dropping to the surface when they see a choice available morsel of baitfish.

Gleeful shouts pepper our twenty-one-foot craft as we stagger for balance in the pitch and rock of the waves. The fish move toward us and then away in predatory packs, marked by gulls and the agitated surface. In between frenzied moments of their activity, we wait at attention, scanning the surface of the water intently, heads swiveling. We're not looking at one another: all eyes are on the gulls and the water. We hold our fly lines at the ready.

Tom and I have brought Brooke along—now seven and a half, too smart for empty promises, too young for no reward—with the tantalizing promise of a boat ride to a tiny "desert island" off the Cape.

Our captain is Tony Biski, a burly, enthusiastic convert to fly fishing, about which he says, "Fly fishing is an art, something to do while you're fishing." Today he is taking us to the flats off Monomoy Point, the thin finger of sand pointing south from the Cape's elbow, home to seabirds, dunes, and many sea disasters of yore. But while we're coming off the high tide, we detour to The Rip where he's just received radio reports of blitzing fish.

My arm is firmly around Brooke's tubby, colorful life preserver. Her Barbie dangles from her hand as we skim over the high tide that covers the miles of undulating white sand we will later walk. Approaching the ocean side of Monomoy we can smell the distinctive oil slick produced by baitfish being shredded, and see gulls circling and diving—two sure indicators of large groups of working fish.

While Tony controls the boat, trying not to drift over the path of the fish, we swiftly lift our rods out of the keepers. Within a couple of casts, Tom hooks and lands two fish, and then—after a drawn-out fight into the backing—lands a twenty-pound striper. I, too, quickly hook a heavy fish and can feel him shaking his head against the line. Pulling him in, we see the flashes of blue—he is a large bluefish—just before he shakes himself one last time and bites off my tippet with his razored teeth.

We wait in a momentary calm, and Tony repositions the boat to where the gulls are working. The brown rolls start in waves towards us, a liquid earthquake, the gulls again fluttering above. Not used to a stripping basket, I have elected to leave my line free and as a result familiarize myself with every protuberance in Tony's boat. As I am having trouble casting any distance with the nine-weight rod into the wind, Tony suggests I use his eight-weight with a sinking line. Instantly my range improves and the deep ache in my shoulder disappears, but because of my excitement, I still cast badly and miss.

Seeing striped bass in such healthy profusion after the decline of the 1970s and 1980s is wild and exhilarating. They arc in chopping circles, swirls of beige backs breaking the surface as they twist and turn in deceptively lazy, vicious packs. Daytime fishing is, obviously, different from night fishing, because here you can see the fish moving up from the murky depths or prowling along the surface. You can see the take or kick yourself about what you're missing.

Of course, night fishing has its particular compensation: the sea's neon phosphorescence lights up the stripers as if they're electric.

And then there's always the indigo night.

⟲⟳

By this time, Brooke's patience is beginning to fray. We have sold this expedition to her based on an island of sand and that is what she wants to see *right now*. Nearly an hour of this pitching and rolling is enough. She begins to complain. "You two are fishing maniacs," she cries with only marginal humor.

Fish are boiling towards us again and our attention is diverted from her crisis. We cast furiously into the watery chaos, hooking or missing as the case may be, forgetting about the small, unhappy member of our quartet. Soon, we hear the sound of pointed foot stamping, harrumphing, and covert groans. We are too preoccupied to respond. Tom hooks a huge striper and our yells of delight set Brooke off in the opposite direction. Never one to hide her feelings, she shouts loudly, "I WANT TO GO TO THE ISLAND NOW!" But my attention shifts to Tom whose face is wreathed with joy as the giant bass runs down into the depths. He sets about bringing it in. Brooke will have no part of it. "NOOO MORE FISSSHHHHINNNGGG!"

To fend off impending disaster, Tom, at the same time he reels in his prize, launches into a long and complicated story involving a cockatiel at a pet store that has amazing adventures. As soon as she hears the magic words, "Once upon a time . . ." Brooke instantly settles into her rapt listening mode, but she is still suspicious enough of her good fortune to give no quarter. When Tom pauses to reel and pump the line and marvel at his luck for a few seconds, Brooke registers immediate vocal displeasure, and Tom resumes, seamlessly, the meandering thread of his story. When the fish is landed and released, the cockatiel's saga continues through my search for my fish ("No, Brooke, we can't leave until Mommy gets *her* fish," Tom explains.)

Mercifully, I finally hook and land a small striper, about twelve pounds, that takes me into the short backing. Tony, the captain, has been feeling the strain. He flicks a drop of sweat from his brow and grins happily. We take a couple of photographs, release the fish, and Tom gives me a kiss and formal congratulations on my first daytime striper. Brooke is moaning insistently. We zoom quickly back to the flats where the tide is receding.

"You've been spoiled, Margot, really spoiled," Tom teases with satisfaction. "You've seen it as good as it gets."

⌒∽⌒

The high tide is on the wane, leaving crescent pillows of fawn-colored sand islands that turn white as they dry. On the horizon the emerald dunes that line Monomoy lend the seascape dimension and color under the reassuring blue dome of this enormous summer sky. Old fishing weirs spike in the distance, like startling, thin, tall fences sticking out of the ocean, grandfathered down in families through the area's salty legacy.

We jump out of the boat into knee-deep, clear ocean water. I strip to my bathing suit and anorak and wade over the firm flats, grateful to sink my feet into the fine, sugar sand. If you didn't know you were on the Massachusetts coast, you could be persuaded this was the Caribbean, so clear is the water, so smooth and white the sand.

In the distance, Tony stalks the flats like a muscular, nut-brown bear, his keen green eyes looking seaward always. Over on the other side of the island, Tom has flipped his stripping basket over his shoulder and is heading away; in one hand he carries his rod and with the other holds the hand of a little girl with a blonde braid who wears a shocking pink bathing suit and carries a bright blue pail, both colors visible at long distance. They range further, getting smaller and vaguer, one looking for shells and crabs, one looking for fish. Ocean treasures.

When we leave later that afternoon, Tony tells me he has named this little island for Brooke.

⌒∽⌒

Several days later, Brooke is invited to play at the beach with friends. At this point in our vacation week, I am numbed from the medical problems of my father, a widowed stroke victim, who lives on the Cape year-round. We have come to visit him only to discover him in medical crisis. Though I have other things on my mind than fishing during this short reprieve from my unofficial nursing duty, I am drawn—hollow as I feel at the moment—to the water. We go again to the sea.

This day we hit low tide right on the nose. Tom and I are now enjoying the company of two Tonys, our captain again, Tony Biski, and our artist friend Tony Stetzko, who in 1981 held the world's record for a surf-caught striper (seventy-three pounds). The sheet of water on the flats we had skimmed over three days ago has now receded, leaving acres of white, rippled sand. Before Tony B. finishes anchoring the boat in the remaining tide, I plunge into the clean, warm ocean, readying my rod with one hand and adjusting a waist pack around my neck with the other. Shouted instructions drift on the wind behind me as the two Tonys rig up their tackle. Tom is out of the boat too, ranging wordlessly and rapidly out to the far flats through the knee-deep water. Tony S. strides out through the water calling eagerly to me, "You're too far, come in on this side of the slough, they're all in here." A pause, then a shout, "LOOK AT THEM . . . SEE THOSE HUGE SHADOWS, THERE THEY GO!"

Behind me there is a close splash, and I hear it and Tony doesn't. I whirl and see the boil and cast and instantly nail a large creature. Plunging, the beast runs out for a while, then eventually turns and bites the hook off.

We wait and shuffle along the slough, this being apparently a slow day on the flats, and Tony teaches me: *See the birds working over there, see the dark edge near the light band, that's where they're coming in, going after the bait, pushing them toward the beach. They like to rub their bellies on the sand, so they come in shallow. They're coming right in.* OH, LOOK AT THEM, OH HERE THEY COME, GET READY, GET READY, THEY'RE MONSTERS, OVER HERE, RIGHT IN FRONT OF . . . (cast, cast, cast, strip, strip, strip).

OH . . . *Oh* . . . *oh* . . . *there they go* . . . Tall and lean, Tony has long, dark Botticelli curls and a small, somewhat dashing scar on his cheek from a boating accident. A friend to all, he boyishly strides the Cape beaches like a great, excited heron.

We walk along the exposed tidal flats of this broad ocean floor, following the little rivers that flow through channels in the dead-low water. Stripers, blues, and maybe bonito are cruising along these miniature rivers, the Tonys explain to us, dining on nature's conveyer belt of sand eels and baitfish.

We come to the convergence of tidal flows where we catch a tidy number of stripers, fishing our striper patterns like nymphs, releasing them all after admiring their size or coloration. Someone brings me a live sand dollar to admire—I had only ever seen their bleached skeletons—and I place the brown-flanneled disk back in the ocean to, I hope, find a mate and make more sand dollars.

Then we amble back to our original starting position before the quickly incoming tide dissipates the still-feeding stripers off Brooke's Island's shores. While we walk back, Tony S. tells me how once he was so excited casting to a night blitz of fish that he dislocated his shoulder—which didn't deter him from completing the evening's fishing.

Now *that's* a fishing maniac.

⌒⌒⌒

By the time we reach the island, my intense need to catch fish has subsided. I have another mission.

After casting without success for a while, I wade back to the anchored boat by myself, grab a sandwich, soda, and a towel, and run back over the humped sand bar to where my carefully placed rod is about to get engulfed by wavelets.

Safely repositioning it in a cradle of dark seaweed near the apex of the island, I spread my towel on the white sand of this crescent island and eat my lunch.

In the distance stand the optimistic, hazy figures of the men poised at the ready in the shimmering ocean. Around me, dunlins and yellowlegs twitter and scurry. As I relax, only the sound of the waves and the wind and the birds fill my ears.

Now it is time. I am overwhelmed trying to spread myself around to all those who need me—my father on the Cape, my husband and daughter, my work. Two households to run, an expanded team of nurses and home health aides' schedules to keep track of. How to keep my father safe and honor his wishes to stay at home when he needs twenty-four-hour care?

At this moment, I just want to run away. The nightmares of aides not showing up have made even my nights heavy. I can't get away from the image of my father's jaw clenched in pain, the helplessness of his frail body. The stuffiness of that old, hot, whaling captain's house.

I wait for the weariness, the confusion, the sadness to be washed out of me by the only salve I know.

The sand crystals coat my hand where it lies on the beach, the terns mew and cry, the sun warms my shoulders. There is a deep throb of a boat on the horizon and the sound of the waves' nurturing constancy as they throw themselves on the beach one after the other. Here, on this little island, miles from the mainland, there is no talking, no demands, no decisions I have to make. I am responsible, at this instant, only for myself. Not a human figure in sight except for the three sympathetic and somewhat protective men who have brought me here and are now gathered on the faraway boat to eat their lunch.

This is my oasis. Brooke's Island. The island of a young girl in a pink bathing suit with a bright blue pail, her blonde hair shining like a beacon.

Here, a bit of wonder returns to pierce my depression. Here, the breeze begins to blow and cleanse. The distant thrum of the boat engine, the calling of the plovers, the sandpipers, the steady fall of the waves, start to nibble at the mounting chaos of schedules, urinals, pain control, and emergency trips to the pharmacy for gauze, saline, rubber gloves, and medicine. I stand up and walk the receding perimeters of this white crescent island, now a mere patch curving out of the encroaching, resolute ocean. I mark off my territory, reclaiming myself from within my father's slow demise. No one is watching me, I am alone. My companions are back out on the flats, ever hopeful, ranging like a small pack of benign wolves.

*He's suffered enough. Twenty-two years of paralysis.*

❧

The rivers of salt water are now slowly narrowing the spit of white sand. Little lapping rivers turn into wide ones, then become bays, and then merge with the ocean. Soon the foam will touch my toes and I will move further up the island.

I can't fill my mind enough with the seascape, the radiating light, the liquid sounds of the sea. But random thoughts intrude: images of the icy February ocean ahead. Worries from life back in Vermont. How in an hour we shall have to leave and I fear I won't be able to return to fish these flats for another year.

Eight long-necked cormorants skim low over the water's surface. They line the tidal islands, some with wings extended, frozen in mid-flap as they dry their feathers. Sandpipers hurry by me along the water's edge like race walkers in the park, beady dark eyes darting nervously. It's gratifying to note their healthy populations.

*All of us have our own rivers,* I remind myself, *with their own beginnings and endings. I am alone on mine, as is my father. I stand in awe of the wonder of circumstance and the mysteries of our lives.*

Tom splashes over with a bottle of mint iced tea and some sugar wafers. "They're *killing* them out in the rip! Wanta go or stay here?"

I elect to stay and he and the two Tonys speed out toward the Atlantic with lots of large hand-waves and big smiles.

I look around. Now I can be by myself on the planet, for this briefest of moments in time. Maybe I'll be lucky and they'll forget me and so I'll have to spend the night on the island.

This idea makes me excited and nervous.

I will bundle up in my windbreaker and towel. I have a Tootsie Pop, Snapple, and a pack of Kleenex in my waist pack, along with a juicy book, pen, and fat notebook. I will watch the glorious Cape Cod sun go down on my now-tiny island of twenty square feet. Then I will huddle and wait for the Perseid meteor shower, the silver dashes flashing so fast in the inky canopy you're not sure you even saw them.

With my rod and only one fly, I will catch a small bluefish, eat sushi, chew on some seaweed. Suck on the last of the lemon drops. Morning will come, a sunrise of indisputable hope and renewal. The striped bass will roil in, just for me, and I shall cast, catch, and release these great creatures from the ocean. Later in the day, the Coast Guard will pick me up on my deserted island, sunburned, thirsty, and I shall have been cleansed by the meteors, the salt winds, the cry of the terns. My fears of death and loss will have been swept away, and I will be ready to return to my father.

I am alone. Peace wraps me like an airy miracle. Slow and light.

⤜⤛

Some time later, the wavelets converge and move more rapidly up the white sand, devouring several inches a minute. I notice an insistent tone to the waves as they get closer. I pick up my gear and move it into the very middle of the exposed sand with a faint feeling of alarm. My crescent island is becoming a fingernail. I am under the assumption that this island stays dry but we are still two hours away from peak high tide. What if this is an abnormal tide? What if my whole island gets swallowed and my companions haven't returned?

I succumb to a brief moment of panic and then happen to glance over to a corner of the island where two seagulls are standing on a tiny crescent island of their own. At the same instant my eyes alight on them, their sliver of sand is being washed over by the first waves. The gulls, looking calmly out to sea, stand knee-deep in the rising tide and then confidently strut about their drowned island.

Again, I patrol my island as the tide comes up. I can measure its width in number of footsteps. And as I walk, I notice that I am not altogether alone. A strange speedboat with one lone occupant has been making a couple of large circles around my island, watching me with craned neck, I now realize. I mildly speculate on what kind of weapon a graphite fly rod would make.

As I complete my tour with hands clasped behind my back, watching my feet making prints in the sand, Tom and the two Tonys suddenly appear, surfing in fast to the island on a big boat wake with anxious looks on their faces. It turns out they couldn't see me from afar, and when they finally spotted my vertical figure on the horizon, it looked as if I was engulfed by water, with that lone boat circling like a shark.

I also learn that my island does *not* remain dry at high tide.

We head for home. The guys are still talking with fevered interest about where the bass are, what and why they do what they do. Tony S. enthuses about plans to bring a mask and a raft the next time, so he "can swim down one of the rivers of eel grass *right next* to the bass." As we gather speed, I look behind me at Brooke's Island. A vessel in full sail moves majestically behind it as the slim patch of sand disappears in the waves.

We hit the rougher water, banging and slamming hard into the waves, the wind whipping strings of my hair into my mouth. Each hard satisfying crash pounds away the remnants of my depression. The pointed white nameless ghosts of a sailing regatta line the haze on the horizon. One has capsized.

Suddenly we are at the harbor mouth. Tony B. cuts the throttle.

The island is nearly underwater by now, but it is a comfort to remember that the tide will eventually turn.

# TRAILING THE SEA-BAT

## CHARLES F. HOLDER

The outer Florida reef, where the army of coral polyps has made its last stand against the Gulf Stream, was lying on the surface of what seemed a sea of molten steel. The wind was lead, and the blue expanse of the gulf had that strange oily appearance so often a characteristic of a dead calm in the tropics. In the west vermilion-tipped clouds—mountains of the air—rose high in the heavens, casting deep shadows over the green-topped creations of the wind, hurricane, or the prevailing tides. The keys appeared to be formed without rhyme or reason, but in reality nature could not have ordered better, as with their outlying banks and reefs they constitute a perfect harbor, a deep blue channel winding clear and distinct against the coral-covered lagoon, completely encircling Garden Key, the headquarters of hunters, sportsmen and anglers who find their way to the outer reef in search of adventure.

Some wit has described fishing in Florida in the summer as sitting in a Turkish bath holding a string, and I think the author of this mot found his inspiration on the reef on a warm day while trailing the sea-bat.

The heat was appalling, pouring down with such intensity that the shallows were too hot for comfort, and thick vaporous clouds waved upward from the bleaching coral sand, distorting every object along shore. For days the dead calm had continued; the long sleepy summer was at its height, and one had to pick his time for sport and diversion. There was an hour or two at sunrise for barracuda spearing, or for the beating jacks; a long siesta at midday, then a while toward evening perhaps when one could lure the dainty gray snapper or test conclusions with the big sharks which swam the blue channel at all times. Then came the night, often cool, to be spent on the water listening to the melody of negro rowers, the weird tales of Chief, a Seminole, who preferred the heat of the outer reef to the mosquitoes of the coast.

On such a night, when the only sound to break the stillness was the distant roar of the surf, there came out of the darkness, near at hand, a rushing, swishing noise; then a clap as of thunder, which seemed to go roaring and reverberating away over the reef, like the discharge of cannon. So startling was the sound, so peculiar, that the negroes stopped rowing, and one or two dropped their oars in consternation.

"Vampa fish, sah," said Paublo, the stroke oar, in a hushed tone, "an he mighty uncomfortable near, sah—jes over yander."

I thought so myself as the eight-oared barge now rocked in the sea made by the fish. In a few moments another jumped some distance away, and we could hear a splashing sound, which Paublo said was caused by the fins as the fish rushed through the water. The darkness was of that quality that could be felt, yet it was that described by Milton as "Dark with expressive bright" as the lagoon scintillated with phosphorescent light; every oar set the sea ablaze with silvery radiance, and ahead of the boat waves of fire seemed to go rippling away. Now another seething, hissing sound was heard, and a blaze of triangular light above some huge, dim fire body below, glided swiftly along; then a volcano seemed to rend the very sea, and out of a blaze of phosphorescent light that sent its radiations in every direction, rose a dim shape, cleaving the air to drop into another volcano, which opened to receive it with loud intonation.

"Sea Vampa, sure," Paublo whispered, as though he feared that the unknown would hear him. "Dey jes wheelin' an' wheelin', leapin', an' I reckon we'se in a bad place."

"Sea bat," grunted Chief, as the ladies expressed alarm. "They jump five, yes, eight feet high."

"How heavy are they?" I asked, thinking of possibilities.

"Three or four tons," replied Chief, sententiously.

This answer was unsatisfactory to some of the party, so we hauled close in shore near Long Key, where we listened to the explosions, as they seemed to be nothing else, caused by the crash of the return of the leaping fish. A school of sea vampires, sea bats, or devil fish, as men call them, had wandered into the lagoon. I knew them by reputation and hearsay, but never had seen one alive; and when I announced that I was going to take one on the following day, if they were still there, the negroes all protested, "One of dem vampas yander is twenty feet wide, 'deed he is. Five years ago a schooner seventy-ton burden, was layin' jes offen de pint yander; de capten had dun done gone ashore an' all de crew ceptin' de cook was a pickin' micramocs on de reef, jes ober yander wha yo' see de ole wrack a-layin', yes sah, jes yander under de cross. All at once dey hear de cook a-hailin' an' screamin' jes lak he crazy, an' lookin' up dere was de schooner, sails furled, anchor down, a-sailin' outen de channel. De cook he ran 'bout lak he crazy; he don' want to jump overboard cause he fraid of de sharks, so he jes yelled; an' de schooner sail on for half a mile, den stop, an' de men what had been follerin', clim board. What done it? why, de vampa fish. Yes, sah, he jes pick up de anchor an' tote it off."

Each man had some particular story to relate as to the dangerous character of the fish and its gigantic size and strength, intended to convince the listener that its capture was impossible. I found that some of these stories were true. A sea bat had towed a schooner up the channel, and while several attempts had been made to take one of these fish, it had never been accomplished in this locality. When I asked for a volunteer, after announcing my intention of trying this sport, the men were strangely silent. There was a superstition among them, that the fish had some demoniac power; that it could seize a man in its claspers and hold him beneath its cloak-like body and smother him. I finally secured the services of Chief and Paublo, and by daylight the following morning we were on the water, the men pulling across the channel to the long lagoon which formed the breakwater of the group to the east.

My boat was a light cedar affair, built in Boston, thoroughly seaworthy and prepared for the rough weather that is often experienced among the keys, by having under her forward and side decks rows of airtight cans, which more than once had proved to be of good service.

For weapons of offense I had the ordinary grains of the reef with which I had often taken large fishes. This harpoon consisted of a two-pronged spear attached to a steel cap which fitted closely upon a long, pliable yellow pine handle. The barbs of the points were movable; when they entered a fish they closed, but when the slightest strain came they opened and prevented the harpoon from tearing out. A stout line or rope was made fast to the grains and led up the pole, and three hundred feet of it coiled forward in a large half barrel. Besides this I had a sharp coral chisel to use as a lance in case of necessity. Thus equipped, we were ready for almost any game, at least of the sea.

The early mornings were usually ushered in by transformation scenes of splendid possibilities—staged in the heavens—and this was no exception. Long before the sun appeared, the east was a mass of crimson clouds; first deep, dark and ominous, gradually increasing in brilliancy, color and tint, until the sun burst forth in all his splendor.

We soon reached the spot where we had heard the thundering of the sea bat the preceding night, but the lagoon was apparently deserted. At Chief suggesting that the fish did not come so far up until full flood tide, we turned and rowed to the south, parallel to the great fringing reef against whose sunken coral rocks the surf broke sullenly. Long Key—a sandy spit since destroyed by a hurricane—Bush Key and the long fringing reef two or three miles in length, formed three sides of the lagoon, which at high water was from ten to twenty feet in depth and through a part of which ran a deep blue channel. Acres were covered with branch coral, while the rest of the bottom was either white sand, or had a scant growth of algae—the home of craw fish, crabs and various shell fish upon which I believed the big rays fed.

The men rowed slowly down the reef by an old ship blown in by a hurricane years before, now lying ghostly and still, with a corporal's guard of pelicans, frigate birds and gulls; down by Bird Key whose population of terns rose high in the air with bewildering cries. I had begun to think that the morning was a poor time for vampire fishing when Chief stopped rowing and pointed to the east. I turned in time to see a black triangular object waved above the surface; it might have been the dorsal fin of a shark, yet no shark had so black a top-gallant sail, or, indeed, so large a one. Paublo was gazing at it; it was a rude awakening for him as I believe he had considered it a forlorn hope, and secretly prayed that we might not see the dreaded fish. I turned the boat in the direction of the fin and bade the men give way. The trim cutter shot through the still water like a gull. Where I had sighted the fish the lagoon began to dip into the deep channel of the Gulf

Stream as it flows between Cuba and the Keys, and until nearly one hundred feet is reached every object on the bottom can be seen, so clear is the water.

We had almost reached the spot when not one, but five or six fins appeared, my exclamation causing the men to look around. I gave the tiller to Paublo, Chief taking the oars, and crept forward. As I picked up the grains I noted that I could see the bottom distinctly thirty-five feet below. We had happened upon a school of the monsters which were indulging in some game of the sea. There were, perhaps, ten or twelve in all, moving in a circle one hundred and fifty feet in diameter, and churning the water into a veritable maelstrom. Chief was slowly and noiselessly propelling the boat ahead, and we drifted about thirty feet from the circumference of the circle.

Surely these fleeting, glistening figures were the witches of the world of fishes, as no more diabolical creature could be imagined. They resembled enormous bats, and in following one another around the circle, raised the inner tip of the long wing-like fin high out of the water in a graceful curve, the other being deeply submerged. Imagine a fish shaped like a bat, the wings ending in graceful points, a vivid black on the upper surface and white beneath, a long whip-like tail, while from near the large and prominent eyes extended forward a pair of writhing, clasping finger-like tentacles three feet in length. Endow such a creature with marvelous activity and a constant desire to change its position and assume some extraordinary attitude, and possibly a faint conception of the actual appearance and personality of these strange creatures circling before me may be obtained.

As we slowly drifted nearer I could see them deep in the water, apparently going through a series of fantastic figures; now gliding down with flying motion of the wings; sweeping, gyrating upward with a twisting vertical motion marvelous in its perfect grace; now they flashed white, again black, so that one would have said they were rolling over and over, turning somersaults, were it possible for so large a fish to accomplish the feat. Since then I have been informed by one who had opportunity to watch them on many occasions, that this is what they were doing, and is really a common practice of the big rays. As I recall this strange performance, the huge creatures would suddenly turn over and shoot along upon their backs, thus displaying the pure white of the ventral surface, then again turning at the surface, move along with the remarkable, undulatory, bird-like motion. All this passed in rapid review, and fearing that they would become alarmed I gave the word, and Chief moved ahead.

I wished to select my game and make the throw as the fish turned, and to accomplish this I waited until several had passed. Finally we drifted directly in the path of the remarkable procession, the fishes paying no attention to the boat. One dived beneath her, another came careening up from below, standing directly on edge, as nearly as I could determine, and fairly exposed its broad back, not ten feet away; and as it glistened in the sun I hurled the grains into it with all my strength. The pine handle seemed shot into the air as it rebounded, then we became witnesses to the extraordinary agility of this monster ray. It appeared to fly into the air, rising, an appalling mass of flesh, out of the seething waters, its side wings beating the heated air as it rose, then falling with a crash and the reverberating sound we had listened to the night before; fell as a square eighteen by ten feet and weighing tons might fall.

As the heavy waves from the impact struck the boat, I stumbled into the bottom, rolling out of the way of the jumping line that was now hissing from the barrel. The fish, after its first leap, had headed directly to the South, or out to sea, and the line was rising upward in coils. The Indian oarsmen rowed the boat ahead to lessen the strain when it should come, but so furious was the rush that I decided to check the fish before the rope was exhausted, and taking a piece of sail-cloth I grasped a coil and held on.

The boat was well under way, but the shock was terrific. Arms and muscles snapped, and for a moment the rope smoked through the cloth; then Chief dropped his oars and took it, and we were under way driving the fish by a single rein. I had used the boat to capture man-eater sharks, and as a precautionary measure to prevent the line from getting over the side, had a deep notch cut in the bow, in which it rested. With no little difficulty we succeeded in lifting it in place, the bow of the boat at the water's edge riding a heavy sea, which rushed ahead of us as an advance guard. In a short time the fish towed us into deep water, and then surged downward, keeping near the bottom, and we were forced as far astern as possible to keep the bow from going under. I noticed that Chief had taken out a big sheath knife, which he habitually carried in a leather scabbard, and held it in his teeth—a significant movement that was not lost on Paublo, whose terrified glance shot from the fast disappearing keys to the hissing line ahead and back again.

We were headed far out into the gulf, and for two miles the ray towed us at rapid pace. It was evident that if something was not done the line would have to be cut away or we would follow our wild steed indefinitely. I therefore directed the men to ship the oars and pull against it while I took a turn with the rope around the forward seat; but this powerful brake had no effect upon the fish. Then I determined to haul in and try to lance it. We were now a mile and a half, perhaps more, to the south of Bird Key in the open gulf and began to feel the long swell that ever rolled in from the west, while an ominous squall cloud as black as night, to the south dead ahead, did not add to the pleasures of the situation. The line was passed astern and we all "boused on," as Paublo expressed it ; now gaining a foot, again slipping back, hauling, straining every muscle, slowly but surely forcing the light boat upon the fish to the accompanying shouts of Paublo and Chief—"ah ho ah," "ah he ho," "all together now," "ah ho!" Then would come a rush; the line would smoke through our fingers for ten or twenty feet, and lying back until the flurry seemed to die away to haul again.

For some time we worked in this way, and I estimated that the fish was not more than twenty feet away, and had crawled out onto the little deck to peer down into the water, when the line rapidly rose, then turned so sharply to the left that I was nearly thrown overboard. The Seminole, who was in the stern, grasped an oar and aided in hauling the boat around; but she yawed and careened so that the water poured in; then the fish appeared at the surface forty feet away, its wing waving in the air like the black piratical flag it was, perhaps in derision, perhaps in defiance, then disappeared. The fish had turned the keeled boat in little more than its length and was now towing us directly back to the reef—a proceeding more than satisfactory as a storm was rapidly coming, and if caught we should have to cut away; so we sat with a turn of the line about the thwart on the alert for any move. Steam could hardly have towed us faster; we flew through the water throwing clouds of spray over the deck, racing with flocks of gulls that eyed us curiously, plunging among schools of Portuguese men of war and velellas, and in a short time without incident entered the lagoon, where I decided to bring matters to a finish and cut away rather than go to sea a second time.

Whether the great fish was accustomed to go to a certain feeding ground and now returned in its terror from mere force of habit, I do not know, but the fact remains that it was up the lagoon between Long Key and the outer fringing reef, into an almost perfect *cul de sac*, the water shallowing at every flap of its wonderful wings. I stood on the little deck and could see every movement of the strange fish, that in swimming over the white sandy bottom in water not over four feet in depth displayed its outline perfectly.

Chief had the oar, steering the boat after the fish, which, it was expected, would turn at any moment, while Paublo stood amidships holding the rope, which had a turn about the seat. The lagoon narrowed rapidly, and at high tide a small boat-channel was formed; at other times being too shallow and easily waded. Perchance the fish having passed this at flood tide, was again making for it, hoping to reach deep water, which was but a stone's throw away. The graceful, bird-like movement of its fins was a fascinating spectacle; a waving, undulatory motion which sent the ray along at a remarkable speed, and the slightest increase of which forced it over the white sand like the shadow of a dark cloud.

We were running parallel to the beach, and some men stopped and waved their hats as we shot by. Suddenly, without the slightest warning, the fish turned. I saw the pointed fin leap into the air until it stood upright, as the fish seemed to breast the water in the turn. I stepped back and shouted a warning to Chief. But it was too late. The bow of the boat was jerked, shivering and trembling, almost completely around, throwing Paublo over the rail into the lagoon, and was away almost before he recovered his feet and stood in water nearly up to his armpits looking at the retreating boat doubtless with amazement seasoned with relief, as he could easily wade to Long Key.

The fish headed for the outer reef, on which a heavy sea was breaking; drawing little or no water it could doubtless plunge over while the boat would either ground, or if it succeeded in making the reef, would doubtless be swamped in the surf. We took the line as Paublo dropped it, and surged upon it with all our strength, and were encouraged by finding that the fish was weakening. But we were rapidly approaching the reef; another haul and we were nearly on top of our quarry, whose long tail was under the boat, the mighty wings pulsating just ahead. A patch of coral now loomed up, and this fortunate obstacle turned the fish and in the whirl the fin seemed to rise almost over the boat, hurling the spray over us, and once more we were off up the lagoon headed for the *cul de sac*.

I gave Chief the rope, and taking the big square-edged lance sent it into the black mass. A cloud of blood followed, while the speed of the fish was increased so that the bow was well under water, flush with the deck. Again and again I lanced the fish, but the blade was a chisel-like affair, and did not penetrate more than five or six inches. There was a duplicate pair of grains in the boat, and this weapon was also hurled into the ray's back, but still it rushed on, seemingly as vigorous as ever. I fully expected to see it turn again, but it held its course, heading directly for the narrow tide channel between Long and Bush keys toward which Paublo was running along the beach of the former key. It was an exciting moment. The fish was alongside, yet we were going, as near as I could judge, at full speed.

Nearer we came, flying over the roots of mangroves, over patches of coral and sea-grass, into a narrow channel hardly four feet deep and not thirty feet wide, with a flat on each side partly bare. Not a tenth of a mile away the sea was beating on the reef, which meant liberty, if not life, to the fish. But fisherman's luck was ours. The tide was so low that it left but two feet in the upper head of the channel into which we ran. The fish discovered its error too late, but made a gamey attempt to rectify it, turning and lifting itself partly out of water, throwing oars, grains, and fishermen into the lagoon.

The turn cost the fish its life, as it ran high on to the narrow mud flat, where it beat the shallow water with its powerful wings, opened its cavernous mouth with great sucking gasps, every moment urging itself further out of its native element. Paublo, who had waded across the little channel in his exuberance, bounded on to the flat back of the monster and waved his hands aloft, while Chief ran in shore with the rope and presently had the fish securely fastened to a mangrove tree not fifty feet away.

We had earned our game and were well exhausted. Had it been high water, and could the ray have gone through the channel, which doubtless it often passed, it would have escaped.

Stretched upon the hot sands beneath the straggling mangroves, Paublo humming a low baccarole of his own invention, Chief silent, but with a long smile fixed upon his countenance, we could not believe but that the writhing black mass was a monstrous bird, one of the uncanny pterodactyls which geologists dream about; yet it was a noble quarry, "the struck eagle stretched upon the plain, no more through rolling clouds to soar again." The weight of the ray we could only conjecture, but it was doubtless several tons; and had this light and airy jumper sprang upon the boat it would have crushed it like paper.

When the tide was at the ebb the black vampire, as the men called it, was high and dry, and was paced off. It was eighteen feet from tip to tip, ten feet long from its mouth to the base of its tail, which was about seven feet in length. It is impossible to convey any adequate idea of the appearance of this devil-fish, sea vampire, this *Mania brevirostra* of science, which is so difficult to take that it more often runs away with boats than is captured, and of whose habits very little is known. Indeed, vampire fishing will never be a popular sport except among those who delight in an element of danger.

Mr. G. E. Northrop, of Chicago, captured a very large sea bat in the Gulf of Mexico in the summer of 1898, and in a letter to the writer described it as remarkable sport. The fish gave a hard fight, towing the heavy boat a long distance. Unfortunately the photographs of this fish turned out unsatisfactorily. In this connection, it is a singular fact that none of the popular works of the day appear to have a thoroughly correct figure of the fish, nor are photographs of it available so far as I know.

The big ray was almost jet black upon its upper surface, the back being rough; the under surface was white, with gray cloud effects here and there, giving it a marbled appearance. Popular fancy has given the fish a sting above the base of the tail, but this is a misnomer; it is without the serrated lance which marks many of the tribe which I took in these waters, one of which wounded a companion by striking its lances across his foot.

The mouth of the ray as we pried it open was of ominous dimensions, and afforded ample room for a man to lie very snugly coiled within. The teeth were very small, but the extraordinary feature of this fish—the one which has given rise to many tales, true and legendary—is its two tentacles or claspers, fleshy objects about four five inches wide and three feet long, which extend outward from each side of the mouth. Their office is undoubtedly to aid in securing food. When the fish is moving they are in constant motion, being whirled about like the tentacles of a squid, and that they are muscular and powerful has been demonstrated on many occasions. The natural movement of the claspers is inward, and when any object strikes between them it is instinctively held—a proceeding which explains the undoubted fact that these fishes can run away with large vessels.

At least five instances of this were heard of on the reef occurring from Tampa Bay to Garden Key, and the Hon. Wm. Elliott, formerly of Beaufort, S. C., a famous hunter of this game, reports two instances from that State. In every case the vessels, always at anchor, suddenly moved off in a mysterious manner and were towed greater or less distances. The ray had collided with the chain, and, true to its instincts, threw its two tentacular feelers or claspers around it and rushed ahead, thus lifting the anchor. That the claspers are very powerful is well shown by the experience of Mr. Elliott, who, in endeavoring to kill a large fish, which he had harpooned and run down, with a knife, felt his arm seized and held so securely that it became numb. He called to the men to hold the fish at all hazards; but it is obvious that if the animal which they had just hauled to the boat had made a rush and broken the harpoon or rope the sportsman would have been carried off in its embrace.

I never heard of an attack being made by the bat on the Florida reef; there it was supposed to catch crayfish, and employ the feelers to whip the food into its mouth.

That so enormous an animal can leap so easily and so high is remarkable, and I believe that this is a common pastime, as in later attempts to follow the fishes at night, I frequently heard the resounding crash that told of the return. The ray which I struck seemed to clear the water three feet, but Chief said that he had seen them jump five feet, while Mr. Elliott, already quoted, states that he has seen them bound ten feet into the air.

On the reef this fish was considered a dangerous animal, and never followed. Some years previous an attempt had been made to catch one which fouled a vessel's cable. The fish became impaled on the anchor, and when brought up broke away. It was then harpooned, but escaped after leaping partly on the boat, breaking the oars on one side, and seriously injuring the crew, who were crushed into the sinking craft. So the sea vampire, which was supposed to suffocate its victims with its cloak-like wings, was dreaded, and that anyone should consider it sport to follow such a creature and hunt it down was more than the ordinary reef negro could understand.

The people of upper Florida, Georgia, and the Carolinas, where the fish is also found, are equally afraid of it; yet, in 1845, to take one of these monsters was considered in these States the highest phase of sport, and the visitor to any of the hospitable plantations near Hilton Head would be sure to be invited to a sea vampire or devil-fish hunt. The sport was followed with great abandon, and one gentleman had a record of sixteen sea vampires taken with the harpoon in one season, the fish towing him from ten to twenty miles and fighting from one to five hours.

The waters of Port Royal Sound were the breeding grounds of the fish, and it is a singular fact that the wild excitement embodied in the sport was discovered in an attempt at retaliation on the part of the planters whose property had been destroyed by the rays. Those whose property abutted the Sound had water fences which marked the limits of their plantations seaward, and some had piers extending out into the water. The heavy posts, which would be in deep water at flood tide, were mysteriously hauled up, and I am informed by a gentleman from this section that the piles of wharves were occasionally similarly treated. For a long time the cause was unexplained, but finally a school of large rays was seen to sweep along and collide with the piles. The fish evidently threw their claspers about them and in the violent struggles which ensued wrenched them loose.

The sportsmen made the attack in eight oared barges propelled by negroes, and when the strike was made the barge rushed away toward the ocean, several other boats being caught as they passed until the fish was towing a procession of craft. This was the initial fish, which measured twenty feet across, and from that time on the exciting pastime became the sport above all others of the Sound region. The catches were marked by many sensational features. On one occasion Mr. T. R. S. Elliott was the harpooner, and when the fish was struck it cleared the water, striking the boat in the bow, sweeping away all the oars on one side, and sending her astern so violently that every man in the barge was thrown from his seat and one or two severely crushed. The man at the helm, James Cuthbert, was pitched headlong on to the deck, while Mr. Elliott took a flying leap into the air, landing upon the back of the struggling fish. He was fortunately hauled aboard before the ray got under way, and stood on the little deck, drenched, and raised a cheer as the boat moved off behind the wild steed.

The legend heard in the Pacific that this fish envelops its prey with its cloak-like wings may be traced to the ancient authors, among whom Oppian writes, "It is the broadest among fishes (*Eurotatos pantessin metichthusin*); and he further describes its habit of seizing mariners, sinking with them and smothering the victim beneath its wings. This belief is still held by the pearl divers off the South Coast. The truth is that while the fish makes a remarkable fight for its liberty, it is timid and never attacks; the fouling of anchors, the leaping upon boats being mere accidents attendant upon the movements of a large fish in agony and fear.

In following this spurt in Port Royal Sound the sharks were often a factor to be dealt with, attacking the wounded sea vampire in such numbers that while being towed by a fish Mr. Elliott took with a line as many as six hammerheads which were following the trail of blood; vicious monsters ranging up to nine feet in length.

In its peculiar somersaults the bat is not unique, as I have repeatedly observed the California banded sheepshead roll over and over; yet in so large a fish it is a remarkable act. Merely venturing an opinion I am inclined to think that this may be a feature of courtship, and nowhere have the strange gambols been so often observed as in Port Royal Sound. Here the fishes were repeatedly seen by Mr. Elliott, as I saw them once in the Gulf of Mexico, swimming in a circle, black and white flashing at intervals as they somersaulted; now swimming upon their backs; now vaulting into the air and while in this position falling upon the back. Sometimes the act would be performed in deep water, the flash of the white ventral side alone telling the story of the turn; again the water would boil at the surface, the horns appear and the huge fish would roll completely over until its tail lashed the air in its descent. So commonly was this trick performed that more than one of the fishes taken by Mr. Elliott was harpooned in the belly.

It is believed that specimens measuring nearly thirty feet across have been seen. Mitchell refers to one caught in the West Indies which required six oxen to drag it up the beach; but the average ray taken on American shores, which the sportsmen may expect to find in the summer months from Port Royal Sound to Garden Key and up the west coast of Florida, and in Lower California, will rarely exceed eighteen or twenty feet in width—large enough to afford some of the most exciting experiences in the annals of sport with the spear at sea.

# BYME-BY-TARPON

## ZANE GREY

To capture the fish is not all of the fishing. Yet there are circumstances which make this philosophy hard to accept. I have in mind an incident of angling tribulation which rivals the most poignant instant of my boyhood, when a great trout flopped for one sharp moment on a mossy stone and then was gone like a golden flash into the depths of the pool.

Some years ago I followed Attalano, my guide, down the narrow Mexican street of Tampico to the bank of the broad Panuco. Under the rosy dawn the river quivered like a restless opal. The air, sweet with the song of blackbird and meadowlark, was full of cheer; the rising sun shone in splendor on the water and the long line of graceful palms lining the opposite bank, and the tropical forest beyond, with its luxuriant foliage festooned by gray moss. Here was a day to warm the heart of any fisherman; here was the beautiful river, celebrated in many a story; here was the famous guide, skilled with oar and gaff, rich in experience. What sport I would have; what treasure of keen sensation would I store; what flavor of life would I taste this day! Hope burns always in the heart of a fisherman.

Attalano was in harmony with the day and the scene. He had cheering figure, lithe and erect, with a springy stride, bespeaking the Montezuma blood said to flow in his Indian veins. Clad in a colored cotton shirt, blue jeans, and Spanish girdle, and treading the path with brown feet never deformed by shoes, he would have stopped an artist. Soon he bent his muscular shoulders to the oars, and the ripples circling from each stroke hardly disturbed the calm Panuco. Down the stream glided long Indian canoes, hewn from trees and laden with oranges and bananas. In the stern stood a dark native wielding an enormous paddle with ease. Wild-fowl dotted the glassy expanse; white cranes and pink flamingoes graced the reedy bars; red-breasted kingfishers flew over with friendly screech. The salt breeze kissed my cheek; the sun shone with the comfortable warmth Northerners welcome in spring; from over the white sand-dunes far below came the faint boom of the ever-restless Gulf.

We trolled up the river and down, across from one rush-lined lily-padded shore to the other, for miles and miles with never a strike. But I was content, for over me had been cast the dreamy, care-dispelling languor of the South.

When the first long, low sell of the changing tide rolled in, a stronger breeze raised little dimpling waves and chased along the water in dark, quick-moving frowns. All at once the tarpon began to show, to splash, to play, to roll. It was as though they had been awakened by the stir and murmur of the miniature breakers. Broad bars of silver flashed in the sunlight, green backs cleft the little billows, wide tails slapped lazily on the water. Every yard of river seemed to hold a rolling fish. This sport increased until the long stretch of water, which had been as calm as St. Regis Lake at twilight, resembled the quick current of a Canadian stream. It was a fascinating, wonderful sight. But it was also peculiarly exasperating, because when the fish roll in this sportive, lazy way they will not bite. For an hour I trolled through this whirlpool of flying spray and twisting tarpon, with many a salty drop on my face, hearing all around me the whipping crash of breaking water.

"Byme-by-tarpon," presently remarked Attalano, favoring me with the first specimen of his English.

The rolling of the tarpon diminished, and finally ceased as noon advanced.

No more did I cast longing eyes upon those huge bars of silver. They were buried treasure. The breeze quickened as the flowing tide gathered strength, and together they drove the waves higher. Attalano rowed across the river into the outlet of one of the lagoons. This narrow stream was unruffled by wind; its current was sluggish and its muddy waters were clarifying under the influence of the now fast-rising tide.

By a sunken log near shore we rested for lunch. I found the shade of the trees on the bank rather pleasant, and became interested in a blue heron, a russet-colored duck, and a brown-and-black snipe, all sitting on the sunken log. Near by stood a tall crane watching us solemnly, and above in the treetop a parrot vociferously proclaimed his knowledge of our presence. I was wondering if he objected to our invasion, at the same time taking a most welcome bite for lunch, when directly in front of me the water flew up as if propelled by some submarine power. Framed in a shower of spray I saw an immense tarpon, with mouth agape and fins stuff, close in pursuit of frantically leaping little fish.

The fact that Attalano dropped his sandwich attested to the large size and close proximity of the tarpon. He uttered a grunt of satisfaction and pushed out the boat. A school of feeding tarpon closed the mouth of the lagoon. Thousands of mullet had been cut off from their river haunts and were now leaping, flying, darting in wild haste to elude the great white monsters. In the foamy swirls I saw streaks of blood.

"Byme-by-tarpon!" called Attalano, warningly.

Shrewd guide! I had forgotten that I held a rod. When the realization dawned on me that sooner or later I would feel the strike of one of these silver tigers a keen, tingling thrill of excitement quivered over me. The primitive man asserted himself; the instinctive lust to conquer and to kill seized me, and I leaned forward, tense and strained with suspended breath and swelling throat.

Suddenly the strike came, so tremendous in its energy that it almost pulled me from my seat; so quick, fierce, bewildering that I could think of nothing but to hold on. Then the water split with a hissing sound to let out a great tarpon, long as a door, seemingly as wide, who shot up and up into the air. He wagged his head and shook it like a struggling wolf. When he fell back with a heavy splash, a rainbow, exquisitely beautiful and delicate, stood out of the spray, glowed, paled, and faded.

Five times he sprang toward the blue sky, and as many he plunged down with a thunderous crash. The reel screamed. The line sang. The rod, which I had thought stiff as a tree, bent like a willow wand. The silver king came up far astern and sheered to the right in a long, wide curve, leaving behind a white wake. Then he sounded, while I watched the line with troubled eyes. But not long did he sulk. He began a series of magnificent tactics new in my experience. He stood on his tail, then on his head; he sailed like a bird; he shook himself so violently as to make a convulsive, shuffling sound; he dove, to come up covered with mud, marring his bright sides; he closed his huge gills with a slap and, most remarkable of all, he rose in the shape of a crescent, to straighten out with such marvelous power that he seemed to actually crack like a whip.

After this performance, which left me in a condition of mental aberration, he sounded again, to begin a persistent, dragging pull which was the most dis-heartening of all his maneuvers; for he took yard after yard of line until he was far away from me, out in the Panuco. We followed him, and for an hour crossed to and fro, up and down, humoring him, responding to his every caprice, as if he verily were a king. At last, with a strange inconsistency more human than fishlike, he returned to the scene of his fatal error, and here in the mouth of the smaller stream he leaped once more. But it was only a ghost of his former efforts—a slow, weary rise, showing he was tired. I could see it in the weakening wag of his head. He no longer made the line whistle.

I began to recover the long line. I pumped and reeled him closer. Reluctantly he came, not yet broken in spirit, though his strength had sped. He rolled at times with a shade of the old vigor, with a pathetic manifestation of the temper that became a hero. I could see the long, slender tip of his dorsal fin, then his broad tail and finally the gleam of his silver side. Closer he came and slowly circled around the boat, eying me with great, accusing eyes. I measured him with a fisherman's glance. What a great fish! Seven feet, I calculated, at the very least.

At this triumphant moment I made a horrible discovery. About six feet from the leader the strands of the line had frayed, leaving only one thread intact. My blood ran cold and the clammy sweat broke out on my brow. My empire was not won; my first tarpon was as if he had never been. But true to my fishing instincts, I held on morosely; tenderly I handled him; with brooding care I riveted my eye on the frail place in my line, and gently, ever so gently, I began to lead the silver king shoreward. Every smallest move of his tail meant disaster to me, so when he moved it I let go of the reel. Then I would have to coax him to swim back again.

The boat touched the bank. I stood up and carefully headed my fish toward the shore, and slid his head and shoulders out on the lily-pads. One moment he lay there, glowing like mother-of-pearl, a rare fish, fresh from the sea. Then, as Attalano warily reached for the leader, he gave a gasp, a flop that deluged us with muddy water, and a lunge that spelled freedom.

I watched him swim slowly away with my bright leader dragging beside him. Is it not the loss of things which makes life bitter? What we have gained is ours; what is lost is gone, whether fish, or use, or love, or name, or fame.

I tried to put on a cheerful aspect for my guide. But it was too soon. Attalano, wise old fellow, understood my case. A smile, warm and living, flashed across his dark face as he spoke:

"Byme-by-tarpon."

Which defined his optimism and revived the failing spark within my breast. It was, too, in the nature of a prophecy.

# SKELTON'S PARTY (SELECTION)

## THOMAS MCGUANE

Skelton followed watching the drawn bow the rod had become, the line shearing water with precision.

"What a marvelously smooth drag this reel has! A hundred smackers seemed steep at the time; but when you're in the breach, as I am now, a drag like this is the last nickel bargain in America!"

Skelton was poling after the fish with precisely everything he had. And it was difficult on the packed bottom with the pole inclining to slip out from under him.

His feeling of hope for a successful first-day guiding was considerably modified by Rudleigh's largely undeserved hooking of the fish. And now the nobility of the fish's fight was further eroding Skelton's pleasure.

When they crossed the edge of the flat, the permit raced down the reef line in sharp powerful curves, dragging the line across the coral. "Gawd, gawd,

gawd," Rudleigh said. "This cookie is stronger than I am!" Skelton poled harder and at one point overtook the fish as it desperately rubbed the hook on the coral bottom; seeing the boat, it flushed once more in terror, making a single long howl pour from the reel. A fish that was exactly noble, thought Skelton, who began to imagine the permit coming out of a deep-water wreck by the pull of moon and tide, riding the invisible crest of the incoming water, feeding and moving by force of blood; only to run afoul of an asshole from Connecticut.

The fight continued without much change for another hour, mainly outside the reef line in the green water over a sand bottom: a safe place to fight the fish. Rudleigh had soaked through his khaki safari clothes; and from time to time Mrs. Rudleigh advised him to "bear down." When Mrs. Rudleigh told him this, he would turn to look at her, his neck muscles standing out like cords and his eyes acquiring broad white perimeters. Skelton ached from pursuing the fish with the pole; he might have started the engine outside the reef line, but he feared Rudleigh getting his line in the propeller and he had found that a large fish was held away from the boat by the sound of a running engine.

As soon as the fish began to show signs of tiring, Skelton asked Mrs. Rudleigh to take a seat; then he brought the big net up on the deck beside him. He hoped he would be able to get Rudleigh to release this hugely undeserved fish, not only because it was undeserved but because the fish had fought so very bravely. No, he admitted to himself, Rudleigh would never let the fish go.

By now the fish should have been on its side. It began another long and accelerating run, the pale sheet of water traveling higher up the line, the fish swerving somewhat inshore again; and to his terror, Skelton found himself poling after the fish through the shallows, now and then leaning over to free the line from a sea fan. They glided among the little hammocks and mangrove keys of Saddlebunch in increasing vegetated congestion, in a narrowing tidal creek that closed around and over them with guano-covered mangroves and finally prevented the boat from following another foot. Nevertheless, line continued to pour off the reel.

"Captain, consider it absolutely necessary that I kill the fish. This one doubles the Honduran average."

Skelton did not reply, he watched the line slow its passage from the reel, winding out into the shadowy creek; then stop. He knew there was a good chance the desperate animal had reached a dead end.

"Stay here."

Skelton climbed out of the boat and, running the line through his fingers lightly, began to wade the tidal creek. The mosquitoes found him quickly and held in a pale globe around his head. He waded steadily, flushing herons out of the mangroves over his head. At one point, he passed a tiny side channel, blocking the exit of a heron that raised its stiff wings very slightly away from its body and glared at him. In the green shadows, the heron was a radiant, perfect white.

He stopped a moment to look at the bird. All he could hear was the slow musical passage of tide in the mangrove roots and the low pattern of bird sounds more liquid than the sea itself in these shallows. He moved away from the side channel, still following the line. Occasionally, he felt some small movement of life in it; but he was certain now the permit could go no farther. He had another thirty yards to go, if he had guessed right looking at Rudleigh's partially emptied spool.

Wading along, he felt he was descending into the permit's world; in knee-deep water, the small mangrove snappers, angelfish, and baby barracudas scattered before him, precise, contained creatures of perfect mobility. The brilliant blue sky was reduced to a narrow ragged band quite high overhead now and the light wavered more with the color of the sea and of estuarine shadow than that of vulgar sky. Skelton stopped and his eye followed the line back in the direction he had come. The Rudleighs were at its other end, infinitely far away.

Skelton was trying to keep his mind on the job he had set out to do. The problem was, he told himself, to go from Point A to Point B; but every breath of humid air, half sea, and the steady tidal drain through root and elliptical shadow in his ears and eyes diffused his attention. Each heron that leaped like an arrow out of his narrow slot, spiraling invisibly into the sky, separated him from the job. Shafts of light in the side channels illuminated columns of pristine, dancing insects.

Very close now. He released the line so that if his appearance at the dead end terrified the permit there would not be sufficient tension for the line to break. The sides of the mangrove slot began to yield. Skelton stopped.

An embowered, crystalline tidal pool: the fish lay exhausted in its still water, lolling slightly and unable to right itself. It cast a delicate circular shadow on the sand bottom. Skelton moved in and the permit made no effort to rescue itself; instead, it lay nearly on its side and watched Skelton approach with a steady, following eye that was, for Skelton, the last straw. Over its broad, virginal sides a lambent, moony light shimmered. The fish seemed like an oval section of sky—yet sentient and alert, intelligent as tide.

He took the permit firmly by the base of its tail and turned it gently upright in the water. He reached into its mouth and removed the hook from the cartilaginous operculum. He noticed that the suddenly loosened line was not retrieved: Rudleigh hadn't even the sense to keep tension on the line.

By holding one hand under the permit's pectoral fins and the other around the base of its tail, Skelton was able to move the fish back and forth in the water to revive it. When he first tentatively released it, it teetered over on its side, its wandering eye still fixed upon him. He righted the fish again and continued to move it gently back and forth in the water; and this time when he released the permit, it stayed upright, steadying itself in equipoise, mirror sides once again purely reflecting the bottom. Skelton watched a long while until some regularity returned to the movement of its gills.

Then he cautiously—for fear of startling the fish—backed once more into the green tidal slot and turned to head for the skiff. Rudleigh had lost his permit.

The line was lying limp on the bottom. Why didn't the fool at least retrieve it? With his irritation Skelton began to return to normal. He trudged along the creek, this time against the tide; and returned to the skiff.

The skiff was empty.

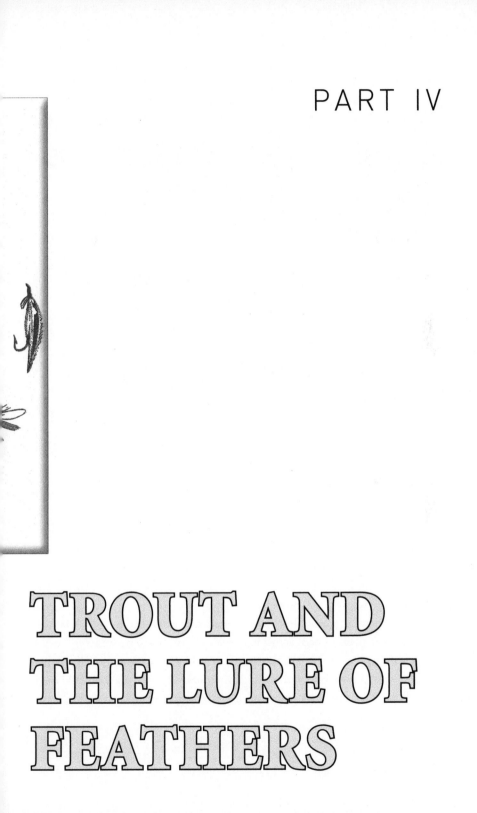

# PART IV

# TROUT AND THE LURE OF FEATHERS

# THE LAKES AT INHLUZANE

## TOM SUTCLIFFE

In those early years we had everything you could want for good stillwater fly fishing; trophy-sized browns and rainbows, even some double-figure trout, sections of lakes where the water dropped away off shelves and ledges and went down three or four meters, tall stands of reeds growing in glassy-green water, acres of waist-deep shallows crossed by old river beds, islands of weed like floating rafts and, in the weeds, the occasional pond-like openings that always held a fish or two.

Then there were countless clear inlet streams we fished as well. They ran in grass-lined, pebbled beds across bare veld, sometimes going underground, or flowing through a necklace of tiny pools roofed by hanging grass, widening as they got closer to the lake, but never getting much wider than you could easily step across. We surprised a lot of fish in these streams, mainly with big, bushy dry flies.

The aquatic life in the lakes was, to put it mildly, abundant. The shallow flats and the inlets and weed margins were alive with dragonfly nymphs, damsels, mayflies, snails, water boatmen, frogs, minnows and, of course, midges. The midge hatches some years were really good. Tall columns of insects would reach into the evening sky like the rising smoke of campfires, occasionally dense enough to just about blot out the setting sun (not really, but that's how we sometimes felt about them). Caddisflies danced erratically over the water along the bank pretty well every mild evening, and mayflies trickled off sporadically mainly in the shallow water around the weedbeds, never dense hatches but always a good filler. We had access to the richest aquatic soup you could dream about and we made the most of it.

We fished just about every way known to modern man—dry flies, emergers, nymphs, wet flies, deeply sunk attractors (we even occasionally trolled, which is one hell of a confession I know, but I can explain it). I suppose we fished nymphs most often, and then again, mostly on sunken weedbeds in waist-deep water—fairly large patterns, though later we got more technical and stand using smaller nymphs hung under tiny strike indicators. There were times that were just perfect for, say, fishing size 16 adult midges on the surface, times when a sunken dragon was exactly the right thing, times when you couldn't go wrong with a twitched DDD, and times, of course, when nothing short of a well-set stick of dynamite would make a trout take notice.

Also, we went through periods sort of obsessing over one or other specific technique. When we would concentrate for months on, say, snails, or emerging caddis pupae, or fishing midges, or imitating flies, ants, whatever, until eventually it slipped out of fashion, lost our exclusive focus and just took its place in our growing armory of strategies. We'd revisit them, sure, but only when conditions were right. The same held for flies. One or other pattern would come into fashion and we'd end up fishing it nearly exclusively for a couple of months, or until we just got tired of it. Then we would break down and go back to our normal philosophy of "fish the water the way that catches fish and stop fooling around trying to be smart."

We learned quite a bit during these academic spells, though. Most of our fads came to us straight out of the pages of the *American Fly Fisherman* and *Fly Rod and Reel*, from the early eighties on. Those two magazines were an inspiration.

But in the Inhluzane there was such a variety of water and such a variety of conditions that you could safely leave any special technique until you ran into exactly the right time to use it. And we got quite good at most techniques. Especially, we got good at casting in wind. You had to, to survive. In the end I felt I could east a fly through a keyhole in a gale from forty paces. Wisely I never put it to the test.

⟡⟡⟡

Float-tubes, when eventually they did come in, opened up even more opportunities. Suddenly we could fish silently just about anywhere we wanted (boats on lakes, on average, are just too noisy), or position ourselves for a perfect drift off structure we couldn't get to before, or even push deep into forests of reeds to locate hidden inner clearings big enough to get a fly into—and never before fished by man. That opened up some of the hottest trout spots I'd ever come across, but it was hard work, and 1 never really figured out how to land the fish I hooked. Over the years I got into some real hogs in these places, but I doubt I landed more than a couple. I settled for thinking it was just good fun hooking them in a place they'd least expected to bump into an angler, and left it at that.

Meanwhile, the Inhluzane's reputation for superb fly fishing grew, and before we knew it there was suddenly a lot more fly-fishing traffic, certainly more than we were used to. Happily, once we got over our resentment at actually having to share the place, there was never more traffic than actually mattered. The fly fishing up there remained a largely remote and authentic experience, likely still is. Generally, now that I think of it, the place at the time was not far short of what, if you happen to enjoy fly fishing, you could loosely call paradise.

⟡⟡⟡

There was one exceedingly remote, small lake on the farm North Star, a mile or so southeast of Hetherdon. A couple of acres of clear water in a sea of rolling grassland, its shallows squeezed up against the edge of a tall forest of wild chestnuts and yellowwoods on the southern slopes of a steep mountainside. We called it the Bush Dam, later just Bush, and it fished well, never any really big fish, but always good to visit. As the crow flies it was only a kilometer or two away, but it took us an hour to get there because the road was rough. In raw weather (which was often the case), it would have made a superb backdrop for one of those frontier-conquering Land Rover ads.

On its north shore a small stream came in cold from under the canopy of trees, and just beyond it there was a second feeder stream, even stronger, making a substantial through-flow of water. There were patches of piquant watercress in the streams and the cold spring water made a perfect mixer for the pale amber stuff, if you were that sort of connoisseur. Personally I didn't notice much difference, but I liked using the watercress in our salads. Mists rolled in any time and without notice and there were days when they got so dense you had to inch your way back to the truck along a fence, or shout for a response to get yourself orientated. Many times the answering shout came from the exact opposite direction you thought it would.

The fish were, still are I'm sure, innocence itself. You could wade out and watch them feeding in clear water less than knee-deep. They were small, maybe a pound or two, very rarely three, smaller anyway than the fish we were used to at Inhluzane. I suspected the little pond might supplement itself with too much natural breeding for its own good, but the place was fine to us the way it was, because you could pretty well bet on getting fish any time you went there. Besides, we visited to experience the setting, as much as for the fishing. And because the fishing was easy, we could relax; just fish off the top of our heads a little (a pleasant change once in a while), and at the same time enjoy the bird life, the tall trees and the wildly-rugged scenery. But the road in was too dodgy for us to make a habit of going there.

I learned the fine art of using a motionless nymph on this lake. You watched a fish working a beat in knee-deep water, waited for a gap, laid out a nymph on a short line, let it settle to the bottom, then lifted the fly up when the trout swam into range. Deadly.

༄

We put in enough time at Inhluzane to start believing we had become masters of stillwater trout. In truth, none of us ever was, though we got pretty serviceable at knowing exactly when to fish and when to home. Like, when light rain fell, or if a warm wind blew out of the west, we were on the water. If the wind got cold and came from the east, we wasted no time pulling our ferrules apart. We had a neat rule of thumb about clouds, too. If they sat motionless over the mountaintops we knew we wouldn't catch much. But we had fishing, week in and week out, on any number of clear lakes, in countryside as pretty as any you could imagine, and we never fussed too much about any sudden change in the weather putting the fish down—we just rode it out. So we cut our stillwater teeth in grand style. We even invented a few flies along the way. One or two have stuck around, like the Zak, the DDD and the Rod-Eye Damsel. But we invented a hundred more that never got further than the edge of the Old Dam and, thinking back on some of them, more's the pity. As I said, you would expect, in time, there wasn't anything left that we didn't know about the trout in that lovely valley, or about fly fishing stillwaters generally.

Not so.

The fact is we learned something new every time we went there. I don't think we got near to actually mastering the fishing, though there were days when we thought we had. Rather, I suppose, we got pretty good at it when the fish were on, and knew more or less how to explain it when they weren't. I suspect that's about the outer limit of what's achievable in any type of fly fishing. About as close as you ever get to being called "an expert," and actually deserving the title. (Frankly, though, I've allways found the term a risky one in fly fishing.)

# 2000 WORDS OF HEARTFELT ADVICE

## VERLYN KLINKENBORG

One spring morning many years ago, I woke up urgently needing to fish with a fly-rod. I'd never been fly fishing, and I hadn't fished at all since I was 12, a boy with a bait rod in a boat. All I remembered about fishing was that sunfish have spines and bullheads have barbels and that it's better to eat lunch as soon as you pull away from the dock, before the sandwiches start to smell like bait. That wasn't much to go on. I called my dad, a longtime fly fisherman. He gave me some good advice. "Start fishing," he said. But I lived in Manhattan. I had little money and no car. All I had was an appetite for an unfamiliar sport, an appetite aroused by the sudden dreamlike memory of sitting on shore when I was very young, watching my dad cast a wet fly in the White River near Meeker, Colorado.

As it happened, I learned to fly fish much as my dad had: I figured it out for myself. But there was a difference. He learned on the high mountain lakes and streams of Colorado. I built a fly rod—it was cheap and I wanted to build one anyway—and took it up to the roof of the building I lived in, which was narrow but nearly a hundred feet long. There in the swirling wind four stories above Third Avenue, I taught myself to cast, using a kiddie pool as my target. I practiced almost every evening for an entire summer. It would have been a ridiculous thing to do, if it hadn't been so effective.

The hardest part about being a beginner in any sport is knowing nothing. The problem isn't just what to learn, it's how to learn, a problem that's even worse in a sport like fly fishing, where a lot of emphasis is laid on tradition and on the supposedly scientific rigor of its best-known modern practitioners. In fact, fly fishing is often presented as a form of connoisseurship, which can be—and is often meant to be—very intimidating. But to some people, the apparent elitism of the sport is part of its attraction. So here's a rule of thumb. If you come across anglers, or angling writers, who make it sound as though the art of the dry fly gets passed down from firstborn to firstborn, ignore them. No one ever inherited a prose style or a casting stroke.

Fly fishing is basically a simple sport, no matter what you hear to the contrary. Casting is easy, not half as hard as learning to swing a golf club or rope a calf. Compared to spin-fishing and bait-casting gear, the equipment is mechanically simple. Fly fishing becomes elitist only if you want to own or lease private water, and in this country that's strictly a matter of cash, not breeding. The thing to remember is this: People spend enormous amounts of money for access to easy fishing. Really hard fishing is usually free. And no matter how far you progress in the sport or how exalted your ambitions become, there's no pleasure in angling as pure as the emotion you feel when you catch your first fish with a fly rod. That moment will echo down your sporting life, whether you find yourself casting for bluegills in a farm pond or for permit on Ascension Bay.

It's natural to want to sign up for fly-fishing school right away, and there are good reasons for doing so. The level of instruction and camaraderie at fishing schools can be very high, even though the enormous network of fly-fishing courses these days resembles a giant intake valve sucking beginners and their cash into the sport. I say, teach yourself instead. You'll be giving the tackle companies enough of your money anyway. Professional instruction can save you some time, but you learn nothing from the mistakes you don't make. Fly fishing isn't a product you consume while worrying about the shortness of time. It's a pursuit that gets interwoven with time itself. Teaching yourself, you learn about the techniques of fly fishing, of course, but, more importantly, you also get a chance to rediscover how you learn. That will be important on the stream. To paraphrase Heraclitus, you can never fish in the same river twice. Conditions are always different, minute by minute, cast by cast, and the ability to adjust to changing conditions—to instruct yourself quickly—is a good measure of an angler's success. If that sounds like mere philosophizing, wait till you find yourself at the onset of a Baetis hatch on the Bighorn River in early May.

Learning isn't just a matter of absorbing information. It's the act of win-nowing information. I think the best, though not the fastest, way to learn to fly fish is to read widely in the literature of the sport, which is a long-lasting plea-sure in itself. Subscribe to the magazines; buy or borrow the books. (Watch the videos too.) Read everything and believe nothing until you've tried it out. Then keep what you can use and throw out the rest. Experience teaches you to read skeptically, and reading makes you a better judge of experience. Practicing on my rooftop long ago, I tried to copy the dissimilar casting styles of Joan Wulff, Lefty Kreh, and Charles Ritz. I also tried to ape every diagram in every fly-casting article I saw. Ultimately the dynamics of the cast itself—how a double haul felt when I did it right—taught me what I needed to know, but by trying out so many different casting styles I discovered that there is no single right way to cast. There is, instead, the broad range of what works.

Over the years, I've spent almost as much time watching anglers as I have fishing. It's a habit I picked up as a beginner, partly because I was lucky enough to be fishing with friends who were, and still are, vastly more skillful than I am. They never gave me advice, and I never asked for it, and yet their example meant everything to me. But in a way I've learned almost as much from watching men and women who were struggling with the sport. In their clumsiness, I could see my own, and I began to correct it little by little. I saw anglers for whom the loss of a fly or a tippet provoked a crisis, because it meant they had to tie an improved clinch knot or, worse, a blood knot. I saw anglers standing in water they should have been casting to, anglers casting to utterly barren stretches of river, anglers lashing the pool behind them with every backcast, anglers hopelessly entangled in the slack they had stripped from their reel, anglers whose rudeness had earned them the contempt of everyone around them.

And what I learned was that there's no substitute for practice or awareness or economy of motion or courtesy. Those are the fundamentals of fly fishing. These days, for instance, it's a fairly common habit to buy prefabricated leaders, knotted or knotless. When I began fly fishing I decided I wanted to tie my own leaders, following the same logic that led me to build my first fly rod and tie my own flies. I bought Art Lee's *Fishing the Dry Fly on Rivers and Streams* and made up a couple of dozen leaders according to his formulas. (Tying leaders in the eve-ning allowed me to pretend that I was fishing.) When I began, a blood knot was merely an aspiration, something I hoped one day to achieve. When I was done tying leaders several nights later, it was an instinct. Now I buy knotless leaders, but I still have a bombproof blood knot. The peculiar thing about learning to fly fish is this: every shortcut you take when you're a beginner ultimately diminishes your feel for the complexity, the subtlety of fly fishing. That's why, if at all possible, you should also learn to tie your own flies. The joy of catching a trout on a fly rod is compounded many times when you do it with a fly of your own making.

When I think back over my fly fishing education—thus far, that is—the single most instructive moment was an evening in June more than a decade ago. I had driven to the Catskills to interview a famous angler, and he invited me to go fishing with him. We drove along the Beaverkill, pausing here and there to look at the stream, and then we parked, geared up, and walked down to the river. I was tense with impatience, with nervousness. I wanted to wade right in and begin to pretend fishing, because, of course, what I really wanted to do was to watch this man fish. Instead, we sat down on a big rock near the high water mark. He didn't say much. He smoked a cigarette all the way down, and then he lit another one. He watched the water, and he tried to help me look where he was looking, although he couldn't actually make me see what he was seeing.

The current ran heavy along the far bank, and the river thinned out over a flat that ended on the near shore, so that most of that broad, beautiful river was in fact very shallow. Well upstream, at a picturesque distance, a couple of anglers were drifting dry flies along the edge of the deep current, a place that looked naturally inviting—to humans, at least. But that wasn't where this man was looking. His gaze ended at a line of rocks in water only a few inches deep, just a dozen yards upstream from us. I can't explain to you how long it seemed before I saw what he was looking at, but when I finally saw it I felt very stupid. It was the tail of a large brown trout, the tail an almost iridescent brown, glowing as it wriggled, half out of water. The fish was nymphing, nosing around in the sediment beneath the rocks. After offering me the chance, the man stood up, paid out line, made a single cast, and caught the fish, which he released.

It wasn't the cast, the catch, or the release that mattered to me, though they were elegant and unhurriedly efficient. It was the lesson about observation. Like most beginners, I had spent so much time thinking about gear and technique that I neglected the most important thing of all: the fact that my real subject was the river. I had watched the water every time I went fishing, watched it as I waded out to what I thought would be a good starting point, watched it as I made my backcast, as my fly drifted downstream. But I had never taken the time to sit down and absorb the river, to realize that what I should really be watching was the way the river differed from itself instant by instant. I had never realized that those differences—in light, in current, in sound—would show me trout, if only I could be patient enough to look for them. It was time to begin fishing in something besides my preconceptions.

That's a hard shift for most of us to make. It's easy enough to emphasize the rituals of fly fishing, its daily and seasonal rhythms, the languorous, almost supplicating beat of a long casting stroke. These are some of the things that make fly fishing a lifelong sport, a sport of ever-deepening complexity. But those rituals and rhythms inevitably belong to the everyday world we inhabit, and they overlay, on the stream, a world we perceive only in flashes, when, for a moment, we're able to concentrate on the swiftness, the abruptness, the almost unimaginable profusion of what nature has laid before us. It is to lengthen those moments of concentration that one goes fly fishing, and a lifetime is barely long enough to learn what they contain.

# FIRST OF APRIL

## WILLIAM SENIOR

What struck me more than anything else, standing by the waterside in the somewhat dull morning of the 1st of April with which I am now concerned, was the extreme backwardness of the season. There was not the slightest spring of grass to be seen in the meadows, and you had to examine very closely to find the signs of budding in the trees. The hawthorns were beginning to shoot, no doubt, and the blackthorns, according to their custom, had flowered. But the clump of willows near which I stood arrested my attention, because I remembered that on the 1st of April of the previous year they were fairly toward development of leaf. Even now they had begun to sprout. But the willow shoots in a curious way, and the sprouting leaf at a little distance looks like something which has decayed, rather than like something which is about to burst into life.

Flowers also were few and far between. I was treading on some ground ivy, which had fairly blossomed, and in the marshy places and near the river, a few celandines had opened their large yellow stars to catch what there was of sun. But, on the whole, it was a very wintry-looking 1st of April prospect, and of course, a moment's reflection would convince one, that this was only natural, for the series of floods had been long and vexatious, and, when the water had gone down, there had supervened nipping frosts and blighting east winds, which had put a strong check upon the forwardness which early in February was being remarked.

But looking about one to make notes of what there was or what there was not in meadow, wood, marsh, or hedgerow was not angling, and in the ten minutes, which I must confess had been spent in the above observations, might probably lose me that fish, of whose existence I was well aware. I knew of his being there during the first week of March. I saw him twice moving about between St. David's Day and Lady Day, and on the previous evening, just before the sun sent down, as I stood on the little wooden bridge spanning a turbulent torrent, which constituted a sort of extra by fall a short distance removed from the weir proper, I was delighted to find that my gentleman had not departed for foreign parts.

A very simple looking man, in that queer combination of nautical and farmyard costume so often to be seen by the riverside, sucked his short black pipe as he leaned upon the rail. He looked so innocent and confiding, and seemed so indifferent to anything connected with the water, gazing as he did at the moment with a far-off style at a distant hill crowned by clumps of trees, that I entered into conversation with him. Yes; he had no doubt there were some trout in the weir pool, and, indeed, he remembered that last year towards the fag end of the season a seven-pounder had been taken between the lasher and weir, and, now he came to think of it, he was also able to state that Tim Bridge, a 'stoopid sort o' feller,' working on the railway, had not more than two months ago been fined by the magistrates thirty shillings for taking a trout out of season from the very weir pool which was thundering in our ears. I was glad to hear that Mr. Bridges had suffered for his breach of the law, although, as the man had gone about from village to village showing his prize, and swiping at each exhibition, it was evident that he was unaware, until too late, of the crime he had wrought. It was a bad case, however, the fish being in miserable condition.

I ought, perhaps to remark that the weir pool at the spot of which I am writing was a very peculiar one. There was the small byfall to which I have referred; there was the weir proper; there was a broadish lasher, the whole between them making a very fair description of tumbling bay, flanked by strong individual streams. A little below, however, there were three small islands ranged at almost equal distances along the bed of the river, and as the bed had silted up between these islands, the stream from the byfall ran swiftly, close under the bank, which was hollowed out and steep. It was in one of the swift streams of this by-water, not far from where it roared under the little bridge, that the trout upon which I had fixed my affections was located.

"There's a pretty good trout feeding yonder," I said to the rustic, who still smoked upon the bridge, with the bowl of his pipe in an inverted position.

"No," he said, "I don't know much about fishing; but you may depend on't there's no trout here."

"Oh," I said, "I beg your pardon, you are mistaken. I have seen him there several times myself, and I mean to get him if I can to-morrow morning."

"Well, sir, I wish yer luck," he replied. "There'll be two or three gents a-fishing, I expect, off the warebeams in the morning. I see 'em going to the White Bull wi' their baskets and rods as I come along just now. You had better be early."

This, I told him, I intended to be, and the civility and intelligence of the man so impressed me that I offered him the choice of any cigar he might fancy from my case. On the morning of April the first I kept the resolution which I had informed my rustic companion I had made, and was at the waterside right early. It was very little after daylight, and, although the wind seemed to be backing a little towards the north, and, although it was a cold air, it was nothing like so piercing as it had been during the previous month.

I soon got to work, spinning over the spot where my trout had taken lodgings, but without success. I worked the stream thoroughly down to the end until breakfast time, toiling hard and executing every dodge with which I was acquainted. My marked trout would have none of me. Then I winced up my line, and disposing safely of the flight, strolled across within hail of two London anglers who had been similarly occupied for three hours over the weir pool. One of them said he had been broken away by a big trout; the other said he had repeated attacks made upon his bleak; but neither had anything to show for their operations. So I left them still trying, and cheering themselves with the interchange of an opinion that the sun would soon shine and infuse something of warmth into the chilly atmosphere.

For myself, I walked back to the White Bull, and resolved that if I could get no trout I would at least get breakfast. I was not a little surprised, though very much delighted, to find that when John, the waiter, with a look of triumph, whipped off the cover from the dish, there lay exposed to view a very shapely

Thames trout that, in the full enjoyment of its physical proportions, would have weighed over three pounds. I asked no questions but attacked the meat, which did not, however, eat with the flavor which betokens the well-conditioned fish. Still, there it was upon the table, as the *pièce de résistance* of the feast, and I did it ample justice.

"Where did you manage to get your trout, John?" I said, as the waiter came to see how I was getting on.

"Well, sir, I cannot exactly say where he came from, but I believe he was caught in the river here this morning."

"Oh, nonsense," I said; "impossible! I was out there at daylight myself, and there was not a soul about at that time, although the gentlemen who are stopping here came down to the weir soon after."

"Well, sir, to tell you the truth, I don't know; but I heard them say that the fish had been caught this morning."

Hereupon, when breakfast was over, I strolled round to the bar and into the smoking-parlor, where, as I expected, I found the landlord. I knew this gentleman of old, and scarcely hoped to receive any information from him; but I felt bound, as a matter of duty, to put him through the leading questions one asks on such an occasion.

"Well, I really don't know," he said. "The trout, of course, has been caught to-day. I shouldn't think of buying a fish out of season, but I never ask any questions. All I can tell you is that the trout was alive when he was brought here."

"What time did you get it?" I inquired.

"I can answer that question very exactly," he replied with a smile, "for the clock in the old church at Longtoncum-Burton was striking seven as I handed over two shillings and took in return the fish, which was still gasping, his gills opening slowly but unmistakably."

"May I ask from whom you bought it?" I then inquired.

"I bought it," he said, "from Bridges."

"What," I said, "do you mean Bridges, the same man that was fined thirty shillings for taking a trout out of season this side of Christmas?"

"Yes," he said, "that is the man, but he learned a lesson that time."

"Do you think Bridges caught the trout?"

"That I cannot say; as I told you, I never ask questions, because I know that if I did, in cases of that kind, I should generally hear lies in answer to them."

I did not quite understand the matter, nor did I feel satisfied about this Thames trout; and as I stood in front of the inn, looking up at the waxen buds which tipped all the branches of the great chestnut tree, and blowing up clouds of tobacco smoke to reach them if they could, I heard the voice of a man who was evidently in some stage of liquor—a voice thick and droning, and the words he spoke, run into each other as they were, at once attracted my attention, for those words were:

"And a blanked good trout it was, I can tell you."

I knew where the voice came from, and strolled round leisurely through the stable-yard, past the kitchen, and so to the taproom, where I saw a laboring man stretched on a settle, with a small measure, apparently of gin, on the table, and an empty glass by its side. There were two other men sitting on each side of the fire smoking stolidly, and not paying, apparently, much attention to the gentleman on the settle. One of them spoke, remarking in a careless sort of tone:

"Well, that is two bob off the thirty, anyhow, Jim."

Here, then, was Mr. Bridges, who had sold the fish; and without beating about the bush, I said, pretending that we were old acquaintances:

"Hallo, Bridges, how are you? That was a good trout you got this morning."

"'Scuse me, sir," he said, "you've got the better on me, for I'm blest if I remember you. Howsomedever, that's neither here nor there; but I didn't catch the trout, you know."

"Who did, then?"

"A man we call Swankey hereabouts."

"A fisherman?"

"Not exactly to say a fisherman—a sort of poacher feller."

"When did he catch it?"

"I should say it was about three this morning he got that trout, but in the most queerest place you'd think on. What Swankey was partickerly pleased about was that one of them swells that is stopping here put him on to the fish last night. Then, d'ye see, Swankey, who never meant to'ed not been gone an hour afore he comes back wi' a bloomin' trout."

The reader will naturally observe at once that the person called Swankey was my innocent friend, to whose agreeable manners I had offered the generous tribute of a good cigar on the previous evening, and who had abused my confidence by slinking out in the raw, dark morning, and capturing the fish upon which I had set my desire for a good month past.

I am too much of a philosopher to fly into a rage over a trifle of this kind; but I must confess, as I took my rod and tackle, and strolled down once more to the river, I felt that Mr. Swankey had got, not only a Thames trout, but a thorough paced April fool in my humble self.

# THE EVOLUTION OF A FLY FISHER

## JOAN SALVATO WULFF

I came into fishing as an innocent: my predatory skills, if I had any, were undeveloped. Loving woods and waters I caught calico bass and perch in the nearby Oldham Pond but, in trout streams, not knowing how to "read" water, nor the comfort, food, and safety needs of trout, I saw only the interesting patterns on the water's surface as if they were art.

If trout were rising I could be effective, but if they were not I became painfully aware of this lack of fishing instinct, especially in the company of anglers whom I think of as "natural born predators." In addition to understanding the hydraulics of the stream, to a man they had exceptional vision, as it related to water, seeing trout under the surface when I could not. A boyfriend, the late Johnny Dieckman, was the first of these and later in life Lee Wulff and Ed Van Put are the two who jump into my mind as always surprising me with their ability to catch fish.

With nothing to start with, I had to substitute my ability to fly cast to unlock the secrets of the stream, covering the water and learning inch by inch.

From this beginning, over the ensuing 70 years, I've been lucky enough to fish for most of the fresh and saltwater species that can be enticed to take a fly. Fishing, and especially fly fishing, has been the constant thread in my life. It's been a wonderful journey and, in the last several years, I have come to realize how differently I see the sport from when I began. It's an evolution I believe I share with others who have a passion for fly fishing.

The early stages of fishing are familiar to most anglers: the focus is on 1) The number. How many did you get? 2) The biggest fish. How big? Show me a photo. And then the most difficult: the wise old brown trout instead of the eternally innocent brookies; permit instead of bonefish. Feeling as if you've learned something.

These three stages play to our competitive nature; measuring ourselves against others whenever there is something to count. And they may stay with us forever in terms of particular species: most, biggest, most difficult. I, for instance, in the latter category, still feel the "need" to catch a 15-20 permit.

After Stage 3 the scope broadens; we enter the stages that are about more than catching fish.

It was Lee who raised my consciousness to Stage 4: giving something back to the resource; looking at the sport from the point of view of the fish. It's about preserving their gene pools as well as their habitat. Lee's wisdom, as early as 1939, that "a good game fish is too valuable to be caught only once" has been the concept that has let growing numbers of anglers enjoy the sport with, perhaps, the same number of fish.

The national conservation organizations are there to lead the way: the Federation of Fly Fishers, Trout Unlimited, the Atlantic Salmon Federation, the International Game Fish Association. I am a member of all of them and find that each group's efforts are distinct and necessary to keep our sport healthy.

In addition to making the sport more meaningful, there is another benefit to "belonging": gatherings of fishing experts willing to share their expertise at conclaves, symposiums, and club programs. It's a win/win situation for anglers of all levels. As involvement grows, your coterie of acquaintances expands and I can easily say that the best people I have ever met have been in this stage of my evolution.

If the first 3 stages are the "youth" of our fishing lives, "giving back" could be considered to be our "middle years," because there *is* more!

The golden years: Stage 5. *Just being there.* When people ask me to name my favorite place to fish, I can only say "wherever I am." And my answer to the question, "which is your favorite fish?" is "whatever I'm fishing for."

Evasive answers? Perhaps. It's just that, as my experience has broadened and I've learned the character of different waters and species of fish, I have come to love and admire them all. It's like partaking of good food. Think of how many different dishes you really love and appreciate each time you have them. Different, but equally wonderful. Remember, I'm talking about a lifetime.

In these years, *catching* fish has become less important; I can be fishless and still have had a good day. I can now fish "through" a companion and be as happy about their catch as they are because I know the challenges, and feelings of joy and satisfaction, that commemorate success.

These years are also a time when I can handicap myself if the fishing is too easy. Lee introduced the idea: "If you catch 3 fish on the same fly, change the fly. See what else they will take." "Reduce your tippet strength." "Use a smaller hook." Lee was an inspiration through the "pureness" of his approach. He always gave the advantage to the fish, through his simple tackle. He used no drag; just a click to keep the reel from overrunning, even with Atlantic salmon and tarpon. And with this tackle, he established a standard: one minute per pound to land the fish. The fish then had to swim away without the need to be revived. Lee's skills in playing fish were legendary.

I love this stage; the pressure is off! Challenge yourself! The competition is now with the fish—not other anglers.

I have one more stage to include in these golden years: #6. Replace yourself. This is about bringing young people into our sport. Unless we do this, our sport will be diminished; first in numbers of anglers and then, with fewer anglers working to preserve the habitat, in quality. Grandkids are the obvious and I am particularly blessed in this regard. I introduced Alex and Andrew to fly fishing when each became 5½ years old with two hands on the rod and a roll cast. They have both caught trout, and Alex has caught Atlantic salmon, on Royal Wulffs. Because I don't tie flies, I gave them fly tying lessons with a professional when they were 7. When I am long gone, they will be fly fishing together.

My cup runneth over.

Old age is approaching but I don't want to limit my enjoyment of the sport by defining it. In these past two years I have caught the largest tarpon of my life (approximately 125 lbs) and enjoyed sailfishing in Guatemala. This summer I was able to fish for steelhead on the Dean River in British Columbia, after hoping to for 40 plus years.

My most memorable fish are those I didn't land: a monster Atlantic salmon on Norway's Alta River, which played *me* for a few minutes, and another huge salmon on New Brunswick's Restigouche. The latter was on my last, "last cast."

It was nearly dark and, having covered the water from 20 feet on out, the cast was the longest I could make. The fish struck and dashed upriver, partly out of the water, which is how we knew he was a big one. Then he turned and raced downriver, into my backing. The guide thought the river was too high to follow the fish in the dark and headed back to shore, in spite of my protests. I found myself unhappily positioned 90 degrees from where the salmon was heading. The end was predictable: the fish never stopped—and nearly emptied my reel before the hook pulled out.

However, the reason I continue to think of this particular fish is not because I lost it, but because of the *wonder* of it all: how *magical* it was to reach out into that enormous river with a tiny artificial offering, when it was dark enough to keep me from seeing the fly land, and actually connect to a wild creature of such a size.

And magical it is. Starting as an innocent, this very ordinary woman has had an extraordinary life through the magic of fly fishing. And I plan to continue. So it's not over till it's over, and this very ordinary woman, having had an extraordinary life through the magic of sport fishing, plans to continue.

# A BIT OF LUCK

## HARRY PLUNKET-GREENE

I had an experience with a trout on the Kennet, which I always associate, quite undeservedly, with "snatching." It was in 1922, and I was staying with Mr. Giveen, who had taken the Mill fishing from Col. Grove-Hills for the latter half of the season. He and I had often stood on the bridge at the top, where the water falls down from the lake of Ramsbury Manor, and hungrily objurgated the great fat three-pounders which laughed at us from beneath. These were rovers by profession, and never stayed long enough in one place to be fished for individually from below; and were up to every trick from above. They would lie with their noses on the ledge immediately underneath us, and dreamily watch the smoke from our pipes ascending to the blue; but the moment the top of a rod appeared over the edge, off they went. We tried concerted action many times, but as soon as ever one of the watchers disappeared from the bridge the pool was abandoned to two-year-olds. On this occasion I was passing by the sluice which forms a small side-carrier to the main fall and I put my head casually over the side, expecting nothing, and there right below me was a big golden trout tucked up under the boards, with his head down-stream and his tail up against the cracks where the water spurted through. He was doing no good there, so I felt it was my duty to get him.

It was an awful prospect. Immediately below him two planks ran across the sluice at intervals of about eight feet, and below them again in the fairway there was a veritable barricade of posts sticking up out of the stream in ragged profusion. There were three on the near side and two on the far side and a gaunt rubbing-post in the middle acting as a buoy, round which every sporting fish was in honor bound to double. Below these again there was another pole running right across the stream only four inches above the water, which swirled under it at a great pace. A more hopeless barbed-wire entanglement it would be hard to imagine to try and fish a fish out of, even if one hooked him. However, he was a beauty, and the fact that he was practically ungetable made it all the more exciting. I had up the ordinary tackle; by all the laws of caution I should have put up a ginger-quill with a No. 1 hook and a May-fly cast, but I reflected that if he got tangled up in the barriers a steel hawser would not hold him, and that if by some amazing fluke he ever came through, the fine tackle would be as good as anything else. Moreover, I should be able to swagger to the others about 4X casts and ooo hooks even more insupportably than before; so I stuck to what I had.

I stood well back where I could just see the tip of his nose and he could not see me, reeled in the line to within six inches of the cast, and gently dropped the fly on to him. It was at once carried out by the stream. I thought it was going to be hopeless, when to my intense delight the back eddy swirled it round at exactly the right moment and brought it over him again. It was then seized once more by the stream and carried off afresh. The process was repeated automatically without my having to do a thing, and there went my fly playing "last across with him," rushing up the backwater, tweaking his nose and dashing off downstream before he could say a word. I was so delighted and laughing so hard that I could not help crawling up to see the fun, and I put my head over to have a look. He was intently absorbed in the game and never saw me. He appeared to take no notice at first and treated it all with dignified unconcern, but as the impudent little beast dashed past him smothering him with insults he began to get impatient, and I saw his tail detach itself from the sluice-board and began to wag. Then he began to shake his head and bunch himself to attack. But nothing happened for a long time and I was just going to give it up, as my arm was getting tired from the unnatural position, when I had a wonderful bit of luck. There was a twig sticking out from the wall on the far side over the back eddy, and the gut caught over it, and, before I knew it, there was the fly bobbing up and down in the water, right in front of him. This was too much. His enemy was delivered into his hands.

He leaped at it, seized it, knew in a moment what had happened, and dashed off down-stream under the planks and through the posts and out into the pool at the bottom. There I had to leave him for a long time to settle himself, with my rod bent double under the first plank. Then the fun began. I cautiously passed it under this with one hand and retrieved it with the other and did the same with the second plank. All idea of keeping the line taut was perforce abandoned. I still had the six upright posts and the flat pole beyond to negotiate. If he once got tangled up in these it would be all over. He was near the top of the pool now, and I lay flat on the ground with the point of the rod out in the space between me and the centre post, terrified lest he should swim up on the near side of A post, catch sight of me, and dash down on the far side or pay a visit to X, Y or Z post. I clung to Mother Earth like a tiger-skin on a polished oak floor. Sure enough, up he came. He swam through the near channel and roamed about under my eyes (or the corner of one of them) for about a fortnight apparently, and then swam slowly back to the pool the same way he had come!

It was almost too good to be true! But the crux was still to be faced—there was still the flat pole to get under. It ran across the top of the pool, with a space of about four inches between it and the water. It was a bare two inches thick and it was quite rotten. I had to get the rod under it somehow (for I could never risk letting him out of the pool again), and I could only just reach it with my hand by holding on to the bank above with my toes and descending apoplectically towards the water. It cracked loudly the moment I touched it. I had to lean hard on the horrible thing with my right hand, pass the rod under with my left, scrabble it out again somehow with my right on the other side, change hands and work myself back up the bank. It groaned and shivered its timbers and fired off shots like a machine-gun—but the little iron-blue had squared it and it held. It was not all over even then, for if the fish had caught sight of me he would have dashed up through the uprights again; so I backed slowly out of sight into a withy-bed and stayed there till there was not a kick left in him. As a matter of fact, he had done it all for me by returning through the posts the same way he had come. The only credit I can take is for keeping out of sight and performing gymnastics with an almost superhuman skill for one of my size and weight. He weighed 2½ lbs.

# FISHING WITH A WORM

## BLISS PERRY

A defective logic is the born fisherman's portion. He is a pattern of inconsistency. He does the things which he ought not to do, and he leaves undone the things which other people think he ought to do. He observes the wind when he should be sowing, and he regards the clouds, with temptation tugging familiarly at his heartstrings, when he might be grasping the useful sickle. It is a wonder that there is so much health in him. A sorrowing political economist remarked to me in early boyhood, as a jolly red-bearded neighbor, followed by an abnormally fat dog, sauntered past us for his nooning: "That man is the best carpenter in town, but he will leave the most important job whenever he wants to go fishing." I stared at the sinful carpenter, who swung along leisurely in the May sunshine, keeping just ahead of his dog. To leave one's job in order to go fishing! How illogical!

Years bring the reconciling mind. The world grows big enough to include within its scheme both the instructive political economist and the truant mechanic. But that trick of truly logical behavior seems harder to the man than to the child. For example, I climbed up to my den under the eaves last night—a sour, black sea-fog lying all about, and the December sleet crackling against the window-panes—in order to varnish a certain fly-rod. Now rods ought to be put in order in September, when the fishing closes, or else in April, when it opens. To varnish a rod in December proves that one possesses either a dilatory or a child-ishly anticipatory mind. But before uncorking the varnish bottle, it occurred to me to examine a dog-eared, water-stained fly-book, to guard against the ravages of possible moths. This interlude proved fatal to the varnishing. A half hour went happily by in rearranging the flies. Then, with a fisherman's lack of sequence, as I picked out here and there a plain snell-hook from the gaudy feathered ones, I said to myself with a generous glow at the heart: "Fly-fishing has had enough sacred poets celebrating it already. Isn't there a good deal to be said, after all, for fishing with a worm?"

Could there be a more illogical proceeding? And here follows the treatise,—a Defense of Results, an Apology for Opportunism,—conceived in agreeable procrastination, devoted to the praise of the inconsequential angleworm, and dedicated to a childish memory of a whistling carpenter and his fat dog.

Let us face the worst at the very beginning. It shall be a shameless example of fishing under conditions that make the fly a mockery. Take the Taylor Brook, "between the roads," on the headwaters of the Lamoille. The place is a jungle. The swamp maples and cedars were felled a generation ago, and the tops were trimmed into the brook. The alders and moosewood are higher than your head; on every tiny knoll the fir balsams have gained a footing, and creep down, impen-etrable, to the edge of the water. In the open spaces the Joe-Pye weed swarms. In two minutes after leaving the upper road you have scared a mink or a rabbit, and you have probably lost the brook. Listen! It is only a gurgle here, droning along, smooth and dark, under the tangle of cedar-tops and the shadow of the balsams. Follow the sound cautiously. There, beyond the Joe-Pye weed, and between the stump and the cedar-top, is a hand's breadth of black water. Fly-casting is impos-sible in this maze of dead and living branches. Shorten your line to two feet, or even less, bait your hook with a worm, and drop it gingerly into that gurgling crevice of water. Before it has sunk six inches, if there is not one of those black-backed, orange-bellied, Taylor Brook trout fighting with it, something is wrong with your worm or with you. For the trout are always there, sheltered by the brushwood that makes this half mile of fishing "not worth while." Below the lower road the Taylor Brook becomes uncertain water. For half a mile it yields only fingerlings, for no explainable reason; then there are two miles of clean fishing through the deep woods, where the branches are so high that you can cast a fly again if you like, and there are long pools, where now and then a heavy fish will rise; then comes a final half mile through the alders, where you must wade, knee to waist deep, before you come to the bridge and the river. Glorious fishing is sometimes to be had here,—especially if you work down the gorge at twilight, casting a white miller until it is too dark to see. But alas, there is a well-worn path along the brook, and often enough there are the very footprints of the "fellow ahead of you," signs as disheartening to the fisherman as ever were the footprints on the sand to Robinson Crusoe.

But "between the roads" it is "too much trouble to fish"; and there lies the salvation of the humble fisherman who disdains not to use the crawling worm, nor, for that matter, to crawl himself, if need be, in order to sneak under the boughs of some overhanging cedar that casts a perpetual shadow upon the sleepy brook. Lying here at full length, with no elbow-room to manage the rod, you must occasionally even unjoint your tip, and fish with that, using but a dozen inches of line, and not letting so much as your eyebrows show above the bank. Is it a becoming attitude for a middle-aged citizen of the world? That depends upon how the fish are biting. Holing a put looks rather ridiculous also, to the mere observer, but it requires, like brook-fishing with a tip only, a very delicate wrist, perfect tactile sense, and a fine disregard of appearances.

There are some fishermen who always fish as if they were being photographed. The Taylor Brook "between the roads" is not for them. To fish it at all is back-breaking, trouser-tearing work; to see it thoroughly fished is to learn new lessons in the art of angling. To watch R., for example, steadily filling his six-pound creel from that unlikely stream, is like watching Sargent paint a portrait. R. weighs two hundred and ten. Twenty years ago he was a famous amateur pitcher, and among his present avocations are violin playing, which is good for the wrist, taxidermy, which is good for the eye, and shooting woodcock, which before the days of the new Nature Study used to be thought good for the whole man. R. began as a fly-fisherman, but by dint of passing his summers near brooks where fly-fishing is impossible, he has become a stout-hearted apologist for the worm. His apparatus is most singular. It consists of a very long, cheap rod, stout enough to smash through bushes, and with the stiffest tip obtainable. The lower end of the butt, below the reel, fits into the socket of a huge extra butt of bamboo, which R. carries unconcernedly. To reach a distant hole, or to fish the lower end of a ripple, R. simply locks his reel, slips on the extra butt, and there is a fourteen-foot rod ready for action. He fishes with a line unbelievably short, and a Kendal hook far too big; and when a trout jumps for that hook, R. wastes no time in maneuvering for position. The unlucky fish is simply "derricked,"— to borrow a word from Theodore, most saturnine and profane of Moosehead guides.

"Shall I play him awhile?" shouted an excited sportsman to Theodore, after hooking his first big trout.

"———no!" growled Theodore in disgust. "Just derrick him right into the canoe!" A heroic method, surely; though it once cost me the best square-tail I ever hooked, for Theodore had forgotten the landing-net, and the gut broke in his fingers as he tried to swing the fish aboard. But with these lively quarter-pounders of the Taylor Brook, derricking is a safer procedure. Indeed, I have sat dejectedly on the far end of a log, after fishing the hole under it in vain, and seen the mighty R. wade downstream close behind me, adjust that comical extra butt, and jerk a couple of half-pound trout from under the very log on which I was sitting. His device on this occasion, as I well remember, was to pass his hook but once through the middle of a big worm, let the worm sink to the bottom, and crawl along it at his leisure. The trout could not resist.

Once, and once only, have I come near equaling R.'s record, and the way he beat me then is the justification for a whole philosophy of worm-fishing. We were on this very Taylor Brook, and at five in the afternoon both baskets were two thirds full. By count I had just one more fish than he. It was raining hard. "You fish down through the alders," said R. magnanimously. "I'll cut across and wait for you at the sawmill. I don't want to get any wetter, on account of my rheumatism."

This was rather barefaced kindness,—for whose rheumatism was ever the worse for another hour's fishing? But I weakly accepted it. I coveted three or four good trout to top off with,—that was all. So I tied on a couple of flies, and began to fish the alders, wading waist deep in the rapidly rising water, down the long green tunnel under the curving boughs. The brook fairly smoked with the rain, by this time, but when did one fail to get at least three or four trout out of this best half mile of the lower brook? Yet I had no luck I tried one fly after another, and then, as a forlorn hope,—though it sometimes has a magic of its own,—I combined a brown hackle for the tail fly with a twisting worm on the dropper. Not a rise! I thought of E. sitting patiently in the saw mill, and I fished more conscientiously than ever.

"Venture as warily, use the same skill,

Do your best, whether winning or losing it,
If you choose to play!—is my principle."

Even those lines, which by some subtle telepathy of the trout brook murmur
themselves over and over to me in the waning hours of an unlucky day, brought
now no consolation. There was simply not one fish to be had, to any fly in the
book, out of that long, drenching, darkening tunnel. At last I climbed out of
the brook, by the bridge. R. was sitting on the fence, his neck and ears carefully
turtled under his coat collar, the smoke rising and the rain dripping from the
inverted bowl of his pipe. He did not seem to be worrying about his rheumatism.

"What luck?" he asked.

"None at all," I answered morosely. "Sorry to keep you waiting."

"That's all right," remarked R. "What do you think I've been doing? I've
been fishing out of the saw-mill window just to kill time. There was a patch
of floating sawdust there,—kind of unlikely place for trout, anyway,—but I
thought I'd put on a worm and let him crawl around a little." He opened his
creel as he spoke. "But I didn't look for a pair of 'em," he added. And there, on
top of his smaller fish, were as pretty a pair of three-quarter-pound brook trout
as were ever basketed.

"I'm afraid you got pretty wet," said R. kindly.

"I don't mind that," I replied. And I didn't. What I minded was the thought
of an hour's vain wading in that roaring stream, whipping it with fly after fly,
while R., the foreordained fisherman, was sitting comfortably in a sawmill, and
derricking that pair of three-quarter-pounders in through the window! I had
ventured more warily than he, and used, if not the same skill, at least the best
skill at my command. My conscience was clear, but so was his; and he had had
the drier skin and the greater magnanimity and the biggest fish besides. There
is much to be said, in a world like ours, for taking the world as you find it and
for fishing with a worm.

One's memories of such fishing, however agreeable they may be, are not to be
identified with a defense of the practice. Yet, after all, the most effective defense
of worm-fishing is the concrete recollection of some brook that could be fished
best or only in that way, or the image of a particular trout that yielded to the
temptation of an angleworm after you had flicked fly after fly over him in vain.
Indeed, half the zest of brook fishing is in your campaign for "individuals,"—as
the Salvation Army workers say,—not merely for a basketful of fish *qua* fish,

but for a series of individual trout which your instinct tells you ought to lurk under that log or be hovering in that ripple. How to get him, by some sportsmanlike process, is the question. If he will rise to some fly in your book, few fishermen will deny that the fly is the more pleasurable weapon. Dainty, luring, beautiful toy, light as thistle-down, falling where you will it to fall, holding when the leader tightens and sings like the string of a violin, the artificial fly represents the poetry of angling. Given the gleam of early morning on some wide water, a heavy trout breaking the surface as he curves and plunges, with the fly holding well, with the right sort of rod in your fingers, and the right man in the other end of the canoe, and you perceive how easy is that Emersonian trick of making the pomp of emperors ridiculous.

But angling's honest prose, as represented by the lowly worm, has also its exalted moments. "The last fish I caught was with a worm," says the honest Walton, and so say I. It was the last evening of last August. The dusk was settling deep upon a tiny meadow, scarcely ten rods from end to end. The rank bog grass, already drenched with dew, bent over the narrow, deep little brook so closely that it could not be fished except with a double-shotted, baited hook, dropped delicately between the heads of the long grasses. Underneath this canopy the trout were feeding, taking the hook with a straight downward tug, as they made for the hidden bank. It was already twilight when I began, and before I reached the black belt of woods that separated the meadow from the lake, the swift darkness of the North Country made it impossible to see the hook. A short half hour's fishing only, and behold nearly twenty good trout derricked into a basket until then sadly empty. Your rigorous fly-fisherman would have passed that grass-hidden brook in disdain, but it proved a treasure for the humble. Here, indeed, there was no question of individually-minded fish, but simply a neglected brook, full of trout which could be reached with the baited hook only. In more open brook-fishing it is always a fascinating problem to decide how to fish a favorite pool or ripple, for much depends upon the hour of the day, the light, the height of water, the precise period of the spring or summer. But after one has decided upon the best theoretical procedure, how often the stupid trout prefers some other plan! And when you have missed a fish that you counted upon landing, what solid satisfaction is still possible for you, if you are philosopher enough to sit down then and there, eat your lunch, smoke a meditative pipe, and devise a new campaign against that particular fish! To get another rise from him after lunch is a triumph of diplomacy, to land him is nothing short of statesmanship. For sometimes he will jump furiously at a fly, for very devilishness, without ever meaning to take it, and then, wearying suddenly of his gymnastics, he will snatch sulkily at a grasshopper, beetle, or worm. Trout feed upon an extraordinary variety of crawling things, as all fishermen know who practice the useful habit of opening the first two or three fish they catch, to see what food is that day the favorite. But here, as elsewhere in this world, the best things lie nearest, and there is no bait so killing, week in and week out, as your plain garden or golf-green angleworm.

Walton's list of possible worms is impressive, and his directions for placing them upon the hook have the placid completeness that belonged to his character. Yet in such matters a little nonconformity may be encouraged. No two men or boys dig bait in quite the same way, though all share, no doubt, the singular elation which gilds that grimy occupation with the spirit of romance. The mind is really occupied, not with the wriggling red creatures in the lumps of earth, but with the stout fish which each worm may capture, just as a saint might rejoice in the squalor of this world as a preparation for the glories of the world to come. Nor do any two experienced fishermen hold quite the same theory as to the best mode of baiting the hook. There are a hundred ways, each of them good. As to the best hook for worm-fishing, you will find dicta in every catalogue of fishing tackle, but size and shape and tempering are qualities that should vary with the brook, the season, and the fisherman. Should one use a three-foot leader, or none at all? Whose rods are best for bait-fishing, granted that all of them should be stiff enough in the tip to lift a good fish by dead strain from a tangle of brush or logs? Such questions, like those pertaining to the boots or coat which one should wear, the style of bait-box one should carry, or the brand of tobacco best suited for smoking in the wind, are topics for unending discussion among the serious minded around the camp-fire. Much edification is in them, and yet they are but prudential maxims after all. They are mere moralities of the Franklin or Chesterfield variety, counsels of worldly wisdom, but they leave the soul untouched. A man may have them at his finger's ends and be no better fisherman at bottom; or he may, like R., ignore most of the admitted rules and come home with a full basket. It is a sufficient defense of fishing with a worm to pronounce the truism that no man is a complete angler until he has mastered all the modes of angling. Lovely streams, lonely and enticing, but impossible to fish with a fly, await the fisherman who is not too proud to use, with a man's skill, the same unpretentious tackle which he began with as a boy.

But ah, to fish with a worm, and then not catch your fish! To fail with a fly is no disgrace: your art may have been impeccable, your patience faultless to the end. But the philosophy of worm-fishing is that of Results, of having something tangible in your basket when the day's work is done. It is a plea for Compromise, for cutting the coat according to the cloth, for taking the world as it actually is.

The fly-fisherman is a natural Foe of Compromise. He throws to the trout a certain kind of lure; and they will take it, so; if not, adieu. He knows no middle path.

"This high man, aiming at a million,
Misses a unit."

The raptures and the tragedies of consistency are his. He is a scorner of the ground. All honor to him! When he comes back at nightfall and says happily, "I have never cast a line more perfectly than I have to-day," it is almost indecent to peek into his creel. It is like rating Colonel Newcome by his bank account.

But the worm-fisherman is no such proud and isolated soul. He is a "low man" rather than a high one; he honestly cares what his friends will think when they look into his basket to see what he has to show for his day's sport. He watches the Foe of Compromise men go stumbling forward and superbly falling, while he, with less inflexible courage, manages to keep his feet. He wants to score, and not merely to give a pretty exhibition of base-running. At the Harvard-Yale football game of 1903 the Harvard team showed superior strength in rushing the ball; they carried it almost to the Yale goal line repeatedly, but they could not, for some reason, take it over. In the instant of absolute need, the Yale line held, and when the Yale team had to score in order to win, they scored. As the crowd streamed out of the Stadium, a veteran Harvard alumnus said: "This news will cause great sorrow in one home I know of, until they learn by to-morrow's papers that the Harvard team acquitted itself creditably." Exactly. Given one team bent upon acquitting itself creditably, and another team determined to win, which will be victorious? The stay-at-homes on the Yale campus that day were not curious to know whether their team was acquitting itself creditably, but whether it was winning the game. Every other question than that was to those young Philistines merely a fine-spun irrelevance. They took the Cash and let the Credit go.

There is much to be said, no doubt, for the Harvard veteran's point of view. The proper kind of credit may be a better asset for eleven boys than any championship; and to fish a bit of water consistently and skillfully, with your best flies and in your best manner, is perhaps achievement enough. So says the Foe of Compromise, at least. But the Yale spirit will be prying into the basket in search of fish; it prefers concrete results. If all men are by nature either Platonists or Aristotelians, fly-fishermen or worm-fishermen, how difficult it is for us to do one another justice! Differing in mind, in aim and method, how shall we say infallibly that this man or that is wrong? To fail with Plato for companion may be better than to succeed with Aristotle. But one thing is perfectly clear: there is no warrant for Compromise but in Success. Use a worm if you will, but you must have fish to show for it, if you would escape the finger of scorn. If you find yourself camping by an unknown brook, and are deputed to catch the necessary trout for breakfast, it is wiser to choose the surest bait. The crackle of the fish in the frying-pan will atone for any theoretical defect in your method. But to choose the surest bait, and then to bring back no fish, is unforgivable. Forsake Plato if you must,—but you may do so only at the price of justifying yourself in the terms of Aristotelian arithmetic. The college president who abandoned his college in order to run a cotton mill was free to make his own choice of a calling; but he was never pardoned for bankrupting the mill. If one is bound to be a low man rather than an impractical idealist, he should at least make sure of his vulgar success.

Is all this but a disguised defense of pot-hunting? No. There is no possible defense of pot-hunting, whether it be upon a trout brook or in the stock market. Against fish or men, one should play the game fairly. Yet for that matter some of the most skillful fly-fishermen I have known were pot-hunters at heart, and some of the most prosaic-looking merchants were idealists compared to whom Shelley was but a dreaming boy. All depends upon the spirit with which one makes his venture. I recall a boy of five who gravely watched his father tramp off after rabbits,—gun on shoulder and beagle in leash. Thereupon he shouldered a wooden sword, and dragging his reluctant black kitten by a string, sallied forth upon the dusty Vermont road "to get a lion for breakfast." That is the true sporting temper! Let there be but a fine idealism in the quest, and the particular object is unessential. "A true fisherman's happiness," says Mr. Cleveland, "is not dependent upon his luck." It depends upon his heart.

No doubt all amateur fishing is but "play,"—as the psychologists soberly term it: not a necessary, but a freely assumed activity, born of surplusage of vitality. Nobody, not even a carpenter wearied of his job, has to go fishing unless he wants to. He may indeed find himself breakfast-less in camp, and obliged to betake himself to the brook,—but then he need not have gone into the woods at all. Yet if he does decide to fish, let him

"Venture as warily, use the same skill,
Do his best, . . ."

whatever variety of tackle he may choose. He can be a whole-souled sportsman with the poorest equipment, or a mean "trout-hog" with the most elaborate.

Only, in the name of gentle Izaak himself, let him be a complete angler; and let the man be a passionate amateur of all the arts of life, despising none of them, and using all of them for his soul's good and for the joy of his fellows. If he be, so to speak, but a worm-fisherman,—a follower of humble occupations, and pledged to unromantic duties,—let him still thrill with the pleasures of the true sportsman. To make the most of dull hours, to make the best of dull people, to like a poor jest better than none, to wear the threadbare coat like a gentleman, to be outvoted with a smile, to hitch your wagon to the old horse if no star is handy,—this is the wholesome philosophy taught by fishing with a worm. The fun of it depends upon the heart. There may be as much zest in saving as in spending, in working for small wages as for great, in avoiding the snapshots of publicity as in being invariably first "among those present." But a man should be honest. If he catches most of his fish with a worm, secures the larger portion of his success by commonplace industry, let him glory in it, for this, too, is part of the great game. Yet he ought not in that case to pose as a fly-fisherman only,—to carry himself as one aware of the immortalizing camera,—to pretend that life is easy, if one but knows how to drop a fly into the right ripple. For life is not easy, after all is said. It is a long brook to fish, and it needs a stout heart and a wise patience. All the flies there are in the book, and all the bait that can be carried in the box, are likely to be needed ere the day is over. But, like the Psalmist's "river of God," this brook is "full of water," and there is plenty of good fishing to be had in it if one is neither afraid nor ashamed of fishing sometimes with a worm.

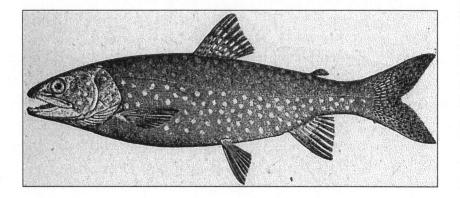

# THE VALUE OF OBSERVATION

## GEORGE M. L. LABRANCHE

Several years ago I was looking on at a tennis match between the champion of America and one of the best men England ever sent to this country, and as I watched their play I could not help but marvel at the accuracy with which the players placed their shots. Their drives were wonderful for direction and speed. On nearly every return the ball barely cleared the net and was seldom more than a few inches above the top as it passed over. A friend who knew many of the experts told me how they attained to their remarkable precision. It was the custom of many of them, he said, when preparing for the big matches, to prac-tice for accuracy by driving the ball against a wall. He said this was particularly true of the American champion, and that it was not unusual for him to use up a dozen or more balls in a day's practice. The wall had painted across its face a line of contrasting color at a height from the ground equivalent to that of the top of a regulation tennis net, and upon the line were painted a number of disks about ten inches in diameter. Standing at a distance from the wall equivalent to the dis-tance of the base-line of a regulation tennis-court from the net, the player would return the ball on its rebound from the wall, striving each time to so place it that it would strike just above the line. The accomplishment of a satisfactory score after a succession of drives would convince the player that he had good control of his stroke, and he would then turn his attention to the disks, against each of which he would drive twenty or more shots, taking them in turn and keeping a record of hits in each case. The accuracy developed by such practice was truly remarkable, and I hesitate to mention the number of times in succession one expert made clean hits—it seemed an incredible number.

I have seen golfers practicing the weak places in their game for hours with as much zeal and earnestness as if they were playing a match, and a polo player of my acquaintance practices his strikes upon a field at his home, riding his ponies as daringly and recklessly as though a championship depended upon his efforts. The devotees of these and similar active sports are keenly alive to the necessity of constant practice, that spirit of competition which is so much a part of them making any endeavor that will aid toward high efficiency or improve game or form, seem worth while. And in all sports, particularly those in which the competition is individual, whenever and wherever opportunity presents itself there will be found hundreds of enthusiasts following every ply of the expert, keenly studying his method, observing his form, and absorbing and storing the knowledge so gained for their own practice later on court or field. So, too, even though competition has no place in fly fishing, and should have none, the angler ought to strive always to "play a good game." He should practice the tactics of his art with the same zeal as do the followers of competitive sports if he hopes ever to become an expert fly fisherman in the highest sense of that misused term.

The casual angler who looks upon fishing as merely incidental to his periods of recreation, during which his chief concern is the recuperation of tired brain and unstrung nerves, may feel that he is making a business of his pleasure by devoting much time to the study of his angling. In a measure this is true, and it would be asking much, indeed, of him who thinks of fly fishing only as a pastime. But to he who realizes that it is a sport—a sport that is also an art—there is no incident, complex or simple, that is unworthy of his attention and consideration. No sport affords a greater field for observation and study than fly fishing, and it is the close attention paid to the minor happenings upon the stream that marks the finished angler. The careless angler frequently overlooks incidents, or looks upon them as merely trivial, from which he might learn much if he would but realize their meaning at the time.

Of greatest importance to the dry fly angler is that mastery of the rod and line that enables him to place his fly lightly and accurately upon the water. I venture to assert that one who has had the advantage of expert instruction in handling a rod, and is thereby qualified to deliver a fly properly, will raise more trout upon his first attempt at fishing a stream than another who, though he knows thoroughly the haunts and habits of the fish, casts indifferently. The contrast between the instructed novice and the uninstructed veteran would be particularly noticeable were they to cast together over the same water in which fish were rising freely. Whether or not the novice would take more fish than the veteran is another question. Lacking experience, the novice would probably hook few fish and land fewer. But he would be starting right, and the necessity of overcoming later on that bad form likely to be acquired by all who begin without competent knowledge of the veteran who would come to him in time.

The beginner should watch the expert and should study particularly the action of the rod. He should note that the power which impels the line forward starts from the butt, travels the entire length of the rod, is applied by a slight forward push rather than by a long sweep, and ends in a distinct snap. He will soon learn that the wrist must do the real work, and no better scheme for teaching this has ever been devised than the time-honored one of holding a fly book or a stone between the casting arm and the body. The proper action of the rod will be best learned if he fasten that part of the butt below the reel to the forearm with a piece of string, a strap of leather, or a stout rubber band, the effect of which device will be to stop the rod in an almost perpendicular position when the line is retrieved. The pull of the line as it straightens out behind him will be distinctly felt, will give him a good idea of the power and action of his rod, and sever as a signal for the forward cast. He should practice casting as often as his spare time will allow—over water when possible, but over grass if necessary. He should not wait until the stream is reached and actual fishing problems begin to press upon his notice for solution. His mind will then be occupied with many other things; hence, the knack of handling the rod should have been already acquired.

After the beginner is satisfied that he can properly place and deliver his fly, he should turn his attention to study of the fish and the currents of the stream. If he has been a wet fly angler his experience will stand him in good stead, as it will qualify him to locate the likely haunts of the fish. Long and varied though his experience may have been, however, the use of the dry fly will open avenues of observation and knowledge that were hidden from him while he practiced the old method. My own experience is responsible for this rather broad statement, but not until after I had become an ardent advocate of the dry fly, and had abandoned the wet fly for good and all, did I realize the truth of it. In the beginning I was ever on the alert for rising fish, and, instead of boldly assailing promising water, wasted much time, on many occasions, scrutinizing the water for some indication that a fish was feeding. In this way I frequently discovered non-feeding fish lying in places where I had not expected to find them. Such fish were then the more easily approached because I was able to assume a position myself that would not disclose my presence. Just as frequently, too, I have seen fine fish cruising about, and have taken many that might have been driven away by the slightest movement on my part. In many cases I have been compelled to remain absolutely motionless for ten or fifteen minutes before a fish would come to rest long enough to make worth while an attempt to get a fly to it. nearly every time, too, that a fish has been hooked I have seen it actually take the fly—an action always instructive, because fish vary greatly in their manner of taking, and interesting, because in it lies one of the real charms of fly fishing.

The continued use of a floating fly upon water where the angler sees no indication of feeding fish, but where experience tells him that they may lie, seems to develop in him a remarkable keenness of vision. This is a direct result, perhaps, of the attention he gives to his fly. My own experience is that while I am watching my fly float down-stream some stone of irregular formation, peculiar color, or difference in size from others about it, lying upon the bottom, arrests my eye, with the effect of making the water appear shallower or clearer than it really is. My fly appears to be the center of a small area upon the surface of the water through which everything is seen as clearly as though through water-glass, the shadow of the fly itself upon the bottom often being plainly discernible. Anglers who fish the dry fly learn to identify the living shadow that appears suddenly under the fly as a trout ready to take it on its next drift down-stream, and to recognize a fish as it sidles out from the bank or swings uncertainly toward the fly just as it passes the boulder that shelters him. In either way an interesting opportunity is afforded, particularly for exercising a very necessary attribute—self-control.

It may be that many happenings I now see upon the stream passed unnoticed when I used the wet fly because of some lack of concentration and observation. If this be so, I have the newer method to thank for the development of those faculties. I have learned not to overlook a single minor happening. Perhaps my keenness to ascribe some meaning to the slightest incident has resulted in the building of many fine structures of theory and dogma upon poor foundations. This may be true, but I am certain that their weaknesses have always become apparent to me in time; and, on the other hand, I am just as certain that I have been greatly benefited by my habit of close attention to the little things that happen on the stream. For instance, I cherished the belief for many years that one advantage of up-stream fishing lay in the fact that when the fly was taken the hook was driven into the fish's mouth instead of being pulled away, as in down-stream fishing. I thought this to be one of the strongest arguments in favor of up-stream fishing, and, theoretically, it is. But I know now that many fish that take a floating do so when they are headed down-stream. While there are still many reasons why up-stream fishing is the better method, this particular argument no longer has weight with me.

As I remember it, the strongest admonition of my early schooling on the stream was never to remain long in one place. I was taught to believe that if a rise was not effected on the first few casts subsequent effort on that water was wasted—that the trout would take the fly at once or not at all. I clung to this belief for years, until one day I saw a fine fish lying in shallow water and took him after casting a dozen or more times. Since then I have taken fish after upwards of fifty casts, and I rarely abandon an attempt for one that I can see if I feel certain that it has not discovered me. Even when I have not actually seen a fish, but have known or believed one to be lying near by, the practice has proven effective. Thus I have had the satisfaction of accomplishing a thing once believed to be impossible; but I have gained more than that: I have learned to be persevering and, what is still more important, deliberate. The man who hurries through a trout stream defeats himself. Not only does he take few fish but he has no time for observation, and his experience is likely to be of little value to him.

The beginner must learn to look with eyes that see. Occurrences of apparently little importance at the moment may, after consideration, assume proportions of great value. The taking of an insect, for instance, may mean nothing more than a rising trout; but the position occupied by this fish may indicate the position taken by others in similar water. The flash of a trout, changing his position preparatory to investigating the angler's fly, will frequently disclose the spot occupied by him before he changed his position; and, later on, when the fish are not in the keenest mood for feeding, a fly presented there accurately may bring a rise. The quick dart up-stream of a small trout from the tail of a pool is a pretty fair indication that a large fish occupies the deeper water above; it indicates just as certainly, however, that the angler has little chance of taking him, the excitement of the smaller fish having probably been communicated to his big relative.

The backwater formed by a swift current on the up-stream side of a boulder is a favorite lurking-place of brown trout. I was fishing such places one day, and found the trout occupying them in rather a taking mood. In approaching a boulder which looked particularly inviting, and while preparing to deliver my fly, I was amazed to see the tail and half the body of a fine trout out of the water at the side of the rock. For a moment I could not believe that I had seen a fish— the movement was so deliberate and I came to the conclusion that it was fancy or that a water-snake, gliding across the stream, had shown itself. Almost immediately, however, I saw the flash of a trout as he left the backwater and dashed pell-mell into the swift water at the side of the boulder. Down-stream he came until he was eight or ten feet below the rock, when, turning sharply and rising to the surface, he took from it some insect that I could not see. Up-stream again he went, and shortly resumed his position in the dead water, showing half his body as he stemmed the current at the side of the rock. Once more this performance was repeated, and I knew I had stumbled upon an interesting experience. Hastily measuring the distance, hoping to get my fly to him before some natural insect might excite him to give another exhibition of gymnastic feeding, I dropped it about three feet above him, and, contrary to my usual method of retrieving it as it floated past the up-stream side of the boulder, I permitted it to come down riding the top of the wave, when the same flash came as the trout dashed after it. The fish could be plainly seen almost directly under the fly. As it reached the rapidly flattening water below the rock, he turned and took it viciously, imme-diately darting up-stream again. He was soundly hooked, however, and I netted a fine fish lacking one ounce of being a pound and a half. My experience hereto-fore had been that if a fly were placed a yard or so above this point and allowed to float down to the rock a feeding fish would rush forward-often as much as two feet-and take it, immediately turning or backing into his position again. I had assumed from this observation when the fly passed the rock or backwater without a rise it should be retrieved and another try made. This fish satisfied me, however, that when really feeding, or when inclined to feed, trout may be lured comparatively long distances by inviting-looking morsels. Either he did not decide to take the fly until just as it was passing him or else he liked the exercise of the chase. In any event, he was not peculiar in his habit, because four more fish were taken in the same manner the same day.

In most cases when the fly is cast above a boulder lying in swift water (which I consider, under certain conditions, one of the best places to look for brown trout) it will be taken as it approaches the rock, the trout darting out and retiring immediately to avoid being caught in the swifter water on either side of his stronghold. But if it is not taken, and is permitted to float down with the current, it may bring a response.

It was a somewhat similar observation which prompted the practice and, I must say, rather dubious development of what some of my friends are pleased to call the "fluttering" or "bounce" cast. This cast is supposed to represent the action of the fluttering insect, the fly merely alighting upon the water, rising, alighting again, repeating the movement three or four times at most; finally coming to rest and being allowed to float down-stream. It rarely comes off, but when it does it is deadly; and, for the good of the sport, I am glad but when it does it is deadly; and, for the good of the sport, I am glad that it is difficult, though sorry, too, for the pleasure of accomplishing it successfully is really greater than that of taking fish with it. The cast is made with a very short line-never over twenty-five feet-and the fly alone touches the water. The action of the fly is very similar to that produced by the method known as "dapping," but instead of being merely dangled from the rod, as is the case when "dapping," the fly is actually cast. It should be permitted to float as far as it will after its fluttering or skipping has ceased. The beginner practicing the cast will do well to cast at right angles to the current, and he should choose rather fast water for his experimenting. The speed of the water will cause the fly to jump, and the action it should have will be the more readily simulated than if the first attempts are made on slow water.

I had made a flying trip to the Brodhead, and, with that strange fatality which seems so often to attend the unfortunate angler rushing off for a weekend in the early season, found the stream abnormally high and horrible weather prevailing. After many attempts to get into the stream, with results equally disastrous to my clothing and temper, I abandoned all idea of wading and walked and crawled along the bank, casting my fly wherever I could but rarely finding good water that could be reached, and rising but a few small fish. As there was a gale blowing in my face directly down-stream, it was practically impossible to place a fly where I wished with any delicacy, and I decided to abandon the sport after trying a pool just above me that I knew contained big fish. My first cast on this water, made during a lull, fell lightly, but brought no response, and after a further half dozen fruitless attempts I began to think of the fine log fire at the house. I made one more cast, however, this time in the teeth of the wind. Using but twenty-five feet of line and a short leader, I was able to straighten both in the air. The wind kept all suspended for an instant, the fly, accompanied by a small part of the leader, finally falling upon the water, where I remained but a fraction of a second, the wind whisking it off and laying it down a foot away. This happened five or six times as the fly came down-stream, and during the time it was traveling a distance of not over eight or ten feet five trout, each apparently over a pound in weight, rose to it, but missed because it was plucked away by the wind just in time to save them. I did not get one of them, and, as it was practically impossible to continue casting under the prevailing conditions, I left the stream. It was brought home solidly to me that day, however, that it was the *action* of the fly alone that moved the fish—and my day was not badly spent. I cannot say as much of the many other days since then that I have spent in what I feel were rather foolish attempts to imitate the effect produced by the wind on that day.

The study of the positions taken by big fish when they are feeding, and those which they occupy when they are not, is an important part in the education of the fly fisher. Each time the angler takes a good fish or sees one feeding, if he will note in his diary its position, the condition of the water, temperature, atmosphere, time of day, and the insect being taken, he will soon have an accumulation of data from which he may learn how to plan a campaign against particular fish at other times. Extremely interesting in itself, the study of insects is of great value to the angler in his attempts at imitation, and the information gleaned from autopsy might not be acquired in any other manner.

It may be said to be an axiom of the fly fisher that where a small trout is seen feeding rarely need a large one be looked for. But the actions of a small fish in sight may sometimes indicate the presence of a larger one unseen. The taking of a fine trout on a certain stream in Sullivan County, on August 27, 1906, after one of those long periods of drought so common in recent years, convinced me of this. I had been waiting for even a slight fall of rain, and, quite a heavy shower having come up the evening before, I started for this stream. Upon my arrival there I was surprised to learn that not a drop of rain had fallen in weeks, and that the shower which had been heavy twenty miles away had not reached the vicinity. While driving from the station to the house at which I was to stop. Along a road that paralleled the stream, the many glimpses I had of the latter filled me with misgivings. At one point the stream and road are very near each other, and, stopping my driver, I got out looking at a famous pool below a dam which had long outlived its usefulness. It was a sizzling-hot day, and at that time—eleven o'clock—the sun was almost directly overhead; yet in the crystal-clear water of this pool, with not a particle of shade to cover him, lay a native trout fourteen inches in length which afterward proved to weigh one pound three ounces. Too fine a fish, I thought, as I clambered back into the carriage, to be occupying such a place in broad daylight, and I promised myself to try for him later in the afternoon. Returning about six o'clock, I found him in the same position, and during the full twenty minutes I watched him, while he appeared to be nervously alert, he never moved. Notwithstanding the fact that everything was against me, and knowing that the chances were more than even that the fish would see me, my rod, or my line, I made plans for approaching him; yet, busy as I was, I could not rid my mind of this ever-recurring thought: with all the known aversion of his kind to heat, and their love of dark nooks, why was this fish out on such a day? Why did he not find a place under the cool shade of the dam? With the instinct strong within him to protect him by hiding, the impulse must have been much stronger that forced him to take so conspicuous a stand—

a mark to the animals which prey upon his kind. As there were absolutely no insects upon the water, and scarcely enough current to bring food of other sort to him, he could not have been feeding. The only reason, then, to account for his being there—the thought struck me forcibly enough—was his fear of a bigger fish. The logical conclusion was that if a fish of his inches (no mean adversary) exposed himself the one that bullied him must be quite solid. I tested this fellow's appetite with a small, pinkish-bodied fly of my own invention, and, standing about forty feet below and considerably to the left, dropped it three or four feet above him; but, although it was certain he could see the fly, he made no attempt to go forward and take it. As it neared him, however, he rushed excitedly to the right and then to the left, taking the fly as it came directly over him, and, before I could realize what had happened, came down-stream toward me at a great rate. As he was securely hooked, I kept him coming, and netted him quietly at the lip of the pool.

That this fish did not take the fly the instant it fell meant to me that he was afraid to go forward into the deeper water which harbored his larger fellow; and his action as the fly appeared over him meant that, while he wanted it badly enough, he would not risk an altercation with the other, which might also have seen it. When he did finally decide that the coast was clear, he took it quickly and rushed down toward the shallower water where he might be secure against sudden attack.

If some of the theories developed in those few moments appear fanciful, it must be remembered that my mind was occupied with the thought that the pool contained a larger fish, and the conclusions based upon the subsequent actions of this smaller one only tended to strengthen this belief. Fanciful or not, I was rewarded a few minutes later by the sight of a monster tail breaking the surface just under the water that trickled over the apron of the dam. Having prepared a gossamer leader, preferring to risk a smash to not getting a rise, I dropped a small Silver Sedge—which I used because it could be more plainly kept in sight—almost immediately in the swirl and was at once fast in a lusty fish. After many abortive attempts to lead him into the diminutive net I had with me, I flung the thing, in disgust, into the woods. I finally beached the fish and lifted him out in my hand. He was a fine brown trout, eighteen and three quarter inches in length, and weighed, the next morning, two pounds nine ounces.

While I was engaged with this fish another rose in practically the same spot under the apron of the dam. Hurriedly replacing the bedraggled fly with a new one, I waited for the trout to show himself, which he did presently, and again I was fast—this time in one of the best fish I have ever seen in these waters. It seemed an interminable length of time, though probably not over ten minutes, that I was engaged with this one, and it was impossible to move him; he kept alternately boring in toward the dam and sulking. In one of the latter fits I urged him toward me somewhat too strongly, and he was off. Immediately I was afforded a sight of what I had lost as he leaped clear of the water in an evident endeavor to dislodge the thing that had fastened to his jaw. The smash made as he struck the water still resounds in my ear, and when I say that this fish would have bone close to five pounds I but exercise the right to that license accorded all anglers to attempt to describe the size of the big ones that get away. Having one good fish in my creel, however, I really had some basis for my calculation—at any rate, he was one of the best fish I have ever risen. Examining my leader, I found it had not broken, but the telltale curl at the end proved that, in the fast-gathering gloom, I had been careless in knotting on the fly.

# TWO OLD TROUT OF THE POOLS, AND THE LITTLE DRY-FLY THAT FINALLY ACCOMPLISHED THEIR RUIN

## EMLYN GILL

The author's early experiences with the floating fly were neither fruitful nor encouraging; but he fully realizes that this lack of success was entirely his own fault, and was due both to a lack of knowledge of dry-fly methods and to an insufficiently aroused interest in them. One day several years ago he saw in a tackle shop some flies different from any in his fly-books, and having been told that they were the English floating flies, laid in a small stock of them, while the tackle-dealer briefly explained how they were used. Afterward these flies were taken on several trips, but were unthought of and unused. One day he met an angler who had used the dry-fly method of fishing and who seemed to be enthusiastic about it. The author made up his mind that he would try the floating fly at the very next opportunity that presented itself. But it must be remembered that he had been a confirmed wet fly fisherman for more than thirty years, and while he had advanced in the wet fly art so far as to use only a single small fly, and leaders fully as fine as those made for dry-fly angling, yet when he reached a stream it was natural for him to think of the lures that had been his companions since boyhood and not to attempt to branch out into new fields.

But one May day, four or five years ago, when on a week's end fishing trip, he was driven to a point verging upon exasperation by a large trout which persisted in rising leisurely from a hole beside an old stump in a pool that had been a favorite of the author's for several years. When its first rise was seen the angler placed over it one of his most attractive wet flies with a feeling of confidence that the trout could not resist it. But resist it he did, not only on the first cast, but on succeeding casts. Then the pool was rested, and another favorite fly was tried with the same result. The trout was still rising occasionally, but paid no attention to the artificial lure; once it arose just as the imitation touched the water and within a few inches of it, apparently entirely unconcerned about the wiles of the angler attempting to lure it to destruction. Again the pool was rested and the trout soon attacked with another pattern. It happened that this was not the first day that the same tactics had been tried both by the writer and his friends, and this particular trout had gained a well-deserved reputation. To make the matter worse, the author, in a fit of vainglorious boasting, had made arrangements at the inn that morning to have this fish cooked for his dinner that very evening.

Finally, having reached a point bordering upon total discouragement, the angler sat down to take a rest and to think things over. In a few minutes there was a "plop," and another big swirl by the stump. The trout was still doing business at the same old stand, but the angler had apparently closed up shop and ceased to take interesting the affairs going on about him.

But in a moment he sat erect, with the appearance of a man who had solved a great and weighty problem. An idea had suddenly flashed through his mind! A tiny japanned vest-pocket eyed-fly box lay open before him, and he was gazing intently at its long neglected contents. There were within this box little whirling duns, Wickham's fancies, Jenny spinners, black gnats and coachmen—all beautifully tied English floating flies. He selected a whirling dun, which has ever since been one of his favorite lures. It was carefully knotted to the filmy leader, and a moment after the next rise of the fish it was floating in the centre of the swirl with wings erect. Then something took place that had not happened before in this spot that season, so far as records showed; the old trout had sucked in the little dun, apparently without the slightest suspicion that it was not a natural insect, and the hook was firmly imbedded in its mouth.

This should have been a lesson to me, but I must confess that it was not. True, I often thought of this episode and admitted that the dry-fly on that occasion had saved the day; furthermore, I listened more attentively when anglers spoke of the floating lure; but the microbe of enthusiasm had not as yet reached its mark.

The following spring I went to the same stream and fully intended to give the dry-fly a thorough try-out. But when the opening day of the season dawned, the morning after my arrival, the habits of a lifetime had full possession of me, and the dry-flies were forgotten. This was in the middle of April. After returning from this trip, there came a feeling of regret that I had not spent at least a part of the time fishing with the floating lure, and so I hurried back to the stream early in May, fully intending that this trip should be devoted exclusively to practice with the dry-fly. The results were neither good nor bad; the fishing seemed to be poor that week, and I used the wet fly and dry-fly alternately, fortune favoring one about as much as the other. I performed one surprising feat, however, with the floating fly that I have always attributed to amazing good luck rather than to particularly good management. It was well known to local and visiting anglers that a large trout occupied an almost impregnable position in the upper part of a long pool above a dam, and it had been considered impossible to reach it with any known lure, without giving it previous warning of danger. It could not be cast for from below, and rocks and bushes made it impossible to assail it from either side; while above, a barrier of rocks was made higher by an old pine tree that had fallen across the stream. Many anglers had schemed to take this trout, but none had succeeded in making even a good attempt at doing so. To make a long story short, I cast a fly from above the fallen pine tree and over it, without even seeing the water in which the fish lay. The floating fly was so cast that it must have drifted down over the trout; in an instant I either heard, or imagined that I heard the "plop" of a rising fish, and we were at once engaged in a struggle, neither of us in sight of the other. How it was possible from that position to "play" this trout to a standstill without getting hopelessly tangled I did not know; but in a short time it showed signs of weakening, and I laid my rod on the top of the barrier formed by the rocks and the pine tree, clambered over as fast as I could, picked up the rod again, and the fish was soon in the net.

By this time I had begun to be somewhat accustomed to the use of the dry-fly, but still lacked the confidence in myself necessary to handle it to the best advantage. The following winter I most fortunately came across Mr. Halford's early books and read them greedily. The naturalness of dry-fly methods as described by him was absolutely convincing, and I became enthusiastic over what I then began to consider the most artistic and beautiful of all methods of angling. Afterward I had the great good fortune to meet some of our dry-fly experts, and now feel competent to go upon the streams alone and at least *learn* new things about this delightful art.

The incidents related have been written so much with the idea of entertaining the reader, as with the hope that they will point a moral to the beginner with dry-fly, with the result that he will start in at once to *master* dry-fly fishing instead drifting along aimlessly until a chance happening compels him to realize the desirability of becoming a skillful dry-fly angler.

At first, if an angler has been a wet fly fisherman all his life, the dry-fly and the methods of its use may seem somewhat strange to him when he takes them up; in other words, he is apt to lack that confidence in himself and the dry-fly that he has when casting the wet fly, to the handling of which he has become thoroughly accustomed. Many are wont to imagine, at first, that there is something more difficult about dry-fly angling than fishing with the sunken lure. This, I think, is not so when one has acquired the knack of it. It may be possible for a bungling fisherman to meet with success in some wilderness waters, or at times in streams nearer civilization when they are high and discolored. But to be a finished wet fly angler one must possess as much skill as the dry-fly fisherman. Nothing but experience can teach a man where the trout lie in the streams; if one starts right, and is shown how, it is comparatively easy to cast a fly skillfully. There are no insurmountable obstacles in the way of becoming a successful dry-fly angler that do not confront the user of the sunken fly.

But *give the dry-fly a chance*; one without previous practice cannot go upon a stream for one day, and meeting with no success rightfully condemn the dry-fly, as has been done the past year by several friends and acquaintances of the author. How many times have not one but many anglers spent an entire week fishing with wet flies on some well-known trout stream, without taking altogether more than a few small fish? My advice to the beginner with the dry-fly is to go ahead and *make* a success of it, without being discouraged by real or fancied obstacles. The first rise to the imitation insect, as it floats down the stream in plain sight of the angler, will give the beginner a thrill he has seldom had when he has felt the tug of a trout taking the sunken fly. The dry-fly game is *worth while*, and no one should hesitate to make any efforts necessary to overcome what may appear to him to be difficulties in the way of becoming an accomplished dry-fly fisherman.

The author is intensely interested in seeing the use of the dry-fly spread in America for several reasons, of which the principal one is, perhaps, that it will give a greatly added pleasure to our anglers. It is a delicate and artistic method of taking trout, and I have found almost without exception that dry-fly experts have such a great love of the game, that a heavy creel at the end of the day is not the principal consideratum. In these days of depleted streams it is most necessary that the doctrine should be spread broadcast that the one pleasure of trout fishing, apart from the joy of being close to nature, is the matching of one's wits against the cunning of the trout. He alone deserves the title of sportsman who returns carefully to the water all trout that he does not need for food; as soon as the fish is taken into the net, all the sport to be had with that particular fish is over, and when killed and put into the creel it has become simply *meat*.

I apprehend that one of the discouragements with which the dry-fly beginner is liable to meet for some time to come will be improper tackle, foisted upon him, unintentionally, perhaps, by dealers who themselves are not familiar with the flies and leaders used by dry-fly experts, and who think that they have made their best efforts to secure a supply of proper tackle. Some friends have complained that dry-flies used by them last season could not be made to float; while I have heard certain dealers recommend leaders almost strong enough for salmon fishing, and yet they did it without intent to deceive. Therefore, whenever he can do so, it will be advisable for the beginner to consult some expert dry-fly angler before purchasing tackle, especially flies and leaders. If the enthusiasm over this method of fishing becomes general among fly-fishermen, as it now bids fair to do, it will be only a short time before all our best tackle dealers have a full and proper equipment of dry-fly necessities.

# THE FINEST TROUT IN THE WORLD

## HARRY PLUNKET-GREENE

It might naturally be supposed that if one had the fishing of a trout-stream like the Bourne one would not leave an inch of it unexplored, but it was a fact that up to this time none of the rods had ever taken the trouble to investigate the top quarter-mile of the water. Savage and Sharkey had somehow got it into their heads that there was nothing worth troubling about above the "lagoon" immediately beyond the viaduct, and as they lived close to the top of the fishing, all the rest of us, myself included, had tacitly accepted this as a matter of fact. Nowadays the whole of this region is a vast watercress bed, and anyone looking out of the window of the train, when passing over the viaduct, would never realize that there was, or ever had been, a river there at all; but in those days there were two streams above, as well as below, the bridge, meeting a little way up and stretching as one, for a quarter of a mile to the end of the fishing.

We had all of us come on occasions as far as the hatch below this final stretch, but, in the belief that the water above was a blank, had always turned back when we got there.

On August 31st of this year, the last day of the season, I found myself at this hatch at about six o'clock in the evening. I had got four fish averaging 1½ lbs., but it had been a bad rising day, cold and windy. At six o'clock it suddenly turned warm and calm, and I was sitting on the hatch smoking a pipe before going home, when I thought that, just for fun, I would walk up to the end of the water. I expected nothing, and had half a mind to leave my rod behind and saunter up with my hands in my pockets. I got over the fence and rolled up on to the bank unconcernedly, and, as I did so, from one weed-patch after another there darted oft a series of two-pounders racing upstream like motor-boats. I dropped like a stone, but the damage was done. I just sat there cursing the day I was born and myself, not only for having lost the chance of a lifetime—for the iron-blues were beginning to come down back—but for having left this gold-mine undiscovered and untouched for two years—and to-day was the last day of the season! If there had been any handy way discovered of kicking oneself physically as well as mentally I should have been unrecognizable when I got home. Every fish was under the weeds long ago, and I might just as well pack up my traps and clear out.

There was an old broken-down footbridge about a hundred yards above me, and I thought that I would go up to it and explore the reach beyond, more with a view to the possibilities of next year than with any hope for present. I got down from the bank and circled round through the meadow. I got to it, and was just picking my way across its rotten planks when under my very feet I saw a small nose appear, followed by a diminutive head and the most enormous shoulder I ever remember to have seen in a chalk stream. I froze stiff where I stood, except that my knees were shaking like aspens, for there right underneath me was gradually emerging the fish of my life. I do not mean to say that I have not caught bigger fish before and since, but this was a veritable star in the dust-heap, a Cinderella stealing out of the kitchen that we all despised, and the romance of the thing put him (*pace* Cinderella) on a pedestal of fame from which I have never taken him down.

It was agonizing work, for he swam up in the most leisurely way at a rate of about an inch in every five seconds, while I was straddled across two wooden planks, either of which might have given way at any moment, and had to pretend that I was part of the landscape. He was immediately under me when he first showed up and I could easily have touched him with my foot. What fish will see and what they will not see will ever remain a mystery! It was then about half-past six (old time), the time of day when one's visibility is most clear, and yet he took not the smallest notice of me. He just strolled up the middle of the stream contentedly as though he were having a smoke after dinner. I can still feel my joints creaking as I sank slowly to my knees and got my line out. It fell just right and he took no more notice of it than of a water-rat, I tried again and again, lengthening the cast as he moved up, and at last he rose towards it, examined it carefully and, horror of horrors!, swam slowly after it downstream through the bridge under my feet! It would have been laughable if it had not been so tragic.

There was I pulling in the slack like a madman, and leaving it in wisps round my knees, scared lest he should see my hand move; and he passed me by without a word and disappeared into the bowels of the bridge.

I just knelt there and swore, trying to look over my shoulder to see if he had gone down below. There was no sign of him, and the situation was painful in the extreme, for my knees were working through the rotten woodwork, and if I tried to ease myself I should either bring the bridge down with a crash or anyway evict Cinderella for good and all.

I bore it as long as I could, and was just going to give it up and scramble out anyhow, when I saw that nose slide out again beneath me, and my old friend started off on his journey up-stream once more.

I began on him with a shorter line this time, and he took the fly at the very first cast like a lamb. If he was a lamb as he took it he was a lion when he had it. Instead of running up-stream, as I hoped and expected he would do, he gave one swish with his tail and bolted down through the bridge, bending the rod double and dragging the point right under. It was done with such lightning speed I had no time to remonstrate. I threw myself flat on my stomach and got the rod sideways over the bridge, and then the fight began. I was on one side of the bridge, and he was half-way to Southampton on the other. He got farther and farther downstream, going from one patch of weeds to the next, and digging and burrowing his nose into the middle of it, while I just hung on, helpless, waiting for the end. He quieted down after a bit, and finding that he could not rub the annoying thing out of his nose on the south side he determined to explore the north, and he began to swim up towards me. I must have been a ridiculous sight, spread-eagled on the rotting planks with splinters digging into my legs and ants and spiders crawling down my neck, vainly endeavoring to hold the rod over the side with one hand, to wind in the line with the other, and to watch him over my shoulder all at the same time. Fortunately, I must have been invisible from below, but the moment he got under the bridge he saw the rod and tore past me upstream with the reel screaming. But now we were on even terms and there was a clear stretch of water ahead, and I was able to play him to a finish. I was really proud of that fight, for, in addition to the cramped style which I was compelled to adopt, it took place in a stream ten feet wide, half-choked with weeds, and I got him on a 000 Ironblue at the end of a 4x point. He weighed 3½ lbs. when I got him home, and I have always bitterly regretted that I did not get him set up, for, with the exception of an 1½-pounder in the hall of Longford Castle, caught in the Avon by one of the family on a "local lure" (the name of which neither fork nor spade would dig from me), he was the most beautiful river-trout in shape, color and proportion I ever saw.

# NOTHING FISHY ABOUT TROUT

## DAVE BARRY

There comes a time when a man must go into the wilderness and face one of Mankind's oldest, and most feared, enemies: trout.

For me, that time came recently in Idaho, where I go every summer. Many people think Idaho is nothing but potato farms, but nothing could be further from the truth: There are also beet farms.

No, seriously, Idaho is a beautiful state that offers—to quote Emerson—"nature out the bazooty." This includes many rivers and streams that allegedly teem with trout. I say "allegedly" because until recently I never saw an actual trout, teeming or otherwise. People were always pointing at the water and saying, "Look! Trout!" But I saw nothing. I wondered if these people were like that creepy little boy in the movie *The Sixth Sense* who had the supernatural ability to see trout.

Anyway, on this Idaho trip my friend Ron Ungerman—and "Ungerman" is NOT a funny name, so let's not draw undue attention to it—persuaded me to go trout fishing. We purchased fishing licenses and hired a guide named Susanne, who is German but promised us that she would not be too strict.

Susanne had me and Ron Ungerman (Ha ha!) put on rubber waders, which serve two important purposes: (1) they cause your legs to sweat; and (2) they make you look like Nerd Boy from the Planet Dork. Then we hiked through roughly 83 miles of aromatic muck to a spot on the Wood River that literally throbbed with trout. I, of course, did not see them, but I did see a lot of blooping on the water surface, which Susanne assured us was caused by trout.

But there was a problem. To catch trout, you have to engage in "fly casting," a kind of fishing that is very challenging, and here I am using "challenging" in the sense of "idiotic." When I was a boy, I fished with a worm on a hook, and it always worked, and I will tell you why: Fish are not rocket scientists. They see a worm, and in their tiny brains they think, "Huh! This is something I have never seen before underwater! I had better eat it!"

But with "fly casting," you wade into the river and attempt to place a "fly"—a furry little hook thingy weighing slightly less than a hydrogen atom— on top of the water right where the trout are blooping. You do this by waving your fishing rod back and forth, using the following rhythm, as explained to us (I am not making this up) by Susanne: "CO-ca CO-la, CO-ca CO-la." On your third CO-la, you point your arm forward, and the "fly," in a perfect imitation of nature, lands on your head. Or sometimes it forms itself into a snarl that cannot be untangled without the aid of a chain saw AND a flamethrower.

At least that's what kept happening to me and my friend Ron Ungerman. (Yes! "Ungerman!") We stood there for hours, waving our rods and going "CO-ca CO-la," but most of the time we were not getting our flies anywhere near the blooping. The trout were laughing so hard at us that they considered evolving legs so they could crawl onto land and catch their breath.

But Susanne was a good teacher, and very patient, and finally, just when I thought I would never ever catch a trout, it happened: I got a citation for not having my fishing license with me. Really. I left the license back in the car. The Idaho Fish and Game official who cited me was very polite, and so was I, because he was wearing a sidearm. I considered asking him if I could borrow it to shoot a trout, but there's probably some rule against THAT, too.

As the day wore on, our efforts—"CO-ca CO-la; CO-ca CO-la"—took on an air of desperation, because it was becoming clear that Susanne, a true professional, was NOT going to let us leave until we caught a blooping fish. So you can imagine how blooping happy we were when Ron (Ungerman) finally managed to haul in a trout. It was not a large trout. It was the length of a standard Cheeto. But it WAS a trout, dammit, and it meant we could stop.

Later, Ron and I agreed that it had been a lot of fun and we would definitely never do it again. So, to any trout reading this column I say: You are safe from us. And to the Idaho Fish and Game Department, I say: You'll never take me alive.

# IN PRAISE OF TROUT—AND ALSO ME

## PAUL O'NEIL

A ngling for the noble trout with an artificial fly is widely defined in literature as an exercise in contentment—a process hardly less stupefying, apparently, than an overdose of goof balls. Bait fishermen consider the practice effete, like tennis as it was played by young females in 1890. Bartenders, undertakers and other sentimental kibitzers assume it denotes high purpose, since fly fishermen—ah damned fool expression!—are alleged to be purists. Fishing experts, and particularly those who write for sporting publications, make fly fishing sound like lion hunting. Experts never have a moment's doubt as to what fly pattern to use, never cast over a trout weighing less than two pounds and never fail to bring the monster to net after 1) a thrilling battle, which went on long after night fell over the clear pool, or 2) a very short tussle, really, due to the fantastic skill with which the quarry was played.

During my twenty years of fishing with a fly, each and every one of these assumptions and definitions has caused me vague hot recurring unease and guilt—the sort of fleeting pangs a second-story man with a hangover might experience at the sound of a Salvation Army band. It seems impossible that there could be a grain of truth in any of them, but the fisherman's handmaiden, alas, is doubt and he is often impelled to ask, "Why am I not a better man?"

The maniac who engineered my worst August afternoon—this was five years ago, but I will remember it if and when I am ninety—typifies the sort of phenomenon which occasions such self-analysis. My first response to his appearance was simple astonishment. He held a wobbling glass rod high in air and, as he lurched slowly downstream, he jiggled and jerked from ankles to head and plucked at his monofilament line—thus activating the lure tied to its end—like Billy Sunday's own bullfiddle player. The man never stopped; he must have trained for his performance as Dempsey trained for Willard or Hackenschmidt trained for Gotch.

"How ya doing?" he cried as he sloshed up, still jerking spastically, to my side. "No good," said I. "Ought to use a minnow," said he, pointing with his chin to his own line. He then shut off his engine for a moment and opened his creel. "Five," said he.

He lied. There were only three. But each beautiful trout was fifteen inches long. I felt—I cannot deny it—like an orphan child at the wading pool.

It was a moment in which it was impossible not to wonder—even though one could pick no worse time for fishing a fly than an August afternoon—whether a real expert would have been standing there, as was I, with an empty creel and an emptier expression being patronized by an inartistic and greed-riddled bait-using cretin. It was also impossible not to wonder, once the first awful shock had passed, whether I would not have reacted more charitably if I had been truly dedicated, truly sporting and pure. I was privy, after all, to fresh air, sunlight, the sight and sound of running water, the loom of green and gentle Catskill heights and the chance to speak generously to a fellow sportsman—all of the ingredients of contentment, certainly, if man ever possessed them. It did no good. I waited steaming with avarice, until the interloper vanished from view and then attached a streamer fly which imitated the minnow he seemed to have used and did my fruitless best to ape his curious style. Ninety per cent of fly fishermen, in my opinion, would have fallen prey to the same lamentable instincts (and would doubtless have failed, as did I) provided they, too, evaded observation by their peers.

It would be incorrect to say that the fly fisherman never enjoys tranquility, never appreciates nature or is incapable of high purpose—even to the point of freeing the trout he has hooked for the masses to snaffle. All are possible as long as the trout are decent enough to rise to the angler's fly in the first place. These conclusions are based, I must confess, on personal speculation, as is my conviction that fly fishermen tend to be competitive, status conscious and crafty types skilled in the low arts of gamesmanship.

I was enormously encouraged in these views, however, by a recent visit—my first—to the gambling hells of Las Vegas. I was startled out of my wits by the boiler factory din—the crash of slot machines, the cries of crap shooters, the sound of music in which I was enveloped at an hour when most people are eating breakfast. But, for all that, the unlikely scene was instantly familiar. Everyone in the big casino—from the old ladies yanking away after jackpots to the high rollers at the dice table—betrayed that complete obliviousness of all other humans and wore that look of mingled cupidity and resignation I had seen on scores of dry-fly pools.

My own case may very well be worse than the average. I not only bear the scars of a thousand old frustrations and anticipate a thousand more but must admit, after a score of years flailing away at streams, that intolerance and prejudice have encroached on my mind as mildew does on last year's cantaloupe. I would rather catch an eight-inch trout than an eight-pound bass. I am incapable, in fact, of understanding why one wants to fish for bass in the first place—or for perch, or for muskellunge, or for pike. Ted Williams seems, at least from afar, to be an absolutely splendid fellow. What impels him to pursue the tarpon—a piscatorial slob with a cheap suit of theatrical armor and a mouth like a vacuum cleaner? Trout, *si*! , Salmon, *si*! you can make fishmeal of the rest for all of me.

I am against roads. I am against detergents. I am against insecticides. I am against logging. I am against flood control. I am not against golf, since I cannot but suspect it keeps armies of the unworthy from discovering trout, but I pity them for playing it when they could be putting a fly on the water.

I have been brought to this condition not only by the beautiful, the disconcerting, the succulent trout, but by the Catskill stream in which I have wooed it—come heat, cold, high water, low water, mud, bulldozers, the New York City Board of Water Supply and locals bent on dumping used tires and old tin cans—for lo these two decades. Esopus Creek is a famous Catskill trout stream; not so famous as its sisters, the Beaverkill and the Neversink, but famous enough, thanks in good part to the fact that fishing writers, like many other kinds of writers, tend to live in New York and to find life there far more significant than life in Colorado, Minnesota or Oregon.

The Esopus rises as a trickle of cold, clear water on the shady slopes of Slide Mountain, the Catskills' highest (4,204 feet) elevation, and ends up, after enduring many lesser indignities, in the faucets, sinks and fire hydrants of the Bronx, Manhattan, Brooklyn, Staten Island and Queens. My addiction to it, nurtured perhaps by some inner masochism, stems from this contrast between promise and fulfillment.

It is a lovely little river. It runs north, then east, then southeast in a twenty-five-mile circle around a cluster of green, ledge-scarred little mountains—Panther, Wittenberg, Terrace, Garfield, Romer, Cross, Pleasant and Cornell—before its broadening valley angles off, still into the east, to blend after another twenty-five miles with the great valley of the Hudson. Its fall is gradual and it presents, mile after mile, that orderly succession of gentle riffles, noisy, boulder-strewn rapids and long, slow pools in which both trout and fisherman are most likely to prosper. It gathers size and authority from two main tributaries as well as dozens of little hollows, cloves and kills; and these brooks—Woodland Valley Creek and Stony Clove Creek—are pleasant trout streams in their own.

The Esopus is an old American landmark. Henry Hudson paused just off the gates of its valley—as he sailed up the Hudson River—in 1609, and there were Dutch and eventually British settlements there from 1614 onward despite bloody raids by the Sopus, a collection of river Indians from whom it got its name. The centuries have left their imprint. State Highway 28 parallels it along the route of an ancient wilderness path and the roadside is littered, between stretches of farmland, with houses, motels, gas stations, stores and little summer resorts. Hamlets with dusty memories—Phoenicia, Boiceville, Shandaken, Allaben, Big Indian—toe up to the highway for the motorist's dollar. But the towns are quiet, comfortably weatherworn and resigned. The summer boarding houses doze amid weedy lawns. Tree-edged meadows often intrude between road and wandering river. The soft mountains, which rise abruptly and overlook all, are clothed in unbroken wilderness.

One can drive from New York City to Phoenicia in just two and a half hours, but deer drink in the mist-hung stream at dawn and the fisherman can wade all through a weekday morning in midsummer and never see another soul. At humid dusk, with the last shine of light on the water, he can fancy that he and the angler silhouetted just upstream are alone on the continent. The Esopus nevertheless can drive him out of his mind. It is victimized so steadily by both man and nature that its wounds, illnesses and distortions of personality, its slow recoveries and its sudden relapses gradually become the major preoccupation of his existence; and he finds himself—even on those rare occasions when the creek is clear, its temperature normal and its water level perfect—cringing in sure anticipation of horrors to come.

The Esopus is tortured by weather. The unprecedented series of hurricanes which belabored the last Coast between 1938 and 1955 almost wrecked its whole system. Tropical deluges accompanied these great storms and roaring, mud-colored floods rolled great boulders down the streambeds, toppled trees, ate out of banks, scoured away insect life and killed thousands and thousands of trout. The scars are still evident along all the creeks. Winter clogs them annually with ice; the snow melt of early spring makes them frigid torrents, and the still of July and August leaves them appallingly low and warm.

Man, meanwhile, labors cheerfully to further the damage. Trout streams are treated with reverence in England and men devote their lives to the art of managing them. But in the U.S. streams are fair game for any lunatic with a bulldozer. Roads are more important. So is a fallacious theory of flood control by which wandering, rock-blocked sections of brooks and rivers—the very sort of water that trout need for their survival—are straightened and flattened into sluices which speed up flow and cause worse damage farther on.

The fisherman can do little in response but fulminate. The creek's torturers are all men of goodwill and are equipped, each and every one, with valid and logical reasons for the depredations—just as were the early tanners who razed the valley's original hemlock forests in the half century after the War of 1812. Only the bark of these great trees was used; the bare hills were left littered, as by endless acres of great bones, with their rotting trunks. New forests of beech, maple, oak and other leafy trees have mercifully replaced them in the last century, but the beds of the streams are given scant chance to recover from the steam shovels and bulldozers of road builders and flood control engineers.

But if the Esopus is endlessly put upon and lamentably accident prone, it has one even more exasperating quality. It is loaded with trout and, though it often makes the fisherman's life a living hell and often seems on the verge of disintegration, he simply cannot—or at any rate *I* simply cannot—walk away and leave it to its own fiendish devices.

The New York City Board of Water Supply dammed its lower valley in 1912 and formed the Ashokan Reservoir, a wide twelve-mile lake into which the stream now empties. In so doing, it inadvertently provided Esopus trout with their own little ocean: a deep, feed-rich haven from which huge rainbows and browns launch themselves, the first in the spring and the latter in the fall, on salmonlike spawning runs to the farthest kills and hollows and to which they return, their genetic duties accomplished, to shelter during the rest of the year. Despite its difficulties, thus, the river stocks itself naturally with wild trout and these progenitors of the big brood fish valiantly defy man's best efforts to eradicate them.

They are benefited, in the process, by the Shandaken Tunnel, an eighteen-mile aqueduct which runs north beneath the hills to tap another Catskill reservoir and which feeds extra water into the Esopus and thence, eventually, into New York's hydrants and dishwashers. This enormous conduit, known locally as the "portal," makes the river unique.

In drought season, when every other Catskill stream—including the upper Esopus and its tributaries—is dreadfully low and warm, the lower river is kept high and cool by the flow from the tunnel mouth. It is kept so high for long periods that, in fact, it can hardly be fished at all; the water department, naturally, is more interested in shooting 500 million gallons a day toward the Bronx than in an angler stranded at streamside by raging rapids. The portal water does ease off in August, it is true, often bringing the fisherman negotiable riffles and slow, gliding pool surfaces. But it brings in late-season silt as well, so that the tantalizing stretches of water, rendered more turbid day by day, are usually the color of bad coffee by the end of the month.

In moments of understandable despond I sometimes think desperately of other trout water—crystalline, virginal, shadowed—and particularly of a little lake hidden high on the northwest's Mount Rainier which I once found by dint of secret directions an old friend cunningly extracted from a knowledgeable ranger. I was the fourth human to fish it. It was rimmed by fir, reflected the great, white dome of the peak like a mirror and, more delightful yet, attracted swarms of flies and bugs from a green marsh which bordered one area of its shoreline. The dry-fly fisherman wants his trout near the surface and I could not see but, in the absolute stillness, could hear the fish splashing away at their insect banquet. They were lovely creatures—a species of cutthroat known as Montana black-spotted trout—with scarlet fins and bellies tinted softly with old rose. But they were also, alas, without discrimination; they took any fly I offered.

There was no trail to the lake. I scared myself half to death working up through vertical cliffs to find it and suffered more grievous fright on the way down; for I was privileged, during the latter process, to look past my shoes at treetops two thousand feet below. But the fishing in itself was simply too easy and, even in memory, does not compete with the Esopus—which not only justifies greed and other less admirable human qualities by its own displays of temper, but makes any minor victory a Roman triumph and provides a steady atmosphere of awful suspense. I could easily drive to the Schoharie, the Beaverkill or the upper Delaware from the rambling and rickety summer house I inhabit in Woodland Valley, but in the last two decades, no matter how disappointing the local fishing, I have never gambled a day on trying them. I have invested so many hours of frustration in the Esopus and its tributaries that the prospect of losing even one unlikely dividend because of absence is more than I can quite bring myself to contemplate.

Water constitutes only one part of the puzzle a fisherman is eternally trying to solve. The other part, of course, is the fish he is trying to extract from it. A trout is not, to put it mildly, gifted with intellect; one would be impelled to say, after the most cursory inspection of his mental apparatus, that he is downright stupid. A great many non-addicts, as a result, find the angler a hilarious spectacle. There he stands, draped in more equipment than a telephone lineman, trying to outwit an organism with a brain no bigger than a breadcrumb, and getting licked in the process. But the fisherman is engaged—or he should be—in a far more complex sort of reasoning. He is trying to understand the trout's environment and to predict the trout's response to it. The trout, if stupid, has his own low cunning—or is equipped, at any rate, with a subtle set of instincts—and he responds to what is happening around him with amazing accuracy. In thus interacting with the stream in which he lives, he creates the illusion of enormous wisdom and instills a sense of gloom and mental inadequacy in his pursuer.

He is both wary and greedy, and the pull of these two aspects of his nature makes him subject to starling alteration of behavior. When the water is full of feed, as during a big hatch of mayflies, nature seems to bet that the benefits of a full stomach far outweigh any danger which may be encountered in achieving it, and the trout will roll and splash recklessly within a yard of a fisherman's waders.

But when he is feeding heavily, he also becomes fantastically selective. He will stuff himself on insects, sometimes so small that they can barely be seen with the naked eye, until he bulges like an Indiana hog, and he will go right on choking them down as long as the supply holds out. Since nature does not want him to waste energy capriciously, however, he will ignore the biggest and most delicious bugs and flies of other species while he is concentrating on the predominant insect of the moment. He will ignore even the tidbits on which he is feeding, if they do not wash almost directly into his mouth, and will hardly move an inch, right or left, while doing so.

When such a big drift of feed ceases, however—and it is a phenomenon which can tail off in a matter of seconds—the trout's *modus operandi* changes completely. As far as the fisherman is concerned he simply seems to vanish, since his natural sense of alarm reasserts itself and he either takes cover behind rocks or in the depths of pools or beneath the distorted light of riffles, or flashes away to such shelter at the first tiny change in the pattern of light or shadow on the water above him. Having retreated, however, he drops his fastidious airs and gulps anything edible which comes his way.

Each of these manifestations of the trout's personality confronts the angler with dilemma. But each presents him, simultaneously, with glorious opportunity. When a trout is feeding selectively, he will refuse any artificial fly which does not duplicate the size, the color and, in an impressionistic sense, the shape of the type upon which he is dining. Give him that, though, and he will grab it with suicidal joy—and so, on the next cast, will the trout who was feeding only a few feet from him. All sorts of little things will disturb him when he is skulking behind a rock; but if he is convinced that he is not being gulled, he will often sip in any old fly the angler puts over him. The practice of fly fishing is based on these twin revelations, and the hopes, the dreams and built-in despondency of the fly fisherman revolve around them.

There are hundred of fly patterns, large and small—dry flies, which float on top of the water, and wet flies and imitations of nymphs, which are induced to wash along under the surface. If a fisherman were able to choose just the right imitation and present it at the right place at the right moment in the right way, he could hook a trout on every cast. He cannot do it. He could not do it with the aid of a computer. But once in a while he can feel himself on the verge of it. If he labors to understand the entomology of streams, keeps notes, memorizes miles of water, always casts with care, fishes continuously and is lucky, he will enjoy occasional brief but dazzling moments of absolute triumph—moments in which he can believe he is the reincarnation of Attila the Hun and the possessor of a mind as penetrating as that of Sherlock Holmes himself. If he enjoys this sort of self-image—and, personally, I find the role of Attila rather attractive—he will be addicted to the fly forever.

He prays for a big hatch of aquatic insects. In the Northeast this usually means a hatch of mayfly, a little creature obviously invented for the fisherman's special benefit. The mayfly spends most of his life as a nymph—an ugly little underwater bug which lives, depending variously on his type, on almost every variety of river bottom. During this phase he does his poor best to keep the trout from eating him. He is finally moved, however, to splendid self-sacrifice. He rises to the surface and changes, in a few seconds, into a dun—a delicate and beautiful little fly with four upright wings, two or three tiny tails and a slender body. The dun bobs on the current like a little sailboat, flutters and, if he is still undevoured, flies slowly upward and away.

In so doing, the mayfly performs several wonderfully unselfish functions. There is no point in fishing a dry fly—or a wet fly either—if no trout can see it; when fish are feeding on the bottom, an angler can beat the water into a froth without attracting their attention. As the nymphs rise, however, the trout rise with them, eating them en route like peanuts. At the surface the fish begin sucking in the floating duns—and are thus positioned to suck in a dry fly which imitates them.

The mayfly is kind enough to engage in these rites on a schedule the fisherman can often anticipate. *Epeorus pleuralis* (often known as Iron Fraudator), the blue-gray mayfly which is first of the species to appear in the spring, may be expected on the water at one o'clock, E.S.T., during the last week in April and the first days of May. The fisherman who is equipped with a dry Quill Gordon, size 12 or 14, can expect to slay trout with ease and precision for fully forty-five minutes.

The Esopus watershed is inhospitable in late April; the hills are rust brown under bare trees, wet snow falls with the rain, and the streams are often too high, too cold or discolored. I find it beautiful. A fly fisherman should think of insects rather than fish, for it is they—since the trout merely respond to their presence—which are the real key to a full creel. The knowledge that Iron Fraudator is absolutely bound to hatch during the week, and at an hour which allows a long, leisurely breakfast, is as bracing as possession of a chart indicating buried treasure.

But the season's exasperations begin in April too. Early mayflies are enormously obliging, but they do not appear simultaneously on the whole river and the fisherman can slop along from pool to pool, maddened by the certainty that duns are appearing somewhere along the stream, and yet never find them—or rising trout—at all. Subspecies of the wonderful insect appear, one after another, through May, June and early July, changing in color from iron blue—through subtle shades and blendings of gray, olive and brown—to creamy yellow forms. Famous old dry fly patterns imitate all the important types; the Hendrickson, the Red Quill, the Grey Fox, the March Brown, the Light Cahill were all invented to match specific mayflies and to take fish when they are hatching. But as the season progresses, the fisherman often finds several different sorts on the water at the same time and can be moved to borderline neurosis while attempting to discover which one predominant insect the trout are actually rating at the moment he casts a fly over them.

There are works of practical entomology (*Matching the Hatch* by Ernest G. Schwiebert, Jr., *Streamside Guide to Naturals and Their Imitations* by Arthur B. Flick) which provide him with thorough background; but he is often balked, nevertheless, as he stands in midstream glaring wildly around him, for clues as to what is going on in the water. Some forms of mayfly—and the artificial flies which imitate them—are remarkably alike. The Hendrickson and Red Quill, in fact, are exactly the same save for the winding on the shank of the hook. But the trout will take one and refuse the other. They not only refuse the fly, they insult the fisherman. A trout will rise within a quarter inch of a fly which is too big or admits light improperly or is slightly off shade and will contemptuously splash water on it. He will jump clear of the surface and land on the other side of it. There are times when he seems to spit on it. But he will not touch it. And he will refuse a fly which matches the emerging duns in every respect if he has decided, for reasons known only to himself, to keep feeding just below the surface on the supply of rising nymphs.

Nature, it must be admitted, has provided the baffled angler with certain helpful signs and portents. A trout usually rises gently if he is feeding on the surface, but tends to splash and roll if he is feeding on nymphs or spent insects floating just beneath it. There are experts who maintain they can identify sixteen different kinds of rises (amongst them the sip, the slash, the double-whorl, the suck, the pyramid, the bulge and hump, and the spotted ring) and instantly announce just how the fish is feeding by noting the way he disturbs the water. But if a man can see dozens of rising trout and cannot make them pay the slightest heed to his artful casting, he has a tendency to quit thinking. Usually he takes refuge in trial and error and begins changing flies at random—a process which involves juggling his rod, a knife, a fly box and a bottle of dope in which he dunks each successive lure to make it float, and doing it all while up to his hips in a turbulent creek.

If he enters into this rigmarole at dusk, he must eventually ask himself an awful question: if he cuts the fly off the end of his leader, will there be light enough to allow his replacing it with another pattern? He can see dim, aluminum-colored flashes where fish are rising in the dark pool. He takes the course of courage and boldness. He cuts. He instantly regrets it. Swarms of no-seeums sift down and bite him like clouds of red-hot pepper. He cannot swat. He is standing motionless, holding a No. 16 Light Cahill toward the dim sky with one hand and trying to poke the invisible end of his synthetic gut leader through its invisible eye with the other. He grunts and sweats. He may even make small moaning sounds. But eventually he admits the cruel truth. He is disarmed. He turns, disconsolately, to wade ashore. At this moment he is subject to a final indignity and, if he is truly unlucky, he will be claimed by it. He slips in the darkness, lurches wildly, tumbles arse over tea kettle. The vehemence, the utter foulness of the profanity which can be induced by this common, even comic little accident is shocking, and the witness who laughs does so at his peril.

But the angler needs more than a knowledge of entomology—although this is a first requirement—to attack trout successfully on streams as cranky as those of the Catskills. He must do more than cast well, too. The fly must be presented correctly, but casting is simply a means to an end and is a far simpler process than is generally believed. After a few months of practice, any fool ought to be able to put a fly within a couple of inches of his target; he should be able to avoid getting hung up in trees and have mastered the trick of dropping loose line on the water to compensate for the drag of current. This is not to say there are no difficult casts. If an angler sees a big fish rising under an overhanging branch and has to reach out to the limit of his rod's power to deliver his fly, there is a very good chance he will manage any number of embarrassing mistakes. But on most water the long, difficult cast is seldom necessary. It is my opinion that motivation is more important than technique and that the successful fisherman catches trout when others do not because he possesses sneaky and atavistic instincts which heighten his perception and his ability to concentrate, and make him respond to all sorts of unkind little signals from his subconscious mind.

Something of this sort occurs in my own case, I believe, out of simple hunger. A great many fishermen are uninterested, or at least profess to be uninterested, in small trout. But in most streams—and certainly in the Esopus, save for the pre-season and postseason spawning runs—there are very few fish of any other kind.

I am an eight-inch trout fisherman. I must admit I enjoy being an eight-inch trout fisherman. I sometimes keep seven-inch trout. A nine- or ten-inch trout looks like an absolute leviathan to me. I admire their beauty. I like the bulge a collection of them makes in my wet canvas creel. I am grateful to them for the fact that they are as selective, if not always as wary, as big trout and that the intellectual problems and gratification involved in luring them at the fly has little to do with their size or weight. But essentially, I like the way they taste and, when I wade into the stream, I am after something special to eat.

This does not mean that I am insensitive to the social delights of landing a big fish. A few big brown trout do skulk in deep holes or beneath boulder-studded white water during the summer and a few more seem to begin their autumnal spawning run as early as August. These monsters—anything longer than sixteen inches or heavier than two pounds is a monster in the Esopus—may rise to the surface for a few minutes during really big spring fly hatches, but mostly they stay deep and invisible, think dour thoughts and eat such minnows and small trout as incautiously invade their lairs. The chances of hooking one of them on a fly are remote in the extreme despite the experts and their interminable creeds about casting. But if the angler wants to be considered absolutely compleat and even perhaps occult—and a fly fisherman would not be a fly fisherman if he did not welcome such rumors—he simply has to produce a monster at least once.

Between May and September real, live, exciting news in Phoenicia concerns only one topic: trout. John McGrath and Joe Holzer who preside over its two grocery stores are fishermen. The Folkerts brothers, Herman and Dick, who run its social center—a combined tackle and golf shop, soda fountain, newspaper stand, bus stop and sporting goods store—are consummate anglers. So is Fred Muehleck, whose racks of ancient Payne, Leonard and Hardy rods are wondrous to behold. So also is Phil Halzell, his Woodland Valley neighbor and stream-side companion of thirty years' standing. Half the inhabitants, in fact, are fishermen and the other half cannot avoid listening to them. Let someone—anyone—catch a monster by whatever means (a construction stiff once lifted a big brown out of Woodland Valley Creek with a clamshell power shovel) and the news flashes up and down the valley roads with the speed of light.

Three summers ago, after going year on year without even seeing a monster, I caught two of them in one three-week period—a two-pounder of 17 inches and a three-pounder which measured 20½ inches. I am willing to admit that I took each of them into town, lugged them through the crowd of people waiting for the Pine Hill-Kingston line bus and thence into Folkerts' tackle shop to be measured, weighed and admired by hangers-on from the soda fountain. While nobody has since spoken of me as a veritable artist with a fly rod, I have reason to believe that I am no longer considered a mere dilettante from New York. I have, in fact, heard several generous remarks about my prey, and one man, whom I did not discourage, seemed to be under the impression that I was able to track down monsters at will.

Honesty compels me to say that I hooked both of them by accident. In each case, a stray current sucked my over fly down deep beside a sunken boulder and presented it to the fish, whose presence I did not remotely suspect, in a completely natural way—an effect no one could have achieved otherwise in a month of trying. Both leviathans, I am sorry to relate, acted like Bowery drunks after I put the iron to them. A three-pound trout, of course, will put a splendid arc in a four-ounce rod, but neither of my fish seemed to have any concept of the thrilling fight which was expected of them. The bigger one ran out of steam after half stranding himself in a shallow riffle while I was trying to lead him into a quiet pool for the big battle. I simply fell on him, wrestled him two out of three falls and carried him ashore. And though both were wrapped in cheesecloth and lovingly poached in a court bouillon, neither of them, alas, tasted very good.

Smaller trout—if they are fat, wild and freshly caught—are something else again. The prospect makes my entire endocrinological system thump, palpitate and clank like a houseful of old-fashioned steam radiators on the first day of winter. It has been my privilege to sample the haute cuisine of Paris, New York, San Francisco and New Orleans, but neither Maxim's nor Le Pavillon have offered me anything to match the tender and delicate taste of these lovely fish, They should, to my mind, be rolled in corn meal, sizzled for four or five minutes in bacon fat (better, for reasons I do not understand, than butter) and served with a fresh green vegetable or salad, a baked potato, or macaroni with a bland cheese sauce. The exterior of the trout, properly done, is crisp and gold; the interior, white, moist and of a flavor, subtle but poignant, as to pierce the very soul. If the air of the dining room is faintly perfumed by fireplace wood smoke, the hilt will taste better: and if one drinks a clear, icy martini while they are cooking and a half bottle of well-chilled Moselle while they are being consumed, he will find himself, when all are gone, sitting mindlessly, happily motionless while his inner being relives and resavors the sensations which have been visited upon it and congratulates itself upon a turn of fortune too splendid to be quite believed.

My memories of such orgies and my unbridled appetite for more of them have a great deal to do, I am convinced, with what successes I may manage in my contest with the Esopus. There are days when some curious perceptiveness—simulated, I can only assume, by messages from my digestive tract—allows me to strike at the split second a trout takes my sunken, drifting nymph, although I can neither see nor feel the fish before it is magically hooked. I am incapable of remembering telephone numbers or even, at times, the names of people I have known for years, but I can visualize miles of stream in infinite detail. The Esopus has its obvious and easily remembered water: the Greeny Deep, Twin Rooks, the Spanish Farm, the Pool-in-Front-of-Bill-McGrath's-House and a succession of noisy cascades known, simply, as Down at Elmer's Diner. But I know hundreds of minor riffles, rock-divided eddies and patches of slack water; I know how they change at various river levels; I remember how fish behave in them and I remember when shadow, if any, falls on them, morning and evening.

The Catskill fisherman needs such information just as the prospector needs an understanding of rock formations—not that the knowledge is likely to produce riches in either case, but because it keeps hope alive. He needs a very good, very expensive fly rod for the same reason, even though in nine hundred ninety-nine out of a thousand situations one can fish just as well with a cheap glass rod.

A fine rod is made of a particularly hard and resilient cane from North Vietnam's Tonkin region. Its delicate sections are machined to tolerances of a thousandth of an inch to produce a specific and particular bending mode or "action." It is simple, exquisitely balanced and beautiful to see—at once an efficient tool and a work of art. The very process of removing a good rod (in my case an eight-foot Orvis) from its aluminum case, of jointing it up and carefully attaching an English reel (no others click so satisfyingly when spun) does something to the spirits comparable, I imagine, to climbing into the cockpit of a Spad or polishing up a set of safecracker's drills. When the fisherman's hand closes on its smooth, cork grip he is armed as Arthur with Excalibur and anticipates triumph almost automatically as he wades into a stream.

Once in a while, furthermore, even on streams as exasperating as the Esopus or its feeders, he will win an enormous victory. I cannot help but feel that my own performance during the hurricane of 1955 was absolutely brilliant. On considering it in retrospect, in fact, I am able to discover in myself qualities so admirable that I would be inclined to discount them were it not for the penetrating, even pitiless, honesty with which I have reviewed the episode. I will go so far as to say that I rose as a phoenix from the ashes of defeat and that I hoped and was rewarded while all others were cast down by despair.

The hurricane and its accompanying deluge made a horrible mess of our Catskill streams; they poured down their valleys under opaque curtains of rain in roaring, muddy floods. It made a mess of my house, too. The roof leaked, and when I put pans under the drips, I was impelled to endure something very like a xylophone concert. Forced into the open by this ungodly racket, I took my rod, drove five miles to the end of the Woodland Valley road and began walking upstream under the trees. I was as wet, in five minutes, as if I had fallen into a swimming pool; but I pressed sternly on and, after two miles, came upon the splendid and gleaming phenomenon I had hoped but not actually expected to find.

Under normal conditions Woodland Valley Creek betrays itself at this high point of its valley only in little skeins and trickles of water among shadowed, mossy rocks. But now it was ten feet wide and, since there were no clay banks to discolor the water, it ran clear as crystal. The native brook trout of the Northeast had been extinct in ninety-five per cent of the Esopus system for a long time— very probably since the tanners cut the hemlocks more than a century ago. But brookies, which had somehow endured year after year in the shadowed trickles of water here, were feeding voraciously in the swollen creek. They were absolutely beautiful fish with a sheen of electric blue, white piped fins, mottled backs and crimson spotted sides. I hooked them for two hours, released all but five of the handsomest, since even a hungry man could hardly deny they had earned the right to freedom, and splashed back down through the rain feeling as though I had discovered the Mother Lode.

Despite such bagman's satisfactions, however, I must confess that my pursuit of artistry, restraint and purity of purpose has progressed very slowly, if at all. But I strive. I have a model: an erect, wispy and grave old gentleman whom I encountered at midday on the Esopus above the portal five years ago and have admired, wistfully, ever since.

The sun was bright. The stream was low and clear. It was not a time to fish at all, for any movement sent trout flashing to cover in the still, brilliantly lighted pools and I was carrying a rod only as insurance against some unlikely opportunity. As I strolled along inspecting a stretch of water I had not seen for a long time, I became conscious of the old gentleman only when I saw him bend, perhaps seventy yards below me, and then straighten, net in hand. But in that instant, even at that distance, I saw that the net contained the dark, curved form of a very big trout—a monster, or, at the very least, a monster junior grade.

When he came slowly upstream, minutes later, I began to understand what a feat he had managed under those absolutely impossible conditions. He did not show me the fish or even allude to it. He had wrapped it in newspaper and had contrived to get most of the resulting package into his creel. If I had not had that glimpse of it in his net, I might not have known he had a fish at all.

He must have been eighty; I doubt if he weighed much more than a hundred pounds and he walked slowly and with care. But I could only assume that he had come to the river with his sheets of old newspaper because he expected to stalk that one particular fish and that he had fully expected to land it. He nodded at me, glanced at my rod and, after reaching into a pocket, produced a roll of leader so fine that it was almost invisible. It must have tested less than a pound. He snapped off two feet of it simply by breaking the fragile stuff between his fingers. "Use this as a tip," he directed. Then he pulled out a plastic box, removed a tiny, curiously bedraggled black fly and handed it to me as well. "Try this," he said. "I tie them during the winter."

This was the fly and this was the weight of leader with which, quite obviously, he had subdued his thick, heavy trout. He had been forced, on such water, to take a long, long, almost impossible cast to avoid frightening his quarry. In teasing up such a fish, indeed, he had very probably had to drop the fly again and again, and each time as lightly as thistledown. And having hooked the monster, he had played it coldly and delicately at the end of that gossamer tip, knowing one slightest false move would lose him the game.

He fixed me with a stern eye until I had tied on his contributions and then, apparently satisfied that he had prepared me, too, for higher things, nodded and turned away toward the road. I knew better—that he had only prepared me for a few fruitless casts on such a day. But I got down on my hands and knees, for all this, to approach a pool formed by the confluence of a little side stream called the West Kill and then, sitting up slowly to avoid alarming its inhabitants, I looked carefully for evidence of opportunity.

The pool was deep, blue and still, but there were gnats dancing over the faint currents at its head and I felt that I saw an occasional tiny disturbance on its surface. I lighted a cigarette, and then made a long cast and promised myself that I would let my fly lie on the quiet water until I had finished smoking. But impatience and lack of faith were soon my undoing. I yanked the line off the water in dissatisfaction after three puffs and cast a foot to the right of its first position. As the line was still in the air, the biggest brown trout I have ever seen broke water like a runaway torpedo and fell back with a shattering splash. "Good Lord!" I cited in astonishment and cupidity—I talk to myself considerably when fishing—and, moved to mindless activity, made still another frantic cast. And this time I saw that my little fly was gone and realized what I had done. The big fish had sucked it in at the split second I had retrieved my line and I had broken off the hairlike leader without the slightest sense of having done so. The monster had jumped because my hook was imbedded in its lip. Had I concentrated, had I waited one second longer . . .

Ah, well. I will, given a bit of luck, be eighty years old myself one day and I like to think a certain improvement in both skill and moral tone will have become evident at that point and that the Esopus—or what is left of it—will yield to the superior man. And, if one matures late, one can always look forward to ninety.

# PART V

# SOME ADVENTURES ON WATER

# THE MIRAMACHI IT AIN'T, SO ALL RIGHT, IT'S 116TH ST.

## JOHN BRYAN

The stretch of the Hudson River that flows past New York City is polluted. Its fish are contaminated with poly-chlorinated biphenyls (PCBs) and its banks are littered with filth. Its few human visitors do not frequent the Miramichi, nor are they familiar with the Gaspé. But the Hudson is a five-minute walk from my apartment on 112th Street in Manhattan, and I have learned to throw flies into its thickness.

On an evening I usually take a dozen or so stripers and snappers or baby bluefish, but occasionally the river whisks me beyond that, directly to Valhalla. As it did one Saturday in late September.

With only three hours before dark, I braved the traffic of the West Side Highway, strung my rod and began to make preliminary casts into the river. My 116th Street beat is a rocky stretch of bank that extends two blocks to a concrete sewer outlet on the left and eight blocks to the right to the bay south of 125th Street. The bank is strewn with man-size rocks, placed there as both highway support and river curb, and the water drops gradually to 30 feet, where stripers and bait-fish cruise. At low tide, the slimy rocks are laden with assorted debris.

I have the 116th Street beat memorized. The boulder with the blue paint. The flat sitting rock where I rest occasionally. The hole with the cable growing from it. The concrete sewage outlet below, and the three sewage pipes above. The tiny "driftwood beach" that I sometimes comb. And the standing rocks that I jump to and from.

I have some of the river's hazards conquered (I hate to say "licked"). Back-casting between traffic. Double-hauling past flotsam. Cleaning my line on every 10th cast.

And I know the river's rhythms. High tide at my beat is 2½ hours later than at the Battery. Change of current takes three hours. Sewage flows often—but not always. Dusk and dawn are the best times, regardless of the tides—unless dead low is combined with a full sewage flow. Then I wouldn't even stick a poacher's line in the river.

That September evening my first casts were downstream, parallel-to-the-bank 50-footers. I was darting a bright weighted streamer—a No. 2 hook with a lot of lead, tinsel and white hair—on a 12-foot leader with a four-pound tip on a sinking line. I retrieved the fly along the rocks as fast as I could yank it.

After five minutes of no fish, I opened my duffel and inflated my raft. Eight minutes of foot-pumping was all it took. A $20 Macy's job, it was similar to the one I used during my school years in North Carolina for floating streams and farm ponds. This one, though, was for the Hudson, for the out-of-casting-distance schools of snappers and stripers that are common to the river. No oars, just a sculling paddle, but with it you can go faster than with oars if you paddle right.

The vinyl raft was large and firm, each of its three compartments perme-ated with the smell of the Hudson. I was now ready for a quick takeoff if far-off stripers were sighted. Until then I would fish the shoreline boulders.

The river was in good condition. The incoming tide, still an hour from high, was clean and relatively free of debris. I say relatively because there is always garbage floating along the banks of the Hudson in Manhattan. Some days it is so bad that it's impossible to retrieve an ungarnished fly. When the tide is dead low and the sewage outlets are active, the water is filled with floating and half-floating objects of every description. The visibility is down to zero and the smell is not pleasant. But that day no sewage was issuing from the outlets and the flotsam was minimal.

On my first upstream cast I got an immediate strike, and I was into a small bass. A 12-incher, silvery with purple-black stripes. I released it and proceeded to catch five more, all small, all in front of the same upriver boulder.

Small stripers are everywhere along the Hudson rocks in the summer (they begin to leave as cold weather arrives). It's easiest to find them with a spinning rod. Just cast along the rocks before and after high tide, retrieving with the current.

Busily releasing small stripers, I scarcely noticed the arrival of the two visitors. When I turned and saw them, they were sitting in my raft in the grass, clutching matching pints of no-name moonshine.

"How ya doin'?" I delicately inquired. "You gonna float around in this thing?" one of them asked.

"Yeah, do this thing hold you up?" said the other.

"Well, for one person it's all right, if you're careful. It can tip over, though, if you don't know what you're doing." I was lying.

"I think we'll take a ride in it," one of them said. "Where's your other oar?"

Tricky situations weren't uncommon on my Upper West Side beat, but this was the first time my raft had been in jeopardy. Both men were bigger than I am, and although they were obviously more than a little drunk, I knew I couldn't stop them if they wanted to take a ride on the raft.

"I'll tell you, right now's not really the best time for a float on the river," I said. "See that log? See how fast it's moving? The currents are really dangerous now. In about an hour the tide will slow down and I'd be glad for you to borrow the raft then. My name's John, and I come down here to fish the river a lot. I've never seen you guys though. What are your names?"

"John, you're my main man. I'm Thomas, and this is my main man Maxwell. You be here in an hour?" I nodded. "Then we'll see you later. We'll float that damn thing all over this damn river."

Thomas and Maxwell wandered off through the screeching traffic. I had lied again. I had no intention of being there when they returned. In a few seconds I was floating upstream with the incoming Hudson tide.

Sculling strongly, I was quickly out toward midriver. I laid down the paddle and cast the streamer toward the edge of one of the many Hudson currents. The river is often like that, like a hundred streams all flowing side by side at different speeds. While rafting, I can adjust my relative speed by entering the various subcurrents, and it is at the junctures of these currents where the fish most often feed. On a calm day you can see snappers working 50 patches across the river. Larger disturbances mean stripers, or sometimes even shad. Once I caught several large shad on my Hudson streamers.

Out away from its shoreline the river is pleasant. With some imagination you can even sense its origins. The Hudson begins 300 miles to the north in the Adirondacks near Mt. Marcy in a fishless two-acre lake called Tear of the Clouds. Spilling gently down, it gradually becomes the wild and rapid upper Hudson, home of native brookies and implanted browns and rainbows that feed on Adirondack mayflies. Stifled at the base of the mountains, the river becomes sluggish, held in check by locks and dams. The trout become carp, and the mayflies houseflies. Pristine tributaries become paper-mill runoffs. Near Troy the sewage takes over. And below the Troy Dam the river first tastes salt and begins to take on the character it has on my beat. The tides extend 154 miles up to Troy and back down past Albany, Kingston, Poughkeepsie, West Point, Croton, Haverstraw Bay, Spuyten Duyvil, the George Washington Bridge, 116th Street. The carp become stripers, the stripers that I was looking for.

Once a school of stripers is located, it pays to move gradually with the current. The baitfish are drifting, and the stripers follow. When I'm bank-fishing and have found a school, I walk slowly along the rocks as I catch and release fish, finally arriving either at the big concrete sewer outlet downriver or the steep gravel bank upriver. Then I return to my starting point to pick up another school.

I sculled the raft, hoping to find a current that would let me drift with some fish. Nearby the surface erupted with six frenzied splashes. Then a smaller splash—my streamer. One strip and a fish was on, pulling hard, taking line, as the raft swung around. The fish was a good one, larger than the 12-inchers I had caught earlier, but not so large that I couldn't slow its runs. Back and forth, the raft rotated with the fish's lunges, zigzagging with the river's flow. I retrieved line gradually, enjoying the bent rod and the tight line. The fish came to the surface 30 feet away and shook its head; a striper. Again it surfaced, and then plunged toward the bottom. But the fish tired, and I soon put my thumb into the jaw of my best Hudson striper. My scale said 3½.

I debated for an instant whether I should keep the bass, for photographs or something. (Hudson River fish shouldn't be eaten because of the high levels of PCBs.) Or to show Steve, my Sheepshead Bay friend who scorns the Hudson, who won't fish my 116th Street retreat with me. But I decided not to bother, and I put the hefty fish back into the river.

Two false casts and the fly was out again. I stripped and felt a tug. Another pleasing battle and another weighed striper. Longer than the first, but thinner and not as heavy.

The next 24 casts produced stripers. I counted. My record had been 39 straight on a rainy Friday in 1975, but they had been 15- and 16-inchers. These were all at the magic three-pound mark. And they were tiring me. An hour and a half of bent graphite had begun to fatigue my forearm. Striper after striper. Schooling 40 feet away from me, moving together with the tide. I wished I had tagging equipment. Each year I resolve that I will tag my next year's fish, but I still hadn't gotten around to it. Beautiful 20-inch fish. But no whoppers. Tugs and pleasure-boaters passing, waving as I landed and released my catch.

More splashing and I flexed the rod for a cast while simultaneously seeing a dozen teenagers on the rocks, each heaving stones in my direction and shouting words I could not understand but which did not sound like pleasantries. My sculling paddle got me out of range without injury, but the stripers were soon behind me, and the record 39 was no longer endangered.

The tide had begun to change and I floated almost motionless amidst the back eddies of the reversing Hudson. Prime time for big stripers. When the high tide comes and lingers for 30 minutes and then begins its retreat, bottom dwellers and baitfish are aroused, and hungry cows supposedly feed.

Small snapper schools pitty-patted gently across the river, but I was looking for splashes, not dimples. I searched the eddies with the streamer, but the next few minutes produced nothing. The teenagers soon tired of their sport, and I moved back to fish near the shoreline. My "main men" weren't there, and I moved north of the 116th Street launching area. I wearily rolled short casts into the rocks as sunset approached, but the fish were apparently somewhere else, and the brief strips produced a half-hour void.

The sun finally dropped into the Jersey bluffs, and I beached the raft near the concrete sewer outlet. I sat dangling my legs from the concrete, slow-pulling the worn-out streamer as I finished the day. Then, a final strike! The fish ran downriver. On my feet, feeling the line through my gloved right hand. Then mono, then Dacron backing. There was no stopping it. The rod was not jerking, just a constant double bend. Line burning across my forefinger.

I held the rod high with both hands at the reel, the buckskinned right hand letting line flow from it. I put pressure, too much pressure, on the line and the fish, but it wouldn't slow. The backing began to vanish and I watched as the reel spool gradually came into view. With only a few feet left, I struck the fish hard, holding the line tightly, bending the rod behind my shoulder. I heard and saw a huge boil 100 yards away where the fish rolled. For a few seconds it stopped, and then with renewed strength moved again. Before I knew it the backing was at its end. The rod strained, the line held for a moment, then parted at its last knot.

The line, the backing, the leader, the fly and the cow bass were gone. As was the day.

After a minute of squeezing a deflating raft, I gathered myself and recrossed the zooming traffic. I walked through Riverside Park, nervously watching for Thomas or Maxwell or the teenagers.

Tired, I leaned forward as I negotiated the 116th Street hill up to Broadway. I watched three street kids playing tag—Shorty, Jolly and Black Lagoon. Black Lagoon was "it." Further up the hill I passed a giant man with a black eye and a bandage around his head. At the top of the hill was Broadway, and it was there that the breeze off the Hudson lost its force. And it was there that I reentered the city of New York, five minutes away from a productive—if somewhat odoriferous—fishing paradise. As usual, I remembered to take a last deep breath of the Hudson before crossing the street to climb the five flights of stairs to my apartment.

# MEMORIES OF MAHSEER

## P. R. BAIRNSFATHER

"CANNY, now! Get him by the gills—that's the lad!"

Then a tremendous heave, a mighty tail outflung, a sickening glimpse of hooks hanging free, and the fish was gone.

"Idiot! what for did ye no take a better grip? I tell you, you'll never see the like o' yon fish again. Man, I would rather have lost my pension!"

In moments of excitement the Colonel always lapsed into broad Doric, and the object of his wrath, his last joined subaltern, stood there dripping mud and water, and with never a word to say. He, too, was suffering as keenly as the other from the despair that comes with such disappointments, and he realized that there was no excuse for having so bungled his share of the disaster. The mahseer that had gone before, needless to say a monster, had been played for hours till it was thought that there was not a kick left in it, and as its captor proudly steered it towards the bank, the subaltern had volunteered to land it, but the last kick had evidently been held in reserve. The boy did what he could to retrieve the position, and flung himself bodily on the top of the fish, and actually held it for a moment in his arms, striving to get firm hold of the slippery scales. But not all the sterling qualities that afterwards won him a well-earned V.C. availed him on this occasion, and so one more great fish went to join the lost legion, and one more fishing story was left minus the dry proof always exacted by them that scoff. Yet, even at the risk to which we fishermen are not insensible, I maintain that this must have been an exceptional mahseer, for it was the talk of the regiment at the time I joined. Moreover, the Colonel was not a man given to exaggeration, and, seeing the fish at close quarters, he stoutly declared that the 6 ft. 1 in. of subaltern were, with reasonable margin, none too much to cover it. The reader, therefore, bearing in mind that a mahseer is, roughly, proportioned much as a salmon, can form some sort of estimate of its probable weight. And at that we must leave it.

Yet surely the most amazing feature of this contest remains to be told, and that is the bait which the mahseer, after much reluctance to feed at all, had at last been induced to take. This was a swallow! Ordinary baits had failed signally; spoon, with minnows both natural and artificial, had been tried without success; and the old Colonel, with his henchman, sat, weary and despondent, on the bank. Suddenly they noticed what appeared to be a fish of unusual size repeatedly coming to the surface of the water just below a neighboring bridge. Some swallows were skimming the water at that spot, and whether the fish was actually attracted by them or not, the incident gave the Colonel the idea which proved an inspiration. The subaltern was told off to shoot a swallow, and it was on this, fitted to a stout triangle, that the lost mahseer had been hooked. That mighty mahseer are occasionally taken is illustrated by one that a friend of mine brought back, not long after the adventure described above, from Tangrot, on the Jhelum, in those days the Mecca of enthusiastic fish men, a fish that measured exactly the same number of inches as his wife—not, it must be confessed, a tall woman, but at any rate not less than five feet. Touching further records of lost giants, I could tell how I once saw a big fish break in a trice, by sheer weight and strength, a four-ply of copper wire between spoon and trace. The line had got caught round the reel-handle in trolling from a boat, and there was no possibility of freeing it before the end came. Not all the monsters have been lost, however, for Mr. Murray Aynsley killed a brace of 104 lb. and 101 lb., both in the Cauvery.

Size and weight are not everything to the true fisherman, who looks for other virtues in his favorites, including a readiness to take some orthodox lure, a spirit of battle when hooked, and a presentable appearance when finally brought to the gaff; and I think that the mahseer can hold its own with some of the best sporting fishes of other lands. Those who have no acquaintance with it may be inclined to underrate its good qualities when they learn that it is a carp, and, like its more homely cousin, a ground-feeder; for the ordinary pond carp undeniably suggests a sluggish quarry entailing hours of waiting beside a float and a hook baited with worm or paste, without in every case much of a struggle at the end. In the case of the carp, the environment of quiet waters may have produced the characteristics that fail to appeal to those who have known better days with salmon and trout, but the mahseer is a very different proposition for the angler to deal with. Living in some of the strongest streams possible for fish life, it too has the qualities of its environment—strength, speed, and dash equal to those of any fresh-run salmon—and its first characteristic rush is such as to inspire a prayer that all is well with the tackle. A carp it may be by race, but to the ordinary carp of our acquaintance the mahseer is as a lean wild boar of the jungle to the fat prize pig in its sty.

Indeed, the mahseer has been styled the Indian salmon, and from the angler's point of view the proud title, is well deserved. It is to be caught in the same kind of rivers and with much the same lures as the salmon, though it must be confessed that it prefers spoon to the fly. It plays in much the same fashion, and the salmon-fisherman's allowance of a minute to the pound would not be excessive with a big mahseer on the rod, while that first wild rush, the invariable opening of the proceedings, is all in the mahseer's favor. In it the fish may fly off at one fell swoop with a hundred yards of line, the leverage on which makes a ten-pounder feel like double the weight. What would Izaak Walton have said to such a fish, seeing that he used no reel, and, when fast to an extra-heavy trout, used to throw his rod into the river and follow as best he could. As a further analogy to the salmon, it should be noted that the mahseer, though it does not, like the other, go down to the sea, has its periods of migration up and down the big Indian rivers, and it was, thanks to his special knowledge of this habit, which he long kept to himself, that a friend of mine used to make sensational catches of mahseer such as turned his brother-fishermen green with envy, his record including over a ton within a month, while on his best day he caught 446 pounds' weight of fish.

There is another advantage which the premier fish of India has over the salmon, and that is that it is never out of season. Owing in all probability to a habit of spawning at various times of year, there are no sluggish autumn fish and no kelts. On the other hand, it is only fair to say that, though eatable soon after capture by sportsmen with a healthy appetite, the mahseer does not compare in this respect with a fresh salmon, though in appearance it suffers little by comparison. We must, however, substitute the larger head and tail, and in place of the beautiful silver of the salmon, suggestive of its stay in the sea, the mahseer's hue is a burnished gold, singularly in keeping with the clear water and fierce sun of its natural haunts.

As I sit over the fire and let my thoughts go back to the pleasant days spent with my old Ringal rod on one or other of the great northern rivers—Ganges, Jumna, Chenab, Beas, or Jhelum—how the memories crowd, and what a remembering of happier things! True, as recalled haphazard, my experiences seem to have been singularly free from sensational episodes, yet they are probably the more typical on that account. These reminiscences seem to centre chiefly round Sialkot, in the north Punjab, where my regiment arrived, one memorable day in 1890, for a three years' spell. I was glad enough to be moved there, for this was the very spot that I had heard of some years earlier from a retired brother officer who had himself enjoyed good sport in the neighboring waters. Here it was that Muchee Bawan might be reached, the very name of which, in the vernacular, signifies home of fish. The best of news awaited me on arrival at our station, for it seemed that the fishing had been utterly overlooked for years, so that those of us who fished had all the satisfaction of rediscovering this once famous ground. It further transpired that, although only thirty miles distant, the road was so troublesome as to be considered next to impossible; but every fisherman will appreciate our satisfaction on learning of this difficulty of approach. From our own bungalow we could plainly see the Pir Punjal mountains, an outlying range of the Himalaya, from which the Tawi River flowed to join the Chenab twelve miles from Sialkot, and Muchee Bawan, the desired, lay somewhere hidden in the misty valley below. Our patience was sorely tried while the cold weather and drill season ran their course, after which, in April, the thermometer steadily rose to punkah heat, and then came the longed-for time for leave. We had arranged to ride as far as possible, camp and baggage being sent forward on camels, which, of course, furnished the usual diversions, one flatly refusing to enter the ferry-boat, and another as obstinately declining to leave it. At long last, however, we pushed on to our journey's end, studiously neglecting a number of attractive pools that we might the sooner make our goal, nothing short of Muchee Bawan itself, unfished these ten years, but previous to that period recognized as incomparable. Our difficulties of transport were by no means light. There was no road, and the only way of getting to the spot was through a deep gorge. There was no footway, and the only mode of travel was by raft. Then where were the raftmen, we asked, only to be told that they were either dead or gone elsewhere. Here, indeed, was an Eastern problem, with, as we surmised, an Eastern solution, for baksheesh ultimately proved the means of producing as many raftmen as we needed, though not before the day was at an end. Daybreak next morning found us at the water's edge, all impatience to be gone; but the raftmen were hurrying matters forward in usual Eastern fashion—that is to say, by sitting round their shriveled goatskins and chattering. It was not, by the way, baksheesh that put new life into the proceedings this time, but anyhow the men quickly and cheerfully grasped what was required of them. The skins were softened in the water and blown up through one of the legs, a rickety old native bedstead lashed to each four skins with odd lengths of string, loin-cloth, or pugaree, and the rafts were ready in reasonable time. An odd procession it was that now started out on the deep, still water of the gorge, the sides of which gradually narrowed till the fairway seemed to end altogether. And the method of propulsion was also curiously simple. The water was too deep for poling, and there would have been no room for paddles, so that four swimmers were allotted to each raft. Naturally the progress was slow, since, with their hands resting on the edge of the raft, they could only use their legs, not in the strong froglike stroke familiar and the weather was normal. We had simply struck an off day on which not a fish could be tempted, and the occasion was at once sadly memorable for the most complete blank I ever scored, but also gloriously associated with what is, perhaps, the reddest-letter day in all my fishing diaries. It fell out in this way. We—that is to say, my good C.O. and myself—had fished three whole days with no result whatever. On the evening of the last day, still doggedly trying every pool we came to, we reached camp, and it was small blame to the C.O. that, having had enough of it, he fell a victim to the lure of tea. Just then, as luck would have it, I noticed some small gulls screaming excitedly over a pool that I knew well some way downstream. It had never been a good pool, and my hopes were not very high; but the birds seemed to mean small fry, and the small fry might mean big fish. Any-how, there were still two clear hours of daylight, and this was our last day, so I resisted the call of tea and set out for the pool. What a sight met my eyes! The water was simply alive with fish, their backs now and then appearing out of water as they dashed after the fry, for all the world like a school of miniature porpoises. So I got to work at once, and the result recalled that first memory of Muchee Bawan. As soon as the spoon touched the water, two or three mahseer would rush for it at once, the best fish generally winning. I was nervous of the result, for it was clearly a case of fishing against time, and I had with me only the light rod and gear. Fish after fish was landed without mishap, and not one of them disgraced its order by omitting that first grand rush and the good fight to follow. Mercifully, the tackle held, and only the coming of night put a stop to the orgy. At length it was no longer possible to see the spoon strike the water, and the sensation of playing the last fish of the day without any notion of the direction in which it was next going to dash provided a fitting climax to a crowded hour. Thirteen fish I had caught in the time, scaling in all just 51 lb. Here, then, was a great happening of the unexpected, the more interesting to me because it had falsified the dictum of our greatest authority on Indian fishing, who holds that any attempt to catch mahseer after sunset is the one thing hopeless. To this generalization my agreeable experience had at any rate furnished a notable exception.

It will not have escaped the reader's notice that the general size of the mahseer that we caught in Muchee Bawan was distinctly mediocre. It must, however, be remembered that the Tawi is only a small tributary stream incapable of raising really big fish, and the charm of the fishing lay in the preference we had for quantity rather than size, as well as for the opportunity of using lighter rods and tackle than are indispensable for mahseer of larger size. For these bigger fish we had to go to the Chenab itself, a much easier jaunt, since the river lay only twelve miles from the station on a good road, so that we could even canter out for an evening's fishing after the day's work and be back the same night. Here it was a matter of trolling from boats with a long line out, the boat being pulled upstream by a rope. On bad days, when the fish were not in the right humour, it was monotonous work, and, as we invariably sat facing the west, the persecuting glare of the sun on the water made us yet more impatient of our ill-luck. Yet there were the other days on which we came in for great reward, for fish weighing from 10 to 50 lb. were quite within the range of moderate expectation, while monsters of far greater weight were known to dwell in the river, and we were ever in hope of hooking one of these. Many we took out of the Chenab in our time, but never the monster. In the end, however, my regiment held the record with a fish of 52 lb., though we were handsomely beaten in actual best take for a single day, for the C.O. of another gallant regiment, able to grant himself leave when we could not get away, and never forgoing the privilege, landed one fine day the much-envied score of sixteen fish to his own rod. Great fish they were, too, the total weight of them being nothing less than 200 lb. No wonder we found some little difficulty in congratulating him!

Here, too, in the Chenab, the conditions under which we caught our fish were ever a mystery. Water, weather and season would be apparently identical on the days of great success and those other days with never a fish. Some days we would troll over the same stretch of water times and again without result. Then, all of a sudden, the fish would come at the bait as if possessed. This was the case on the day that gave me my first forty-pounder. My companion, already into one which proved almost as heavy, had landed in order the better to play his fish, and I, resisting the usual temptation of offering good advice, essayed to prove my pet theory, that mahseer have a certain moment at which they must feed, by taking a cast from the shore. The theory held good in practice, for, sure enough, next moment I had him, and then came a splendid fight. It was a strenuous dance he led me up and down the bank for thirty-five glorious if anxious minutes. Happily, the channel was clear, and there was little or no danger from rapid or snag, yet, with such a heavy fish in play, no minute was free from anxiety, and every mad rush seemed to mark the end. When at last the fish took to rolling over and over far out in the stream, it seemed impossible that the gut could bear the strain, and, as a matter of fact, my misgivings on the subject proved well-founded, for, as I afterwards discovered, the gut was actually severed and disaster had been averted only by its having jammed so tightly between the treble hooks as to hold the great fish in its final struggles. It was a good thing that I was spared this knowledge until the fish was safe on the bank, else I might not have had the courage to go through with it. Three more, all of them good fish, we got out of that reach, and the luck was such as to carry us through many another less successful day.

These were great times no doubt, yet I wonder whether, after all, the simpler incidents much earlier in my Indian days were not even happier! There was the far-off time, for instance, when, under the spell of my first introduction to mahseer, I would gallop out a good nine miles on a hot weather morning, starting at 3 AM so as to be on the water an hour or so before sunrise. The ignoble bait used on these occasions was nothing more than a pellet of dough, and the one pool had to be assiduously groundbaited for days before my visit. Not a fish would move after the sun was once on the water, so the sport had to be short and sharp, and it was fun of the best while it lasted, for I never once remember drawing blank. A few lumps of dough were thrown into the pool on arrival, just to attract and locate the fish, after which came the cast, a rush from all directions, and a fish on the rod, its size depending on which first got to the bait. The madness of the first rush was particularly noticeable here, probably owing to the eagerness of the fish to make good its prize in presence of so much competition. Half a dozen would be the usual morning's take, and I was able to get back in good time to provide fresh fish for the mess breakfast. True, these fish never exceeded a weight of from one to five pounds, but even that was satisfactory when contrasted with my previous experience of nothing but small trout at home. In the more sophisticated moods of after years, such sport would have seemed too trivial to be thought of, but in those early days it was very welcome.

It was about that period that there befell me one of those incidents which the fisherman never forgets. I was not actually on a fishing trip, but had been told by an old hand that at a certain spot on the marching road to Cashmere, whither I was bound after ibex, a small stream joined the Jhelum River, and that if I were to try a cast or two at the junction, I might reasonably look forward to hooking something enormous. The rod was therefore taken along and the expert's instructions obeyed to the letter. A frog was to be the lure on this occasion, and it was, indeed, about the only sort of bait appropriate to this season of dirty flood water, though I never again fell thus far. At any rate, the result warranted the experiment, for I had not been fishing more than ten minutes when the jerk came and the mahseer was off in its proverbial non-stop rush, fortunately upstream and in the slacker current above the tributary. I could form no estimate of its size, but I knew that I had never felt anything like it before. It was absolutely beyond control, though I could plainly see that if the fish once got out in the mainstream, it would be all over in a moment. Up and down the water it raced, backwards and forwards, with nearly all my line out, alarmingly close to the main current, yet mercifully turning just at the crucial spot, wholly of its own sweet will, for I had no control over its movements whatever. Ten minutes of this followed, and then the fish suddenly determined to go downstream. It showed no sign of tiring, and of course I was brought up all standing by the tributary stream, too deep to be crossed except by swimming. This was out of the question, as I could never have got across while holding on to the rod with such a fish at the other end. Then it was that my young attendant, whom I had so far overlooked, had an inspiration.

"Give me the rod, Sahib," he said. "I can easily take it over, while you run round by the bridge."

This suggested a happy solution of the difficulty, and, after warning the youngster to hold on like grim death, I raced for the bridge. The young fellow swam like a duck, and the mahseer behaved just as I could have wished. Feeling it once again at the end of the rod, when I took it from the native, I all but laughed aloud in the certainty of success. Alas! Whether its anger had been roused by the unavoidable jerking of the rod during the swim, or whether it simply judged the time had come to put an end to such fooling and get to business, the grim fact remains that, within a few moments of my recovering the rod, the fish dashed off downstream and out in the middle. No check was possible, and, as the mahseer lurched and struggled, borne down by the irresistible current, I got one unforgettable glimpse of its proportions. I rushed madly down the bank, helplessly watching the line disappear off the reel until it was all out. Then came one final pull, and the fish of my life was gone.

Here, then, though it ended in dismal failure, was the greatest moment in all my memories of mahseer. Yet, as has been said, it was but one of many happy fishing episodes, and it would be hard to say whether, if there is any comparison between the two, it really gave me more excitement than that remote triumph when, as a boy, I successfully guddled an enormous half-pound trout while the other boy, more mindful of home instructions, dutifully paused to remove his boots. I wonder!

# THE ONE THAT GOT AWAY
# (SELECTION)

### HOWELL RAINES

N o, I was oppressed by the sheer weight of something more personal—my own amateurishness in the face of this new kind of fly fishing. I had gotten cocky about my ability to catch trout and bass, including some large ones. But in saltwater environments, the heavy rods and lines, the persistent winds, the greater distances needed even in routine casts—all these factors converged to form a nexus of neuromuscular chaos. Whenever it was mentioned that I had written a book about fishing, I made a point of telling people that my skills were modest. Then I would pick up a rod and prove it.

But hell's hammers, I didn't want to think of myself as clumsy, either. Somehow the abundance of Christmas Island, where it is possible to catch plenty of easy fish, sharpened the contrast between those fish and the hard ones that Lefty or the other experts might catch. I'm talking about the ghostly torpedoes you sometimes glimpsed on the turbulent rim of the islands, where the easeful shallows brushed up against the fertile, brutal surge of the blue Pacific. I particularly liked these ocean flats, which were bands of shallow, protected water between the coral reef and the shore. It is an environment of great violence, beauty and motion: gulls, terns, pipers zipping by within inches of your head, angelfish and blacktip reef sharks at your feet, and always the big combers marching in to die in shuddering explosions against the coral ramparts of the barrier reef. Fishing those flats, with the cannonade of the waves always in your ears and the spirals of white spume leaping incessantly toward the sky, was a little like standing behind a fortified line during a battle, protected improbably from a world of violence that stretched to the horizon. In those spots, if you trained your eyes on the area where the clear water stranded off into the deeper green underbelly of the incoming waves, you'd see the most intimidating bonefish, the sovereign loners, a full yard long, which didn't need to slide into the knee-deep flats to nibble little stuff. In their passing, these fish put me in mind of what Isak Dinesen said about elephants. They moved along as if they had an appointment at the end of the world.

In the precincts of such fish, one day Tabaki spoke.

"Big bone. He's coming along the edge of the deep water."

Sure enough, moving steadily through the green murk was a gray shape five or six times the size of the fish we had been catching in droves in a long march across an amiable flat.

"You can't reach him from here. Let's move out. Don't splash."

We took an intersecting line to try to get ahead of the fish. It was coming steadily on an unveering course, out there in about four feet of water.

"Cast now, as far as you can," Tabaki said, in that voice guides use when they suddenly care whether a particular fish is caught. It is a voice very different from the one they use when they are saying, in effect, you paid your money, here's your shot, I do this every day.

He was watching the relationship between my false casts and the fish. On the fourth or fifth stroke, he said, "Let it go."

I did. To my surprise, the fly landed in the edge of the deep water. Maybe my best cast ever. Not dead-on, but plausible.

"Let it sink," Tabaki said. "He might see it."

I let it sink without hope, satisfied simply that the cast had not been a humiliation.

"Now, strip, strip," he said.

Dear hearts, I wish to tell you that this lordly fish swung toward the fly as inexorably as doom's pendulum, not hastening in the least until the last instant, when it closed on the fly in a rush and took it and was the biggest fish of our trip and one of the biggest ever taken at Christmas Island, where a seven- or eight-pound fish is a large one.

I wish to tell you that and I suppose I could, but it did not happen.

The cast was not quite good enough, or my luck was not the supremely obliterating luck you need to make up for a cast that is not quite good enough. A few times in a fishing life that kind of luck will come along, but it did not come to me on this day in the Republic of Kiribati.

Nor was my casting good enough for the other edge-cruising gorillas we spotted on the ocean flats where the big ones would from time to time come looming along under the combers. Just as well, Tabaki explained, since a bonefish that strong and that close to the reef will simply bore over the edge and cut you off on the coral and that would break your heart more cleanly than a bad cast. I would have been willing to take my chances on that kind of heartbreak.

PART VI

# ANGLERS ALL—AND MATTERS PHILOSOPHIC

# THE MAN WHO LIVED TWO LIVES IN ONE: ZANE GREY

## ROBERT H. BOYLE

There never has been anyone quite like Zane Grey. Famed as the author of *Riders of the Purple Sage* and fifty-seven other Westerns tinged with purple prose, Grey ranks as the greatest bestselling novelist of his time. For years the total sales of his books fell behind only the Holy Bible and McGuffey Readers. At his death in 1939 his novels had sold more than 15 million copies in the United States alone, and thirty years later they were still selling at the rate of 750,000 to a million books a year. Magazines paid Grey as much as $85,000 for the serial rights to a single work, and Hollywood transferred epic after epic to the silver screen. Gary Cooper, Cary Grant, Warner Baxter, Warner Oland, Richard Arlen, Richard Dix, Randolph Scott, Wallace Beery, Roscoe Karns,

Harry Carey, William Powell, Jack Holt, Jack LaRue, Billie Dove, Lili Damita, Fay Wray, Jean Arthur and Buster Crabbe are among the stars who got their start in Zane Grey movies.

On film or in print Grey's Westerns enthralled the public. The books were stilted, awkward and stuffed with painful dialogue ("If you think I'm wonderful and if I think you're wonderful—it's all really very wonderful, isn't it?"), but they throbbed with the narrative drive of a true storyteller and the fervor of a moralist who made certain that virtue triumphed over evil on the range. "Never lay down your pen, Zane Grey," John Wanamaker, the white-haired merchant prince, once advised, putting a friendly hand on the novelist's shoulder. "I have given away thousands of your books and have sold hundreds of thousands. You are distinctively and genuinely American. You have borrowed none of the decadence of foreign writers . . . The good you are doing is incalculable."

Grey received acclaim and money (and some critical brickbats) for his writings, but in another field his distinction was almost beyond compare—he was one of the finest fishermen the world has ever known. In the words of Ed Zern, who edited the anthology *Zane Grey's Adventures in Fishing*, "It is reasonable to assume that no one will ever challenge his right to be known as the greatest fisherman American has ever produced." It has been said that the dream of many American males is to have $1 million and go fishing. "Well," writes Zern, "Zane Grey had $1 million, and he really went fishing."

Grey is the classic case of the compulsive angler. He was truly obsessed by fish. "Not many anglers, perhaps, care for the beauty of a fish," Grey wrote in *Tales of Fishes*, one of his eight books on angling, "but I do." He would rhapsodize on the beauty of a huge tuna that "blazed like the sword of Achilles" or marvel over the shimmering colors of a dolphin, only to feel a pang because the dolphin was dying and he was "the cause of the death of so beautiful a thing." The leaping of fish absolutely fascinated him, and even fish fins and fishtails had what he called, with a flourish, "a compelling power to thrill and excite me."

From black bass to blue marlin, Grey pursued fish the world over with unmatched avidity. He explored and established new fishing grounds and techniques in Florida, California, Nova Scotia, New Zealand and Australia. He took great delight in fishing where no one had ever fished before, and his sense of anticipation was so keen that even arranging tackle for a trip gave him exquisite pleasure. He was the first man to catch a fish weighing more than 1,000 pounds on rod and reel. In his day he held most world records: 582-pound broadbill swordfish; 171-pound Pacific sailfish; 758-pound bluefin tuna; 318-pound yellowfin tuna; 1,040-pound striped marlin; 1,036-pound tiger shark;

618-pound silver marlin; 111-pound yellowtail; and a 63-pound dolphin. The record for the yellowtail and the yellowfin tuna have not been beaten since the International Game Fish Association began keeping records in 1938. Grey was held in such high regard that the Pacific sailfish was named for him, *Istiophom greyi*. Hardy's in England manufactured a Zane Grey reel, while in the United States there was a Zane Grey bass bug, a Zane Grey steelhead fly and a Zane Grey teaser.

Grey had his bad days fishing—he once passed 88 days without a strike—but he remained enthusiastic. "The enchantment never palls," he wrote. "Years on end I have been trying to tell why, but that has been futile. Fishing is like Jason's quest for the Golden Fleece . . . something evermore is about to happen." When something did, Grey wrote about it exuberantly. If he made an unusual catch he would wire *The New York Times*. There were some critics who thought him guilty of exaggeration. A friend, Robert H. Davis, the editor of *Munsey's Magazine*, wrote Grey, "If you went out with a mosquito net to catch a mess of minnows your story would read like Roman gladiators seining the Tigris for whales." Davis added, "You say, 'the hard diving fight of a tuna liberates the brute instinct in a man.' Well, Zane, it also liberates the qualities of a liar!" Grey cheerfully reported these comments himself in *Tales of Fishes*. Such criticisms did not bother him. But he was vexed and angered when his sportsmanship was called into question, as it was on a couple of occasions.

Zane Grey's passion for fishing, which, by his own admission, grew stronger through the years, started in his childhood. "Ever since I was a little tad I have loved to chase things in the water," he wrote. He was born in Zanesville, Ohio, on January 31, 1872. His Christian name was actually Pearl, and the family name was spelled Gray. After college he dropped Pearl in favor of his middle name of Zane, and he changed spelling of Gray to Grey. He also shaved three years off his age, according to Norris F. Schneider, the foremost authority on Grey, and on his death obituaries reported he had been born in 1875.

Grey came from pioneer stock. His great grandfather, Colonel Ebenezer Zane, settled what is now Wheeling, West Virginia, in 1770 and moved into Ohio after the Revolution. Zanesville is named for him. Grey's father, Dr. Lewis Gray, was a farmer and a preacher who eventually became a dentist with a practice in the Terrace section of Zanesville.

The oldest of five children, young Pearl was so mischievous that he was known as "the terror of the Terrace." On one occasion he destroyed a bed of imported tulips planted in front of the Zanesville Historical and Art Institute. The name Pearl, especially in conjunction with the name Gray, apparently bothered him considerably. The only time he ever liked it was during his adolescent years, when he strove to dramatize himself by dressing in pearl-gray suits.

He was six when he saw his first fish. "Looking down from my high perch into the clear pool directly under me, I saw something that transfixed me with a strange rapture. Against the sunlit amber depths of the little pool shone a wondrous fish creature that came to the surface and snapped at a bug. It flashed silver and rose." The experience stayed with him. In school and church Pearl Gray was a dreamer. "I dreamed, mostly of fields, hills and streams . . . As I grew older, and learned the joys of angling, I used to run away on Sunday afternoons. Many a time have I come home late, wet and weary after a thrilling time along the river or stream, to meet with severe punishment from my outraged father. But it never cured me. I always went fishing on Sunday. It seemed the luckiest day." Dr. Gray told Pearl the only good fishermen who had ever lived were Christ's disciples, but the boy paid no heed; and he became the admirer of a local bum named Muddy Mizer who was always fishing on the Muskingum River.

Besides fishing, Pearl's other love was baseball, a sport at which he and his brother Romer, called R.C., excelled. Pearl was a pitcher, and he and R.C. played semipro ball around Ohio. Dr. Gray wanted Pearl to become a dentist, and he had him start by polishing sets of false teeth on a lathe. His pitching arm stood him in good stead. When the family moved to Columbus, Pearl unofficially went into practice on his own, pulling teeth in Frazeysburg until the Ohio Dental Association compelled him to stop. He continued playing baseball, and after one game a scout from the University of Pennsylvania offered him a scholarship. His father allowed him to accept it on the condition that he major in dentistry.

At Penn, Grey was at first highly unpopular. Ignorant of student traditions, he accidentally entered the upper class section of a lecture hall one day and triggered a riot in which his clothes were torn off and the room wrecked. After another contretemps he was chased by sophomores into a stairwell, where he managed to hold them off by hurling potatoes. His name and his refusal to go along with the crowd, to smoke, to drink or to gamble, made him the butt of jokes, and he escaped by spending most of his time reading in the library and playing baseball. He proved to be so good a ballplayer that, as he wrote later, "The bitter loneliness of my college days seemed to change. Wilborn, captain of the track team, took me up; Danny Coogan, the great varsity catcher, made me a member of Sigma Nu; Al Bull, the center on the famous football team that beat Yale and Princeton and Harvard, took me as a roommate."

Grey played left field for Penn. His one lapse came in a game against Harvard, when he accidentally stepped into a hole and a fly ball hit him on the head, allowing the winning run to score. Ordinarily his fielding was excellent. He once made a catch that helped Penn beat the Giants at the Polo Grounds. In his senior year he came to bat in the ninth inning against the University of Virginia with Penn trailing by a run. There were two outs and a man on second. A verbose professor shouted, "Grey, the honor of the University of Pennsylvania rests with you!" Grey homered to win the game.

Grey was graduated with a diploma in dentistry in 1896. He opened an office in Manhattan on the West Side, and there he languished. He did not like the city, and he got away whenever possible. He played baseball for the Orange Athletic Club in New Jersey, and he became the youngest member of the Camp Fire Club. There a fellow member suggested that Grey write a story about his bass fishing on the Delaware. He did, and the story—his first effort—was published in *Recreation* in May 1902. The appearance of the article gave him direction, and he began writing an historical novel about his ancestor, Betty Zane, who carried gunpowder to her brother, Colonel Zane, during the siege of Fort Henry in the Revolution. All winter Grey labored over the book in a dingy flat. Upon completing it he drew the cover and inside illustrations. No publisher would accept *Betty Zane,* and, after a wealthy patient offered to back it, Grey had it printed privately. Sales were nil, but in a visit to Zanesville in 1904, Grey grandly announced that he given up dentistry to devote himself "exclusively to literature."

In 1905 Grey married Lina Roth of New York, whom he had met a few years earlier while he was canoeing down the Delaware in one of his escapes from dentistry. She had faith in her husband and a bit of money to boot, and he gave up his practice to write while living in a house overlooking the Delaware in Lackawaxen, Pennsylvania. There he wrote, hunted, fished and savored "the happiness that dwells in wilderness alone." R.C., by now a professional ballplayer, chipped in with an occasional dollar, and Zane later repaid him by making him his official secretary and constant fishing companion.

Grey followed up *Betty Zane* by writing a couple of other books about the Ohio frontier, *The Spirit of the Border* and *The Last Trail*, which the A. L. Burt Company eventually published. They were flops. But Grey hung on, and in 1907 he went west with one Buffalo Jones, visiting the wilder parts of Utah and Arizona. Jones had a ranch on the rim of the Grand Canyon, where he was hybridizing black Galloway cattle with buffalo and calling the offspring cattalo. In his spare time he liked to lasso mountain lions. Grey loved it all, and, upon returning to the East, he wrote a book about Jones, *The Last of the Plainsmen*, which he took to Harper, a firm that had rebuffed him previously.

Eagerly he awaited word and, hearing none, he visited the publishing house, where an editor coldly informed him, "I don't see anything in this to convince me that you can write either narrative or fiction." It was the bleakest moment in Grey's life. He was 36 years old, he had abandoned dentistry, his wife was pregnant with their first child and he had failed again. "When I staggered down the old stairway and out into Pearl Street I could not see," he later recalled. "I had to hold on to an iron post at the corner, and there I hung fighting such misery as I had never known. Something came to me there. They had all missed it. They did not know . . . and I went back to Lackawaxen to the smile and encouragement that never failed me."

He promptly wrote his first Western novel, *The Heritage of the Desert.* Harper yielded and published it in 1910—the year of the birth of his first son, Romer—and Grey thought he was at last on his way. Quickly he wrote *Riders of the Purple Sage*, but Harper rejected it as too "bulgy." Grey asked a vice-president of the firm to read the manuscript. He liked the novel, and so did his wife, who stayed up until three in the morning to finish it. The book was published, and Grey was permanently established. In fifteen years *Riders of the Purple Sage* sold two million copies. Grey also turned out half a dozen juveniles, many of them dealing with his baseball experiences. In *The Young Pitcher* he wrote of the potato episode at Penn and drew himself as Ken Ward, the hero. His brother, R.C., also called Reddy, was Reddy Ray, spark plug of the team. In *The Shortstop*, Grey named the hero after Chase Alloway, a professional player he had known in Ohio. (In the Western *The Lone Star Ranger* Grey named one of the villains Chess Alloway.)

Although comfortably off, Grey continued to write feverishly. He could not abide waste of time. As a writer and as an angler Grey was a finisher, and he followed both callings to the hilt. "It is so easy to start anything, a fishing jaunt or a career," he wrote, "but it is an entirely different matter to finish. The men who fail to finish in any walk of life, men who have had every opportunity . . . can be numbered by the millions." At top speed, Grey found he could write 100,000 words a month. He would pen himself up in his study, where he would sit in a Morris chair, writing in longhand on a lapboard, furiously chewing the top of a soft No. 1 pencil when a sentence failed him. He compiled notebooks of vivid phrases and expressions, and he often thumbed a worn copy of a book, *Materials and Methods of Fiction*, by Clayton Milton. Grey's son Romer said, "That was father's bible. It had a greater influence on his writing than any other work." Grey wrote only one draft of a book; he left the finishing of the manuscript to his wife. When not writing he fished. He knew a long stretch of the Delaware by memory. "I own nearly a thousand acres of land on it," he wrote. "I have fished it for ten years. I know every rapid, every eddy, almost, I might say, every stone from Callicoon to Port Jervis. This fifty-mile stretch of fast water I consider the finest bass ground I have ever fished." In July, when the river was low, he would scout the water for big bass by going upstream and drifting face down on a raft. "I see the bottom everywhere, except in rough water. I see the rocks, the shelves, the caverns. I see where the big bass live. And I remember." When the time came to fish, Grey became part of the landscape; he trod the slippery stones "as if I were a stalking Indian. I knew that a glimpse of me, or a faint jar vibrating under the water, or an unnatural ripple on its surface, would be fatal to my enterprise." Not every visiting angler exalted the fishing; some referred to Lackawaxen Creek as the Lackanothing or Lackarotten.

With money coming in, Grey and R.C. began fishing in Florida. They went after bonefish, snook and tarpon. Grey was among the first to go after sailfish, and he did so well that other fishermen flocked to the Gulf Stream. He was intrigued by wahoo, then seldom caught, reasoning that they could be taken because "all fish have to eat." He caught wahoo, and he helped put the Keys on the map. Wherever he went, he fished. On a trip to Mexico to gather material for a novel, his train chanced to pass by a jungle river, the Santa Rosa. Immediately Grey wondered, "Where did that river go? How many waterfalls and rapids hastened its journey to the Gulf? What teeming life inhabited its rich banks? How wild was the prospect! It haunted me!" In time he made the trip in a flat-bottom boat. On a trip to Yucatán, he happened to hear of "the wild and lonely Alacranes Reef where lighthouse keepers went insane from solitude, and where wonderful fishes inhabited the lagoons. That was enough for me. Forthwith I meant to go to Alacranes." Forthwith he did. There he met a little Englishman, Lord L., and "it was from him I got my type for Castleton, the Englishman, in *The Light of the Western Stars*. I have been told that never was there an Englishman on earth like the one I portrayed in my novel. But my critics never fished with Lord L."

Grey never lost any time. On a fishing trip he was up before everyone at four in the morning, transcribing the adventures of the previous day. If fishing was slack, he worked on a book until breakfast. He wrote much of *The Drift Fence* and *Robbers' Roost* at sea, and he piled up such a backlog of books that *Boulder Dam*, which he wrote while off on a trip in the 1930s, was not published by Harper until 1963.

In 1914 Grey started going west to Catalina each summer, where he tried swordfishing. In his first year he spent over three weeks at sea, trolling a total of 1,500 miles. Grey saw nineteen swordfish but did not get one strike. Instead of becoming discouraged, he was pleased. "By this time," he wrote, "I had realized something of the difficult nature of the game, and I had begun to have an inkling of what sport it might be." On the twenty-fifth day Grey sighted a swordfish, which he hooked. But the fish broke away, and Grey was sick at heart. The following summer found him back in Catalina. "I was crazy on swordfish," he admitted. To get his arms, hands and back into fighting trim, he rowed a boat for weeks on end. His patience and training were rewarded—he set a record by catching four swordfish in one day.

Between gathering material for novels and advising on movies and fishing, Grey began to visit Southern California so frequently that he moved his family to Los Angeles in 1918. Two years later he bought the small estate in Altadena that now serves as the headquarters of Zane Grey, Inc. Once established on the West Coast, Grey took up steelhead fishing in Oregon, and on a trip down the Rogue River he ran into a prospector who offered to sell his shack and land. Grey bought the place at Winkle Bar as offhandedly as he would buy a dozen new rods. He also owned some land and a small hunting lodge in Arizona. He shuttled from one place to another, writing, fishing, hunting, and gathering material. "[The year] 1923 was typical of what I do in the way of work and play," he replied to an admirer who had asked what a typical year was like.

The pleasant paradox, however, is that my play turns out to be valuable work. January and February I spent at Long Key, Florida, where I wrote, read, fished and wandered along the beach. The spring I spent with my family in Altadena, California, where I wrote and studied, and played with my family. Tennis is my favorite game. During this season I motored with Mrs. Grey down to San Diego and across the mountains to El Centro and Yuma, through the wonderful desert land of Southern California. June found me at Avalon, Catalina Island, a place I have found as inspiring as Long Key, and infinitely different. Here I finished a novel, and then began my sword-fishing on the Pacific. My brother, R.C., and I roamed the sea searching for giant swordfish. Sometimes we ran a hundred miles in a day. The sea presents a marvelous contrast to the desert. It inspires, teaches, subdues, uplifts, appalls and remakes me. There I learned more of nature than on land. Birds and fishes, strange sea creatures, are always in evidence. In September I took Mr. [Jesse] Lasky and his [Paramount] staff to Arizona to pick out locations for the motion picture, *The Vanishing American.* Upon the return I parted with the Lasky outfit at the foot of Navajo Mountains . . . I, with my guide Wetherill, with selected cowboys and horses, tried for the third time to reach Wild Horse Mesa. In October I went to my hunting lodge in the Tonto Basin, where the magnificent forests of green pine and silver spruce and golden aspen soothed my eyes after the long weeks on sea and desert. Here I hunted and rode the lonely leaf-covered trails, lay for hours on the Rim, listening to the bay of hounds, and spent many a pleasant evening round the camp-fire, listening to my men, the gaunt long-legged and lead-faced backwoodsmen of the Tonto Basin. November and December found me back again at Altadena, hard as nails, brown as an Indian, happy to be home with my family, keen for my study with its books and pictures, and for the long spell of writing calling me to its fulfillment.

Grey always had some new adventure going. A Norwegian named Sievert Nielsen, a sailor turned prospector, read Grey's novel *Desert Gold* and wrote to him under the misapprehension that the story of the treasure in the farfetched plot was true. Grey was so charmed with the letter that he invited Nielsen to see him. They became friends and hiked across Death Valley for the thrill of it.

Grey's success at landing big fish prompted a correspondence with Captain Laurie Mitchell of Liverpool, Nova Scotia. Mitchell, who was to become one of Grey's fishing companions, was enthusiastic about giant bluefin tuna off Nova Scotia. He himself had landed only one—it happened to be a world-record 710 pounds—and had lost between fifty and sixty of the big fish. Other anglers had caught perhaps a total of ten. The fish were simply too tough for ordinary tackle. This was just the sort of challenge that appealed to Grey, who promptly began laying plans to fish in Nova Scotia. He reasoned that his swordfish tackle would be adequate for the tuna, provided that the boat from which he was fishing was fast and maneuverable. He had two light skiffs built in Nova Scotia, and from Florida he ordered a special launch, twenty-five feet long and equipped with two engines capable of doing eighteen miles an hour. The launch was so designed that at full speed it could turn on its own length. Grey installed Catalina fighting chairs in each boat.

Within a couple of weeks Grey proved his strategy to be right. He hooked three tuna and landed two, one of which was a world-record 758 pounds and the largest fish of any species ever caught on rod and reel.

Before leaving Nova Scotia, Grey fulfilled a boyhood dream of buying "a beautiful white ship with sails like wings to sail into tropic seas." The three-masted schooner, which he called *Fisherman*, held the record for the run from Halifax to New York City. Grey scrupulously made certain she never had been used as a rumrunner; ever the teetotaler, he would not have a bootlegger's boat as a gift. He had *Fisherman* outfitted with all the tackle that "money could buy and ingenuity devise," and, with R.C. and Romer, he set sail for Galápagos, Cocos Island, the Gulf of Panama and the Pacific coast of Mexico. On this trip he caught a 135-pound Pacific sailfish, the first known to science, but otherwise fishing conditions were not good because of an abundance of sharks.

Broadbill swordfish remained Grey's great love. In 1926 at Catalina, he and his brother caught a total of 10, including Zane's world-record 582-pounder. In that same year R.C. caught five marlin, all weighing more than 300 pounds. No other angler had then caught more than one 300-pound fish, and the 354-pounder taken by R.C. was a world record. It was a great year for the brothers, and, as Grey wrote, "Not the least pleasure in our success was to run back to Avalon with the red flag flying at the masthead, to blow a clarion blast from the boat's whistle, and to see the pier filled with excited spectators. Sometimes thousands of visitors massed at the end of the pier to see the swordfish weighed and photographed. On these occasions R.C. and I would have to stand the battery of hundreds of cameras and shake hands until we broke away from the pier."

Not everyone cheered Grey. He and R.C. broke early with members of the Catalina Tuna Club over Grey's choice of tackle. Although a light-tackle man in freshwater, Grey used very heavy tackle for big game fish. He argued that fish that broke off light tackle either became prey to sharks or died.

Grey accepted the invitation of the New Zealand government to investigate the big-game fishing possibilities in that country. Captain Mitchell and R.C. went with him. They revolutionized local practices; instead of fishing with bait deep down, they took fish by trolling. Grey caught a world-record 450-pound striped marlin and a record 111-pound yellowtail, while Captain Mitchell set a record with a 976-pound black marlin. Grey's greatest pleasure, however, was finding copies of Westerns in even the remotest homes he visited. "This was surely the sweetest and most moving of all the experiences I had; and it faced me again with the appalling responsibility of a novelist who in these modern days of materialism dares to foster idealism and love of nature, chivalry in men and chastity in women."

Back home, Grey had difficulties in Arizona. In 1930 the state passed game laws and established seasons, and Grey, accustomed to hunting bears whenever the mood was on him, was angered. He felt that he was entitled to hunt year round, because he had put Arizona on the map. When a warden refused to issue him a resident license Grey was "grossly insulted," and he gave up his lodge in the Tonto Basin. "In twelve years my whole bag of game has been five bears, three bucks and a few turkeys," he said. "I have written fifteen novels with Arizona background. Personally it cost me $30,000 to get material for one book *To the Last Man*. My many trips all over the state have cost me $100,000. So in every way I have not been exactly an undesirable visitor." He was so indignant he said he would never return and, as a parting shot, he said that the game commission and the Forest Service had sold out to "the commercial interest." As a case in point, he cited the north rim of the Grand Canyon as nothing more than a "tin-can gasoline joint." Grey felt strongly about the Grand Canyon, so much so that he could not bring himself to write about it. It was simply too marvelous to describe.

Fishing in the Pacific lured him more and more. He revisited New Zealand and Tahiti, where he caught his record 1,040-pound striped marlin. The fish was mutilated by sharks; had it not been, it would have weighed 200 pounds more. When the Australian government asked him to explore big-game fishing there, Grey went to Australia and landed his record tiger shark off Sydney Heads. Always the unknown beckoned. He spent $40,000 for a steel-hulled schooner originally built for the Kaiser, and another $270,000 went into refurbishing the ship, which he named *Fisherman II*. His dream of dreams was to fish the waters of Christmas Island off Madagascar, where there were reports of sailfish twenty-two feet long. Equipped with six launches, *Fisherman II* embarked for Christmas Island on a round-the-world cruise. The ship was 195 feet long, but she had a narrow twenty-eight-foot beam and she rolled, even in a calm sea. Even Grey got sick. "We had so much trouble it was unbelievable," said his young son, Loren. "We got as far as Totoya in the Fijis. The captain was ill. The chief engineer had appendicitis. We were there for over a month or more with costly repairs. Father finally called the trip off because of a pressing business matter with his publisher." Eventually Grey gave up on the ship, and she ended her days as a cannery tender for a West Coast tuna fleet.

While steelhead fishing in Oregon in 1937 Grey suffered a stroke. Romer and a guide carried him to a car and got him home, where he recuperated. Within a year he seemed recovered. He went to Australia to fish and then back to Altadena to write, before going on to Oregon for steelhead. There he insisted that Loren and three friends fish "not only all day, but every day in the week," said Loren, who became a professor of education at San Fernando Valley State College. "We finally had a big fight with him and said we wanted to go home.

If he wouldn't let us go home, would he at least let us go into town on weekends and live it up a little bit? He finally gave in, so we'd fish just five days a week."

Determined to make a complete recovery, Grey worked out with a rod in a fighting chair set on the porch of the west wing of his house. Every day Grey would battle imaginary fish, pumping the rod perhaps 200 times before calling it quits. He was getting ready for the next expedition. It never came. On October 23, 1939 Zane Grey died. His workouts in the fighting chair apparently had been too much for him. He once wrote, in his younger days, "There is only one thing wrong with a fishing day—its staggering brevity. If a man spent all his days fishing, life would seem to be a swift dream." For Zane Grey, compulsive angler, the swift dream was over.

# THE ANGLER

## WASHINGTON IRVING

It is said that many an unlucky urchin is induced to run away from his family, and betake himself to a seafaring life, from reading the history of Robinson Crusoe; and I suspect that, in like manner, many of those worthy gentlemen who are given to haunt the sides of pastoral streams with angle rods in hand, may trace the origin of their passion to the seductive pages of honest Izaak Walton. I recollect studying his *Compleat Angler* several years since, in company with a knot of friends in America, and moreover that we were all completely bitten with the angling mania. It was early in the year; but as soon as the weather was auspicious, and the spring began to melt into the verge of summer, we took rod in hand and sallied into the country, as stark mad as was ever Don Quixote from reading books of chivalry.

One of our party had equaled the Don in the fullness of his equipments: being attired *cap-à-pie* for the enterprise. He wore a broad-skirted fustian coat, perplexed with half a hundred pockets; a pair of stout shoes, and leathern gaiters; a basket slung on one side for fish; a patent rod, a landing net, and a score of other inconveniences, only to be found in the true angler's armory. Thus harnessed for the field, he was as great a matter of stare and wonderment among the country folk, who had never seen a regular angler, as was the steel-clad hero of La Mancha among the goatherds of the Sierra Morena.

Our first essay was along a mountain brook, among the highlands of the Hudson; a most unfortunate place for the execution of those piscatory tactics which had been invented along the velvet margins of quiet English rivulets. It was one of those wild streams that lavish, among our romantic solitudes, unheeded beauties, enough to fill the sketch-book of a hunter of the picturesque. Sometimes it would leap down rocky shelves, making small cascades, over which the trees threw their broad balancing sprays, and long nameless weeds hung in fringes from the impending banks, dripping with diamond drops. Sometimes it would brawl and fret along a ravine in the matted shade of a forest, filling it with murmurs; and, after this termagant career, would steal forth into open day with the most placid demure face imaginable; as I have seen some pestilent shrew of a housewife, after filling her home with uproar and ill-humor, come dimpling out of doors, swimming and curtseying, and smiling upon all the world.

How smoothly would this vagrant brook glide, at such times, through some bosom of green meadow-land among the mountains: where the quiet was only interrupted by the occasional tinkling of a bell from the lazy cattle among the clover, or the sound of a woodcutter's axe from the neighboring forest.

For my part, I was always a bungler at all kinds of sport that required either patience or adroitness, and had not angled above half an hour before I had completely "satisfied the sentiment," and convinced myself of the truth of Izaak Walton's opinion, that angling is something like poetry—a man must be born to it. I hooked myself instead of the fish; tangled my line in every tree; lost my bait; broke my rod; until I gave up the attempt in despair, and passed the day under the trees, reading old Izaak; satisfied that it was his fascinating vein of honest simplicity and rural feeling that had bewitched me, and not the passion for angling. My companions, however, were more persevering in their delusion. I have them at this moment before my eyes, stealing along the border of the brook, where it lay open to the day, or was merely fringed by shrubs and bushes. I see the bittern rising with hollow scream as they break in upon his rarely-invaded haunt; the kingfisher watching them suspiciously from his dry tree that overhangs the deep black mill-pond, in the gorge of the hills; the tortoise letting himself slip sideways from off the stone or log on which he is sunning himself; and the panic-struck frog plumping in headlong as they approach, and spreading an alarm throughout the watery world around.

I recollect also, that, after toiling and watching and creeping about for the greater part of a day, with scarcely any success, in spite of all our admirable apparatus, a lubberly country urchin came down from the hills with a rod made from a branch of a tree, a few yards of twine, and, as Heaven shall help me! I believe, a crooked pin for a hook, baited with a vile earthworm—and in half an hour caught more fish than we had nibbles throughout the day!

But, above all, I recollect, the "good, honest, wholesome, hungry" repast, which we made under a beech-tree, just by a spring of pure sweet water that stole out of the side of a hill; and how, when it was over, one of the party read old Izaak Walton's scene with the milkmaid, while I lay on the grass and built castles in a bright pile of clouds, until I fell asleep. All this may appear like mere egotism; yet I cannot refrain from uttering these recollections, which are passing like a strain of music over my mind, and have been called up by an agreeable scene which I witnessed not long since.

In a morning's stroll along the banks of the Alun, a beautiful little stream which flows down from the Welsh hills and throws itself into the Dee, my attention was attracted to a group seated on the margin. On approaching, I found it to consist of a veteran angler and two rustic disciples. The former was an old fellow with a wooden leg, with clothes very much but very carefully patched, betokening poverty, honestly come by, and decently maintained. His face bore the marks of former storms, but present fair weather; its furrows had been worn into a habitual smile; his iron-gray locks hung about his ears, and he had altogether the good-humored air of a constitutional philosopher who was disposed to take the world as it went. One of his companions was a ragged wight, with the skulking look of an arrant poacher, and I'll warrant could find his way to any gentleman's fish-pond in the neighborhood in the darkest night. The other was a tall, awkward, country lad, with a lounging gait, and apparently somewhat of a rustic beau. The old man was busy in examining the maw of a trout which he had just killed, to discover by its contents what insects were seasonable for bait; and was lecturing on the subject to his companions, who appeared to listen with infinite deference. I have a kind feeling towards all "brothers of the angle," ever since I read Izaak Walton. They are men, he affirms, of a "mild, sweet, and peaceable spirit;" and my esteem for them has been increased since I met with an old *Tretyse of Fishing with the Angle*, in which are set forth many of the maxims of their inoffensive fraternity. "Take good hede," sayeth this honest little tretyse, "that in going about your disportes ye open no man's gates but that ye shet them again. Also ye shall not use this forsayd crafti disport for no covetousness to the encreasing and sparing of your money only, but principally for your solace, and to cause the helth of your body and specyally of your soule."

I thought that I could perceive in the veteran angler before me an exemplification of what I had read; and there was a cheerful contentedness in his looks that quite drew me towards him. I could not but remark the gallant manner in which he stumped from one part of the brook to another; waving his rod in the air, to keep the line from dragging on the ground, or catching among the bushes; and the adroitness with which he would throw his fly to any particular place; sometimes skimming it lightly along a little rapid; sometimes casting it into one of those dark holes made by a twisted root or overhanging bank, in which the large trout are apt to lurk. In the meanwhile he was giving instructions to his two disciples; showing them the manner in which they should handle their rods, fix their flies, and play them along the surface of the stream. The scene brought to my mind the instructions of the sage Piscator to his scholar. The country around was of that pastoral kind which Walton is fond of describing. It was a part of the great plain of Cheshire, close by the beautiful vale of Gessford, and just where the inferior Welsh hills begin to swell up from among fresh-smelling meadows. The day, too, like that recorded in his work, was mild and sunshiny, with now and then a soft-dropping shower, that sowed the whole earth with diamonds.

I soon fell into conversation with the old angler, and was so much entertained that, under pretext of receiving instructions in his art, I kept company with him almost the whole day; wandering along the banks of the stream, and listening to his talk. He was very communicative, having all the easy garrulity of cheerful old age; and I fancy was a little flattered by having an opportunity of displaying his piscatory lore; for who does not like now and then to play the sage?

He had been much of a rambler in his day, and had passed some years of his youth in America, particularly in Savannah, where he had entered into trade, and had been ruined by the indiscretion of a partner. He had afterwards experienced many ups and downs in life, until he got into the navy, where his leg was carried away by a cannon ball, at the battle of Camperdown. This was the only stroke of real good fortune he had ever experienced, for it got him a pension, which, together with some small paternal property, brought him in a revenue of nearly forty pounds. On this he retired to his native village, where he lived quietly and independently; and devoted the remainder of his life to the "noble art of angling."

I found that he had read Izaak Walton attentively, and he seemed to have imbibed all his simple frankness and prevalent good-humor. Though he had been sorely buffeted about the world, he was satisfied that the world, in itself, was good and beautiful. Though he had been as roughly used in different countries as a poor sheep that is fleeced by every hedge and thicket, yet he spoke of every nation with candor and kindness, appearing to look only on the good side of things: and, above all, he was almost the only man I had ever met with who had been an unfortunate adventurer in America, and had honesty and magnanimity enough to take the fault to his own door, and not to curse the country. The lad that was receiving his instructions, I learnt, was the son and heir apparent of a fat old widow who kept the village inn, and of course a youth of some expectation, and much courted by the idle gentlemanlike personages of the place. In taking him under his care, therefore, the old man had probably an eye to a privileged corner in the tap-room, and an occasional cup of cheerful ale free of expense.

There is certainly something in angling, if we could forget, which anglers are apt to do, the cruelties and tortures inflicted on worms and insects, that tends to produce a gentleness of spirit, and a pure serenity of mind. As the English are methodical even in their recreations, and are the most scientific of sportsmen, it has been reduced among them to perfect rule and system. Indeed it is an amusement peculiarly adapted to the mild and highly-cultivated scenery of England, where every roughness has been softened away from the landscape. It is delightful to saunter along those limpid streams which wander, like veins of silver, through the bosom of this beautiful country; leading one through a diversity of small home scenery; sometimes winding through ornamented grounds; sometimes brimming along through rich pasturage, where the fresh green is mingled with sweet-smelling flowers; sometimes venturing in sight of villages and hamlets, and then running capriciously away into shady retirements. The sweetness and serenity of nature, and the quiet watchfulness of the sport, gradually bring on pleasant fits of musing; which are now and then agreeably interrupted by the song of a bird, the distant whistle of the peasant, or perhaps the vagary of some fish, leaping out of the still water, and skimming transiently about its glassy surface. "When I would beget content," says Izaak Walton, "and increase confidence in the power and wisdom and providence of Almighty God, I will walk the meadows by some gliding stream, and there contemplate the lilies that take no care, and those very many other little living creatures that are not only created, but fed (man knows not how) by the goodness of the God of nature, and therefore trust in him."

I cannot forbear to give another quotation from one of those ancient champions of angling, which breathes the same innocent and happy spirit:

Let me live harmlessly, and near the brink
Of Trent or Avon have a dwelling-place,
Where I may see my quill, or cork, down sink,
With eager bite of pike, or bleak, or dace;
And on the world and my Creator think:
Whilst some men strive ill-gotten goods t' embrace;
And others spend their time in base excess
Of wine, or worse, in war, or wantonness.
Let them that will, these pastimes still pursue,
And on such pleasing fancies feed their fill;
So I the fields and meadows green may view,
And daily by fresh rivers walk at will,
Among the daisies and the violets blue,
Red hyacinth and yellow daffodil.

On parting with the old angler I inquired after his place of abode, and happening to be in the neighborhood of the village a few evenings afterwards, I had the curiosity to seek him out. I found him living in a small cottage, containing only one room, but a perfect curiosity in its method and arrangement. It was on the skirts of the village, on a green bank, a little back from the road, with a small garden in front, stocked with kitchen herbs, and adorned with a few flowers. The whole front of the cottage was overrun with a honeysuckle. On the top was a ship for a weather-cock. The interior was fitted up in a truly nautical style, his ideas of comfort and convenience having been acquired on the berth-deck of a man-of-war. A hammock was slung from the ceiling, which, in the daytime, was lashed up so as to take but little room. From the centre of the chamber hung a model of a ship, of his own workmanship. Two or three chairs, a table, and a large sea-chest, formed the principal movables. About the wall were stuck up naval ballads, such as "Admiral Hosier's Ghost," "All in the Downs," and "Tom Bowline," intermingled with pictures of sea-fights, among which the battle of Camperdown held a distinguished place. The mantel-piece was decorated with sea-shells; over which hung a quadrant, flanked by two wood-cuts of most bitter-looking naval commanders. His implements for angling were carefully disposed on nails and hooks about the room. On a shelf was arranged his library, containing a work on angling, much worn, a Bible covered with canvas, an odd volume or two of voyages, a nautical almanac, and a book of songs.

His family consisted of a large black cat with one eye, and a parrot which he had caught and tamed, and educated himself, in the course of one of his voyages; and which uttered a variety of sea phrases with the hoarse brattling tone of a veteran boatswain. The establishment reminded me of that of the renowned Robinson Crusoe; it was kept in neat order, every thing being "stowed away" with the regularity of a ship of war; and he informed me that he "scoured the deck every morning, and swept it between meals."

I found him seated on a bench before the door, smoking his pipe in the soft evening sunshine. His cat was purring soberly on the threshold, and his parrot describing some strange evolutions in an iron ring that swung in the centre of his cage. He had been angling all day, and gave me a history of his sport with as much minuteness as a general would talk over a campaign; being particularly animated in relating the manner in which he had taken a large trout, which had completely tasked all his skill and wariness, and which he had sent as a trophy to mine hostess of the inn.

How comforting it is to see a cheerful and contented old age; and to behold a poor fellow, like this, after being tempest-tost through life, safely moored in a snug and quiet harbor in the evening of his days! His happiness, however, sprung from within himself, and was independent of external circumstances; for he had that inexhaustible good-nature, which is the most precious gift of Heaven; spreading itself like oil over the troubled sea of thought, and keeping the mind smooth and equable in the roughest weather.

On inquiring further about him, I learned that he was a universal favorite in the village, and the oracle of the taproom; where he delighted the rustics with his songs, and, like Sinbad, astonished them with his stories of strange lands, and shipwrecks, and sea-fights. He was much noticed too by gentlemen sportsmen of the neighborhood; had taught several of them the art of angling; and was a privileged visitor to their kitchens. The whole tenor of his life was quiet and inoffensive, being principally passed about the neighboring streams, when the weather and season were favorable; and at other times he employed himself at home, preparing his fishing tackle for the next campaign, or manufacturing rods, nets, and flies, for his patrons and pupils among the gentry.

He was a regular attendant at church on Sundays, though he generally fell asleep during the sermon. He had made it his particular request that when he died he should be buried in a green spot, which he could see from his seat in church, and which he had marked out ever since he was a boy, and had thought of when far from home on the raging sea, in danger of being food for the fishes—it was the spot where his father and mother had been buried.

I have done, for I fear that my reader is growing weary; but I could not refrain from drawing the picture of this worthy "brother of the angle"; who has made me more than ever in love with the theory, though I fear I shall never be adroit in the practice of his art; and I will conclude this rambling sketch in the words of honest Izaak Walton, by craving the blessing of St. Peter's master upon my reader, "and upon all that are true lovers of virtue; and dare trust in his providence; and be quiet; and go a angling."

# WHAT AND WHO IS AN ANGLER?

## THADDEUS NORRIS

I t is not my intention to offer any remarks on the antiquity of angling, or say
much in its defense. Dame Juliana Berners, Izaak Walton, and more recent
authors, have discoursed learnedly on its origin, and defended it wisely and valiantly from the aspersions and ridicule of those who cannot appreciate its quiet
toys, and who know not the solace and peace it brings to the harassed mind, or
how it begets and fosters contentment and a love of nature.

I ask any caviller to read Dr. Bethune's Bibliographical Preface to his edition Walton; and then Father Izaak's address to the readers of his discourse,
"but especially to THE HONEST ANGLER," and accompany him in spirit,
as Bethune by the quiet Lea, or Cotton by the bright rippling Dove; and if he be
not convinced of the blessed influences of the "gentle art," or if his heart is not
warmed, or no recollections of his boyish days come back to him, I give him up
without a harsh word, but with a feeling of regret, that a lifetime should be spent
without attaining so much of quiet happiness that might have been so easily

possessed, and quoting a few sad words from Whittier's Maud Muller, only say "it might have been."

Many anglers, such as Sir Humphrey Davy and Sir Joshua Reynolds, besides some of my own acquaintance, have sought its cheering influences in advanced life. I know of one whose early manhood and maturer years were spent on the boisterous deep, and who, though now past eighty, is still an ardent, but quiet angler; and when no better spot can be found, he will even fish through the ice in winter for roach. No doubt his days have been lengthened out, and the burden of life lightened, by his love of angling.

But how sweetly memories of the past come to one who has appreciated and enjoyed it from his boyhood, whose almost first penny, after he wore jacket and trousers, bought his first fish hook; whose first fishing line was twisted by mother or sister; whose float was the cork of a physic vial, and whose sinkers were cut from the sheet lead of an old tea chest! Thus rigged, with what glad anticipations of sport, many a boy has started on some bright Saturday morning, his gourd, or old cow's horn of red worms in one pocket, and a jackknife in the other, to cut his alder pole with, and wandered "free and far" by still pool and swift waters, dinnerless—except perhaps a slight meal at a cherry tree, or a handful of berries that grew along his path—and come home at night weary and footsore, but exulting in his string of chubs, minnows, and sunnies, the largest as broad as his three fingers! He almost falls asleep under his Saturday night scrubbing, but in the morning, does ample justice to his "catch," which is turned out of the pan, crisp and brown, and matted together like a pancake.

In *my* school days, a boy might have been envied, but not loved for proficiency in his studies; but he was most courted, who knew the best fishing holes; who had plenty of powder and shot; the best squirrel dog, and the use of his father's long flintlock gun. And I confess, as I write these lines with my spectacles on, that I have still a strong drawing toward this type of a boy, whether I meet him in my lonely rambles, or whether he dwells only in my memory.

Sometimes the recollection of our boyish sports comes back to us after manhood, and one who has been "addicted" to fishing relapses into his old "ailment"; then angling becomes a pleasant kind of disease, and one's friends are apt to become inoculated with the virus, for it is contagious. Or men are informally introduced to each other on the stream, by a good-humored salutation, or an inquiry of "*What luck?*" or a display of the catch, or the offer of a cigar, or the flask, or a new fly; and with such introduction have become fast friends, from that affinity which draws all true anglers together.

But let me ask what is an angler, and who is a true angler? One who fishes with nets is not, neither is he who spears, snares, or dastardly uses the crazy bait to get fish, or who catches them on set lines; nor is he who is boisterous, noisy, or quarrelsome; nor are those who profess to practice the higher branches of the art, and affect contempt for their more humble brethren, who have not attained to their proficiency, imbued with the feeling that should possess the true angler.

Nor is he who brings his ice chest from town, and fishes all day with worm or fly, that he may return to the city and boastingly distribute his soaked and tasteless trout among his friends and brag of the numbers he has basketed, from fingerlings upwards.

Anglers may be divided into almost as many genera and species as the fish they catch, and engage in the sport from as many impulses. Let me give, "en passant," a sketch of a few of the many I have met with.

There is the Fussy Angler, a great bore; of course you will shun him. The Snob Angler, who speaks confidently and knowingly on a slight capital of skill or experience. The Greedy, Pushing Angler, who rushes ahead and half fishes the water, leaving those who follow in doubt as to whether he has fished a pool or rift carefully, or slurred it over in his haste to reach some well-known place down the stream before his companions. The company of these, the quiet, careful angler will avoid.

We also meet sometimes with the Spick-and-Span Angler, who has a highly varnished rod, and a superabundance of useless tackle; his outfit is of the most elaborate kind as regards its finish. He is a dapper "well got up" angler in all his appointments, and fishes much indoors over his claret and poteen, when he has a good listener. He frequently displays bad taste in his tackle, intended for fly-fishing, by having a thirty-dollar multiplying reel, filled with one of Conroy's very best relaid sea-grass lines, strong enough to hold a dolphin. If you meet him on the teeming waters of northern New York, the evening's display of his catch depends much on the rough skill of his guide.

The Rough-and-Ready Angler, the opposite of the aforenamed, disdains all "tomfoolery," and carries his tackle in an old shot bag, and his flies in a tangled mass.

We have also the Literary Angler, who reads Walton and admires him hugely; he has been inoculated with the sentiment only; the five-mile walk up the creek, where it has not been fished much, is very fatiguing to him; he "did not know he must wade the stream," and does not until he slips in, and then he has some trouble at night to get his boots off. He is provided with a stout bass rod, good strong leaders of salmon gut, and a stock of Conroy's "journal flies," and wonders if he had not better put on a shot just above his stretcher fly.

The Pretentious Angler, to use a favorite expression of the lamented Dickey Riker, once Recorder of the city of New York, is one "that prevails to a great extent in this community." This gentleman has many of the qualities attributed by Fisher, of the "Angler's Souvenir," to Sir Humphrey Davy. If he has attained the higher branches of the art, he affects to despise all sport which he considers less scientific; if a salmon fisher, he calls trout "vermin"; if he is a trout fly-fisher, he professes contempt for bait fishing. We have talked with true anglers who were even disposed to censure the eminent Divine, who has so ably, and with such labor of love, edited our American edition of Walton, for affectation, in saying of the red worm, "our hands have long since been washed of the dirty things." The servant should not be above his master, and certainly "Iz. Wa.," whose disciple the Doctor professed to be, considered it no indignity to use them, nor was he disgusted with his "horn of gentles." But the Doctor was certainly right in deprecating the use of ground bait in reference to trout, when the angler can with a little faith and less greed soon learn the use of the fly.

The *Shad-roe Fisherman.*—The habitat of this genus (and they are rarely found elsewhere) is Philadelphia. There are many persons of the aforesaid city, who fish only when this bait can be had, and an idea seems to possess them that fish will bite at no other. This fraternity could have been found some years back, singly or in pairs, or little coteries of three or four, on any sunshiny day from Easter to Whitsuntide, heaving their heavy dipsies and horsehair snoods from the ends of the piers, or from canal boats laid up in ordinary—the old floating bridge at Gray's Ferry was a favorite resort for them. Sometimes the party was convivial, and provided with a junk bottle of what they believed to be *old rye*.

Before the gas works had destroyed the fishing in the Schuylkill, I frequently observed a solitary individual of this species, wending his way to the river on Sunday mornings, with a long reed pole on his shoulder, and in his hand a tin kettle of shad roe; and his "prog," consisting of hard-boiled eggs and crackers and cheese, tied up in a cotton bandana handkerchief. Toward nightfall "he might have been seen" (as James the novelist says of the horseman), trudging homeward with a string of pan rock and white perch, or "catties" and eels, his trousers and coat sleeves well plastered with his unctuous bait, suggesting the idea of what, in vulgar parlance, might be called "a very nasty man."

But let us not turn up our scientific noses at this humble brother; nor let the home missionary or tract distributor rate him too severely, if he should meet with him in his Sunday walks; for who can tell what a quiet day of consolation it has been to him; he has found relief from the toils and cares of the week, and perhaps from the ceaseless tongue of his shrewish "old woman." If his sport has been good, he follows it up the next day, and keeps "blue Monday."

We have seen some very respectable gentlemen in our day engaged in fishing with shad roe at Fairmount Dam. The bar even had its representative, in one of our first criminal court lawyers. He did not "dress the character" with as much discrimination as when he lectured on Shakespeare, for he always wore his blue coat with gilt buttons: he did not appear to be a successful angler. "Per contra" to this was a wealthy retired merchant, who used to astonish us with his knack of keeping this difficult bait on his hooks, and his skill in hooking little white perch. Many a troller has seen him sitting bolt upright in the bow of his boat on a cool morning in May, with his overcoat buttoned up to his chin, his jolly spouse in the stern, and his servant amidship, baiting the hooks and taking off the lady's fish. The son also was an adept as well as the sire. Woe to the perch fisher, with his bait of little silvery eels, if these occupied the lower part of the swim, for the fish were all arrested by the stray ova that floated off from the "gobs" of shad roe.

As we love contrasts, let us here make a slight allusion to that sensible "old English gentleman," the Admiral, who surveyed the northwest coast of America to see, if in the contingency of the Yankees adhering to their claim of "fifty-four forty," the country about Vancouver's Island was worth contending for. He was an ardent angler, and it is reported, that on leaving his ship he provided stores for a week, which comprised of course not a few drinkables; as well as salmon rods and other tackle, and started in his boats to explore the rivers and tributaries, which, so goes the story, were so crammed in many places with salmon, that they could be captured with a boat hook; and still with all the variety of salmon flies and the piscatory skill of the admiral and his officers, not a fish could be induced to rise at the fly. He returned to his ship disheartened and disgusted, averring that the country was not worth contending for; that the Yankees might have it and be——; but it would be indecorous to record the admiral's mild expletive.

The True Angler is thoroughly imbued with the spirit of gentle old Izaak. He has no affectation, and when a fly cast is not to be had, can find amusement in catching sunfish or roach, and does not despise the sport of any humbler brother of the angle. With him, fishing is a recreation, and a "calmer of unquiet thoughts." He never quarrels with his luck, knowing that satiety dulls one's appreciation of sport as much as want of success, but is ever content when he has done his best, and looks hopefully forward to a more propitious day. Whether from boat or rocky shore, or along the sedgy bank of the creek, or the stony margin of the mountain brook, he deems it an achievement to take fish when they are difficult to catch, and his satisfaction is in proportion. If he is lazy, or a superannuated angler, he can even endure a few days' trolling on an inland lake, and smokes his cigar, chats with the boatman, and takes an occasional "nip," as he is rowed along the wooded shore and amongst the beautiful islands.

A true angler is generally a modest man; unobtrusively communicative when he can impart a new idea; and is ever ready to let a pretentious tyro have his say, and good-naturedly (as if merely suggesting how it should be done) repairs his tackle, or gets him out of a scrape. He is moderately provided with all tackle and "fixins" necessary to the fishing he is in pursuit of. Is quietly self-reliant and equal to almost any emergency, from splicing his rod or tying his own flies, to trudging ten miles across a rough country with his luggage on his back. His enjoyment consists not only in the taking of fish: he draws much pleasure from the soothing influence and delightful accompaniments of the art.

With happy memories of the past summer, he joins together the three pieces of his fly rod at home, when the scenes of the last season's sport are wrapped in snow and ice, and renews the glad feelings of long summer days. With what interest he notes the swelling of the buds on the maples, or the advent of the bluebird and robin, and looks forward to the day when he is to try another cast! and, when it comes at last, with what pleasing anticipations he packs up his "traps," and leaves his business cares and the noisy city behind, and after a few hours' or few days' travel in the cars, and a few miles in a rough wagon, or a vigorous tramp over rugged hills or along the road that leads up the banks of the river, he arrives at his quarters! He is now in the region of fresh butter and mealy potatoes—there are always good potatoes in a mountainous trout country. How pleasingly rough everything looks after leaving the prim city! How pure and wholesome the air! How beautiful the clumps of sugar maples and the veteran hemlocks jutting out over the stream; the laurel; the ivy; the moss-covered rocks; the lengthening shadows of evening! How musical the old familiar tinkling of the cow-bell and the cry of the whippoorwill! How sweetly he is lulled to sleep as he hears

The waters leap and gush
O'er channelled rock and broken bush!

Next morning, after a hearty breakfast of mashed potatoes, ham and eggs, and butter from the cream of the cow that browses in the woods, he is off, three miles up the creek, a cigar or his pipe in his mouth, his creel at his side, and his rod over his shoulder, chatting with his chum as he goes; free, joyous, happy; at peace with his Maker, with himself, and all mankind; he should be grateful for this much, even if he catches no fish. How exhilarating the music of the stream! how invigorating its waters, causing a consciousness of manly vigor, as he wades sturdily with the strong current and casts his flies before him! When his zeal abates, and a few of the speckled lie in the bottom of his creel, he is not less interested in the wild flowers on the bank, or the scathed old hemlock on the cliff above, with its hawk's nest, the lady of the house likely inside, and the male proprietor perched high above on its dead top and he breaks forth lustily—the scene suggesting the song—

> The bee's on its wing, and the hawk on its nest,
> And the river runs merrily by.

When noon comes on, and the trout rise lazily or merely rip, he halts "sub tegmine fagi," or under the shadow of the dark sugar maple to build a fire and toast trout for his dinner, and wiles away three hours or so. He dines sumptuously, straightens and dries his leader and the gut of his dropper, and repairs all breakage. He smokes leisurely, or even takes a nap on the greensward or velvety moss, and resumes his sport when the sun has declined enough to shade at least one side of the stream, and pleasantly anticipates the late evening on the still waters far down the creek. God be with you, gentle angler, if actuated with the reeling of our old master! whether you are a top fisher or a bottom fisher; whether your bait be gentles, brandling, grub, or red worm; crab, shrimp, or minnow; caddis, grasshopper, or the feathery counterfeit of the ephemera. May your thoughts be always peaceful, and your heart filled with gratitude to Him who made the country and the rivers; and "may the east wind never blow when you go a-fishing!"

# NOTE TO *DON JUAN*, CANTO XIII

## LORD BYRON

And angling, too, that solitary vice,
Whatever Izaak Walton sings or says;
The quaint, old, cruel coxcomb, in his gullet
Should have a hook, and a small trout to pull it.

It would have taught him humanity at least. This sentimental savage, whom it is a mode to quote (among the novelists) to show their sympathy for innocent sports and old songs, teaches how to sew up frogs, and break their legs by way of experiment, in addition to the art of angling, the cruelest, the coldest, and the stupidest of pretended sports. They may talk about the beauties of Nature, but the angler merely thinks about his dish of fish; he has no leisure to take his eyes from off the streams, and a single *bite* is worth to him more than all the scenery around. Besides, some fish bite best on a rainy day. The whale, the shark, and the tunny fishery have somewhat of noble and perilous in them; even net fishing, trawling, etc., are more humane and useful. But angling!—No angler can be a good man.

# A PAINTER, AN ANGLER, AND SOME
# OTHERS

### WILLIAM SCROPE

Exploring one morning the upper parts of the river, with my trout rod in my hand, I came to a little meadow in a vale where the stream played in mazes beneath hanging coppices. In this sequestered spot, I espied a gentle angler—I may say particularly gentle. His mode of fishing appeared so novel, that I was induced to pry a little into it; so I ventured to approach him, and asked what sport he had been having.

"Oh, glorious, glorious—perfectly enchanting! All Paradise is around me!"

I took notice, however, that although he held his rod pretty much in the usual piscatorial position of altitude, his fly was by no means on the water, but lay very comfortably dry upon the furze on the bank side, and that, whatever his hand might pretend to be doing, his mind was not at that moment particularly bent upon a capture. Whilst he stood entranced, I took the liberty of lifting up the lid of his basket, in which I descried nothing but a pair of gloves—not a fish reposed in it. It was clean, new, and Cockney-like, and I ventured to give him a hint to this effect.

"Well now I declare, sir, that is very singular; because I certainly caught two trout, and put them into my creel. But I dare say you are a little absent, and did not notice them; I am somewhat absent myself occasionally."

He examined the basket, and found only gloves by themselves—gloves.

"Where can I have put them?"

"Indeed I can't guess, sir."

He then began to shuffle about and examine his waistcoat pockets and those of his pantaloons, nay, actually his fob.

"Perhaps, sir, you did not find quite room enough in your fob, and put them into your coat pocket for fear they should soil the basket."

"Bless me! so I did; and here they are, truly. I see now how it is; in a hurry, and whilst I was wrapt in admiration of the scenery, I put the gloves where the fish should have been, and *vice versa*—nothing could be more natural."

This he said with simplicity worthy of the golden age. But he declared that although he was not at that moment very intent on the sport, he did like the fishing exceedingly. "Because," said he, "it requires no parade of attendance, like other field sports; it leads to the most beautiful spots; and I take up my rod and my painting box at any hour I please, and saunter over the flowery meads, in a state of tranquil enjoyment, amidst all the most pleasing images of rural life."

I observed there was considerable excitement in fishing occasionally, as well as tranquility. "For instance, now," said I, "there is a sea trout in that run of water that will make your heart dance, if you should happen to hook him; I saw him put his head up at the cheek of the current, and he had a willful look, and is likely to make most pernicious runs when hooked; for these sort of fish are very active and strong. If you will give me leave, I will change your trout fly for a larger one, and instruct you how to proceed, as from the nature of your tackle I conclude you are not accustomed to fish of this description. There now—go a little higher up the stream; throw above him, and bring the fly gently round; and if he comes at it, do not strike him too hard, or you will break your slender tackle. If you get hold of him, we shall see how he is to be managed; he will put your tranquility to the test, I promise you."

He grasped the rod, and held it aloft; then, after a considerable pause, "He is exactly in the right spot," said he. "Precisely," I replied.

"What a rich red tone of color he has—how well it tells in the shadow! He will come in capitally."

"He is not red, I assure you, but clear as silver, and I wish he may come in capitally."

"Bless me! he looks red to me, and I must take him immediately; he is exactly the thing I wanted." So saying, to my amazement, he dropped the rod, and pulled out a sketch book, in which he began painting a red cow in water colors that was reposing under a hawthorn bush on the opposite bank, just beyond the stream where the fish was lying, and which had been the real object of his remarks. When he had done with the cow, however, I put the rod once more into his hands, and reminded him of the fish.

"Now throw a few yards above the spot where you see the water boiling around the large blue stone. Very well; advance a step every time you throw. Capital! Now you are precisely at the fish. Strike him gently if he rises. Well done!—by Paul Potter you have him! Hold up the top of your rod, and keep an even steady pull upon him."

"How can I keep a steady pull upon such a wild animal? Why he springs out of the water, and whizzes about in it, like that fire-work called a serpent."

"Be steady—be steady, or he will whiz you about with a witness. Shorten your line; get into the water, and follow him."

"What a cruel speech! Why I never learned to swim. You are exceedingly inconsiderate indeed, sir."

"Swim! why the water on this channel is scarcely over your ankles, and I will help you if you should happen to stumble."

"Then we should both meet a watery grave together. I have often read of such calamities."

"In with you—in with you, I say, or he will be off. There, I told you so; he has broke your line; and, pray pardon me, but pretty work you have made of it with your tranquility."

"Well, as it seems to make you so uneasy, I will go a little way into the water, though I shall not enjoy it."

"Why, what is the use of wetting yourself, now, you have lost the fish?"

"True, true—I did not sufficiently consider that; so now I will go back, and see if I can improve my cow."

This was abundantly philosophical; but intelligible enough to me, who being very much addicted to painting myself, know how absorbing a passion it is.

The cow was a good cow—drawn in a clean and decisive manner, with a correct knowledge of the anatomy of the animal. I praised accordingly, and we began naturally enough to talk upon the principles of landscape painting; and as we both agreed pretty well as to those principles, so we both laid down the law with as much confidence as if we were the lineal descendants of Zeuxis or Apelles—a fashion, I must observe, most particularly prevalent at the present day. I fear it is not worth while to notice our remarks . . .

Then, having beguiled the attention of Mr. Tintern (for that was the stranger's name) from the summits in which he had been soaring, I found him quite ready to receive an impression of a more humble kind, and he attended me in my walk, nothing loth. I was very much gratified with his company; for, besides his talent and simplicity of character, there was such an appearance of benevolent feeling in much of his conversation, which I have not thought it necessary to mention, that no one could avoid being taken with him.

I commenced operation at the Carry-wheel, which is nearly at the head of the Pavilion-water, and had not made four casts before I hooked a fish. He was evidently diminutive; but, dwarf as he was, he thought a good deal of himself, and was prodigal of the little strength which nature had given him. I thought him conceited, and so hauled him on shore at once without any ceremony. He proved to be a river trout of four pounds—a silly-looking creature enough.

Well, I went forward and caught a few gilses and salmon in the upper Pavilion-water, not worth mentioning, except as the sport had the effect of rousing my new friend from his abstraction; indeed I met with nothing remarkable till I came to the Kingswell Lees. Now every one knows that the Kingswell Lees, in fisherman's phrase, fishes off land; so there I stood on *terra durra* amongst the rocks that dip down to the water's edge. Having executed one or two throws, there comes to me a voracious fish, and makes a startling dash at "Meg with the muckle mouth." Sharply did I strike the caitiff; whereat he rolled round disdainful, making a whirl in the water of prodigious circumference: it was not exactly Charybdis, or the Maelstrom, but rather more like the wave occasioned by the sudden turning of a man-of-war's boat. Being hooked, and having by this turn set his nose peremptorily down the stream, he flashed and whizzed away like a rocket. My situation partook of the nature of a surprise. Being on a rocky shore, and having a bad start, I lost ground at first considerably; but the reel sang out joyously, and yielded a liberal length of line, that saved me from the disgrace of being broke. I got on the best pace I was able, and was on good ground just as my line was nearly all run out. As the powerful animal darted through Meg's Hole, I was just able to step back and wind up a few yards of line; but he still went a killing pace, and when he came near Melrose Bridge he evinced a distressing preference for passing through the farther arch, in which case my line would have been cut by the pier. My heart sunk with apprehension, for he was near the opposite bank. Purdie, seeing this, with great presence of mind took up some stones from the channel, and threw them one by one between the fish and the said opposite bank. This naturally brought Master Salmo somewhat nearer; but still for a few moments we had a doubtful struggle for it. At length, by lowering the head of the rod, and thus not having so much of the ponderous weight of the fish to encounter, I towed him a little sideways; and so advancing towards me with propitious fin, he shot through the arch nearest me.

Deeply immersed, I dashed after him as best I might; and arriving on the other side of the bridge I floundered out upon dry land, and continued the chase. The salmon, "right orgillous and presumptive," still kept the strength of the stream, and abating nothing of his vigor, went swiftly down the Whirls; then through the Boat shiel, and over the shallows, till he came to the throat of the Elmwheel, down which he darted amain. Owing to the bad ground, the pace here became exceedingly distressing. I contrived, however, to keep company with my fish, still doubtful of the result, till I came to the bottom of the long cast in question, when he still showed fight, and sought the shallows below. Unhappily the alders prevented my following by land, and I was compelled to take water again, which slackened my speed. But the stream soon expanding, and the current diminishing, my fish likewise traveled more slowly; so I gave a few sobs and recovered my wind a little, gathered up my line, and tried to bring him to terms. But he derided my efforts, and dashed off for another burst, triumphant. Not far below lay the rapids of the Saughterford: he would soon gain them at the pace he was going, that was certain; see, he is there already! But I back out again on dry land, nothing loth, and have a fair race with him. Sore work it is. I am a pretty fair runner, as has often been testified; but his velocity is surprising. On, on—still he goes, ploughing up the water like a steamer. "Away with you, Charlie! Quick, quick, man—quick for your life! Loosen the boat at the Cauld Pool, where we shall soon be." And so indeed we were, when I jumped into the said craft, still having good hold of my fish.

The Tweed is here broad and deep, and the salmon at length had become somewhat exhausted; he still kept in the strength of the stream, however, with his nose seawards, and hung heavily. At last he comes near the surface of the water. See how he shakes his tail and digs downwards, seeking the deep profound—that he will never gain. His motions become more short and feeble; he is evidently doomed, and his race well-nigh finished. Drawn into the hare water, and not approving of the extended cleik, he makes another swift rush, and repeats this effort each time that he is towed to the shallows. At length he is cleiked in earnest, and hauled to shore: he proves one of the grey scull, newly run, and weighs somewhat about twenty pounds. The hook is not in his mouth, but in the outside of it; in which case a fish being able to respire freely, always shows extraordinary vigor, and generally sets his head down the stream.

During the whole period of my experience in fishing, though I have had some sharp encounters, yet I never knew any sport equal to this. I am out of breath even now whenever I think of it. I will trouble any surveyor to measure the distance from the Kingswell Lees, the starting spot, above Melrose Bridge, to the end of the Cauld Pool, the death place, by Melrose Church, and to tell me how much less it is than a mile and three-quarters—I say I will trouble him to do so; and let him be a lover of the angle, that he may rather increase than diminish the distance, as in good feeling and respect for the craft it behooves him to do. I will likewise thank my contemporaries and posterity to bear in mind that the distance about to be measured by this able surveyor was run at an eclipse pace, always allowing for some slight abatement in speed pending our immersion.

Whilst I was taking a rest on the greensward, the heated face of my excellent new friend appeared through the alders. He could not, however, be fairly said to be in at the death; the *coup de grace* having been already given about five minutes. He expressed the greatest astonishment at the swiftness and result of the race, and at the power of the fish, who had been able to distress two full-grown men so completely. He owned he was much excited, but thought fishing for salmon would be too turbulent an amusement for him; though perhaps he might have kept up with a good pony, had the ground been passable by such a beast. Poussin, Virgil, the Apennines, all were forgotten; and he began to enter warmly into the spirit of the present, and was curious to know by what particular tactics one can contrive to get the better of such a large furious monster, as he expressed it, with such apparently inadequate means, when a small sea trout broke him with all the ease imaginable. As I now reckoned upon his attention, I told him as follows—how to manage a large salmon, and how a large salmon may manage us:—

"When you get hold of a *monstrum horrendum ingens* of a fish, say of some five and forty pounds, you must anticipate a very long and severe battle. If, therefore, you have a disposable Gilly with you, despatch him instantly for some skilful fisherman, as well to assist you when you are exhausted with fatigue, as to bring your dinner and supper; not forgetting a dark lantern, that you may not be beaten by the shades of night—a circumstance by no means improbable. At the first onset you will probably be obliged to keel) your arms and rod aloft, in order to steer clear of the rocks. This action, with a heavy rod and large fish on your

line, is very distressing, if continued even for a short time; and it will be necessary to repeat it often, if the channel is not very favorable; and in that case your
muscles will ache insupportably, if they at all resemble those of other men. The
easiest position, when it is safe to use it, is to place the butt of your rod against the
stomach as a rest, and to bring the upper part of the arm and the elbow in close
contact with the sides, putting on at the same time an air of determination.

"If your leviathan should be superlatively boisterous, no one knows what
may happen. For instance, should you be in a boat, and he should shoot away
down the river, you must follow rapidly; then, when he again turns upwards,
what a clever fellow your fisherman must be, to stop a boat that has been going
down a rapid stream at the rate of eight miles an hour, and bring it round all of a
sudden in time to keep company with the fish, who has taken an upward direction! And what a clever fellow a piscator must be, if he can prevent twenty yards
of his line, or more, from hanging loose in the stream! These sort of things will
happen, and they are ticklish concerns. All I can do is to recommend caution and
patience; and the better to encourage you in the exercise of these virtues, I will
recount what happened to Duncan Grant in days of yore.

"First, you must understand that what is called 'preserving the river' was
formerly unknown, and every one who chose to take a cast did so without let or
hindrance.

"In pursuance of this custom, in the month of July, some thirty years ago,
one Duncan Grant, a shoemaker by profession, who was more addicted to fishing
than to his craft, went up the way from the village of Aberlour, in the north, to
take a cast in some of the pools above Elchies Water. He had no great choice
of tackle, as may be conceived; nothing, in fact, but what was useful, and scant
supply of that.

"Duncan tried one or two pools without success, till he arrived at a very
deep and rapid stream, facetiously termed '*the Mountebank*': here he paused, as if
meditating whether he should throw his line or not. 'She is very big,' said he to
himself, 'but I'll try her; if I grip him he'll be worth the handing.' He then fished
it, a step and a throw, about half way down, when a heavy splash proclaimed that
he had raised him, though he missed the fly. Going back a few paces, he came
over him again, and hooked him. The first tug verified to Duncan his prognos-
tication, that if he was there 'he would be worth the handing'; but his tackle
had thirty plies of hair next the fly, and he held fast, nothing daunted. Give and
take went on with dubious advantage, the fish occasionally sulking. The thing at
length became serious; and, after a succession of the same tactics, Duncan found
himself at the Boat of Aberlous, seven hours after he had hooked his fish, the said

fish fast under a stone, and himself completely tired. He had some thoughts of breaking his tackle and giving the thing up; but he finally hit upon an expedient to rest himself, and at the same time to guard against the surprise and consequence of a sudden movement of the fish.

"He laid himself down comfortably on the banks, the butt end of his rod in front; and most ingeniously drew out part of his line, which he held in his teeth. 'If he tugs when I'm sleeping,' said he, 'I think I'll find him noo'; and no doubt it is probable that he would. Accordingly, after a comfortable nap of three or four hours, Duncan was awoke by a most unceremonious tug at his jaws. In a moment he was on his feet, his rod well up, and the fish swattering down the stream. He followed as best he could, and was beginning to think of the rock at Craigellachie, when he found to his great relief that he could 'get a pull on him.' He had now comparatively easy work; and exactly twelve hours after hooking him, he cleiked him at the head of Lord Fife's water: he weighed fifty-four pounds, Dutch, and had the tide lice upon him."

Thus Duncan Grant has instructed us how to manage a large salmon. Let us now see how a large salmon may manage us.

In the year 1815, Robert Kerse hooked a clean salmon of about forty pounds in the Makerstoun Water, the largest, he says, he ever encountered; sair work he had with him for some hours; till at last Rob, to use his own expression, was "clean dune out." He landed the fish, however, in the end, and laid him on the channel; astonished, and rejoicing at his prodigious size, he called out to a man on the opposite bank of the river, who had been watching him for some time.

"Hey, mon, sic a fish!"

He then went for a stone to fell him with; but as soon as his back was turned, the fish began to wamble towards the water, and Kerse turned, and jumped upon it; over they both tumbled, and they, line, hook, and all went into the Tweed. The fish was too much for Rob, having broke the line, which got twisted round his leg, and made his escape, to his great disappointment and loss, for at the price clean salmon were then selling, he could have got five pounds for it.

Thus you see how a large fish may manage us.

I must tell you that the above-mentioned Robert Kerse has long been a distinguished character on the Tweed. At a secluded spot, where the woods and rocks dip down to the margin of the river, and where its current is opposed by a rocky barrier through which it has worn its way in frightful gorges, the gaunt figure of Auld Rob of the Troughs has been seen any time these forty years. He is very tall and bony, and when working his boat with the canting pole amongst the rapids, or looking down aloft ready to strike, he cuts a most formidable

Salvator Rosa-like appearance. Rob is now highly seasoned with the saltiness of time, being nearer eighty than seventy years old; drinks whiskey like water, his native element; and to this day runs after the hounds, when they come near, like a boy of fifteen. He is a genuine lover of all sports, and has begot numerous sons and daughters: of the former, four are game-keepers, and fishermen on Tweed, Tiviot, and Ettrick, to the Duke of Bubbleuch, Lord Lothian, and Lord Home. They are remarkable as claiming a regular descent from Saxon ancestors in the most remote times, and are an active, athletic, clean-limbed race of men, keen of eye, and swift of foot, of good pluck, and altogether amphibious, loving the heather and mountain flood better than the street and servants' hall. Stalwart men would they have been in a Border Foray had they lived in the time of Johnny Armstrong. Such and so great are the Kerses; but they will not go down to posterity like the Purdies, "carent quia Vate sacro"; neither could the old river god Rob himself contend with the otter so valiantly as Charlie Purdie. Whether it was that he had a sort of fellow-feeling for an animal that was amphibious like himself, and followed the same profession, or from what other cause I cannot say, but Rob did not particularly shine in a fair stand-up otter fight, as you shall hear.

In the latter end of September, 1839, Kerse had set a cairn net at the Clippers, "a little below Makerstoun House, but on the bank of the river opposite to it; and on going to the cairn to examine the net, he saw a young otter sitting on, and entangled in it; he threw more of the net over it, whilst drawing it to the land, and when he had caught hold of the tail, and was carrying it off, a large otter, which he described as "a she ane," five feet in length, jumped out of the water, ran up the bank after him to use his own words, "like a mad bear," and commenced a furious attack upon hint. Rob had nothing to defend himself with but his hat; and as he was holding the young one with one hand, he found he was likely to have the worst of it, and to be bitten by the one animal or the other. So he threw the whelp to the old one, saying, "Ay, ye she devil, ye may get her, twae to ane is odds." They both swam away; that is, the two otters, not Kerse.

On looking after them he saw two other young ones trying to make past the point of the cairn, which, owing to the strength of the current, they seemed unable to effect: Kerse thought he would try the thing again, so he laid hold of one of them and pulled it out also by the tail; scarce had he done this, and had begun to take to his heels, ere out again jumped the old one, and attacked him; but this time Rob had provided himself with a large stone, and hit the old beast on the back, when he again set off and carried the young one with him which was afterwards given to Lord John Scott. During the whole contest, says Rob, "the auld beast keepit squeeling, and makin' a noise something like a horse, when he gies a snore."

# FISHING

### REVEREND THOMAS BASTARD

Fishing, if I, a fisher, may protest
Of pleasures is the sweet'st, of sports the best,
Of exercises the most excellent,
Of Recreations the most innocent.
But now the sport is marred, and wot ye why?
Fishes decrease, and fishers multiply.

# CRAZY FOR RIVERS (SELECTION)

## BILL BARICH

That autumn, I went a little crazy for rivers. The weather was unusually mild in northern California, where I live, and I had some time to spare and couldn't imagine a better way to spend it than in the high mountain country as the leaves began to fall. I fished the Merced and the Stanislaus, the Kings and the North Yuba, and I had some luck on them all and might have fished the Tuolumne, too, if nature hadn't dealt me a setback. It was a good period in my life, calm and reflective, even happy. The days flowed by unbroken, in perfect sunlight, and often I found myself thinking back over the years and thanking the heavens I'd come to be where I was, knee-deep in a trout stream with a fly rod in my hand.

Some people are born anglers, but I was not, even though my father had a passion for fishing. When I was a boy, I used to hear him complain about his distance from a decent lake as he dodged the traffic between our Long Island home and his office in Manhattan. He'd grown up in rural Michigan, the last of twelve children. His older brothers had taught him to love the outdoors, so he came by his longing honestly. His father—my grandfather, a stocky Slav always dressed for a wedding in a three-piece wool suit from Dubrovnik—was fond of the woods, as well, and saw no irony in decorating the tavern he owned with his cherished forest creatures (deer, moose, even hawks) stuffed and mounted.

For some reason, I'd met only a couple of my paternal uncles, so I enjoyed being told stories about them, especially about John, the eldest, who was a legendary hunter. He had shared a bed with my father for a while. That wasn't uncommon in large families in those days, and it might never have been mentioned at all, except that John talked and hunted in his sleep. In the middle of the night, he'd sit bolt upright in a trance, grab my father by the shoulders, shake him, and shout, "There's a bear in the room! Oh, no! He's going to attack us!" My father never saw the bear, of course, but it seemed real to him, and he would shiver and whimper until John stuck out an arm like a rifle, took deliberate aim, and fired a fatal shot.

"Blam! Got 'im!" he'd cry. "We're saved!" Then he would roll over and go back to sleep.

Though I couldn't have known it then, not when I was still a child myself, I understood later that my father told such stories because he missed the folks on the Upper Peninsula and felt nostalgic for his youth and its sporting pursuits. His success in business had separated him from much that he cared about and had affection for, so every summer he would saddle up his family for a two-week vacation at a fishing resort, ordinarily in Minnesota—my mother was from there—but once in darkest Maine, at Sebago Lake, where I was puzzled and a bit frightened by the taciturn, stiff-spined, pipe-smoking men in flannel shirts, who were already cutting firewood in July.

I got my first fishing lessons on those trips, but I was a lackluster student. I could swing a Louisville Slugger with aplomb and even hit the long ball, but I was terribly awkward with a spin rod. Whenever I snarled my line or tossed a Jitterbug into a tree, my father would become flustered, carrying on about the minutes he was losing as he untied the knots and retrieved the plugs from limbs. He had a temper back then and lacked the patience to be a sympathetic teacher. We hardly ever caught any fish, either, so my brother, David, and I, being enterprising lads, would amuse ourselves by liberating minnows from the minnow bucket, shooting at squirrels with a Whammo slingshot, and conducting stupid giggling fits whose sole purpose was to further annoy the old man.

The only rewarding fishing I ever had on vacation, in fact, was courtesy of Carl Peterson, my mother's father, who guided us kids around Paradise Lake in a rowboat, in 1956. Carl managed an apartment building in St. Paul and bought me my first official cowboy outfit—chaps, spurs, boots, the works. I liked him a lot, although not as much as I liked my Uncle Ned, a former star player in a semi-pro baseball league, who worked as a mailman and let me walk his route with him sometimes. Ned always had a powerful thirst, and if the weather happened to be humid, we would be forced to stop at a few saloons along the way, where my uncle would polish off a quick draft beer, often paid for by an admiring fan, while I thumped the pinball machine and developed bad habits at an early age.

Carl Peterson didn't fish much himself, but he had patience in his favor and knew that children in boats are most content when they have something to do. He let us fish for easy-to-catch crappies instead of the tricky bass or pike my father went after, and we hauled in so many of them so fast that we got our picture in the local paper holding up a stringer to show off our forty or fifty victims. It still astonishes me to see how proud I look, a sophisticated East Coast youth of thirteen with his hair styled in a fashionable "Hollywood" crew cut (flat on top and slicked back at the sides), secretly imagining his future as a rock-and-roll star, even as he poses with a bunch of dead crappies at Paradise Lake.

I really hated fishing by the time I turned sixteen. I rebelled against the entire concept of a family vacation and whined and protested until my parents agreed to let me stay home alone. (Not incidentally, that was the summer I lost my virginity to a lusty cheerleader in my very own upstairs bedroom, treating her to an ice-cream pop from a circling Good Humor truck immediately afterward because I had no idea what else to do.) I thought that sitting in a boat in the middle of nowhere was the dumbest activity known to mankind and swore I would never fish again—and I might have kept my promise, too, if my brother hadn't intervened by accident, thirteen years later.

I had taken Horace Greeley's advice by then and migrated west to seek my fortune, although not to *work* for it. I was living in San Francisco, in a spacious Haight-Ashbury Victorian that we renters failed to dust even once during our tenancy. My hair, suffice it to say, was not in a Hollywood crew cut anymore, and I'd mastered the fine art of slacking. As for David, he had what we referred to as a "straight" job (book salesman in Manhattan), but he'd managed to finagle a transfer to California so he could savor the hippie glories I'd described to him. On a whim, he brought some of my father's old tackle with him, and we passed a comical evening sorting through it, laughing as we dredged up the names of the long-forgotten lures—Hawaiian Wigglers in lurid purple skirts, an evil black Sonic, a wacky Crazy Crawler, and a single Lazy Ike, yellow with bright-red polka dots.

We stored the tackle in the basement, where it languished. It might have stayed there forever, or at least until our landlord evicted us, if I hadn't fallen for a new girlfriend and invited her on a romantic trip to the Sierra Nevada. Not that I'd ever been to the Sierra Nevada myself, but that hardly matters when you're wild about someone. I studied the maps and made the plans and knew in my heart that we would be all right wherever we landed, as long as the place had a bed. After packing the car and loading the cooler, I went downstairs at the last minute and grabbed one of the vintage spin rods and a reel, South Bend and Zebco respectively, although I wasn't truly conscious of why I might be doing it and moved about as a person does in a daze or a dream.

We wound up in a rustic cabin on Stuart Fork of the Trinity River, in the shadow of the Trinity Alps. The cabin resembled a packing crate inside and had an icebox instead of a fridge, but it fronted on the river and was blessed with an open-air porch, where we slept on a lumpy mattress and gazed up at the brilliant stars and moonlit peaks and felt that we must be the most fortunate couple on earth. We went hiking, played games of cribbage, and cooked steaks over the coals, and yet not once did it occur to me that I was reliving the family vacation. I was still very young then and blind to so many things, and I didn't realize how a past experience can touch us deeply, can shatter us or set us free, even though we've never reckoned with its power. But I know it now. The past is never wholly gone.

Those days in the mountains were glorious days. It was late in September, but the afternoons were still blazing hot, and we liked nothing better than a nap on the porch after lunch, with the sun falling all around us and the air rich with the scent of sun-warmed pines. One afternoon, I woke before my girlfriend and stood looking at the river, so low and clear I could count the pebbles of the streambed. Trout in there? I doubted it, but I rigged up the rod for fun, rolled up my jeans, and waded barefoot into the water. I could see the sun glinting off the spoon I'd bought at the resort's store and could hear some Steller's jays bickering in the tall trees, and I drifted so far away from Stuart Fork that when a fish hit my lure, it had the effect of yanking me out of the clouds and back into my body.

High up leaped a silvery little rainbow, as hooked in the moment as I was.

# A RIVER RUNS THROUGH IT
# (SELECTION)

## NORMAN MACLEAN

We somehow couldn't get started that morning. After Paul and I had left home, Father put away his fishing tackle, probably thinking he was putting it away for good, so now he couldn't remember where. Mother had to find most of the things for him. She knew nothing about fishing or fishing tackle, but she knew how to find things, even when she did not know what they looked like.

Paul, who usually got everyone nervous by being impatient to be on the stream, kept telling Father, "Take it easy. It's turned cooler. We'll make a killing today. Take it easy." But my father, from whom my brother had inherited his impatience to have his flies on water, would look at me visibly loathing himself for being old and not able to collect himself.

My mother had to go from basement to attic and to most closets in between looking for a fishing basket while she made lunches for three men, each of whom wanted a different kind of sandwich. After she got us in the car, she checked each car door to see that none of her men would fall out. Then she dried her hands in her apron, although her hands were not wet, and said, "Thank goodness," as we drove away.

I was at the wheel, and I knew before we started just where we were going. It couldn't be far up the Blackfoot, because we were starting late, and it had to be a stretch of water of two or three deep holes for Paul and me and one good hole with no bank too steep for Father to crawl down. Also, since he couldn't wade, the good fishing water had to be on his side of the river. They argued while I drove, although they knew just as well as I did where we had to go, but each one in our family considered himself the leading authority on how to fish the Blackfoot River. When we came to the side road going to the river above the mouth of Belmont Creek, they spoke in unison for the first time. "Turn here," they said, and, as if I were following their directions, I turned to where I was going anyway.

The side road brought us down to a flat covered with ground boulders and cheat grass. No livestock grazed on it, and grasshoppers took off like birds and flew great distances, because on this flat it is a long way between feeding grounds, even for grasshoppers. The flat itself and its crop of boulders are the roughly ground remains of one of geology's great disasters The flat may well have been the end of the ice age lake, half as big as Lake Michigan, that in places was two thousand feet deep until the glacial dam broke and this hydraulic monster of the hilts charged out on to the plains of eastern Washington High on the mountains above where we stopped to fish are horizontal scars slashed by passing icebergs.

I had to be careful driving toward the river so I wouldn't high-center the car on a boulder and break the crankcase. The flat ended suddenly and the river was down a steep bank, blinking silver through the trees and then turning to blue by comparing itself to a red and green cliff. It was another world to see and feel, and another world of rocks. The boulders on the flat were shaped by the last ice age only eighteen or twenty thousand years ago, but the red and green precambrian rocks beside the blue water were almost from the basement of the world and time.

We stopped and peered down the bank. I asked my father, "Do you remember when we picked a lot of red and green rocks down there to build our fireplace? Some were red mudstones with ripples on them."

"Some had raindrops on them," he said. His imagination was always stirred by the thought that he was standing in ancient rain spattering on mud before it became rocks.

"Nearly a billion years ago," I said, knowing what he was thinking.

He paused. He had given up the belief that God had created all there was, including the Blackfoot River, on a six-day work schedule, but he didn't believe that the job so taxed God's powers that it took Him forever to complete.

"Nearly half a billion years ago," he said as his contribution to reconciling science and religion. He hurried on, not wishing to waste any part of old age in debate, except over fishing. "We carried those big rocks up the bank," he said, "but now I can't crawl down it. Two holes below, though, the river comes out in the open and there is almost no bank. I'll walk down there and fish, and you fish the first two holes. I'll wait in the sun. Don't hurry."

Paul said, "You'll get 'em," and all of a sudden Father was confident in himself again. Then he was gone.

We could catch glimpses of him walking along the bank of the river which had been the bottom of the great glacial lake. He held his rod straight in front of him and every now and then he lunged forward with it, perhaps reenacting some glacial race memory in which be speared a hairy ice age mastodon and ate him for breakfast.

Paul said, "Let's fish together today." I knew then that he was still taking care of me, because we almost always split up when we fished. "That's fine," I said. "I'll wade across and fish the other side," he said. I said, "Fine," again, and was doubly touched. On the other side you were backed against cliffs and trees, so it was mostly a roll-casting job, never my specialty. Besides, the river was powerful here with no good place to wade, and next to fishing Paul liked swimming rivers with his rod in his hand. It turned out he didn't have to swim here, but as he waded sometimes the wall of water rose to his upstream shoulder while it would be no higher than his hip behind him. He stumbled to shore from the weight of water in his clothes, and gave me a big wave.

I came down the bank to catch fish. Cool wind had blown in from Canada without causing any electric storms, so the fish should be off the bottom and feeding again. When a deer comes to water, his head shoots in and out of his shoulders to see what's ahead, and I was looking all around to see what fly to put on. But I didn't have to look further than my neck or my nose. Big clumsy flies bumped into my face, swarmed on my neck and wiggled in my underwear. Blundering and soft-bellied, they had been born before they had brains. They had spent a year under water on legs, had crawled out on a rock, had become flies and copulated with the ninth and tenth segments of their abdomens, and then had died as the first light wind blew them into the water where the fish circled excitedly. They were a fish's dream come true—stupid, succulent, and exhausted from copulation. Still, it would be hard to know what gigantic portion of human life is spent in this same ratio of years under water on legs to one premature, exhausted moment on wings.

I sat on a log and opened my fly box. I knew I had to get a fly that would match these flies exactly, because when a big hatch like this or the salmon fly is out, the fish won't touch anything else. As proof, Paul hadn't had a strike yet, so far as I could see.

I figured he wouldn't have the right fly, and I knew I had it. As I explained earlier, he carried all his flies in his hat-band. He thought that with four or five generals in different sizes he could imitate the action of nearly any aquatic or terrestrial insect in any stage from larval to winged. He was always kidding me because I carried so many flies. "My, my," he would say, peering into my fly box, "wouldn't it be wonderful if a guy knew how to use ten of all those flies." But I've already told you about the Bee, and I'm still sure that there are times when a general won't turn a fish over. The fly that would work now had to be a big fly, it had to have a yellow, black-banded body, and it had to ride high in the water with extended wings, something like a butterfly that has had an accident and can't dry its wings by fluttering in the water.

It was so big and flashy it was the first fly I saw when I opened my box. It was called a Bunyan Bug, tied by a fly tyer in Missoula named Norman Means, who ties a line of big flashy flies all called Bunyan Bugs. They are tied on big hooks, No. 2's and No. 4's, have cork bodies with stiff horsehair tied crosswise so they ride high in the water like dragonflies on their backs. The cork bodies are painted different colors and then are shellacked. Probably the biggest and flash-iest of the hundred flies my brother made fun of was the Bunyan Bug No. 2.

I took one look at it and felt perfect. My wife, my mother-in-law, and my sister-in-law, each in her somewhat obscure style, had recently redeclared their love for me. I, in my somewhat obscure style, had returned their love; I might never see my brother-in-law again. My mother had found my father's old tackle and once more he was fishing with us. My brother was taking tender care of me, and not catching any fish. I was about to make a killing.

It is hard to cast Bunyan Bugs into the wind because the cork and horsehair make them light for their bulk. But, though the wind shortens the cast, it acts at the same time to lower the fly slowly and almost vertically to the water with no telltale splash. My Stone Fly was still hanging over the water when what seemed like a speedboat went by it, knocked it high into the air, circled, opened the throttle wide on the returning straight away, and roared over the spot marked X where the Stone Fly had settled. Then the speedboat turned into a submarine, disappearing with all on board including my fly, and headed for deep water. I couldn't throw line into the rod fast enough to keep up with what was disappearing and I couldn't change its course. Not being as fast as what was under water, I literally forced it into the air. From where I was I suppose I couldn't see what happened, but my heart was at the end of the line and telegraphed back its impressions as it went by. My general impression was that marine life had turned into a rodeo. My particular information was that a large Rainbow had gone sunfishing, turning over twice in the air, hitting my line each time and tearing loose from the fly which went sailing out into space. My distinct information was that it never looked around to see. My only close-at-hand information was that when the line was reeled in, there was nothing on the end of it but some cork and some hairs from a horse's tail.

The stone flies were just as thick as ever, fish still swirled in quiet water, and I was a little smarter. I don't care much about taking instructions, even from myself, but before I made the next cast I underlined the fact that big Rainbows sometimes come into quiet waters because aquatic insects hatch in or near quiet waters. "Be prepared," I said to myself, remembering an old war song. I also accepted my own advice to have some extra coils of line in my left hand to take some of the tension off the first run of the next big Rainbow swirling in quiet water.

So on this wonderful afternoon when all things came together it took me one cast, one fish, and some reluctantly accepted advice to attain perfection. I did not miss another.

From then on I let them run so far that sometimes they surged clear across the river and jumped right in front of Paul. When I was young, a teacher had forbidden me to say "more perfect" because she said if a thing is perfect it can't be more so. But by now I had seen enough of life to have regained my confidence in it. Twenty minutes ago I had felt perfect, but by now my brother was taking off his bat and changing flies every few casts. I knew he didn't carry any such special as a Bunyan Bug No. 2 Yellow Stone Fly. I had five or six big Rainbows in my basket which began to hurt my shoulder so I left it behind on shore. Once in a while I looked back and smiled at the basket. I could hear it thumping on the rocks and falling on its side. However I may have violated grammar, I was feeling more perfect with every Rainbow.

Just after my basket gave an extra large thump there was an enormous splash in the water to the left of where I was casting. "My God," I thought before I could look, "there's nothing that big that swims in the Blackfoot," and, when I dared look, there was nothing but a large circle that got bigger and bigger. Finally the first wave went by my knees. "It must be a beaver," I thought I was waiting for him to surface when something splashed behind me. "My God," I said again, "I would have seen a beaver swim by me under water." While I was wrenching my neck backwards, the thing splashed right in front of me, too close for comfort but close enough so I could watch what was happening under water. The silt was rising from the bottom like smoke from the spot where lightning had struck. A fair-sized rock was sitting in the spot where the smoke was rising.

While I was relating my past to the present rock, there was another big splash in front of me, but this time I didn't bother to jump. Beaver, hell! Without looking, I knew it was my brother. It didn't happen often in this life, only when his fishing partner was catching fish and he couldn't. It was a sight, however rare, that he could not bear to watch. So he would spoil his partner's hole, even if it was his brother's. I looked up just in time to see a fair-sized boulder come out of the sky and I ducked too late to keep it from splashing all over me.

He had his hat off and he shook his fist at me. I knew he had fished around his hat band before he threw the rocks. I shook my fist back at him, and waded to shore, where my basket was still thumping. In all my life, I had got the rock treatment only a couple of times before. I was feeling more perfect than ever.

I didn't mind that he spoiled the hole before I had filled my basket, because there was another big hole between us and father. It was a beautiful stretch of water, against cliffs and in shadows. The hole I had just fished was mostly in sunlight—the weather had become cooler, but was still warm enough so that the hole ahead in shadows should be even better than the one in sunlight and I should have no trouble finishing off my basket with a Bunyan Bug No. 2 Yellow Stone Fly.

Paul and I walked nearly the length of the first hole before we could hear each other yell across the river. I knew he hated to be heard yelling, "What were they biting on?" The last two words, "biting on," kept echoing across the water and pleased me.

When the echoes ceased, I yelled back, "Yellow stone flies." These words kept saying themselves until they subsided into sounds of the river. He kept turning his hat round and round in his hands.

I possibly began to get a little ashamed of myself. "I caught them on a Bunyan Bug," I yelled. "Do you want one?"

"No," he yelled before "want one" had time to echo. Then "want one" and "no" passed each other on the back turns.

"I'll wade across with one," I said through the cup of my hands. That's a lot to say across a river, and the first part of it returning met the last part of it just starting. I didn't know whether he had understood what I had said, but the river still answered, "No."

While I was standing in quiet, shady water, I half noticed that no stone flies were hatching, and I should have thought longer about what I saw but instead I found myself thinking about character. It seems somehow natural to start thinking about character when you get ahead of somebody, especially about the character of the one who is behind. I was thinking of how, when things got tough, my brother looked to himself to get himself out of trouble. He never looked for any flies from me. I had a whole round of thoughts on this subject before I returned to reality and yellow stone flies. I started by thinking that, though he was my brother, he was sometimes knot-headed. I pursued this line of thought back to the Greeks who believed that not wanting any help might even get you killed. Then I suddenly remembered that my brother was almost always a winner and often because he didn't borrow flies. So I decided that the response we make to character on any given day depends largely on the response fish are making to character on the same day. And thinking of the response of fish, I shifted rapidly back to reality, and said to myself, "I still have one more hole to go."

I didn't get a strike and I didn't see a stone fly and it was the same river as the one above, where I could have caught my limit a few minutes before if my brother hadn't thrown rocks in it. My prize Bunyan Bug began to look like a fake to me as well as to the fish. To me, it looked like a floating mattress. I cast it upstream and let it drift down naturally as if it had died. Then I popped it into the water as if it had been blown there. Then I made it zigzag while retrieving it, as if it were trying to launch itself into flight. But it evidently retained the appearance of a floating mattress. I took it off, and tried several other flies. There were no flies in the water for me to match, and by the same token there were no fish jumping.

I began to cast glances across the river under my hat brim. Paul wasn't doing much either. I saw him catch one, and he just turned and walked to shore with it, so it couldn't have been much of a fish. I was feeling a little less than more perfect.

Then Paul started doing something he practically never did, at least not since he had been old enough to be cocky. He suddenly started fishing upstream, back over the water he had just fished. That's more like me when I feel I haven't fished the hole right or from the right angle, but, when my brother fished a hole, he assumed nothing was left behind that could be induced to change its mind.

I was so startled I leaned against a big rock to watch.

Almost immediately he started hauling them in. Big ones, and he didn't spend much time landing them either. I thought he gave them too little line and took them in too fast, but I knew what he was up to. He expected to make a killing in this hole, and he wasn't going to let any one fish thrash around in the water until it scared the rest off. He had one on now and he held the line on it so tight he was forcing it high in the air. When it jumped, he leaned back on his rod and knocked the fish into the water again. Full of air now, it streaked across the top of the water with its tail like the propeller of a seaplane until it could get its submarine chambers adjusted and submerge again.

He lost a couple but he must have had ten by the time he got back to the head of the hole.

Then he looked across the river and saw me sitting beside my rod. He started fishing again, stopped, and took another look. He cupped his hands and yelled, "Do you have George's No. 2 Yellow Hackle with a feather not a horse-hair wing?" It was fast water and I didn't get all the words immediately. "No. 2" I caught first, because it is a hell of a big hook, and then "George," because he was our fishing pal, and then "Yellow." With that much information I started to look in my box, and let the other words settle into a sentence later.

One bad thing about carrying a box loaded with flies, as I do, is that nearly half the time I still don't have the right one. "No," I admitted across the water, and water keeps repeating your admissions.

"I'll be there," he called back and waded upstream.

"No," I yelled after him, meaning don't stop fishing on my account. You can't convey an implied meaning across a river, or, if you can, it is easy to ignore. My brother walked to the lower end of the first hole where the water was shallow and waded across.

By the time he got to me, I had recovered most of the pieces he must have used to figure out what the fish were biting. From the moment he had started fishing upstream his rod was at such a slant and there was so much slack in his line that he must have been fishing with a wet fly and letting it sink. In fact, the slack was such that he must have been letting the fly sink five or six inches. So when I was fishing this hole as I did the last one—with a cork-body fly that rides on top of the water—I was fighting the last war. "No. 2" hook told me of course it was a hell of a big insect, but "yellow" could mean a lot of things. My big question by the time he got to me was, "Are they biting on some aquatic insect in a larval or nymph stage or are they biting on a drowned fly?"

He gave me a pat on the back and one of George's No. 2 Yellow Hackles with a feather wing. He said, "They are feeding on drowned yellow stone flies."

I asked him, "How did you think that out?"

He thought back on what had happened like a reporter. He started to answer, shook his head when he found he was wrong, and then started out again. "All there is to thinking," he said, "is seeing something noticeable which makes you see something you weren't noticing which makes you see something that isn't even visible."

I said to my brother, "Give me a cigarette and say what you mean."

"Well," he said, "the first thing I noticed about this hole was that my brother wasn't catching any. There's nothing more noticeable to a fisherman than that his partner isn't catching any.

"This made me see that I hadn't seen any stone flies flying around this hole."

Then he asked me, "What's more obvious on earth than sunshine and shadow, but until I really saw that there were no stone flies hatching here I didn't notice that the upper hole where they were hatching was mostly in sunshine and this hole was in shadow."

I was thirsty to start with, and the cigarette made my mouth drier so I flipped the cigarette into the water.

"Then I knew," he said, "if there were flies in this hole they had to come from the hole above that's in the sunlight where there's enough heat to make them hatch.

"After that, I should have seen them dead in the water. Since I couldn't see them dead in the water, I knew they had to be at least six or seven inches under the water where I couldn't see them. So that's where I fished."

He leaned against a big rock with his hands behind his head to make the rock soft "Wade out there and try George's No. 2," he said, pointing at the fly he had given me.

I didn't catch one right away, and I didn't expect to. My side of the river was the quiet water, the right side to be on in the hole above where the stone flies were hatching, but the drowned stone flies were washed down in the powerful water on the other side of this hole. After seven or eight casts, though, a small ring appeared on the surface. A small ring usually means that a small fish has risen to the surface, but it can also mean a big fish has rolled under water. If it is a big fish under water, he won't look so much like a fish as an arch of a rainbow that has appeared and disappeared.

Paul didn't even wait to see if I landed him. He waded out to talk to me. He went on talking as if I had time to listen to him and land a big fish. He said, "I'm going to wade back again and fish the rest of the hole." Sometimes I said, "Yes," and when the fish went out of the water, speech failed me, and when the fish made a long run I said at the end of it, "You'll have to say that over again."

Finally, we understood each other. He was going to wade the river again and fish the other side. We both should fish fairly fast, because Father probably was already waiting for us. Paul threw his cigarette in the water and was gone without seeing whether I landed the fish.

Not only was I on the wrong side of the river to fish with drowned stone flies, but Paul was a good enough roll caster to have already fished most of my side from his own. But I caught two more. They also started as little circles that looked like little fish feeding on the surface but were broken arches of big rainbows under water. After I caught these two, I quit. They made ten, and the last three were the finest fish I ever caught. They weren't the biggest or most spectacular fish I ever caught, but they were three fish I caught because my brother waded across the river to give me the fly that would catch them and because they were the last fish I ever caught fishing with him.

After cleaning my fish, I set these three apart with a layer of grass and wild mint.

Then I lifted the heavy basket, shook myself into the shoulder strap until it didn't cut any more, and thought, "I'm through for the day. I'll go down and sit on the bank by my father and talk." Then I added, "If he doesn't feel like talking, I'll just sit."

I could see the sun ahead. The coming burst of light made it look from the shadows that I and a river inside the earth were about to appear on earth. Although I could as yet see only the sunlight and not anything in it, I knew my father was sitting somewhere on the bank. I knew partly because he and I shared many of the same impulses, even to quitting at about the same time. I was sure without as yet being able to see into what was in front of me that he was sitting somewhere in the sunshine reading the New Testament in Greek. I knew this both from instinct and experience.

Old age had brought him moments of complete peace. Even when we went duck hunting and the roar of the early morning shooting was over, he would sit in the blind wrapped in an old army blanket with his Greek New Testament in one hand and his shotgun in the other. When a stray duck happened by, he would drop the book and raise the gun, and, after the shooting was over, he would raise the book again, occasionally interrupting his reading to thank his dog for retrieving the duck.

The voices of the subterranean river in the shadows were different from the voices of the sunlit river ahead. In the shadows against the cliff the river was deep and engaged in profundities, circling back on itself now and then to say things over to be sure it had understood itself. But the river ahead came out into the sunny world like a chatterbox, doing its best to be friendly. It bowed to one shore and then to the other so nothing would feel neglected.

By now I could see inside the sunshine and had located my father. He was sitting high on the bank. He wore no hat. Inside the sunlight, his faded red hair was once again ablaze and again in glory. He was reading, although evidently only by sentences because he often looked away from the book. He did not close the book until some time after he saw me.

I scrambled up the bank and asked him, "How many did you get?" He said, "I got all I want." I said, "But how many did you get?" He said, "I got four or five." I asked, "Are they any good?" He said, "They are beautiful."

He was about the only man I ever knew who used the word "beautiful" as a natural form of speech, and I guess I picked up the habit from hanging around him when I was little.

"How many did you catch?" he asked. "I also caught all I want," I told him. He omitted asking me just how many that was, but he did ask me, "Are they any good?" "They are beautiful," I told him, and sat down beside him.

"What have you been reading?" I asked. "A book," he said. It was on the ground on the other side of him. So I would not have to bother to look over his knees to see it, he said, "A good book."

Then he told me, "In the part I was reading it says the Word was in the beginning, and that's right. I used to think water was first, but if you listen carefully you will hear that the words are underneath the water."

"That's because you are a preacher first and then a fisherman," I told him. "If you ask Paul, he will tell you that the words are formed out of water."

"No," my father said, "you are not listening carefully. The water runs over the words. Paul will tell you the same thing. Where is Paul anyway?"

I told him he had gone back to fish the first hole over again. "But he promised to be here soon," I assured him. "He'll be here when he catches his limit," he said. "He'll be here soon," I reassured him, partly because I could already see him in the subterranean shadows.

My father went back to reading and I tried to check what we had said by listening. Paul was fishing fast, picking up one here and there and wasting no time in walking them to shore. When he got directly across from us, he held up a finger on each hand and my father said, "He needs two more for his limit."

I looked to see where the book was left open and knew just enough Greek to recognize λόγος as the Word. I guessed from it and the argument that I was looking at the first verse of John. While I was looking, Father said, "He has one on."

It was hard to believe, because he was fishing in front of us on the other side of the hole that Father had just fished. Father slowly rose, found a good-sized rock and held it behind his back. Paul landed the fish, and waded out again for number twenty and his limit. Just as he was making the first cast, Father threw the rock. He was old enough so that he threw awkwardly and afterward had to rub his shoulder, but the rock landed in the river about where Paul's fly landed and at about the same time, so you can see where my brother learned to throw rocks into his partner's fishing water when he couldn't bear to see his partner catch any more fish.

Paul was startled for only a moment. Then he spotted Father on the bank rubbing his shoulder, and Paul laughed, shook his fist at him, backed to shore and went downstream until he was out of rock range. From there he waded into the water and began to cast again, but now he was far enough away so we couldn't see his line or loops. He was a man with a wand in a river, and whatever happened we had to guess from what the man and the wand and the river did.

As he waded out, his big right arm swung back and forth. Each circle of his arm inflated his chest. Each circle was faster and higher and longer until his arm became defiant and his chest breasted the sky. On shore we were sure, although we could see no line, that the air above him was singing with loops of line that never touched the water but got bigger and bigger each time they passed and sang. And we knew what was in his mind from the lengthening defiance of his arm. He was not going to let his fly touch any water close to shore where the small and middle-sized fish were. We knew from his arm and chest that all parts of him were saying, "No small one for the last one." Everything was going into one big cast for one last big fish.

From our angle high on the bank, my father and I could see where in the distance the wand was going to let the fly first touch water. In the middle of the river was a rock iceberg, just its tip exposed above water and underneath it a rock house. It met all the residential requirements for big fish—powerful water carrying food to the front and back doors, and rest and shade behind them.

My father said, "There has to be a big one out there."

I said, "A little one couldn't live out there."

My father said, "The big one wouldn't let it."

My father could tell by the width of Paul's chest that he was going to let the next loop sail. It couldn't get any wider. "I wanted to fish out there," he said, "but I couldn't cast that far."

Paul's body pivoted as if he were going to drive a golf ball three hundred yards, and his arm went high into the great arc and the tip of his wand bent like a spring, and then everything sprang and sang.

Suddenly, there was an end of action. The man was immobile. There was no bend, no power in the wand. It pointed at ten o'clock and ten o'clock pointed at the rock. For a moment the man looked like a teacher with a pointer illustrating something about a rock to a rock. Only water moved. Somewhere above the top of the rock house a fly was swept in water so powerful only a big fish could be there to see it.

Then the universe stepped on its third rail. The wand jumped convulsively as it made contact with the magic current of the world. The wand tried to jump out of the man's right band. His left hand seemed to be frantically waving goodbye to a fish, but actually was trying to throw enough line into the rod to reduce the voltage and ease the shock of what had struck.

Everything seemed electrically charged but electrically unconnected. Electrical sparks appeared here and there on the river. A fish jumped so far downstream that it seemed outside the man's electrical field, but, when the fish had jumped, the man had leaned back on the rod and it was then that the fish had toppled back into the water not guided in its reentry by itself. The connections between the convulsions and the sparks became clearer by repetition. When the man leaned back on the wand and the fish reentered the water not altogether under its own power, the wand recharged with convulsions, the man's hand waved frantically at another departure, and much farther below a fish jumped again. Because of the connections, it became the same fish.

The fish made three such long runs before another act in the performance began. Although the act involved a big man and a big fish, it looked more like children playing. The man's left hand sneakily began recapturing line, and then, as if caught in the act, threw it all back into the rod as the fish got wise and made still another run.

"He'll get him," I assured my father.

"Beyond doubt," my father said. The line going out became shorter than what the left hand took in.

When Paul peered into the water behind him, we knew he was going to start working the fish to shore and didn't want to back into a hole or rock. We could tell he had worked the fish into shallow water because he held the rod higher and higher to keep the fish from bumping into anything on the bottom. Just when we thought the performance was over, the wand convulsed and the man thrashed through the water after some unseen power departing for the deep.

"The son of a bitch still has fight in him," I thought I said to myself, but unmistakably I said it out loud, and was embarrassed for having said it out loud in front of my father. He said nothing.

Two or three more times Paul worked him close to shore, only to have him swirl and return to the deep, but even at that distance my father and I could feel the ebbing of the underwater power. The rod went high in the air, and the man moved backwards swiftly but evenly, motions which when translated into events meant the fish had tried to rest for a moment on top of the water and the man had quickly raised the rod high and skidded him to shore before the fish thought of getting under water again. He skidded him across the rocks clear back to a sandbar before the shocked fish gasped and discovered he could not live in oxygen. In belated despair, he rose in the sand and consumed the rest of momentary life dancing the Dance of Death on his tail.

The man put the wand down, got on his hands and knees in the sand, and, like an animal, circled another animal and waited. Then the shoulder shot straight out, and my brother stood up, faced us, and, with uplifted arm proclaimed himself the victor. Something giant dangled from his list. Had Romans been watching they would have thought that what was dangling had a helmet on it.

"That's his limit," I said to my father.

"He is beautiful," my father said, although my brother had just finished catching his limit in the hole my father had already fished. This was the last fish we were ever to see Paul catch. My father and I talked about this moment several times later, and whatever our other feelings, we always felt it fitting that, when we saw him catch his last fish, we never saw the fish but only the artistry of the fisherman.

While my father was watching my brother, he reached over to pat me, but he missed, so he had to turn his eyes and look for my knee and try again. He must have thought that I felt neglected and that he should tell me he was proud of me also but for other reasons.

It was a little too deep and fast where Paul was trying to wade the river, and he knew it. He was crouched over the water and his arms were spread wide for balance. If you were a wader of big rivers you could have felt with him even at a distance the power of the water making his legs weak and wavy and ready to swim out from under him. He looked downstream to estimate how far it was to an easier place to wade.

My father said, "He won't take the trouble to walk downstream. He'll swim it." At the same time Paul thought the same thing, and put his cigarettes and matches in his hat.

My father and I sat on the bank and laughed at each other. It never occurred to either of us to hurry to the shore in case he needed help with a rod in his right hand and a basket loaded with fish on his left shoulder. In our family it was no great thing for a fisherman to swim a river with matches in his hair. We laughed at each other because we knew he was getting damn good and wet, and we lived in him, and were swept over the rocks with him and held his rod high in one of our hands.

As he moved to shore he caught himself on his feet and then was washed off them, and, when he stood again, more of him showed and he staggered to shore. He never stopped to shake himself. He came charging up the bank showering molecules of water and images of himself to show what was sticking out of his basket, and he dripped all over us, like a young duck dog that in its joy forgets to shake itself before getting close.

"Let's put them all out on the grass and take a picture of them," he said. So we emptied our baskets and arranged them by size and took turns photographing each other admiring them and ourselves. The photographs turned out to be like most amateur snapshots of fishing catches—the fish were white from overexposure and didn't look as big as they actually were and the fishermen looked self-conscious as if some guide had to catch the fish for them.

However, one closeup picture of him at the end of this day remains in my mind, as if fixed by some chemical bath. Usually, just after he finished fishing he had little to say unless he saw he could have fished better. Otherwise, he merely smiled. Now flies danced around his hatband. Large drops of water ran from under his hat on to his face and then into his lips when he smiled.

At the end of this day, then, I remember him both as a distant abstraction in artistry and as a closeup in water and laughter.

My father always felt shy when compelled to praise one of his family, and his family always felt shy when he praised them. My father said, "You are a fine fisherman."

My brother said, "I'm pretty good with a rod, but I need three more years before I can think like a fish."

Remembering that he had caught his limit by switching to George's No. 2 Yellow Hackle with a feather wing, I said without knowing how much I said, "You already know how to think like a dead stone fly."

We sat on the bank and the river went by. As always, it was making sounds to itself, and now it made sounds to us. It would be hard to find three men sitting side by side who knew better what a river was saying.

# ON NORMAN MACLEAN

## JOHN MACLEAN

When I was a teenager, finally big enough to keep up with my father on the Big Blackfoot River, he and I spent several summers alone in Montana at our cabin on Seeley Lake. We once fished 31 days in a row, filling the cabin's freezer with milk cartons that had big fishtails sticking out the top. There was no catch-and-release ethic in those days, and our idea of conservation was to catch-and-give-away to the non-fisher folk in the town of Seeley Lake, who appreciated the protein.

My father, Norman Maclean, fished with too many great fly fishermen to think he was the best, though at some aspects of the game he was better than anyone he fished against.

Once he had a fish on, he almost never lost it. He was a careful and patient player of trout: The throb of the fish running through the light wand connected him to the natural world he worshipped even as his own father worshipped the natural and supernatural worlds, mingling the two. As you can tell from his book, *A River Runs Through It,* he fished waters deeper than the river in front of him.

After my father finally slid a fish onto the bank, rushing only at the end when the fish tired and its head could be held out of water, he would muse out loud for a while, especially if it were a big fish. He liked an audience, even if only one teenaged son, though it was clear he addressed a broader public even then.

Standing on the bank with the fish in his hand like a teacher holding out a text, he would recount the details of the battle. Inevitably he turned to what his brother and father would have thought if they had seen the show. His brother, Paul, was one helluva fisherman.

His brother told him, he often said in his muse, that there was nobody as good as Norman Maclean at landing a fish, though Paul criticized him for lacking his, Paul's, aggressiveness in going after fish in difficult spots. Paul became a presence with us on the river, a broad-shouldered figure with a slouch Stetson who would stop for a moment to admire my dad for his artfulness in playing a fish, but who was happy in the knowledge that his creel was heavier and fuller, and always would be.

The old man, my father's father, was a Scottish Presbyterian minister who believed that only God and big fish merited veneration. In his muse, my dad wondered what his father would have thought of him; no answer came back. The old man was an austere presence, watching from atop the high cutbanks as we—dad, Paul and I—cast for a prize.

I am sorry my dad cannot be here tonight to accept this prestigious prize. He has become an old man himself now, and at 86 years of age can no longer climb the high cutbanks. But after many years of musing, he landed the big one in the end: He got all the stories down the right way in one place. He has left his own presence in the remarkable book for which you honor him.

Now instead of being only with me when ghosts arise along the river, he will be among us all, as long as men fish and read books.

# A SINGLE STEP

### GEORGE REIGER

Once, while poking along the recently flood-ravaged banks of Rock Creek in the District of Columbia, I came across two men and a boy fishing by the dam below Oakhill Cemetery. When I asked the age-old question, "How's fishing?" their replies were sufficiently evasive to encourage me to linger.

Sure enough, first the boy, then one of the men, got bites. They flicked their rod tips as nonchalantly as possible, but the resulting liveliness of their lines made further subterfuge futile. Each landed a channel catfish of about a pound and a half. When I asked whether they'd caught others, pride overcame discretion, and each angler hoisted a stringer of channel cats, bullheads, and sunfishes.

Meanwhile, not many yards away, car-imprisoned commuters crawled by, unaware of our presence, eyes fixed on the bumpers and tail-lights of the vehicles ahead of them. If and when Washington commuters go fishing, most drive to the trout streams of western Maryland and Pennsylvania; or down to the salty waters bracketing the Delmarva Peninsula. Although many of their children become fishermen in their own right, who's to say they're more worthy anglers than those who learn their craft by the less than pristine waters of Rock Creek?

Non-anglers assume that fishing is entirely about catching fish. Catching is important, of course. It's all that matters to beginners, and if veteran anglers didn't at least occasionally find their quarry in a feeding mood, they'd take up some related pastime, like the study of plasma physics. But veterans also know that as we grow older, fishing becomes as much about ritual and memory as putting new notches on the reel.

Many non-anglers, especially those who've come of age in the past quarter-century, think fishing is a spectator sport dominated by tournaments and dependant on high-tech equipment. Yet even competition fishermen know that angling means participation, not voyeurism, and that the most successful anglers have knowledge and special skills superceding gadgetry. Ultimately, each and every fishing trip begins with the individual making a single step from the shore into the water, or from the dock onto a boat, where he or she hopes and expects the anxieties of ordinary life to seep away on the current and tides, allowing him or her to become someone better.

Herbert Hoover observed that all men are equal before fish, and surely the boy with a menial summer job, casting into the dawn, believes that something wonderful is about to happen; the woman whose reality has not quite matched the bright expectations of college is renewed by the sight of birds far out over the waves; and for the troubled man, each moment of fishing dilutes his old sins and fresh suffering.

Philip Wylie once wrote that all anglers are philosophers, not because of our alleged patience—the usual explanation—but because we understand, even as children, that angling is lifelong recreation. Whitewater kayaking and mountaineering are sports for youth alone. Time may alter the kind or quantity of angling we do, but it never ends our opportunity. The old man casting over a darkening pool and the white-haired lady watching her sand-spiked rod nod to the surf are only variations on the little boy who once chased suckers in the shallows or the little girl who collected shells along the beach. The ghosts of who we were commune over increasing seasons with whom we are today. We're humbled by this, and some are even made wiser by the eternal nature of the fact that angling—like every epic journey—begins with but a single step.

# THE EVEN-TEMPERED ANGLER
# (SELECTION)

### LOUIS RUBIN

The real test of which kind of fishing one prefers above all other forms is probably that of the association of ideas. When you hear the word "fishing," what image comes into your mind? Doubtless for the trout or salmon fisherman the picture that "fishing" conveys involves standing, feet braced against the current, in a stream of cold rushing water, up to one's waist and with the water swirling outside one's waders, while expertly dropping a dry fly across fifty feet of water so that it settles without a ripple upon the surface where a trout has been feeding.

For the black-bass fisherman, the image that is summoned by the word "fishing" must be the exploding force of a huge largemouth—a lunker or hawg, the B.A.S.S. Masters call it—as it breaks the surface of the lake to grab a plug tossed skillfully to within a foot of the bank, and the tautness of the monofilament as the rod is lifted to halt it.

The offshore fisherman, moving along the edge of the Gulf Stream in a powerful boat and taking the light swells easily, must surely dream of the leap, high above the spray, of the billfish while the fisherman strains to hold the bending rod in its socket. For the inshore fisherman trolling for kings and big blues, there is the moment when the rod bends in a wide bow, the click mechanism on the reel rasps and the drag hisses as the line is stripped from the reel, followed by the rush to pick up the rod and to feel, transmitted along its length, the plunging weight of a big fish.

For myself, however much I enjoy those kinds of fishing, and however much I crave going after flounder with live shrimp in the tidal creeks of the coastal salt marsh that I have watched and loved watching since my boyhood, the word "fishing," uttered abruptly and without particular context, means something else.

It is the month of August, in Gloucester County, Virginia. I am anchored in a motorboat in twenty feet of water, inshore from the red nun buoy opposite the Naval Weapons Station just upstream from Yorktown on the York River. An hour earlier the buoy was slanted upstream from the force of the incoming tide; now it floats upright. I have caught a half-dozen good gray trout, and I am waiting for another, but there has been a hiatus in the fishing. I know that other fish will come along presently and am content to wait.

Everything is still. The gulls are at rest. They are perched on the stakes of an old fish trap in toward shore. The grass of the tidal marsh, the foliage of the trees on the shoreline beyond them, a quarter mile away, are in full green. Yet there seems in that greenness shading that is too fulfilled for the green growth of the spring and earlier summer, a ripening beyond the point of greatest strength and beginning to shade into decline.

There is the sound of a boat, a gasoline engine over across the way. A white boat, low and slender, is easing downstream—a crab boat heading home after working upriver. So far away on the water is it that it seems to have no wake, no waves, sliding across the water as if in a tableau. The sky overhead is remote and endless, a blue canopy with indifferent clouds.

A breeze picks up, lightly patterns the surface of the river into lines and shapes. The slight waves come slapping against the sides of the boat, making a low, hollow tapping sound. A gull lifts itself from its fellows and swings off in a wide arc; its white wings propel it across the river toward the shore. Its sharp cry interrupts the silence as it trails off, disappears. There is crying among the remaining gulls, but not one rises to follow.

The calling subsides, the gulls sit quietly and wait. The breeze falls off. The surface of the water is still. The crab boat is so far away that its engine makes no sound at all. All things are at rest.

It cannot last. It must not. The tide must change, the wind pick up, to blow away the stillness, the gulls rise to their scavenging, the world get on with its affairs. Soon we will be leaving for home, and the green of the marsh and trees will turn yellow as the summer sun recedes and autumn comes.

Not once does the season stop, for all that it seems now to suspend itself. It was passing by all the time, and what seems rest is only the momentary consciousness of its movement on its regular, methodical course. As surely as the gull rises into the air and swerves away, the tide is flowing and the earth tilting away from the sun.

Yet they seem to have stopped this day, as if the summer, and the season, and the sun were like a steel ball rolling up an incline, propelled by its own momentum, further and further—until the force of inertia moves to equalize the momentum, and asserts itself, and prevails.

For a moment, before the downward plummet, at the very top of the ultimate forward ascent, the one force is countered by the other, and summer seems, here on the river, to have stopped in midflight.

It is then, just then, that another fish bites.

# WHAT'S IN A NAME?

## HOWARD FRANK MOSHER

*"Name children some names and see what you do."*

—"Maple," Robert Frost

It was the summer of 1969, and I had just made a monumentally foolish mistake. Imagining that there were shortcuts to learning how to write and publish fiction, I accepted a creative writing fellowship at the University of California at Irvine and lit out with my wife, from our home in Vermont, for the Pacific coast. Along the way, we fished. We fished in the Upper Peninsula of Hemingway's Michigan, in Norman Maclean's Montana, up in the mountains of Alberta. We fished in Washington and Oregon, and then we hit southern California, where there were no trout, just automobiles and palm trees.

One afternoon a week or so after we'd arrived, I stopped at the intersection of Hollywood and Vine, where a man in a gorilla suit was busily directing traffic. A guy in a phone company truck pulled up beside me. He must have noticed my green license plate because he rolled down his window and called out, in a deadly serious voice, "I'm from Vermont, too. Go home while you still can."

So, missing the mountains, the farms and the woods I'd begun to write about, and, not least of all, the fishing, that's exactly what we did. Three days later we were back in northern Vermont. I had no writing degree, no job, no prospects. There were two small consolations. We'd gotten home just in time for the fall brown trout run, and the brook trout fishing in the beaver bogs was just starting to pick up again.

"What have you done for work before?" Jake Blodgett asked me on the morning after my somewhat less than triumphal return to New England.

Standing on the falling-in door stoop of the tall, white-haired logger and former whiskey runner, feeling his pale-blue stare cut through me like a chainsaw, I admitted that all I'd ever done was to teach school, but hearing that he needed a helper, I was hoping to get some "real-life" experience.

Jake thought about this proposition. Then he said, "Well, schoolteacher. How much would you want for pay?"

Now it was my turn to think. Finally, I said that I'd never worked in the woods before, and suggested that Jake try me out for a few days, then pay me what I was worth to him.

"That wouldn't be much," he said, and it wasn't. But for the rest of that fall and on into the winter, I worked with Jake, up in the mountains near the Canadian border, skidding the logs he cut out to a clearing with his ancient lumbering horse.

After work and on Sundays, we fished the brooks and rivers of the border country. When the lakes froze, we went ice fishing. Over lunch in the woods, and on our fishing expeditions, Jake told me stories of his wild, Prohibition-era days, running Canadian booze, making moonshine, outwitting game wardens. He was the best fisherman I'd ever known, with a sixth sense of where trout lay and how to entice them to strike, and a sixth sense, too, for telling a good story. During the course of that fall and winter, the Vermont woods became my graduate school, Jake Blodgett my literary mentor.

One day in a snowstorm he asked me if I'd ever write about his life. I told him yes.

Jake nodded. "Well, schoolteacher," he said, "then you better get on with it."

I love Labrador. I love its big, wild lakes, its unexplored whitewater rivers, its northern lights flaring up pink and silver and blue across the entire night sky. Most of all, I love its brook trout. In 1992, my 20-year-old son, Jake, and I stood by a nameless Labrador river we'd walked over a nameless mountain to reach. I was upstream from Jake a hundred yards or so, and we were both catching brookies from three to five pounds, as fast as we could land them.

"What have you got on there?" I called out to Jake over the rapids. "A whale?"

"No, a two-pound brook trout," he called back.

"That's no brook trout. That fish you're fighting is huge."

"Oh, that," Jake said. "That's the twenty-pound lake trout that has my two-pound brook trout in its mouth and won't let go."

Thinking how much my son's logger-whiskeyrunner-fisherman namesake would have enjoyed being here to see this, I began to laugh. Jake, in the meantime, handed me his fly rod, walked into the river, wrapped his arms about that monstrous laker and picked it up out of the rushing water, with the brook trout still in its jaws.

At that moment, I had a father's, and a fisherman's, epiphany. I realized, standing in the last wilderness of eastern North America, one hundred miles from the nearest settlement, that like his namesake, my son was attuned and connected to big woods and wild rivers, and the wild animals and fish that lived in them, in a way I could only marvel at. That, too, would have delighted my old bootlegger friend, and so would Jake's reply when I asked him what he was going to do with his unusual two-for-one catch.

"Put them back where they belong and fish some more," Jake said, and that, of course, is just what we proceeded to do.

# THE SOLITARY AND FRIENDLY SPORT

## R. PALMER BAKER, JR.

In this story three fishermen stop their car at a crossroad and ask a woodsman the way to Beaver Creek.

"What you fellers lookin' for?"

They say they are going fishing. Trout fishing.

In due course the backwoodsman tells them the way. "You fellers got any whiskey with you?"

They say no.

"How about a little 'baccy?" They say they don't smoke.

"Well, now," says the backwoodsman, "I thought you fellers said you was goin' fishin'."

There is something to this story. Trout fishing is the most solitary yet the most companionable of sports. It can be very elegant and very disreputable. One of my companions was equally devoted to dry fly fishing and bridge. His idea of a successful trip was to play cards most of the night, fish in the morning, sleep away the afternoon, and then fish the evening rise. When he died, at a sadly early age, his friends knew that this was his idea of heaven. He used to admire and not just laugh at Webster's wonderful cartoon of the four salmon fishermen playing bridge in a hut near the river. Outside, another member of the party staggers under the weight of an enormous fish and calls for attention. "George, you're a dummy," says one of the players, "you go look at the damn fish."

On a Thursday before Decoration Day, the bridge master and I left the city with two other friends to fish the New York waters of the Battenkill. One member of our party did not have a license, so we looked for the file office of the town clerk at the county seat. Misdirected, we entered a lawyer's office. After learning of our mistake and apologizing to his secretary, we said—three of the party being lawyers—that we should like to meet him. This was not possible; she told us. This was the month of May, and every Thursday afternoon he went fishing.

The afternoon was a fine one, and we got out on the stream as quickly as we could, knowing that a long evening of bridge lay ahead of us. Cahills were coming off the water in numbers, and the trout were taking them with regularity. Our bridge master was in his element. He caught and released one fish after another. Downstream, a worm fisherman could contain himself no longer. He came up along the bank, just as another trout was landed.

"Hey, mister! What bait you usin'?" The bridge master drew himself up.

"My dear fellow," he said, "this is a dry fly." Then retribution followed. Turning toward shore, he stepped into a hole. Quietly the bridge master went under, holding his Leonard aloft like Excalibur. His fishing hat gently floated downstream, and a moment later, walruslike, he emerged.

This companionable kind of fishing is one of the happiest aspects of the sport. Yet it is also rewarding now and then to fish by yourself. Solitude, particularly for the city man, is at the heart of fishing for trout.

The best times for this are days stolen from work, the beginnings of vacations, the end of some sustained endeavor. I remember one day at the close of college, when I was released—how temporarily!—from intellectual bondage. It was on the Vermont–New York line, and I did not have a care in the world. Early in the morning a big trout kept rising at the center of the biggest pool in the river. I almost drowned trying to reach him with the fly, but he was much too far out for me. At that time I eschewed the wearing of waders, and when I came out of the water I was numb with cold; but neither this nor the failure to catch the trout diminished the pleasure of the morning.

In the afternoon I fished a meadow tributary. The best pools were open and without cover, so it was necessary to cast while lying almost prone. If the fly landed properly, the trout jumped when they took it.

After the war I returned to the river again, staying with my wife's sister, who was opening her country house for the summer. At six o'clock, the June morning was glorious. Since I did not have my license, I had to wait until after breakfast before fishing, so I dressed and walked through the village and across the fields to look at the stream before the household was awake.

The nearest pool was bordered on one side by hayfields and on the other by the slope of a wooded hill. Seated on a tree root at the head of the pool, comfortably smoking his pipe, was a local fisherman of great repute. He had been fishing with minnows and was through for the day. Together, the two trout in his basket weighed at least five pounds. I admired them with envy and delight.

The rest of the day was like standing at the gates of paradise. In the morning we bought the license, did the shopping, and got the house ready for the summer. At noon neighbors insisted on having us for lunch. In the afternoon we had to follow a golf tournament. But then my hostess took pity.

After the tournament, we ate an early supper and drove quickly back to the house. While we were passing a graveyard I was told to hold my breath and make a wish. "Now," she said, as I drew my breath, "you will catch your trout."

There were two good hours of daylight ahead of me. Off I went, through the village and across the fields, with my rod.

At dusk the swallows began to dive and circle, feeding on the mayflies that were coming off the water. The little trout started splashing at the flies on the surface.

Then two bigger fish began to rise steadily in a little bay at the head of the pool. The current swirled there against a high grassy bank where two Guernsey cows were feeding, now and then lifting their heads to look with curiosity at the fisherman below them. Each time a mayfly drifted along this bank there was a dimple on the surface and the insect disappeared.

Kneeling on a gravel bar, I was able to get very close to this location and, for once, to float my fly, a Cahill, without drag to one of the rising trout. He took it with a dimple, followed the pressure of the line, and allowed himself to be landed in the pool below the gravel bar. He was a brook trout, not too common in this part of the river, June-fat and a foot long.

The second trout along the bank took the fly in the same way. It was a brown trout, almost identical in size, and so I had a good brace. Having been defeated by this river more than once, I placed the fish in my bag and walked back to the house with satisfaction.

My hostess and her husband were standing in the kitchen. When I held the two fish out to her, one in each hand, she said, "My goodness, they're still alive; they're quivering."

"No," I said. "That's me." And I thanked her for the graveyard wish and what had turned out to be a perfect day.

When you are fishing alone, you had better bring your fish home if you want your friends and family to believe you. On the other hand, the return of a large trout to the stream without a witness can result in a fine sense of moral superiority.

The fact is that the fly-fisherman is likely to raise his biggest and most difficult trout when he is on the stream alone, concentrating and undisturbed. One spring morning, when I looked from the office window, the sun was sparkling on the waters of the North River, the city plane trees were green, and the pigeons were wheeling on a fresh west wind. The thought of that day wasted in the city was intolerable. I closed my desk and left.

Two hours later I was on one of the streams in the Croton watershed. Although heavily fished at the beginning of the season, some of these are good brown trout waters. They have a cool and constant flow from the reservoir outlets and their banks are shaded and protected from siltation. Most of the fish are stocked, but now and then the fly-fisherman takes a wild trout, and once in a while a big one comes up from the reservoir below.

This was one of those occasions—an escape from the city—when solitude is a joy. I walked upstream for fifteen minutes before making the first cast. Violets were blooming along the edge of the woods. The red-winged blackbirds called to each other as they nested at the edges of the swamp. Presently I was walking in a grove of hemlocks, approaching the first pool.

The first attempt was made with a dun variant, a smoky-gray fly with a long hackle. Immediately two little trout splashed and jumped over it. At about the same time, a hatch of small red-gray flies was seen coming off the water. When the fly was changed to a Red Quill, one of the little trout took it at once. He was returned to his family and I proceeded upstream.

None of the rising fish was of any size, but one came up in virtually every pool. When I came to one of the larger pools I fished the lower end carefully, but there was no response. This was odd. There should have been several small trout at the tail of the pool. Then I looked upstream, to the very head of the pool, where the current flowed between two big rocks. There was a tiny splash in the current.

On another occasion I had seen a splash like this and later had been able to identify it. The splash was caused not by a little fish but by the flick of a big trout's tail as it turned in the current. Suddenly I was convinced that this was a similar occasion, particularly since the absence of small fish at the tail indicated that a big one might have driven them off.

The Red Quill was dried, oiled, and dipped in the stream to wash off the excess dressing. I got it into the air and began lengthening the cast. Back and forth went the line, along the side of the pool so as not to throw its shadow over the trout. In a moment all was in readiness for the final delivery when the back cast hung solidly up in a hemlock branch.

Good-bye, Red Quill; good-bye, leader. At this point I was not going to move from my position and disturb the pool. After drawing the line tight and cursing a little, I broke off the fly and the first tippet of the leader. With shaking hands I finally succeeded in tying on a new tippet and another Red Quill.

This time more care was used with the back cast. The fly landed in the current between the rocks, floated two inches, and simply disappeared.

If I had not already been sure, I would have known this was a big fish when I tightened on the line. For a moment he did not move. Then he jumped. He jumped six times. He was certainly fifteen inches long—a monster for the stream. He began to run up and down the pool, powerfully, frantically. Because I was now standing at the tail, he turned each time he saw me. He wanted badly to go downstream toward the reservoir from which he no doubt had recently come.

Now he raced upstream, into the current between the rocks where he had taken the fly, and in an instant he was fighting in the pool above me. Then I made the mistake of stepping out on the bank to follow. I am convinced that he saw me. He came back downstream with a leap, raced through the pool, and was into the fast water below me. When I stripped in line and snubbed him he jumped one more time and was gone

There is a catharsis in this kind of experience. The next day I was again prepared for work. My angling friends who know the stream nod their heads and say they believe me when I tell the story. I think some do. And some may not.

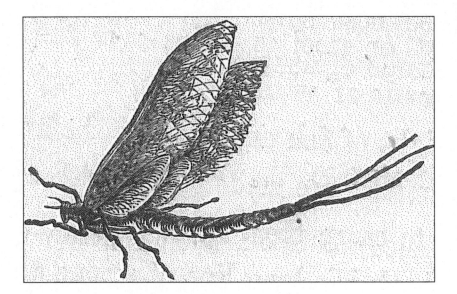

# MIDSTREAM CRISIS

## LAMAR UNDERWOOD

As the year began, I decided to embrace the advice of my friend Sparse Grey Hackle, who told me: "Let the wolf out!" He was dead right. It was the only way to go. No more Mister Nice Guy!

My New Year's resolution was a notice served on all creatures, great and small, that in the open seasons ahead I was going to fill my hand. I was fed up with two-trout days, three-bass weekends and no-deer vacations. I'd had it with calling to bird dogs that wouldn't stand still and turkeys that would (two ridges away!). I didn't want to see another pheasant getting up 200 yards away down a corn row or another bay full of ducks and geese rafted up and preening their feathers under skies that had flown in from Palm Springs.

Government wags told me that in the previous season some 2.5 million hunters had shot 12 million ducks. The calculator that lives beside my checkbook told me that works out to five or six ducks per hunter. I didn't get any five ducks! Who the hell shot my ducks?

All around, the previous year had not just been bad; it had been a disaster. I zigged when they zagged. The northeasters and I booked into the same places at the same times. I frightened the spots off brown trout while bass slept through my offerings. The deer left the mountain country I hunt, but those from the woods alongside my house found my tulips and peas in the spring, then shredded two young pines during rubtime in the fall. Plenty of geese crossed the pit blinds I hunkered in all season, but they were so high they were a menace to aviation—and they held express tickets.

My dismal performances afield forced me to face what the late John Foster Dulles called "an agonizing reappraisal." Clearly, my tactics were lousy; my timing stank, my equipment belonged in a museum.

I knew better than to seek some all-embracing formula as my game plan. Each subject would have to be tackled separately, tactics and gear made precise. The geese, I felt, would be the simplest problem to deal with. I began squirreling away the bucks to purchase a 10-gauge magnum automatic, with which I intended to wreak havoc on the Eastern Shore. My more immediate problem—and infinitely more complex—was what to do about those trout.

Since the Romans knew nothing about splitcane rods and matching the hatch, they invented a calendar that starts the new year off from the pit of winter. For me and millions of other fishermen the real new year begins on the opening day of trout season. My usual opening-day scenario looked like this:

An already-pudgy figure, bulked further by enough clothes to outfit the Klondike gold rush, stands hip-deep in a flow of black water torn into sudsy rips by protruding rocks and bearing of the countryside what the winter snows have been holding in storage: sticks, leaves, tires, a bloated cat, the occasional beer can. Overhead the sky is a glowering mass of putty, against which the bare branches of the trees snap and creak with iron-hard stiffness as blasts of wind arrive from Siberia. For hours our man alternates making casts, peering intently at the jaunty little flies that ride the current like miniature galleons, and fumbling stiff fingers through his flybox in search of new offerings. To find a greater fool, you would have to look inside an ice fishing shanty.

The bottom of a trout stream is its food factory, and on this day it will not be violated by anything except the soles of el piscator's waders. Although he will soon abandon his dry flies (how quickly the credo fades: "I'd rather catch one on top than five down deep"), our man will make only tentative probes into the depths. His wet flies, streamers and nymphs will sweep harmlessly over the heads of the stone-hugging trout. Troutless by 3 o'clock, he will seek the solace of the lodge where fire, firewater and kindred snake-bit companions will be waiting with tales of woe and livers in various stages of distress.

Long before opening day dawned last season, I was determined to never again be a part of this demented tableau.

For weeks I hit the books with an intensity seldom mounted in my professional life. Schwiebert, Whitlock, Marinaro, Swisher-Richards, Cucci-Nastasi—the great masters of flyfishing for trout were devoured. Their instruction manifested itself in a barrage of catalogs and small packages of flies arriving daily from every comer of troutdom. My wading vest bulged with trinkets. Latin names of bugs came trippingly off the tongue.

Opening day, I stood thigh-deep at the head of a pool of black water, frigid and swollen with runoff. Coming to the stream, I had received the usual assortment of reports that the fish were in a coma. The voice on the car radio had said something about snow. None of these things intimidated me at all. This year I was ready.

To meet this early and elemental trouting condition, I pried open a box of nymphs. These were not ordinary nymphs, but masterpieces of illusion—caterpillar-like, hairy-leggy-juicy-looking. Each was weighted with enough piano wire to outfit a Steinway. Never mind that they would hit the water with the finesse of a slam-dunk. They would go down, my friend, down, down to the very noses of these frozen wisenheimers. I would fish these creations with a leader hacked to three feet. (Long leaders, I had learned, rise in the pushing and swelling of the current.) The whole outfit would ride down with high-density sinking line topped by a fluorescent strike indicator to tell me when I had a customer.

You don't cast such a rig. What you do is sort of heave the whole mess out and to one side, paying close attention that a hook in the ear is not the immediate result of the effort.

I watched the curls of line and leader straighten downstream toward a boulder that slashed the smooth flow. I tried to form a mental image of what the nymph was doing—sinking, tumbling, ticking over rocks. The line straightened past the boulder. I paid out three more long pulls from the reel, watching the strike indicator bob on downstream.

Suddenly I thought I saw it dart forward. I came back with rod and line and felt the weight of a trout. As the brown—a lovely 15-incher—darted and splashed on the way to the net, my elation soared. My patience and virtue and hard study were to be rewarded. The masters of the game were indeed wise and learned men.

After that, you can imagine my heart-hammering excitement when the next 30 minutes yielded two more fish, about the same size as the first.

Then the devil sent his disciples to descend upon me, like a plague of locusts. First one, then two, then three other anglers were crowding into my stretch of water. Not one asked what I was using. They simply assumed I had found "The Place."

Never mind, I told myself. You can afford to be generous. I waded from the stream and pointed up toward uninhabited water. In a few minutes I was sloshing, much too fast, through a bouldery run of pocket water when I felt my right foot sliding down an eel-slick ledge. I lurched hard to the left, but that leg would not bear the burden. I went down into the water on my back with a teeth-jarring crash. Totally submerged for a second, I stood up and cursed my luck and the worn felt soles of my waders. I was drenched, achingly cold, and clearly out of action for the rest of the day.

As I waded to the edge of the stream, I discovered another result of my accident with dramatic suddenness. As I made a little sideways move with my left leg to step around a rock, I felt a nauseating wave of pain. I did not want to feel such a shock again, ever, so now I picked my way gingerly along, trying to protect the knee.

Yuk! Yuk! See the man all soaking wet and limping toward his car. Fat-ass must've fallen in. Yuk! Yuk!

A prominent physician whom I trust sentenced the knee to six weeks of healing. Because I could not wade the stream, I could not fish for trout. The great fly hatches of early spring for which I had prepared myself so diligently came and went: the Blue Quills, the Hendericksons, the Grannon caddis, the March Browns.

My mood was foul and depressed. Without my jogging program, with which I had successfully been losing weight, I quickly regained ten pounds. Going to work in New York on the train one day I was struck by a thought as morbid as any I've ever had: The obituary page of the *New York Times* named very few males in their 90s. No, the ages of the boys getting their names in the paper were in the 70s and 80s. At age 45 I had the startling realization that in all likelihood I was more than halfway to the barn. Life begins at 80? Give me a break!

Okay, my somber mood told me, so you've lost some of your good moves and speed. You can't hit a 60-yard mallard or sink a three-foot putt. On the tennis court children who can't get into an R-rated film have you gasping like a beached whale. The guide can show you a tarpon at 60 feet, and you may or may not be able to get the fly to it (probably not, given any kind of wind). But relax, buster. For the years have given you wisdom. Look at what you did with those opening-day trout!

I was still clinging to this slightly uplifting notion when I finally got back to the river in late May. One of the year's best hatches remained. According to the grapevine, the Sulphurs had arrived in tentative numbers two days earlier, and all signs pointed to their major emergence late that evening.

The hatch of *Ephemerella dorothea,* which goes on with diminishing consistency for about six weeks on good eastern streams, ranks as a favorite because it stirs smart, self-respecting trout into an unusual orgy of gluttony. Unlike some mayfly hatches, which deliver more sizzle than steak, the appearance of the No. 16 yellow-and-dun flies in the last hour before darkness produces fishing so fast and exciting that it is the stuff for cool hands and stout hearts.

My favorite slick-water was flat empty that evening. My recent misfortune was all forgotten as I waded into position and made a few desultory casts while waiting for the hatch to begin. The air was heavy with humidity, and low clouds on the ridges promised that darkness would come early and perhaps a thunderstorm with it.

The time that passed seemed interminable. Nothing came off the darkening water, not even caddis. A kingfisher flew upstream, scolding my presence. I heard a great homed owl up on the mountain and an answering cry from nearby. Then I saw the first delicate yellow mayfly climbing steeply toward the trees. In a few moments there was another, then another, then another, and then I actually saw one in the instant it left the water—and beyond it the swirl of a trout.

My line arched through the growing dusk. I saw my artificial Sulphur begin its jaunty ride down the feeding lane where the trout had swirled. It floated on downstream unharmed. There were other rises all over the pool now—not splashy water-throwing slaps, but subtle bulges and swirls.

I really started worrying when my bogus Sulphur made three more rides through the melee without interesting a trout. What was wrong? The fly? The leader? My thoughts screamed as I watched the hatch and rises go on: You've been out of action so long you don't know what you're doing.

In the middle of this burst of self-condemnation I saw something—flashes of darting trout just beneath the surface. That was it! The trout were not taking the surface duns! They were nymphing, gulping the insects as they rose to the surface and in the film as they emerged into winged shape.

I was prepared for this, but my hands trembled as I opened the flybox and got out a floating nymph. The light was going fast, but I managed to tie on the fly without digging out my night light. In my excitement, however, I dropped my reading half-glasses into the stream. Klutz! Fool! I should have had them on a cord around my neck.

No matter. I had the right ammo now, and the fish were still going strong as I roll-cast the nymph to the top of the pool. Instantly a trout was on, and I felt a flush of ultimate satisfaction.

The fish was a strong pulsating weight as it struggled upstream for a few seconds. Then the line went slack as the trout bolted downstream almost past my legs, a momentary shadow that caused me to gasp: I was into my largest trout ever.

The reel screamed appropriately as the fish bolted downstream. He reached the lip of the falls that terminated the pool and turned to face the current. The steady pressure on the 5X felt unbelievable. I had the feeling of the fish backing up, backing to the edge of the tumbling water. He was going to be washed over the lip! I had to do something! I palmed the flange of the reel, increasing the drag, and thereby succeeded in instantly breaking off the trout as surely as though I'd been trying to.

I reeled in the sickeningly slack line and looked at the 5X tippet. So many trout were still taking the sulphur nymphs all over the pool that the excitement smothered the loss of the big fish. I quickly had another floating nymph out, ready to tie on. I felt my shirt pocket for my reading glasses and remembered where they had gone. I held the fly at arm's length against the gloom of the darkening sky. No way. I could not thread the eye of the hook in that dimness.

No problem. My night light had a magnifying glass that fit over the top of the light. No sweat, just stay cool.

I was deeply aware of the rises continuing all over the pool as I pulled the light out and draped its cord around my neck. I felt deeper into the pocket for the magnifying glass. It wasn't there! I flipped the switch on the light. Nothing! *Click, click. Click, click.* Still nothing! Okay, the batteries are dead. You're on your own. Now just hold the fly very still against what is left of the sky and tie it on.

My panic rose as I tried unsuccessfully to tie on the No. 16 Sulphur. I tied a No. 14. It would not go. In a final burst of madness and inspiration, I dug out a No. 10 Blonde Wulff, the biggest fly in my vest. Maybe it would work on these feeding fish.

Perhaps it would have. I don't know. I never got the Wulff tied on. My vision is 20-20, but at age 45 I could not see close up well enough to tie on a fly and resume fishing a hatch that I had waited for all winter.

I reeled in slowly, felt the end of the leader reach the reel, then broke down my rod. The splashes of feeding trout popped out from the darkness. I could not see the rises now, but they were distinctive above the murmur the current made as it tailed from the pool downstream.

Slowly the disappointment drained away. The easy moves, the good speed. Going, going with the years. Yet it was true: You were wiser, vastly richer in the things you knew. Such as realizing right now that what made fishing so great was that on any given outing, things could happen that you would remember all of your days. Few other times in life could offer that. That is the easy part of change—the knowing, the feeling. The other side is that you have left something precious behind—something you had used up and would have to go on without.

Flashes of lightning came across the ridgetop, then the roll of advancing thunder. The feeding grew quieter, then died out completely. The bursts of lightning helped me find my way up the hillside to the lane that led back to the car.

I did not know if I had reached the end of something or the beginning.

The wind blew on the high ridges, gusting along the slopes, coming down to the river.

# BLUE DUN

## FRANK MELE

It is natural, I think, for beginnings to be arbitrary. Even human lives, it seems, can begin somewhat capriciously. Any account of inceptions is therefore apt to be treacherous, or at best, unreliable—especially so, if one seeks for causes to satisfy the human prerequisite to Effect. How to enter into even the merest thumbnail history of an attitude compounded from flowing waters, bankside dawdlers, bamboo, cock's hackles, and a certain color of indeterminate hue, and to give some intimation of their genesis, is a task for wiser heads than mine.

I suppose I could say, for example, that the glowing vision of a Blue Dun cape materialized one night as my pregnant mother knelt at prayer before her little Madonna. But this would be sheer fabrication, and even worse, an affront to the quality of her fervor, for she wanted her unborn son to be a violinist. In her frame of mind, the Blue Dun cape would have been taken for some harping angel in miniature, or a biblical dove with Blue Dun feathers appropriate to the sky of Heaven.

Now, all this might ingratiate me to the good folks of the world, but I would be answerable to the few who know that it is from just such compromises that many a potent myth has had its start. Caught thus, between the half-truths of our salty worthies and the gem-hard unpleasantries of the few, I could try to salvage some of my peace of mind by affirming that since myths appear to be as necessary as breathing to the run-of-the-mill of the species, I shall not try to discredit them, since, by acquiescing to that grand old custom, there is the chance of an absolution of anglers. In other words, if what is sauce for the goose, et cetera, there is no longer ground for casting aspersions on anglers. And no need to take their redemption any farther. For all that anglers' myths tend to fragility, they are still a good deal less vulnerable than the contrivances of ordinary men. I trust that now I can get on with the narrative without ransacking my racial memory for some specious cause—say, an angling ancestor who might justify the events to follow.

There was little in my childhood that might have cast any significant shadows before, unless it was a predilection for puddles. Later, in boyhood, when great and sudden rainstorms magically transformed the city streets into brooks, an unexplainable ecstasy would drive me out of doors to hover dreamy-eyed about the curbstone banks of the new rivulets. To this day, when a muskrat clambers out to some riverbank, I am reminded of the rats that scrambled out of the flooded sewer drains and went scurrying over the great cobblestones of the street.

Some years later, done with early studies, well past the intermediate stage, and reeking with the faint, musty odor of the mud, weeds, and pickerel of the farmland streams near my native Rochester, I went to Syracuse to find new ways for scaling the higher reaches of violin playing. That I had already been one of the youngest members of the Rochester Philharmonic Orchestra did not seem to me as impressive, honorable, or profitable as to have the inner beauty of a musical phrase revealed to me by a gaunt and profane master, Andre Polah, my teacher, an artist of stature—one of the elect, whose career had been stifled by an ironic accident.

An ominous silence had settled over the nation. And when in its deepest recesses, a cataclysmic bomb exploded, shattering the national economy, the country reeled and staggered in a state of shock. Life went on, but with empty pockets and, quite often, an empty belly—that is, among the laboring classes and those of us in the arts. And when, against the protestations and vilifications of outraged Pilgrims, who had acquired affluence presumably without the help of God, a crippled and compassionate President decreed the Work Projects, we musicians filed due notice of bona fide indigence, cut the fringes from our trouser cuffs, and began to use our professional skills as members of the new symphony orchestra. It was held to be one of the more contemptible projects, in that men were getting paid, however minimally, for merely making great music.

Andre was a gifted conductor as well, and when he was appointed director of the orchestra he set about reconciling his passion for a high standard of performance, as much as his choleric nature would permit, with the inevitable quota of mediocrities that were better suited to vaudeville than to Mozart, Brahms, Debussy, and yes, even Stravinsky. There was now relief from want, but not from the humiliation that attended its formalities; and what shreds of dignity had survived the stigma attached to the projects were annihilated by a jibing press and the indignation of the good burghers of upper New York State. Those were gloomy days, scarcely relieved by the pall of grime that hung over the scabrous public buildings. The drabness of that city was exceeded only by a pervasive meanness of spirit. But redemption could be found in the beauty of its countryside. Out beyond the green drumlins, among the valleys to the northeast and south, beautiful streams with Indian names beckoned, inviting heavy hearts to lightness, and corroded hopes to a good burnishing at the hands of waterside alders.

Andre was a fly-fisher, and when this mad Dutchman adopted me as his fishing companion, my hopes began to soar as an early zeal for bait casting got transposed to the fly rod. As in violin playing, I sought out the masters, ransacking the shelves of the university and public libraries for books on flyfishing. In the stacks I found Emlyn Gill, Bergman, Hewitt, Southard, Lord Grey. I saved enough to send to Paul Young for his *Making and Using the Fly and Leader.* And then I began to tie flies, buying hooks by the dozen when I could afford them. Certain exotic materials could only be purchased. Others I begged. And many I borrowed from an environment that had taken on a new depth. A rich world of texture and color had opened to me. For the first time I saw the extraordinary range of color in dogs, cats, pet and wild rabbits, monkeys, mice, squirrels, ducks, geese, and fowl of all kinds. My visits to the zoo now had a vibrant urgency that gave pause to children and made the keepers nervous. And when the orchestra played at a county fair that was famous for its yearly exhibit of rare fowl, and I found the attendant away for lunch, my head swam. In the operation that followed, a dizziness nearly overcame me, fearing that at any moment the uproar would fetch a guard.

One morning at rehearsal a new man came in dragging a cello by the scruff of the neck. Andre had briefed me about him over the previous day's intermission coffee. In the excitement Andre's English, normally unpredictable, had slipped a few cogs and was being ground up by Dutch, French, and German accents. Under those great eyebrows of Holland straw his blue eyes were gleaming wolfishly. In a gravelly bass he told me the news. "This man is un maker of rodts! Un goddamt specialiste von fly rodts! Dry-fly rodts!" I could not have been more impressed had Andre announced the entry of Pablo Casals into our ranks. Our rods were of poor quality, soft as willow. Andre's treasured rods and reels by Hardy had been stolen from his car years ago.

Andre's words were still reverberating in my ear as Brenan took his place at the rear of the cello section. As he began to tune his cello he looked so unprofessional that I began to get faintly sick. But shortly I saw something that made me close my eyes in blessed relief. There would not be, could not be, any repercussion from the podium. Hopelessly out of practice after years of rodmaking, Brenan had sacked valor for a plausible discretion. It would have been difficult for him to have made an audible mistake. He was bowing away impassively, in step with the others, the bow hair hovering over the treacherous rapids then settling down agreeably in the more navigable runs, glides, and pools. It was a stroke of true wisdom, appreciated none the less by Andre than by me. One day, Brenan invited me to his shop.

Coming in to the warmth of a little world of bamboo out of the whiplashing snows and icy sidewalks of Syracuse was no less than a bit of parochial magic, bringing easement and balm to a troubled soul. The shop's mood was a mélange of violinmaker's shop and tackle store, sources both for repose and wonder. There I saw and fondled my first dry-fly rods. Had Brenan had an apprenticeship or a family tradition there would not have been any flaw of workmanship. If imperfect, they were superb in action; I have had a few in hand since then that were comparable to his best rods, and many that were inferior. However prudent a cellist, Dan was an adventurous rodmaker; and in the matter of rod design for the dry fly he was ahead of his time.

A blackboard with the chalked heading, "Days to Opening Day" read "63," awaiting the first of the coterie to come in to roost out of the waning afternoon, leaving the gloom, chill, and snow to the defeated day. By five-thirty the blackboard read "62." I basked in the warmth of talk that diverted the winter stream to its summer course on the shop's floor. Rods sprang to life. Lines darted and looped under the soiled sky of the ceiling. At a bench to one side sat Bill, Dan's son, at his afterwork vise, contriving a better bivisible fly than the last. Flies whisked about. A great trout rose to McBride's fly of last summer, then plunged downward to sulk in the depths of the floor below. It was the rite of the Waiting Men enduring their season of work with invocations to a reluctant spring—not a whit less primitive than the crude and basic formalities of their remote ancestors. From a judicial chamber, from a locomotive's cab, from symphony hall, office, machine shop, barroom, laboratory, they had come to improvise upon their truth, which was the Dry Fly.

Later, at a nearby tavern, Dan, mellowing in whisky, would hold forth for the hardier few. A gifted writer on many aspects of the sport, Dan had an extensive correspondence with leading figures in the field. His knowledge of angling history of the Catskill and Adirondack mountains was imposing and intimate; and the names I culled out of those benign extemporizations sounded like a roll call of latter-day saints: Theodore Gordon, La Branche, Hewitt, Holden, of the "Idyll of the Split Bamboo," Izaak Walton (no less a figure than Dante), Halford, the English Prince of the True Faith, and then the glorious school of Catskill fly-tyers who had received Gordon's afflatus at death: Rueben Cross, Herman Christian, the Darbees, Walt Dette. By now Dan had become for me the arbiter of all things piscatorial, and an inexhaustible source of fishing lore.

One afternoon at the tavern Dan had soared to really admirable form, and was weaving in and out of the key of Dry Fly Major with the skill of an Irish Bach when, at once, he struck an arresting chord. "The Quill Gordon fly," said Dan, "was the great turning point in American dry-fly fishing. Gordon's creativity in his choice of materials and his ingenuity in determining a just style for our waters set the pattern that was to become our tradition. After an extensive correspondence with the mighty Halford, and a cordial exchange of flies, he departed once and for all from the English tradition, retaining only that which could be adapted to his concept of a fly that could dance on our broken waters, and which, on our long glides and pools, looked like a newly hatched dun. It is therefore *de rigueur*, mandatory, that this fly be tied with the natural Blue Dun hackle! Else it is not a true Quill Gordon fly!" By now Dan's voice had the ring of One Hundred Proof. "For that matter," he added, "no fly could rightfully bear the name Dun unless it was tied in the natural color!"

There it was. With four words Dan had wakened me out of a deep sleep, only to plunge me into a nightmare of frustration at the thought of all those Quill Gordon flies I had tied from a very well dyed cock's neck of excellent quality. I had traded a Pernambuco violin bow for it to a greedy dealer in fly-tying materials. The fact that the bow was not a true Pernambuco was small consolation. The neck was not a true Blue Dun. Dan's words resolved all doubts that I had had from time to time about those flies. Their color was inert. They reminded me of ash. Dan's incantation had at once set me before the Veil that concealed a great Mystery. What the revelation could conceivably be was as yet only a strange stirring of blood in my head. This color, Blue Dun, would I know it were I to come suddenly face to face with it? What could there be about it which had set it apart so remotely yet compellingly on a mountain peak in my mind?

"Well, Frankie," said Dan. "I can only say that there is nothing quite like it. I don't know how to describe it. One simply has to see the natural Blue Dun for himself, with his own eyes. Only then can he understand. It is one of Nature's rare moods. It is color and light making their ways out of chaos and darkness." For the moment I had to content myself with this Hibernian tune from the Prophet. Had Dan had access then to Gordon's letters to the great English angler, G. E. M. Skues, he would have quoted:

"My farmer friend and I have been trying to breed good dun hackles, but the cocks are turning out poorly."

Later: "I found a blue cock of the year yesterday and hope that I will succeed in buying the bird—the neck is of such a lovely color—"

And six years later: "It seems too bad when we consider how rarely one finds a cock with blue dun hackles." Even then, it seems, the natural color was painfully scarce.

Dan, I am sure, was not aware of what was happening to me, else he would have modified his dictum from unalterable law to permissible deviation. He had a deep respect for my skill as a violinist, and a personal liking that probably set me only a cut or two below Theodore Gordon, for Dan adored great music. But I do believe that had he altered his pronunciamento out of care for my peace of mind, and that of my family's, I doubt that it would have greatly diverted the course of the future. Blue Dun was now a fever in my brain.

The violence of my reaction and its later consequences cannot be entirely ascribed to Dan, with all due respect to his eloquence and imagery. Later events tend to suggest that the occasion triggered something deep within, well beyond normal reach, well to the other side of any intimation, even, of its existence; for I had yet to see a single feather of natural Blue Dun.

Then, streambound early one Sunday morning, as the car was hurtling over the road, the irascible Marcel gave me what appears now to be the first lucid description of the color Blue Dun. This taut but amiable Frenchman, a hairdresser, was a passionate angler whose fly casting was a model of elegance and precision. He was singing obscene French songs, by way, I thought, of exorcising the previous day's ordeal with fat and fretful matrons. When he had finished still another classic of the latrine I put the question to him. He was a knowledgeable and meticulous fly-tyer.

"Marcel. What is the real Blue Dun like? The natural—you know-"

"Ah, *mon cher*," he replied. "That? What can I say? It is like nothing else, and everything. It is not blue, like the flag blue. It is something that is always— How shall I say? Becoming?"

Late that afternoon at Marcel's home I saw my first natural Blue Dun neck. I was silent a long time. It was real, and it was there. But it was unreal; and it was somewhere else. Marcel was right. It was in the act of becoming. I raised my eyes at last and spoke.

"Marcel. Where is Blue Dun?"

"Ah." Marcel canted his head a bit to one side. "That is a difficult question. How shall I tell you? That it is where you find it? Yes. To find it. Until then it is like the—like the smoke—"

"In search of the sky."

"Yes! Exactly!" Marcel nodded sharply, then suddenly fixed me with a curious look followed by an expression of bewilderment, as of a spirit scurrying through the ages.

"But how did you know?" he asked, from a great distance.

"I'm not sure," I said, my words sounding from afar. "You may have said it once before, and I remembered it."

Hairdressers, I believe, are masters of applied psychology. Marcel had read something in my face that was unintentional, of which I was not aware. "What size do you tie the Quill Gordon?" he asked.

"Twelve."

He riffled affectionately through the quivering hackles, then carefully plucked out two and gave them to me. It was an act of superlative generosity, well beyond friendship. I had heard it said that the French were stingy. I say that they are selectively extravagant. On that occasion it was nothing less than a minor sacrifice, which only a cynic can make without pomp. "Bon!" concluded Marcel. "You are now fit to enter the Beaverkill. You are going next week with Dan?"

"Yes. Dan is taking three of us. It will be my very first time. I have never seen it, except in dreams."

"Ah," sighed Marcel. "It is a dream within a dream."

On a fresh summer morning a week later, as Blue Dun was rising in the east, a Ford went wheezing toward the valleys where the sacred rivers ran. Under the wise and gentle guidance of Dan, the Prophet, three of us were to have our baptism at last in the Beaverkill River.

Hours later, when the southern hills had greatened to Catskill massiveness, we descended a long, winding grade and the Ford stopped, heaving and burbling in exhaustion at the bank of a majestic pool. We alighted. The Prophet turned to us, intoned the keynote and conducted an impromptu cantata, the hymn, "Praise God from Whom All Blessings Flow." It was an unlikely chorus: a nominal Protestant, a fled Catholic, a remoted Jew, and an atheist. But it was in time, and fervent. In a many-celled fly box, squatting in its own special compartment, the fly with the mystical color listened, awaiting its first flight over the holy waters.

If memory serves me, and often it doesn't, we camped near to the Mountain Pool. Darkness was nigh, and wood was fetched at Dan's request for a fire big enough to conjure up the Spirits of the River, that he might transpose the secrets that passed back and forth from the distant rapids to the crackling flames. As the night deepened, the thin, reedy chords of a harmonica floated in and out of the conversational murmur. It was a nostalgic whimper before the fact of small-ness beneath a firmament of stars—the Aeolian harp of the Catskills singing of humility and peace, and gratitude to the great Unknown.

Later, two figures materialized from the outer world of darkness and entered the glow of the fire to bring their hands to Dan's. Gladness and surprise were in the Prophet's greetings, and through their fullness there ran a finely gleaming thread of respect. One of them was Reuben Cross, the greathearted and improvident master of fly-making who was already a legend, and with him was Alfred W. Miller, the Sparse Grey Hackle of the genial writings that were enriching Beaverkill lore.

In the early morning I entered the waters, rod in hand. I do not remember how many trout rose to my fly—or whether, indeed, any did. But I shall not forget that I moved as in a dream, hearing the voices of the river rising and falling with mysterious clarity through the hovering mists. And I remember the crystalline water that seemed to magnify the purity of the rocks, and the cool green darkness of the ferns, a profusion of frail, lush arches in the shadowed banks; and as the mist began to rise, a doe and her fawn crossed the pool below.

In the ensuing years, my work as a symphonist took me to various parts of the country for the fall, winter, and spring months. As each music season rounded its peak, and spring was faintly visible in the distant valley, the voice of a wakened obsession would begin loudening to a command to action. The trail was faint, often washed out. But, like a stubborn hound, I would return to certain crossways, hoping for a cold scent that would lead miraculously to a Blue Dun cape of quality that had fallen asleep in mid-flight. When the orchestra played "The Moldau," a tone poem which the Bohemian Smetana had distilled from the sounds of a great river, my left-hand fingers would scurry agreeably with the riffles at its headwaters, but the bow had become a fly rod in the other hand. The fly was, appropriately, a Blue Dun, since I had long ago formulated the theory that the natural Dun-hackled fly would take trout anywhere in the world at one time or another.

On nights off, a few of us would meet to play chamber music. The music we made, mostly for ourselves, was the most rewarding of all in terms of personal fulfillment. And if a pianist and a bassist were present, no great persuasion was needed for them to join us in a reading of Schubert's "Trout" Quintet, a tribute to that noble fish by the Austrian genius. As in the song that had inspired the

Quintet, the measured, buoyant cheer of its theme would have been perfect incidental music to the ballet of a stately brown swirling at his feast of mayfly nymphs aspiring to dunhood. Later, in the quiet of the Pittsburgh night, I would write another of those ritual letters—this time to a house in England: "Gentlemen, would you by chance have a cock's cape of natural Blue Dun of good quality to offer? I am aware of the rarity of this color and am, accordingly, prepared to consider the payment of a premium. I would be most grateful—"

I suppose it was inevitable that I should one day settle in the Catskills. I had had as much as I wanted of the unquiet life, and one year I returned, not merely for the summer, but to stay, in a village within twenty minutes' drive of the Esopus, a river proud and mighty still, its spirit unbroken after years of torment by water-greedy Manhattan. My community had a rich and highly respected tradition of the arts, offering scope for playing in a summer series of distinction and a likely potential for students of the violin and viola. Then, within one to two hours' reach there flowed the great rivers of angling history, allegedly tired, but still alluring and productive in their classically temperamental fashion. These were the Schoharie, the Delawares, East and West, the Willowemoc, and the Neversink and Beaverkill rivers.

My decision, however, had come at a time when, for perhaps too many reasons, mind and body had wandered off into a twilight world. There is a withering hostility in the winter Catskills, a taut suspension of life outdoors that can drive men's backs against their own walls. There is beauty, too; and joy may be found or contrived. But the gnawings of a marginal life can dispose a man toward the consolations of the jug. The cheapness and goodness of native applejack made it possible to appease a growing congenital thirst, transporting me to an inner island so beguiling that I did not want to leave. I was unable to. Years drifted by. Then, shambling one day through the familiar vapors, I stumbled over my persistent little man again, the one I had ignored and even insulted so often in the past. This time I heard him out; I believed him, and together we managed to stop it once and for all. I did not know it then, but he was congenital, too.

As I improved I began reconstituting the sport, and shortly began to hear the distant crowing of Blue Dun roosters again. The awakening was owing in part to the interest and kindness of Preston Jennings, who had recently retired to nearby Bearsville. His classic *A Book of Trout Flies* was, for me, the first truly significant work on angling entomology and dry-fly design for Eastern streams. It brought order to the chaos of a still rather wayward tradition of American dry-fly fishing and carried it to solid ground. It was issued in a limited edition by a private press in elegant format and was, ironically, remaindered. Its cost at the time was one factor. The other may have been the cool objectivity of a style uninviting to those American anglers who were still disposed toward boyish writings on fishing. However, by now the book had reemerged as a rare find, commanding premium prices—and it was very scarce. All told, it amounted very nearly to a conspiracy. Accordingly, Jennings was not awarded the honor due him in his lifetime. His genius is reflected in another work, the *Streamside Guide*, by Arthur Flick; and Jennings may be said to have been godfather to this indispensable little book.

Curiously, I found that Jennings' passion for the stream had also entered a state of suspension, although unlike mine, his was marked by sobriety, tinged however, with disillusion. Some causes for the latter have been implied. Then, too, Bobby was a man of sensibility, intelligence, and aesthetic awareness, all of which together can incline one to vulnerability. Such persons must stand on reserve or perish, at risk of incurring a judgment of pride. But such was not the case, and I like to think that I may have played a small part in his reconciliation to the Catskill streams, for which I think he was glad, or so it seemed as I watched him flexing his beloved Payne rod over a rifflehead, proving the potency of his Blue Dun Variant in conjuring a fifteen-inch brown out of its depths.

At his home one evening, Bobby brought out a small box and opened it with a reverence. Suggestive of a collector opening to some fabulous diamond. In it were dry flies which had been tied by Herman Christian and Theodore Gordon. I could not imagine them more perfect had they been tied that morning. One of the original models for the Quill Gordon fly was among them. Its form and color engraved themselves in my mind and thereafter became the model for my own imitations. I have since seen other flies allegedly by Gordon, but none had the finesse or the buoyant elegance.

As a tyer, Bobby was a superior artist, and his materials were the finest I had ever seen, or have ever seen since. Among his necks were Blue Duns as fine as I ever hope to see. Jennings was also inclined to the artist's brush and palette, and I believe that this, together with a related color-study, in which he had been absorbed for some time, had drawn him and his gracious wife to an artistic environment. His experience with salmon flies while fishing the great coastal rivers of the East had led to an inquiry into the reasons for the effectiveness of the many-hued salmon fly; and that to a study of the prismatic effect given off by the tiny bubbles of air formed about the microscopic filaments or hairs on the body of a rising nymph. Further inquiry had suggested that the salmon's memory held an indelible association of these colors with the food nymphs of its grilsehood.

All told, his efforts had begun to yield up a logical case for the salmon fly and its seemingly irrational gaudiness.

I felt pleased, even honored by Jennings' friendship, but in a rather vague, disembodied way. For those were difficult days—days in which the slow withdrawal of the alcohol had brought to view the shambles of a once productive life, and of a collective fruitfulness reduced to abject singleness. Vaguely aware of trudging forward, I was mostly conscious of a mouthful of ashes, of a battered spirit which had barely averted bankruptcy. But, as I have since gathered, my outer aspect was one of calm bordering on indifference, occasionally rising to arrogance. How far this was from the actual inward state would be a volume in itself, a compact little book, some of whose contents Bobby may have discerned; for one evening, in his studio, as he was delving into a drawer, he turned suddenly to me with a smile. In his outstretched hand was a superb cape of natural Blue Dun. For reasons that have never been clear, I declined it, with a thick murmur of thanks. I doubt whether I could have offended him more. I had virtually spit into the face of a noble gesture, one prompted by the purest motive of intuitive sensibility. Apparently, my reconstruction still had a long way to go. It is not surprising then, that after an unfortunate misunderstanding, we never saw each other again.

An offer came from an orchestra in Texas. Glad for the opportunity of relief from the aftermath of recent history, I accepted. Far from the Catskills, far from trout, my bewildered fly rods huddling in a friend's closet, I entered into the symphonic world again under the benevolent auspices of a mild Texas winter. But when the last Norther had subsided to spring, the old song of the quest began humming in my head again—and the voices of the rivers that flowed under the distant silhouettes of my mountains. I began to write letters that were utterly incongruous with that flat and surly land: "Gentlemen, would you by chance—Blue Dun? I would be most grateful—"

Returned to a comparatively tranquil and ordered life in the Catskills, I found it necessary from time to time to suspend the attrition of the long, bitter winters with occasional jaunts to Jerusalem. Together with my angling companions of some years we found respite from the winter jitters by observing, from time to time, one of a number of what may be called "Darbee Days." I suppose that, given other circumstances, they may have been called "Walt Dette," "Bill Kelly," or "Roy Steenrod" Days, for they, too, were a part of the angling-conservation custodianship at the banks of the great tradition. They were the Keepers of the Gate. But the Darbees were friends of long standing; and then—well, yes, there was also the little matter of their Blue Dun fowl, a strain of their own breeding that glared peevishly out the many cages in the back yard. Inside, we basked in the homemade sunlight of hackles, hooks, furs, rods, reels, lines, leaders, nets, selecting materials with which to tie flies at home later, by way of preserving our sanities during the deserted time of the year. There was talk of flies, of streams, of the men who lived for them, of books in which the waters ran, and where now and then one found a superior music which had been inspired by the trout, a simple vertebrate, but with this difference: That it stirred a mystery in the deepest recess of our beings, a primal nostalgia that quickened in the sight of its brilliant spots and bands of iridescence where gulps of moonlight had congealed to color. Padding in with feminine unobtrusiveness, the First Lady of American fly-tying gave greeting and passed to some other phase of sorting. Held by some to be, craftwise, the better half of the Darbee legend, Elsie would have disdained and Harry confirmed it. Actually, the difference, if any, was beyond the ken of niggling amateurs. Above the genial drone of Harry's voice on the trail of a point of conservation there sounded the faint, rhythmical fanfare of Blue Dun cocks, proud in their little beaked trumpets.

Later, on the long drive home, fly life hatched and surfaced in the murmuring car, and the unheard litanies to a reluctant spring that sang under our words must surely have been noted under the thick ice of Pepacton Reservoir and commented upon with frigid bubbles by the huge trout which had greatened in it within a few miles of its source, the self-renouncing Delaware.

Came the fall of another year, and Fate took one of us for a disastrous ride. For two weeks Jim Mulligan lay in a coma. Waking, he was to lie for two years in a veterans hospital bed until the one half of his body could support the paralyzed half. How many connivances and fabrications that Joe Nazzaro and I dreamed up en route to the hospital I cannot remember; nor how many precious days of liberty that Joe, and I, too, gave up that we might bring the stream to the distant bedside where our shattered friend lay.

But mercy, however capricious, will also have its say; and in having regained the use of one half of his body, Jim, a distinguished cartoonist, set himself the formidable task of transferring the skill of a now inert hand to the strong but untrained one. There came a winter's day at last when the inroads of "cabin fever" decreed a Darbee Day. Once again, with our valiant but unsteady Jim, we set off on wings of Blue Dun.

At Margaretville we crossed the upper Delaware and shortly were following the shoreline road of the severely beautiful Pepacton. Later, turning away from the reservoir, we began the long ascent, then down to Roscoe; and when we crossed the upper Beaverkill I doffed the only hat for the three of us. Shortly beyond the village, on the Manor road, we skirted the Willowemoc, greenbubbling at its icy lips and winter-dark in the upper pool. In the riffles above, a cold fire flared under a shaft of brilliant sunlight from a rift in the gray clouds.

Time has not perceptibly dimmed my memory of Darbee's greeting to the man whom destiny had banged on the brain; nor the implication that it had done so ineffectively. Out the candor of his blue eyes, out the heart of a rich experience, came the blessing of man's humanity to man: a beckoning to Jim to search and find a wholeness of his own. Before we left he gave Jim the token that would articulate his wish for many a year. It was in a paper sack.

As the car was cantering home along the Pepacton road Jim opened the paper sack with his good hand. In the waning light of the afternoon we saw the Blue Dun cape glowing. As he turned it we saw the component glints in the light from the reflecting whiteness of the reservoir. Visibly moved by his great good fortune, Jim's speech, till now painfully laborious, made a curious modulation and he said, slowly but clearly, "It seems to have other meanings."

In my cabinet of fly materials there is a special drawer. Lying in it is a small number of Blue Dun capes of varying shades nestling about each other in all the glory of their muted iridescence. They were all acquired more or less honorably: that is, in the sense that legitimacy and honesty are terms subject to parochial rules, and that it takes a good deal of imagination to transcend our little moral geographies.

I will not say how many there are, because I want to be surprised each time I count them. And when I do so, it is less to affirm my possessiveness than the privilege of their custody. That they are only a small part of countless numbers of shades and attitudes of color piques me, but it does not disturb me, for the ones allotted to me all have their special meaning. Each is a memento of a particular quest. They invite, of course, to other quests, but I really need not undertake them, because each day the colors are a little bit different, as each day is different; and thus they multiply in my mind's eye. Through their difference, as in the multicolored variants of Bach's great "Chaconne," there runs the somber strain of the fact that I grow older, and soon the fiddle strings will fray out and their sound must fade. But the colors will not, for Blue Dun waits upon other questions, whose answers, even more than mine, will disavow finality. As for instance, "Why is Blue Dun?"

One could as well ask: "Why is Love?" Or, indeed, "Why is Life?"

PART VII

CLASSIC
FISHING
STORIES

# STORYTELLING ON THE THAMES

## JEROME K. JEROME

The neighborhood of Streatley and Goring is a great fishing center. There is some excellent fishing to be had here. The river abounds in pike, roach, dace, gudgeon, and eels, just here; and you can sit and fish for them all day.

Some people do. They never catch them. I never knew anybody catch anything, up the Thames, except minnows and dead cats, but that has nothing to do, of course, with fishing! The local fisherman's guide doesn't say a word about catching anything. All it says is the place is "a good station for fishing"; and, from what I have seen of the district, I am quite prepared to bear out this statement.

There is no spot in the world where you can get more fishing, or where you can fish for a longer period. Some fishermen come here and fish for a day, and others stop and fish for a month. You can hang on and fish for a year, if you want to: it will be all the same.

The *Angler's Guide to the Thames* says that "jack and perch are also to be had about here," but there the *Angler's Guide* is wrong. Jack and perch may be about there. Indeed, I know for a fact that they are. You can see them there in shoals, when you are out for a walk along the banks: they come and stand half out of the water with their mouths open for biscuits. And, if you go for a bathe, they crowd round, and get in your way, and irritate you. But they are not to be "had" by a bit of worm on the end of a hook, nor anything like it—not they!

I am not a good fisherman myself. I devoted a considerable amount of attention to the subject at one time, and was getting on, as I thought, fairly well; but the old hands told me that I should never be any real good at it, and advised me to give it up. They said that I was an extremely neat thrower, and that I seemed to have plenty of gumption for the thing, and quite enough constitutional laziness. But they were sure I should never make anything of a fisherman. I had not got sufficient imagination.

They said that as a poet, or a shilling shocker, or a reporter, or anything of that kind, I might be satisfactory, but that, to gain any position as a Thames angler, would require more play of fancy, more power of invention than I appeared to possess.

Some people are under the impression that all that is required to make a good fisherman is the ability to tell lies easily and without blushing; but this is a mistake. Mere bald fabrication is useless; the veriest tyro can manage that. It is in the circumstantial detail, the embellishing touches of probability, the general air of scrupulous—almost of pedantic—veracity, that the experienced angler is seen.

Anybody can come in and say, "Oh, I caught fifteen dozen perch yesterday evening," or "Last Monday I landed a gudgeon, weighing eighteen pounds, and measuring three feet from the tip to the tail."

There is no art, no skill, required for that sort of thing. It shows pluck, but that is all.

No; your accomplished angler would scorn to tell a lie, that way. His method is a study in itself.

He comes in quietly with his hat on, appropriates the most comfortable chair, lights his pipe, and commences to puff in silence. He lets the youngsters brag away for a while, and then, during a momentary lull, he removes the pipe from his mouth, and remarks, as he knocks the ashes out against the bars:

"Well, I had a haul on Tuesday evening that it's not much good my telling anybody about."

"Oh! why's that?" they ask.

"Because I don't expect anybody would believe me if I did," replies the old fellow calmly, and without even a tinge of bitterness in his tone, as he refills his pipe, and requests the landlord to bring him three of Scotch—cold.

There is a pause after this, nobody feeling sufficiently sure of himself to contradict the old gentleman. So he has to go on by himself without any encouragement.

"No," he continues thoughtfully; "I shouldn't believe it myself if anybody told it to me, but it's a fact, for all that. I had been sitting there all the afternoon and had caught literally nothing—except a few dozen dace and a score of jack; and I was just about giving it up as a bad job when I suddenly felt a rather smart pull at the line. I thought it was another little one, and I went to jerk it up. Hang me, if I could move the rod! It took me half an hour—half an hour, sir!—to land that fish; and every moment I thought the line was going to snap! I reached him at last, and what do you think it was? A sturgeon! A forty-pound sturgeon! Taken on a line, sir! Yes, you may well look surprised—I'll have another three of Scotch, landlord, please."

And then he goes on to tell of the astonishment of everybody who saw it; and what his wife said, when he got home, and of what Joe Buggles thought about it.

I asked the landlord of an inn up the river once, if it did not injure him, sometimes, listening to the tales that the fishermen about there told him; and he said:

"Oh, no; not now, sir. It did used to knock me over a bit at first, but, lor love you! me and the missus we listens to 'em all day now. It's what you're used to, you know. It's what you're used to."

I knew a young man once, he was a most conscientious fellow, and, when he took to fly fishing, he determined never to exaggerate his hauls by more than twenty-five per cent.

"When I have caught forty fish," said he, "then I will tell people that I have caught fifty, and so on. But I will not lie any more than that, because it is sinful to lie."

But the twenty-five per cent plan did not work well at all. He never was able to use it. The greatest number of fish he ever caught in one day was three, and you can't add twenty-five per cent to three—at least, not in fish.

So he increased his percentage to thirty-three and a third; but that, again, was awkward, when he had caught only one or two; so, to simplify matters, he made up his mind to just double the quantity.

He stuck to this arrangement for a couple of months, and then he grew dissatisfied with it. Nobody believed him when he told them that he only doubled, and he, therefore, gained no credit that way whatever, while his moderation put him at a disadvantage among the other anglers. When he had really caught three small fish, and said he had six, it used to make him quite jealous to hear a man, who he knew for a fact had caught only one, going about telling people he had landed two dozen.

So, eventually, he made one final arrangement with himself, which he has religiously held to ever since, and that was to count each fish that he caught as ten, and to assume ten to begin with. For example, if he did not catch any fish at all, then he said he had caught ten fish—you could never catch less than ten fish by his system; that was the foundation of it. Then, if by any chance he really did catch one fish, he called it twenty, while two fish would count thirty, three forty, and so on.

It is a simple and easily worked plan, and there has been some talk lately of its being made use of by the angling fraternity in general. Indeed, the Committee of the Thames Anglers' Association did recommend its adoption about two years ago, but some of the older members opposed it. They said they would consider the idea if the number were doubled, and each fish counted as twenty.

If ever you have an evening to spare, up the river, I should advise you to drop into one of the little village inns, and take a seat in the taproom. You will be nearly sure to meet one or two old rodmen, sipping their toddy there, and they will tell you enough fishy stories, in half an hour, to give you indigestion for a month.

George and I—I don't know what had become of Harris; he had gone out and had a shave, early in the afternoon, and had then come back and spent full forty minutes in pipe-claying his shoes, we had not seen him since—George and I, therefore, and the dog, left to ourselves, went for a walk to Wallingford on the second evening, and, coming home, we called in at a little riverside inn, for a rest and other things.

We went into the parlor and sat down. There was an old fellow there, smoking a long clay pipe, and we naturally began chatting.

He told us that it had been a fine day today, and we told him that it had been a fine day yesterday, and then we all told each other that we thought it would be a fine day tomorrow; and George said the crops seemed to be coming up nicely.

After that it came out, somehow or other, that we were strangers in the neighborhood, and that we were going away the next morning. Then a pause ensued in the conversation, during which our eyes wandered round the room. They finally rested upon a dusty old glass case, fixed very high up above the chimney piece, and containing a trout. It rather fascinated me, that trout; it was such a monstrous fish. In fact, at first glance, I thought it was a cod.

"Ah!" said the old gentleman, following the direction of my gaze, "fine fellow that, ain't he?"

"Quite uncommon," I murmured; and George asked the old man how much he thought it weighed.

"Eighteen pounds six ounces," said our friend, rising and taking down his coat. "Yes," he continued, "it wur sixteen year ago, come the third o' next month, that I landed him. I caught him just below the bridge with a minnow. They told me he wur in the river, and I said I'd have him, and so I did. You don't see many fish that size about here now, I'm thinking. Good night, gentlemen, good night."

And out he went, and left us alone.

We could not take our eyes off the fish after that. It really was a remarkably fine fish. We were still looking at it, when the local carrier, who had just stopped at the inn, came to the door of the room with a pot of beer in his hand, and he also looked at the fish.

"Good-sized trout, that," said George, turning round to him.

"Ah! you may well say that, sir," replied the man; and then, after a pull at his beer, he added, "Maybe you wasn't here, sir, when that fish was caught?"

"No," we told him. We were strangers in the neighborhood.

"Ah!" said the carrier, "then, of course, how should you? It was nearly five years ago that I caught that trout."

"Oh! was it you who caught it, then?" said I.

"Yes, sir," replied the genial old fellow. "I caught him just below the lock—leastways, what was the lock then—one Friday afternoon; and the remarkable thing about it is that I caught him with a fly. I'd gone out pike fishing, bless you, never thinking of a trout, and when I saw that whopper on the end of my line, blest if it didn't quite take me aback. Well, you see, he weighed twenty-six pound. Good night, gentlemen, good night."

Five minutes afterward, a third man came in, and described how he had caught it early one morning, with bleak; and then he left, and a stolid, solemn-looking, middle-aged individual came in, and sat down over by the window.

None of us spoke for a while; but at length, George turned to the newcomer and said:

"I beg your pardon, I hope you will forgive the liberty that we—perfect strangers in the neighborhood—are taking, but my friend here and myself would be much obliged if you would tell us how you caught that trout."

"Why, who told you I caught that trout!" was the surprised query. We said that nobody had told us so, but somehow or other we felt instinctively that it was he who had done it.

"Well, it's a most remarkable thing—most remarkable," answered the stolid stranger, laughing: "because, as a matter of fact, you are quite right. I did catch it. But fancy your guessing it like that. Dear me, it's really a most remarkable thing."

And then he went on, and told us how it had taken him half an hour to land it, and how it had broken his rod. He said he had weighed it carefully when he reached home, and it had turned the scale at thirty-four pounds.

He went in his turn, and when he was gone, the landlord came in to us. We told him the various histories we had heard about his trout, and he was immensely amused, and we all laughed very heartily.

"Fancy Jim Bates and Joe Muggles and Mr. Jones and old Billy Maunders all telling you that they had caught it. Ha! ha! ha! Well, that is good," said the honest old fellow, laughing heartily. "Yes, they are the sort to give it me, to put up in my parlor, if they had caught it, they are! Ha! ha! ha!"

And then he told us the real history of the fish. It seemed that he had caught it himself, years ago, when he was quite a lad; not by any art or skill, but by that unaccountable luck that appears to always wait upon a boy when he plays the wag from school, and goes way out fishing on a sunny afternoon, with a bit of string tied onto the end of a tree.

He said that bringing home that trout had saved him from a whacking, and that even his schoolmaster had said it was worth the rule of three and practice put together.

He was called out of the room at this point, and George and I again turned our gaze upon the fish.

It really was a most astonishing trout. The more we looked at it, the more we marveled at it.

It excited George so much that he climbed up on the back of a chair to get a better view of it.

And then the chair slipped, and George clutched wildly at the trout case to save himself, and down it came with a crash, George and the chair on top of it.

"You haven't injured the fish, have you?" I cried in alarm, rushing up.

"I hope not," said George, rising cautiously and looking about.

But he had. That trout lay shattered into a thousand fragments—I say a thousand, but they may have been only nine hundred. I did not count them.

We thought it strange and unaccountable that a stuffed trout should break up into little pieces like that.

And so it would have been strange and unaccountable, if it had been a stuffed trout, but it was not.

That trout was plaster of Paris.

# OL' SETTLER OF DEEP HOLE

## IRVING BACHELLER

Uncle Eb was a born lover of fun. But he had a solemn way of fishing that was no credit to a cheerful man. It was the same when he played the bass viol, but that was also a kind of fishing at which he tried his luck in a roaring torrent of sound. Both forms of dissipation gave him a serious look and manner, that came near severity. They brought on his face only the light of hope and anticipation the shadow of disappointment.

We had finished our stent early the day of which I am writing. When we had dug our worms and were on our way to the brook with pole and line a squint of elation hold of Uncle Eb's face. Long wrinkles deepened as he looked into the sky for a sign of the weather, and then relaxed a bit as he turned his eyes upon the smooth sward. It was no time for idle talk. We tiptoed over the leafy carpet of the woods. Soon as I spoke he lifted his hand with a warning "Sh-h!" The murmur of the stream was in our ears. Kneeling on a mossy knoll we baited the hooks; then Uncle Eb beckoned to me.

I came to him on tiptoe.

"See thet there foam 'long side o' the big log?" he whispered, pointing with his finger.

I nodded.

"Cre-e-ep up jest as ca-a-areful as ye can," he went on whispering. "Drop in a leetle above an' let'er float down."

Then he went on, below me, lifting his feet in slow and stealthy strides.

He halted by a bit of drift wood and cautiously threw in, his arm extended, his finger alert. The squint on his face took a firmer grip. Suddenly his pole gave a leap, the water splashed, his line sang in the air and fish went up like a rocket. As we were looking into the tree tops it thumped the shore beside him, quivered a moment and flopped down the bank. He scrambled after it and went to his knees in the brook coming up empty handed. The water was slopping out of his boot legs.

"Whew!" said he, panting with excitement as I came over to him. "Reg'lar ol' he one," he added, looking down at his boots. "Got away from me—consarn him! Hed a leetle too much power in the arm."

He emptied his boots, baited up and went back to his fishing. As I looked up at him he stood leaning over the stream jiggling his hook. In a moment I saw a tug at the line. The end of his pole went under water like a flash. It bent double as Uncle Eb gave it a lift. The fish began to dive and rush. The line cut the water in a broad semicircle and then went far and near with long, quick slashes. The pole nodded and writhed like a thing of life. Then Uncle Eb had a look on him that is one of the treasures of my memory. In a moment the fish went away with such a violent rush, to save him, he had to throw his pole into the water.

"Heavens an' airth!" he shouted, "the ol' settler!"

The pole turned quickly and went lengthwise into the rapids. He ran down the bank and I after him. The pole was speeding through the swift water. We scrambled over logs and through bushes, but the pole went faster than we. Presently it stopped and swung around. Uncle Eb went splashing into the brook. Almost within reach of the pole he dashed his foot upon a stone falling headlong in the current. I was close upon his heels and gave him a hand. He rose hatless, dripping from head to foot and pressed on. He lifted his pole. The line clung to a snag and then gave way; the tackle was missing. He looked at it silently, tilting his head. We walked slowly to the shore. Neither spoke for a moment.

"Must have been a big fish," I remarked.

"Powerful!" said he, chewing vigorously on his quid of tobacco as he shook his head and looked down at his wet clothing. "In a desp'rit fix ain't I?"

"Too bad!" I exclaimed.

"Seldom ever hed sech a disapp'intment," he said. "Ruther counted on ketchin' thet fish—he was s' well hooked!"

He looked longingly at the water a moment. "If I don't go hum," said he, "an' keep my mouth shet I'll say sumthin' I'll be sorry fer."

He was never quite the same after that. He told often of his struggle with this unseen, mysterious fish and I imagined he was a bit more given to reflection. He had had hold of the "ol' settler of Deep Hole,"—a fish of great influence and renown there in Faraway. Most of the local fishermen had felt him tug at the line one time or another. No man had ever seen him for the water was black in Deep Hole. No fish had ever exerted a greater influence on the thought, the imagination, the manners or the moral character of his contemporaries. Tip Taylor always took off his hat and sighed when he spoke of the "ol' settler." Ransom Walker said he had once seen his top fin and thought it longer than a razor. Ransom took to idleness and chewing tobacco immediately after his encounter with the big fish, and both vices stuck to him as long as he lived. Everyone had his theory of the "ol' settler." Most agreed he was a very heavy trout. Tip Taylor used to say that in his opinion " 'Twas nuthin' more'n a plain, overgrown, common sucker," but Tip came from the Sucker Brook country where suckers lived in colder water and were more entitled to respect.

Mose Tupper had never had his hook in the "ol' settler" and would believe none of the many stories of adventure at Deep Hole that had thrilled the township.

"Thet fish hes made s' many liars 'round here ye dunno who t' b'lieve," he had said at the corners one day, after Uncle Eb had told his story of the big fish. "Somebody 't knows how t' fish hed oughter go 'n ketch him fer the good o' the town—thet's what I think."

Now Mr. Tupper was an excellent man but his incredulity was always too bluntly put. It had even led to some ill feeling.

He came in at our place one evening with a big hook and line from "down east"—the kind of tackle used in salt water.

"What ye goin' t' dew with it?" Uncle Eb inquired. "Ketch thet fish ye talk s' much about—goin' t' put him out o' the way."

" 'Taint fair," said Uncle Eb, "it's leading a pup with a log chain."

"Don't care," said Mose, "I'm goin' t' go fishin' t'morrer. If there reely is any sech fish—which I don't believe there is—I'm goin' t' rassle with him an' mebbe tek him out o' the river. Thet fish is sp'ilin' the moral character o' this town. He oughter be rode on a rail—thet fish hed."

How he would punish a trout in that manner Mr. Tupper failed to explain, but his metaphor was always a worse fit than his trousers and that was bad enough.

It was just before haying and, there being little to do, we had also planned to try our luck in the morning. When, at sunrise, we were walking down the cow path to the woods I saw Uncle Eb had a coil of bed cord on his shoulder.

"What's that for?" I asked.

"Wall," said he, "goin' t' hev fun anyway. If we can't ketch one thing we'll try another."

We had great luck that morning and when our basket was near full we came to Deep Hole and made ready for a swim in the water above it. Uncle Eb had looped an end of bed cord and tied a few pebbles on it with bits of string.

"Now," said he presently, "I want t' sink this loop t' the bottom an' pass the end o' the cord under the drift wood an' we can fetch it 'crost under water."

There was a big stump, just opposite, with roots running down the bank into the stream. I shoved the line under the drift with a pole and then hauled it across where Uncle Eb drew it up the bank under the stump roots.

"In 'bout half an hour I cal'late Mose Tupper'll be 'long," he whispered. "Wisht ye'd put on yer clo's an' lay here back o' the stump an' hold on t' the cord. When ye feel a bite give a yank er two an' haul in like Sam Hill—fifteen feet er more quicker'n scat. Snatch his pole right away from him. Then lay still."

Uncle Eb left me, shortly, going up stream. It was near an hour before I heard them coming. Uncle Eb was talking in a low tone as they came down the other bank.

"Drop right in there," he was saying, "an' let her drag down, through the deep water, deliberate like. Git clus t' the bottom."

Peering through a screen of bushes I could see an eager look on the unlovely face of Mose. He stood leaning toward the water and jiggling his hook along the bottom. Suddenly I saw Mose jerk and felt the cord move. I gave it a double twitch and began to pull. He held hard for a jiffy and then stumbled and let go yelling like mad. The pole hit the water with a splash and went out of sight like a diving frog. I brought it well under the foam and drift wood. Deep Hole resumed its calm, unruffled aspect. Mose went running toward Uncle Eb.

" 'S a whale!" he shouted. "Ripped the pole away quicker'n lightnin'."

"Where is it?" Uncle Eb asked.

"Tuk it away f' me," said Mose. "Grabbed it jes' like thet," he added with a violent jerk of his hand.

"What d' he dew with it?" Uncle Eb inquired.

Mose looked thoughtfully at the water and scratched his head, his features all a tremble.

"Dunno," said he. "Swallered it mebbe."

"Mean t' say ye lost hook, line, sinker 'n pole?"

"Hook, line, sinker 'n pole," he answered mournfully. "Come nigh haulin' me in tew."

" 'Taint possible," said Uncle Eb.

Mose expectorated, his hands upon his hips, looking down at the water.

"Wouldn't eggzac'ly say 'twas possible," he drawled, "but 'twas a fact."

"Yer mistaken," said Uncle Eb.

"No I haint," was the answer, "I tell ye I see it."

"Then if ye see it the nex' thing ye orter see 's a doctor. There's sumthin' wrong with you sumwheres."

"Only one thing the matter o' me," said Mose with a little twinge of remorse. "I'm jest a natural born perfect durn fool. Never c'u'd b'lieve there was any sech fish."

"Nobody ever said there was any sech fish," said Uncle Eb. "He's done more t' you 'n he ever done t' me. Never served me no sech trick as thet. If I was you I'd never ask nobody t' b'lieve it. 'S a leetle tew much."

Mose went slowly and picked up his hat. Then he returned to the bank and looked regretfully at the water.

"Never see the beat o' thet," he went on. "Never see sech power 'n a fish. Knocks the spots off any fish I ever hearn of."

"Ye riled him with that big tackle o' yourn," said Uncle Eb. "He wouldn't stan' it."

"Feel jest as if I'd hed holt uv a wil' cat," said Mose. "Tuk the hull thing— pole an' all—quicker 'n lightnin'. Nice a bit o' hickory as a man ever see. Gol' durned if I ever heern o' the like o' that, ever."

He sat down a moment on the bank.

"Got t' rest a minute," he remarked. "Feel kind o' wopsy after thet squabble."

They soon went away. And when Mose told the story of "the swallered pole" he got the same sort of reputation he had given to others. Only it was real and large and lasting.

"What d' ye think uv it?" he asked, when he had finished.

"Wall," said Ransom Walker, "wouldn't want t' right out plain t' yer face."

" 'Twouldn't be p'lite," said Uncle Eb soberly.

"Sound a leetle ha'sh," Tip Taylor added.

"Thet fish has jerked the fear o' God out he way it looks t' me," said Carlyle Barber.

"Yer up 'n the air, Mose," said another. "Need a sinker on ye."

They bullied him—they talked him down, demurring mildly, but firmly.

"Tell ye what I'll do," said Mose sheepishly, "I'll b'lieve you fellers if you'll b'lieve me."

"What, swop even? Not much!" said one, with emphasis. " 'Twouldn't be fair. Ye've ast us t' b'lieve a genuwine out 'n out impossibility."

Mose lifted his hat and scratched his head thoughtfully. There was a look of embarrassment in his face.

"Might a ben dreamin'," said he slowly. "I swear it's gittin' so here 'n this town a feller can't hardly b'lieve himself."

"Fur's my experience goes," said Ransom Walker, "he'd a fool 'f he did."

" 'Minds me o' the time I went fishin' with Ab Thomas," said Uncle Eb. "He ketched an ol' socker the fust thing. I went off by myself 'n got a good sized fish, but 'twant s' big 's hisn. So I tuk 'n opened his mouth 'n poured in a lot o' fine shot. When I come back Ab he looked at my fish 'n begun t' brag. When we weighed 'em mine was leetle heavier.

" 'What!' says he. ' 'Tain't possible thet leetle cuss uv a trout 's heavier 'n mine.'

" ' 'Tis sartin,' I said.

" 'Dummed deceivin' business,' said he as he hefted 'em both. 'Gittin' so ye can't hardly b'lieve the stillyurds.' "

# THE LUCY COFFIN

## W. D. WETHERELL

My father, so long a distinguished member of the Philadelphia bar, was totally incapable of making up a story. His clients were expected to tell him in simple words what had happened, and then he would try to shape the plain words, the unadorned facts, into an argument a jury would find compelling. Imagination, exaggeration, hyperbole—he actively disapproved of all three. This was bad luck for me, since I was born with an oversupply of each, something he blamed on heredity, a great-uncle who wrote advertisements for Florida real estate back in the Twenties, and, before me, was the closest thing to a writer the family had.

So the one story Dad told me I listened to very closely. It was a fish story of course. Fly fishing was Dad's one vulnerability, the only thing we could tease him about, or theme his birthday presents around, or, on great occasions, actually share with him out on the water.

He was good at it, he fished all over the world, and his eyes came alive on a river in a way they didn't even in the courtroom. He never had the usual fisherman's virtue of patience . . . he despised patience, considered it the most mediocre of virtues . . . but what he had instead was endurance, getting out on the water before anyone else in camp and coming back far later. And he looked the part, too, once he started putting some years on. Wrinkles made him more handsome, not less. People always imagined him with a pipe in his mouth, squinting toward the sunset, though the truth is he never smoked.

That this passion was fueled in part by a rather dry, stiff, passionless marriage should perhaps come as no surprise. There were lots of dry, stiff, passionless marriages in the Philadelphia of those years. My parents didn't divorce, they had old-fashioned notions about what was owed their children, and I don't remember any particular arguments. Mother went her way, Dad went his, at least until her last years, when there was a softening, a drawing together, that surprised no one more than them.

I'm not sure when I first heard Dad's one and only story—there doesn't seem to be a place in memory where I didn't know it. He was just old enough to have served in the last days of the war, and it wasn't until almost a year after it ended that he was discharged. He went back to law school and graduated quickly—which means the story begins in the late spring of 1948.

He decided that before starting his practice he would treat himself to one grand fishing expedition. He would take a train to Vermont, then spend the summer hiking and hitchhiking through the hills, fishing every single stream and pond he came upon, boarding at farmhouses where he could find them, or camping rough in the woods. For three months, he would care about nothing except fishing, think about nothing except fishing, press the summer so deep in his memory it would never shake loose.

And that's pretty much the way it turned out. He traveled north along the Connecticut River, and when he came to a tributary, he would fish upstream toward the west, then strike out cross-country and follow the next tributary downstream to its junction with the big river—a back and forth, weaving kind of progression that meant there was very little water he missed. The days of the log drives were over, but there were plenty of old-time rivermen left who were more than happy to tell him where the big trout were hiding—and they weren't often wrong.

Back in the Depression, tramps and hobos had been distrusted, even feared here, but once the farm wives realized Dad was just fishing, a veteran, he was often given a room free of charge. In the morning, there would be chores he could help out with, and afternoons he would spend chasing the browns and rainbows that lived in the deep pools, or fishing for wild brook trout in the beaver ponds where most of these rivers had their starts, wading in the muck if he had to, sometimes taking all day to build a raft.

Thanks to his zigzag pattern, his getting stuck on rivers he loved best, it took him June and a good part of July to advance northwards sixty miles. There was still a lot of Vermont left to go before he hit Canada, but suddenly, between one tributary and the next, the landscape dramatically changed. The Connecticut veered away into New Hampshire, and the rivers flowed north towards Quebec and the St. Lawrence. The forest, instead of being dominated by maple and pine, was now mostly spruce, with boreal swamps and undulating sheets of pewter-colored rock. The farms were few and far between and mostly failed— this was a land of empty farmhouses where ghostly curtains blew out through shattered glass.

The first part of the story, the background, my father told quickly, with a lawyer's fine sense for how much he could ask of a jury's patience. But he would always hesitate here, take his glasses off and put them back on again, look out the nearest window, smile ruefully, then turn back again, his voice pitched now to a lower key.

"And then something odd happened, something I hadn't counted on. You have to understand that I was pretty cocky in those days. I thought, when it came to fly fishing, I was the hottest thing to ever hit Vermont. But once I got into the deep woods, the lonely country, things changed. I couldn't catch a fish, no matter how hard I tried. Not a trout, not a sucker, not even a chub. They all had locks on their jaws and for the life of me I couldn't find the key."

It was late August now, hot, with low water in all the streams. He slept in the woods most nights, though when it rained he found shelter in abandoned logging camps set in pockets against the ridges. On one nameless stream, fishing through a tunnel of alders, his leather wallet of flies, his best flies, dropped into the water and floated away, so he was down now to his rejects and spares.

"For the first time all summer, I began feeling sorry for myself. A thunderstorm hit me that night, so I was a pretty sorry sight once morning came. The only thing keeping me from heading to the train station and home was that the terrain was growing gentle again, with those beautiful open hillsides similar to what I had seen further south. I'll fish one more river, I decided. Just one more and then I'm done."

He was walking along, drying out in the sunshine, when he came upon an iron bridge with unusually elaborate scrollwork, and past it, a tree with a crudely-painted sign. *Hand Tied Flies!* It read. In that lonely countryside, it startled him; it could have said *Hand Cut Diamonds* and he wouldn't have been more surprised. There was an arrow pointing uphill along a road so rough a mule would have turned around in disgust. Figuring he had nothing to lose, he started up it—and that's when he had his second surprise.

On the top of the hill, set under a grove of ancient maple, was a small white farmhouse with an attached red barn. It wasn't derelict or abandoned like so many of the highest places but well-cared for, neat, even prim. Holsteins had trampled the yard up, but there was a garden surrounded by a picket fence, and it wasn't a vegetable garden either, but a flower garden, with tall showy gladiolas that were obviously meant to be cut and brought inside.

There was no one around, at least not at first, but when my father circled behind the barn he came upon a tool shed where a husky young man sat on a wicker chair listening to the Red Sox game on the radio. On the workbench beside him were piles of chicken feathers and Christmas tinsel and small black hooks. It was as if, my father said, the man knew he was coming and wanted to get right down to business.

"I saw your sign," my father said.

The young man looked Dad over. "Fly fisherman?"

"I try to be."

"Then you'll want six of these."

He handed over a Prince Albert tobacco tin. Inside were half a dozen of the rattiest looking, most outlandish flies Dad had ever seen. There looked to be muskrat fur in it, and duck quill, and a huge shank of rooster hackle—and Dad's first temptation was to laugh out loud.

"How much?" he asked carefully, not wanting to offend him.

"A dollar for the six."

"Does it have a name?"

"No. Well, sure. The Lucy Coffin. There, I just named it. You try that, fish it up on top slathered in fly dope, and if you use anything else you ain't as smart as you look."

Those of you who know fish stories can sense where this is headed. Dad stuffed those flies in his pocket, then forgot all about them. The last river he fished in Vermont was the Willoughby. As with all the other places he fished in August, he couldn't find a way to get the trout to rise—until, desperate, he remembered the Lucy Coffin. Tying one on, he threw it out there with a why-not kind of cast—and promptly rose a three-pound brown that fought him stubbornly for a good half hour. Six more fish followed, each almost as big, and when he finally gave up because of darkness, trout were still jumping toward it out of the black. For the last week of his trip, he fished nothing else—and everywhere it immediately resulted in the same kind of triumphs.

That was Dad's story, his one and only. Even as a kid, I wondered about it, not so much whether it was true or not . . . since Dad didn't make anything up, I knew it was true . . . but at the sweetness that would come into his tone, especially during the last part about that lonely, forgotten farm. It seemed more wistfulness than the summer really warranted, though obviously, being alone like that, at a time when a place was at its most beautiful and forgotten, had left an enduring impression.

I'd like to say, as a kid, I never tired of hearing him tell this story, but the truth is, I did get tired, particularly when I reached my teens. A magic fly? A fly that worked miracles? Sure, Dad. Right. Anything you say.

And then, from a storyteller's point of view, he made a smart move. The summer I was sixteen, driving me back from a camp counselor job I had in Maine, he detoured over to show me Vermont. We fly fished several of the streams he discovered in 1948; Dad, unlike most men who are experts at something, was more than willing to let me go off and learn on my own, playing dumber than he really was, knowing I would either fall in love with it on my own or it wouldn't take.

We only had four days. On the third, I suddenly woke up to the fact we were now doing more driving than fishing, going off on dirt roads that led away from the rivers uphill. All these detours seemed of the same pattern. "We're low on flies," Dad would announce, then suddenly swerve the wheel to the right. We would drive to the top of the hill where the road gave out into ruts, Dad would get out, look over the abandoned field going back to brush, maybe take a few steps toward what remained of a farmhouse . . . a cellar hole, a blackened chimney . . . then come back to the car shaking his head.

"Well, it was around here somewhere. Things have changed, all this forest. I was on foot, never bothered with maps. Half the streams I didn't even know what their names were. Being lost was part of the adventure."

I tried to be helpful. "Maybe it was over by that river we fished yesterday? I saw a lot of old farms."

My father considered this, then shook his head. "Well, maybe, but I don't think so, Paul. I searched there pretty thoroughly last time."

"Last time?"

He smiled, shyly. "Oh, I had a business trip to Boston a couple years back. Came over here for a few days, looked around. It wasn't fishing season. Mud season, so I couldn't get very far." He raised himself up on tiptoes, put his hands around his eyes like binoculars. "See that open meadow over there? Let's see if we can find a road, then, if it's not there, we'll do some fishing."

He was quiet driving home. It was by far the best four days together we ever had, it got me started fly fishing, but I was confused at how silent he seemed, how disappointed. If we hadn't found his fly shop, that was okay by me. The Lucy Coffin? Hell, we caught plenty of trout without it—which is what I wanted to tell him, but he had his lawyer's face on now, his *losing* lawyer's face, and I knew that was something I couldn't dent.

When my mother died three years ago, Dad took it harder than any of us would have expected. As I said, during her last years their dependence on each other kept growing as their friends and colleagues one by one disappeared. Passion Dad had missed out on in life, but at least he found a quiet warmth, and losing that, at his age, hurt him deeply.

When I first broached the idea of a fishing trip, Dad was hesitant. He still fished, but mostly in ponds now, trolling streamers from a rowboat. I made it sound like I was the one who badly needed to get away . . . I had just finished a book; I was worn out, in need of a change . . . and, though he could see right through my stratagems, Dad wasn't immune to what June was doing to the air, even in suburban Philadelphia.

But he still hesitated; there was a meeting at his retirement community he was supposed to chair, and I had to come out with the argument I'd been saving as my clincher.

"We'll go and see if we can find the old place where you bought the Lucy Coffin. Maybe even find the same man."

"Dead," Dad grunted.

"How do you know that? You said he was about your own age, didn't you? He could still be tying flies. And even if he's gone, we'll make a real effort to locate where that farm was, that shouldn't be impossible."

"It's vanished. I couldn't find it last time."

"You had me in tow."

"Well no. The time after that, I searched pretty hard."

"You went back again?"

"Four or five times now."

"Four or five times?"

I'd been on the lookout for signs of dotage, but still this surprised me—he said it in a sly, secretive way, like he'd admitted sneaking off to Las Vegas. I didn't know the story had such a hold on him still. For me, it was nostalgic, going back up there, and I suppose I expected it was merely that for him, a story that sleeps wherever stories sleep in men his age, not something that actively burned.

He was waiting for me in the parking lot when I got there Thursday morning—the leathery, craggy-looking version of Dad, a rod tube sticking out from his ancient duffel bag, his waders slung around his shoulders like a bandolier.

Our drive north was on the quiet side—except for grandkids, none of the subjects we came up with seemed to take hold. Always before we could fall back on politics, me kidding him about being a Republican, him teasing me about being a Democrat, but that kind of teasing isn't possible anymore. Only once did he broach anything even remotely serious. We were up in Massachusetts, we had just gone through a long stretch of malls, and he waved his hand around, as if indicating, not just what we could see out the window, but the deeper, more essential part we could only sense.

"Countries are like old men, Paul. They get ugly when they get old . . ." and the truth of that, the doubled truth, kept things pretty quiet until we hit Vermont.

It was much better after that. The long evening shadows cut across the interstate, there were caddis flies dancing like flames around the top of the highest birches, and when we got out of the car at our motel the smell of late-blooming lilac made us look at each other and smile. Next morning, up early, we drove into the mountains, and the farther we drove the younger and fresher the land seemed. I got Dad to tell his story again, not the end he always rushed toward, but the earlier part, those June weeks when he had wandered around the foothills with no motive in life other than catching rainbows, brookies and browns.

We fished some of the same streams. Dad took forever stringing up his rod and pulling on his waders, but once in the river he did fine, not shuffling along like an old man in slippers, but high-stepping like a stork. We both caught trout. They weren't the natives he remembered, they were probably two weeks off the stock truck, but the rivers rushed the same way they always rushed, the willows danced the same dance in the wind, and there were afternoon hatches of mayflies we did very well with, fishing deep into dark. If anything, Dad seemed to have more energy and pep at the end of the day than he had when we began.

"Rhubarb pie," he said, taking a deep sniff of evening air. "I can still smell it. All these farm wives baked great rhubarb pies."

We spent the next day on a little tributary that wasn't on the map. I had to peel the alders back so Dad could enter the best pool, but when he did he caught three wild brookies, the last, for that water, a real monster, pushing fifteen inches. We admired it for the few seconds he took to let it slip back from his hand to the water. "One to quit on," I said, not really thinking about my words. "Yes, one to quit on," Dad said softly, thinking about them hard.

That night we found an old tourist home, the kind you wouldn't think existed anymore. *Titus Takes Tourists* read the sign out front—and Titus turned out to be even older than my father, with a thick mountain accent I could barely understand. But Dad could understand—he and Titus sat up talking half the night. "Twenty bucks!" his wife said, when it was time to leave. She acted embarrassed to ask so much, so, at least in this respect, we were back in 1948 at last.

But it was time to go home now. I had a book signing scheduled in Washington and Dad still wanted to chair his meeting. I had big ideas about driving it all in one day, so we left early, when the fog still lay clotted on the river. We crossed on an old iron bridge, and instead of a regular paved roadbed, there were thick old beams that made it bumpy. Something about the bumps, or the smell of creosote, or the lacy pattern of the metal got Dad thinking.

"Is there a road up here to the right?" he asked, before we were all the way over.

"It doesn't look like much of a road, Dad." I pointed in the vague direction of Philadelphia. "We've got a long drive ahead of us."

"Is there an old barn? Small, like it was made for miniature cows? Two gables, crazy windows?"

He was looking directly at me when he asked this—he was testing himself by not looking out the window.

"What's left of a barn, yes. There, you look yourself. Underneath all that poison ivy."

Dad nodded without looking, as if I were telling him nothing he didn't already know. "Turn right," he said, with a strange tremor in his voice—and then he closed his eyes, as if only by doing so could he find the right way. "There should be a bog in half a mile, then an apple orchard, then a small wooden dam."

Maybe there were those things—the washouts and ruts kept my attention fixed on the driving. A switchback got us onto an easier grade, and the upper part went under a tunnel of purple lilacs that must have been the last to bloom in the entire state. They don't grow wild, someone had once planted them, so maybe we were on the right track after all—and yet no mental effort I was capable of making could make that thick forest disappear, picture this as ever having been open.

The road ended in at a washout that could have swallowed a tank. I parked on its lip. Dad, without saying anything, opened his door and started striding through the trees. Certainty—his whole posture was shaped to it—and though I was a long way from feeling this myself, I started after him.

I caught up pretty fast. There were some spruce, then a band of dying birch, and I remembered that birch were the trees that grew first on abandoned land, and just when I was trying to figure out how many years this could take, I came into a little clearing in the middle of which stood a house.

It was standing, I'll say that much for it. The tin roof seemed pinned by rusty lightning rods to the simple Cape that stood beneath. The siding had long ago been weathered into bone color, hunters had riddled much of it with bullets, and the windows were starred with broken glass. In front was a porch that had once faced the road, but its supports had collapsed and the gingerbread trim, algae-covered and blistered, lay in pieces in the tall grass that licked the sides.

Dad stood staring down at something, and when I came up to him he pointed, bent stiffly, reached out his hand. Below a broken window the planks had been replaced with fresh, clean pine, making it look as if someone had chosen this spot to begin their renovations. Had they started, then, faced with the enormity of the job, given up? Except for that and a deflated soccer ball we found near the pyramid-heaped ruins of the barn, there were no signs of recent life.

Some of the debris had been pulled over to where an enormous apple tree had muscled out its own clearing. Dad reached down to turn through the planks. The third or fourth had purple lettering burned into its side like an old tattoo—he held it up to the light so we could read it—but it seemed an advertisement for seed or fertilizer, and didn't say anything about hand-tied flies.

"Is this it?" I asked.

I stood there staring toward the farmhouse, trying to imagine paint on it, a shiny new roof, curtains, flowers. I don't know what Dad saw. Again, as with the forest, the hand of time was too heavy for me to lift.

Dad's voice, when he started, was pitched very soft, like the voice a gentle man uses when someone is sleeping in the next room. And he touched the apple tree while he talked. That seemed important to him, the simple rough contact.

"What I'll never forget is how she was standing there waiting at the top of the road. Not waiting for me—waiting for anyone, their life was so lonely. I remember thinking how the sign for flies was their way of luring strangers just so they could have a little talk with someone besides themselves. If so, it was a good lure—it caught me easily enough."

A brown and shriveled apple, last year's, clung to the branch. He reached his hand toward it, and the motion alone was enough to make it fall.

"There was just the two of them. Her brother was seventeen—heavy, strong, and so round-shouldered he was nearly humpbacked. He could take care of cows all right, and winter he worked with the loggers. Their father had gone off to a defense plant after Pearl Harbor and that's the last they ever saw of him. Their mother died of cervical cancer a few years later. Lucy had the care of her, there was no one else. The parents or grandparents were either very brave or very stupid to have made a farm so high. The boy's name was Ira and her name was Lucy. Lucy Coffin."

The name, which I expected and didn't expect, seemed to come out of him hard. He coughed, or pretended to, and I followed his eyes back to the road.

He remembered what she looked like that first evening, he said. A young woman his own age standing there with an apron on, staring intently toward the dusk, wiping, with a wonderfully impatient gesture, the curly red hair that fell down across her eyes. She was beautiful, of course, though not in a way he had ever learned to see as beautiful before. He thought first of a tomboy, someone freckled and athletic, but she was past that stage now, and the chores hadn't yet roughened her skin. In the brief interval of grace that lay between he saw a girl so fresh and brave and natural it took his breath away, right from that first moment.

"I ended up staying with them for two weeks—they were absurdly grateful for my company. It was like they lived on an island and I had brought them news of the outside world. It was incredibly hard, the life they led, especially during the war years. It was thirty-five miles to the nearest movie house, and they told me how they would use horses to get down their road, then shovel out their old Ford from the snow, push and shove it to get it going, putting on chains when they got to macadam, then drive all that way just to see a double feature, getting back after midnight so they could tend to the cows. Ira liked fishing, so we hit it off pretty quick. He tied flies, sold a few now and then down in town, but they were cheap, gaudy things, nothing special. He really didn't understand what was happening between Lucy and me. Her bedroom faced the barn, and I remember waking up with her, getting out of bed quietly, pulling on my sweater, walking over to the window and seeing Ira stripped to the waist chopping away at five in the morning, and then at night he still wouldn't be finished, all the work he had."

Neither one of them knew much about anything except work. Once a month there were those expeditions to go see Clark Gable or Bette Davis, but except for these their life had few ornaments. Dad explained how he found an old kite in the barn leftover from when they were little, but neither one remembered how to fly it, and when he tied a tail on, got it up in the air, they thought he was a magician. And a picnic—they had never thought it possible, to go somewhere pretty and eat outside just for fun. At night, the three of them sat by the radio listening to the Red Sox and then Jack Benny. When Ira trudged off exhausted to bed, he and Lucy would walk outside together with a blanket and lie under the stars.

Neither one of them was a hick, he wanted to make sure I understood that. Lucy had an energy and directness nothing could stop, except for the one great bafflement that had her in its grip—how to be brave and deal with what life had brought her without her bravery digging a trap for her, making the loneliness even worse. For all the harshness in her life, she had a wonderful laugh and once started it would run away with her, set him laughing, too—laughing so much they cried. And silence—how many other girls her age knew how to make silence say everything? If he could teach her about kites and picnics, she could teach him about sweetness . . . never before had he suspected life was capable of being so sweet . . . and, in the end, what sadness was, too.

One afternoon they helped Ira finish his chores so they could all go fishing. Ira fished hard, but without much skill, and spent most of the time admiring my father's little Payne fly rod. After their picnic, he and Lucy walked upstream toward a waterfall. She had borrowed Ira's hat for the sun, a battered old porkpie with flies tucked in the band, and before long, that's pretty much all she was wearing, that floppy red hat. He laughed over that, and she laughed, too, bending over a little pool where the water was so thin it acted like a mirror.

My father explained all this while holding onto the apple tree, but now he stepped away, seemed actually to break that invisible cord, and walked slowly back to where I stood in the center of those rotting old planks. He looked old . . . I was startled at how old he suddenly looked . . . and maybe it was the dark evening shadows doing that, or maybe it was the contrast with the young man I followed so intently in his story. Time had stopped while he was telling it, but it was ticking again, and, judging by the way he closed his eyes, Dad felt the rush of those minutes even more than I did.

"I thought about asking her to come away with me—I thought about nothing else that last week. Would she have come? It would have broken her brother's heart. Still, I think if I had pressed her she would have come. Our worlds were so different. When I asked her about her future, she wouldn't tell me about any dreams or plans, but then right toward the end she did. 'I'd like to be in pictures,' she said. Out of all her loneliness, she could come up with nothing else."

My father's voice deepened—it was like he was struggling to recapture his lawyer's tone, get back into that safety zone where words expressed simple, incontrovertible facts.

"Lucy is one day younger than I am. She was born on October seventh and I was born on October sixth, and I teased her about how much younger she was, how much wiser I was. Every single birthday since I've thought about where she might be, what life has brought her. I've always wondered if we kept pace somehow, she in her world, me in mine . . . I got up in the middle of the night, being careful not to wake her. I didn't leave a note for her, but I left one for Ira on the kitchen table, along with that little Payne fly rod. I walked down the road in the moonlight, and never before had I seen anything so beautiful, and yet every step was torture. I can feel this even now, understand that Paul? Arthritis, that young doctor of mine says whenever I got for my checkup. But that's not what a man my age feels in his knees. It's all those times you walked away from someone you should never have walked away from."

I went over and took his arm, since he actually seemed faltering now, and there were those roots and rocks to navigate before we got back to the car.

"So there wasn't a fly?" I said. "No Lucy Coffin?"

"Oh, there was a fly all right." He reached into his pocket, brought out his leather fly book, the one he used for his very best flies. He opened it, held it toward the keyhole of light still visible in the west.

"Ira could tie in a clumsy, self-taught way. He gave me some Black Gnats before I left. Six of them. Years when the memory hurt worst, I would take one out and tie it on. I have one left. Here, open your hand."

I felt something sharp and tickly against my palm; I folded my fist tight to make sure it stayed there, that it didn't drop loose. *Mine now.* I didn't say it, but, like a small child accepting a present, that's what I felt.

"Yours now," my father said, reading my thoughts. He smiled—not a happy smile, not a sad smile either, but one that seemed pressed into the thin, permeable layer that lies in between. I could see him stare toward the first stars, sensed him using the silence to set up a line to go out on, like an old experienced storyteller from way back when, not someone who just had the one.

"I fished Ira's fly pretty hard all those two weeks, and never caught a thing on it, but for once in my life I didn't care."

# CROCKER'S HOLE

## R. D. BLACKMORE

The Culm, which rises in Somersetshire, and hastening into a fairer land (as the border waters wisely do) falls into the Exe near Killerton, formerly was a lovely trout stream, such as perverts the Devonshire angler from due respect toward Father Thames and the other canals round London. In the Devonshire valleys it is sweet to see how soon a spring becomes a rill, and a rill runs on into a rivulet and a rivulet swells into a brook; and before one has time to say, "What are you at?"—before the first tree it ever spoke to is a dummy, or the first hill it ever ran down has turned blue, here we have all the airs and graces, demands and assertions of a full-grown river.

But what is the test of a river? Who shall say? "The power to drown a man," replies the river darkly. But rudeness is not argument. Rather shall we say that the power to work a good undershot wheel, without being dammed up all night in a pond, and leaving a tidy back stream to spare at the bottom of the orchard, is a fair certificate of river-hood. If so, many Devonshire streams attain that rank within five miles of their spring; aye, and rapidly add to it. At every turn they gather aid, from ash-clad dingle and aldered meadow, mossy rock and ferny wall, hedge-trough-roofed with bramble netting, where the baby water lurks, and lanes that coming down to ford bring suicidal tribute. Arrogant, all-engrossing river, now it has claimed a great valley of its own; and whatever falls within the hill scoop sooner or later belongs to itself. Even the crystal "shutt" that crosses the farmyard by the woodrick, and glides down an aqueduct of last year's bark for Mary to fill the kettle from; and even the tricklets that have no organs for telling or knowing their business, but only get into unwary oozings in and among the water grass, and there make moss and forget themselves among it—one and all, they come to the same thing at last, and that is the river.

The Culm used to be a good river at Culmstock, tormented already by a factory, but not strangled as yet by a railroad. How is it now the present writer does not know, and is afraid to ask, having heard of a vile "Culm Valley Line." But Culmstock bridge was a very pretty place to stand and contemplate the ways of trout; which is easier work than to catch them. When I was just big enough to peep above the rim, or to lie upon it with one leg inside for fear of tumbling over, what a mighty river it used to seem, for it takes a treat there and spreads itself. Above the bridge the factory stream falls in again, having done its business, and washing its hands in the innocent half that has strayed down the meadows. Then under the arches they both rejoice and come to a slide of about two feet, and make a short, wide pool below, and indulge themselves in perhaps two islands, through which a little river always magnifies itself and maintains a mysterious middle. But after that, all of it used to come together, and make off in one body for the meadows, intent upon nurturing trout with rapid stickles, and buttercuppy corners where fat flies may tumble in. And here you may find in the very first meadow, or at any rate you might have found, forty years ago, the celebrated "Crocker's Hole."

The story of Crocker is unknown to me, and interesting as it doubtless was, I do not deal with him, but with his Hole. Tradition said that he was a baker's boy who, during his basket rounds, fell in love with a maiden who received the cottage loaf, or perhaps good "Households" for her master's use. No doubt she was charming, as a girl should be, but whether she encouraged the youthful baker and then betrayed him with false role, or whether she "consisted" throughout— as our cousins across the water express it—is known to their *manes* only. Enough that she would not have the floury lad; and that he, after giving in his books and money, sought an untimely grave among the trout. And this was the first pool below the bread walk deep enough to drown a five-foot baker boy. Sad it was; but such things must be, and bread must still be delivered daily.

A truce to such reflections—as our foremost writers always say, when they do not see how to go on with them—but it is a serious thing to know what Crocker's Hole was like; because at a time when (if he had only persevered, and married the maid, and succeeded to the oven, and reared a large family of short-weight bakers) he might have been leaning on his crutch beside the pool, and teaching his grandson to swim by precept (that beautiful proxy for practice)—at such a time, I say there lived a remarkable fine trout in that hole. Anglers are notoriously truthful, especially as to what they catch, or even more frequently have not caught. Though I may have written fiction, among many other sins—as a nice old lady told me once—now I have to deal with facts; and foul scorn would I count it ever to make believe that I caught that fish. My length at that time was not more than the butt of a four-jointed rod, and all I could catch was a minnow with a pin, which our cook Lydia would not cook, but used to say, "Oh, what a shame, Master Richard! They would have been trout in the summer, please God! if you would only a' let 'em grow on." She is living now and will bear me out in this.

But upon every great occasion there arises a great man; or to put it more accurately, in the present instance, a mighty and distinguished boy. My father, being the parson of the parish, and getting, need it be said, small pay, took sundry pupils, very pleasant fellows, about to adorn the universities. Among them was the original "Bude Light," as he was satirically called at Cambridge, for he came from Bude, and there was no light in him. Among them also was John Pike, a born Zebedee if ever there was one.

John Pike was a thickset younker, with a large and bushy head, keen blue eyes that could see through water, and the proper slouch of shoulder into which great anglers ripen; but greater still are born with it; and of these was Master John. It mattered little what the weather was, and scarcely more as to the time of year, John Pike must have his fishing every day, and on Sundays he read about it, and made flies. All the rest of the time he was thinking about it.

My father was coaching him in the fourth book of *The Aeneid* and all those wonderful species of Dido, where passion disdains construction; but the only line Pike cared for was of horsehair. "I fear, Mr. Pike, that you are not giving me your entire attention," my father used to say in his mild dry way; and once when Pike was more than usually abroad, his tutor begged to share his meditations. "Well, sir," said Pike, who was very truthful, "I can see a green drake by the strawberry tree, the first of the season, and your derivation of 'barbamus' put me in mind of my barberry dye." In those days it was a very nice point to get the right tint for the mallard's feather.

No sooner was the lesson done than Pike, whose rod was ready upon the lawn, dashed away always for the river, rushing headlong down the hill, and away to the left through a private yard, where "No Thoroughfare" was put up and a big dog stationed to enforce it. But Cerberus himself could not have stopped

John Pike; his conscience backed him up in trespass the most sinful when his heart was inditing of a trout upon the rise.

All this, however, is preliminary, as the boy said when he put his father's coat upon his grandfather's tenterhooks, with felonious intent upon his grandmother's apples; the main point to be understood in this, that nothing—neither brazen tower, hundred-eyed Argus, nor Cretan Minotaur—could stop John Pike from getting at a good stickle. But, even as the world knows nothing of its greatest men, its greatest men know nothing of the world beneath their very nose, till fortune sneezes dexter. For two years John Pike must have been whipping the water as hard as Xerxes, without having ever once dreamed of the glorious trout that lived in Crocker's Hole. But why, when he ought to have been at least on bowing terms with every fish as long as his middle finger, why had he failed to know this champion? The answer is simple—because of his short cuts. Flying as he did like an arrow from a bow, Pike used to hit his beloved river at an elbow, some furlong below Crocker's Hole, where a sweet little stickle sailed away downstream, whereas for the length of a meadow upward the water lay smooth, clear, and shallow; therefore the youth, with so little time to spare, rushed into the downward joy.

And here it may be noted that the leading maxim of the present period, that man can discharge his duty only by going counter to the stream, was scarcely mooted in those days. My grandfather (who was a wonderful man, if he was accustomed to fill a cart in two days of fly fishing on the Barle) regularly fished downstream; and what more than a cartload need anyone put into his basket?

And surely it is more genial and pleasant to behold our friend the river growing and thriving as we go on, strengthening its voice and enlarging its bosom, and sparkling through each successive meadow with richer plenitude of silver, than to trace it against its own grain and good will toward weakness, and littleness, and immature conceptions.

However, you will say that if John Pike had fished upstream, he would have found this trout much sooner. And that is true; but still, as it was, the trout had more time to grow into such a prize. And the way in which John found him out was this. For some days he had been tormented with a very painful tooth, which even poisoned all the joys of fishing. Therefore he resolved to have it out and sturdily entered the shop of John Sweetland, the village blacksmith, and there paid his sixpence. Sweetland extracted the teeth of the village, whenever they required it, in the simplest and most effectual way. A piece of fine wire was fastened round the tooth, and the other end round the anvil's nose, then the sturdy blacksmith shut the lower half of his shop door, which was about breast-high, with the patient outside and the anvil within; a strong push of the foot upset the anvil, and the tooth flew out like a well-thrown fly.

When John Pike had suffered this very bravely, "Ah, Master Pike" said the blacksmith, with a grin, "I reckon you won't pull out thic there big vish"—the smithy commanded a view of the river—"clever as you be, quite so peart as thiccy."

"What big fish?" asked the boy, with deepest interest, though his mouth was bleeding fearfully.

"Why, that girt mortial of a vish as hath his hover in Crocker's Hole. Zum on 'em saith as a' must be a zammon."

Off went Pike with his handkerchief to his mouth, and after him ran Alec Bolt, one of his fellow pupils, who had come to the shop to enjoy the extraction.

"Oh, my!" was all that Pike could utter, when by craftily posting himself he had obtained a good view of this grand fish.

"I'll lay you a crown you don't catch him!" cried Bolt, an impatient youth, who scorned angling.

"How long will you give me?" asked the wary Pike, who never made rash wagers.

"Oh! till the holidays if you like; or, if that won't do, till Michaelmas?"

Now the midsummer holidays were six weeks off—boys used not to talk of "vacations" then, still less of "recesses."

"I think I'll bet you," said Pike, in his slow way, bending forward carefully, with his keen eyes on this monster, "but it would not be fair to take till Michaelmas. I'll bet you a crown that I catch him before the holidays—at least, unless some other fellow does?"

The day of that most momentous interview must have been the 14th day of May. Of the year I will not be so sure; for children take more note of days than of years, for which the latter have their full revenge thereafter. It must have been the 14th, because the morrow was our holiday, given upon the 15th of May, in honor of a birthday.

Now, John Pike was beyond his years wary as well as enterprising, calm as well as ardent, quite as rich in patience as in promptitude and vigor. But Alec Bolt was a headlong youth, volatile, hot, and hasty, fit only to fish the Maelstrom, or a torrent of new lava. And the moment he had laid that wager he expected his crown piece; though time, as the lawyers phrase it, was "expressly of the essence of the contract." And now he demanded that Pike should spend the holiday in trying to catch that trout.

"I shall not go near him" that lad replied, "until I have got a new collar." No piece of personal adornment was it, without which he would not act, but rather that which now is called the fly cast, or the gut cast, or the trace, or what it may be. "And another thing," continued Pike, "the bet is off if you go near him, either now or at any other time, without asking my leave first, and then only going as I tell you."

"What do I want with the great slimy beggar?" the arrogant Bolt made answer. "A good rat is worth fifty of him. No fear of my going near him, Pike. You shan't get out of it that way."

Pike showed his remarkable qualities that day, by fishing exactly as he would have fished without having heard of the great Crockerite. He was upon and away upon the millstream before breakfast; and the forenoon he devoted to his favorite course—first down the Craddock stream, a very pretty confluent of the Culm, and from its junction, down the pleasant hams, where the river winds toward Uffculme. It was my privilege to accompany this hero, as his humble Sancho; while Bolt and the faster race went up the river ratting. We were back in time to have Pike's trout (which ranged between two ounces and one half pound) fried for the early dinner; and here it may be lawful to remark that the trout of the Culm are of the very purest excellence, by reason of the flinty bottom, at any rate in these the upper regions. For the valley is the western outlet of the Black Down range, with the Beacon hill upon the north, and the Hackpen long ridge to the south; and beyond that again the Whetstone hill, upon whose western end wark portholes scarped with white grit mark the pits. But flint is the staple of the broad Culm Valley under good, well-pastured loam; and here are chalcedonies and agate stones.

At dinner everybody had a brace of trout—large for the larger folk, little for the little ones, with coughing and some patting on the back for bones. What of equal purport could the fierce rat hunter show? Pike explained many points in the history of each fish, seeming to know them none the worse, and love them all the better, for being fried. We banqueted, neither a whit did soul get stinted of banquet impartial. Then the wielder of the magic rod very modestly sought leave of absence at the teatime.

"Fishing again, Mr. Pike, I suppose," my father answered pleasantly; "I used to be fond of it at your age; but never so entirely wrapped up in it as you are."

"No, sir; I am not going fishing again. I want to walk to Wellington, to get some things at Cherry's."

"Books, Mr. Pike? Ah! I am very glad of that. But I fear it can only be fly books."

"I want a little Horace for eighteenpence—the Cambridge one just published, to carry in my pocket—and a new hank of gut."

"Which of the two is more important? Put that into Latin, and answer it."

"*Utrurn pluris facio? Placcurn flocd. Viscera magni.*" With this vast effort Pike turned as red as any trout.

"After that who could refuse you?" said my father. "You always tell the truth, my boy, in Latin or in English."

Although it was a long walk, some fourteen miles to Wellington and back, I got permission to go with Pike; and as we crossed the bridge and saw the tree that overhung Crocker's Hole, I begged him to show me that mighty fish.

"Not a bit of it," he replied. "It would bring the blackguards. If the blackguards once find him out, it is all over with him."

"The blackguards are all in factory now, and I am sure they cannot see us from the windows. They won't be out till five o'clock."

With the true liberality of young England, which abides even now as large and glorious as ever, we always called the free and enlightened operatives of the period by the courteous name above set down, and it must be acknowledged that some of them deserved it, although perhaps they poached with less of science than their sons. But the cowardly murder of fish by liming the water was already prevalent.

Yielding to my request and perhaps his own desire—manfully kept in check that morning—Pike very carefully approached that pool, commanding me to sit down while he reconnoitered from the meadow upon the right bank of the stream. And the place which had so sadly quenched the fire of the poor baker's love filled my childish heart with dread and deep wonder at the cruelty of women. But as for John Pike, all he thought of was the fish and the best way to get at him.

Very likely that hole is "holed out" now, as the Yankees well express it, or at any rate changed out of knowledge. Even in my time a very heavy flood entirely altered its character; but to the eager eye of Pike it seemed pretty much as follows, and possibly it may have come to such a form again:

The river, after passing through a hurdle fence at the head of the meadow, takes a little turn or two of bright and shallow indifference, then gathers itself into a good strong slide, as if going down a slope instead of steps. The right bank is high and beetles over with yellow loam and grassy fringe; but the other side is of flinty shingle, low and bare and washed by floods. At the end of this rapid, the stream turns sharply under an ancient alder tree into a large, deep, calm repose, cool, unruffled, and sheltered front the sun by branch and leaf—and that is the hole of poor Crocker.

At the head of the pool (where the hasty current rushes in so eagerly, with noisy excitement and much ado) the quieter waters from below, having rested and enlarged themselves, come lapping up round either curve, with some recollection of their past career, the hoary experience of foam. And sidling toward the new arrival of the impulsive column, where they meet it, things go on which no man can describe without his mouth being full of water. A *V* is formed, a fancy letter *V*, beyond any designer's tracery and even beyond his imagination, a perpetually fluctuating limpid wedge, perpetually creneled and rippled into by little ups and downs that try to make an impress but can only glide away upon either side or sink in dimples under it. And here a gray bough of the ancient alder stretches across, like a thirsty giant's arm, and makes it a very ticklish place to throw a fly. Yet this was the very spot our John Pike must put his fly into, or lose his crown.

Because the great tenant of Crocker's Hole, who allowed no other fish to wag a fin there, and from strict monopoly had grown so fat, kept his victualing yard—if so low an expression can be used concerning him—without above a square yard of this spot. He had a sweet hover, both for rest and recreation, under the bank, in a placid antre, where the water made no noise, but tickled his belly in digestive ease. The loftier the character is of any being, the slower and more dignified his movements are. No true psychologist could have believed—as Sweetland the blacksmith did, and Ms. Pook the tinman—that this trout could ever be the embodiment of Crocker. For this was the last trout in the universal world to drown himself for love; if truly any trout has done so.

"You may come now, and try to look along my back," John Pike, with a reverential whisper, said to me. "Now, don't be in a hurry, young stupid; kneel down. He is not to be disturbed at his dinner, mind. You keep behind me, and look along my back; I never clapped eyes on such a whopper."

I had to kneel down in a tender reminiscence of pastureland and gaze carefully; and not having eyes like those of our Zebedee (who offered his spine for a camera, as he crawled on all fours in front of me), it took me a long time to descry an object most distinct to all who have that special gift of piercing with their eyes the water. See what is said upon this subject in that delicious book, *The Gamekeeper at Home*.

"You are no better than a muff," said Pike, and it was not in my power to deny it.

"If the sun would only leave off," I said. But the sun, who was having a very pleasant play with the sparkle of the water and the twinkle of the leaves, had no inclination to leave off yet, but kept the rippling crystal in a dance of flashing facets, and the quivering verdure in a steady flush of gold.

But suddenly a May fly, a luscious gray drake, richer and more delicate than canvasback or woodcock, with a dart and a leap and a merry zigzag, began to enjoy a little game above the stream. Rising and falling like a gnat, thrilling her gauzy wings, and arching her elegant pellucid frame, every now and then she almost dipped her three long tapering whisks into the dimples of the water.

"He sees her! He'll have her as sure as a gun!" cried Pike, with a gulp, as if he himself were "rising." "Now can you see him, stupid?"

"Crikey, crokums!" I exclaimed, with classic elegance; "I have seen that long thing for five minutes; but I took it for a tree."

"You little"—animal quite early in the alphabet—"now don't you stir a peg, or I'll dig my elbow into you."

The great trout was stationary almost as a stone, in the middle of the *V* above described. He was gently fanning with his large clear fins, but holding his own against the current mainly by the wagging of his broad-fluked tail. As soon as my slow eyes had once defined him, he grew upon them mightily, molding himself in the matrix of the water, as a thing put into jelly does. And I doubt whether even John Pike saw him more accurately than I did. His size was such, or seemed to be such, that I fear to say a word about it; not because language does not contain the word, but from dread of exaggeration. But his shape and color may be reasonably told without wounding the feeling of an age whose incredulity springs from self-knowledge.

His head was truly small, his shoulders vast; the spring of his back was like a rainbow when the sun is southing; the generous sweep of his deep elastic belly, nobly pulped out with rich nurture, showed what the power of his brain must be, and seemed to undulate, time for time, with the vibrant vigilance of his large wise eyes. His latter end was consistent also. An elegant taper run of counter, coming almost to a cylinder, as a mackerel does, boldly developed with a hugeous spread to a glorious amplitude of swallowtail. His color was all that can well be desired, but ill described by any poor word palette. Enough that he seemed to tone away from olive and umber, with carmine stars, to glowing gold and soft pure silver, mantled with a subtle flush of rose and fawn and opal.

Swoop came a swallow, as we gazed, and was gone with a flick, having missed the May fly. But the wind of his passage, or the skit of wing, struck the merry dancer down, so that he fluttered for one instant on the wave, and that instant was enough. Swift as the swallow, and more true of aim, the great trout made one dart, and a sound, deeper than a tinkle, but as silvery as a bell, rang the poor ephemerid's knell. The rapid water scarcely showed a break; but a bubble sailed down the pool, and the dark hollow echoed with the music of a rise.

"He knows how to take a fly," said Pike; "he has had too many to be tricked with mine. Have him I must; but how ever shall I do it?"

All the way to Wellington he uttered not a word, but shambled along with a mind full of care. When I ventured to look up now and then, to surmise what was going on beneath his hat, deeply set eyes and a wrinkled forehead, relieved at long intervals by a solid shake, proved that there are meditations deeper than those of philosopher or statesman.

Surely no trout could have been misled by the artificial May fly of that time, unless he were either a very young fish, quite new to entomology; or else one afflicted with a combination of myopy and bulimy. Even now there is room for plenty of improvement in our counterfeit presentment; but in those days the body was made with yellow mohair, ribbed with red silk and gold twist and as thick as a fertile bumblebee. John Pike perceived that to offer such a thing to Crocker's trout would probably consign him—even if his great stamina should overget the horror—to an unbeatable death, through just and natural indignation. On the other hand, while the May fly lasted, a trout so cultured, so highly refined, so full of light and sweetness, would never demean himself to low bait, or any coarse son of a maggot.

Meanwhile, Alec Bolt allowed poor Pike no peaceful thought, no calm absorption of high mind into the world of flies, no placid period of cobbler's wax, floss silk, turned hackles, and dubbing. For in making of flies John Pike had his special moments of inspiration, times of clearer insight into the everlasting verities, times of brighter conception and more subtle execution, tails of more elastic grace and heads of a neater and nattier expression. As a poet labors at one immortal line, compressing worlds of wisdom into the music of ten syllables, so toiled the patient Pike about the fabric of a fly comprising all the excellence that ever sprang from maggot. Yet Bolt rejoiced to jerk his elbow at the moment of sublimest art. And a swarm of flies was blighted thus.

Peaceful, therefore, and long-suffering, and full of resignation as he was, John Pike came slowly to the sad perception that arts avail not without arms. The elbow, so often jerked, at last took a voluntary jerk from the shoulder, and Alec Bolt lay prostrate, with his right eye full of cobbler's wax. This put a desirable check upon his energies for a week or more, and by that time Pike had flown his fly.

When the honeymoon of spring and summer (which they are now too fashionable to celebrate in this country), the heyday of the whole year marked by the budding of the wild rose, the start of the wheat ear from its sheath, the feathering of the lesser plantain, and flowering of the meadowsweet, and, foremost for the angler's joy, the caracole of May flies—when these things are to be seen and felt (which has not happened at all this year), then rivers should be mild and bright, skies blue and white with fleecy cloud, the west wind blowing softly, and the trout in charming appetite.

On such a day came Pike to the bank of Culm, with a loudly beating heart. A fly there is, not ignominious, or of cowdab origin, neither gross and heavy-bodied, from cradlehood of slimy stones, nor yet of menacing aspect and suggesting deeds of poison, but elegant, bland, and of sunny nature, and obviously good to eat. Him or her—why quest we which?—the shepherd of the dale, contemptuous of gender, except in his own species, has called, and as long as they two coexist will call, the Yellow Sally. A fly that does not waste the day in giddy dances and the fervid waltz, but undergoes family incidents with decorum and discretion. He or she, as the case may be—for the natural history of the river-bank is a book to come hereafter, and of fifty men who make flies not one knows the name of the fly he is making—in the early morning of June, or else in the second quarter of the afternoon, this Yellow Sally fares aboard, with a nice well-ordered flutter.

Despairing of the May fly, as it still may be despaired of, Pike came down to the river with his masterpiece of portraiture. The artificial Yellow Sally is generally always—as they say in Cheshire—a mile or more too yellow. On the other hand, the Yellow Dun conveys no idea of any Sally. But Pike had made a very decent Sally, not perfect (for he was young as well as wise), but far above any counterfeit to be had in fishing-tackle shops. How he made it, he told nobody. But if he lives now, as I hope he does, any of my readers may ask him through the G. P. O. and hope to get an answer.

It fluttered beautifully on the breeze, and in such living form that a brother or sister Sally came up to see it, and went away sadder and wiser. Then Pike said: "Get away, you young wretch," to your humble servant who tells this tale; yet, being better than his words, allowed that pious follower to lie down upon his digestive organs and with deep attention watch. There must have been great things to see, but to see them so was difficult. And if I huddle up what happened, excitement also shares the blame.

Pike had fashioned well the time and manner of this overture. He knew that the giant Crockerite was satiate now with May flies, or began to find their flavor failing, as happens to us with asparagus, marrow-fat peas, or strawberries, when we have had a month of them. And he thought that the first Yellow Sally of the season, inferior though it were, night have the special charm of novelty. With the skill of a Zulu, he stole up through the branches over the lower pool till he came to a spot where a yard-wide opening gave just space for spring of rod. Then he saw his desirable friend at dinner, wagging his tail, as a hungry gentleman dining with the Lord Mayor agitates his coat. With one dexterous whirl, untaught by any of the many books upon the subject, John Pike laid his Yellow Sally (for he cast with one fly only) as lightly as gossamer upon the rapid, about a yard in front of the big trout's head. A moment's pause, and then too quick for words was the thing that happened.

A heavy plunge was followed by a fearful rush. Forgetful of the current the river was ridged, as if with a plow driven under it; the strong line, though given out as fast as might be, twanged like a harp string as it cut the wave, and then Pike stood up, like a ship dismasted, with the butt of his rod snapped below the ferrule. He had one of those foolish things, just invented, a hollow butt of hickory; and the finial ring of his spare top looked out, to ask what had happened to the rest of it. "Bad luck!" cried the fisherman; "but never mind, I shall have him next time, to a certainty."

When this great issue came to be considered, the cause of it was sadly obvious. The fish, being hooked, had made off with the rush of a shark for the bottom of the pool. A thicket of saplings below the alder tree had stopped the judicious hooker from all possibility of following; and when he strove to turn him by elastic pliance, his rod broke at the breach of pliability. "I have learned a sad lesson," said John Pike, looking sadly.

How many fellows would have given up this matter, and glorified themselves for having hooked so grand a fish, while explaining that they must have caught him, if they could have done it! But Pike only told me not to say a word about it, and began to make ready for another tug of war. He made himself a splice rod, short and handy, of well-seasoned ash, with a stout top of bamboo, tapered so discreetly, and so balanced in its spring, that verily it formed an arc, with any pressure on it, as perfect as a leaf poplar in a stormy summer. "Now break it if you can," he said, "by any amount of rushes; I'll hook you by your jacket collar; you cut away now, and I'll land you."

This was highly skillful, and he did it many times; and whenever I was landed well, I got a lollipop, so that I was careful not to break his tackle. Moreover he made him a landing net, with a kidney-bean stick, a ring of wire, and his own best nightcap of strong cotton net. Then he got the farmer's leave, and lopped obnoxious bushes; and now the chiefest question was: What bait, and when to offer it? In spite of his sad rebuff, the spirit of John Pike had been equable. The genuine angling mind is steadfast, large, and self-supported, and to the vapid, ignominious chaff; tossed by swine upon the idle wind, it pays as much heed as a big trout does to a dance of midges. People put their fingers to their noses and said: "Master Pike, have you caught him yet?" and Pike only answered: "Wait a bit." If ever this fortitude and perseverance is to be recovered as the English Brand (the one thing that has made us what we are, and may yet redeem us from niddering shame), a degenerate age should encourage the habit of fishing and never despairing. And the brightest sign yet for our future is the increasing demand for hooks and gut.

Pike fished in a manlier age, when nobody would dream of cowering from a savage because he was clever at skulking; and when, if a big fish broke the rod, a stronger rod was made for him, according to the usage of Great Britain. And though the young angler had been defeated, he did not sit down and have a good cry over it.

About the second week in June, when the May fly had danced its day and died—for the season was an early one—and Crocker's trout had recovered from the wound to his feelings and philanthropy, there came a night of gentle rain, of pleasant tinkling upon window ledges, and a soothing patter among young leaves, and the Culm was yellow in the morning. "I mean to do it this afternoon," Pike whispered to me, as he came back panting. "When the water clears there will be a splendid time."

The lover of the rose knows well a gay voluptuous beetle, whose pleasure is to lie embedded in a fount of beauty. Deep among the incurving petals of the blushing fragrance, he loses himself in his joys sometimes, till a breezy waft reveals him. And when the sunlight breaks upon his luscious dissipation, few would have the heart to oust him, such a gem from such a setting. All his back is emerald sparkles, all his front red Indian gold, and here and there he grows white spots to save the eye from aching. Pike put his finger in and fetched him out, and offered him a little change of joys, by putting a Limerick hook through his thorax, and bringing it out between his elytra. *Cetonia aurata* liked it not, but pawed the air very naturally, and fluttered with his wings attractively.

"I meant to have tried with a fern web," said the angler; "until I saw one of these beggars this morning. If he works like that upon the water, he will do. It was hopeless to try artificials again. What a lovely color the water is! Only three days now to the holidays. I have run it very close. You be ready, younker."

With these words he stepped upon a branch of the alder, for the tone of the waters allowed approach, being soft and sublustrous, without any mud. Also Master Pike's own tone was such as becomes the fisherman, calm, deliberate, free from nerve, but fall of eye and muscle. He stepped upon the alder bough to get as near as might be to the fish, for he could not cast this beetle like a fly; it must be dropped gently and allowed to play. "You may come and look," he said to me; "when the water is so, they have no eyes in their tails."

The rose beetle trod upon the water prettily, under a lively vibration, and he looked quite as happy and considerably more active, than when he had been cradled in the anthers of the rose. To the eye of a fish he was a strong individual, fighting courageously with the current, but sure to be beaten through lack of fins; and mercy suggested, as well as appetite, that the proper solution was to gulp him.

"Hooked him in the gullet. He can't get off!" cried John Pike, laboring to keep his nerves under. "Every inch of tackle is as strong as a bell pull. Now, if I don't land him, I will never fish again!"

Providence, which had constructed Pike, foremost of all things, for lofty angling—disdainful of worm and even minnow—Providence, I say, at this adjuration, pronounced that Pike must catch that trout. Not many anglers are heaven-born; and for one to drop off the hook halfway through his teens would be infinitely worse than to slay the champion trout. Pike felt the force of this, and rushing through the rushes, shouted: "I am sure to have him, Dick! Be ready with my nightcap."

Rod in a bow like a springle riser; line on the hum, like the string of Paganini; winch on the gallop, like a harpoon wheel, Pike, the headcenter of everything, dashing through thick and thin, and once taken overhead—for he jumped into the hole, when he must have lost him else, but the fish too impetuously towed him out, and made off in passion for another pool, when, if he had only retired to his hover, the angler might have shared the baker's fate—all these things (I tell you, for they all come upon again, as if the day were yesterday) so scared me of my never very steadfist wits, that I could only holloa! But one thing I did, I kept the nightcap ready.

# A FATAL SALMON

## FRANK FORESTER

It was as fair a morning of July as ever dawned in the blue summer sky; the sun as yet had risen but a little way above the waves of fresh green foliage which formed the horizon of the woodland scenery surrounding Widecomb Manor; and his heat, which promised ere mid-day to become excessive, was tempered now by the exhalations of the copious night-dews, and by the cool breath of the western breeze, which came down through he leafy gorges, in long, soft swells from the open moorlands.

All nature was alive and joyous; the air was vocal with the piping melody of the blackbirds and thrushes, caroling in every brake and bosky dingle; the smooth, green lawn before the windows of the old hall was peopled with whole tribes of fat, lazy hares, limping about among the dewy herbage, fearless, as it would seem, of man's aggression; and to complete the picture, above, a score of splendid peacocks were strutting to and fro on the paved terraces, or perched upon the carved stone balustrades, displaying their gorgeous plumage to the early sunshine.

The shadowy mists of the first morning twilight had not been dispersed from the lower regions, and were suspended still in the middle air in broad fleecy masses, though melting rapidly away in the increasing warmth and brightness of the day.

And still a fain blue line hovered over the bed of the long rocky gorge, which divided the chase from the open country, floating about it like the steam of a seething caldron, and rising here and there into tall smoke-like columns, probably where some steeper cataract of the mountain-stream sent its foam skyward.

So early, indeed, was the hour, that had my tale been recited of these degenerate days, there would have been no gentle eyes awake to look upon the loneliness of a new-awakened nature.

In the good days of old, however, when daylight was still deemed to be the fitting time for labor and for pastime, and night the appointed time for natural and healthful sleep, the dawn was wont to brighten beheld by other eyes than those of clowns and milkmaids, and the gay songs of the matutinal birds were listened to be ears that could appreciate their untaught melodies.

And now, just as the stable clock was striking four, the great oaken door of the old Hall was thrown open with a vigorous swing that made it rattle on its hinges, and Jasper St. Aubyn came bounding out into the fresh morning air, with a foot as elastic as that of the mountain roe, singing a snatch of some quaint old ballad.

He was dressed simply in a close-fitting jacket and tight hose of dark-green cloth, without any lace or embroidery, light boots of untanned leather, and a broad-leafed hat, with a single eagle's feather thrust carelessly through the band. He wore neither cloak nor sword, though it was a period at which gentlemen rarely went abroad without these, their distinctive attributes; but in the broad black belt which girt his rounded waist he carried a stout wood-knife with a buckhorn hilt; and over his shoulder there swung from a leathern thong a large wicker fishing-basket.

Nothing, indeed, could be simpler or less indicative of any particular rank or station in society than young St. Aubyn's garb, yet it would have been a very dull and unobservant eye which should take him for aught less than a high-born and high-bred gentleman.

His fine intellectual face, his bearing erect before heaven, the graceful ease of his every motion, as he hurried down the flagged steps of the terrace, and planted his light foot on the dewy greensward, all betokened gentle birth and gentle associations.

But he thought nothing of himself, nor cared for his advantages, acquired or natural. The long and heavy salmon-rod which he carried in his right hand, in three pieces as yet unconnected, did not more clearly indicate his purpose than the quick marking glance which he cast toward the half-veiled sun and hazy sky, scanning the signs of the weather.

"It will do, it will do," he said to himself, thinking as it were aloud, "for three or four hours at least; the sun will not shake off those vapors before eight o'clock at the earliest, and if he do come out than hot and strong, I don't know but the water is dark enough after the late rains to serve my turn a while longer. It will blow up, too, I think, from the westward and there will be a brisk curl on the pools. But come, I must be moving, if I would reach Darringford to breakfast."

And as he spoke he strode out rapidly across the park toward the deep chasm of the stream, crushing a thousand aromatic perfumes from the dewy wild-flowers with his heedless foot, and thinking little of the beauties of nature, as he hastened to the scene of his loved exercise.

It was not long, accordingly, before he reached the brink of the steep rocky bank above the stream, which he proposed to fish that morning, and paused to select the best place for descending to the water's edge.

It was, indeed, as striking and romantic a scene as ever met the eye of painter or of poet. On the farther side of the gorge, scarcely a hundred yards distant, the dark limestone rocks rose sheer and precipitous from the very brink of the stream, rifted and broken into angular blocks and tall, columnar masses, from the clefts of which, wherever they could find oil enough to support their scanty growth, a few stunted oaks shot out almost horizontally with their gnarled arms and dark-green foliage, and here and there the silvery bark and quivering tresses of the birch relieved the monotony of color by their gay brightness. Above, the cliffs were crowned with the beautiful purple heather, now in its very glow of summer bloom, about which were buzzing myriads of wild bees, sipping their nectar from its cups of amethyst.

The hither side, though rough and steep and broken, was not, in the place where Jasper stood, precipitous; indeed it seemed as if at some distant period a sort of landslip had occurred, by which the summit of the rocky wall had been broken into massive garments, and hurled down in an inclined plane into the bed of the stream, on which it had encroached with its shattered blocks and rounded boulders.

Time, however, had covered all this abrupt and broken slope with a beautiful growth of oak and hazel coppice, among which, only at distant intervals, could the dun weather-beaten flanks of the great stones by discovered.

At the base of this descent, a hundred and fifty feet perhaps below the stand of the young sportsman, flowed the dark arrowy stream—a wild and perilous water. As clear as crystal, yet as dark as the brown cairngorm, it came pouring down among the broken rocks with a rapidity and force which showed what must be its fury when swollen by a storm among the mountains, here breaking into wreaths of rippling foam where some unseen ledge chafed its current, there roaring and surging white as December's snow among the great round-headed rocks, and there again wheeling in sullen eddies, dark and deceitful, round and round some deep rock-rimmed basin.

Here and there, indeed, it spread out into wide, shallow, rippling rapids, filling the whole bottom of the ravine from side to side, but more generally it did not occupy above the fourth part of the space below, leaving sometimes on this margin, sometimes on that, broad pebbly banks, or slaty ledges, affording an easy footing and a clear path to the angler in its troubled waters.

After a rapid glance over the well-know scene, Jasper plunged into the coppice, and following a faint track worn by the feet of the wild-deer in the first instance, and widened by his own bolder tread, soon reached the bottom of the chasm, though not until he had flushed from the dense oak covert two noble black cocks with their superb forked tails, and glossy purple-lustered plumage, which soared away, crowing their bold defiance, over the heathery moorlands.

Once at the water's edge, the young man's tackle was speedily made ready, and in a few minutes his long line went whistling through the air, as he wielded the powerful two-handed rod, as easily as if it had been a stripling reed, and the large gaudy peacock-fly alighted on the wheeling eddies, at the tail of a long arrowy shoot, as gently as it if had settled form too long a flight. Delicately, deftly, it was made to dance and skim the clear, brown surface, until it had crossed the pool and neared the hither bank; then again, obedient to the pliant wrist, it arose on glittering wing, circled half around the angler's head, and was sent fifteen yards aloof, straight as a wild bee's flight, into the little mimic whirlpool, scarce larger than the hat of the skilful fisherman, which spun around and round just leeward of a gray ledge of limestone. Scarce had it reached its mark before the water broke all round it, and the gray deceit vanished, the heavy swirl of the surface, as the break was closing, indicating the great size of the fish which had risen. Just as the swirl was subsiding, and the forked tail of the monarch of the stream was half seen as he descended, that indescribably but well-know turn of the angler's wrist fixed the barded hook and taught the scaly victim the nature of the prey he had gorged so heedlessly.

With a wild bound he threw himself three feet out of the water, showing his silver sides, with the sea-lice yet clinging to his scales, a fresh sea-run fish of fifteen, ay, eighteen pounds, and perhaps over.

On his broad back he strikes the water, but not as he meant the tightened line; for as he leaped the practiced hand had lowered the rod's tip, that it fell in a loose bight below him. Again! again! again! And yet a fourth time he bounded into the air with desperate and vigorous *soubresaults*, like an unbroken steed that would dismount his rider, lashing the eddies of the dark stream into the bright bubbling streaks, and making the heart of his captor beat high with anticipations of the desperate struggle that should follow, before the monster should lie panting and exhausted on the yellow sand or moist greensward.

Away! with the rush of an eagle through the air, he is gone like an arrow down the rapids—how the reel rings, and the line whistles from the swift working wheel; he is too swift, too headstrong to be checked as yet; tenfold the strength of that slender tackle might not control him in his first fiery rush.

But Jasper, although young in years, was old in the art, and skilful as the craftiest of the gentle craftsmen. He gives him the butt of his rod steadily, trying the strength of his tackle with a delicate and gentle finger, giving him line at every rush, yet firmly, cautiously, feeling his mouth all the while, and moderating his speed even while he yields to his fury.

Meanwhile, with the eye of intuition, and the nerve of iron, he bounds along the difficult shore, he leaps from rock to rock, alighting on their slippery tops with the firm agility of the rope-dancer, he splashes knee-deep through the slippery shallows, keeping his line ever taught, inclining his rod over his shoulder, bearing in his fish ever with a killing pull, steering him clear of every rock or stump against which he would fain smash the tackle, and landing him at length in a fine open roomy pool, at the foot of a long stretch of white and foamy rapids, down which he has just piloted him with the eye of faith, and the foot of instinct.

And now the great Salmon has turned sulky; like a piece of lead he has sunk to the bottom of the deep black pool, and lies on the gravel bottom in the sullenness of despair.

Jasper stooped, gathered up in his left hand a heavy pebble, and pitched it into the pool, as nearly as he could guess to the whereabout of his game— another—and another! Aha! that last has roused him. Again he throws himself clear out of water, and again foiled in his attempt to smash the tackle, dashes away down stream impetuous.

But his strength is departing—the vigor of his rush is broken. The angler gives him the butt abundantly, strains on him with a heavier pull, yet ever yields a little as he exerts his failing powers; see, his broad, silver side has thrice turned up, even to the surface, and though each time he was recovered himself, each time it has been with a heavier and more sickly motion.

Brave fellow! his last race is run, his last spring sprung—no more shall he disport himself in the bright reaches of the Tamar; no more shall the Naiads wreathe his clear silver scales with river-greens and flowery rushes.

The cruel gaff is in his side—his cold blood stains the eddies for a moment—he flaps out his death-pang on the hard limestone.

"Who-whoop! a nineteen-pounder!"

Meantime the morning had worn onward, and ere the great fish was brought to the basket, the sun had soared clear above the mist-wreaths, and had risen so high into the summer heaven that his slant rays poured down into the gorge of the stream, and lighted up the clear depths with a luster so transparent that ever pebble at the bottom might have been discerned, with the large fish here and there floating mid-depth, with their heads upstream, their gills working with a quick motion, and their broad tails vibrating at short intervals slowly but powerfully, as they lay motionless in opposition to the very strongest of the swift current.

The breeze had died away, there was no curl upon the water, and the heat was oppressive.

Under such circumstances, to whip the stream was little better than mere loss of time, yet as he hurried with a fleet foot down the gorge, perhaps with some ulterior object, beyond the mere love of sport, Jasper at times cast his fly across the stream, and drew it neatly, and, as he thought, irresistibly, right over the recusant fish; but though once or twice a large lazy Salmon would sail up slowly from the depths, and almost touch the fly with his nose he either sunk down slowly in disgust, without breaking the water, or flapped his broad tail over the shining fraud as if to mark his contempt.

It had now got to be near noon, for, in the ardor of his success, the angler had forgotten all about his intended breakfast; and, his first fish captured, had contented himself with a slender meal furnished from out his fishing-basket and his leathern bottle.

Jasper had traversed by this time some ten miles in length, following the sinuosities of the stream, and had reached a favorite pool at the head of along, straight, narrow trench, cut by the waters themselves in the course of time, through the hard schistous rock which walls the torrent on each hand, not leaving the slightest ledge or margin between the rapids and the precipice.

Through his wild gorge of some fifty yards in length, the river shoots like an arrow over a steep inclined plane of limestone rock, the surface of which is polished by the action of the water, till it is as slippery as ice, and at the extremity of leaps, down a sheer descent of some twelve feet into a large, wide basin, surrounded by softly swelling banks of greensward, and a fair amphitheater of woodland.

At the upper end this pool is so deep as to be vulgarly deemed unfathomable; below, however, it expands yet wider into a shallow rippling ford, where it is crossed by the high-road, down stream of which again there is another long, sharp rapid, and another fall, over the last steps of the hills; after which the nature of the stream becomes changed, and it murmurs gently onward through a green pastoral country, unrippled and uninterrupted.

Just in the inner angle of the high-road, on the right hand of the stream, there stood an old-fashioned, low-browed, thatch-covered stone cottage, with a rude portico of rustic woodwork overrun with jasmine and virgin-bower, and a pretty flower-garden sloping down in successive terraces to the edge of the basin. Beside this, there was no other house in sight, unless it were part of the roof of a mill which stood in the low ground on the brink of the second fall, surrounded with a mass of willows. But the tall steeple of a country church, raising itself heavenward above the brow of the hill, seemed to show that, although concealed by the undulations of the ground, a village was hard at hand.

The morning had changed a second time, a hazy film had crept up to the zenith, and the sun was now covered with a pale golden veil, and a slight current of air down the gorge ruffled the water.

It was a capital pool, famous for being the temporary haunt of the very finest fish, which were wont to lie there awhile, as if to recruit themselves after the exertions of leaping the two falls and stemming the double rapid, before attempting to ascend the stream farther.

Few, however, even of the best and boldest fishermen, cared to wet a line in its waters, in consequence of the supposed impossibility of following a heavy fish through the gorge below, or checking him at the brink of the fall. It is true, that throughout the length of the pass, the current was broken by bare, slippery rocks peering above the waters, at intervals, which might be cleared by an active cragsman; and it had been in fact reconnoitered by Jasper and others in cool blood, but the result of the examination was that it was deemed impassable.

Thinking, however, little of striking a large fish, and perhaps desiring to waste a little time before scaling the banks and merging on the high-road, Jasper threw a favorite fly of peacock's hurl and gold tinsel lightly across the water; and, almost before he had time to think, had hooked a monstrous fish, which, at the very first leap, he set down as weighing at least thirty pounds.

Thereupon followed a splendid display of piscatory skill. Well knowing that his fish must be lost if he once should succeed in getting his head down the rapid, Jasper exerted every nerve, and exhausted every art to humor, to meet, to retrain, to check him. Four times the fish rushed for the pass, and four times Jasper met him so stoutly with the butt, trying his tackles to the very utmost, that he succeeded in forcing him from the perilous spot. Round and round the pool he had piloted him, and had taken post at length, hoping that the worst was already over, close to the opening of the rocky chasm.

He was gone—but Jasper's blood was up, and thinking of nothing but his sport, he dashed forward, and embarked, with a fearless foot, into the terrible descent.

Leap after leap he took with beautiful precision, alighting firm and erect on the centre of each slippery block, and bounding thence to the next with unerring instinct, guiding his fish the while with consummate skill through the intricacies of the pass.

There were now but three more leaps to be taken before he would reach the flat table-rock above the fall, which once attained, he would have firm foothold and a fair field; already he rejoiced, triumphant in the success of his bold attainment, and confident in victory, when a shrill female shriek reached his ears from the pretty flower-garden; caught by the sound, he diverted his eyes, just as he leaped, toward the place thence it came; his foot slipped and the next instant he was flat on his back in the swift stream, where it shot the most furiously over the glassy rock. He struggled manfully, but in vain. The smooth, slippery surface afforded no purchase to his gripping fingers, no hold to his laboring feet. One fearful, agonizing conflict with the wild waters, and he was swept helplessly over the edge of the fall, his head, as he glanced down foot foremost, striking the rocky brink with fearful violence.

He was plunged into the deep pool, and whirled round and round by the dark eddies long before he rose, but still, though stunned and half-disabled, he strove terribly to support himself, but it was all in vain.

Again he sunk and rose once more, and as he rose that wild shriek again reached his ears, and his last glance fell upon a female form wringing her hands in despair on the bank, and a young man rushing down in wild haste from the cottage on the hill.

He felt that aid was at hand, and struck out again for life—for dear life!

But the water seemed to fail beneath him.

A slight flash sprang across his eyes, his brain reeled, and all was blackness.

He sunk to the bottom, spurned it with his feet, and rose once more, but not to the surface.

His quivering blue hands emerged alone above the relentless waters, grasped for a little moment at empty space, and then disappeared.

The circling ripples closed over him, and subsided into stillness.

He felt, know, suffered nothing more.

His young, warm heart was cold and lifeless—his soul had lost its consciousness—the vital spark had faded into darkness—perhaps was quenched forever.

# A GALLANT POACHER

## JOHN BUCHAN

When the Hispana crossed the Bridge of Larrig His Majesty's late Attorney-General was modestly concealed in a bush of broom on the Crask side, from which he could watch the sullen stretches of the Lang Whang. He was carefully dressed for the part in a pair of Wattie Lithgow's old trousers much too short for him, a waistcoat and jacket which belonged to Sime the butler and which had been made about the year 1890, and a vulgar flannel shirt borrowed from Shapp. He was innocent of a collar, he had not shaved for two days, and as he had forgotten to have his hair cut before leaving London his locks were of a disreputable length. Last, he had a shocking old hat of Sir Archie's from which the lining had long since gone. His hands were sun-burned and grubby, and he had removed his signet-ring. A light ten-foot greenheart rod lay beside him, already put up, and to the tapered line was fixed a tapered cast ending in a strange little cocked fly. As he waited he was busy oiling fly and line.

His glass showed him an empty haugh, save for the figure of Jimsie at the far end close to the Wood of Larrigmore. The sun-warmed waters of the river drowsed in the long dead stretches, curled at rare intervals by the faintest western breeze. The banks were crisp green turf, scarcely broken by a boulder, but five yards from them the moss began—a wilderness of hags and tussocks.

Somewhere in its depths he knew that Benjie lay coiled like an adder, waiting on events.

Leithen's plan, like all great strategy, was simple. Everything depended on having Jimsie out of sight of the Lang Whang for half an hour. Given that, he believed he might kill a salmon. He had marked out a pool where in the evening fish were usually stirring, one of those irrational haunts which no piscatorial psychologist has ever explained. If he could fish fine and far, he might cover it from a spot below a high bank where only the top of his rod would be visible to watchers at a distance. Unfortunately, that spot was on the other side of the stream. With such tackle, landing a salmon would be a critical business, but there was one chance in ten that it might be accomplished; Benjie would be at hand to conceal the fish, and he himself would disappear silently into the Crask thickets. But every step bristled with horrid dangers. Jimsie might be faithful to his post—in which case it was hopeless; he might find the salmon dour, or a fish might break him in the landing, or Jimsie might return to find him brazenly tethered to forbidden game. It was no good thinking about it. On one thing he was decided: if he were caught, he would not try to escape. That would mean retreat in the direction of Crask, and an exploration of the Crask coverts would assuredly reveal what must at all costs be concealed. No. He would go quietly into captivity, and trust to his base appearance to be let off with a drubbing.

As he waited, watching the pools turn from gold to bronze, as the sun sank behind the Glenraden peaks, he suffered the inevitable reaction. The absurdities seemed huge as mountains, the difficulties innumerable as the waves of the sea. There remained less than an hour in which there would be sufficient light to fish—Jimsie was immovable (he had just lit his pipe and was sitting in medita-tion on a big stone)—every moment the Larrig waters were cooling with the chill of evening. Leithen consulted his watch, and found it half-past eight. He had lost his wrist-watch, and had brought his hunter, attached to a thin gold chain. That was foolish, so he slipped the chain from his button-hole and drew it through the arm-hole of his waistcoat.

Suddenly he rose to his feet, for things were happening at the far side of the haugh. Jimsie stood in an attitude of expectation—he seemed to be hearing something far upstream. Leithen heard it too, the cry of excited men . . . Jimsie stood on one foot for a moment in doubt; then he turned and doubled towards the Wood of Larrigmore . . . The gallant Crossby had got to business and was playing hare to the hounds inside the park wall. If human nature had not changed, Leithen thought, the whole force would presently join the chase—Angus and Lennox and Jimsie and Dave and doubtless many volunteers. Heaven send fleetness and wind to the South London Harrier, for it was his duty to occupy the interest of every male in Strathlarrig till such time as he subsided with angry expostulation into captivity.

The road was empty, the valley was deserted, when Leithen raced across the bridge and up the south side of the river. It was not two hundred yards to his chosen stand, a spit of gravel below a high bank at the tail of a long pool. Close to the other bank, nearly thirty yards off, was the shelf where fish lay of an evening. He tested the water with his hand, and its temperature was at least 60 degrees. His theory, which he had learned long ago from the aged Bostonian, was that under such conditions some subconscious memory revived in salmon of their early days as parr when they fed on surface insects, and that they could be made to take a dry fly.

He got out his line to the required length with half a dozen casts in the air, and then put his fly three feet above the spot where a salmon was wont to lie. It was a curious type of cast, which he had been practicing lately in the early morning, for by an adroit check he made the fly alight in a curl, so that it floated for a second or two with the leader in a straight line away from it. In this way he believed that the most suspicious fish would see nothing to alarm him, nothing but a hapless insect derelict on the water.

Sir Archie had spoken truth in describing Leithen to Wattie Lithgow as an artist. His long, straight, delicate casts were art indeed. Like thistledown the fly dropped, like thistledown it floated over the head of the salmon, but like thistledown it was disregarded. There was indeed a faint stirring of curiosity. From where he stood Leithen could see that slight ruffling of the surface which means an observant fish . . .

Already ten minutes had been spent in this barren art. The crisis craved other measures.

His new policy meant a short line, so with infinite stealth and care Leithen waded up the side of the water, sometimes treading precarious ledges of peat, sometimes waist deep in mud and pond-weed, till he was within twenty feet of the fishing-ground. Here he had not the high bank for a shelter, and would have been sadly conspicuous to Jimsie, had that sentinel remained at his post. He crouched low and cast as before with the same curl just ahead of the chosen spot.

But now his tactics were different. So soon as the fly had floated past where he believed the fish to be, he sank it with a dexterous twist of the rod-point, possible only with a short line. The fly was no longer a winged thing; drawn away under water, it roused in the salmon early memories of succulent nymphs . . . At the first cast there was a slight swirl, which meant that a fish near the surface had turned to follow the lure. The second cast the line straightened and moved swiftly up-stream.

Leithen had killed in his day many hundreds of salmon—once in Norway a notable beast of fifty-five pounds. But no salmon he had ever hooked had stirred in his breast such excitement as this modest fellow of eight pounds. "'Tis not so wide as a church-door,'" he reflected with Mercutio, "'but 'twill suffice'—if I can only land him." But a dry-fly cast and a ten-foot rod are a frail wherewithal for killing a fish against time. With his ordinary fifteen-footer and gut of moderate strength he could have brought the little salmon to grass in five minutes, but now there was immense risk of a break, and a break would mean that the whole enterprise had failed. He dared not exert pressure; on the other hand, he could not follow the fish except by making himself conspicuous on the greensward. Worst of all, he had at the best ten minutes of the job.

Thirty yards off an otter slid into the water. Leithen wished he was King of the Otters, as in the Highland tale, to summon the brute to his aid.

The ten minutes had lengthened to fifteen—nine hundred seconds of heart-disease—when, wet to the waist, he got his pocket-gaff into the salmon's side and drew it on to the spit of gravel where he had started fishing. A dozen times he thought he had lost, and once when the fish ran straight up the pool his line was carried out to its last yard of backing. He gave thanks to high Heaven, when, as he landed it, he observed that the fly had all but lost its hold and in another minute would have been free. By such narrow margins are great deeds accomplished.

He snapped the cast from the line and buried it in mud. Then cautiously he raised his head above the bank. The gloaming was gathering fast, and so far as he could see the haugh was still empty. Pushing his rod along the ground, he scrambled on to the turf.

There he had a grievous shock. Jimsie had reappeared, and he was in full view of him. Moreover, there were two men on bicycles coming up the road, who, with the deplorable instinct of human nature, would be certain to join in any pursuit. He was on turf as short as a lawn, cumbered with a tell-tale rod and a poached salmon. The friendly hags were a dozen yards off, and before he could reach them his damning baggage would be noted.

At this supreme moment he had an inspiration, derived from the memory of the otter. To get out his knife, cut a ragged wedge from the fish, and roll it in his handkerchief was the work of five seconds. To tilt the rod over the bank so that it lay in the deep shadow was the work of three more . . . Jimsie had seen him, for a wild cry came down the stream, a cry which brought the cyclists off their machines and set them staring in his direction. Leithen dropped his gaff after the rod, and began running towards the Larrig bridge—slowly, limpingly, like a frightened man with no resolute purpose of escape. And as he ran he prayed that Benjie from the deeps of the moss had seen what had been done and drawn the proper inference.

It was a bold bluff, for he had decided to make the salmon evidence for, not against him. He hobbled down the bank, looking over his shoulder often as if in terror, and almost ran into the arms of the cyclists, who, warned by Jimsie's yells, were waiting to intercept him. He dodged them, however, and cut across to the road, for he had seen that Jimsie had paused and had noted the salmon lying blatantly on the sward, a silver splash in the twilight. Leithen doubled up the road as if going towards Strathlarrig, and Jimsie, the fleet of foot, did not catch up with him till almost on the edge of the Wood of Larrigmore. The cyclists, who had remounted, arrived at the same moment to find a wretched muddy tramp in the grip of a stalwart but breathless gillie.

"I tell ye I was daein' nae harm," the tramp whined. "I was walkin' up the water-side—there's nae law to keep a body frae walkin' up a water-side when there's nae fence—and I seen an auld otter killin' a saumon. The fish is there still to prove I'm no leein'."

"There is a fush, but you wass thinkin' to steal the fush, and you would have had it in your breeks if I hadna seen you. That is poachin' ma man, and you will come up to Strathlarrig. The master said that anyone goin' near the watter was to be lockit up, and you will be lockit up. You can tell all the lees you like in the mornin'."

Then a thought struck Jimsie. He wanted the salmon, for the subject of otters in the Larrig had been a matter of dispute between him and Angus, and here was evidence for his own view.

"Would you two gentlemen oblige me by watchin' this man while I rin back and get the fush? Bash him on the head if he offers to rin."

The cyclists, who were journalists out to enjoy the evening air, willingly agreed, but Leithen showed no wish to escape. He begged a fag in a beggar's whine, and, since he seemed peaceable, the two kept a good distance for fear of infection. He stood making damp streaks in the dusty road, a pitiable specimen of humanity, for his original get-up was not improved by the liquefaction of his clothes and a generous legacy of slimy peat. He seemed to be nervous, which indeed he was, for if Benjie had not seized his chance he was utterly done, and if Jimsie should light upon his rod he was gravely compromised.

But when Jimsie returned in a matter of ten minutes he was empty-handed.

"I never kenned the like," he proclaimed. "That otter has come back and gotten the fush. Ach, the maleecious brute!"

The rest of Leithen's progress was not triumphant. He was conducted to the Strathlarrig lodge, where Angus, whose temper and wind had alike been ruined by the pursuit of Crossby, laid savage hands upon him, and frog-marched him to the back premises. The head-keeper scarcely heeded Jimsie's tale. "Ach, ye poachin' va-aga-bond. It is the jyle ye'll get," he roared, for Angus was in a mood which could only be relieved by violence of speech and action. Rumbling Gaelic imprecations, he hustled his prisoner into an outhouse, which had once been a larder and was now a supplementary garage, slammed and locked the door, and, as a final warning, kicked it viciously with his foot, as if to signify what awaited the culprit when the time came to sit on his case.

Early next morning, when the great door of Strathlarrig House was opened and the maids had begun their work, Oliphant, the butler—a stately man who had been trained in a ducal family—crossed the hall to connoiter the outer world. There he found an under-housemaid, nursing a strange package which she averred she had found on the doorstep. It was some two feet long, swathed in brown paper, and attached to its string was a letter inscribed to Mr. Junius Bandicott.

The parcel was clammy and Oliphant handled it gingerly. He cut the cord, disentangled the letter, and revealed an oblong of green rushes bound with string. The wrapping must have been insecure, for something forthwith slipped from the rushes and flopped on the marble floor, revealing to Oliphant's disgusted eyes a small salmon, blue and stiff in death.

At that moment Junius, always an early bird, came whistling downstairs. So completely was he convinced of the inviolability of the Strathlarrig waters that the spectacle caused him no foreboding.

"What are you flinging fish about for, Oliphant?" he asked cheerfully.

The butler presented him with the envelope. He opened it and extracted a dirty half-sheet of notepaper, on which was printed in capitals, "With the compliments of John Macnab."

Amazement, chagrin, amusement followed each other on Junius's open countenance. Then he picked up the fish and marched out of doors shouting "Angus" at the top of a notably powerful voice. The sound brought the scared face of Professor Babwater to his bedroom window.

Angus, who had been up since four, appeared from Lady Maisie's Pool, where he had been contemplating the waters. His vigil had not improved his appearance or his temper, for his eye was red and choleric and his beard was wild as a mountain goat's. He cast one look at the salmon, surmised the truth, and held up imploring hands to Heaven.

"John Macnab!" said Junius sternly. "What have you got to say to that."

Angus had nothing audible to say. He was handling the fish with feverish hands and peering at its jaws, and presently under his fingers a segment fell out.

"That fush was cleekit," observed Lennox, who had come up. "It was never catched with a flee."

"Ye're a leear," Angus roared. "Just tak a look at the mouth of it. There's the mark of the huke, ye gommeril. The fush was took wi' a rod and line."

"You may reckon it was," observed Junius. "I trust John Macnab to abide by the rules of the game."

Suddenly light seemed to break in on Angus's soul. He bellowed for Jimsie, who was placidly making his way towards the group at the door, lighting his pipe as he went.

"Look at that, James Mackenzie. Aye, look at it. Feast your een on it. You wass tellin' me there wass otters in the Larrig and I said there wass not. You wass tellin' me there wass an otter had a fush last night at the Lang Whang. There's your otter and be damned to ye!"

Jimsie, slow of comprehension, rubbed his eyes. "Where wass you findin' the fush? Aye, it's the one I seen last night. That otter must be wrang in the heid."

"It is not wrang in the heid. It's you that are wrang in the heid, James Mackenzie. The otter is a ver-ra clever man, and its name will be John Macnab." Slowly enlightenment dawned on Jimsie's mind.

"He wass the tramp," he ingeminated. "He wass the tramp."

"And he's still lockit up," Angus cried joyfully. "Wait till I get my hands on him." He was striding off for the garage when a word from Junius held him back.

"You won't find him there. I gave orders last night to let him go. You know, Angus, you told me he was only a tramp that had been seen walking up the river."

"We will catch him yet!" cried the vindictive head-keeper. "Get you on your bicycle, Jimsie, and away after him. He'll be on the Muirtown road . . . There's just the one road he can travel."

"No, you don't," said Junius. "I don't want him here. He has beaten us fairly in a match of wits, and the business is finished."

"But the thing's no possible," Jimsie moaned. "The skeeliest fisher would not take a saumon in the Lang Whang with a flee . . . And I wasna away many meenutes . . . And the tramp was a poor shilpit body—not like a fisher or any kind of gentleman at all—at all . . . And he hadna a rod . . . The thing's no possible.

"I think it was the Deevil."

# BRANNIGAN'S TROUT

## NICK LYONS

After the crack up, he was hospitalized for six months. Twice the doctors warned Jane that they might lose him. Then, when they saved him, they warned that there was probably brain damage. When he was released, in November, they told him he'd be paralyzed on his right side for life. Four doctors confirmed the verdict.

There was nothing for it.

Perhaps there was a slight chance, but not likely, that regular exercise, steady exercise over a period of several years, might restore some small portion of his mobility. Not much. Possibly none. Frankly, Brannigan was not inclined to try. Why go through all the effort? So he sat silent and sullen in the wheelchair that grey afternoon and allowed the men in white to push him to the car, lift and place him into the front seat, collapse the chair and put it in the back, then tell Jane how he was to get in and out, how she was to rig the contraption and place it for him. Like a baby.

He said not a word on the long trip through the sere, dead countryside. Jane told him about the boys, and which friends had called; Mike Novak might come over that evening. He didn't even nod. His great black-haired head thrown back and tilted to one side, he watched with dead eyes the fleeting fields of withered cornstalks, leafless trees, dark scudding clouds. There was nothing for it. He was forty-six and it was over. He couldn't sell books or anything else anymore; he didn't know whether he could drink beer with his friends, chop wood, tend his garden, drive, smoke, sing, read, write; and certainly the fishing season was over for him. Permanently.

The crash in all its stark detail, the fluky chance of it, kept flashing through his brain: Johnny Wohl driving, across the seat from him saying, seconds before, "Well, Billy, we made a day of it, didn't we? I never saw the river so alive." And Mike in the back. Laughing wildly and about to say something about having caught three Hendricksons. Then the rasp of brakes, the black car coming just that moment smoothly out of the side road, the jolt of fear, his hands flying up, his back thrusting backward against the seat, the hurtling forward—and darkness, and stabbing, raw pain in his shoulders, his head. Then nothing. Johnny Wohl and the two teenagers in the black car had been killed instantly. Mike came out of it with his right pinky broken. Well, good for him. Good for old Mike.

As for himself, it would have been better to have had it over then, right then when it happened. Quick. No more pain to die than to live, then. He need merely not have come out of the coma. After that first, searing pain, poof. For good. And they all said he's only lived because he wanted to live. So he lived—like a half-squashed worm.

He saw suddenly in his mind the 20-guage shotgun in the cabinet in his den. Would Jane have removed it? This was no time to ask. That night, when the boys were doing their homework, he'd wheel in by himself and just take a look-see. He'd take it out, break it open . . . take a look-see.

At dinner, Jane talked constantly—about the Murphy's new Brittany spaniel; the good batch of slab wood Frank had hauled from the lumber yard, piece by piece, and cut himself; the threat of an early snow. Brannigan looked up now and then from his plate, spread his lips slightly in the best he could do for a smile, and nodded. He said nothing. He was still not sure what the cracked, alien sound of his voice—what remained of speech—would be to these people, whether he could put together all the words needed for one whole sentence. Whenever he raised his head and looked toward one of his sons, Frank to his right, fifteen, Junior on his left, a year older and dark-haired too, rebellious, they were looking at their own plates. They knew everything. When he looked back at his own plate and prepared his next strategy to get a piece of meat to his mouth, he thought he saw, peripherally, their heads raise slightly and turn toward him. He didn't think he could bear it. Not that. He'd come through Normandy without a scratch; he'd never been seriously ill in his life.

Working diligently with the fork in his left hand, like they'd taught him in the hospital, he speared a piece of the steak Jane had cut for him, shifted the fork carefully in his hand, and brought it to his mouth. He chewed the meat slowly for a few moments, then lowered the fork to get another. But the prongs pressed against the gristle, slipped, and flicked the chunk of meat onto the floor. Brannigan looked after it, heard Jane say, "I'll pick it up later, dear," then slammed the fork down on his plate. Frank and Junior raised their hunched shoulders and looked up sharply. Jane took a deep breath.

"Nuff," muttered Brannigan. "Nuff." He pushed the wheelchair away, turning it, and, his hand on the wheel-rail, glided into the living and toward his den—hearing Frank say something low that ended with "like that," and Junior's heavier voice, and then Jane telling them in a normal voice to finish quickly and go upstairs: they'd talk of it later.

He negotiated the living room and came to the door of his den. His room. The door was closed but he came against it sideways, took his left hand from the wheel-rail and reached out for the knob. As he did so, the chair slipped back a few inches and he was only able to touch a bit of the knob. He gritted his teeth, pounded his left hand down on the armrest, wheeled himself close again, and tried another time. Again the chair slipped back a bit and he couldn't, hard as he strained, even touch the knob. *Damned. Damned.* He sat in the chair, breathing heavily for a few moment, then tried again, got it, flung the door open, gave the wheel-rail a sharp thrust forward, and was in his room. *His* room.

God, how many good hours he'd spent there. The soft old armchair. His own mount of the four-pound brook trout he's caught in Canada that summer with Mike and Johnny. The humidor with those long black dago-ropes he loved so much. Fireplace. Little fly-tying table—just like he'd left it. Silver rod cases in the cabinet he'd built himself. The old black-bear rug he'd bought, over Jane's hilarious objections. *His room.*

It was a room to which he slunk after a knockdown argument with Jane, a lousy road trip; he went there to plan his selling strategies, realign the world, read quietly in the evening or tie flies. He'd had most of his serious talks with his boys in this room; and he'd laughed and drunk beer and told stories half the night with Johnny and Mike here. Useless now. There was not one thing in the room, as he looked around, that he wanted.

*The shotgun.*

His eyes shifted sharply to the oak cabinet with the V-back that fitted into the corner so snugly. It was there. He went to his fly-tying table, opened the middle drawer, and felt with his hand among the capes and bobbins until his fingers found and closed tightly around the long brass key. Then, holding the key in the palm of his left hand, he used his fingers to push the chair over to the cabinet.

He had only that one gun, a beautiful 20-gauge with polished walnut stock, grey shoulder cushion, twin slate-grey barrels. He liked the feel of it in his hands, the power with which it jerked back when he shot. He'd gotten his first grouse with it last winter. Sam, Johnny's Brittany, had frozen on point, Johnny had called for the flush, and the grouse, a single, had exploded with a whirr from the underbrush. "Yours!" shouted Mike, and he'd swung, led, and watched the bird pause, sputter, and fall. He remembered the deep satisfaction he'd felt from that connection, that force which shot out from him and dropped that bird.

*The shotgun.*

Another moment and he'd have it in his hands, feel its sleek powerful lines, its smooth stock. The gun held power, energy, force; merely to have it in your hands was to feel some electrical current, some charge of strength shot into your veins, your body. "Look-see," he said, flinching at the cracked, strange sound of his voice, inserting the key into the lock and turning, then opening the cabinet door slowly.

It was not there. The cabinet was empty.

His eyes blazed and he slammed the door shut. It was not there. She had taken it. Grasping the wheel-rail he thrust downward and began to roll across the carpet toward the closed door to the living room. She had taken it. "Gun," he said, his voice a rasping growl. "Gun. Gun." Then, opening the door, he let his head fall, and he muttered, "Did she . . . really . . . think . . ."

"So the point is that *I* asked Jane for your goddamn shotgun because mine is at the gunsmith and I ain't got one to use next week," Mike said ten minutes later when they were alone in the den. "She didn't want to let me have it. Nope. 'Mike,' she says, 'Billy loves that rifle.' That's what she called it, a rifle, 'and I don't think I can let you have it.'"

Brannigan frowned. He looked intently at the bronze, hearty face of his friend, that bullish chest above toothpick legs, the straight black, always greasy and carefully combed hair, the mechanic's hands, stained black.

"I says: 'Look, Janie, he may not be out until after Christmas and I know he'd want me to put a few notches on it for him. One thing about Billy, he don't like a good rod or shotgun lying around. Offends his Scotch-Irish blood.'"

"Lie."

"I was going to take it out to the range, test it on some clays, but if you'd like it back, got some special use for it, I'll . . ." He broke off, lowered his voice, and said: "It's been rough, ain't it, kiddo?"

"Ruh-uf."

"Yeah, said Mike, turning his back and walking across the room to look at the big, bright male brook trout on the wall. "Remember when you got that one, Billy?" he said without turning around. "You'd cast that big funny fly from New Zealand, the Red Setter, looked like a whore's hairdo, into the swirls below the falls. I was behind you. I'd gotten one about three pounds that morning and you was burning mad. Didn't even speak to me at lunch. Well, maybe I was being a bit rotten about it." He came and sat down in the soft old armchair. "I must've turned and the next thing I know your rod's bent like a crescent moon and you're yelling like a banshee. Johnny thinks you've fallen in or got bit by a snake, so he comes running up, and by this time there's the goddamnedest smug look on your face! You've got the fish well hooked, you've seen him roll, and you know the size of him—and you know you got the greatest audience any mug ever had."

He watched Brannigan's eyes. They changed as he told the story.

"You're using this ten-pound-test leader and can't possibly lose that fish unless it gets into the rapids, and you're acting just as cockeyed cool as a cock of the roost. Johnny and me, we may be a little green around the gills but we're sitting polite as you please, murmuring a few friendly words of praise now and then—like, 'Did *that* lemon have to get it?'—and you keep playing him gently, making maybe a bit too much of a show of fear when it heads downstream. Cool. Very cool, Billy. And when Johnny wants to net him for you, with the big net, what do you do? Wave him away, and fuss with that minnow net you carry."

The faintest trace of a smile began to struggle around the corners of Brannigan's twisted mouth and eyes.

"So this absolute monster of a brookie, the biggest trout any of us has ever seen, is beat, and over on its side, and you're swiping at it with your net—probably trying to get it to rush off so's the show can go on—and first you get the tail in, right?"

Brannigan nodded.

"Then when it flops out, you try to bend it in, from the middle, but the monster won't be bent, so you go for the head, which barely fits into that guppy net, and then you've got it head first to about the gills and sort of clamp your hand down on the rest and come yelping out of the water, the line and rod and net and you all tangled together, and you fall on it. God, that fish was gorgeous—and there he is. That the way it happened, Billy? Something like that?"

Brannigan raised his left hand in a little shrug. "Ha-pinned . . . like . . . that."

"So the point is, you got one. You got one bigger than any of us ever got, even Johnny, God rest his soul, and now you figure, 'The big bird's crapped on me. I've caught my last big fish and shot my last grouse.' That it?"

"That-z-it."

"Johnny doesn't make it and you ain't satisfied to be here. Instead of being pleased I come tonight, passing up some very possible quail, you're going to stew in your own bile, right?"

"Rrr-ight."

"There's no one in particular to hate for it, so you figure you'll spread the hate around, to Jane and the boys, and especially yourself, and maybe you'll get lucky and not be around too much longer to be a burden to anyone. Well, I see your point, Brannigan. Lot of logic to it. Then say maybe there's a chance in a couple hundred thousand that you get anything back on that right side, so you say, 'Bad odds.'" He walked to the fly-tying table, picked up one of the capes, a pale ginger, and bent back the hackle of one feather. "A good one, Billy. First-rate dry-fly neck. Good small size, too." Then he went to the humidor and drew out one of the twisted black cigars. "You don't mind?" Brannigan, watching him closely, did not change his expression. Mike put the cigar in the center of his mouth, struck a match, and got the tip of the cigar glowing like a little coal. "Good cigar, Billy." He puckered his lips, held the cigar in three fingers, and took a long puff.

Brannigan kept watching him. He had not moved his chair from the moment Mike had come in. *Quail. Big trout. A grouse or two. Lives for that. Two wives, maybe have ten more. Funny guy. The way he holds that cigar—like he owned the world, all of it. Shotgun. Ask.*

"So the point is, it would break my sweet heart if you wasn't around, kiddo. Know what I mean? You know what I did when they told me you was"—he put out his hand, palm down, and rocked it slightly—"maybe not going to make it? I prayed. Me. Prayed. I said, 'Oh, God, let old Billy come through with *anything*, any goddamnit thing at all, so long as he's here and I can brag to him now and then about what quail I'm snatching—anything, God, just so long as he's here where I can see his ugly black-haired head now and then'"—he puffed hard at the cigar—"when the quail ain't flying and the trout is down. It's rough, right?"

*Ask about shotgun.*

"Suddenly the rules is all changed."

*The gun.*

"So the point is," he said, puffing hard, exhaling three times in rapid succession—"Hell, I don't know what the point is, Billy, but it will be awfully lonely next May when the Hendricksons start popping not to . . . Here, catch this"—and he tossed a softball, underhand, directly at Brannigan's chest. The left hand went up and forced the ball against the right shoulder. The right shoulder, limp and loose, twitched ever so slightly toward the ball. Brannigan held the ball for a moment, then took it in his left hand and tossed it back. Then he left his right shoulder and slowly dug his fingers into the muscle. "Not . . . much left."

"You'll cast lefty," said Mike. "Once knew an old poacher name of Sven who had to learn because there was bad brush on the right side. Dry-fly purist of a poacher." And the story went on for twenty minutes, and included a patrol dog named Wolf, five pound rainbows, two delicious young women, the true origin of "Sven's left curve drop cast," which only lefties could use, and then, just before the point of it all, Mike simply said, "It's eleven. The quail will have flown. I'll bring the 20-gauge tomorrow, eh?"

Brannigan smiled, a slow, deep smile that spread into his cheeks and eyes, and stayed, even when the twitch started. He nudged his right hand out with his left, so Mike could take and hold it, and Mike took it and held it in both of his own, rubbing the lifeless thing vigorously, then turning quickly for the door. Before he got there, Brannigan said: "The gun . . . yours."

*The limbs remember,* he thought, working the rake lightly across the soil he'd just fitted with seed, *and so does the earth. It remembers what it must do to these seeds, and the seeds, someplace deep within them, knew what they must do.*

Back and forth he moved the rake, holding it firmly in his left hand, using his nearly useless right to steady it. The May sun was warm but not bright, and kneaded his broad naked shoulders. He could walk without the cane now—somewhat. With that bizarre arc. His hair had gone snow white, which he liked, but otherwise, if he didn't move and didn't talk, he looked nearly the same.

Everyone else had planted a week or two ago but he'd worked more slowly, as he had to—long patient hours, setting his fertilizer, running the hand plow steadily across the small garden he'd staked out last spring, seeding the soil. This would be a good year. He could feel it. He's learned how to coax green from the brown soil, how important it was, always, to be patient—to lay the proper foundation, however long that took, before you could expect anything to grow. Tomatoes, cucumbers, carrots, radishes, onions—he'd had these last year; now he added kale, zucchini, tarragon, other herbs. Each day now he would work on his garden for several hours, bending down to it, plucking, feeling, watering, watching. It all mattered. Even the watching. Every day. He'd increased the size of his garden by a third this year. It would require more work but he could do it. He still forgot many things—names, events, people he had known; but he forgot nothing connected to his garden. It would be a good garden this year, as fruitful as anyone's garden. Maybe better.

*Got it all now*, he thought, leaning against the rake, *and Mike will be here soon to take us a-fishing.* It would be good to be in the car, on a trip, listening to Mike's excited patter, it would be good to try the river again. Mike had said the Hendricksons had started.

Three years. Days, weeks, months had ticked by, minute by minute, and imperceptibly the changes had come. The insurance had kept them from bankruptcy, Jane had begun to work for a real-estate agent in town—and had blossomed with it. Junior was earning his way in college, his own man, and Frank was a senior in high school and working part-time at Mike's garage. They didn't need what he'd once earned; he knew that what they needed most he could give them only after he had given it to himself.

He had done the exercises the men in white advised, with barbells and bicycle—over and over and again; he hated to do them and stopped when it came time to work in his garden. Several times last spring Mike had taken him to the West Branch, which they'd often fished together, before he got wracked. At first he merely found a rock, sat down, and watched. But he had not been able to resist the tug, deep inside him, to be on the stream, part of it, fishing. Wasn't that *really* why he'd done all those endless, tedious exercises, up and down, back and forth, hour after hour, all those months?

It had been impossible at first, after nearly two years. He had slipped twice on the rocks before he even reached the river. Even with the cane his right leg would not hold on broken terrain. Then he slipped again when he took his first tentative step into the water, careening badly, catching himself on his left arm. "No help, no help," he'd said when Mike stepped toward him. Then he'd been unable to strip line and cast left-handed, and finally, after several mad minutes he had given it up and fallen again on his way out, slamming his chin into a rock, cutting it sharply. No. It was not possible. He could not do it.

But it was a warm May morning and Mike would be there soon and it would be better this year. He'd earned it. Perhaps he'd even take his first trout since the crash.

Mike came promptly at twelve, and in a few minutes they were in the car racing toward the West Branch. "Magnificent day, Billy," Mike said, pushing the pedal harder. "The Hendricksons will be on in all their glory. They'll be popping out and the birds will be working, and we're going to get us a few. The cornfield run. I can feel a certain fat old brownie just waiting for you there today."

Mike parked along a small dirt turnoff and they got out and began to rig their rods, put on the waders. Mike was suited up and ready before Brannigan had worked on leg into his hip boots. "Go on, Mike. I'll be there . . . when I'm there."

"So you're tired of my company. Fine. I'm going upstream, you take the middle of the run. Where the current slows. Take your time: we're a half hour early. Lousy luck, kiddo."

Brannigan watched him stride off, his bull back bouncing even in waders. Then he finished raising his boots, strapped them to his belt, and got out his vest. He could use his right hand as a support now, to hold one section of the rod firmly enough for his left to insert the other section; he managed it, with guides aligned, on only the second try. Then he strung the line slowly through the guides until the end of the fly line and all of the leader were outside the tip top. It was well he had practiced all winter.

He got out a Hendrickson he'd tied before the crash, kept in mothballs, and held it as firmly as he could with his right fingers. Then he tried to insert the point of the leader. It would not go. He kept shoving it off to the side, or shaking the fly. Finally he dropped the fly in the grass and had to bend down, slowly, to look for it. When he found it, he stayed on the ground in the shadow of the car and held the fly up to the sky so that the light-blue would show through the hole and he could better fit in the leader. The operation took him five minutes.

As he began to walk along the edge of the cornfield toward the river, his right leg came up in a large, jerky arc, and then down again, one step after the other. Slowly. There was no rush. There was plenty of time. Mike had coaxed him out several more times last summer and fall, and each time he fell but there was some slight improvement. Not much. Not enough for him to know he could do it, like he could garden, not enough to get a line out far enough to tempt a trout—but some. You had to connive. You had to be cunning and crafty, and to forget how it once was. You had to remember always that it would not all come back, not ever. You had to work within the fixed knowledge that you continue to improve, always, and that this counted, but that even at your very best, some day, you would be, by the world's standards, a lemon.

Perhaps he'd get one today. His first. It would be wonderful if he could get into a really large trout, perhaps seventeen or eighteen inches. You didn't have to make many casts, just the right one at the right time. He'd practiced on the lawn and he knew he now could get enough distance to reach the lip of the current in the cornfield pool. He'd once fished it many times. There was room for a decent backcast, and the shallow bar on his side of the run was hard earth and rubble, with only a few rocks that might trip him up. Mike had made a good choice; he'd be fishing upstream, in the fast water where the Hendricksons hatched, but there'd be plenty of fish falling back into the pool to pick up the duns as they floated down, especially once the hatch really got going

One step at a time—the right leg out first, and down, out and down. No hurry. You couldn't rush a walk anymore than you could a garden. You couldn't rush anything. Anyway, you saw more when you walked this slow—those crows pecking at corn seeds, that huge growth of skunk cabbage, lush and green and purple, the fuzzy green on the boughs of the willows. A gorgeous day, only slightly overcast now, perfect for Hendricksons.

As he neared the row of trees that bordered the river, he could see Mike upstream, wading deep; his rod was held high and had a sharp arc. *Good old Mike. Got one already.* Up and out, then down. Then again. And again. He worked his way through the alders to the edge of the river. The water was perfect—dark and alive, flecked with bubbles and eddies where the current widened and slowed. Like he'd dreamed it all winter. Yes, that was a fish. And another. He looked to the sky and saw four or five tan flies flutter and angle off into the trees. *Yes. Yes.*

He took a tentative step into the water and felt a touch of fear as he left the firmness of the earth. No matter. It would pass. All the old feeling was there; he could still feel, deep within him, something in him reaching out to the life of the river—its quick faceted run above the long flat pool below; its translucent dark green and gliding shadows. Flowing, always moving. Changing. The same and not the same. He picked out a dun and watched it bound, like a tiny tan sailboat, over the tail of the riffle, then swirl and float into slower water where it vanished in a sudden pinching of the surface.

Yes, they were moving today. He could see six, seven fish in fixed feeding positions, rising steadily. There was plenty of time. *Don't rush. Do it very, very slowly.* They'd be going good for another hour; he wanted to pick out one good fish, near enough for him to reach with his short cast. Only one good fish. He didn't want a creelful. Only one.

Upstream, Mike was into another trout, and a few minutes later while Brannigan still eased slowly, steadily into deeper water, inch by inch, Mike had another. *We've caught one of those magical days*, he thought. *Another foot or so* . . . At last, deep as he dared go, he stood on firm hard rubble in water up to his thighs. He stripped line deliberately by raising and lowering his right hand; then, holding the loose line as best he could, he made an extremely short cast. *Good. Much better this year.* Then he stood, rod poised, watching the spreading circles of feeding fish. There were two twelve-inchers in the middle current lane, feeding freely, and two small fish back ten feet; he couldn't reach any of those anymore, though they'd once have been easy enough casts. He could never have finished to that rise in the far eddy, though: the currents were too tricky, the cast too long. Too bad. That was a large fish.

Then he saw the steady sipping rise directly upstream from him, not thirty feet away. Sometimes the largest fish rose like that, but so did fingerlings. It was time to try. He could reach that fish.

His first cast was too short and too hard. His next was off to the right and too hard. The next two were not bad but the fish both times rose to a natural a second before his fly floated past. On his next cast, the trout rose freely, took, and, gripping line and handle with his left hand, as he'd practiced, he struck and had the fish on. A good one. A bright, large leaper that came out, shaking its spots at him and falling back, and then streaking up into the current, across to the far bank, boring deep, and then leaping again.

"Mike!" He usually didn't talk while he fished but he wanted his friend to see this. He hadn't shouted very loud and above him, Mike, busy with still another fish, did not hear. Again the fish came out. "A beauty," he said audibly. "A fine brown." Again the fish raced across the current, stripping line from the reel, arching the rod sharply. *Got to get it. Can't lose this one.*

In ten minutes he could tell the trout was tiring. But it was still on the opposite side of the current. As he began to retrieve the line slowly, the fish came into the current and allowed itself to be carried downstream. Then, suddenly, it bolted directly toward him and the like went slack. "No, no," he said, struggling but unable to strip back line quickly enough.

When he regained control, the fish was gone. He drew the line back slowly until he could see the bedraggled fly. The fish had merely pulled out on the slack line—because of his goddam right arm. His right arm—which might as well not be there.

He was sitting in the car, all his equipment packed away, when Mike came back. Mike had caught seven fish, all of size but none as large as the one Brannigan had lost, and said it was the best day he could remember, except of course the day he'd gotten the three-pound brookie in Canada and Brannigan that lucky male. Brannigan offered a weak smile but said nothing, and Mike looked at him and then said nothing as he took off his vest and waders.

In the car, heading home, he turned to Brannigan and asked quietly, "How'd you do, Billy? Take any?"

"I lost one . . . Mike. Pretty good fish. Then I decided I'd better quit because at least I hadn't fallen in. Like every other time. So I headed . . . out. Slowly. Praising myself all the time . . . that at least I hadn't taken . . . a bath this time."

"You took some bad ones last year, Billy."

"I'd lost a good one, a really good fish, and that didn't make . . . me feel too cheery . . . Yet I'd hooked it and played it a long time . . . which I . . . never did before, not since I got wrecked, and I figured . . . if I could get out without a spill, I'd . . . still be ahead."

"Was it really a good fish, Billy?"

"Big. Very big brown."

"Sixteen inches."

"More."

"That's a big fish."

"So I was one step or two from the bank, smiling and praising myself . . . that I . . . hadn't fallen, when . . . I went into a pothole."

"Hell!"

"So I went down and over, ass . . . over teakettle. Almost drowned."

"Billy!"

"Almost. My head went under . . . and I was on my right side and couldn't . . . get leverage, and sort of forced my head out, and went under again, and gagged. Know I was going to die. I felt the grasp of brakes . . . in my brain. I suddenly . . . did not want to die. They water was shallow . . . but it was deep enough. Deep enough. Mike. I did not want to die," he said quietly. "So finally I managed to twist over onto my left side. Broke my rod. Slammed my bone badly. Barely . . . got out of it."

Mike looked over at this friend who had lost his fish, nearly ended it all. He had not one word to cheer him with. Brannigan was sitting in the same seat he'd been in when the accident smashed him, and there was a curious grin on his face. "Maybe we . . . really shouldn't go anymore, Billy," Mike said soberly. "Know what I mean?" He had hoped desperately that Brannigan would get one good trout, that this day might be a new beginning. He had for three years said everything he knew to say. He had no words left.

Faintly, as a slight pressure first and then a firm grip, Mike felt his friend's left hand on his shoulder. "No," he heard Brannigan say. And when he turned: "We're going . . . to keep going . . . back."

# A FATAL SUCCESS

## HENRY VAN DYKE

Beekman De Peyster was probably the most passionate and triumphant fisherman in the Petrine Club. He angled with the same dash and confidence that he threw into his operations in the stock-market. He was sure to be the first man to get his flies on the water at the opening of the season. And when we came together for our fall meeting, to compare notes of our wanderings on various streams and make up the fish-stories for the year, Beekman was almost always "high hook." We expected, as a matter of course, to hear that he had taken the most and the largest fish.

It was so with everything that he undertook, he was a masterful man. If there was an unusually large trout in a river, Beekman knew about it before any one else, and got there first, and came home with the fish. It did not make him unduly proud, because there was nothing uncommon about it. It was his habit to succeed, and all the rest of us were hardened to it.

When he married Cornelia Cochrane, we were consoled for our partial loss by the apparent fitness and brilliancy of the match. If Beekman was a masterful man, Cornelia was certainly what you might call a mistressful woman. She had been the head of her house since she was eighteen years old. She carried her good looks like the family plate; and when she came into the breakfast-room and said good-morning, it was with an air as if she presented every one with a check for a thousand dollars. Her tastes were accepted as judgments, and her preferences had the force of laws. Wherever she wanted to go in the summer-time, there the finger of household destiny pointed. At Newport, at Bar Harbor, at Lenox, at Southampton, she made a record. When she was joined in holy wedlock to Beekman De Peyster, her father and mother heaved a sigh of satisfaction, and settled down for a quiet vacation in Cherry Valley.

It was in the second summer after the wedding that Beekman admitted to a few of his ancient Petrine cronies, in moments of confidence (unjustifiable, but natural), that his wife had one fault.

"It is not exactly a fault," he said, "not a positive fault, you know. It is just a kind of a defect, due to her education, of course. In everything else she's magnificent. But she doesn't care for fishing. She says it's stupid,—can't see why any one should like the woods,—calls camping out the lunatic's diversion. It's rather awkward for a man with my habits to have his wife take such a view. But it can be changed by training. I intend to educate her and convert her. I shall make an angler of her yet."

And so he did.

The new education was begun in the Adirondacks, and the first lesson was given at Paul Smith's. It was a complete failure.

Beekman persuaded her to come out with him for a day on Meacham River, and promised to convince her of the charm of angling. She wore a new gown, fawn-color and violet, with a picture-hat, very taking. But the Meacham River trout was shy that day; not even Beekman could induce him to rise to the fly. What the trout lacked in confidence the mosquitoes more than made up. Mrs. De Peyster came home much sunburned, and expressed a highly unfavorable opinion of fishing as an amusement and of Meacham River as a resort.

"The nice people don't come to the Adirondacks to fish," said she; "they come to talk about the fishing twenty years ago. Besides, what do you want to catch that trout for? If you do, the other men will say you bought it, and the hotel will have to put in a new one for the rest of the season."

The following year Beekman tried Moosehead Lake. Here he found an atmosphere more favorable to his plan of education. There were a good many people who really fished, and short expeditions in the woods were quite fashionable. Cornelia had a camping-costume of the most approved style made by Dewlap on Fifth Avenue,—pearl-gray with linings of rose-silk,—and consented to go with her husband on a trip up Moose River. They pitched their tent the first evening at the mouth of Misery Stream, and a storm came on. The rain sifted through the canvas in a fine spray, and Mrs. De Peyster sat up all night in a waterproof cloak, holding an umbrella. The next day they were back at the hotel in time for lunch.

"It was horrid," she told her most intimate friend, "perfectly horrid. The idea of sleeping in a shower-bath, and eating your breakfast from a tin plate, just for sake of catching a few silly fish! Why not send your guides out to get them for you?"

But, in spite of this profession of obstinate heresy, Beekman observed with secret joy that there were signs, before the end of the season, that Cornelia was drifting a little, a very little but still perceptibly, in the direction of a change of heart. She began to take an interest, as the big trout came along in September, in the reports of the catches made by the different anglers. She would saunter out with the other people to the corner of the porch to see the fish weighed and spread out on the grass. Several times she went with Beekman in the canoe to Hardscrabble Point, and showed distinct evidences of pleasure when he caught large trout. The last day of the season, when he returned from a successful expedition to Roach River and Lily Bay, she inquired with some particularity about the results of his sport; and in the evening, as the company sat before the great open fire in the hall of the hotel, she was heard to use this information with considerable skill in putting down Mrs. Minot Peabody of Boston, who was recounting the details of her husband's catch at Spencer Pond. Cornelia was not a person to be contented with the back seat, even in fish-stories.

When Beekman observed these indications he was much encouraged, and resolved to push his educational experiment briskly forward to his customary goal of success.

"Some things can be done, as well as others," he said in his masterful way, as three of us were walking home together after the autumnal dinner of the Petrine Club, which he always attended as a graduate member. "A real fisherman never gives up. I told you I'd make an angler out of my wife; and so I will. It has been rather difficult. She is 'dour' in rising. But she's beginning to take notice of the fly now. Give me another season, and I'll have her landed."

Good old Beekman! Little did he think—But I must not interrupt the story with moral reflections.

The preparations that be made for his final effort at conversion were thorough and prudent. He had a private interview with Dewlap in regard to the construction of a practical fishing-costume for a lady, which resulted in something more reasonable and workmanlike than had ever been turned out by that famous artist. He ordered from Hook & Catchett a lady's angling-outfit of the most enticing description,—a split-bamboo rod, light as a girl's wish, and strong as a matron's will; an oxidized silver reel, with a monogram on one side, and a sapphire set in the handle for good luck; a book of flies, of all sizes and colors, with the correct names inscribed in gilt letters on each page. He surrounded his favorite sport with an aureole of elegance and beauty. And then he took Cornelia in September to the Upper Dam at Rangeley.

She went reluctant. She arrived disgusted. She stayed incredulous. She returned—Wait a bit, and you shall hear how she returned.

The Upper Dam at Rangeley is the place, of all others in the world, where the lunacy of angling may be seen in its incurable stage. There is a cozy little inn, called a camp, at the foot of a big lake. In front of the inn is a huge dam of gray stone, over which the river plunges into a great oval pool, where the trout assemble in the early fall to perpetuate their race. From the tenth of September to the thirtieth, there is not an hour of the day or night when there are no boats floating on that pool, and no anglers trailing the fly across its waters. Before the late fishermen are ready to come in at midnight, the early fishermen may be seen creeping down to the shore with lanterns in order to begin before cock-crow. The number of fish taken is not large,—perhaps five or six for the whole company on an average day,—but the size is sometimes enormous,—nothing under three pounds is counted, and they pervade thought and conversation at the Upper Dam to the exclusion of every other subject. There is no driving, no dancing, no golf, no tennis. There is nothing to do but fish or die.

At first, Cornelia thought she would choose the latter alternative. But a remark of that skilful and morose old angler, McTurk, which she overheard on the verandah after supper, changed her mind.

"Women have no sporting instinct," said he. "They only fish because they see men doing it. They are imitative animals."

That same night she told Beekman, in the subdued tone which the architectural construction of the house imposes upon all confidential communications in the bedrooms, but with resolution in every accent, that she proposed to go fishing with him on the morrow.

"But not on that pool, right in front of the house, you understand. There must be some other place, out on the lake, where we can fish for three or four days, until I get the trick of this wobbly rod. Then I'll show that old bear, McTurk, what kind of an animal woman is."

Beekman was simply delighted. Five days of diligent practice at the mouth of Mill Brook brought his pupil to the point where he pronounced her safe.

"Of course," he said patronizingly, "you haven't learned all about it yet. That will take years. But you can get your fly out thirty feet, and you can keep the tip of your rod up. If you do that, the trout will hook himself, in rapid water, eight times out of ten. For playing him, if you follow my directions, you'll be all right. We will try the pool tonight, and hope for a medium-sized fish."

Cornelia said nothing, but smiled and nodded. She had her own thoughts.

At about nine o'clock Saturday night, they anchored their boat on the edge of the shoal where the big eddy swings around, put out the lantern and began to fish. Beekman sat in the bow of the boat, with his rod over the left side; Cornelia in the stern, with her rod over the right side. The night was cloudy and very black. Each of them had put on the largest possible fly, one a "Bee-Pond" and the other a "Dragon;" but even these were invisible. They measured out the right length of line, and let the flies drift back until they hung over the shoal, in the curly water where the two currents meet.

There were three other boats to the left of them. McTurk was their only neighbor in the darkness on the right. Once they heard him swearing softly to himself, and knew that he had hooked and lost a fish.

Away down at the tail of the pool, dimly visible through the gloom, the furtive fisherman, Parsons, had anchored his boat. No noise ever came from that craft. If he wished to change his position, he did not pull up the anchor and let it down again with a bump. He simply lengthened or shortened his anchor rope. There was no click of the reel when he played a fish. He drew in and paid out the line through the rings by hand, without a sound. What he thought when a fish got away, no one knew, for he never said it. He concealed his angling as if it had been a conspiracy. Twice that night they heard a faint splash in the water near his boat, and twice they saw him put his arm over the side in the darkness and bring it back again very quietly.

"That's the second fish for Parsons," whispered Beekman, "what a secretive old Fortunatus he is! He knows more about fishing than any man on the pool, and talks less."

Cornelia did not answer. Her thoughts were all on the tip of her own rod. About eleven o'clock a fine, drizzling rain set in. The fishing was very slack. All the other boats gave it up in despair; but Cornelia said she wanted to stay out a little longer, they might as well finish up the week.

At precisely fifty minutes past eleven, Beekman reeled up his line, and remarked with firmness that the holy Sabbath day was almost at hand and they ought to go in.

"Not till I've landed this trout," said Cornelia.

"What? A trout! Have you got one?"

"Certainly; I've had him on for at least fifteen minutes. I'm playing him Mr. Parsons' way. You might as well light the lantern and get the net ready; he's coming in towards the boat now."

Beekman broke three matches before he made the lantern burn; and when he held it up over the gunwale, there was the trout sure enough, gleaming ghostly pale in the dark water, close to the boat, and quite tired out. He slipped the net over the fish and drew it in—a monster.

"I'll carry that trout, if you please," said Cornelia, as they stepped out of the boat; and she walked into the camp, on the last stroke of midnight, with the fish in her hand, and quietly asked for the steelyard.

Eight pounds and fourteen ounces,—that was the weight. Everybody was amazed. It was the "best fish" of the year. Cornelia showed no sign of exultation, until just as John was carrying the trout to the ice-house. Then she flashed out:

"Quite a fair imitation, Mr. McTurk,—isn't it?"

Now McTurk's best record for the last fifteen years was seven pounds and twelve ounces.

So far as McTurk is concerned, this is the end of the story. But not for the De Peysters. I wish it were. Beekman went to sleep that night with a contented spirit. He felt that his experiment in education had been a success. He had made his wife an angler.

He had indeed, and to an extent which he little suspected. That Upper Dam trout was to her like the first taste of blood to the tiger. It seemed to change, at once, not so much her character as the direction of her vital energy. She yielded to the lunacy of angling, not by slow degrees, (as first a transient delusion, then a fixed idea, then a chronic infirmity, finally a mild insanity,) but by a sudden plunge into the most violent mania. So far from being ready to die at Upper Dam, her desire now was to live there and to live solely for the sake of fishing— as long as the season was open.

There were two hundred and forty hours left to midnight on the thirtieth of September. At least two hundred of these she spent on the pool; and when Beekman was too exhausted to manage the boat and the net and the lantern for her, she engaged a trustworthy guide to take Beekman's place while he slept. At the end of the last day her score was twenty-three, with an average of five pounds and a quarter. His score was nine, with an average of four pounds. He had succeeded far beyond his wildest hopes.

The next year his success became even more astonishing. They went to the Titan Club in Canada. The ugliest and most inaccessible sheet of water in that territory is Lake Pharaoh. But it is famous for the extraordinary fishing at a certain spot near the outlet, where there is just room enough for one canoe. They camped on Lake Pharaoh for six weeks, by Mrs. De Peyster's command; and her canoe was always the first to reach the fishing-ground in the morning, and the last to leave it in the evening.

Some one asked him, when he returned to the city, whether he had good luck.

"Quite fair," he tossed off in a careless way; "we took over three hundred pounds."

"To your own rod?" asked the inquirer, in admiration.

"No-o-o," said Beekman, "there were two of us."

There were two of them, also, the following year, when they joined the Natasheebo Salmon Club and fished that celebrated river in Labrador. The custom of drawing lots every night for the water that each member was to angle over the next day, seemed to be especially designed to fit the situation. Mrs. De Peyster could fish her own pool and her husband's too. The result of that year's fishing was something phenomenal. She had a score that made a paragraph in the newspapers and called out editorial comment. One editor was so inadequate to the situation as to entitle the article in which he described her triumph "The Equivalence of Woman." It was well-meant, but she was not at all pleased with it.

She was now not merely an angler, but a "record" angler of the most virulent type. Wherever they went, she wanted, and she got, the pick of the water. She seemed to be equally at home on all kinds of streams, large and small. She would pursue the little mountain-brook trout in the early spring, and the Labrador salmon in July, and the huge speckled trout of the northern lakes in September, with the same avidity and resolution. All that she cared for was to get the best and the most of the fishing at each place where she angled. This she always did.

And Beekman,—well, for him there were no more long separations from the partner of his life while he went off to fish some favorite stream. There were no more home-comings after a good day's sport to find her clad in cool and dainty raiment on the verandah, ready to welcome him with friendly badinage. There was not even any casting of the fly around Hardscrabble Point while she sat in the canoe reading a novel, looking up with mild and pleasant interest when he caught a larger fish than usual, as an older and wiser person looks at a child playing some innocent game. Those days of a divided interest between man and wife were gone. She was now fully converted, and more. Beekman and Cornelia were one; and she was the one.

The last time I saw the De Peysters he was following, her along the Bea-verkill, carrying a landing-net and a basket, but no rod. She paused for a moment to exchange greetings, and then strode on down the stream. He lingered for a few minutes longer to light a pipe.

"Well, old man," I said, "you certainly have succeeded in making an angler of Mrs. De Peyster."

"Yes, indeed," he answered,—"haven't I?" Then he continued, after a few thoughtful puffs of smoke, "Do you know, I'm not quite so sure as I used to be that fishing is the best of all sports. I sometimes think of giving it up and going in for croquet."

# ON DRY-COW FISHING AS A FINE ART

## RUDYARD KIPLING

It must be clearly understood that I am not at all proud of this performance. In Florida men sometimes hook and land, on rod and tackle a little finer than a steam-crane and chain, a mackerel-like fish called "tarpon," which sometime run to 120 pounds. Those men stuff their captures and exhibit them in glass cases and become puffed up. On the Columbia River sturgeon of 150 pounds weight are taken with the line. When the sturgeon is hooked the line is fixed to the nearest pine tree or steamboat-wharf, and after some hours or days the sturgeon surrenders himself, if the pine or the line do not give way. The owner of the line then states on oath that he has caught a sturgeon, and he, too, becomes proud.

These things are mentioned to show how light a creel will fill the soul of a man with vanity. I am not proud. It is nothing to me that I have hooked and played seven hundred pounds weight of quarry. All my desire is to place the little affair on record before the mists of memory breed the miasma of exaggeration.

The minnow cost eighteenpence. It was a beautiful quill minnow, and the tackle-maker said that it could be thrown as a fly. He guaranteed further in respect to the triangles—it glittered with triangles—that, if necessary, the minnow would hold a horse. A man who speaks too much truth is just as offensive as a man who speaks too little. None the less, owing to the defective condition of the present law of libel, the tackle-master's name must be withheld.

The minnow and I and a rod went down to a brook to attend to a small jack who lived between two clumps of flags in the most cramped swim that he could select. As a proof that my intentions were strictly honorable, I may mention that I was using a light split-cane rod—very dangerous if the line runs through the weeds, but very satisfactory in clean water, inasmuch as it keeps a steady strain on the fish and prevents him from taking liberties. I had an old score against the jack. He owed me two live-bait already, and I had reason to suspect him of coming up-stream and interfering with a little bleak-pool under a horse-bridge which lay entirely beyond his sphere of legitimate influence. Observe, therefore, that my tackle and my motives pointed clearly to jack, and jack alone; though I knew that there were monstrous big perch in the brook.

The minnow was thrown as a fly several times, and, owing to my peculiar, and hitherto unpublished, methods of fly throwing, nearly six pennyworth of the triangles came off, either in my coat-collar, or my thumb, or the back of my hand. Fly fishing is a very gory amusement.

The jack was not interested in the minnow, but towards twilight a boy opened a gate of the field and let in some twenty or thirty cows and half-a-dozen cart-horses, and they were all very much interested. The horses galloped up and down the field and shook the banks, but the cows walked solidly and breathed heavily, as people breathe who appreciate the Fine Arts.

By this time I had given up all hope of catching my jack fairly, but I wanted the live-bait and bleak-account settled before I had quite made up my mind to borrow a tin of chloride of lime from the farm-house—another triangle had fixed itself in my fingers—I made a cast which for pure skill, exact judgment of distance, and perfect coincidence of hand and eye and brain, would have taken every prize at a bait-casting tournament. That was the first half of the cast. The second was postponed because the quill minnow would not return to its proper place, which was under the lobe of my left ear. It had done thus before, and I supposed it was in collision with a grass tuft, till I turned around and saw a large red and white bald faced cow tying to rub what would be withers in a horse with her nose. She looked at me reproachfully, and her look said as plainly as words: "The season is too far advanced for gadflies. What is this strange disease?"

I replied, "Madam, I must apologize for an unwarrantable liberty on the part of my minnow, but if you will have the goodness to keep still until I can reel in, we will adjust this little difficulty."

I reeled in very swiftly and cautiously, but she would not wait. She put her tail in the air and ran away. It was a purely involuntary motion on my part: I struck. Other anglers may contradict me, but I firmly believe that if a man had foul-hooked his best friend through the nose, and that friend ran, the man would strike by instinct. I struck, therefore, and the reel began to sing just as merrily as though I had caught my jack. But had it been a jack, the minnow would have come away. I told the tackle-maker this much afterwards, and he laughed and made allusions to the guarantee about holding a horse.

Because it was a fat innocent she-cow that had done me no harm the minnow held—held like an anchor-fluke in coral moorings—and I was forced to dance up and down an interminable field very largely used by cattle. It was like salmon fishing in a nightmare. I took gigantic strides, and every stride found me up to my knees in marsh. But the cow seemed to skate along the squashy greens by the brook, to skim over the miry backwaters, and to float like a mist through the patches of rush that squirted black filth over my face. Sometimes we whirled through a mob of her friends—there were no friends to help me—and they looked scandalized; and sometimes a young and frivolous cart-horse would join in the chase for a few miles, and kick solid pieces of mud into my eyes; and through all the mud, the milky smell of kine, the rush and the smother, I was aware of my own voice crying: "Pussy, pussy, pussy! Pretty pussy! Come along then, puss-cat!" You see it is so hard to speak to a cow properly, and she would not listen—no, she would not listen.

Then she stopped, and the moon got up behind the pollards to tell the cows to lie down; but they were all on their feet, and they came trooping to see. And she said, "I haven't had my supper, and I want to go to bed, and please don't worry me." And I said, "The matter has passed beyond any apology. There are three courses open to you, my dear lady. If you'll the common sense to walk up to my creel I'll get my knife and you shall have all the minnow. Or, again, if you'll let me move across to your near side, instead of keeping me so coldly on your off side, the thing will come away in one tweak. I can't pull it out over your withers. Better still, go to a post and rub it out, dear. It won't hurt much, but if you think I'm going to lose my rod to please you, you are mistaken." And she said, "I don't understand what you are saying. I am very, very unhappy." And I said, "It's your fault for trying to fish. Do go to the nearest gate-post, you nice fat thing, and rub it out."

For a moment I fancied she was taking my advice. She ran away and I followed. But all the other cows came with us in a bunch, and I thought of Phaeton trying to drive the Chariot of the Sun, and Texan cowboys killed by stampeding cattle, and "Green Grow the Rushes, O!" and Solomon and Job, and "loosing the bands of Orion," and hooking Behemoth, and Wordsworth who talks about whirling around with stones and rocks and trees, and "Here we go round the Mulberry bush," and "Pippin Hill," and "Hey Diddle Diddle," and most especially the top joint of my rod. Again she stopped—but nowhere in the neighborhood of my knife—and her sisters stood moonfaced round her. It seemed that she might, now, run towards me, and I looked for a tree, because cows are very different from salmon, who only jump against the line, and never molest the fisherman. What followed was worse than any direct attack. She began to buckjump, to stand on her head and her tail alternately, to leap to the sky, all four feet together, and to dance on her hind legs. It was so violent and improper, so desperately unladylike, that I was inclined to blush, as one would blush at the sight of a prominent statesman sliding down a dire escape, or a duchess chasing her cook with a skillet. That flop-some abandon might go on all night in the lonely meadow among the mists, and if it went on all night—this was pure inspiration—I might be able to worry through the fishing line with my teeth.

Those who desire an entirely new sensation should chew with all their teeth, and against time, through a best waterproofed silk line, one end of which belongs to a mad cow dancing fairy rings in the moonlight; at the same time keeping one eye on the cow and the other on the top joint of a split-cane rod. She buck-jumped and I bit on the slack just in front of the reel; and I am in a position to state that that line was cored with steel wire throughout the particular section which I attacked. This had been formally denied by the tackle-maker, who is not to be believed.

The wheep of the broken line running through the rings told me that henceforth the cow and I might be strangers. I had already bidden good-bye to some tooth or teeth; but not price is too great for freedom of the soul.

"Madam," I said, "the minnow and twenty feet of very superior line are your alimony without reservation. For the wrong I have unwittingly done to you I express my sincere regret. At the same time, may I hope that Nature, the kindest of nurses, will in due season—"

She or one of her companions must have stepped on her spare end of the line in the dark, for she bellowed wildly and ran away, followed by all the cows. I hoped the minnow was disengaged at last; and before I went away looked at my watch, fearing to find it nearly midnight. My last cast for the jack was made at 6:23 PM There lacked still three and a-half minutes of the half-hour; and I would have sworn that the moon was paling before the dawn!

"Simminly someone were chasing they cows down to bottom o' Ten Acre," said the farmer that evening. "'Twasn't you, sir?"

"Now under what earthly circumstances do you suppose I should chase your cows? I wasn't fishing for them, was I?"

Then all the farmer's family gave themselves up to jam-smeared laughter for the rest of the evening, because that was a rare and precious jest, and it was repeated for months, and the fame of it spread from the farm to another, and yet another at least three miles away, and it will be used again for the benefit of visitors when the freshets come down in spring.

But to the greater establishment of my honor and glory I submit in print this bald statement of fact, that I may not, through forgetfulness, be tempted later to tell how I hooked a bull on a Marlow Buzz, how he ran up a tree and took to water, and how I played him along the London-road for thirty miles, and gaffed him at Smithfield. Errors of this kind may creep in with the lapse of years, and it is my ambition ever to be a worthy member of that fraternity who pride themselves on never deviating by one hair's breadth from the absolute and literal truth.

# THE HOLE

## GUY DE MAUPASSANT

"Cuts and wound that caused death"—That was the heading of the charge which brought Leopold Renard, upholsterer, before the Assize Court.

Round him were the principal witnesses, Madame Flameche, widow of the victim, Louis Ladureau, cabinetmaker, and Jean Durdent, plumber.

Near the criminal was his wife, dressed in black, a little ugly woman, who looked like a monkey dressed as a lady.

This is how Renard described the drama:

"Good heavens, it is a misfortune of which I am the first and last victim, and with which my will has nothing to do. The facts are their own commentary, Monsieur le President. I am an honest man, a hard-working man, an upholsterer in the same street for the last sixteen years, known, liked, respected, and esteemed by all, as my neighbors have testified, even the porter, who is not folatre every day. I am fond of work, I am fond of saving, I like honest men, and respectable pleasures. That is what has ruined me, so much the worse for me; but as my will had nothing to do with it, I continue to respect myself.

"Every Sunday for the last five years, my wife and I have spent the day at Passy. We get fresh air, not to say that we are fond of fishing—as fond of it as we are of small onions. Melie inspired me with that passion, the jade; she is more enthusiastic than I am, the scold, and all the mischief in this business is her fault, as you will see immediately.

"I am strong and mild-tempered, without a pennyworth of malice in me. But she, oh la la! She looks insignificant, she is short and thin, but she does more mischief than a weasel. I do not deny that she has some good qualities; she has some, and those very important to a man in business. But her character! Just ask about it in the neighborhood; even the porter's wife, who has just sent me about my business—she will tell you something about it.

"Every day she used to find fault with my mild temper: 'I would not put up with this! I would not put up with that.' If I had listened to her, Monsieur le President, I should have had at least three bouts of fisticuffs a month."

Madame Renard interrupted him: "And for good reasons too; they laugh best who laugh last."

He turned toward her frankly: "Oh! very well, I can blame you, since you were the cause of it."

Then, facing the President again he said:

"I will continue. We used to go to Passy every Saturday evening, so as to be able to begin fishing at daybreak the next morning. It is a habit which has become second nature with us, as the saying is. Three years ago this summer I discovered a place, oh! such a spot! There, in the shade, were eight feet of water at least and perhaps ten, a hole with a retour under the bank, a regular retreat for fish and a paradise for any fisherman. I might look upon that hole as my property, Monsieur le President, as I was its Christopher Columbus. Everybody in the neighborhood knew it, without making any opposition. They used to say: 'That is Renard's place'; and nobody would have gone to it, not even Monsieur Plumsay, who is renowned, be it said without any offense, for appropriating other people's places.

"Well, I went as usual to that place, of which I felt as certain as if I had owned it. I had scarcely got there on Saturday, when I got into Delila, with my wife. Delila is my Norwegian boat, which I had built by Fourmaise, and which is light and safe. Well, as I said, we got into the boat and we were going to bait, and for baiting there is nobody to be compared with me, and they all know it. You want to know with what I bait? I cannot answer that question; it has nothing to do with the accident; I cannot answer, that is my secret. There are more than three hundred people who have asked me; I have been offered glasses of brandy and liquors, fried fish, matelotes, to make me tell! But just go and try whether the chub will come. Ah! they have patted my stomach to get at my secret, my recipe. Only my wife knows, and she will not tell it, any more than I shall! Is not that so, Melie?"

The President of the Court interrupted him:

"Just get to the facts as soon as you can."

The accused continued: "I am getting to them; I am getting to them. Well, on Saturday, July 8, we left by the five twenty-five train, and before dinner we went to ground-bait as usual. The weather promised to keep fine, and I said to Melie: 'All right for to-morrow!' And she replied: 'It looks like it.' We never talk more than that together.

"And then we returned to dinner. I was happy and thirsty, and that was the cause of everything. I said to Melie: 'Look here Melie, it is fine weather, so suppose I drink a bottle of Casque a meche. That is a little white wine which we have christened so, because if you drink too much of it prevents you from sleeping and is the opposite of a nightcap. Do you understand me?

"She replied: 'You can do as you please, but you will be ill again, and will not be able to get up to-morrow.' That was true, sensible, prudent, and clear-sighted, I must confess. Nevertheless, I could not withstand it, and I drank my bottle. It all comes from that.

"Well, I could not sleep. By Jove! It kept me awake till two o'clock in the morning, and then I went to sleep so soundly that I should not have heard the angel shouting at the Last Judgment.

"In short, my wife woke me at six o'clock and I jumped out of bed, hastily put on my trousers and jersey, washed my face and jumped on board Delila. But it was too late, for when I arrived at my hole it was already taken! Such a thing had never happened to me in three years, and it made me feel as if I were being robbed under my own eyes. I said to myself, Confound it all! confound it! And then my wife began to nag at me. 'Eh! What about your Casque a meche! Get along, you drunkard! Are you satisfied, you great fool?' I could say nothing, because it was all quite true, and so I landed all the same near the spot and tried to profit by what was left. Perhaps after all the fellow might catch nothing, and go away.

"He was a little thin man, in white linen coat and waistcoat, and with a large straw hat, and his wife, a fat woman who was doing embroidery, was behind him.

"When she saw us take up our position close to their place, she murmured: 'I suppose there are no other places on the river!' And my wife, who was furious, replied: 'People who know how to behave make inquiries about the habits of the neighborhood before occupying reserved spots.'

"As I did not want a fuss, I said to her: 'Hold your tongue, Melie. Let them go on, let them go on; we shall see.'

"Well, we had fastened Delila under the willow-trees, and had landed and were fishing side by side, Melie and I, close to the two others; but here, Monsieur, I must enter into details.

"We had only been there about five minutes when our male neighbor's float began to go down two or three times, and then he pulled out a chub as thick as my thigh, rather less, perhaps, but nearly as big! My heart beat, and the perspiration stood on my forehead, and Melie said to me: 'Well, you sot, did you see that?'

"Just then, Monsieur Bru, the grocer of Poissy, who was fond of gudgeon fishing, passed in a boat, and called out to me: So somebody has taken your usual place, Monsieur Renard? And I replied: 'Yes, Monsieur Bru, there are some people in this world who do not know the usages of common politeness.'

"The little man in linen pretended not to hear, nor his fat lump of a wife, either."

Here the President interrupted him a second time: "Take care, you are insulting the widow, Madame Flameche, who is present.

Renard made his excuses: "I beg your pardon, I beg your pardon, my anger carried me away . . . Well, not a quarter of an hour had passed when the little man caught another chub and another almost immediately, and another five minutes later.

"The tears were in my eyes, and then I knew that Madame Renard was boiling with rage, for she kept on nagging at me: 'Oh! how horrid! Don't you see that he is robbing you of your fish? Do you think that you will catch anything? Not even a frog, nothing whatever. Why, my hands are burning, just to think of it.'

"But I said to myself: 'Let us wait until twelve o clock. Then this poaching fellow will go to lunch, and I shall get my place again. As for me, Monsieur le President, I lunch on the spot every Sunday; we bring our provisions in 'Delila.' But there! At twelve o'clock, the wretch produced a fowl out of a newspaper, and while he was eating, actually he caught another chub!

"Melie and I had a morsel also, just a mouthful, a mere nothing, for our heart was not in it.

"Then I took up my newspaper, to aid my digestion. Every Sunday I read the Gil Blas in the shade like that, by the side of the water. It is Columbine's day, you know, Columbine who writes the articles in the Gil Blas. I generally put Madame Renard into a passion by pretending to know this Columbine. It is not true, for I do not know her, and have never seen her, but that does not matter; she writes very well, and then she says things straight out for a woman. She suits me, and there are not many of her sort.

"Well, I began to tease my wife, but she got angry immediately, and very angry, and so I held my tongue. At that moment our two witnesses, who are present here, Monsieur Ladureau and Monsieur Durdent, appeared on the other side of the river. We knew each other by sight. The little man began to fish again, and he caught so many that I trembled with vexation, and his wife said: 'It is an uncommonly good spot, and we will come here always, Desire.' As for me, a cold shiver ran down my back, and Madame Renard kept repeating: 'You are not a man; you have the blood of a chicken in your veins'; and suddenly I said to her: 'Look here, I would rather go away, or I shall only be doing something foolish.'

"And she whispered to me as if she had put a red-hot iron under my nose: 'You are not a man. Now you are going to run away, and surrender your place! Off you go, Bazaine!'

"Well, I felt that, but yet I did not move, while the other fellow pulled out a bream, Oh! I never saw such a large one before, never! And then my wife began to talk aloud, as if she were thinking, and you can see her trickery. She said: 'That is what one might call stolen fish, seeing that we baited the place ourselves. At any rate, they ought to give us back the money we have spent on bait.'

"Then the fat woman in the cotton dress said in turn: 'Do you mean to call us thieves, Madame?' And they began to explain, and then they came to words. Oh! Lord! those creatures know some good ones. They shouted so loud, that our two witnesses, who were on the other bank, began to call out by way of a joke: 'Less noise over there; you will prevent your husbands from fishing.'

"The fact is that neither of us moved any more than if we had been two tree-stumps. We remained there, with our noses over the water, as if we had heard nothing, but by Jove, we heard all the same. 'You are a mere liar.'

" 'You are nothing better than a street-walker.'

" 'You are only a trollop.'

" 'You are a regular strumpet.'

"And so on, and so on; a sailor could not have said more.

"Suddenly I heard a noise behind me, and turned round. It was the other one, the fat woman who had fallen on to my wife with her parasol. Whack! Whack! Melie got two of them, but she was furious, and she hits hard when she is in a rage, so she caught the fat woman by the hair and then, thump, thump. Slaps in the face rained down like ripe plums. I should have let them go on—women among themselves, men among themselves—it does not do to mix the blows, but the little man in the linen jacket jumped up like a devil and was going to rush at my wife. Ah! no, no, not that, my friend! I caught the gentleman with the end of my fist, crash, crash, one on the nose, the other in the stomach. He threw up his arms and legs and fell on his back into the river, just into the hole.

"I should have fished him out most certainly, Monsieur le President, if I had had the time. But unfortunately the fat woman got the better of it, and she was drubbing Melie terribly. I know that I ought not to have assisted her while the man was drinking his fill, but I never thought that he would drown, and said to myself: 'Bah, it will cool him.'

"I therefore ran up to the women to separate them, and all I received was scratches and bites. Good Lord, what creatures! Well, it took me five minutes, and perhaps ten, to separate those two viragoes. When I turned round, there was nothing to be seen, and the water was as smooth as a lake. The others yonder kept shouting: 'Fish him out!' It was all very well to say that, but I cannot swim and still less dive!

"At last the man from the dam came, and two gentlemen with boat-hooks, but it had taken over a quarter of an hour. He was found at the bottom of the hole in eight feet of water, as I have said, but he was dead, the poor little man in his linen suit! There are the facts, such as I have sworn to. I am innocent, on my honor."

The witnesses having deposed to the same effect, the accused was acquitted.

# THE LADY OR THE SALMON?

## ANDREW LANG

The circumstances which attended and caused the death of the Hon. Houghton Grannom have not long been known to me, and it is only now that, by the decease of his father, Lord Whitchurch, and the extinction of his noble family, I am permitted to divulge the facts. That the true tale of my unhappy friend will touch different chords in different breasts, I am well aware. The sportsman, I think, will hesitate to approve him; the fair, I hope, will absolve. Who are we, to scrutinize human motives, and to award our blame to actions which, perhaps, might have been our own, had opportunity beset and temptation beguiled us? There is a certain point at which the keenest sense of honor, the most chivalrous affection and devotion, cannot bear the strain, but break like a salmon line under a masterful stress. That my friend succumbed, I admit; that he was his own judge, the severest, and passed and executed sentence on himself, I have now to show.

I shall never forget the shock with which I read in the "Scotsman," under "Angling," the following paragraph:

"Tweed.—Strange Death of an Angler.—An unfortunate event has cast a gloom over fishers in this district. As Mr. K-, the keeper on the B- water, was busy angling yesterday, his attention was caught by some object floating on the stream. He cast his flies over it, and landed a soft felt hat, the ribbon stuck full of salmon-flies. Mr. K- at once hurried up-stream, filled with the most lively apprehensions. These were soon justified. In a shallow, below the narrow, deep and dangerous rapids called "The Trows," Mr. K- saw a salmon leaping in a very curious manner. On a closer examination, he found that the fish was attached to a line. About seventy yards higher he found, in shallow water, the body of a man, the hand still grasping in death the butt of the rod, to which the salmon was fast, all the line being run out. Mr. K- at once rushed into the stream, and dragged out the body, in which he recognized with horror the Hon. Houghton Grannom, to whom the water was lately let. Life had been for some minutes extinct, and though Mr. K- instantly hurried for Dr. -, that gentleman could only attest the melancholy fact. The wading in "The Trows" is extremely dangerous and difficult, and Mr. Grannom, who was fond of fishing without an attendant, must have lost his balance, slipped, and been dragged down by the weight of his waders. The recent breaking off of the hon. gentleman's contemplated marriage on the very wedding-day will be fresh in the memory of our readers."

This was the story which I read in the newspaper during breakfast one morning in November. I was deeply grieved, rather than astonished, for I have often remonstrated with poor Grannom on the recklessness of his wading. It was with some surprise that I received, in the course of the day, a letter from him, in which he spoke only of indifferent matters, of the fishing which he had taken, and so forth. The letter was accompanied, however, by a parcel. Tearing off the outer cover, I found a sealed document addressed to me, with the superscription, "Not to be opened until after my father's decease." This injunction, of course, I have scrupulously obeyed. The death of Lord Whitchurch, the last of the Grannoms, now gives me liberty to publish my friend's *Apologia pro morte et vita sua*.

"Dear Smith" (the document begins), "Before you read this—long before, I hope—I shall have solved the great mystery—if, indeed, we solve it. If the water runs down to-morrow, and there is every prospect that it will do so, I must have the opportunity of making such an end as even malignity cannot suspect of being voluntary. There are plenty of fish in the water; if I hook one in "The Trows," I shall let myself go whither the current takes me. Life has for weeks been odious to me; for what is life without honor, without love, and coupled with shame and remorse? Repentance I cannot call the emotion which gnaws me at the heart, for in similar circumstances (unlikely as these are to occur) I feel that I would do the same thing again.

"Are we but automata, worked by springs, moved by the stronger impulse, and unable to choose for ourselves which impulse that shall be? Even now, in decreeing my own destruction, do I exercise free-will, or am I the sport of hereditary tendencies, of mistaken views of honor, of a seeming self-sacrifice, which, perhaps, is but selfishness in disguise? I blight my unfortunate father's old age; I destroy the last of an ancient house; but I remove from the path of Olive Dunne the shadow that must rest upon the sunshine of what will eventually, I trust, be a happy life, unvexed by memories of one who loved her passionately. Dear Olive! how pure, how ardent was my devotion to her none knows better than you. But Olive had, I will not say a fault, though I suffer from it, but a quality, or rather two qualities, which have completed my misery. Lightly as she floats on the stream of society, the most casual observer, and even the enamored beholder, can see that Olive Dunne has great pride, and no sense of humor. Her dignity is her idol. What makes her, even for a moment, the possible theme of ridicule is in her eyes an unpardonable sin. This sin, I must with penitence confess, I did indeed commit. Another woman might have forgiven me. I know not how that may be; I throw myself on the mercy of the court. But, if another could pity and pardon, to Olive this was impossible. I have never seen her since that fatal moment when, paler than her orange blossoms, she swept through the porch of the church, while I, disheveled, mud-stained, half-drowned—ah! that memory will torture me if memory at all remains. And yet, fool, maniac, that I was, I could not resist the wild, mad impulse to laugh which shook the rustic spectators, and which in my case was due, I trust, to hysterical but NOT unmanly emotion. If any woman, any bride, could forgive such an apparent but most unintentional insult, Olive Dunne, I knew, was not that woman. My abject letters of explanation, my appeals for mercy, were returned unopened. Her parents pitied me, perhaps had reasons for being on my side, but Olive was of marble. It is not only myself that she cannot pardon, she will never, I know, forgive herself while my existence reminds her of what she had to endure. When she receives the intelligence of my demise, no suspicion will occur to her; she will not say "He is fitly punished;" but her peace of mind will gradually return.

It is for this, mainly, that I sacrifice myself, but also because I cannot endure the dishonor of a laggard in love and a recreant bridegroom.

So much for my motives: now to my tale.

"The day before our wedding-day had been the happiest in my life. Never had I felt so certain of Olive's affections, never so fortunate in my own. We parted in the soft moonlight; she, no doubt, to finish her nuptial preparations; I, to seek my couch in the little rural inn above the roaring waters of the Budon.

Move eastward, happy earth, and leave
Yon orange sunset fading slow;
From fringes of the faded eve
Oh, happy planet, eastward go,

I murmured, though the atmospheric conditions were not really those described by the poet.

Ah, bear me with thee, smoothly borne,
Dip forward under starry light,
And move me to my marriage morn,
And round again to—

"River in grand order, sir," said the voice of Robins, the keeper, who recognized me in the moonlight. "There's a regular monster in the Ashweil," he added, naming a favorite cast; "never saw nor heard of such a fish in the water before."

"Mr. Dick must catch him, Robins," I answered; "no fishing for me tomorrow."

"No, sir," said Robins, affably. "Wish you joy, sir, and Miss Olive, too. It's a pity, though! Master Dick, he throws a fine fly, but he gets flurried with a big fish, being young. And this one is a topper."

With that he gave me good-night, and I went to bed, but not to sleep. I was fevered with happiness; the past and future reeled before my wakeful vision. I heard every clock strike; the sounds of morning were astir, and still I could not sleep. The ceremony, for reasons connected with our long journey to my father's place in Hampshire, was to be early—half-past ten was the hour. I looked at my watch; it was seven of the clock, and then I looked out of the window: it was a fine, soft grey morning, with a south wind tossing the yellowing boughs. I got up, dressed in a hasty way, and thought I would just take a look at the river. It was, indeed, in glorious order, lapping over the top of the sharp stone which we regarded as a measure of the due size of water.

The morning was young, sleep was out of the question; I could not settle my mind to read. Why should I not take a farewell cast, alone, of course? I always disliked the attendance of a gillie. I took my salmon rod out of its case, rigged it up, and started for the stream, which flowed within a couple of hundred yards of my quarters. There it raced under the ash tree, a pale delicate brown, perhaps a little thing too colored. I therefore put on a large Silver Doctor, and began steadily fishing down the ash-tree cast. What if I should wipe Dick's eye, I thought, when, just where the rough and smooth water meet, there boiled up a head and shoulders such as I had never seen on any fish. My heart leaped and stood still, but there came no sensation from the rod, and I finished the cast, my knees actually trembling beneath me. Then I gently lifted the line, and very elaborately tested every link of the powerful casting-line. Then I gave him ten minutes by my watch; next, with unspeakable emotion, I stepped into the stream and repeated the cast. Just at the same spot he came up again; the huge rod bent like a switch, and the salmon rushed straight down the pool, as if he meant to make for the sea. I staggered on to dry land to follow him the easier, and dragged at my watch to time the fish; a quarter to eight. But the slim chain had broken, and the watch, as I hastily thrust it back, missed my pocket and fell into the water. There was no time to stoop for it; the fish started afresh, tore up the pool as fast as he had gone down it, and, rushing behind the torrent, into the eddy at the top, leaped clean out of the water. He was 70 lbs. if he was an ounce. Here he slackened a little, dropping back, and I got in some line. Now he sulked so intensely that I thought he had got the line round a rock. It might be broken, might be holding fast to a sunken stone, for aught that I could tell; and the time was passing, I knew not how rapidly. I tried all known methods, tugging at him, tapping the butt, and slackening line on him. At last the top of the rod was slightly agitated, and then, back flew the long line in my face. Gone! I reeled up with a sigh, but the line tightened again. He had made a sudden rush under my bank, but there he lay again like a stone. How long? Ah! I cannot tell how long! I heard the church clock strike, but missed the number of the strokes. Soon he started again down-stream into the shallows, leaping at the end of his rush—the monster. Then he came slowly up, and "jiggered" savagely at the line. It seemed impossible that any tackle could stand these short violent jerks. Soon he showed signs of weakening. Once his huge silver side appeared for a moment near the surface, but he retreated to his old fastness. I was in a tremor of delight and despair. I should have thrown down my rod, and flown on the wings of love to Olive and the altar. But I hoped that there was time still—that it was not so very late! At length he was failing. I heard ten o'clock strike. He came up and lumbered on the surface of the pool. Gradually I drew him, plunging ponderously, to the graveled beach, where I meant to "tail" him. He yielded to the strain, he was in the shallows, the line was shortened. I stooped to seize him. The frayed and overworn gut broke at a knot, and with a loose roll he dropped back towards the deep. I sprang at him, stumbled, fell on him, struggled with him, but he slipped from my arms. In that moment I knew more than the anguish of Orpheus. Orpheus! Had I, too, lost my Eurydice? I rushed from the stream, up the steep bank, along to my rooms. I passed the church door. Olive, pale as her orange-blossoms, was issuing from the porch. The clock pointed to 10.45. I was ruined, I knew it, and I laughed. I laughed like a lost spirit. She swept past me, and, amidst the amazement of the gentle and simple, I sped wildly away. Ask me no more. The rest is silence."

Thus ends my hapless friend's narrative. I leave it to the judgment of women and of men. Ladies, would you have acted as Olive Dunne acted? Would pride, or pardon, or mirth have ridden sparkling in your eyes? Men, my brethren, would ye have deserted the salmon for the lady, or the lady for the salmon? I know what I would have done had I been fair Olive Dunne. What I would have done had I been Houghton Grannom I may not venture to divulge. For this narrative, then, as for another, "Let every man read it as he will, and every woman as the gods have given her wit."

# FISH ARE SUCH LIARS!

## ROLAND PERTWEE

There had been a fuss in the pool beneath the alders, and the small rainbow trout, with a skitter of his tail, flashed upstream, a hurt and angry fish. For three consecutive mornings he had taken the rise in that pool, and it injured his pride to be jostled from his drift just when the May fly was coming up in numbers. If his opponent had been a half-pounder like himself, he would have stayed and fought, but when an old hen fish, weighing fully three pounds, with a mouth like a rat hole and a carnivorous, cannibalistic eye rises from the reed beds and occupies the place, flight is the only effective argument.

But Rainbow was very much provoked. He had chosen his place with care. Now the May fly was up, the little French chalk stream was full of rising fish, and he knew by experience that strangers are unpopular in that season. To do one's self justice during a hatch, one must find a place where the fly drifts nicely overhead with the run of the stream, and natural drifts are scarce even in a chalk stream. He was not content to leap at the fly like a hysterical youngster who measured his weight in ounces and his wits in milligrams. He had reached that time of life which demanded that he should feed off the surface by suction rather than exertion. No living thing is more particular about his table manners than a trout, and Rainbow was no exception.

"It's a sickening thing," he said to himself, "and a hard shame." He added: "Get out of my way," to a couple of fat young chug with big mouths who were bubbling the surface in the silly, senseless fashion of their kind.

"Chub indeed!"

But even the chub has a home and he had none—and the life of a homeless river dweller is precarious.

"I will not and shall not be forced back to midstream," he said.

For, save at eventide or in very special circumstances, trout of personality do not frequent open water where they must compete for every insect with the wind, the lightning-swift sweep of swallows and martins, and even the laborious pursuit of predatory dragon-flies with their bronze wings and bodies like rods of colored glass. Even as he spoke he saw a three-ouncer leap at a dapping May fly which was scooped out of his jaws by a passing swallow. Rainbow heard that tiny click as the May fly's body cracked against the bird's beak. A single wing of yellowy gossamer floated downward and settled upon the water. Under the shelving banks to right and left, where the fly, discarding its nymph and still too damp for its virgin flight, drifted downstream, a dozen heavy trout were feeding thoughtfully and selectively.

"If only some angler would catch one of them, I might slip in and occupy the place before it gets known there's a vacancy."

But this uncharitable hope was fulfilled, and with another whisk of his tail he propelled himself into the unknown waters upstream. A couple of strands of rusty barbed wire, relic of the war, spanned the shallows from band to bank. Passing beneath them he came to a narrow reach shaded by willows, to the first of which was nailed a board bearing the words Pêche Réservée. He had passed out of the communal into private water—water running languidly over manes of emerald weed between clumps of alder, willow herb, tall crimson sorrel and masses of yellow iris. Ahead, like an apple-green rampart, rose the wooded heights of a forest; on either side were flat meadows of yellowing hay. Overhead, the vast expanse of blue June sky was tufted with rambling clouds. "My scales!" said Rainbow. "Here's water!"

But it was vain to expect any of the best places in such a reach would be vacant, and to avoid a recurrence of his unhappy encounter earlier in the morning, Rainbow continued his journey until he came to a spot where the river took one of those unaccountable right-angle bends which result in a pool, shallow on the one side, but slanting into deeps on the other. Above it was a water break, a swirl, smoothing, as it reached the pool, into a sleek, swift run, with an eddy which bore all the lighter floating things of the river over the calm surface of the little backwater, sheltered from above by a high shelving bank and a tangle of bramble of herb. Here is this backwater the twig, the broken reed, the leaf, the cork, the fly floated in suspended activity for a few instants until drawn back by invisible magnetism to the main current.

Rainbow paused in admiration. At the tail of the pool two sound fish were rising with regularity, but in the backwater beyond the eddy the surface was still and unbroken. Watching open-eyed, Rainbow saw not one but a dozen May flies, fat, juicy, and damp from the nymph, drift in, pause, and carried away untouched. It was beyond the bounds of possibility that such a place could be vacant, but there was the evidence of his eyes to prove it; and nothing if not a tryer, Rainbow darted across the stream and parked himself six inches below the water to await events.

It so happened that at the time of his arrival the hatch of fly was temporarily suspended, which gave Rainbow leisure to make a survey of his new abode. Beyond the eddy was a submerged snag—the branch of an apple tree borne there by heavy rains, water-logged, anchored, and intricate—an excellent place to break an angler's line. The river bank on his right was riddled under water with old rat holes, than which there is not better sanctuary. Below him and to the left was a dense bed of weeds brushed flat by the flow of the stream.

"If it comes to the worst," said Rainbow, "a smart fish could do a get-away here with very little ingenuity, even from a cannibalistic old hen like—hullo!"

The exclamation was excited by the apparition of a gauzy shadow on the water, which is what a May fly seen from below looks like. Resisting a vulgar inclination to leap at it with the violence of a youngster, Rainbow backed into the correct position which would allow the stream to present the morsel, so to speak, upon a tray. Which it did—and scarcely a dimple on the surface to tell what had happened.

"Very nicely taken, if you will accept the praise of a complete stranger," said a low, soft voice, one inch behind his line of sight.

Without turning to see by whom he had been addressed, Rainbow flicked a yard upstream and came back with the current four feet away. In the spot he had occupied an instant before lay a great old trout of the most benign aspect, who could not have weighed less than four pounds.

"I beg your pardon," said Rainbow, "but I had no idea that any one—that is, I just dropped in en passant, and finding an empty house, I made so bold—"

"There is no occasion to apologize," said Old Trout seductively. "I did not come up from the bottom as early to-day as is my usual habit at this season.

Yesterday's hatch was singularly bountiful and it is possible I did myself too liberally."

"Yes, but a gentleman of your weight and seniority can hardly fail to be offended at finding—"

"Not at all," Old Trout broke in. "I perceive you are a well-conducted fish who does not advertise his appetite in a loud and splashing fashion."

Overcome by the charm of Old Trout's manner and address, Rainbow reduced the distance separating them to a matter of inches.

"Then you do not want me to go?" he asked.

"On the contrary, dear young sir, stay by all means and take the rise. You are, I perceive, of the rainbow or, as they say here in France, of the *Arc-en-ciel* family. As a youngster I had the impression that I should turn out a rainbow, but events proved it was no more than the bloom, the natural sheen of youth."

"To speak the truth, sir," said Rainbow, "unless you had told me to the contrary, I would surely have thought you one of us."

Old Trout shook his tail. "You are wrong," he said. "I am from Dulverton, an English trout farm on the Exe, of which you will have heard. You are doubtless surprised to find an English fish in French waters."

"I am indeed," Rainbow replied, sucking in a passing May fly with such excellent good manners that it was hard to believe he was feeding. "Then you, sir," he added, "must know all about the habits of men."

"I may justly admit that I do," Old Trout agreed. "Apart from being hand-reared, I have in my twelve years of life studied the species in moods of activity, passivity, duplicity, and violence."

Rainbow remarked that such must doubtless have proved of invaluable service. It did not, however, explain the mystery of his presence on a French river.

"For, sir," he added, "Dulverton, as once I heard when enjoying 'A Chat about Rivers,' delivered by a much-traveled sea trout, is situated in the west of England, and without crossing the Channel I am unable to explain how you arrived here. Had you belonged to the salmon family, with which, sir, it is evident you have no connection, the explanation would be simple, but in the circumstances it baffles my understanding."

Old Trout waved one of his fins airily. "Yet cross the Channel I certainly did," said he, "and at a period in history which I venture to state will not readily be forgotten. It was during the war, my dear young friend, and I was brought in a can, in company with a hundred yearlings, to this river, or rather the upper reaches of this river, by a young officer who wished to further an entente between English and French fish even as the war was doing with the mankind of these two nations."

Old Trout sighed a couple of bubbles and arched his body this way and that.

"There was a gentleman and a sportsman," he said. "A man who was acquainted with our people as I dare to say very few are acquainted. Had it ever been my lot to fall victim to a lover of the rod, I could have done so without regret to his. If you will take a look at my tail, you will observe that the letter W is perforated on the upper side. He presented me with this distinguishing mark before committing me, with his blessing, to the water."

"I have seldom seen a tail more becomingly decorated," said Rainbow. "But what happened to your benefactor?"

Old Trout's expression became infinitely sad. "If I could answer that," said he, "I were indeed a happy trout. For many weeks after he put me into the river I used to watch him in what little spare time he was able to obtain, casting a dry fly with the exquisite precision and likeness to nature in all the likely pools and runs and eddies near his battery position. Oh, minnows! It was a pleasure to watch that man, even as it was his pleasure to watch us. His bravery, too! I call to mind a dozen times when he fished unmoved and un-startled while bullets from machine guns were packing at the water like herons and thudding into the mud banks upon which he stood."

"An angler!" remarked Rainbow. "It would be no lie to say I like him the less on that account."

Old Trout became unexpectedly stern.

"Why so?" he retorted severely. "Have I not said he was also a gentleman and a sportsman? My officer was neither a pot-hunter nor a beast of prey. He was a purist—a man who took delight in pitting his knowledge of nature against the subtlest and most suspicious intellectual forces of the wild. Are you so young as not yet to have learned the exquisite enjoyment of escaping disaster and avoiding error by the exercise of personal ingenuity? Pray, do not reply, for I would hate to think so hard a thing of any trout. We as a race exist by virtue of our brilliant intellectuality and hypersensitive selectivity. In waters where there are no pike and only an occasional otter, but for the machinations of men, where should we turn to school our wits? Danger is our mainstay, for I tell you, Rainbow, that trout are composed of two senses—appetite, which makes of us fools, and suspicion, which teaches us to be wise."

Greatly chastened not alone by what Old Trout had said but by the forensic quality of his speech, Rainbow rose short and put a promising May fly onto the wing.

"I am glad to observe," said Old Trout, "that you are not without conscience."

"To tell you the truth, sir," Rainbow replied apologetically, "my nerve this morning has been rudely shaken, but for which I should not have shown such want of good sportsmanship."

And with becoming brevity he told the tale of his eviction form the pool downstream. Old Trout listened gravely, only once moving, and that to absorb a small blue dun, an insect which he keenly relished.

"A regrettable affair," he admitted, "but as I have often observed, women, who are the gentlest creatures under water in adversity, are a thought lacking in moderation in times of abundance. They are apt to snatch."

"But for a turn of speed, she would certainly have snatched me," said Rainbow.

"Very shocking," said Old Trout. "Cannibals are disgusting. They destroy the social amenities of the river. We fish have but little family life and should therefore aim to cultivate a freemasonry of good-fellowship among ourselves. For my part, I am happy to line up with other well-conducted trout and content myself with what happens along with my own particular drift. Pardon me!" he added, breasting Rainbow to one side. "I invited you to take the rise of May fly, but I must ask you to leave the duns alone." Then, fearing this remark might be construed to reflect adversely upon his hospitality, he proceeded: "I have a reason which I will explain later. For the moment we are discussing the circumstances that led to my presence in this river."

"To be sure—your officer. He never succeeded in deluding you with his skill?"

"That would have been impossible," said Old Trout, "for I had taken up a position under the far bank where he could only have reached me with a fly by wading in a part of the river which was in view of a German sniper."

"Wily!" Rainbow chuckled. "Cunning work, sir."

"Perhaps," Old Trout admitted, "although I have since reproached myself with cowardice. However, I was at the time a very small fish and a certain amount of nervousness is forgivable in the young."

At this gracious acknowledgement the rose-colored hue in Rainbow's rainbow increased noticeably—in short, he blushed.

"From where I lay," Old Trout went on, "I was able to observe the maneuvers of my officer and greatly profit thereby."

"But excuse me, sir," said Rainbow, "I have heard it said that an angler of the first class is invisible from the river."

"He is invisible to the fish he is trying to catch," Old Trout admitted, "but it must be obvious that he is not invisible to the fish who lie beside or below him. I would also remind you that during the war every tree, every scrap of vegetation, and every vestige of natural cover had been torn up, trampled down, razed. The river banks were as smooth as the top of your head. Even the buttercup, that very humorous flower that tangles up the back cast of so many industrious anglers, was absent. Those who fished on the Western Front had little help from nature."

Young Rainbow sighed, for, only a few days before, his tongue had been badly scratched by an artificial alder which had every appearance of reality.

"It would seem," he said, "that this war had its merits."

"My young friend," said Old Trout, "you never made a greater mistake. A desire on the part of our soldiery to vary a monotonous diet of bully beef and biscuit often drove them to resort to villainous methods of assault against our kind."

"Nets?" gasped Rainbow in horror.

"Worse than nets—bombs," Old Trout replied. "A small oval black thing called a Mills bomb, which the shameless fellows flung into deep pools."

"But surely the chances of being hit by such a—"

"You reveal a pathetic ignorance," said Old Trout. "There is no question of being hit. The wretched machine exploded under water and burst our people's insides or stunned us so that we floated dead to the surface. I well remember my officer coming upon such a group of marauders one evening—yes, and laying about him with his fists in defiance of King's Regulations and the Manual of Military Law. Two of them he seized by the collar and the pants and flung into the river. Spinning minnow, that was a sight worth seeing! 'You low swine,' I heard him say; 'you trash, you muck! Isn't there enough carnage without this sort of thing?' Afterward he sat on the bank with the two dripping men and talked to them for their soul's sake.

"'Look ahead, boys. Ask yourselves what are we fighting for? Decent homes to live in at peace with one another, fields to till and forests and rivers to give us a day's sport and fun. It's our rotten job to massacre each other, but, by gosh, don't let's massacre the harmless rest of nature as well. At least, let's give 'em a running chance. Boys, in the years ahead, when all the mess is cleared up, I look forward to coming back to this old spot, when there is alder growing by the banks, and willow herb and all reeds and the drone of insects instead of the rumble of those guns. I don't want to come back to a dead river that I helped to kill, but to a river ringed with rising fish—some of whom were old comrades of the war.' He went on to tell of us hundred Dulverton trout that he had marked with the letter W. 'Give 'em their chance,' he said, 'and in the years to come those beggars will reward us a hundred times over. They'll give us a finer thrill and put up a cleaner fight than old Jerry ever contrived.' Those were emotional times, and though you may be reluctant to believe me, one of those two very wet men dripped water from his eyes as well as his clothing.

"'Many's the 'appy afternoon I've 'ad with a roach pole on Brentford Canal,' he sniffed, 'though I've never yet tried m' hand against a trout.' 'You shall do it now,' said my officer, and during the half-hour that was left of daylight that dripping soldier had his first lesson in the most delicate art in the world. I can see them now—the clumsy, wet fellow and my officer timing him, timing him— 'one and two, and one and two, and—' The action of my officer's wrist with its persuasive flick was the prettiest thing I have ever seen."

"Did he carry out his intention and come back after the war?" Rainbow asked.

"I shall never know," Old Trout replied. "I do not even know if he survived it. There was a great battle—a German drive. For hours they shelled the river front, and many falling short exploded in our midst with terrible results. My own bank was torn to shreds and our people suffered. How they suffered! About noon the infantry came over—hordes in field gray. There were pontoons, rope bridges and hand-to-hand fights on both banks and even in the stream itself."

"And your officer?"

"I saw him once, before the water was stamped dense into liquid mud and dyed by the blood of men. He was in the thick of it, unarmed, and a German officer called on him to surrender. For answer he struck him in the face with a light cane. Ah, that wrist action! Then a shell burst, smothering the water with clods of fallen earth and other things."

"Then you never knew?"

"I never knew, although that night I searched among the dead. Next day I went downstream, for the water in that place was polluted with death. The bottom of the pool in which I had my place was chocked with strange and mangled tenants that were not good to look upon. We trout are a clean people that will not readily abide in dirty houses. I am a Dulverton trout, where the water is filtered by the hills and runs cool over stones."

"And you have stayed here ever since?"

Old Trout shrugged a fin. "I have moved with the times. Choosing a place according to the needs of my weight."

"And you have never been caught, sir, by any other angler?"

"Am I not here?" Old Trout answered with dignity.

"Oh, quite, sir. I had only thought, perhaps, as a younger fish enthusiasm might have resulted to your disadvantage, but that, nevertheless, you had been returned."

"Returned! Returned!" echoed Old Trout. "Returned to the frying-pan! Where on earth did you pick up that expression? We are in France, my young friend; we are not on the Test, the Itchen, or the Kennet. In this country it is not the practice of anglers to return anything, however miserable in size."

"But nowadays," Rainbow protested, "there are Englishmen and Americans on the river who show us more consideration."

"They may show you more consideration," said Old Trout, "but I am of an importance that neither asks for nor expects it. Oblige me by being a little more discreet with your plurals. In the impossible event of my being deceived and caught, I should be introduced to a glass case with an appropriate background of rocks and reeds."

"But, sir, with respect, how can you be so confident of our unassailability?" Rainbow demanded, edging into position to accept an attractive May fly with yellow wings that was drifting downstream toward him.

"How?" Old Trout responded. "Because—" Then suddenly: "Leave it, you fool!"

Rainbow had just broken the surface when the warning came. They yellow-winged May fly was wrenched off the water with a wet squeak. A tangle of limp cast lapped itself round the upper branches of a willow far upstream and a raw voice exclaimed something venomous in French. By common consent the two fish went down.

"Well, really," expostulated Old Trout, "I hoped you were above that kind of thing! Nearly to fall victim to a downstream angler. It's a little too much! And think of the effect it will have on my prestige. Why, that incompetent fool will go about boasting that he rose me. Me!"

For some minutes Rainbow was too crestfallen even to apologize. At last: "I am afraid," he said, "I was paying more heed to what you were saying than to my own conduct. I never expected to be fished from above. The fly was on uncommonly good imitation and it is a rare thing for a Frenchman to use Four-X gut."

"Rubbish," said Old Trout testily. "These are mere half-pound arguments. Four-X gut, when associated with a fourteen-stone shadow, should deceive nothing over two ounces. I saved your life, but it is all very provoking. If that is a sample of your general demeanor, it is improbable that you will ever reach a pound."

"At this season we are apt to be careless," Rainbow wailed. "And nowadays it is so hard, sir, to distinguish the artificial fly from the real."

"No one expects you to do so," was the answer, "but common prudence demands that you should pay some attention to the manner in which it is presented. A May fly does not hit the water with a splash, neither is it able to sustain itself in midstream against the current. Have you ever seen a natural insect leave a broadening wake of cutwater behind its tail? Never mind the fly, my dear boy, but watch the manner of its presentation. Failure to do that has cost many of our people their lives."

"You speak," said Rainbow, a bit sulkily, "as though it were a disgrace for a trout ever to suffer defeat at the hands of an angler."

"Which indeed it is, save in exceptional circumstances," Old Trout answered. "I do not say that a perfect upstream cast from a well-concealed angler, when the fly alights dry and cocked and dances at even speed with the current, may not deceive us to our fall. And I would be the last to say that a grasshopper skillfully dapped on the surface through the branches of an overhanging tree will inevitably bring about our destruction. But I do most emphatically say that in such a spot as this, where the slightest defect in presentation is multiplied a hundredfold by the varying water speeds, a careless rise is unpardonable. There is only one spot—and that a matter of twelve yards downstream—from which a fly can be drifted over me with any semblance to nature. Even so, there is not one angler in a thousand who can make that cast with success, by reason of a willow which cramps the back cast and the manner in which these alders on our left sprawl across the pool."

Rainbow did not turn about to verify these statements because it is bad form for a trout to face downstream. He contented himself by replying, with a touch of acerbity: "I should have thought, sir, with the feelings you expressed regarding sportsmanship, you would have found such a sanctuary too dull for your entertainment."

"Every remark you make serves to aggravate the impression of your ignorance," Old Trout replied. "Would you expect a trout of my intelligence to put myself in some place where I am exposed to the vulgar assaults of every amateur upon the bank? Of the green boy who lashes the water into foam, of the purblind peasant who slings his fly at me with a clod of earth or a tail of weed attached to the hood? In this place I invite attention from none but the best people—the expert, the purist."

"I understood you to say that there were none such in these parts," grumbled Rainbow.

"There are none who have succeeded in deceiving me," was the answer. "As a fact, for the last few days I have been vastly entranced by an angler who, by any standard, is deserving of praise. His presentation is flawless and the only fault I can detect in him is a tendency to overlook piscine psychology. He will be with us in a few minutes, since he knows it is my habit to lunch at noon."

"Pardon the interruption," said Rainbow, "but there is a gallant hatch of fly going down. I can hear your two neighbors at the tail of the pool rising steadily."

Old Trout assumed an indulgent air. "We will go up if you wish," said he, "but you will be well advised to observe my counsel before taking the rise, because if my angler keeps his appointment you will most assuredly be meunièred before nightfall."

At this unpleasant prophecy Rainbow shivered. "Let us keep to weed," he suggested.

But Old Trout only laughed, so that bubbles from the river bed rose and burst upon the surface.

"Courage," said he; "it will be an opportunity for you to learn the finer points of the game. If you are nervous, lie nearer to the bank. The natural fly does not drift there so abundantly, but you will be secure from the artificial. Presently I will treat you to an exhibition of playing with death you will not fail to appreciate." He broke off and pointed with his eyes. "Over you and to the left."

Rainbow made a neat double rise and drifted back into line. "Very mellow," he said—"very mellow and choice. Never tasted better. May I ask, sir, what do you mean by piscine psychology?"

"I imply that my angler does not appreciate the subtle possibilities of our intellect. Now, my officer concerned himself as vitally with what we were thinking as with what we were feeding upon. This fellow, secure in the knowledge that this presentation is well-nigh perfect, is content to offer me the same variety of flies day after day, irrespective of that fact that I have learned them all by heart. I have, however, adopted the practice of rising ever now and then to encourage him."

"Rising? At an artificial fly? I never heard such temerity in all my life," gasped Rainbow.

Old Trout moved his body luxuriously. "I should have said, appearing to rise," he amended. "You may have noticed that I have exhibited a predilection for small duns in preference to the larger Ephemeridae. My procedure is as follows: I wait until a natural dun and his artificial May fly are drifting downstream with the smallest possible distance separating them. Then I rise and take the dun. Assuming I have risen to him, he strikes, misses, and is at once greatly flattered and greatly provoked. By this device I sometimes occupy his attention for over an hour and thus render a substantial service to others of my kind who would certainly have fallen victim to his skill."

"The river is greatly in your debt, sir," said Young Rainbow, with deliberate satire.

He knew by experience that fish as well as anglers are notorious liars, but the exploit his host recounted was a trifle too strong. Taking a sidelong glance, he was surprised to see that Old Trout did not appear to have appreciated the subtle ridicule of his remark. The long, lithe body had become almost rigid and the great round eyes were focused upon the surface with an expression of fixed concentration.

Looking up, Rainbow saw a small white-winged May fly with red legs and a body the color of straw swing out from the main stream and describe a slow circle over the clam surface above Old Trout's head. Scarcely an inch away a tiny blue dun, its wings folded as closely as the pages of a book, floated attendant. An upward rush, a sucking kerr-rop, and when the broken water had calmed, the dun had disappeared and the May fly was dancing away downstream.

"Well," said Old Trout, "how's that, my youthful skeptic? Pretty work, eh?"

"I saw nothing in it," was the impertinent reply. "There is not a trout on the river who could not have done likewise."

"Even when one of those two flies was artificial?" Old Trout queried tolerantly.

"But neither of them was artificial," Rainbow retorted. "Had it been so, the angler would have struck. They always do."

"Of course he struck," Old Trout replied.

"But he didn't," Rainbow protested. "I saw the May fly go down with the current."

"My poor fish!" Old Trout replied. "Do you presume to suggest that I am unable to distinguish an artificial from a natural fly? Are you so blind that you failed to see the prismatic colors in the water from the paraffin in which the fly had been dipped? Here you are! Here it is again!"

Once more the white-winged insect drifted across the backwater, but this time there was no attendant dun.

"If that's a fake I'll eat my tail," said Rainbow.

"If you question my judgment," Old Trout answered, "you are at liberty to rise. I dare say, in spite of a shortage of brain, that you would eat comparatively well."

But Rainbow, in common with his kind, was not disposed to take chances.

"We may expect two or three more casts from this fly and then he will change it for a bigger. It is the same program every day without a variation. How differently my officer would have acted. By now he would have discovered my little joke and turned the tables against me. Aye me, but some men will never learn! Your mental outfit, dear Rainbow, is singularly like a man's," he added. "It lacks elasticity."

Rainbow made no retort and was glad of his forbearance, for every word Old Trout had spoken was borne out by subsequent events. Four times the white-winged May fly described an arc over the backwater, but in the absence of duns Old Trout did not rise again. Then came a pause, during which, through a lull in the hatch, even the natural insect was absent from the river.

"He is changing his fly," said Old Trout, "but he will not float it until the hatch starts again. He is casting beautifully this morning and I hope circumstances will permit me to give him another rise."

"But suppose," said Rainbow breathlessly, "you played this game once too often and were foul hooked as a result?"

Old Trout expanded his gills broadly. "Why, then," he replied, "I should break him. Once round a limb of that submerged apple bough and the thing would be done. I should never allow myself to be caught and no angler could gather up the slack and haul me into midstream in time to prevent me reaching the bough. Stand by."

The shadow of a large, dark May fly floated cockily over the backwater and had almost returned to the main stream when a small iron-blue dun settled like a puff of thistledown in its wake.

The two insects were a foot nearer the fast water than the spot where Old Trout was accustomed to take the rise. But for the presence of a spectator, it is doubtful whether he would have done so, but Young Rainbow's want of appreciation had excited his vanity, and with a rolling swoop he swallowed the dun and bore it downward.

And then an amazing thing happened. Instead of drifting back to his place as was expected, Old Trout's head was jerked sideways by an invisible force. A thin translucent thread upcut the water's surface and tightened irresistibly. A second later Old Trout was fighting, fighting, fighting to reach the submerged apple bough with the full weight of the running water and the full strength of the finest Japanese gut strained against him.

Watching, wide-eyed and aghast, from one of the underwater rat holes into which he has hastily withdrawn, Rainbow saw the figure of a man rise out of a bed of irises downstream and scramble upon the bank. In his right hand, with the wrist well back, he held a light split-cane rod whose upper joint was curved to a half-circle. The man's left hand was detaching a collapsible landing net from the ring of his belt. Every attitude and movement was expressive of perfectly organized activity. His mouth was shut as tightly as a steel trap, but a light of happy excitement danced in his eyes.

"No, you don't, my fellar," Rainbow heard him say. "No, you don't. I knew all about that apple bough before ever I put a fly over your pool. And the weed bed on the right," he added, as Old Trout made a sudden swerve half down and half across stream.

Tucking the net under his arm the man whipped up the slack with a light-ning-like action. The maneuver cost Old Trout dear, for when, despairing of reaching the weed and burrowing into it, he tried to regain his old position, he found himself six feet farther away from the apple bough than when the battle began.

Instinctively Old Trout knew it was useless to dash downstream, for a man who could take up slack with the speed his adversary had shown would profit by the expedient to come more quickly to term with him. Besides, lower down there was broken water to knock the breath out of his lungs even where he lay straining and slugging this way and that, the water was pouring so fast into his open mouth as nearly to drown him. His only chance of effecting a smash was by a series of jumps, followed by quick dives. Once before, although he had not confessed it to Rainbow, Old Trout had saved his life by resorting to this expe-dient. It takes the strain off the line and returns it so quickly that even the finest gut is apt to sunder.

Meanwhile, the man was slowly approaching, winding up as he came. Old Trout, boring in the depths, could hear the click of the check reel with increasing distinctness. Looking up, he saw that the cast was almost vertical above his head, which meant that the moment to make the attempt was at hand. The tension was appalling, for ever since the fight began his adversary had given him the butt unremittingly. Aware of his own weight and power, Old Trout was amazed that any tackle could stand the strain.

"Now's my time," he thought, and jumped.

It was no ordinary jump, but an aerial rush three feet out of the water, with a twist at its apex and a cutting lash of the tail designed to break the cast. But his adversary was no ordinary angler, and at the first hint of what was happening he dropped the point of the rod flush with the surface.

Once and once more Old Trout flung himself into the air, but after each attempt he found himself with diminishing strength and with less line to play with.

"It looks to me," said Rainbow mournfully, "as if my unhappy host will lose this battle and finish up in that glass case to which he was referring a few minutes ago." And greatly affected, he burrowed his nose in the mud and wondered, in the event of this dismal prophecy coming true, whether he would be able to take possession of the pool without molestation.

In consequence of these reflections he failed to witness the last phase of the battle when, as will sometimes happen with big fish, all the fight went out of Old Trout, and rolling wearily over and over, he abandoned himself to the clinging embraces of the net. He never saw the big man proudly carry Old Trout back into the hayfield, where, before proceeding to remove the fly, he sat down beside a shallow dike and lit a cigarette and smiled largely. Then, with an affectionate and professional touch, he picked up Old Trout by the back of the neck, his forefinger and thumb sunk firmly in the gills.

"You're a fine fellar," he said, extracting the fly; "a good sportsman and a funny fish. You fooled me properly for three days, but I think you'll own I outwitted you in the end."

Rummaging in his creel for a small rod of hard wood that he carried for the purpose of administering the quietus, he became aware of something that arrested the action. Leaning forward, he stared with open eyes at a tiny W perforated in the upper part of Old Trout's tail.

"Shades of the war! Dulverton!" he exclaimed. Then with a sudden warmth: "Old chap, old chap, is it really you? This is red-letter stuff. If you're not too far gone to take another lease of life, have it with me."

And with the tenderness of a woman, he slipped Old Trout into the dike and in a tremble of excitement hurried off to the auberge where the fishermen lodged, to tell a tale no one even pretended to believe.

For the best part of an hour Old Trout lay in the shallow waters of the dike before slowly cruising back to his own place beneath the overhanging bank. The alarming experience through which he had passed had made him a shade forgetful, and he was not prepared for the sight of Young Rainbow rising steadily at the hatch of fly.

"Pardon me, but a little more to your right," he said, with heavy courtesy.

"Diving otters!" cried Young Rainbow, leaping a foot clear of the water. "You, sir! You!"

"And why not?" Old Trout replied. "Your memory must be short if you have already forgotten that this is my place."

"Yes, but—" Rainbow began and stopped.

"You are referring to that little circus of a few minutes ago," said Old Trout. "It is possible you failed to appreciate the significance of the affair? I knew at once it was my dear officer when he dropped the artificial dun behind the natural May fly. In the circumstances I could hardly do less than accept his invitation. Nothing is more delightful than a reunion of comrades of the war." He paused and added: "We had a charming talk, he and I, and I do not know which of us was the more affected. It is a tragedy that such friendship and such intellect as we share cannot exist in common element."

And so great was his emotion that Old Trout dived and buried his head in the weeds. Whereby Rainbow did uncommonly well during the midday hatch.

# A WEDDING GIFT

## JOHN TAINTOR FOOTE

George Baldwin Potter is a purist. That is to say, he either takes trout on a dry fly or he does not take them at all. He belongs to a number of fishing clubs, any member of which might acquire his neighbor's wife, beat his children, or poison a dog and still cast a fly, in all serenity, upon club waters; but should he impale on a hook a lowly though succulent worm and immerse the creature in those same waters it would be better that he send in his resignation at once, sooner than face the shaken committee that would presently wait upon him.

George had become fixed in my mind as a bachelor. This, of course, was a mistake. I am continually forgetting that purists rush into marriage when approaching or having just passed the age of forty. The psychology of this is clear.

For twenty years, let us say, a purist's life is completely filled by his efforts to convert all reasonable men to his own particular method of taking trout. He thinks, for example, that a man should not concern himself with more than a dozen types of standard flies. The manner of presenting them is the main consideration. Take any one of these flies, then, and place, by means of an eight-foot rod, a light, tapered line, and a mist-colored leader of reasonable length, on fast water—if you want trout. Of course, if you want to listen to the birds and look at the scenery, fish the pools with a long line and an eight-foot leader. Why, it stands to reason that—

The years go by as he explains these vital facts patiently, again and again, to Smith and Brown and Jones. One wet, cold spring, after fighting a muddy stream all day, he re-explains for the better part of an evening and takes himself, somewhat wearily upstairs. The damp and chill of the room at whatever club he may be fishing is positively tomblike. He can hear the rain drumming on the roof and swishing against the windows. The water will be higher than ever tomorrow, he reflects, as he puts out the lights and slides between the icy sheets. Steeped to the soul in cheerless dark, he recalls numbly that when he first met Smith and Brown and Jones they were fishing the pools with a long line. That was, let's see—fifteen—eighteen—twenty years ago. Then he must be forty. It isn't possible! Yes, it is a fact that Smith and Brown and Jones are still fishing the pools with a long line.

In the first faint light of dawn he falls into an uneasy, muttering slumber. The dark hours between have been devoted to intense thought and a variety of wiggles which have not succeeded in keeping the bedclothes against his shoulder blades.

Some time within the next six months you will remember that you have forgotten to send him a wedding present.

George, therefore, having arrived at his fortieth birthday, announced his engagement shortly thereafter. Quite by chance I ran across his bride-to-be and himself a few days before the ceremony, and joined them at lunch. She was a blonde in the early twenties, with wide blue eyes and a typical rose-and-white complexion. A rushing, almost breathless account of herself, which she began the moment we were seated, was curious, I thought. It was as though she feared an interruption at any moment. I learned that she was an only child, born and reared in Greater New York; that her family had recently moved to New Rochell; that she had been shopping madly for the past two weeks; that she was nearly dead, but that she had some adorable things.

At this point George informed me that they would spend their honeymoon at a certain fishing club in Maine. He then proceeded to describe the streams and lakes in that section at some length-during the rest of the luncheon, as a matter of fact. His fiancée, who had fallen into a wordless abstraction, only broke her silence with a vague murmur as we parted.

Owing to this meeting I did not forget to send a wedding present. I determined that my choice should please both George and his wife through the happy years to come.

If I had had George to consider, I could have settled the business in two minutes at a sporting-goods store. Barred from these for obvious reasons, I spent a long day in a thoroughly exhausting search. Late in the afternoon I decided to abandon my hopeless task. I had made a tremendous effort and failed. I would simply buy a silver doodad and let it go at that.

As I staggered into a store with the above purpose in view, I passed a show case devoted to fine china, and halted as my eyes fell on a row of fish plates backed by artfully rumpled blue velvet. The plates proved to be hand painted. On each plate was one of the different varieties of trout, curving up through green depths to an artificial fly just dropping on the surface of the water.

In an automatic fashion I indicated the plates to a clerk, paid for them, gave him my card and the address, and fled from the store. Some time during the next twenty-four hours it came to me that George Potter was not among my nearest and dearest. Yet the unbelievable sum I had left with that clerk in exchange for those fish plates could be justified in no other way.

I thought this fact accounted for the sort of frenzy with which George flung himself upon me when next we met, some two months later. I had been week-ending in the country and encountered him in the Grand Central Station as I emerged from the lower level. For a long moment he wrung my hand in silence, gazing almost feverishly into my face. At last he spoke:

"Have you got an hour to spare?"

It occurred to me that it would take George an hour at least to describe his amazed delight at the splendor of my gift. The clock above Information showed that it was 12:45. I therefore suggested that we lunch together.

He, too, glanced at the clock, verified its correctness by his watch, and seized me by the arm.

"All right," he agreed, and was urging me toward the well-filled and some-what noisy station café before I grasped his intention and tried to suggest that we go elsewhere. His hand only tightened on my arm.

"It's all right," he said; "good food, quick service—you'll like it."

He all but dragged me into the café and steered me to a table in the corner. I lifted my voice above an earnest clatter of gastronomical utensils and made a last effort.

"The Biltmore's just across the street."

George pressed me into my chair, shoved a menu card at me and addressed the waiter.

"Take his order." Here he jerked out his watch and consulted it again. "We have forty-eight minutes. Service for one. I shan't be eating anything; or, no—bring me some coffee—large cup—black."

Having ordered mechanically, I frankly stared at George. He was dressed, I now observed, with unusual care. He wore a rather dashing gray suit. His tie, which was an exquisite shade of gray-blue, was embellished by a handsome pearl. The handkerchief, appearing above his breast pocket, was of the same delicate gray-blue shade as the tie. His face had been recently and closely shaven, also powdered; but above that smooth whiteness of jowl was a pair of curiously glittering eyes and a damp, beaded brow. This he now mopped with his napkin.

"Good God," said I, "what is it, George?"

His reply was to extract a letter from his inside coat pocket and pass it across the table, his haunted eyes on mine. I took in its few lines at a glance:

"Father has persuaded me to listen to what you call your explanation. I arrive Grand Central 2:45, daylight saving, Monday." Isabelle.

Poor old George, I thought; some bachelor indiscretion; and now, with his honeymoon scarcely over, blackmail, a lawsuit, heaven only knows what.

"Who," I asked, returning the letter, "is Isabelle?"

To my distress, George again resorted to his napkin. Then, "My wife," he said.

"Your wife!"

George nodded.

"Been living wither people for the last month. Wish he'd bring that coffee. You don't happen to have a flask with you?"

"Yes, I have a flask." George brightened. "But it's empty. Do you want to tell me about your trouble? Is that why you brought me here?"

"Well, yes," George admitted. "But the point is—will you stand by me? That's the main thing. She gets in"—here he consulted his watch—"in forty-five minutes, if the train's on time." A sudden panic seemed to seize him. His hand shot across the table and grasped my wrist. "You've got to stand by me, old man—act as if you knew nothing. Say you ran into me here and stayed to meet her. I'll tell you what—say I didn't seem to want you to stay. Kid me about wanting her all to myself, or something like that. Get the point? It'll give me a chance to sort of—well, you understand."

"I see what you mean, of course," I admitted. "Here's your coffee. Suppose you have some and then tell me what this is all about—if you care to, that is."

"No sugar, no cream," said George to the waiter; "just pour it. Don't stand there waving it about—pour it, pour it!" He attempted to swallow a mouthful of steaming coffee, gurgled frightfully and grabbed his water glass. "Great jumping Jehoshaphat!" he gasped, when he could speak, and glared at the waiter, who promptly moved out into the sea of diners and disappeared among a dozen of his kind.

"Steady, George," I advised as I transferred a small lump of ice from my glass to his coffee cup.

George watched the ice dissolve, murmured "Idiot" several times, and presently swallowed the contents of the cup in two gulps.

"I had told her," he said suddenly, "exactly where we were going. She mentioned Narragansett several times—I'll admit that. Imagine—Narragansett! Of course I bought her fishing things myself. I didn't buy knickers or woolens or flannel shirts—naturally. You don't go around buying a girl breeches and underwear before you're married. It wouldn't be—well, it isn't done, that's all. I got her the sweetest three-ounce rod you ever held in your hand. I'll bet I could put out sixty feet of line with it against the wind. I got her a pair of English waders that didn't weigh a pound. They cost me forty-five dollars. The rest of the outfit was just as good. Why, her fly box was a Truxton. I could have bought an American imitation for eight dollars. I know a lot of men who'll buy leaders for themselves at two dollars apiece and let their wives fish with any kind of tackle. I'll give you my word I'd have used anything I got for her myself. I sent it all out to be packed with her things. I wanted her to feel that it was her own—not mine. I know a lot of men who give their wives a high-class rod or an imported reel and then fish with it themselves. What time is it?"

"Clock right up there," I said. But George consulted his watch and used his napkin distressingly again.

"Where was I?"

"You were telling me why you sent her fishing things out to her."

"Oh, yes! That's all of that. I simply wanted to show you that from the first I did all any man could do. Ever been in the Cuddiwink district?"

I said that I had not.

"You go in from Buck's Landing. A lumber tug takes you up to the head of Lake Owonga. Club guides meet you there and put you through in one day—twenty miles by canoe and portage up the west branch of the Penobscot; then nine miles by trail to Lost Pond. The club's on Lost Pond. Separate cabins, with a main dining and loafing camp, and the best squaretail fishing on earth—both lake and stream. Of course, I don't fish the lakes. A dry fly belongs on a stream and nowhere else. Let me make it perfectly clear."

George's manner suddenly changed. He hunched himself closer to the table, dropped an elbow upon it and lifted an expository finger.

"The dry fly," he stated, with a new almost combative ring in his voice, "is designed primarily to simulate not only the appearance of the natural insect but its action as well. This action is arrived at through the flow of the current. The moment you move a fly by means of leader you destroy the—

I saw that an interruption was imperative.

"Yes, of course," I said; "but your wife will be here in—"

It was pitiful to observe George. His new-found assurance did not flee—flee suggests a withdrawal, however swift—it was immediately and totally annihilated. He attempted to pour himself some coffee, take out his watch, look at the clock, and mop his brow with his napkin at one and the same instant.

"You were telling me how to get to Lost Pond," I suggested.

"Yes, to be sure," said George. "Naturally you go in light. The things you absolutely have to have—rods, tackle, waders, wading shoes, and so forth, are about all a guide can manage at the portages in addition to the canoe. You pack in extras yourself—change of underclothes, a couple of pairs of socks, and a few toilet articles. You leave a bag or trunk at Buck's Landing. I explained this to her. I explained it carefully. I told her either a week-end bag or one small trunk. Herb Trescott was my best man. I left everything to him. He saw us on the train and handed me tickets and reservations just before we pulled out. I didn't notice in the excitement of getting away that he'd given me three trunk checks all stamped 'Excess.' I didn't notice it till the conductor showed up, as a matter of fact. Then I said, 'Darling, what in heaven's name have you brought three trunks for?' She said—I can remember her exact words—'Then you're not going to Narragansett?'

"I simply looked at her. I was too dumbfounded to speak. At last I pulled myself together and told her in three days we'd be whipping the best squaretail water in the world. I took her hand, I remember, and said, 'You and I together, sweetheart,' or something like that."

George sighed and lapsed into a silence which remained unbroken until his eye happened to encounter the face of the clock. He started and went on:

"We got to Buck's Landing, but way of Bangor, at six in the evening of the following day. Buck's Landing is a railroad station with grass growing between the ties, a general store and hotel combined, and a lumber wharf. The store keeps canned peas, pink-and-white candy, and felt boots. The hotel part is—well, it doesn't matter except that I don't think I ever saw so many deer heads; a few stuffed trout but mostly deer heads. After supper the proprietor and I got the three trunks up to the largest room: We just go them in and that was all. The tug left for the head of the lake at seven next morning. I explained this to Isabelle. I said we'd leave the trunks there until we came out, and offered to help her unpack the one her fishing things were in. She said, 'Please go away!' So I went away. I got out a rod and went down to the wharf. No trout there, I knew; but I thought I'd limber up my wrist. I put on a Cahill Number Fourteen—or was it Sixteen—"

George knitted his brows and stared intently but unseeingly at me for some little time.

"Call it a Sixteen," I suggested.

George shook his head impatiently and remained concentrated in thought.

"I'm inclined to think it was a Fourteen," he said at last. "But let it go; it'll come to me later. At any rate, the place was alive with big chub—a foot long, some of 'em. I'll bet I took fifty—threw 'em back, of course. They kept on rising after it got dark. I'd tell myself I'd go after one more cast. Each time I'd hook a big chub, and—well, you know how the time slips away.

"When I got back to the hotel all the lights were out. I lit matches until I got upstairs and found the door to the room. I'll never forget what I saw when I opened that door—never! Do you happen to know how many of the kind of things they wear a woman can get into one trunk? Well, she had three and she'd unpacked them all. She had used the bed for the gowns alone. It was piled with them—literally piled; but that wasn't a starter. Everywhere you looked was a stack of things with ribbons in 'em. There were enough shoes and stockings for a girl's school; silk stockings, mind you, and high-heeled shoes and slippers." Here George consulted clock and watch. "I wonder if that train's on time," he wanted to know.

"You have thirty-five minutes, even if it is," I told him; "go right ahead."

"Well, I could see something was wrong from her face. I didn't know what, but I started right in to cheer her up. I told her all about the chub fishing I'd been having. At last she burst into tears. I won't go into the scene that followed. I'd ask her what was the matter and she'd say, 'Nothing,' and cry frightfully. I know a lot of men who would have lost their tempers under the circumstances, but I didn't; I give you my word. I simply said, 'There, there,' until she quieted down. And that isn't all. After a while she began to show me her gowns. Imagine—at eleven o'clock at night, at Buck's Landing! She'd hold up a dress and look over the top of it at me and ask me how I liked it, and I'd say it was all right. I know a lot of men who wouldn't have sat there two minutes.

"At last I said, 'They're all all right, darling,' and yawned. She was holding up a pink dress covered with shiny dingle-dangles, and she threw the dress on the bed and all but had hysterics. It was terrible. In trying to think of some way to quiet her it occurred to me that I'd put her rod together and let her feel the balance of it with the feel I'd bought her—a genuine Fleetwood, mind you—attached. I looked around for her fishing things and couldn't find them. I'll tell you why I couldn't find them." George paused for an impressive instant to give his next words the full significance due them. "They weren't there!"

"No?" I murmured weakly.

"No," said George. "And what do you suppose she said when I questioned her? I can give you her exact words—I'll never forget them. She said, 'There wasn't any room for them.'" Again George paused. "I ask you," he inquired at last, "I ask you as man to man; what do you think of that?"

I found no adequate reply to this question and George, now thoroughly warmed up, rushed on.

"You'd swear I lost my temper then, wouldn't you? Well, I didn't. I did say something to her later, but I'll let you be the judge when we come to that. I'll ask you to consider the circumstances. I'll ask you to get Old Faithful in your mind's eye."

"Old Faithful?" I repeated. "Then you went to the Yellowstone later?"

"Yellowstone! Of course not! Haven't I told you we were already at the best trout water in America? Old Faithful was a squaretail. He'd been in the pool below Horseshoe Falls for twenty years, as a matter of record. We'll come to that presently. How are we off for time?"

"Thirty-one minutes," I told him. "I'm watching the clock—go ahead."

"Well, there she was, on a fishing trip with nothing to fish with. There was only one answer to that—she couldn't fish. But I went over everything she'd brought in three trunks and I'll give you my word she didn't have a garment of any sort you couldn't see through.

"Something had to be done and done quick, that was for sure. I fitted her out from my own things with a sweater, a flannel shirt, and a pair of knickerbockers.

Then I got the proprietor up and explained the situation. He got me some heavy underwear and two pairs of woolen stockings that belonged to his wife. When it came to shoes it looked hopeless, but the proprietor's wife, who had got up, too, by this time, thought of a pair of boy's moccasin's that were in the store and they turned out to be about the right size. I made arrangements to rent the room we had until we came out again to keep her stuff in, and took another room for the night—what was left of it after she'd repacked what could stay in the trunks and arranged what couldn't so it wouldn't be wrinkled.

"I got up early, dressed, and took my duffle down to the landing. I wakened her when I left the room. When breakfast was ready I went to see why she hadn't come down. She was all dressed, sitting on the edge of the bed. I said, 'Breakfast is ready, darling,' but I saw by her face that something was wrong again. It turned out to be my knickers. They fitted her perfectly—a little tight in spots—except in the waist. They would simply have fallen off if she hadn't held them up.

"Well, I was going in so light that I only had one belt. The proprietor didn't have any—he used suspenders. Neither did his wife—she used—well, whatever they use. He got me a piece of clothesline and I knotted it at each and ran it through the what-you-may-call-'ems of the knickers and tied it in front. The knickers sort of puckered all the way around, but they couldn't come down—that was the main thing. I said, 'There you are, darling.' She walked over and tilted the mirror of the bureau so that she could see herself from head to foot. She said, 'Who are going to be at this place where we are going?' I said, 'Some of the very best dry-fly men in the country.' She said, 'I don't mean them; I mean the women. Will there be any women there?'

"I told her, certainly there would be women. I asked her if she thought I would take her into a camp with nothing but men. I named some of the women: Mrs. Fred Beal and Mrs. Brooks Carter and Talcott Ranning's sister and several more.

"She turned around slowly in front of the mirror, staring into it for a minute. Then she said, 'Please go out and close the door.' I said, 'All right, darling; but come right down. The tug will be here in fifteen minutes.'

"I went downstairs and waited for ten minutes, then I heard the tug whistle for the landing and ran upstairs again. I knocked at the door. When she didn't answer I went in. Where do you suppose she was?"

I gave it up.

"In bed!" said George in an awe-struck voice. "In bed with her face turned to the wall; and listen, I didn't lose my temper as God is my judge. I rushed down to the wharf and told the tug captain I'd give him twenty-five dollars extra if he'd hold the boat till we came. He said all right and I went back to the room.

"The breeches had done it. She simply wouldn't wear them. I told her that at a fishing camp in Maine clothes were never thought of. I said, 'No one thinks of anything but trout, darling.' She said, 'I wouldn't let a fish see me looking like that.'" George's brow beaded suddenly. His hands dived searchingly into various pockets. "Got a cigarette? I left my case in my other suit."

He took a cigarette from me, lighted it with shaking fingers and inhaled deeply.

"It went on like that for thirty minutes. She was crying all the time, of course. I had started down to tell the tug captain it was all off, and I saw a woman's raincoat hanging in the hall. It belonged to someone up in one of the camps, the proprietor told me. I gave him seventy-five dollars to give to whoever owned it when he came out, and took it upstairs. In about ten minutes I persuaded her to wear it over the rest of her outfit until we got to camp. I told her one of the women would be able to fix her up all right when we got there. I didn't believe it, of course. The women at camp were all old-timers; they'd gone in as light as the men, but I had to say something.

"We had quite a trip going in. The guides were at the head of the lake all right—Indian Joe and a new man I'd never seen, called Charlie. I told Joe to take Isabelle—he's one of the best canoemen I ever saw. I was going to paddle bow for my man, but I'd have to bet a cookie Indian Joe could stay with us on any kind of water. We had to beat it right through to make camp by night. It's a good stiff trip, but it can be done. I looked back at the other canoe now and then we struck about a mile of white water that took all I had. When we were through the other canoe wasn't in sight. The river made a bend there, and I thought it was just behind and would show up any minute.

"Well, it didn't show up and I began to wonder. We hit our first portage about ten o'clock and landed. I watched downstream for twenty minutes, expecting to sight the other canoe every instant. Then Charlie, who hadn't opened his head, said, 'Better go back,' and put the canoe in again. We paddled downstream for all that was in it. I was stiff with fright. We saw 'em coming about three miles lower down and back-paddled till they came up. Isabelle was more cheerful-looking than she'd been since we left New York, but Joe had that stony face an Indian gets when he's sore.

"I said, 'Anything wrong?' Joe just grunted and drove the canoe past us. Then I saw it was filled with wild flowers. Isabelle said she'd been picking them right off the banks all the way long. She said she'd only had to get out of the boat once, for the blue ones. Now, you can't beat that—not in a thousand years. I leave it to you if you can. Twenty miles of stiff current, with five portages ahead of us and a nine-mile hike at the end of that. I gave that Indian the devil for letting her do such a thing, and tipped the flowers into the Penobscot when we unloaded for the first portage. She didn't speak to me on the portage, and she got into her canoe without a word.

"Nothing more happened going in, except this flower business had lost us two hours, and it was so dark when we struck the swamp at Loon Lake that we couldn't follow the trail well and kept stumbling over down timber and stepping into bog holes. She was about fagged out by then, and the mosquitoes were pretty thick through there. Without any warning she sat down on the trail. She did it so suddenly I nearly fell over her. I asked her what was the matter and she said, 'This is the end'—just like that—'this is the end!' I said, 'The end of what, darling?' She said, 'Of everything!' I told her if she sat there all wet and muddy she'd catch her death. She said she hoped so. I said, 'It's only two miles more, darling. Just think, tomorrow we'll be on the best trout water in the world!' With that she said, 'I want my mother, my darling mother,' and bowed her head in her hands. Think it over, please; and remember, I didn't lose my temper. You're sure there's nothing left in your flask?"

"Not a drop more, George," I assured him. "Go ahead; we've only twenty-five minutes."

George looked wildly at the clock, then at his watch.

"A man never has it when he wants it most. Have you noticed that? Where was I?"

"You were in the swamp."

"Oh, yes! Well, she didn't speak after that, and nothing I could say would budge her. The mosquitoes had got wind of us when we stopped and were coming in swarms. We'd be eaten alive in another ten minutes. So I told Joe to give his pack to Charlie and help me pick her up and carry her. Joe said, 'No, by damn!' and folded his arms. When an Indian gets sore he stays sore, and when he's sore he's stubborn. The mosquitoes were working on him good and plenty, though, and at last he said, 'Me carry packs. Charlie help carry—that.' He flipped his hand over in the direction of Isabelle and took the pack from Charlie.

"It was black as your hat by now, and the trail through there was only about a foot wide with swamp on each side. It was going to be some job getting her out of there. I thought Charlie and I would make a chair of our arms and stumble along with her some way; but when I started to lift her up she said, 'Don't touch me!' and got up and went on. A blessing if there ever was one. We got to camp at ten that night.

"She was stiff and sore the next morning—you expect it after a trip like that—besides, she'd caught a little cold. I asked her how she felt, and she said she was going to die and asked me to send for a doctor and her mother. The nearest doctor was at Bangor and her mother was in New Rochelle. I carried her breakfast over from the dining camp to our cabin. She said she couldn't eat any breakfast, but she did drink a cup of coffee, telling me between sips how awful it was to die alone in a place like that.

"After she'd had the coffee she seemed to feel better. I went to the camp library and got *The Dry Fly on American Waters*, by Charles Darty. I considered him the soundest man in the country. He's better than Pell or Fawcett. My chief criticism of him is that in his chapter on Streams East of the Alleghenies—east of the Alleghenies, mind you—he recommends the Royal Coachman. I consider the Lead-Wing Coachman a serviceable fly on clear, hard-fished water; but the Royal—never! I wouldn't give it a shade over the Professor or the Montreal. Just consider the body alone of the Royal Coachman—never mind the wings and hackle—the body of the Royal is—"

"Yes, I know, George," I said; "but—"

I glanced significantly at the clock. George started, sighed, and resumed his narrative.

"I went back to the cabin and said, 'Darling, here is one of the most intensely interesting books ever written. I'm going to read it aloud to you. I think I can finish it to-day. Would you like to sit up in bed while I read?' She said she hadn't strength enough to sit up in bed, so I sat down beside her and started reading. I had read about an hour, I suppose, when she did sit up in bed quite suddenly. I saw she was staring at me in a queer, wild way that was really startling. I said, 'What is it, darling?' She said, 'I'm going to get up. I'm going to get up this instant.'

"Well, I was delighted, naturally. I thought the book would get her by the time I'd read it through. But there she was, as keen as mustard before I'd got well into it. I'll tell you what I made up my mind to do, right there. I made up my mind to let her use my rod that day. Yes, sir—my three-ounce Spinoza, and what's more, I did it."

George looked at me triumphantly, then lapsed into reflection for a moment.

"If ever a man did everything possible to—well, let it go. The main thing is, I have nothing to reproach myself with—nothing. Except—but we'll come to that presently. Of course, she wasn't ready for dry flies yet. I borrowed some wet flies from the club steward, got some cushions for the canoe and put my rod together. She had no waders, so a stream was out of the question. The lake was better, anyway, that first day; she'd have all the room she wanted for her back cast.

"I stood there on the landing with her before we got into the canoe and showed her just how to put out a fly and recover it. Then she tried it." A sort of horror came into George's face. "You wouldn't believe any one could handle a rod like that," he said huskily. "You couldn't believe it unless you'd seen it. Gimme a cigarette.

"I worked with her a half hour or so and saw no improvement—none whatever. At last she said, 'The string is too long. I can't do anything with such a long string on a pole.' I told her gently—gently, mind you—that the string was an eighteen-dollar double-tapered Hurdman line, attached to a Gebhardt reel on a three-ounce Spinoza rod. I said, 'We'll go out on the lake now. If you can manage to get a rise, perhaps it will come to you instinctively.'

"I paddled her out on the lake and she went at it. She'd spat the flies down and yank them up and spat them down again. She hooked me several times with her back cast and got tangled up in the line herself again and again. All this time I was speaking quietly to her, telling her what to do. I give you my word I never raised my voice—not once—and I thought she'd break the tip every moment.

"Finally she said her arm was tired and lowered the rod. She'd got everything messed up with her last cast and the flies were trailing just over the side of the canoe. I said, 'Recover your cast and reel in, darling.' Instead of using her rod, she took hold of the leader close to the flies and started to pull them into the canoe. At that instant a little trout—couldn't have been over six inches—took the tail fly. I don't know exactly what happened, it was all over so quickly. I think she just screamed and let go of everything. At any rate, I saw my Spinoza bounce off the gunwale of the canoe and disappear. There was fifty feet of water just there. And now listen carefully: not one word did I utter—not one. I simply turned the canoe and paddled to the landing in absolute silence. No reproaches of any sort. Think that over!"

I did. My thoughts left me speechless. George proceeded:

"I took out a guide and tried dragging for the rod with a gang hook and heavy sinker all the rest of the day. But the gangs would only foul on the bottom. I gave up at dusk and paddled in. I said to the guide—it was Charlie—I said, 'Well, it's all over, Charlie.' Charlie said, 'I brought Mr. Carter in and he had an extra rod. Maybe you could borrow it. It's a four-ounce Meecham.' I smiled. I actually smiled. I turned and looked at the lake. 'Charlie,' I said, 'somewhere out there in that dark water, where the eye of man will never behold it again, is a three-ounce Spinoza—and you speak of a Meecham.' Charlie said, 'Well, I just thought I'd tell you.' I said, 'That's all right, Charlie. That's all right.' I went to the main camp, saw Jean, the head guide and made arrangements to leave the next day. Then I went to our cabin and sat down before the fire. I heard Isabelle say something about being sorry. I said, 'I'd rather not talk about it, darling. If you don't mind, we'll never mention it again.' We sat there in silence, then, until dinner.

"As we got up from dinner, Nate Griswold and his wife asked us to play bridge with them that evening. I'd told no one what had happened, and Nate didn't know, of course. I simply thanked him and said we were tired, and we went back to our cabin. I sat down before the fire again. Isabelle seemed restless. At last she said, 'George.' I said, 'What is it, darling?' She said, 'Would you like to read to me from that book?' I said, 'I'm sorry, darling; if you don't mind I'll just sit here quietly by the fire.'

"Somebody knocked at the door after a while. I said, 'Come in.' It was Charlie. I said, 'What is it, Charlie?' Then he told me that Bob Frazer had been called back to New York and was going out the next morning. I said, 'Well, what of it?' Charlie said, 'I just thought you could maybe borrow his rod.' I said, 'I thought you understood about that, Charlie.' Charlie said, 'Well, that's it. Mr. Frazer's rod is a three-ounce Spinoza.'

"I got up and shook hands with Charlie and gave him five dollars. But when he'd gone I began to realize what was before me. I'd brought in a pint flask of prewar Scotch. Prewar—get that! I put this in my pocket and went over to Bob's cabin. Just as I was going to knock I lost my nerve. I sneaked away from the door and went down to the lake and sat on the steps of the canoe landing. I sat there for quite a while and took several nips. At last I thought I'd just go and tell Bob of my loss and see what he said. I went back to his cabin and this time I knocked. Bob was putting a few odds and ends in a shoulder pack. His rod was in its case, standing against the wall.

"I said, 'I hear you're going out in the morning.' He said, 'Yes, curse it, my wife's mother has to have some sort of damned operation or other.' I said, 'How would a little drink strike you, Bob?' He said, 'Strike me! Wait a minute! What kind of drink?' I took out the flask and handed it to him. He unscrewed the cap and held the flask to his nose. He said, 'Great heavens above, it smells like—' I said, 'It is.' He said, 'It can't be!' I said, 'Yes, it is.' He said, 'There's a trick in it somewhere.' I said, 'No, there isn't—I give you my word.' He tasted what was in the flask carefully. Then he said, 'I call this white of you, George,' and took a good stiff snort. When he was handing back the flask he said, 'I'll do as much for you some day, if I ever get the chance.' I took a snifter myself.

"Then I said, 'Bob, something awful has happened to me. I came here to tell you about it.' He said, 'Is that so? Sit down.' I sat down and told him. He said, 'What kind of rod was it?' I said, 'A three-ounce Spinoza.' He came over and gripped my hand without a word. I said, 'Of course, I can't use anything else.' He nodded, and I saw his eyes flicker toward the corner of the room where his own rod was standing. I said, 'Have another drink, Bob.' But he just sat down and stared at me. I took a good stiff drink myself. Then I said, 'Under ordinary circumstances, nothing on earth could hire me to ask a man to—' I stopped right there.

"Bob got up suddenly and began to walk up and down the room. I said, 'Bob, I'm not considering myself—not for a minute. If it was last season, I'd simply have gone back to-morrow without a word. But I'm not alone any more. I've got the little girl to consider. She's never seen a trout taken in her life—think of it, Bob! And here she is, on her honeymoon, at the best water I know of. On her honeymoon, Bob!' I waited for him to say something, but he went to the window and stared out, with his back to me. I got up and said good-night and started for the door. Just as I reached it he turned from the window and rushed over and picked up his rod. He said, 'Here, take it,' and put the rod case in my hands. I started to try to thank him, but he said, 'Just go ahead with it,' and pushed me out the door."

The waiter was suddenly hovering above us with his eyes on the dishes.

"Now what do you want?" said George.

"Never mind clearing here," I said. "Just bring me the check. Go ahead, George."

"Well, of course, I can't any more than skim what happened finally, but you'll understand. It turned out that Ernie Payton's wife had an extra pair of knickers and she loaned them to Isabelle. I was waiting outside the cabin while she dressed next morning, and she called out to me, 'Oh, George, they fit!' Then I heard her begin to sing. She was a different girl when she came out to go to breakfast. She was almost smiling. She'd done nothing but slink about the day before. Isn't it extraordinary what will seem important to a woman? Gimme a cigarette."

"Fifteen minutes, George," I said as I supplied him.

"Yes, yes, I know. I fished the Cuddiwink that day. Grand stream, grand. I used a Pink Lady—first day on a stream with Isabelle—little touch of senti-ment—and it's a darn good fly. I fished it steadily all day. Or did I try a Seth

Green about noon? It seems to me I did, now that I recall it. It seems to me that where the Katahdin brook comes in I—"

"It doesn't really matter, does it, George?" I ventured.

"Of course, it matters!" said George decisively. "A man wants to be exact about such things. The precise details of what happens in a day's work on a stream are of real value to yourself and others. Except in the case of a record fish, it isn't important that you took a trout; it's exactly how you took him that's important."

"But the time, George," I protested.

He glanced at the clock, swore softly, mopped his brow—this time with the blue-gray handkerchief—and proceeded.

"Isabelle couldn't get into the stream without waders, so I told her to work along the bank a little behind me. It was pretty thick along there, second growth and vines mostly; but I was putting that Pink Lady on every foot of good water and she kept up with me easily enough. She didn't see me take many trout, though. I'd look for her, after landing one, to see what she thought of the way I'd handled the fish, and almost invariably she was picking the ferns or blueberries, or getting herself untangled from something. Curious things, women. Like children, when you stop to think of it."

George stared at me unseeingly for a moment.

"And you never heard of Old Faithful?" he asked suddenly. "Evidently not, from what you said a while ago. Well, a lot of people have, believe me. Men have gone to Cuddiwink district just to see him. As I've already told you, he lay beside a ledge in the pool below Horseshoe Falls. Almost nothing else in the pool. He kept it cleaned out. Worst sort of cannibal, of course—all big trout are. That was the trouble—he wanted something that would stick to his ribs. No flies for him. Did his feeding at night.

"You could see him dimly if you crawled out on a rock that jutted above the pool and looked over. Hey lay in about ten feet of water, right by his ledge. If he saw you he'd back under the ledge, slowly, like a submarine going into dock. Think of the biggest thing you've ever seen, and that's the way Old Faithful looked, just laying there as still as the ledge. He never seemed to move anything, not even his gills. When he backed in out of sight he seemed to be drawn under the ledge by some invisible force.

"Ridgway—R. Campbell Ridgway—you may have read his stuff. Brethren of the Wild, that sort of thing—claimed to have seen him move. He told me about it one night. He said he was lying with just his eyes over the edge of the rock, watching the trout. Said he'd been there an hour, when down over the falls came a young red squirrel. It had fallen in above and been carried over. The squirrel was half drowned, but struck out feebly for shore. Well, so Ridgway said—Old Faithful came up and took Mister Squirrel into camp. No hurry; just came drifting up, sort of inhaled the squirrel and sank down to the ledge again. Never made a ripple, Ridgway said; just business.

"I'm telling you all this because it's necessary that you get an idea of that trout in your mind. You'll see why in a minute. No one ever had hold of him. But it was customary, if you fished the Cuddiwink, to make a few casts over him before you left the stream. Not that you ever expected him to rise. It was just a sort of gesture. Everybody did it.

"Knowing that Isabelle had never seen trout taken before, I made a day of it—naturally. The trail to camp leaves the stream just at the falls. It was pretty late when we got to it. Isabelle had her arms full of—heaven knows what— flowers and grass and ferns and fir branches and colored leaves. She'd lugged the stuff for hours. I remember once that day I was fighting a fourteen-inch blackberry—I think it was—she'd found. How does that strike you? And listen! I said, 'It's a beauty, darling.' That's what I said—or something like that . . . Here, don't you pay that check! Bring it here, waiter!"

"Go on, George!" I said. "We haven't time to argue about the check. You'd come to the trail for camp at the falls."

"I told Isabelle to wait at the trail for a few minutes, while I went below the falls and did the customary thing for the edification of Old Faithful. I only intended to make three or four casts with the Number Twelve Fly and the hair-fine leader I had on, but in getting down to the pool I hooked the fly in a bush. In trying to loosen it I stumbled over something and fell. I snapped the leader like a thread, and since I had to put on another, I tied on a fairly heavy one as a matter of form.

"I had reached for my box for a regulation fly of some sort when I remembered a fool thing that Billy Roach had given me up on the Beaverkill the season before. It was fully two inches long; I forget what he called it. He said you fished it dry for bass or large trout. He said you worked the tip of your rod and made it wiggle like a dying minnow. I didn't want the contraption, but he'd borrowed some fly oil from me and insisted on my taking it. I'd stuck it in the breast pocket of my fishing jacket and forgotten it until then.

"Well, I felt in the pocket and there it was. I tried it on and went down to the pool. Now let me show you the exact situation." George seized a fork. "This is the pool." The fork traced an oblong figure on the tablecloth. "Here is Old Faithful's ledge." The fork deeply marked this impressive spot. "Here are the falls, with white water running to here. You can only wade to this point here, and then you have an abrupt six-foot depth. 'But you can put a fly from here to here with a long line,' you say. No, you can't. You've forgotten to allow for your back cast. Notice this bend here? That tells the story. You're not more than twenty feet from a lot of birch and whatnot, when you can no longer wade. 'Well then, it's impossible to put a decent fly on the water above the sunken ledge,' you say. It looks like it, but this is how it'd done: right here is a narrow point running to here, where it dwindles off to a single fat rock. If you work out on the point you can jump across to this rock—situated right here—and there you are, with about a thirty-foot cast to the sunken ledge. Deep water all around you, of course, and the rock is slippery; but—there you are. Now notice this small cove, right here. The water from the falls rushes past it in a froth, but in the cove it forms a deep eddy, with the current moving round and round like this." George made a slow circular motion with the fork. "You know what I mean?"

I nodded.

"I got out on the point and jumped to the rock; got myself balanced, worked out the right amount of line and cast the dungaree Bill had forced on me, just above the sunken ledge. I didn't take the water lightly and I cast again, but I couldn't put it down decently. It would just flop in—too much weight and too many feathers. I suppose I cast it a dozen times, trying to make it settle like a fly. I wasn't thinking of trout—there would be nothing in there except Old Faithful—I was just monkeying with this doodle-bug thing, now that I had it on.

"I gave up at last and let it lie out where I had cast it. I was standing there looking at the falls roaring down, when I remembered Isabelle, waiting up on the trail. I raised my rod preparatory to reeling in and the what-you-may-call-'em made a kind of dive and wiggle out there on the surface. I reached for my reel handle. Then I realized that the thingamajig wasn't on the water. I didn't see it disappear, exactly; I was looking at it, and then it wasn't there. 'That's funny,' I thought, and struck instinctively. Well, I was fast—so it seemed—and no snags in there. I gave it the butt three or four times, but the rod only bowed and nothing budged. I tried to figure it out. I thought perhaps a water-logged timber had come diving over the falls and upended right there. Then I noticed the rod take more of a bend and the line began to move through the water. It moved out slowly, very slowly, into the middle of the pool. It was exactly as though I was hooked on to a freight train just getting under way.

"I knew what I had hold of then, and yet I didn't believe it. I couldn't believe it. I kept thinking it was a dream, I remember. Of course, he could have gone away with everything I had any minute if he'd wanted to, but he didn't. He just kept moving slowly, round and round the pool. I gave him what pressure the tackle would stand, but he never noticed a little thing like that; just kept moving around the pool for hours, it seemed to me. I'd forgotten Isabelle; I admit that. I'd forgotten everything on earth. There didn't seem to be anything else on earth, as a matter of fact, except the falls and the pool and Old Faithful and me. At last Isabelle showed up on the bank above me, still lugging her ferns and whatnot. She called down to me above the noise of the falls. She asked me how long I expected her to wait alone in the woods, with night coming on.

"I hadn't had the faintest idea how I was going to try to land the fish until then. The water was boiling past the rock I was standing on, and I couldn't jump back to the point without giving him slack and perhaps falling in. I began to look around and figure. Isabelle said, 'What on earth are you doing?' I took off my landing net and tossed it to the bank. I yelled, 'Drop that junk quick and pick up that net!' She said, 'What for, George?' I said, 'Do as I tell you and don't ask questions!' She laid down what she had and picked up the net and I told her to go to the cove and stand ready.

"She said, 'Ready for what?' I said, 'You'll see what presently. Just stand there.' I'll admit I wasn't talking quietly. There was the noise of the falls to begin with, and—well, naturally, I wasn't.

"I went to work on the fish again. I began to educate him to the lead. I thought if I could lead him into the cove he would swing right past Isabelle and she could net him. It was slow work—a three-ounce rod—imagine! Isabelle called, 'Do you know what time it is?' I told her to keep still and stand where she was. She didn't say anything more than that.

"At last the fish began to come. He wasn't tired—he'd never done any fighting, as a matter of fact—but he'd take a suggestion as to where to go from the rod. I kept swinging him nearer and nearer the cove each time he came around. When I saw he was about ready to come I yelled to Isabelle. I said, 'I'm going to bring him right past you, close to the top. All you have to do is to net him.'

"When the fish came round again I steered him into the cove. Just as he was swinging past Isabelle the stuff she'd been lugging began to roll down the bank. She dropped the landing net on top of the fish and made a dive for those leaves and grasses and things. Fortunately the net handle lodged against the bank, and after she'd put her stuff in a nice safe place she came back and picked up the net again. I never uttered a syllable. I deserve no credit for that. The trout had made a surge and shot out into the pool and I was too busy just then to give her any idea of what I thought.

"I had a harder job getting him to swing in again. He was a little leery of the cove, but at last he came. I steered him toward Isabelle and lifted him all I dared. He came up nicely, clear to the top. I yelled, 'Here he comes! For God's sake, don't miss him!' I put everything on the tackle it would stand and managed to check the fish for an instant right in front of Isabelle.

"And this is what she did: it doesn't seem credible—it doesn't seem humanly possible; but it's a fact that you'll have to take my word for. She lifted the landing net above her head with both hands and brought it down on top of the fish with all her might!"

George ceased speaking. Despite its coating of talcum powder, I was able to detect an additional pallor in his countenance.

"Will I ever forget it as long as I live?" he inquired at last.

"No, George," I said, "but we've just exactly eleven minutes left."

George made a noticeable effort and went on.

"By some miracle the fish stayed on the hook; but I got a faint idea of what would have happened if he'd taken a real notion to fight. He went around the pool so fast it must have made him dizzy. I heard Isabelle say, 'I didn't miss him, George'; and then—well, I didn't lose my temper; you wouldn't call it that exactly. I hardly knew what I said. I'll admit I shouldn't have said it. But I did say it; no doubt of that; no doubt of that whatever."

"What was it you said?" I asked.

George looked at me uneasily.

"Oh, the sort of thing a man would say impulsively—under the circumstances."

"Was it something disparaging about her?" I inquired.

"Oh, no," said George, "nothing about her. I simply intimated—in a somewhat brutal way, I suppose—that's she'd better get away from the pool—er—not bother me any more is what I meant to imply."

For the first time since George had chosen me for a confidant I felt a lack of frankness on his part.

"Just what did you say, George?" I insisted.

"Well, it wasn't altogether my words," he evaded. "It was the tone I used, as much as anything. Of course, the circumstances would excuse—Still, I regret it. I admit that. I've told you so plainly."

There was no time in which to press him further.

"Well, what happened then?" I asked.

"Isabelle just disappeared. She went up the bank, of course, but I didn't see her go. Old Faithful was still nervous and I had to keep my eye on the line. He quieted down in a little while and continued to promenade slowly around the pool. I suppose this kept up for half an hour more. Then I made up my mind that something had to be done. I turned very carefully on the rock, lowered the tip until it was on the line with the fish, turned the rod under my arm until it was pointing behind me and jumped.

"Of course, I had to give him slack; but I kept my balance on the point by the skin of my teeth, and when I raised the rod he was still on. I worked to the bank, giving out line, and crawled under some bushes and things and got around to the cove at last. Then I started to work again to swing him into the cove, but absolutely nothing doing. I could lead him anywhere except into the cove. He'd had enough of that; I didn't blame him, either.

"To make a long story short, I stayed with him for two hours. For a while it was pretty dark; but there was a good-sized moon that night, and when it rose it shone right down on the pool through a gap in the trees fortunately. My wrist was gone completely, but I managed to keep some pressure on him all the time, and at last he forgot about what had happened to him in the cove. I swung him in and the current brought him past me. He was on his side by now. I don't think he was tired even then—just discouraged. I let him drift over the net, heaved him out on the bank and sank down beside him, absolutely all in. I couldn't have got to my feet on a bet. I just sat there in a sort of daze and looked at Old Faithful, gleaming in the moonlight.

"After a half-hour's rest I was able to get up and go to camp. I planned what I was going to do on the way. There was always a crowd in the main camp living room after dinner. I simply walked into the living room without a word and laid Old Faithful on the center table.

"Well, you can imagine faintly what happened. I never got any dinner— couldn't have eaten any, as a matter of fact. I didn't even get a chance to take off my waders. By the time I'd told just how I'd done it to one crowd, more would come in and look at Old Faithful; and then stand and look at me for a while; and then make me tell it all over again. At last everybody began to dig up anything they had with a kick in it. Almost every one had a bottle he'd been hoarding. There was Scotch and gin and brandy and rye and a lot of experimental stuff. Art Bascom got a tin dish pan from the kitchen and put in on the table beside Old Faithful. He said, 'Pour your contributions right in here, men.' So each man dumped whatever he had into the dish pan and everybody helped himself.

"It was great, of course. The biggest night of my life, but I hope I'll never be so dog-tired again. I felt as though I'd taken a beating. After they'd weighed Old Faithful—nine pounds five and a half ounces; and he'd been out of water two hours—I said I had to go to bed, and went.

"Isabelle wasn't in the cabin. I thought, in a hazy way, that she was with some of the women, somewhere. Don't get the idea I was stewed. But I hadn't had anything to eat, and the mixture in that dish pan was plain TNT.

"I fell asleep as soon as I hit the bed; slept like a log till daylight. Then I half woke up, feeling that something terrific had happened. For a minute I didn't know what; then I remember what it was. I had landed Old Faithful on a three-ounce rod!

"I lay there and went over the whole thing from the beginning, until I came to Isabelle with the landing net. That made me look at where her head should have been on the pillow. It wasn't there. She wasn't in the cabin. I thought perhaps she'd got up early and gone out to look at the lake or the sunrise or something. But I got up in a hurry and dressed.

"Well, I could see no signs of Isabelle about camp. I ran into Jean just coming from the head guide's cabin and he said, 'Too bad about your wife's mother.' I said, 'What's that?' He repeated what he'd said, and added, 'She must be an awful sick woman.' Well, I got out of him finally that Isabelle had come straight up from the stream the evening before, taken two guides and started for Buck's Landing. Jean had urged her to wait until morning, naturally; but she'd told him she must get to her mother at once, and took on so, as Jean put it, that he had to let her go.

"I said, 'Let me have Indian Joe, stern, and a good man, bow. Have 'em ready in ten minutes.' I rushed to the kitchen, drank two cups of coffee and started for Buck's Landing. We made the trip down in seven hours, but Isabelle had left with her trunks on the 10:40 train.

"I haven't seen her since. Went to her home once. She wouldn't see me; neither would her mother. Her father advised not forcing things—just waiting. He said he'd do what he could. We'll, he's done it—you read the letter. Now you know the whole business. You'll stick, of course, and see me through just the first of it, old man. Of course, you'll do that, won't you? We'd better get down to the train now. Track nineteen."

"George," I said, "one thing more: just what did you say to her when she—"

"Oh, I don't know," George began vaguely.

"George," I interrupted, "no more beating about the bush. What did you say?"

I saw his face grow even more haggard, if possible. Then it mottled into a shade resembling the brick on an old colonial mansion.

"I told her—" he began in a low voice.

"Yes?" I encouraged.

"I told her to get the hell out of there."

And now a vision was presented to my mind's eye; a vision of twelve fish plates, each depicting a trout curving up through green waters to an artificial fly. The vision extended on through the years. I saw Mrs. George Baldwin Potter ever gazing upon those rising trout and recalling the name on the card which had accompanied them to her door.

I turned and made rapidly for the main entrance of the Grand Central Station. In doing so I passed the clock above Information and saw that I still had two minutes in which to be conveyed by a taxicab far, far from the entrance to Track Nineteen.

I remember hearing the word "quitter" hurled after me by a hoarse, despairing voice.

# MR. THEODORE CASTWELL

## G. E. M. SKUES

Mr. Theodore Castwell, having devoted a long, strenuous and not unenjoyable life to hunting to their doom innumerable salmon, trout, and grayling in many quarters of the globe, and having gained much credit among his fellows for his many ingenious improvements in rods, flies, and tackle employed for that end, in the fullness of time died and was taken to his own place.

St. Peter looked up from a draft balance sheet at the entry of the attendant angel.

"A gentleman giving the name of Castwell. Says he is a fisherman, your Holiness, and has 'Fly-Fishers' Club, London' on his card."

"Hm-hm," says St. Peter. "Fetch me the ledger with his account." St. Peter perused it.

"Hm-hm," said St. Peter. "Show him in."

Mr. Castwell entered cheerfully and offered a cordial right hand to St. Peter.

"As a brother of the angle—" he began.

"Hm-hm," said St. Peter. "I have been looking at your account from below."

"I am sure I shall not appeal to you in vain for special consideration in connection with the quarters to be assigned to me here."

"Hm-hm," said St. Peter.

"Well, I've seen worse accounts," said St. Peter. "What sort of quarters would you like?"

"Do you think you could manage something in the way of a country cottage of the Test Valley type, with modern conveniences and, say, three quarters of a mile of one of those pleasant chalk streams, clear as crystal, which proceed from out the throne, attached?"

"Why, yes," said St. Peter. "I think we can manage that for you. Then what about your gear? You must have left your fly rods and tackle down below. I see you prefer a light split cane of nine foot or so, with appropriate fittings. I will indent upon the Works Department for what you require, including a supply of flies. I think you will approve of our dresser's productions. Then you will want a keeper to attend you."

"Thanks awfully, your Holiness," said Mr. Castwell. "That will be first-rate. To tell you the truth, from the Revelations I read, I was inclined to fear that I might be just a teeny-weeny bit bored in heaven."

"In h-hm-hm," said St. Peter, checking himself.

It was not long before Mr. Castwell found himself alongside an enchantingly beautiful clear chalk stream, some fifteen yards wide, swarming with fine trout feeding greedily: and presently the attendant angel assigned to him had handed him the daintiest, most exquisite, light split-cane rod conceivable—perfectly balanced with the reel and line—with a beautifully damped tapered cast of incredible fineness and strength, and a box of flies of such marvelous tying as to be almost mistakable for the natural insects they were to simulate.

Mr. Castwell scooped up a natural fly from the water, matched it perfectly from the fly box, and knelt down to cast to a riser putting up just under a tussock ten yards or so above him. The fly lit like gossamer, six inches above the last ring; and next moment the rod was making the curve of beauty. Presently, after an exciting battle, the keeper netted out a beauty of about two and a half pounds.

"Heavens," cried Mr. Castwell. "This is something like."

"I am sure his Holiness will be pleased to hear it," said the keeper.

Mr. Castwell prepared to move upstream to the next riser when he noticed that another trout had taken up the position of that which he had just landed, and was rising. "Just look at that," he said, dropping instantaneously to his knee and drawing off some line. A moment later an accurate fly fell just above the neb of the fish, and instantly Mr. Castwell engaged in battle with another lusty fish. All went well, and presently the landing net received its two and a half pounds.

"A very pretty brace," said Mr. Castwell, preparing to move on to the next string of busy nebs which he had observed putting up around the bend. As he approached the tussock, however, he became aware that the place from which he had just extracted so satisfactory a brace was already occupied by another busy feeder.

"Well, I'm damned," said Mr. Castwell. "Do you see that?"

"Yes, sir," said the keeper.

The chance of extracting three successive trout from the same spot was too attractive to be forgone, and once more Mr. Castwell knelt down and delivered a perfect cast to the spot. Instantly it was accepted and battle was joined. All held, and presently a third gleaming trout joined his brethren in the creel.

Mr. Castwell turned joyfully to approach the next riser round the bend. Judge, however, his surprise to find that once more the pit beneath the tussock was occupied by a rising trout, apparently of much the same size as the others.

"Heavens," exclaimed Mr. Castwell. "Was there ever anything like it?"

"No, sir," said the keeper.

"Look here," said he to the keeper, "I think I really must give this chap a miss and pass on to the next."

"Sorry, it can't be done, sir. His Holiness would not like it."

"Well, if that's really so," said Mr. Castwell, and knelt rather reluctantly to his task.

Several hours later he was still casting to the same tussock.

"How long is this confounded rise going to last?" inquired Mr. Castwell. "I suppose it will stop soon."

"No, sir," said the keeper.

"What, isn't there a slack hour in the afternoon?"

"No afternoon, sir."

"What? Then what about the evening rise?"

"No evening rise, sir," said the keeper.

"Well, I shall knock off now. I must have had about thirty brace from that corner."

"Beg pardon, sir, but his Holiness would not like that."

"What?" said Mr. Castwell. "Mayn't I even stop at night?"

"No night here, sir," said the keeper.

"Then do you mean that I have got to go on catching these damned two-and-a-half-pounders at this corner forever and ever?"

The keeper nodded.

"Hell!" said Mr. Castwell.

"Yes," said his keeper.

# ACKNOWLEDGMENTS

A ll the excerpts used in this book are used by permission of the author, the author's estate, or by statute unless otherwise noted.

Where works have been reprinted recently, the last known edition is indicated for the reader's benefit.

"The Primitive Fish-Hook" by Barnet Phillips. From *The Century*. "Ælian—The Macedonian Invention, or the First Mention of an Artificial Fly" by William Radcliffe. From *Fishing from the Earliest Times* (Ares Publishers Inc., 1974). "The Compleat Angler" by Izaak Walton and Charles Cotton. From *The Compleat Angler: Or, The Contemplative Man's Recreation* (Modern Library, 1998.) "Trout: Meeting Them on the 'June Rise'" by "Nessmuk." From *Fishing with a Fly*, eds. Charles F. Orvis and A. Nelson Cheney (Book Sales, 1990). "Trouting Along the Catasauqua" by Frank Forester. From *Frank Forester's Fugitive Sporting Sketches*. "The Boy and the Angle" by Rowland E. Robinson. From *Silver Fields and Other Sketches of a Farmer-Sportsman* (Houghton Mifflin Company). "Some Memories of Early Days" by Lord Grey of Falloden. From *Fly Fishing* (The Lyons Press, 1985). "Fishing with My Daddy" by Jimmy Carter. From *An Outdoor Journal* (University of Arkansas Press, 1988). "The River God" by Roland Pertwee. From

Miramichi it ain't, so all right, it's 116th St." by John Bryan. From *Sports Illustrated* (October 17, 1977). "Memories of Mahseer" by P. R. Bairnsfather. From *A Book of Fishing Stories*, ed. F. G. Aflalo (Dent & Sons, Ltd., 1913). "The One That Got Away" (selection) by Howell Raines. From *The One That Got Away: A Memoir* (Scribner, 2006). "The Man Who Lived Two Lives in One: Zane Grey" by Robert H. Boyle. From *Sports Illustrated* (April 29, 1960). "The Angler" by Washington Irving. From *Roger Caras' Treasury of Great Fishing Stories* (Galahad Books, 1999). "What and Who Is an Angler?" by Thaddeus Norris. From *The Armchair Angler*, eds. Terry Brykcyznski and David Reuther (BBS Publishing Corporation, 1994). "A Painter, an Angler, and Some Others" by William Scrope. From *Days and Nights of Salmon Fishing in the Tweed* (The Mercat Press, 1975). "Fishing" by Reverend Thomas Bastard (1498). "Crazy for Rivers" (selection) by Bill Barich (The Lyons Press, 1999). "A River Runs Through It" (selection) by Norman Maclean (University of Chicago Press, 1976). "On Norman Maclean" by John Maclean (from *Fly Rod & Reel*, 1990). "A Single Step" by George Reiger. From *The Washington Post*. "The Even-Tempered Angler" (selection) by Louis Rubin (Winchester Press, 1983). "What's in a Name?" by Howard Frank Mosher. "The Solitary and Friendly Sport" by R. Palmer Baker Jr. From *The Armchair Angler*, eds. Terry Brykcyznski and David Reuther (BBS Publishing Corporation, 1994). "Midstream Crisis" by Lamar Underwood. From *Editors in the Stream* (Halo Books, 1992). "Blue Dun" by Frank Mele. From *Small in the Eye of a River* (Paul Pursell, 1988). "Storytelling on the Thames" by Jerome K. Jerome. From *Three Men in a Boat* (Viking, 1978). "Ol' Settler of Deep Hole" by Irving Bacheller. From *Eben Holden: A Tale of the North Country* (Dodo Press, 2006). "The Lucy Coffin" by W.D. Wetherell. "A Fatal Salmon," Frank Forester. From *A Creelful of Fishing Stories: A Pastime Book*, ed. Henry van Dyke (Charles Scribner's Sons, 1932). "A Gallant Poacher" by John Buchan. From *John Mcnab* (The Houghton Mifflin Company, 1925). "Brannigan's Trout" by Nick Lyons. From *Full Creel* (Grove Atlantic, 2001). "A Fatal Success" by Henry van Dyke. From *Fisherman's Luck* (Indypublish.com, 2002). "On Dry-Cow Fishing as a Fine Art" by Rudyard Kipling. From *The Fishing Gazette* (December 1890). "The Hole" by Guy de Maupassant. From *Selected Short Stories* (Penguin, 1987). "The Lady or the Salmon?" by Andrew Lang. From *Angling Sketches* (Kensing Publishing, 2006). "Fish Are Such Liars!" (selection) by Roland Pertwee. From *Fish are Such Liars!* (Livingston Publishers, 1972). "A Wedding Gift" by John Taintor Foote. From *A Wedding Gift* (The Lyons Press, 1992). "Mr. Theodore Castwell" by G. E. M. Skues. From *Side-Lines, Side-Lights & Reflections* (Seeley Service & Co., Ltd., 1932).